HOWARD HUGHES

HIS LIFE & MADNESS

Also By Donald L. Barlett and James B. Steele

Forevermore: Nuclear Waste in America

America: What Went Wrong?

America: Who Really Pays the Taxes?

America: Who Stole the Dream?

The Great American Tax Dodge

HOWARD HUGHES

HIS LIFE & MADNESS

By Donald L. Barlett
and James B. Steele

W. W. Norton & Company
New York   London

Manufacturing by The Haddon Craftsmen, Inc.

Library of Congress Cataloging–in–Publication Data

Barlett, Donald L.
[Empire]
Howard Hughes : his life and madness / Donald L. Barlett and James B. Steele.
p. cm.
Originally published as: Empire. 1st ed. c1979.
Includes bibliographical references and index.
ISBN 0-393-32602-0 (pbk.)
1. Hughes, Howard, 1905–1976. 2. Celebrities—United States—Biography.
3. Businesspeople—United States—Biography. 4. Millionaires—United States—Biography.
I. Steele, James B. II. Title.
CT275.H6678B37 2004
338.7'67'092—dc22
[B]   2004050138

W. W. Norton & Company, Inc.
500 Fifth Avenue, New York, N.Y. 10110
www.wwnorton.com

W. W. Norton & Company Ltd.
Castle House, 75/76 Wells Street, London W1T 3QT

1 2 3 4 5 6 7 8 9 0

For
Nancy, Eileen, Matthew, and Allison

CONTENTS

PREFACE

FEW, if any, figures in American history have provoked so many suspicions, stirred so much curiosity, inspired so many images, and been so greatly misunderstood as Howard Robard Hughes, Jr.

Such was the mystery and power surrounding his life that when he was pronounced dead on arrival at Methodist Hospital in Houston, Texas, on April 5, 1976, his fingerprints were lifted by a technician from the Harris County Medical Examiner's Office and forwarded to the Federal Bureau of Investigation in Washington. Secretary of the Treasury William E. Simon, for federal tax purposes, wanted to be sure that the dead man was indeed Howard Hughes. After comparing the fingerprints with those taken from Hughes in 1942, the FBI confirmed the identity.

The public life of Hughes was itself enough to ensure the spinning of a certain mythology. He was a record-setting aviator cut from a heroic mold on the Lindbergh model. His amorous adventures with some of Hollywood's leading ladies and his eccentric lifestyle were the stuff that sold newspapers. His fabulous wealth and his reputed genius at the business of making ever-greater amounts of money only heightened public curiosity.

As the years wore on, Hughes became in the public mind what his public-relations apparatus wanted him to be. In this, the publicists did not lack assistance. All who had known Hughes, and many who only claimed to, had a story to tell about the reclusive industrialist. And so the legend grew, embroidered, indeed made possible by Hughes's pathological obsession with secrecy and seclusion.

So completely was truth distorted that Hughes could lose tens of millions of dollars for more than thirty consecutive years in one of his companies and yet be named one of America's ten greatest businessmen. So impenetrable was the curtain of secrecy that Jean Peters, invariably pictured as a deeply involved Mrs. Howard Hughes, only saw her husband by appointment.

So it is that any serious biography of Howard Hughes must surmount and remold the legend given currency, and all but petrified, by years of repetition. This task is both aided and impeded by the size of the public record, which runs to hundreds of thousands of pages of documents relating to Hughes and his empire. It is clear to the authors, after four years of research, that the record spawned by Hughes is rivaled in size by few men of modern times. Because this material is not found in any central location, but rather is scattered from coast to coast, only bits and pieces have found their way into the public print. As a result, the full story has gone untold. Spanning the whole of Hughes's life, we have compiled the single largest collection of Hughes documents and records outside the Hughes organization itself, the largest and most powerful privately controlled business empire in the country. We examined more than a quarter-million pages of records and documents, from which we reproduced, or in some instances handcopied, some fifty thousand pages. The material was gathered from sources in more than fifty cities in twenty-three states and five foreign countries, from Bayonne, New Jersey, to Santa Ana, California, from Nassau to Tokyo. The papers were drawn from nearly fifty different offices, agencies, and departments of local, state, and federal governments, from the Los Angeles Police Department to the Department of Defense, from the Nevada Gaming Commission to the Quebec Securities Commission.

These papers include thousands of Hughes's handwritten and dictated memoranda, family letters, CIA memoranda, FBI reports, contracts with nearly a dozen departments and agencies of the federal government, loan agreements, hundreds of memoranda and reports prepared by Hughes executives and lawyers, deeds, mortgages, lease agreements, corporate charters, census reports, college records, federal income-tax returns, Oral History transcripts, partnership agreements, autopsy reports, birth and death records, marriage license applications, divorce records, naturalization petitions, bankruptcy records, corporation annual reports, stock offering circulars, real estate assessment records, notary public commissions, applications for pilot certificates, powers of attorney, minutes of the board meetings of Hughes's companies, police records, transcripts of Securities and Exchange Commission proceedings, genealogical records, government audit reports, voter registration records, annual assessment work affidavits, transcripts of Civil Aeronautics Board proceedings, the daily logs of Hughes's activities, hearings and reports of committees of the House of Representatives and Senate, transcripts of Federal Communications Commission proceedings, wills, estate records, grand jury testimony, trial transcripts, civil and criminal court records.

None of this is to suggest that all information appearing in an official government document or legal record is the whole truth. Obviously, such is not the case. Long before Clifford Irving appeared with his spurious autobiography of Hughes, forged documents, although uncommon, were not unknown in the Hughes empire. A fake memorandum bearing Hughes's name, submitted to McGraw-Hill by Irving as "evidence" of the authenticity of his manuscript, was not the first—or last—time that Hughes's signature was forged. Nor was it the last time that someone prepared a bogus Hughes memorandum. Moreover, thousands of critical documents once in the possession of the Hughes organization have been destroyed as no longer necessary—or to avoid embarrassment or conceal wrongdoing. Other documents are being withheld from public inspection by United States government agencies for possibly the same reasons. And other Hughes documents have been stolen. The records that are available, however, provide a rich source of new information and enable one to establish what is fraudulent or fiction, substantiate what actually was, and bring one closer to the truth. Because so much misinformation has already been published, we have attempted to reduce speculation to a minimum, to speculate only when the evidence warrants, and to lay out the facts to allow the reader to reach conclusions, to make judgments.

Much of the material presented here, especially covering the last twenty years of Hughes's life, has become available only since his death, and particularly within the past year as courts in Houston, Las Vegas, Los Angeles, and Wilmington have been inundated in an ongoing flood of paperwork growing out of the administration of the Hughes estate. In addition, there has been a series of civil lawsuits involving Hughes companies that have yielded a similar volume of paperwork. Businesses are seldom willing to open their corporate files for historians. But because of the legal actions brought by and against Hughes companies, there now is available an unprecedented accumulation of records and documents that set forth the inner workings of the billion-dollar empire.

For much of his life, everything that Hughes said, everything that he did, was duly recorded in a memorandum, as were many of the actions of his staff and executives. Although he seldom wrote a personal letter—the best estimate is fewer than a dozen over the last half century of his life—he was a prolific memorandum writer, some weeks writing or dictating hundreds of pages, and in the process revealing as much about himself as about his businesses. Indeed, perhaps no other man has poured out so many business communications that told, also, so much about his most personal thoughts and beliefs. These documents, too, have become available in increasing numbers over the past year.

Only this wealth of fresh, inimitable material has made our book possible. But even so, we have not answered each question, explored every road in Howard Hughes's life. No single book could do that. What we have sought to do here is to set down, for the first time, the story of a powerful and curious American who has rightly—if for many of the wrong reasons—fascinated our age.

ACKNOWLEDGMENTS

MANY obligations are incurred in a research project of four years' duration. The following list, therefore, is not intended to be all-inclusive, but rather an indication of the extent of our debt and a symbol of our gratitude to all who assisted.

We would first like to extend our deepest appreciation to those persons who, for one reason or another, must remain anonymous. They are the past and present employees of the Hughes organization and persons who have had extensive dealings with the Hughes organization, from lawyers to government officials to legal secretaries.

We are beholden to many librarians at private, public, and university libraries across the country, including the Academy of Motion Picture Arts and Sciences Library, Barker Texas History Center Library and Archives of the University of Texas, Cambria County (Pennsylvania) Library, Case Western Reserve University Libraries, Clark County (Nevada) Library, Cleveland Public Library, Dallas Public Library, Houston Public Library, Library of Congress, Los Angeles Public Library, Miami Public Library, Museum of Modern Art Library, National Archives and Records Service, New York Public Library, Northrop University Library, Oral History Research Office of Columbia University, and the Scotland County (Missouri) Library. We would especially like to recognize the unfailing cooperation of Clifford Crowers and his staff in the government publications room, as well as Geraldine Duclow, Bernard Pasqualini, and Vilma Wallis, all of the Free Library of Philadelphia; Betty Metz at the Jenkins Memorial Law Library of the Philadelphia Bar Association; Albert Vara at the Samuel Paley Library of Temple University; and John Merkel and Barbara Metz at the University of Pennsylvania Libraries.

Librarians at many newspapers were also most helpful, including the *Albuquerque Journal, Austin American–Statesman, Boston Globe, Cleveland*

Plain Dealer, Detroit Free Press, Honolulu Star–Bulletin, Kansas City Star, Los Angeles Times, Miami Herald, Nevada State Journal and *Gazette, Phoenix Republic* and *Gazette, Seattle Times, Toronto Star, Tulsa World* and *Tribune,* and *Vancouver Sun.* We would especially like to thank for all their kindnesses Julia Vance, librarian at the *Houston Post,* and Ernest Perez, librarian at the *Houston Chronicle.* We are most deeply indebted to the library staff of the *Philadelphia Inquirer*—whose years of dedication have produced a superb newspaper library—Joe DiMarino, Frank Donahue, Frank Gradel, Joe Gradel, Mary Holland, Gene Loielo, Bill Matthaeus, Ron Taylor, and Mary Taffe.

Clerks in a number of state and federal courts responded with both patience and diligence to our repeated requests for court records, including the Arizona Superior Court in Phoenix, Harris County (Texas) Probate Court, Lee County (Iowa) Probate Court, Los Angeles County Superior Court, San Francisco County Superior Court, Scotland County (Missouri) Probate Court, and the Wayne County Circuit Court. Special thanks are due to Richard Johnson at the United States District Court in Los Angeles, Elda Hanks and the staff at the Eighth Judicial District Court of Clark County in Las Vegas, Ted Kast at the United States District Court in San Francisco, the staff of Basil R. Battaglia at the New Castle County Chancery Court in Wilmington, and Grover Luttrell and his staff at the New Castle County Register of Wills Office.

There were many in government agencies who also responded most generously and graciously to our frequent requests, especially Colonel Fletcher Elder at the Department of Defense in Washington, Marisue Prince and Ed Green at the FAA Aeronautical Center in Oklahoma City, Pat Thompson at the GSA in Washington, Larry Batdorf at the IRS in Washington, Charles H. Powers at the IRS District Office in Philadelphia, and Tom Horton at the SEC in Washington.

A number of authorities in various professions were unstinting in making their expertise available to us, but we would especially like to recognize Thomas F. Field of Tax Analysts and Advocates for taking the time to make complex tax laws understandable.

We would also like to express our deepest appreciation to Ed Barber, our editor at W. W. Norton, not only for his counsel, which contributed so much to the shaping of this book, but for his patience in seeing this project through; Fred Bidgood, our meticulous copy editor at Norton; Mary Lowe Kennedy, copy desk chief at the *Philadelphia Inquirer,* who read the manuscript and offered suggestions which, as usual, improved it immeasurably; and Maureen and Bryan Meehan who gave a hand with the typing when it was desperately needed. And finally, a special word of thanks to Gene Roberts, the executive editor of the *Philadelphia Inquirer,* who originally suggested that we conduct an in-depth study of the Hughes empire, and then allowed us the time and freedom to carry it out. The resultant 20,000-word series, published in the *Inquirer* in December of 1975, became the springboard for this book.

Although many contributed to this effort, any errors in fact or interpretation, and we hope they are few, are ours alone.

HOWARD HUGHES

HIS LIFE & MADNESS

PROLOGUE

DEATH IN MEXICO

A COOL tropical breeze blew from the sea, gently swaying the palm trees and curtains in the open lobby. Dancers in Tiffany's, the hotel's lavish discotheque, were unlimbering, preparing to make a long night of it. In El Grotto, the swim bar just beyond the lobby, a dozen or so couples splashed about in the glowing pool, sipping drinks or quietly slipping through the cascading waterfall to the artificial cave that lay beyond it.

Twenty stories above, on the top floor of the Acapulco Princess Hotel, Chuck Waldron hunched over a desk, making entries in the day's log. From the adjoining room, he heard Hughes call. Irritated, Waldron shoved the papers aside and went into the room. The old man was really being a nuisance tonight.

"Pour me some water," Hughes said.[1]

Waldron took a bottle of water from the refrigerator in the adjoining room and poured a fresh glass. Hughes raised the glass slowly to his lips but did not drink. Waldron watched the old man set the glass on the night table and went back to his desk. It was his job to file memoranda, letters, reports, work schedules, and other communications. No one had assigned these tasks; they were just things he felt compelled to do. He usually found the desk strewn with papers when he reported for duty because none of the other men felt the same need. Waldron was fastidious; he liked everything in its place. Hughes called again and Waldron returned to the bedroom.

"Some water."[2]

"You've got some," Waldron told him.[3] Four partly filled glasses stood on the nightstand next to the old man's bed.

"Well, that's warm now," he complained feebly.[4]

Waldron took the glasses, emptied them, and poured Hughes another. Sitting down at his desk, once more he heard the high-pitched quavering voice.

Waldron was running out of patience. There had been no peace tonight. He must have poured thirty glasses of water, and the old man had barely touched any of them. He seemed to want Waldron in the room with him all the time.

"You don't need any water," Waldron called out in irritation and bent again to his work.[5] Now Hughes fell quiet.

At 4 A.M., about halfway through his eight-hour shift, Waldron brought in a strawberry tart and a cup of milk and set them down on the tray in front of Hughes, who looked at the food impassively.

"I want you to eat it," Waldron said.

"Not now."

"No, I want you to eat it," Waldron said firmly.

"Well, leave it and I'll . . ." The voice trailed off in midsentence, as though Hughes could not put together what he wanted to say.[6] In a little while, the old man ate a bite of the tart and took a sip of milk before sinking back onto the pillow behind him. Waldron returned to his desk.

Hughes now lay still. Outside it was dark, but inside the room day and night looked the same. Thick draperies were taped over the windows to seal out the light. The passage of time was marked only by the three shift changes in the next room as Hughes's aides came and went. From his hospital bed at one end, Hughes could see a bench, a luggage rack, and two chairs near the center of the room, and a chest of drawers along one wall. To one side of the bed were a movie projector and an amplifier. On either side of him were heavy rectangular nightstands. Atop one was a small metal box. At the far end of the room, near the movie screen, he could see the door to the hotel hallway. It was boarded shut, secured by a two-by-four attached to metal brackets.

The old man must have felt terrible. His mouth and throat were dry. He had sores on his back, and the left side of his head hurt from the time he had fainted and fallen over onto the nightstand. He felt a constant urge to urinate. He was listless and sometimes lay motionless in the bed for hours. Now, lying in the dark, hovering near unconsciousness, he mustered the energy to move.

Reaching for the metal box on the nightstand, his hand fumbled inside it and pulled out a syringe filled with a pale white liquid—codeine. He called the needle his plaything and he longed for those moments when he could stick it in his arm, depress the plunger only part of the way to send a little of the liquid into his body, humming and singing to it as it dangled from his arm, then depress the plunger again, releasing the rest of the liquid while he sang over and over, "Hey bob a ree bop, hey bob a ree bop."[7] A few weeks before, when he was living in the Bahamas, he was told his needles would be taken away unless he moved to Mexico. He was told there was no more codeine in the Bahamas, but in Mexico there would be more codeine than ever before. The old man had agreed. Now he was silent as he took the syringe from the box. He only popped the needle into his arm and pushed.

Hughes had stopped eating. Every day they brought him food and every day he turned it away. It was not the first time he had refused to eat. They had seen him go without food for days at a time. Sometimes he simply stopped eating as a reaffirmation of his powerful will. But this time it had nothing to do with will.

About 7:30, Jim Rickard came on duty and Waldron spent a few minutes briefing him. Then he left and Rickard went into the bedroom and saw Hughes propped up, dozing. Hughes always slept that way, not liking to be in a supine position. He looked tired and worn, his long gray hair and beard unkempt and scraggly. Rickard could not remember a time when Hughes had slept as much as he was sleeping now. Perhaps he should let Los Angeles know how sick the old man was. It was not really Rickard's place to say anything; he was the junior member of the group. But Hughes had not eaten any substantial food in nearly two weeks.[8] Before his shift ended, Rickard put in the call to Los Angeles.

At 4 P.M., George Francom came on duty. It was his first shift back after two weeks of leave in St. George, Utah. Francom had never understood the reason for the sudden move to Mexico. It had made no sense to him to move a failing man from the Bahamas, where they had everything they needed, to Acapulco, where nothing seemed to work, where there were few supplies, and where none of them could even speak the language. No one had asked his opinion, of course. Acapulco was one headache after another. The electricity and air conditioning were inconstant. They had difficulty importing supplies. They had to change cooks. Hughes was upset by the slightest variation in routine, and these disruptions had made him moody and cantankerous.

He did not eat for the next three days. Francom did get him to drink a little milk, but that was all. Dr. Norman Crane, one of two personal physicians then on duty in the penthouse, went in to see him a few times, but other than recommending that Hughes should eat and drink more, there was no treatment. Growing steadily weaker, Hughes spent his days sleeping or lingering in a semiconscious state. In his rare wakeful moments, he was confused, disoriented, and often incoherent.

Jack Real, a Hughes executive and one of Hughes's oldest associates, later said that he put in a telephone call to Logan, Utah, for Dr. Wilbur Thain, the physician who had overall responsibility for Hughes's medical care. As Real recalled the conversation:

"I don't want to play doctor, Wilbur, but your patient is dying," Real said.

"Well, goddamn it, you are playing doctor and mind your own business," Dr. Thain said.

"Wilbur, you need to get here," Real repeated.

"I've got a party in the Bahamas and I'll come over after that," Dr. Thain said.[9]

Hughes's decline was making all of them uneasy. They had wondered for years what would happen when he sank to this stage. Putting him in a hospital was not an appealing option, but in the past they had at least been close to good hospitals. Now they were hundreds of miles from one, and without an airplane.

The organization had airplanes all over the world, yet none had been sent to Mexico. But whatever was done with the old man would not be decided by the men in the penthouse. They knew this was a decision for Los Angeles.

When Francom came on to relieve John Holmes at 4 P.M. Saturday afternoon, April 3, 1976, Hughes was delirious. He spoke very slowly, each word a struggle, and put together the words only made gibberish. Hughes was trying to tell Francom something, but he could not make out what it was. Something about an insurance policy.[10] Hughes kept repeating, "insurance policy, insurance policy." Francom's inability to understand frustrated the old man, and he called Holmes back into the bedroom. Then, as both stood next to the bed, Hughes launched into the same disjointed monologue, saying over and over something about an insurance policy. Holmes also failed to understand; he and Francom stared uncomprehendingly at each other as the old man mumbled on.

The doctors drew a blood sample from him that afternoon. They usually had to beg. He did not like to be touched. Now, in his weakness, he put up little resistance when they inserted the needle. The blood, and a urine specimen, were sent to a local laboratory. The results were mixed—"numerosos" red and white blood cells in the urine and slightly elevated levels of glucose, uric acid, and creatinine in the blood.[11] None of these readings was especially serious. But the report also showed an exceptionally high urea level—104.5 milligrams—a strong indication that dehydration was becoming critical.[12] A normal adult count ranges from 20 to 38 milligrams.

On Saturday evening, Francom came into the room and saw a hypodermic syringe dangling from Hughes's arm. Hughes was now so feeble he could no longer insert the needle and depress the plunger. He had broken off half a dozen needles in both arms trying to give himself shots.[13] When the syringe fell from his arm and dropped to the floor, Hughes motioned for Francom to give him the injection.[14] Francom refused. Hughes was not in pain. What he needed, desperately, was fluids, not a fix. Francom called Dr. Crane. When Crane arrived, he put the syringe in Hughes's arm and injected the codeine[15] and Hughes dozed off. That night, one of the men spoke again to Los Angeles and gave a full report on the old man. There was still no decision on what to do, where to take him.

At midnight, when Waldron relieved Francom, Hughes was awake and delirious. Waldron had hoped to get the old man to do a little work that night. He took a document into the bedroom for him to sign. It was a proxy authorizing more people to draw checks on Hughes's personal account. Hughes would not take it; he mumbled something about having other papers to sign. Waldron was puzzled. What other documents could Hughes be talking about? Waldron kept track of the papers and there was nothing else for him to sign except the proxy relating to his checking account. Hughes was now back to his litany about an insurance policy. Waldron thought he understood him to say it was a policy covering Waldron and his children, but there was no such insurance policy.

Hughes grew weaker during the night. By the next day he could no longer talk, and that afternoon he slipped into a coma. When Francom came on duty, Hughes was lying motionless in bed, staring blankly ahead, looking pale and wasted. Once in a while he would slowly close his eyes, then reopen them. Francom noticed something else he had never seen before. Hughes's face and neck were twitching.

In the office next to the bedroom, calls were going back and forth to Los Angeles. Still no decision, but the men were told that Dr. Thain would be flying in the next day.

At midnight on Sunday, April 4, when Waldron reported for his shift, Francom told him that the old man was worse. During his shift, Francom had anxiously summoned another of Hughes's personal physicians, Dr. Lawrence Chaffin, to the bedroom. Waldron looked in. Hughes was propped up in bed unconscious, his face and neck twitching uncontrollably. Dr. Chaffin sat at his bedside. Sometime after midnight Chaffin came out of the bedroom and asked Francom and Waldron to summon Dr. Thain to Acapulco at once.[16] There was another flurry of telephone calls to Los Angeles. Thain was tracked down by phone an hour later. A small, private air ambulance had been hired from a Fort Lauderdale company. The plane would pick up Thain in a few hours and bring him to Mexico.

At dawn on Monday, April 5, Thain had not yet arrived, so Chaffin put in a hurried call to an Acapulco doctor, asking him to come to the Princess Hotel to examine a patient who was very ill.[17] Dr. Victor Manuel Montemayor responded quickly, and by 5:45 A.M. he had ascended in the service elevator of the Princess to the penthouse and made his way first into Room 2008, then Room 2010, and finally Room 2012, the bedroom.

The man lying in the hospital bed appeared to be suffering from a seizure. When Dr. Montemayor pulled back the sheet to begin his examination, he was appalled at the body underneath, a long skeleton clad in wrinkled, wasted flesh. The sick man was tall, over six feet, but he weighed less than a hundred pounds. A tumor gaped open on the left side of his scalp. His forearms were splotchy with black, blue, and yellow marks. His left shoulder was bruised and swollen. Bedsores covered his back. Needle tracks ran up and down both arms and thighs. What Dr. Montemayor could not see was that enough codeine circulated inside the body to kill an ordinary man.

As he took the man's blood pressure, felt his pulse, and listened to his heart, Dr. Montemayor could not understand why this patient was not in a hospital. Money could not be the reason. This was the most expensive suite in the most expensive hotel in Acapulco, yet this man was starving, dying of neglect like a beggar. The seizure, Montemayor soon diagnosed, was caused in part by the failure of the brain to receive enough blood—a condition made worse because the patient's head was raised. After making his tests, Dr. Montemayor concluded that the man was suffering from severe dehydration and should be given oxygen and intravenous fluids immediately.[18]

Dr. Montemayor looked up from the bed and asked the two doctors why the man was not in a hospital. They answered that he was a very difficult patient who did not like hospitals. Looking down at the helpless, unconscious wreck before him, Dr. Montemayor was puzzled by the explanation.

"This man should be in a good hospital," Montemayor told Chaffin. "As a friend, I'm telling you, don't stay here in Mexico to find a hospital. Take him back to the States."[19] Packing his bag to leave, Montemayor took one last look at the old man on the bed, concluding that although seriously ill, the man need not die if he were taken immediately to a hospital and given proper care.[20]

In the office next to the bedroom, word came in—Los Angeles had decided. Hughes was to be taken to a hospital. Several locations had been considered: Salt Lake City, Miami, the Bahamas, even London. In the end, they had settled on Houston. The plane bringing Dr. Thain to Mexico was to carry Hughes back to the city of his birth, and the city he had avoided since the deaths of his parents fifty years before. One of the men in the office telephoned the Manzanaris Funeral Parlor in Acapulco and ordered an ambulance.

It was after 7 A.M. that Monday morning before Dr. Thain finally arrived. Instead of going immediately to see Hughes, Real said Dr. Thain moved into the office next to the bedroom and began rummaging through the filing cabinets, pulling out papers that had flowed between Acapulco and Los Angeles, feeding them into a shredder.[21] To Jack Real, it seemed that Thain spent two hours destroying documents before he went in to examine Hughes.[22] Then he wrote a prescription and asked one of the men to have it filled. When the medicine arrived a few minutes later, Thain used it to give Hughes several injections.[23] As he was giving him the shots, he mentioned to the others in the bedroom that sometimes it took a while for the medicine to produce a reaction. As the minutes ticked by, Hughes showed no change. He lay in a trancelike state, oblivious to everything around him, breathing with great difficulty.

At 10:30, the men began preparing to take him to the plane. The hotel security chief was alerted to make the service elevator available and to clear the ground floor near the elevator doors of onlookers. An aide left for the airport to make sure the airplane was in the proper location and ready. Another went in search of carts sturdy enough to handle the oxygen tanks and other medical equipment.

At 11 A.M. they lifted Hughes out of bed, placed him on a stretcher, and carried him down the hall to the elevator, which took them straight to the lobby. The doors opened and they quickly carried him through a cordoned-off section and out the rear door into the parking lot. The ambulance driver leaped out to help load the old man and the equipment into the rear.

At the airport, far from the terminals bustling with tourists, a small white jet sat parked. The men got out of the car and lifted Hughes from the ambulance, carrying him up the steps of the plane. As they took Hughes aboard, his lips moved slightly. The oxygen tanks came next, but in the small cabin there was scant room for the cylinders; several minutes elapsed before the oxygen system was operating again. Dr. Thain, Dr. Chaffin, and Holmes went aboard, the door closed behind them, and the plane taxied into position at the end of the runway. At 11:30, the control tower gave clearance for takeoff and the jet moved smoothly forward.

It rose sharply over the face of the Sierra Madre del Sur, the rugged coastal range that defines Mexico's southern coast, before passing the crest and leveling off. The pilot set a northeasterly course for Houston. The day was bright and clear, with good visibility and moderate winds. Below were Mexico's jagged peaks, lush forests and valleys, and sun-bleached villages white against the green hills. It was a perfect day for flying, the kind of day when Howard Hughes had loved to be at the controls.

In the cabin, the old man's pulse and heart grew weaker. His life signs were barely detectable. An hour out of Acapulco, where the foothills of the Sierra gave way to the flat, desertlike terrain of northern Mexico, Hughes's breathing became more erratic. His chest rose and fell in forced gasps under the bright yellow blanket pulled up to his bearded chin. Then, at 1:27 P.M., his heart stopped. Behind the plane, glistening in the afternoon sun, was the wide, brown swirl of the Rio Grande. Howard Hughes had finally come home to Texas.

CHAPTER 1

THE EARLY YEARS

THE FAMILY

ALL his life, Howard Hughes stood in awe of his father, the tall, handsome, flamboyant man who endowed him with a flair for the dramatic, a love of things mechanical, and one of the great industrial creations of the twentieth century. Springing from Hughes Sr.'s labor, ingenuity, and vision, the Hughes Tool Company was an achievement that shadowed Howard's own career, even as the world sang his praises. In the eyes of the world he had more than matched his father's stride, but in his own mind he never did. Perhaps, then, the best place to begin the story of Howard Hughes is with his remarkable paternal forebears.

The Hughes clan traced their origins in the New World to the very beginning of colonial America, when Jesse Hughes, of English-Welsh ancestry, settled in Powhatan County, Virginia, a few years after Jamestown was founded in 1607. They were a big-boned people with large ears and long, gangly limbs, often afflicted with hearing impairments, crippling arthritis, and irascible temperaments.[1] As America moved west, so did they—first to Kentucky, then to Illinois, and finally, in 1853, to northeast Missouri.

The federal government had given Howard Hughes's great-grandfather, Joshua W. Hughes, forty acres in Scotland County, Missouri, for his services in fighting Indians in Illinois. On this rolling, but "none too prosperous" piece of land, Joshua built a simple log house and settled down to raise a family.[2] Felix, his oldest son, who was Howard Hughes's grandfather, was expected to farm, but showing a determination that would guide him through life, he opted for another course—teaching school—and thus the family ties to the land were broken.

After serving in the Union Army during the Civil War, Felix returned to

Scotland County to "read law," and later to practice it, in nearby Lancaster, Missouri, population five hundred. He soon married Jean Amelia Summerlin, who, like Felix, had been raised on a Scotland County farm. Their marriage would last sixty-one years, but it was not without its tempestuous moments. Felix was a Yankee, but Jean held an "unconquerable loyalty to the South," owing to her Virginia ancestry.[3] She was in fact ashamed to have been born in Iowa, a hopelessly northern state. They were opposites in other ways too. Felix was practical, down-to-earth. Jean was dreamy, romantic, and eccentric, a girl who composed long novels in her head, who climbed on summer days into a big cherry tree on her parents' farm and, "sitting among the branches, would think out elaborate chapters in an endless romance."[4]

While Felix poured out his energies building a successful law practice, Jean lavished all her attention on their four children. Rural Missouri was not an environment conducive to a classical education, but Jean nevertheless raised her children "with artistic ideals and passions."[5] Mimi, as they called her, taught them "the names of Greek sculptors and Italian renaissance painters from infancy."[6] She also implanted in them a drive to excel. "My mother instilled the ambitions," Rupert, her third-born, wrote later. "My father found the funds."[7]

Felix "found the funds" by being Lancaster's superintendent of schools, by trying both civil and criminal cases, and by gradually building himself into a pillar of the small town. By 1880, his adroit legal work on behalf of powerful railroad syndicates in Missouri earned him the presidency of the Keokuk & Western Railway, and the family moved seventy-five miles east to Keokuk, Iowa, then a thriving little city of fifteen thousand. Well on his way to becoming a moderately wealthy man and a respected civic leader (he would eventually be elected Keokuk's mayor and a judge), Felix could now provide even more money for Mimi to educate their precocious children.

She sent them to the best tutors and schools. Greta, the oldest child, born in 1867, was determined to be an opera star, and she was sent to Chicago, then New York, and finally to Paris for the finest training. Rupert, born in 1872, dubbed "History" because of his scholarly face, wrote his first poem when he was seven, and after taking degrees at Adelbert College in Cleveland and at Yale, set forth on a writing career that made him internationally famous as an author of popular novels. Felix Jr., the youngest, born in 1874 and also musically inclined, was soon packed off to Europe to study.

Only Howard, the second of the four children, born in 1869, remained, seemingly a misfit, unable to find his niche. It was not that he lacked talent. He had, in fact, a "marked genius" for taking apart intricate mechanisms.[8] He spent hours tinkering with watches, clocks, and engines of every sort "to see what made them go."[9] But for all his native mechanical ability, he seemed unable to channel energy constructively. Instead, he was restless and sometimes worse. He charged candy at the corner store, then failed to pay for it. Although he had been forbidden to do so by his father, he staged a cockfight behind the family home, then slapped his brother when Rupert tattled on him to their father. By the time he was a youth, Howard Hughes Sr. had earned an "unsavory reputation" in Keokuk.[10]

Nevertheless, the family stood by him—especially his mother. Jean Hughes had nothing but pride for her tall, handsome son. She blamed his troubles on others: "Howard was never expelled from a school that was worthy of him."[11] As he approached college age, he temporarily buckled down and was accepted by Harvard College for the fall term of 1893. Felix Hughes had long hoped that his oldest son would follow him into law, and Harvard was a logical first step. But Howard botched that opportunity as well, dropping out after a year to return to Iowa. To soften this blow to the family, Howard enrolled in the law school of Iowa State University, but again the tedious demands of education proved unendurable. "Too impatient to await the course of graduation," he immediately took the Iowa bar examination, passed it, and joined his father's law firm without completing his studies.[12]

No sooner had Howard Hughes Sr. occupied a desk in his father's downtown Keokuk law office than his spirit rebelled again. He quickly found the law "too-exacting a mistress."[13] Whatever Felix's hopes had once been, he now realized that Howard was not cut out for the profession. By mutual agreement, Howard quit the practice and, apparently to his father's relief, quit Keokuk as well sometime in 1895.

If Howard Hughes Sr. had a clear notion of what he intended to do with his life when he left home, it is not evident in the story of the next few years. His life followed the pattern of his adolescence. Abounding in nervous energy, he flitted from one hotbed of mining activity to the next—low-grade silver mining in the Colorado mountains, zinc mining in the wilds of Indian Territory (now Oklahoma), and lead mining in rural southwestern Missouri— seeking his fortune "under the surface of the earth."[14] He did not find it, but his wanderings were not a loss. "If I accomplished nothing more," he wrote later, "I at least learned something of the art of drilling wells with cable tools."[15] It was a knowledge he would put to fabulous use.

In each place, Hughes Sr. plunged into the thick of mining, discarding his good clothes for the greasy uniform of a field worker, rubbing shoulders with the roughest, most hardened men of his time. Hughes saw himself as much an explorer as a fortune hunter. Robert E. Peary and men like him were finding the few undiscovered lands on the earth's surface. For Hughes Sr., the new frontier lay not beyond the horizon but below it. The outermost ends of the world were being rapidly explored, but "the road towards the center is still Virgin soil."[16]

While mining for lead near Joplin, Missouri, in January 1901, Hughes got word of a great discovery in Texas. On January 10, 1901, Captain Anthony Francis Lucas, a mining engineer, drilled into the Texas prairie near Beaumont and struck oil. With a mighty roar, it gushed forth in a 150-foot arc over the surrounding plain. For nine days the well ran wild before Lucas could cap it. Spindletop, as it was called, was the greatest oil well of its time, and dramatic evidence of the incredible wealth that lay buried in the Texas soil. Thousands of men, moved by the vision of the Lucas gusher, streamed into East Texas. Hughes Sr. later wrote about his reaction when he learned of the Spindletop discovery:

I heard the roar in Joplin and made for the seat of disturbance. Beaumont in those days was no place for a divinity student. The reek of oil was everywhere. It filled the air, it painted the houses, it choked the lungs and stained men's souls. Such another excitement will not be seen for a generation. It will take that length of time to get together an equal number of fools and "come-on's" at one spot. I turned greaser and sank into the thick of it. Rough neck, owner, disowner, promoter, capitalist and "mark" —with each I can claim kin, for I have stood in the steps of each.[17]

From Spindletop, Hughes followed the crowd from one strike to another, learning the ins and outs of the young industry and applying the rudimentary knowledge of drilling he had picked up in mining ore to tap oil reservoirs. Although he was for once sticking to a line of work, his fortunes fluctuated as wildly as ever. "One year he had fifty thousand in the bank," Rupert wrote later. "The next he owed the bank fifty thousand."[18] He survived these reversals mostly because of his "uncanny gift for extracting money from my father for his wildest schemes."[19] And Hughes might have gone on wandering aimlessly from one oil field to the next had he not met Allene Stone Gano.

Hughes was hardly an attractive marriage prospect. He had no steady income. His future was uncertain. His past was marked by chronic instability. He was thirty-four years old and no closer to success in the oil business than the day he had abandoned law nine years before. But he did have his fine points. He was well-dressed, charming, and educated—qualities in short supply in turn-of-the-century Texas. Allene Gano found him appealing. The daughter of a prominent Dallas judge, she had been raised in a cultured, refined atmosphere. Whatever else he might be, Howard Hughes Sr. was a gentleman.

Like the Hugheses, the Ganos went back a long way in America. But they had a somewhat more illustrious past. The first Ganos were French Huguenots who settled in New York in the seventeenth century after fleeing religious persecution in France. In the Revolutionary War, the Reverend John Gano was chaplain of the Continental Army, and was said to have converted George Washington to the Baptist faith. Howard Hughes's great-grandfather on his mother's side was General Richard Montgomery Gano, a dashing soldier who gave up a medical practice for the nomadic, grueling life of a Confederate cavalry officer in the Civil War. He fought in more than seventy battles, was said to have won all but four, had five horses shot from beneath him, and was wounded only once. After the war he settled in Dallas, where he raised thoroughbred horses, preached the gospel, and surveyed uncharted regions of Texas. The general rolled several careers into one, as an entry in his daily journal attests: "Today I surveyed 16 sections and saved 16 souls."[20] Before his death, the general was credited with "saving" sixteen thousand fellow Texans.

General Gano's son William Beriah Gano—the maternal grandfather of Howard Hughes Jr.—was a graduate of Harvard Law School. He rose quickly in Dallas's legal fraternity from practicing attorney to judge. (Howard Hughes Jr., who would spend so much of his later life defying court orders, thus had judges as grandfathers on both sides of the family.) W.B.—he disliked the name Beriah and preferred to go by his initials—married Jeanette de Lafayette Grissim, a doctor's daughter and also a descendant of an old Huguenot family. Nettie, as an early Dallas social directory described her, was a graduate of Wellesley College and of the Musical Conservatory of Cincinnati, a student of "belles-lettres," and a "musician of marked ability."[21] Like the Hughes household in Keokuk, the Gano home in Dallas was filled with music and literature.

Allene, born in 1883, was the oldest of four children. Tall, well-formed, and dark-haired like all the Ganos, she was a quiet, soft-spoken, and refined young woman. A relative who remembered her years later said Allene "looked and acted like a queen."[22] She was calm and not easily ruffled except when a cat came into the same room with her. She had an intense fear of the animals and was known to faint when one came near.[23] Not much is known of Howard Hughes Sr.'s courtship with Allene Gano except that it was apparently short. On May 24, 1904, the couple were married at the bride's home on Master Street in Dallas. They made a handsome pair: Allene, tall and graceful, with a beautifully formed face set off by high cheekbones against rich, dark-brown hair; Hughes, straight-backed, proud, slender, slightly ascetic-looking, with a long angular face and deep brown eyes. They left immediately after the marriage on a long tour of Europe. That Hughes did not have the money to spare for such an extravagant wedding present did not stop him. It was typical of the flamboyant gestures by which Howard Hughes's father lived his life.

Months later, after traveling through England, France, and Germany, the couple settled in Houston, where Hughes could be near the "oil game."[24] Once a sleepy, semitropical southern community, Houston was being transformed by the oil rush. It was not so much a city as an overgrown town. Old, sprawling southern homes dozed alongside new Victorian mansions with ornate turrets and circular rooms. Office buildings rose up six or more stories next door to stucco hovels of another century. The streets were still mostly dirt; only a few were paved with crushed shell, asphalt, or limestone slabs, which glistened like marble in the rain. On Buffalo Bayou, the city's serpentine link to the sea, the lonely horns of oceanbound steamers sounded all day long and far into the night.

In the city's center, on a hill above the bayou, rose the two Romanesque towers of City Hall. Anchored firmly in Market Square, the massive brick-and-stone edifice was Houston's marvel. Punctuated by the two richly ornamented towers and capped by an imposing clock whose bell tolled devotedly every half hour, City Hall was something to behold: soaring arches, delicately sculptured figures, exquisitely inlaid tiles, and resplendent public rooms. Outside in the dusty square, life went forward on a more primitive level. Vendors hawked fresh vegetables, fruits, and rabbits from the backs of mule-drawn carts. People strolled by displays of fresh partridge, sandhill crane, and snipe, tied neatly in bundles at the neck. Saloons never closed, and around the corner from City Hall an ounce of cocaine was as easily bought as a glass of beer or a woman.

By the hour, or so it seemed, passenger trains streamed into Houston. Smoke billowed from beneath the immense wooden shed at Grand Central Station, where trains from all points ground to a halt and discharged their thousands of weary riders into the humid Gulf Coast air. Officially, Houston had sixty thousand people in 1905. But it seemed like more.

The lure was oil. After Spindletop in 1901, there were other great finds in East Texas, some on the outskirts of Houston itself. The region was becoming the oil capital of the nation. No early-day H. L. Hunt had emerged as the archetypal Texas oilman, but men such as William Stamps Farish, a small-town Mississippi lawyer, had come to Texas after Spindletop and parlayed a modest stake into a fortune drilling for oil. Petroleum companies with names like the Lucky Strike Oil Company and Slow Poke Oil Company came into being overnight. As more and more oil flowed from the ground, surged through pipelines to Houston, and emptied into steamers bound for ports around the world, money gushed into Houston itself.

When Allene and Howard Hughes Sr. settled down in 1905, they lived at 1404 Crawford Street, a few blocks east of what is today downtown Houston. The house has long since disappeared, as have most of the other dwellings in the near eastside neighborhood. It was a modest area of frame houses bordering both sides of a crude lane, in keeping with the family's means at the time. Here Howard Robard Hughes, Jr., was born on Christmas Eve of 1905. The birth was so difficult for Allene that although she was only twenty-two years old and in good health, the attending physician, Dr. Oscar L. Norsworthy, advised her not to have any more children.[25]

Howard Hughes came into the world as mysteriously as he left it. No birth certificate has survived. Dr. Norsworthy was one of the city's most respected doctors and presumably would have completed and filed it with authorities. Nevertheless, there is no trace of Hughes's birth certificate at either the Houston Board of Health or the Texas Division of Vital Statistics in Austin. Thirty-six years later, at the outbreak of the Second World War, this would present a problem for Hughes when he had to authenticate his age. In the absence of a document, an aunt, Annette Gano Lummis, and Estelle Sharp, the mother of one of Hughes's childhood friends, signed an affidavit attesting to where and when he was born. To this day, it is the only official record of his birth.

Howard would have no memory of the little house where he was born. His early life was transient and unsettled as his father followed the oil rush from one strike to the next. Sometimes Howard and his mother would go along on these expeditions, but most of the time the conditions in the field were too rough for a young mother and child, and they stayed behind in Houston. When Howard was about eighteen months old, the family moved to northern Louisiana, then a new hotbed for oil exploration. They settled temporarily in a little town called Oil City, twenty-five miles north of Shreveport. From this grimy petroleum outpost, Hughes Sr. traveled out into the adjoining fields to wildcat

Allene Gano Hughes with Howard,
about 1910.
Liberty Library Corporation

for oil. Back in town, he doubled as postmaster and deputy sheriff of Oil City
to help make ends meet.

THE ROCK EATER

By the time Hughes Sr. moved to Louisiana, he had a partner, Walter Bedford
Sharp, a brilliant oilman of slight build and tireless energy who was one of the
most respected oil operators in Texas. Although he disliked partners and was
usually too independent-minded to work with anyone, Hughes's decision to
team up with Sharp was one of the smartest moves he ever made. Sharp had
an uncanny nose for oil, and was already on his way to riches. He was also
knowledgeable about oil-field technology and, like Hughes, was interested in
improving drilling methods. He had patented a process for injecting com-
pressed air into deficient oil wells to make them flow artificially.

Even with Sharp as a partner, Hughes made no spectacular breakthrough
as an oilman in Louisiana. He continued to earn a respectable living as a
wildcatter, but there were no significant finds. Nevertheless, the Louisiana
interlude changed his life. As he and Sharp drilled for oil, they became increasingly frustrated over their inability to penetrate thick rock formations and
hard, sandy soil that perhaps shielded vast oil deposits. The most popular drill
in those days—the fishtail drill, so named for its shape—was maddeningly
inadequate. It bore smoothly through dirt, mud, and soft sand, but when its
cutting edges encountered rock or hard sand, progress became painfully slow.
Oilmen were forced to use cable drills literally to hammer their way through
hard formations. When the process worked at all, it took days or weeks.

By 1908, Sharp and Hughes were spending more and more time on attempts to come up with a drill that could bore through solid rock. Before the year was out they had done it. Known as the Hughes rock bit, it would have a sweeping effect on the development of the oil industry and would make Hughes, and later his son, Howard Jr., incredibly wealthy. The story of how the bit was designed and came into use is, like so many aspects of the Hughes legacy, shrouded in mystery. The Hughes Tool Company and the members of the Hughes family have insisted that the drill was solely the product of Howard Robard Hughes, Sr.'s inventive mind. The widow of Walter Sharp—who died a few years after the drill was invented—contended that her husband helped develop it. The full story will probably never be known, but one of its missing chapters may be found in the obscure memoir of a little-known oil-industry pioneer.

The man, Granville A. Humason, an adventurous young millwright who left Mississippi in 1908 to seek work in the northern Louisiana oil fields, met Hughes Sr. one night in a Shreveport bar and showed him a model of a crudely fashioned drill bit made of wooden spools. Its main features were two cone-shaped cutters that continued to rotate when they touched a surface. Humason had gotten the idea for it one morning while grinding coffee and he had tried to sell it to several oil-well drillers. No one would listen. Hughes, however, listened closely and decided to buy Humason's spools on the spot, offering $150, which Humason accepted. Delighted at finally having sold his idea, Humason celebrated by spending $50 on drinks for the "oil boys" who were

Howard Robard Hughes, Sr.,
about 1910.
Texas State Archives

crowded into the saloon. He then left with Hughes to visit Walter Sharp at the nearby Phoenix Hotel. Hughes showed his partner the spools he had just purchased and told him, "Sharp, give me fifteen hundred dollars. I'll give you a half interest."[26]

"What," exclaimed Sharp, puzzled, "[in] those spools?" Hughes pulled his partner aside for a few minutes of private conversation and afterward Sharp handed over $1,500 to Hughes. Leaving $500 with his wife, Hughes "jumped on the train" to go to Washington, where he planned to have the drill patented.[27] Actually, Hughes jumped on the train to Keokuk, turning, as he often did when he needed financial help, to his father, who hired a leading St. Louis patent lawyer, Paul Bakewell, to file the necessary papers with the patent office in Washington. Hughes Sr. apparently made the final drawings for the drill in the family home in Keokuk. Rupert Hughes later wrote that his brother had "called for a breadboard from the kitchen, fastened paper on it, and, sitting at a dining room table, began to sketch his model. He emerged from the family dining room with an Archimedean cry of 'Eureka' and the picture of a bit that had no less than 166 cutting edges!"[28] To go along with the design, Hughes Sr. wrote a lengthy technical description of the bit. On November 20, 1908, Bakewell filed Hughes's application for two patents covering the drill with the U.S. Patent Office. Calling his invention a "new and useful Improvement in Drills," Hughes listed himself as the sole inventor.[29]

While waiting for Washington to act, Hughes took his drawings to a machine shop and had a prototype of his drill manufactured. In June of 1909, he and Sharp brought the newly cast steel bit by horse-drawn wagon to an oil field at Goose Creek, Texas. Stopping at an oil well that had defied conventional drills, they ordered field hands away from the site, secretly brought the drill bit out from under wraps, and attached it to the pipe stem of a conventional rotary drilling rig. For the next eleven hours, the drill bore through fourteen feet of solid rock, a feat so miraculous for the time that drillers dubbed the mysterious device the "rock eater."[30] The success of the field test made Hughes all the more eager to secure his patents. When a delay developed in the application, a Washington lawyer was hired to shepherd the request through the Patent Office bureaucracy. On August 10, 1909, the Patent Office granted Hughes patents 930,758 and 930,759 on his rock bit. The foundation of the Hughes fortune had been laid.*

---

*Exactly what role, if any, Humason's spools may have played in the final design of the rock bit which Hughes patented is impossible to determine today. For many years, inventors had experimented with rolling cutter bits and had secured patents. Hughes Sr. was no doubt familiar with their work. In fact, the Patent Office, in reviewing Hughes's application, rejected many of his claims as "nothing patentable" over features found in other drills. Nevertheless, the Hughes rock bit, while in part a synthesis of current ideas, also had its unique features and became, in the words of an authoritative history of oil-well drilling by J. E. Brantly, "one of the great inventions and developments of the entire oil well drilling industry." Although others had designed similar drills, Hughes's rock bit proved to be far superior. Through what Brantly called

In 1909, when Howard was three years old, the family moved back to Houston. With the patents secured, Hughes Sr. and Sharp went into business, leasing the rock bit to other oilmen. They formed the Sharp–Hughes Tool Company, a partnership, and rented a corner of the Houston Car Wheel & Machine Company as the tool company's first shop. For all practical purposes, the job of managing the fledgling company and promoting the rock bit was left to Hughes. Although he and Sharp were equal partners, Sharp continued to concentrate on exploring for oil. It was a wise division of duties. Sharp had few peers as an oilman and Hughes Sr. was an exceptional salesman. In the beginning the response to the drill was not especially enthusiastic. But in time that would change.

Until now, the Hugheses had lived near the stagnant, mosquito-infested waters of the Houston bayous, which often became a health hazard in the summer. Now it was time to move to the south side, a burgeoning mecca for the city's rich and powerful. Although they were not yet rich, or even well-off, Allene and Howard Hughes were very much a part of Houston's elite. They were members of Christ Church Cathedral, the city's leading Episcopal church and the most prestigious congregation in the city. They belonged to the Houston Country Club. And when young Howard was old enough to go to school, they enrolled him at Prosso's Academy, a private school then "catering to the upper crust."[31]

At Prosso's, Howard was an average student. Like his father, he had little interest in school. But Howard's case was complicated by another handicap. He was quiet and shy, a boy who did not make friends easily. Consequently, he spent a great deal of time alone. Instead of concentrating on his schoolwork, Howard preferred to tinker with mechanical gadgets, taking them apart and reassembling them. He even built a makeshift radio sending set, lifting most of the working parts from the family doorbell. Years later, Hughes would recall that one of the "greatest thrills" of his life was when his homemade radio set actually worked.[32]

Howard's father was pleased by his son's budding interest in electronics and mechanics. It mirrored his own interests. Hughes Sr. hoped that Howard would one day become an engineer. He helped his son build a motorbike, one of the first in Houston, rigging a small gasoline engine to a conventional bicycle. Although the machine could not have gone very fast, Howard's motorized bicycle delighted him and struck terror into the hearts of neighboring parents, who had never seen such a contraption and feared for their children. Hughes Sr. also set up a worktable at the tool company's plant, where Howard passed the time learning about machines and working with tools.

The neighborhood where Howard grew up abounded in children his own

---

an "ingenious mounting of the cone cutters," the drill had revolutionary power and thrust, and could shear smoothly through solid rock without grinding itself up in the process. Over the years, the Hughes rock bit has been refined and improved, but its main features have remained unchanged from 1909 to the present.

age, but he had only one friend—Dudley C. Sharp, the son of his father's partner. In many ways the two boys were opposites. Howard was thin and sickly looking; Dudley was well-built, robust, the picture of health. Howard was shy, quiet, and withdrawn; Dudley was outgoing, talkative, and made friends easily. Yet, the two became fast friends. Howard was envious of Dudley's ability to make friends, and Dudley admired the determination that enabled Howard, when motivated, to undertake a project and stick to it. Both of them started taking saxophone lessons at about the same time. Dudley, convinced that he would never be very good at the instrument, quickly lost interest. But Howard, determined to master the instrument at all costs, practiced and practiced, and in doing so "drove his family almost insane with his tootlings."[33]

With each year, the family grew more prosperous. The Sharp–Hughes Tool Company, now a major supplier of drill bits to the oil industry, had its own two-story building at Second and Girard Streets, where the precious bits were packaged and shipped out to oilmen around the world. Largely because of Hughes Sr.'s promotional efforts, the rock bit was gaining wide acceptance in the oil fields. Hughes was also determined to stay abreast of the drilling industry's needs. He set up a galvanized metal shed next to the plant where he and his engineers devised and tested new drills. A stickler for detail, Hughes had rock shipped from all parts of the country to be used in the tests. When a new bit was considered satisfactory, he immediately applied for a patent. Hughes also bought up patents on other rock bits, some predating his own, and filed lawsuits to frighten off competitors who tried to introduce drills that he felt in any way infringed on his patents. Less than five years after the tool company was founded, Hughes had not only made an impressive start on sewing up the American drilling market but had also patented his rock bit in at least thirteen foreign countries. In doing so, he was laying the groundwork that would one day give the company a near worldwide monopoly in supplying drill bits to the oil industry.

On November 28, 1912, Walter Sharp, long plagued by ill health, died at the age of forty-two. He left his half interest in the tool company to his wife, Estelle. Early in 1913 the growing company was formally incorporated. The Sharp–Hughes name was retained, and capital stock of $300,000 was issued, evenly divided between Hughes Sr. and Sharp's heirs. Estelle Sharp and Allene Hughes were the best of friends and constant companions, but Estelle and her business managers soon became alarmed over the way Hughes Sr. was running the company. "He was spending money faster than the tool company could make it," Dudley Sharp contended.[34] Although he was obviously a gifted promoter, Hughes was not much of a manager, and Estelle feared that he might one day bankrupt the company. Hughes thought nothing, for instance, of renting an entire wing of a hotel to throw a lavish party for a prospective customer. He often shipped his big cabin cruiser, *Rollerbit*, to California by rail when he wanted to entertain West Coast oilmen. When Hughes's spending sprees put the company in the red, it fell to Estelle to make up the deficits,[35]

The original cone bit
that launched the Hughes
fortune.
Wide World Photos

The Sharp–Hughes Tool
Company in Houston,
about 1910. *United
Press International*

and two years later, she sold her interest for $65,000 to Ed Prather, an oilman and friend of both Hughes Sr. and Walter Sharp. On February 3, 1915, the name of the company was changed to the Hughes Tool Company, but as it turned out, Prather had no more success in controlling Hughes Sr. than Estelle Sharp, and within three years he would sell out too. This time there was no new partner. Hughes bought out Prather, gaining 100 percent control.

MOTHER

Young Howard, or Sonny, as he was called to distinguish him from his father, grew up under the eye of his mother. Since his father traveled much of the time, to California, to New York, to Louisiana—wherever necessary to promote his rock bit—the task of raising Howard fell to Allene, who made it a full-time job. His mother, in fact, smothered Howard Jr. with care. She forced him to take mineral oil nightly. She watched for the slightest change in his physical condition. If she detected any abnormality in his feet, teeth, digestion, or bowels, she whisked him off to a doctor for an examination. During outbreaks of infectious diseases, the two of them often left Houston for some distant, uncontaminated place.

Relatives who saw Howard and Allene Hughes together felt the boy "idolized" his mother. "Howard and his mother were very close," said Mrs. Martha Potts, a cousin. "Howard didn't treat his mother the way all of us treated our mothers. When we wanted to hug our mothers, we would just rush up into their arms. Howard was more formal." Mrs. Potts remembered one time in particular when she and several of her cousins from Dallas were visiting Howard and his mother in Houston. "Allene drove us down to Galveston to see the houses and the sea. We drove back to Houston. We all just started to scatter to our rooms when Howard came up to his mother and said, 'Thank you, mother, for so much fun today.' It made the rest of us feel impolite, like country bumpkins. Howard was so well-behaved, patient, and attentive."[36]

When Howard was about ten, he was officially welcomed into the society for which his mother had so conscientiously been preparing him by being crowned "king" of the Christ Church Cathedral May Fete, an annual spring rite staged for the children of the elite congregation. A photograph of Howard and his "court" has survived. About a dozen children are seated cross-legged, in flowing white togas. Twenty more are standing behind them similarly garbed, peering intently into the camera. At the top, taller than the others, a pointed paper crown resting to one side of his head, is Howard, surveying his court, tight-lipped and aloof.[37]

Howard did not spend a night away from his mother until he was ten years old. In the summer of 1916, his parents sent him away to camp. A neighbor, Lewis Thompson, had recommended a boys' camp in the Pocono Mountains of northeastern Pennsylvania. Camp Teedyuskung was operated by Daniel Carter Beard, one of the founders in 1910 of the Boy Scouts of America.

At Dan Beard's Outdoor School, youthful campers, or "Buckskin Men," as they were called, were schooled in outdoor living and nature. Mostly from affluent eastern families, the boys learned to live in tents, to make fires without matches, to flip flapjacks in a skillet over an open fire, and to identify local flora and fauna. The regimen was broken by pleasant boat rides on Lake Teedyuskung at dusk or by overnight hikes into the lush Pennsylvania woods. Allene Hughes felt that the camp would be an ideal place to help Howard build up his fragile health. On June 14, 1916, she wrote Beard:

My dear Mr. Beard:

I have received your catalogue and letter of May 29th and we have heard much of your camp from Mr. Thompson and his boys. Mr. Hughes and I feel that the life at your camp and your personal influence will be of great benefit to Howard and [we] are enclosing his application for entrance this summer. There are a few questions we want to ask and will very much appreciate your answering by wire. Do you take boys as young as Howard? How many boys near his age will you probably have in camp? What will your total enrollment be? This will be Howard's first experience away from his family and we think it desirable to place him in a rather small camp for this year at least.[38]

Beard's reply was satisfactory to Allene Hughes, and she made plans to take Howard to New York in late June, where they would meet Hughes Sr., who was in the city on business. From there, Allene planned to escort her son the eighty miles northwest to Beard's camp. On June 23, 1916, Hughes Sr., at the Vanderbilt Hotel on Park Avenue, sent a brief note to Beard:

My dear Sir:

Enclosed please find Boy Scouts Measurement Blank filled in with my dear boy's dimensions. I trust you will be able to get his suit without serious delay and that Howard will outgrow the shirt during the eight weeks. When Mrs. Hughes arrives in New York we will communicate with you at once and obtain final directions. Please advise me at once your camp telephone number.[39]

On June 28, Howard and his mother arrived at the camp, and Howard was assigned to his own "stockade." Allene Hughes looked over the grounds and was given a briefing by Beard and his assistants on what her son would be doing for the next eight weeks during his stay, then returned to New York. A few days later, Hughes Sr. wrote Beard:

My dear Mr. Beard:

I am taking the liberty of enclosing several newspaper clippings showing the rapid spread of infantile paralysis in Brooklyn and elsewhere.

Mrs. Hughes has told me one of your boys is in a hospital in Brooklyn having his throat treated who is soon to return to your camp where our boy is.

I thought these clippings might be of interest as the clippings show how easily the violent germs are carried even by a well person.[40]

On July 11, to reassure Howard's parents that their son would not be exposed to any harmful germs, Beard wrote the couple at the Vanderbilt that the boy referred to in their letter would be placed in "quarantine" as soon as he returned to camp and "will not be allowed to enter his own tent until the doctor thinks it safe for him to do so." Beard went on to give the parents a report on Howard. "Your boy seems to be holding his own here in camp. He is an interesting little chap, full of fun and well liked. Please tell his mother that the last time I saw him he did not look a bit like he was going to cry. His mouth was open and he was yelling, but he was yelling to the rest of the stockade to hurry up, and get a move on. In fact he has shown no signs of homesickness at all and seems very happy."[41]

A month later, Beard sent along to Howard's parents various reports he was receiving from the camp doctor and wildlife instructors on their son's progress. "So that you may have a clear understanding," Beard wrote, "I am giving you the reports just as they come into me. Such reports to me are always more harsh than when written for the fond parent's eyes.

"Doctor's report: —Physical condition, bowels, feet, O.K. General appearance, better than when he first entered camp. Heart, much better now. First Aid Mark A.

"Instructor's report: —He cannot stick to one thing very long, but is doing fairly well in scoutcraft and never gives us any trouble. In birds his effort and deportment is [sic] good. In his other studies he is trying hard, but is easily discouraged. Needs someone to show him how and then make him do it."[42]

Back in New York, Allene Hughes was finding it hard to be separated from her son. At the beginning of the summer she had been worried about how Howard would get along without her. All the reports indicated he was doing fine, but Allene was nevertheless filled with anxiety. She and Hughes Sr. had hoped to pick up Howard about mid-August, but Hughes was running behind schedule in New York. This gave her the option of leaving Howard at the camp for a few more days. Before making a decision, she wanted to see her son. On August 9, 1916, the day she received Beard's latest report on Howard, Allene sat down at her desk at the Vanderbilt and wrote a reply in her elegant, flowing handwriting. Thanking Beard for giving them a "frank report" on Howard's classwork rather than one "written to please," she quickly moved on to the subject that was troubling her:

We had expected to go to Shawnee, Pa. this week and after two weeks there come over to camp for Howard but Mr. Hughes has again been delayed and doesn't know just when he can leave so we are delighted that there may be an opportunity for Howard to stay longer with you. Before deciding definitely however I would very much like to talk to him. Do you think it could be safely arranged, in any way, so that I could see him for a few minutes? I would not come to camp of course. Please wire me what you think about it and I will come up at once and return the same day. His letters are so short and unsatisfactory that I feel I must talk to him if it is possible before I can decide about leaving him longer.[43]

Whether Howard's mother carried off her secret rendezvous with her son is not known, but less than two weeks later she abruptly took him out

Daniel Carter Beard, "Chief"
of Camp Teedyuskung.
Boy Scouts of America

of the camp anyway. The reason for the sudden move was a polio scare in the East. On August 21, 1916, she wrote Beard from the Buckwood Inn at Shawnee-on-Delaware, in Pennsylvania, about thirty miles from the camp:

"We will come up for Howard the latter part of the week and I think I will take him straight to Cleveland. Mr. Hughes' brother has a big place at Euclid Heights and I think Howard would be safer there than anywhere around here. I am afraid of the trip on the train but it seems to me less risky than trying to go in a car and stopping at various hotels. I wanted to ask you to [get] from the doctor the proper health certificates if possible so I won't have any trouble on the train."[44]

On August 26, Allene picked up Howard at the camp and left immediately for Cleveland and the home of Hughes Sr.'s youngest brother Felix. Then a teacher of light opera, Felix and his musically talented wife Adella lived in a spacious home in the city's exclusive Cleveland Heights section. Howard's aunt was busily engaged in efforts that would lead to the formation of the Cleveland Orchestra. Allene and Howard stayed there until she felt the polio scare had passed.

Howard had enjoyed his short stay at camp and looked forward to returning. On November 27, 1916, "Chief" Beard wrote Howard that Teddy Roosevelt himself was expected to visit the camp the next season and urged Howard to bring a friend with him. On December 29, 1916, five days after his eleventh birthday, Howard wrote back.

Dear Chief,

I was glad to get your letter, and I hope that I can come to your camp next year, and bring my friend Dudley Sharp. I have joined the Y.M.C.A. and like it very much.

Enclosed please find my Buckskin Badge. I have returned it on account of eating some candy.

> With love from,
> Howard

> P.S. I hope that you and Mrs. Beard and Bartlett and Barbara have a Happy New Year.[45]

As much as Howard wanted to return to the Pennsylvania woods the next summer, for a while it seemed unlikely. On April 22, 1917, he and his mother wrote individual letters and sent them off together to Beard.

"I don't think that I will be able to come up to camp this summer although I would like it very much," Howard wrote the Chief. "We have just bought a boat and I think that we will stay here all summer except about one or two months. I hope that the camp is as nice this summer as it was last summer."[46]

Allene Hughes explained that the family planned to stay "close at home" this summer.[47] But soon afterward Howard fell sick. He lost seven or eight pounds, had problems with his digestion, and missed school. His mother began to feel that the crisp mountain air of northeastern Pennsylvania might be the tonic needed to restore her son's health. On June 19, 1917, Howard wrote Beard: "I may be able to come up to camp after all. Mother has thought it over and she says that if Daddy thinks it is all right I can surely come. If I come I will bring my friend Dudley also but we will not be able to come up until the 10th of July. We will want to be put in Luitenant Oris's [*sic*]* stockade. We will also want to room together, and what about that stockade you promised me? Answer soon."[48]

Eager for a summer in the wild, Howard and Dudley arrived at the camp on Monday afternoon, July 16, 1917. In a letter that followed the next day, Allene Hughes asked Chief Beard to pay special attention to Howard's health: "I hope the doctor will keep an eye on him, watching his feet and teeth, and see that he takes his Russian oil every night. I put a large bottle of it in his suitcase, but I am sure he was tempted to throw it out of the car window and he may have done it." She asked Beard to make sure that neither Howard nor Dudley took a long hike right away, which might tax their resistance, or to eat any of the camp's "precious" flapjacks.[49]

Howard's mother also wrote directly to his stockade leader, Lieutenant Aures:

*Lieutenant Aures was a stockade leader at Dan Beard's Outdoor School.

I am afraid that you may not have realized when you promised to take Howard under your wing and into your stockade that your promise entailed writing me every now and then to let me know just how he is getting along. I am trying hard to overcome too much anxiety over my one chick but don't seem to make much headway. As I wrote Chief, he has not been at all well this spring and ever since he left camp last year he has been having trouble with the soles of his feet. Please if you notice any of his shoes getting run over *throw* them away. I started him off with two pairs of doctored up old shoes which may be too small to wear with scout stockings but might be alright with his ordinary hose. I have ordered two larger pairs which I will send as soon as the heels are fixed according to the doctor's directions.

I am afraid you will find him pretty nervous this year. He was so much improved in that respect by last year's camp that I hoped he was outgrowing it and his supersensitiveness but it seems to have all come back this spring since he has not been so well. That is one reason I was particularly glad for you to have him in your stockade. I think you understand him well enough to help him over the many times he gets his feelings hurt. . . . If you can help Howard to take the teasing without getting hurt and resentful we will surely be lastingly in your debt. Dudley makes friends so much more easily than Howard does and Howard feels that keenly too. . . . If you can help him to forget himself, get along better with boys and perhaps teach him to keep his hut in order, I ask for nothing else.[50]

Howard was glad to be back in the familiar rustic surroundings of Chief Beard's camp, but the summer was not as pleasant for him as the year before. The United States' entry into the First World War had deprived Beard of some of his more experienced instructors, and the men who took their place were not all of the same caliber. Also, a small group of older bullies at the camp made life uncomfortable for some of the young woodcrafters like Howard. A few days after his arrival at camp, Howard spoke to his mother by phone and complained of "bad dreams," of "not sleeping well," and of "feeling tired all the time."[51] Allene Hughes asked the camp office to have the doctor examine Howard immediately. On July 27, Beard cabled a brief medical report to her in Houston: "Doctor reports eyes, ears, nose, throat, lungs, heart OK. Digestion all right. No restrictions. Letter follows."[52]

Despite all of Allene's fears for her son's health, she was delighted with the way he looked when he returned to Houston later that summer. "He is in better condition, I think, than he has ever been," she wrote Beard. "His cheeks are round and fat and rosy and he is full of 'pep.' We think you are largely responsible for this and hope he can be with you next summer."[53]

A few days after Howard returned from camp, Houston was convulsed by a race riot. On the night of August 23, 1917, a contingent of black soldiers who were part of a national guard unit camped outside the city rioted over the way Houston police had earlier manhandled a black fellow soldier. Arming themselves with revolvers and rifles, the soldiers marched toward downtown Houston, indiscriminately shooting whites who tried to stop them. Before police could halt their advance and take them into custody, seventeen persons had been killed. Thirteen black soldiers later were executed.

The riot made an indelible impression on Howard. Although he lived miles away from the scene of the killings, he later wrote that he had been "right in the middle" of the riot.[54] Gruesome stories spread through Houston's white community about atrocities allegedly committed by black soldiers. Howard was caught up in the anti-Negro frenzy sweeping the town, instilling in him a lifelong bias against blacks. Fifty years later he cited the 1917 riot as the reason his Las Vegas casinos should never give in to pressure from blacks for more jobs.

Early in 1918, the family moved into a new house in Houston. The year before, Hughes Sr. had bought a corner lot at 3921 Yoakum Boulevard, in the exclusive Montrose section north of Rice Institute, and began building an imposing two-story brick house. Despite Hughes Sr.'s extravagant business practices, the tool company was returning ever-greater profits. The house Hughes built was in keeping with his growing stature as one of the city's leading businessmen.

Howard's room was on the second floor, facing north. There he assembled his shortwave radio equipment and, using his call number, 5CY, spent hours flashing messages to amateur operators all over the country and to ships at sea. With fellow radio enthusiasts, he formed the Radio Relay League, a local organization of young amateurs like himself. Since Howard had the latest equipment, the boys usually met in his room.

Despite that interest, the winter and spring of 1918, when he was twelve, was an unhappy time for Howard. He was sick and spent a good deal of time confined to his bedroom. When he got back to school, he found himself hopelessly behind the rest of the class and was forced to spend all his time trying to catch up. His illness served to alienate him further from education. As the summer months approached, Chief Beard began writing Howard, urging him to sign up for camp that year. Although Howard still had an uneasy feeling about the camp because of the way he had been bullied by older boys the summer before, he thought about going back, and when he found out that Dudley had already signed up, he made up his mind. On May 4, 1918, Allene Hughes sent his application and a note along to Chief Beard, with the inevitable concerns:

"As the time approaches he always wants to go back tho' I don't think he was very happy while there last year. We are very glad that he does want to go back because there is no doubt of the benefit that he receives. I wish you would write me more of the camp as it is to be this summer." Allene asked Beard if he intended to appoint Howard a stockade leader this summer. "Please don't think from this question that I want him to be one unless in your judgment he should be. I surely want to know so that I can save his being disappointed when he gets to camp by telling him before he goes. Last year he thought because he was a second year boy and a buckskin that he would surely be a stockade leader and it was a bitter blow when he found out that he wasn't."[55]

On May 9, Beard replied that all the unruly pupils and faculty had been "eliminated" from the camp and that Howard would undoubtedly have a more enjoyable time this year. Beard said he had always intended to appoint Howard a stockade leader, but he could not guarantee him the position before the summer session began: "I do not like to make a positive promise because many things may arise to upset my plans," Beard wrote. "I may have more leaders than stockades. However, rest assured we will do all in our power to make Howard happy, and I think the main thing to do is to make him healthy."[56] Howard made plans to go, even to setting a date for his arrival, but for some reason the trip was cancelled at the last minute. He never returned to Dan Beard's Outdoor School.

During Howard's childhood, Allene Hughes exerted an overpowering influence on his development. She was obsessed with her son's physical and emotional condition. If she was not worried about his digestion, feet, teeth, bowels, color, cheeks, weight, or proximity to others with contagious diseases, she was anxious about what she called his "supersensitiveness," nervousness, and inability to make friends with other boys. If Howard had no inherent anxieties in those directions as a small boy, he certainly had them by the time he reached adolescence. His mother helped instill in him lifelong phobias about his physical and mental state. Howard also learned from her that the best way to attract attention or to escape unpleasant situations was to complain of illness. The slightest whimper from him would unleash a wave of smothering attention from Allene Hughes, and throughout his life he would pretend to be sick when he wanted to avoid responsibility or elicit sympathy.

TRAGEDY

Even though Howard was no longer going to camp, Allene Hughes still arranged for him to get away from Houston during the summer when danger from disease was at a height. Sometimes the two of them went to resorts like the Greenbrier, in White Sulfur Springs, West Virginia, where Howard could play golf, one of his new interests. Other times he went alone to visit his grandparents in Keokuk. Hughes Sr. had built his mother, Jean, a handsome white frame "summer" home on a bluff high above the Mississippi. In the evening, one could gaze out across the great river from the screened-in back porch and bask in the solitude of the midwestern night. But the visits were not always happy for Howard. His grandparents' differences had hardened with time. They quarrelled more than ever. Felix was nearly deaf, and Jean had developed a phobia about bugs, refusing to allow closets to be built in her new home for fear insects would nest in them. At night, she dined regularly on a spartan meal of buttermilk and cornbread. Occasionally a neighbor child, like pert Mary Hollingsworth, five years older than Howard, was conscripted to take him to a movie. But much of the time he was alone with his cantankerous grandparents.

One spring day in 1919, when Howard was thirteen, he suddenly could not walk. His panic-stricken parents feared that he had contracted polio. Houston doctors confirmed that his illness had all the signs of infantile paralysis and Howard was confined to a wheelchair. Hughes Sr. frantically telephoned the Rockefeller Institute for Medical Research in New York and pleaded with the director, Dr. Simon Flexner, a pioneer in polio and meningitis research, to come to Houston. Dr. Flexner sent an associate, Dr. H. T. Chickering. After examining Howard, Dr. Chickering was not certain of the cause of the boy's illness, but was confident that he would recover. Dr. Chickering attended Howard for two weeks in Houston, then spent four more weeks with him and his mother on Mackinac Island in Michigan. Finally, after more than two months in a wheelchair, Howard was able to walk again. By summer he had begun to "pick up," as his father wrote later, "and become a perfectly normal boy."[57] The cause of the illness remained a mystery.

That fall, Howard enrolled in South End Junior High School (now San Jacinto High) in Houston and continued his lackluster academic ways, to the discomfort of his father. Although he had been the bane of many a teacher himself, Hughes Sr. now firmly believed in education. In spite of his son's mediocre showing, he was determined to send him to the best schools. While he himself had found Harvard stifling, Hughes Sr. hoped to send Howard there. To prepare for that, he enrolled his son in the exclusive Fessenden School, in West Newton, Massachusetts. In the fall of 1920, when he was fourteen, Howard boarded the train for Boston.

At Fessenden, Howard was thrown in with the sons of other wealthy parents who were counting on the school to polish their boys into suitable Ivy League material. Founded in 1903, Fessenden was situated on a rolling, lush tract in the midst of one of Boston's oldest suburbs. Every facility from a sports arena to a library could be found on the grounds. There was even a nine-hole golf course.

For the first time in his life, Howard studied hard. The following June, he was cited for "outstanding industry and attention to studies."[58] According to the school, Howard's academic records have long since been destroyed, but Percy Williams, briefly a roommate, recalled that Howard was a "hard worker" who achieved good marks.[59] "He was a good mathematician," said Williams, "and he was fairly good in languages, French comes to mind."[60] Howard also amused some of his classmates with a scheme that enabled him to pick up spare change, even though his parents kept him plentifully supplied with cash. Frequently receiving shipments of fresh grapefruit from Texas, Howard took what he needed for himself and sold the rest to his classmates at a nickel apiece.

Howard still remained shy and withdrawn at Fessenden. "He didn't get involved in too many social things," Williams said.[61] The school sponsored joint dances with girls' schools in the area, but "I don't recall him coming to those dances."[62] Even so, Howard tended to stand out. He was growing into an exceptionally tall, handsome young man. Williams remembered him as the tallest boy in their class of thirty. Despite his shyness, he usually sat near the front of his classes, probably an early indication of hearing difficulty. Hughes insisted years later that his hearing had been damaged in a childhood swimming accident. A more logical explanation is that he was suffering from the same hearing defect that had plagued the Hughes family for generations. His father, both his uncles, and his grandfather on his father's side were all hard of hearing. His Uncle Rupert, in fact, had been denied overseas service in the First World War in part because of growing deafness.

While Howard's grades at Fessenden were good compared to his past marks, he excelled at only one thing—golf. In fact, he was becoming a fanatic about the game. There was not as much time to play in Boston as there had been in Houston, but Howard spent every possible minute on Fessenden's course. In the spring he entered a school tournament, losing the championship by only one stroke.

During the year, Hughes Sr. dropped by the school and took Howard to the Harvard–Yale boat races in New London, Connecticut. As a loyal Harvard man, he was rooting, of course, for the Crimson and promised Howard that he could have anything he wanted if Harvard won. When Harvard did win, Howard told his father he wanted to take a ride in an airplane. On the way into New London he had seen a Curtiss seaplane tied up to a bulkhead in the Thames River advertising rides for five dollars a head. Hughes Sr. was not

Class of 1921, Fessenden School, West Newton, Massachusetts. Hughes is fourth from right, third row. *Wide World Photos*

happy at the idea of his only son thus risking his neck, but Howard was insistent. His father gave in and paid the ten dollars, and the two of them went up for a brief flight, which, though uneventful, was a turning point in Howard Hughes's life. Those few minutes in the Curtiss seaplane fired his fascination with airplanes and marked the beginning of a lifelong love affair with aviation, his most enduring passion.

In June of 1921, Howard was graduated from Fessenden's sixth form, a level roughly equivalent to eighth grade in public school. The class prophet wrote: "Howard Hughes has a large ranch in Texas where he raises toothless cows. The advantage of those animals over any others is beyond the human mind with Hughes' excepted."[63] The class historian summed up Fessenden's ambivalent attitude toward the young man: "Howard Robard Hughes comes from just where you would expect: Texas. But we are not sure just where he will go."[64] As the boys prepared to go home for the summer, Percy Williams asked Howard to sign his yearbook. In one column where Hughes was to list his ambition, he wrote, "yegg," then a popular slang term meaning criminal or thug. In another column entitled Happy Thoughts, Howard wrote in French, *"Il n'y a pas"*—none.[65]

Instead of sending Howard on to one of the well-known eastern prep schools, Hughes decided to enroll his son in the Thacher School in Ojai, California, near Santa Barbara. The family was spending more time in Los Angeles—Hughes had opened a branch of the tool company there to serve California oilmen, who had embraced the rock bit with even more enthusiasm than their counterparts in Texas—and Howard's parents wanted him in a school nearby so they could be with him more often.

But getting Howard admitted to Thacher was no simple matter. The school was small and in the summer of 1921 when Hughes tried to enroll his son for the fall, he found out that Thacher was already full. Hughes personally appealed to Sherman Day Thacher, the school's founder and president, saying he was deeply discouraged, but had not given up hope that his son might indeed be admitted. "My own life has been a constant uphill fight," he wrote Thacher, "and I never like to give up once I start to accomplish any definite thing. Right now, this is one of the deepest regrets [I] have had to face."[66]

To induce Thacher to make a place for his son, Hughes offered to build an addition to the school's dormitory. Whether the school accepted is not clear, but Hughes's persistence paid off: Howard was admitted to Thacher that fall.

With an enrollment of only sixty students, Thacher was smaller and more intimate than Fessenden, but this had no effect on Howard's shy behavior. Once he played a detective in a school play, walking around the stage whispering to other characters his true identity, then imploring them to keep the information a secret. But mostly he shunned group activities. He bought a horse and rode for hours alone in the hills near the school. As usual, his mother worried about him.

On October 19, 1921, less than two months after Howard had entered the school, Allene Hughes wrote Sherman Thacher inquiring about her son. She told the headmaster that Howard seemed to like Thacher, but rarely mentioned any other boys. "I think it is awfully hard," she wrote, "for an only child to adjust himself well in school and make friends as he should, and I am very interested to hear from you about him."[67]

During the spring semester, Allene Hughes entered Baptist Hospital in Houston for minor surgery. The operation was a curettement, usually performed to remove growths or abnormal tissues from the uterus or to stop excessive hemorrhaging, although in her case the exact reason for the surgery was not disclosed. She went into the hospital the afternoon of March 29, 1922, planning to return home a few hours later. Instead, she never regained consciousness from the anesthetic. At thirty-nine, Allene Hughes was dead. Her death devastated Howard's father. In his despair, he sent off two telegrams— one to Howard in Ojai and the other to his brother Rupert, who was living in Los Angeles where he was writing screenplays for Sam Goldwyn. Rupert later wrote:

I received one night a heartbroken telegram from my brother, saying that Allene, his wife, had died suddenly. He had telegraphed young Howard at Ojai, telling him merely that his mother was ill and he had better come home. My brother asked me to meet the boy when he came down from Ojai and put him on the first train for Texas.

Young Howard, then just sixteen, arrived in great anxiety and suspense. I hesitated a long while over telling him the bitter truth. My poor brother, I knew, had suffered so much in the death of his beloved and beautiful wife that telling his son the news would be too much to put upon him. So I steeled myself, told young Howard the truth, and tried to uphold him in his first great tragedy.[68]

However much anguish and pain his mother's death caused him, Howard never discussed it. Grief, like so many facets of his personality, was a very private matter for him. It was not so with his father. Howard Hughes Sr. was permanently shaken by the premature death of his wife. He used any excuse to stay away from Houston. The city that had given rise to his growing fortune and had been the scene of many warm memories now became too painful to endure, and he spent his time traveling to New York, Los Angeles, wherever a convenient excuse led him. On his rare trips to Houston, he could not bear even to set foot in the family home on Yoakum Boulevard.[69]

To look after Howard, he turned to Annette Gano, a younger sister of Allene, who had lived in the Yoakum house since 1919 and was already a full-fledged member of the family. Tall, dark, and outgoing, Annette had been graduated from Wellesley College, then enlisted in the Red Cross in the First World War and sailed to Europe to serve coffee and doughnuts to Allied troops on the Western Front. After the war, she had become active in civic and charitable work in Houston. At the time Allene died, the thirty-one-year-old Annette was on the verge of marrying a prominent Houston physician. Hughes begged her not to get married, but instead to devote her life to raising Howard. Hughes was "possessed," as Annette recalled, by the notion that she should bring up his son. "I told him that I would give him one year and live with Sonny," she said later. "Then I was going to get married. I thought it was not good to have Sonny live with a little old lady."[70]

Soon after Allene's death, Hughes Sr., Howard, and Annette left Houston for the West Coast "to get away from Yoakum."[71] Howard and Annette settled in a cottage at the Vista del Arroyo, a hotel in Pasadena, while Hughes stayed most of the time at the Ambassador Hotel in Los Angeles. Howard returned to Thacher that fall, but his stay was even shorter than that of the year before. Early in 1923, shortly after Howard turned seventeen, Hughes informed Sherman Thacher that he was taking his son out of the school. After saying that he thought Howard needed special tutoring, Hughes disclosed the real reason for the move. In a candid, moving admission, Hughes explained that he was desperately lonely and had been unable to get a grip on himself since his wife's death. Perhaps with Howard with him in Los Angeles, he told Thacher, he could cure his loneliness and fill the emptiness in his life.[72] Although sympathetic to Hughes, Thacher gently urged him to leave Howard in school until the end of the year:

[Howard] needs more than most boys the contact with other fellows such as he gets in school; and I think your desire and tendency to indulge him in every way would probably be very hard for him to resist and probably not at all good for him. I feel quite sure that the fact is that it is not the best thing for a boy to be held in constant sympathetic association with those of an older generation, even his own father and mother. Nature seems to insist on a certain kind of separation between the generations, and the child seems to develop abnormally and not quite wholesomely if we attempt to vary this order of nature. We have to be content with rather slender associations and intimacies and ready to look on at a respectful distance while the young people work out their own problems and carry on their development among their own contemporaries.[73]

Thacher told Hughes he did not believe his son needed special tutoring:

I think he needs to be treated like any other boy and to learn more about how to carry himself among other fellows, and I think he himself really feels conscious of this although I believe he is full of sympathy for you and most desirous of contributing in every way that he can to your contentment during these hard days.[74]

All of this had a serious effect on Howard. Whether he was torn between wanting to stay at Thacher or go to his father is not clear. In any event, he became ill with a headache and cold, and spent several days in bed. Thacher wrote Hughes on January 17 that his son had been sick, but was recovering.

A few days later, Howard went to Los Angeles to visit his father and never returned to Thacher. Now that the issue was settled, Sherman Thacher wrote Howard: "I have every confidence that you are making the right decision in staying with your father, and I hope that you will get every kind of advantage out of your life in Pasadena and the intimacy with him which I know will give him great satisfaction and be a very great comfort to him at the same time."[75]

Even though he had taken his son out of high school prematurely, Hughes still had high hopes that Howard would be able to go to college. No sooner was Howard back at the Vista del Arroyo with Annette than he worked out an arrangement for Howard to attend classes at the California Institute of Technology in Pasadena. Howard's lack of a high school diploma did not deter his father. In return for letting Howard attend classes at Cal Tech, Hughes Sr. made a contribution of an undisclosed amount to the school's scholarship fund. As Annette bluntly put it later, "they were bribed to let him in."[76] Even though Cal Tech agreed to allow Howard to attend, it apparently did not go so far as to give him credit for the courses he took. The school has no formal record of Hughes's attendance. The only indication that he even went there is a brief note in the school's files that a Cal Tech upperclassman tutored Howard in solid geometry in 1923.

Annette's feelings toward Howard would cool over the years, but in 1923, while he was going to Cal Tech and she was looking after him at the Vista del Arroyo, she saw him as a model nephew: "He was perfectly beautiful, and he was a charming young boy, and that year I was with him in California he couldn't have been more thoughtful. We ate dinner together every night."[77]

Howard and his father often spent Sundays at the home of Hughes Sr.'s brother Rupert, who lived in a gabled, Gothic mansion on South Western Avenue. Hughes Sr. was fascinated by the new motion-picture industry and was eager to produce films himself. It was an interest no doubt sparked by Rupert, who, after a highly successful career in New York, including a stint as an editor of the *Encyclopaedia Britannica* and as a writer of dozens of bestselling popular novels, had been lured west by Sam Goldwyn to turn his most popular tales into wildly successful silent movies. Since his arrival in Hollywood in 1919, Rupert had taken the budding film capital by storm, and by the early 1920s he was one of the town's most talked-about celebrities, earning upward of $125,000 a year.

Rupert's Hollywood Sunday brunches were an institution. Famous actresses, actors, and directors met and mingled on the grounds to eat, drink, and talk about motion pictures. Hughes Sr. was a regular participant and he usually brought Howard along. At one party, Howard met Eleanor Boardman, who was starring in *Souls for Sale,* a movie being directed by Rupert. Howard was immediately infatuated with the twenty-three-year-old hazel-eyed actress, but the feeling was not mutual. Eleanor found Howard "very unattractive, very shy, hard of hearing, difficult."[78] Too shy to ask her for a date, Howard sought his father's help. As Miss Boardman later remembered, "he tried to sell me young Howard . . . by telling me he was going to be so rich."[79] For Miss Boardman, who would become one of the reigning queens of the silent screen and marry the director King Vidor, money was insufficient incentive.

In the summer of 1923, Annette Gano's year of solicitude to Howard ended and she went back to Houston to marry her fiancé, Dr. Frederick Rice Lummis, a member of the family that had founded Rice Institute. Although

Hughes Sr. still opposed the marriage, he promised to return to Houston to give Annette away. But on her wedding day he failed to appear. Shortly after Annette and her husband moved into their first apartment, Hughes Sr. asked her if she would move back to Yoakum. Howard, he explained, would be returning to Houston to attend classes at Rice. By some means, Hughes had managed to persuade the school to enroll his son as a freshman that fall, even though he still had no high school diploma. Annette talked it over with her husband and agreed. "My husband was a saint," she recalled. "[We] closed our apartment, packed everything up and moved to Yoakum so Sonny could go to Rice."[80]

Hughes Sr. continued to shun Houston. His absence had no effect on the tool company, for Hughes had little taste anyway for the day-to-day grind of managing a business, and over the years he had installed a competent group of managers to oversee the company. He had especially come to rely on the leadership of his general manager, R. C. Kuldell, a former army colonel whom he had recruited after the First World War. But even so, there were a few meetings too important to be missed, and in January of 1924 he made one of his rare visits to the city.

On the afternoon of January 14, while meeting with S. P. Brown, the tool company's sales manager, Hughes Sr. "suddenly rose to his feet, grasped at the desk before him convulsively, and fell to the floor."[81] At fifty-four, Howard Robard Hughes, Sr., was dead of a heart attack. For Howard, Jr., as Annette later recalled, the news was a "horrible blow."[82] His father's death was as unexpected and traumatic as his mother's had been less than two years earlier. One moment each had been alive and seemingly healthy; the next moment they were dead.

On January 16, at the funeral held in the Hughes house on Yoakum, the rich and powerful of Houston turned out to pay tribute to the man who had revolutionized the oil industry with the rock bit. They also paid homage to him as a friend. "There is no man in the oil industry who was more endeared, no matter what his station or rank," contended one oil journal.[83] That afternoon, with Dr. Peter Gray Sears of Christ Church Cathedral presiding, Hughes Sr. was buried next to his wife at Glenwood Cemetery. For eighteen-year-old Howard, it was a time of great loneliness, sorrow, and grief. It was also the end of his boyhood.

The premature death of both parents had a profound psychological effect on Howard. Raised to believe in his own delicate nature and in the grave danger of being exposed to germs, he became obsessed about his health, and feared that he too was destined for an early death. The slightest change in his physical condition or the mildest illness now threw him into a panic. He began to take pills and resort to all sorts of precautions to insulate himself from disease and illness. It was an obsession that would grow with time.

POWER PLAY

At the time of his father's death, Howard did not have the slightest notion of what to do in life. His parents had always planned his every move. His father had enrolled him in the best schools with hopes that he would become an engineer. Howard despised school and was at best lukewarm to the idea of becoming an engineer, but he was an obedient, acquiescent son who did what he was told. Hughes Sr. had hardly been a stern taskmaster, but Howard revered his father and wanted to please him. Insecure about his own drives and ambitions, he had gone along with his father's goals. One searches his youth in vain for a trace of the individualism and rock-hard independence that would govern him as a man and make him a cult hero to millions. As a youth, Howard was nothing more than a jumble of possibilities, none of them very promising.

All that began to change with his father's death. Less than a month after Hughes Sr. died, Howard dropped out of Rice. College had been his father's idea, not his. In the months ahead, more signs of his growing independence appeared, sometimes to the despair of his relatives. Free of his father's overpowering personality, Howard began to think for himself. There was another reason for his new independence: his father's death had made him an extraordinarily rich and powerful young man.

Under the terms of Hughes Sr.'s will, Howard was the major beneficiary of the estate. The will, dated eleven years earlier, left half the estate to Howard's mother and one-fourth to Howard. (Since Allene Hughes had already died, her share passed automatically to her son.) The remaining one-fourth was divided equally among Howard's grandfather, grandmother, and Uncle Felix. Rupert, who was already earning a sizable income, was not included. Hughes Sr.'s sister Greta had died of tuberculosis in 1916. Shortly before Hughes Sr. died, he had drafted a revised will, which gave a higher percentage of the estate to his parents and brothers. But he never signed it. Had he done so, Howard's career might have been quite different; at least he would not have started it with a supply of money that seemed virtually endless.

True to his spendthrift ways to the end, Hughes Sr. left little cash. Most of the estate was represented by 1,500 shares of stock in the Hughes Tool Company. The value of the company stock was conservatively estimated at $750,000 for inheritance-tax purposes. The company, which was then returning yearly profits of several hundred thousand dollars, was in fact worth many times that amount. Overall, the estate was appraised at $861,518. Once Hughes Sr.'s debts had been paid, the net figure was reduced to $607,606.[84] Theoretically, Howard was worth three-fourths of that amount, or about $450,000. In fact, at eighteen years of age, he was a millionaire.

Shortly after the funeral, Howard left for Los Angeles to visit Rupert and his grandparents, who had been unable to attend the funeral because of their advanced ages. Felix Sr., at eighty-five, and Jean, now eighty-two, had left Keokuk the year before to escape the rugged midwestern winters. At the time of their son's death they were staying with Rupert in Los Angeles. Howard found the house, the scene of such lively gatherings in years gone by, shrouded in gloom.

The grandparents were overcome with grief. Jean Hughes, still erect and proud, wore black in memory of her dead son. If she had had a favorite child, it was Howard Sr. "I am so desolate," she wrote a friend after her son's death. "Life is so dark and cold. That precious Howard was my idol, more to me than all the world. But why try to tell you. For you must realize that all my heart was given to that precious child. My life is finished. Nothing left."[85]

Howard's stay with his relatives was a disaster, and a turning point in his relationship with his father's side of the family. Not long after Howard arrived, he and Rupert began to quarrel. At issue was Howard's future. Rupert felt obligated to take Howard under his wing and offer guidance. He suggested that he should be named Howard's guardian until he reached twenty-one. Howard viewed this as an attempt by Rupert to grab control of his inheritance. Rupert also thought Howard should go back to school and complete his studies, a view shared by the rest of the family. It was also one of Howard Sr.'s wishes, as spelled out in his will. But Howard had other ideas.

He told Rupert and his grandparents that he did not need a guardian, did not want to return to school, and instead wanted to take over his father's company. Coming from an eighteen-year-old boy, this must have sounded preposterous. Exactly what occurred next is not clear, but both sides clearly staked out positions, refusing to budge, and the visit degenerated into a series of ugly scenes. Within a few weeks, Howard returned to Houston "very bitter" toward Rupert, as Dudley Sharp recalled.[86]

In Houston, Howard received little support for his plans from his aunt, Annette. "I told him he ought to finish Rice and have a degree before he got too independent," she remembered. "He paid no attention to me."[87] Instead, Howard was now more than ever determined to free himself from any strings to his relatives, and he decided to buy out their minority interest in the tool company. As he explained later, "The thing I knew was that I would never be able to get along with my relations and that's why I was determined to buy them out and go it alone."[88] Howard told the officers of the tool company to open negotiations with his grandparents and uncle to acquire their 25 percent interest. They were not eager to sell, but in May of 1924, just four months after Howard Sr.'s death, they reluctantly agreed to do so. The purchase price was $325,000. To raise the cash, the tool company dipped into its own reserves— a move that left it dangerously close to insolvency for a year. But it was a risk Howard was willing to take to go it alone.

In doing so, he cut forever most of his family ties, leaving nothing but bitterness between himself and his father's relatives. Howard blamed all the trouble on Rupert, whom he believed had organized the other relatives against him. Jean Hughes, Howard's sensitive grandmother, suffered most from the breach and went to her grave bitter toward Howard. Her will, signed a few months before her death in 1928, left her estate to her two surviving sons,

Rupert Hughes,
Howard's uncle.
Pach Brothers

Rupert and Felix Jr. In Article 4, she singled out her only grandson for special notice: "I mention the name of my grandson, Howard R. Hughes Jr. to show that I have not forgotten him and that I purposely have not given him anything in this my Last Will and Testament."[89]

By buying out his relatives, Howard had consolidated his hold on the Hughes Tool Company less than six months after his father died. The only barrier between him and absolute control was his age—he was a minor and would not be truly his own man until he was twenty-one. But he soon saw a way to overcome that obstacle.

Howard had learned that under Texas law a minor can, at age nineteen, petition the courts to remove his disabilities as a minor and be declared an adult. That done, Howard could acquire virtually all the rights and privileges of an adult and assume full control of the tool company. He could hold the stock in his own name. He could oversee his financial affairs without the need of a court-appointed guardian, thus circumventing Rupert. Annette Lummis, with whom Howard was still living, did not like this idea any better than her nephew's earlier decision to drop out of college. But Howard, she said, was "just possessed to be declared an adult," and he went ahead with his plan over her objections.[90]

Howard could not actually file the legal application until December 24, 1924—his nineteenth birthday. In the meantime, he campaigned hard with Judge Walter Montieth to act favorably on the request when it reached his court. All through the fall, Howard was one of the judge's golfing partners at the Houston Country Club. Now an excellent golfer, Howard had done some homework about the tool company. "Walter Montieth said he couldn't ask him any question that Howard didn't know the answer," Annette remembered.[91] Although he had no intention of going back to college, Howard promised the judge that if he was declared an adult, the next fall he would go to Princeton University, where his friend Dudley was then enrolled, and finish his education.[92] All of this made a favorable impression on the judge and on December 24, when Howard's application was filed with the court, it was a foregone conclusion that Judge Montieth would act in his favor. Two days later he signed an order removing the young man's "disabilities of minority" and declaring him of "full age."[93] With that signature, Howard Hughes became master of his own future.

Even though Hughes now had full control of the tool company, he took no step to interfere in its day-to-day operations. Like his father, he had little interest in them, and, in Howard's case there was an added reason: he considered it his "father's monument"—to be preserved, protected, and left alone.[94] Thus he suppressed his instinct to meddle in a way he was never able to do again. For Hughes, there would be other worlds to conquer, although he still did not have a clear notion of what they would be. He experimented with a steam-powered car, talked to Annette about going west to produce motion pictures, and that spring began wooing a young woman named Ella Rice.

She was two years older than Hughes, dark-haired with soft features and an aristocratic air, and a sense of belonging among society people who made Hughes feel uncomfortable and out of place. The daughter of a wealthy businessman, Ella was a grand-niece of William Marsh Rice, the founder of Rice Institute. In Houston, there was no better name than Rice. Hughes had known Ella since childhood, when both had attended Christ Church Cathedral. As they grew up, their paths diverged. Howard was something of a flop with girls and not much interested in the city's social life. His wealth and dark good looks should have made him an appealing young man about town, but he had few dates, and when he did go out, to functions like the debutante balls, he often showed up alone. Ella, on the other hand, was the wheel around which young Houston society turned, forever surrounded by suitors and very much in demand.

Annette later recalled that Howard saw Ella at a social affair at Christ Church in which she was crowned queen and "apparently he was in love with her from then on."[95] As it had been earlier with Eleanor Boardman, the infatuation was one-sided, at least at first. Ella did not pay much attention to Hughes's overtures. As time went by they dated, and Hughes became all the more determined to win her hand. He wanted Ella to marry him and to come with him to California. But when he asked her to do so, she refused. For help, Hughes turned to his aunt Annette, who was related by marriage to Ella's parents:

[He] came to me and asked me to go and convince Aunt Mattie [Ella's mother] to let Ella marry him, and I was against it. . . . I didn't think he ought to. I thought he ought to go to Rice . . . but I went and asked her. . . . I convinced Aunt Mattie she ought to let Ella marry Howard. I said, "I can't send him with all that money to California with all those vampire movie people." And Aunt Mattie she agreed with me, and Ella and Howard were married.[96]

The wedding was scheduled for June 1, 1925. In the weeks leading up to the ceremony, Hughes did not throw himself into the traditional round of bachelor parties or merry prenuptial celebrations. Instead, he wrote his will:

I give . . . to my friend Dudley C. Sharp . . . the sum of Ten Thousand Dollars; to my uncle, Chilton Gano, Fifteen Thousand Dollars; to my aunt, Mrs. James P. Houstoun, Twenty-Five Thousand Dollars; to my aunt, Mrs. Fred R. Lummis, One Hundred

Ella Rice, Hughes's first wife, in 1938.
Bettmann Archive

Thousand Dollars and my home on Yoakum Boulevard; . . . to my wife, Ella Rice Hughes, the sum of Five Hundred Thousand Dollars in first class, high-grade securities, to be delivered to her by my Executors as soon after my death as can conveniently be arranged. . . . To Lily Adams and John Farrell (my colored household servants) . . . a weekly pension of Twenty Dollars each. . . .

To six executives of the tool company he bequeathed a percentage of the company's dividends: S. P. Brown, 1 percent; Matt Boehm, C. S. Johnson, and H. W. Fletcher, 2 percent each; Arch A. MacDonald, 3 percent; and R. C. Kuldell, 5 percent. Conspicuously absent from the last will and testament of nineteen-year-old Howard Hughes was any bequest or reference to his uncle Rupert, his uncle Felix, his grandparents, Felix and Jean Hughes, or any other relative on his father's side of the family. For the remaining assets of his estate, Hughes had special plans:

As soon after my death as practicable, my Executors shall cause to be created a corporation, to be known as HOWARD R. HUGHES MEDICAL RESEARCH LABORATO- RIES, the objects and purposes of which shall be the prosecution of scientific research for the discovery and development of antitoxins for the prevention, and specific reme- dies for the cure, of the most important and dangerous diseases to which this section of the country may be subjected. Said Laboratories shall be located in Harris County, Texas [Houston]. It shall not be a school for the education of doctors, nor of those desiring medical education, but shall be a LABORATORY devoted to the discovery and development of ways, means, antitoxins, and specifics for the prevention and curing of the most serious diseases with which this country may from time to time be afflicted, and shall be devoted to the search for and development of the highest scientific methods for the prevention and treatment of diseases.

The laboratories were to be headed by a three-man board of trustees— Frank Andrews, the tool company's lawyer; Dr. Fred Lummis, Annette's husband; and Frederick C. Proctor, a family friend. The same three were also to serve as executors of Hughes's estate. They would have the power to establish the laboratories, make bylaws, and oversee their operations. Hughes directed that as soon as the conditions of his estate would permit, the trustees should

acquire a proper site in the vicinity of the city of Houston and proceed with the construction of proper buildings for the scientific research herein provided for. I espe- cially direct that they shall construct and build the very finest and most highly scientific LABORATORIES for such research work that may be obtained, and that they shall employ, to the extent of the means available for that purpose, a few of the most noteworthy scientists and doctors available for the particular line of work. I do not desire a large number of scientific men employed, but I do desire the very best available for the particular subjects which my Trustees may from time to time have under investigation.

In the last part of the will, Hughes wrote a tribute to his father and a plea that his father's creation—the tool company—be preserved after his own death:

It is my will and desire that my Trustees shall continue the operation of Hughes Tool Company as far as practicable as now carried on. This institution was founded by my father and promoted through his genius and ability, to the success which it now enjoys, and it is my purpose and intention, so long as I shall live, to continue its development and progress, by following out the policies practiced by my father; and it is my will and desire that my Trustees, so far as practicable, shall continue the same course after my death, thus building to my father a permanent monument marking his initiative, judgment and foresight in the founding and upbuilding of a great business. My Executors and Trustees shall never pledge the stock of said company. They shall never sell the same so long as said company may be profitably operated; and it is my will and desire that they shall exhaust every means to see that its profitable operation is continued. If they fail in this, they may sell the physical properties, or sell the stock, as an entirety, and devote the proceeds of such sale to the objects and purposes expressed in this will in founding HOWARD R. HUGHES MEDICAL RESEARCH LABORATORIES.[97]

After working for weeks on the will with Frank Andrews, once his father's lawyer and now his, Hughes signed the ten-page document on May 30, 1925, two days before he was married.

The wedding took place at seven o'clock on the evening of June 1 in the rose garden of the home of Ella's sister, Libby Farish, at 10 Remington Lane in Shadyside, the luxurious walled enclave of the Houston aristocracy bordering Rice Institute. The *Houston Chronicle* called the wedding a "notable event of the year on the social calendar."[98] Little Martha Farish, Ella's niece, and five-year-old Janet Houstoun, who was the daughter of Hughes's other maternal aunt, Martha Houstoun, were flower girls. Dudley Sharp, just back from his freshman year at Princeton, was best man. As the women in their long white gowns and the men in their white linen suits sweltered in the humid evening, Dr. Peter Gray Sears of Christ Church solemnized the marriage of Ella Rice, twenty-one, and Howard Hughes Jr., nineteen.

In the short space of the year and a half since his father's death, young Howard Hughes had asserted himself in ways no one in the family could have foretold. The obedient boy had given way to an aggressive, rebellious young man. He had broken with his relatives, grabbed control of a fortune, and taken a wife at an age when most of his peers were completing their first year of college. Yet where was this flash of independence leading him? He was still not sure, but he had decided that his future lay beyond Houston, his father's town.

After a leisurely summer of playing golf, working on his steam-powered car, and taking his wife to Dallas to show her off to his Gano cousins, Hughes was ready to move on. He and Ella packed and took the train to California. By then, Hollywood had come to represent for spirited young men what Spindletop had meant a generation before: adventure, excitement, and wealth. Hughes had no need for money, but he did have a need to prove himself. Perhaps in the slightly unreal, but vibrant world of Hollywood he would find a way to do that.

CHAPTER 2

HOLLYWOOD

THE LEGEND BEGINS

"HOLLYWOOD," wrote one contemptuous critic in 1923, "is wherever the young and the ignorant expect to get the triumph without the toil, the reputation without the virtues, the fame without the achievement."[1] If the young Howard Hughes had left home intending to achieve instant recognition, he could not have selected a better place.

He and Ella took up residence late in 1925 at the Ambassador Hotel, the same luxurious manor where Hughes's father had stayed on visits to the Coast. The Ambassador was situated in its own tropical park far from downtown, only a short walk from the Cocoanut Grove nightclub and near the movie studios that attracted Hughes. He had vague ideas about producing movies. Hughes Sr. had run with the movie crowd, and after his death, Howard's only relief from the oppressive gloom at Uncle Rupert's had been occasional visits to the Goldwyn Studios in Culver City. In the shadow of the sets, amid the clutter of cameras and props, the shouts of actors and directors, and the general confusion of the place, Hughes watched in fascination as silent movies were made.

For his first film venture, Hughes teamed up with Ralph Graves, an actor whom Hughes Sr. had once placed on the tool company's payroll. Graves had acquired a story called *Swell Hogan* that he was convinced would make a great movie. Hughes invested about sixty thousand dollars and let Graves do the rest. The finished product was so bad it was never released.[2] For all its opportunity, Hollywood also had its pitfalls, and Hughes was pressured by his family, notably Rupert, to abandon movies lest he squander his inheritance. Their opposition made him all the more determined to succeed.

On his next try, Hughes was more fortunate. The director was Marshall Neilan, an old friend of Hughes Sr., and the film, a comedy called *Everybody's*

Acting, was not only well received by critics, but made a modest profit. California began to seem more permanent. Hughes and Ella moved out of the Ambassador and into a spacious Spanish-style house at 211 Muirfield Road in the Hancock Park section, where many of the movie people were settling down. The back of the house looked out across the fairways of the Wilshire Country Club, where Hughes played golf. The verdant landscape, thick with plants and trees, sheltered the house from the semitropical sun. First leasing the house, Hughes eventually bought it for $135,000. As further evidence of his desire to stay in California, he amended the charter of a tool-company subsidiary, the Caddo Rock Drill Bit Company of Louisiana, to allow it to make movies as well as lease drill bits. Caddo thus became the vehicle for all his early films. Offices were established in the Taft Building at Hollywood and Vine. To oversee Caddo's Hollywood operations, Hughes picked Noah Dietrich, a stocky, gruff-talking former accountant and semiprofessional racing car driver he had hired late in 1925. The son of a poor Wisconsin minister, Dietrich was sixteen years older than Hughes and had worked as a bank teller, auditor, and certified public accountant. Starting as Hughes's personal financial adviser on the West Coast, Dietrich gradually received more assignments of an administrative nature from his youthful employer and, a shrewd and ambitious man, he gladly accepted the new role. He was cut out for more than balancing Hughes's checkbook.

Notwithstanding the success of *Everybody's Acting,* nobody took Hughes seriously as a moviemaker except Hughes himself. To most, he was an amateur destined to be devoured by the charlatans and hucksters of Hollywood. Yet the twenty-one-year-old Texas millionaire continued to confound them. In the fall of 1926, he had another success. Lewis Milestone, an iron-willed and talented Russian-born director, had broken bitterly with Warner Brothers and refused to report for work. When the studio sued, seeking $200,000 in damages, Milestone moved to escape both his contract and the judgment by submitting to the claim and then filing for bankruptcy. Inevitably, "no other studio would hire him," and Milestone was preparing to go to Europe for work when he received a mysterious call from an intermediary of a wealthy producer who was looking for a director.[3] Milestone met with Neil S. McCarthy, a Los Angeles lawyer representing Hughes's interests in California, and was signed to a three-year contract by Caddo, a deal that eventually paid off for everyone. The film was *Two Arabian Knights,* a comedy set in the trenches of the Western Front about a feuding sergeant and a private "who play out their miniature war against a world-war background."[4] Costing five hundred thousand dollars, it was a grand departure from Hughes's earlier low-budget films and a spectacular box-office success in 1927–28. It made stars of the two leading men, Louis Wolheim and William Boyd, later more popular for his movie and television role as Hopalong Cassidy, and launched Milestone on a great career that included *All Quiet on the Western Front* and *Of Mice and Men.* For his work in directing *Two Arabian Knights,* Milestone won an Academy Award in 1928, the second year of the awards.

Beyond his role as financier, Hughes played little part in the award-winner, and the accolades properly fell on the cast and director. To Hollywood, Hughes was still a neophyte, "the sucker with the money," as Ben Hecht would later call him facetiously.[5] He only occasionally visited the set and even then, according to what is probably an apocryphal story by the film's leading lady, Mary Astor, he "couldn't understand where 'the fourth wall' was."[6] This was a gross misjudgment. Whatever others might think of his ability, Howard Hughes was quietly absorbing the technical side of filmmaking. In his next effort, he would step out of the shadows.

Never one to think small, Hughes had in mind nothing less than an epic, a movie that would celebrate on a grand scale the deeds and valor of First World War airmen. It was a subject close to his heart. Always fascinated by airplanes, he had learned to fly and by 1928 he was an expert pilot. Many an afternoon was spent making lazy circles over Southern California in his snug Waco, swooping low over Malibu Beach, reveling in the sense of freedom that only flying afforded him. Hughes had long admired the Royal Air Force aces and he wanted to portray their exploits on film. His director friend Marshall Neilan had supplied a fitting title—*Hell's Angels.*

Neilan agreed to direct. A team of scriptwriters was put to work on a story. Ben Lyon and James Hall were placed under contract to play the roles of two brothers who fall in love with the same girl, played by a statuesque Norwegian blonde, Greta Nissen. Neilan, however, soon had a falling-out with Hughes, who had strong opinions on how the movie should be shot. So Hughes borrowed director Luther Reed, an aviation enthusiast and former aviation editor of the *New York Herald Tribune,* who was under contract to Paramount. But Reed was no more able to get along with Hughes than Neilan had been. Irritated by constant interference, he resigned in disgust after only two months, telling Hughes: "If you know so much, why don't you direct it yourself?"[7]

Hughes did just that. On October 31, 1927, he began shooting the indoor scenes at Metropolitan Studio at Romaine Street and Cahuenga Avenue in Hollywood, and within two months had completed them. If the silent era had one great advantage for producers, it was that retakes were never required for flubbed lines. Hughes then moved into the phase of *Hell's Angels* he relished above all—filming the aerial sequences.

For these, Hughes assembled props and manpower on a scale that impressed even Hollywood. He wanted the aerial shots to be realistic, and the only way to achieve that was to use actual First World War fighter planes. For months, his scouts toured Europe rounding up relics from the war—Spads, SE-5s, Sopwith Camels, Fokkers. In all, he acquired or leased eighty-seven vintage planes, giving him command of the largest private air force in the world. He spent more than five hundred thousand dollars on aircraft. To fly them, he hired war aces like Roscoe Turner and daredevil stunt pilots. A ground crew of more than a hundred mechanics serviced the aircraft. In January 1928, the airplanes and men assembled at Mines Field in Inglewood, the site of present-day Los Angeles International Airport, to begin the aerial scenes.

As Hughes watched the classic planes soaring in the blue California sky, he could not resist the temptation to take one up himself. Against the advice of other pilots, he went for a "little hop" in a Thomas Morse scout plane, a ship he had never flown before.[8] Four hundred feet off the ground, he banked left and the rotary-powered Morse flipped into a "dangerous flat spin."[9] Pilots, stuntmen, and mechanics watched in horror as the airplane crashed to earth. The story was put out that Hughes crawled from the wreckage unhurt, "combing pieces of motor out of his hair."[10] Actually, Hughes was pulled unconscious from the crumpled plane, one cheekbone crushed. He spent days in hospitals and underwent facial surgery. But his face, at least according to Noah Dietrich, was never the same. Where the cheekbone had been "there was an indentation."[11] Even so, Hughes was luckier than some of his pilots. Three died in fiery accidents during the filming.

As Hughes's air force grew, he moved operations to a more spacious location in the San Fernando Valley and continued to shoot through the summer of 1928, sparing no expense. *Hell's Angels* served almost as a hiring hall for cameramen, who were forever running into fellow technicians on Hollywood Boulevard during a movieland depression and greeted with: "Are you out of work or are you on *Hell's Angels?*"[12] Dozens of them were kept busy shooting the same scenes over and over again to gain the realism he wanted. The sequence portraying London being bombed by a zeppelin was reshot more than a hundred times. Often this striving for effect bordered on recklessness. In one scene, a fighter plane was ordered to fly so low over stationary cameras that it actually hit one.[13] Nothing deterred Hughes. He wanted the aerial scenes shot against a backdrop of puffy white clouds, but Southern California had none to offer. Hughes waited in vain. Finally, he shifted operations to northern California, where the sky might prove more cooperative. On the eve of his departure for the San Francisco Bay area, Ella walked out on him.

It had never been a good marriage. Hughes was too much of a loner to share life with another person. Besides that, he had made a miserable existence for Ella in California. He spent all his time with movie people, but refused to allow her to socialize with them. "I don't think Howard thought they were her equal," Annette Lummis said later. "I think he tried to keep Ella where she belonged, in the Pasadena social group."[14] *Hell's Angels* was the final indignity. Making the movie was the first great obsession of Hughes's life. He had thrown himself into the production with a zeal that excluded all else, and it was not uncommon for him to work twenty-four to thirty-six hours at a stretch. He devoted himself to it with a ruthless determination that frightened even him. "Many times," he said later, "I thought I'd never live to see the finish."[15] With Hughes absent from Muirfield Road for days at a time, Ella felt completely shut out of his life. In October of 1928, she quietly went home to Houston for a trial separation.

Two weeks after she left, Hughes signed over his Yoakum Boulevard house in Houston to his aunt, Annette Lummis, who had been living there with her husband and growing family. Hughes did this after he learned that Annette and her husband were planning to build their own house. Even though he no longer used the place, Hughes was upset that it might be vacated, and he pleaded with Annette to stay, telling her he would give her the house and build a swimming pool in the yard if she would remain. Annette replied that she did not want a pool; she wanted more room. Hughes readily agreed to finance an addition. Faced with such an appealing offer, the Lummises abandoned the idea of moving.

It was a generous gift, but Hughes's act had more to do with his own sentimental feeling than with concern for Annette. Within a few months, when he rewrote his will, he excluded her and all his mother's relatives from his estate. Since he had cut his father's side out in 1925, this meant that Hughes had no plans to leave any of his fortune to relatives. Instead, he wanted the bulk of it to go to medical research. No copy of this second will has survived, but Ella, too, was undoubtedly excluded. After their separation, they headed for a final break. Later, in November of 1929, she filed for divorce in Houston, charging Hughes with "excesses and cruel treatment."[16] He did not contest, and the divorce was formally granted on December 9, 1929.

With Ella gone, Hughes pursued his true love, the concluding scenes of *Hell's Angels.* In Oakland, he found the clouds he wanted as a backdrop for an aerial dogfight, involving some forty airplanes, that would make the film a masterpiece of action cinema. Back in Los Angeles, there was one last scene to shoot. To viewers who later saw it on the screen, it was a brilliant stroke. A large German Gotha bomber, the terror of the Luftwaffe, is hit by Allied fire. The plane spins out of control, crashes, and burns, symbolizing the destruction of the Hun menace. Most viewers probably did not know as they watched the scene that a hapless mechanic had been trapped in the plane when it dived to earth.

As Hughes prepared to film the bomber scene, his pilots urged him to abandon his plan for the plane to actually spin. They thought it was too dangerous. But Hughes insisted. The plane had to spin. The movie required it. Despite the danger, one adventurous pilot, Al Wilson, volunteered to fly the mission. To produce the effect on screen of a burning plane, Hughes needed someone to lie in the fuselage near the plane's rear to work a series of smoke pots. He found his man in Phil Jones, an enthusiastic grease monkey who had been pestering Hughes for a year to let him fly. Both pilot and mechanic were fitted with parachutes and told to bail out when the plane went into the spin.

They took their positions in the Gotha (which was actually a Sikorsky disguised to resemble the German plane) and took off. With Hughes watching from aloft in a small plane, Wilson kicked the bomber into a spin at five thousand feet and bailed out. For some reason, Jones either missed the signal or was unable to get out of the plane. The bomber screamed to earth and crashed in a plowed field. Hughes made an emergency landing near the wreck,

Above: Plotting an aerial sequence for *Hell's Angels* with Harry Perry, chief camera-man.   *The Museum of Modern Art/Film Stills Archives*

Below: On a Hollywood set about 1930.   *Philadelphia Inquirer*

"his propeller casting clouds of weed tops, and rushed to the burning plane to get Jones out."[17] The mechanic was already dead. Wilson's pilot's license was temporarily revoked by the Department of Commerce, and the Professional Pilots' Association demanded his resignation. Hughes had a scene for *Hell's Angels* that no one would ever forget.

It was 1929. The movie was now nearly finished and, suddenly, quite obsolete. In October of 1927, Al Jolson had startled the world when he brought sound to the movies in *The Jazz Singer.* At first, Hollywood treated sound as a passing fad, but not the public. The public loved the talkies and demanded more. Hughes had already invested more than $2 million in *Hell's Angels,* an incredible sum for those days of cheap labor and low overhead, but the sound revolution doomed it to an ignominious failure. Hughes felt he had no choice but to reshoot the dialogue scenes with sound and dub in audio for the aerial sequences.

To write a new script, Hughes borrowed Joseph Moncure March, a poet then under contract to MGM. Except for the air scenes and the final sequence, where one brother kills the other, March thought the silent version of *Hell's Angels* was "depressingly bad."[18] He knew Hughes had been deeply involved in its writing, but even so, he recommended that the old script be scrapped and a new one written. Hughes agreed, and in ten days March had roughed out a script that Hughes liked. Ben Lyon and James Hall would still be perfect for the two lead male roles. But Greta Nissen, who spoke English with a Norwegian accent, would be ludicrous as the seductive English girl wooed by both brothers.

So Hughes opened his search for a replacement. Dozens of young women paraded into Metropolitan Studio for screen tests. Meanwhile, production started with orders to shoot around the leading lady as Hughes struggled "to make up his mind."[19]

Late one afternoon, as the film crews turned off the lights on a set depicting an RAF mess hall in France and began packing their cameras for the day, a feisty theatrical agent, Arthur Landau, reminded the head cameraman that he had a prospect waiting for a screen test. Grumbling, the cameramen restored the lights and cameras and in walked a young woman with "almost albino blonde hair" and a "puffy somewhat sulky little face."[20] Her name was Harlean Carpenter, but she went by the stage name of Jean Harlow.

Landau had noticed her at a drinking fountain at Hal Roach studios. What caught his eye were her "high firm breasts" and her "astonishingly blonde hair, unnaturally light and brushed back from her high forehead."[21] As Landau studied her movements, he observed to a companion that he thought she was not wearing a bra.

"She never does," answered his friend. "It's her advertisement."[22]

Convinced that he had a product of simmering sexuality, Landau had lined up a screen test with Hughes. But as the blue-eyed, eighteen-year-old stepped onto the Metropolitan set, she looked as though she were auditioning for a slapstick part in a Laurel and Hardy comedy—which she had played—

rather than the *femme fatale* called for in *Hell's Angels.* Her dress fit poorly. It was too snug around the bodice and hips. Joseph March, the screenwriter, took one look at the latest candidate and muttered: "My God, she's got a shape like a dustpan."[23]

The screen test was a disaster. Harlow was in tears half the time. At one point, she pleaded with the dialogue director, James Whale, who had become increasingly impatient with her, "Tell me, tell me exactly how you want me to do it."

"I can tell you how to be an actress," he answered, "but I cannot tell you how to be a woman."[24]

When Hughes saw the screen test, he grimaced and told Landau: "In my opinion, she's nix."[25]

Never one to take no for an answer, Landau argued with Hughes, raving about her hair, her acting ability, her sensuality. She was the perfect combination of "good kid and tramp" to make the role a success.[26]

"She's a broad and willing to put out for the fliers," he contended. "But she knows that after she's made them forget the war for a little while, they still have to take off and they might never come back. So her heart's breaking while she's screwing them."[27] Perhaps sensing the appeal of Landau's argument, Hughes slowly came around. The agent said that Hughes could have Harlow for $1,500 a week for a six-week minimum.

"I ought to keep you around for laughs," Hughes answered. "I'll give her $1,500 for the whole six weeks and don't argue."[28] Hughes insisted in addition that she sign a long-term contract with Caddo. Landau, quietly bursting with glee, consented.

As it turned out, Jean Harlow, with her "slightly lazy sexual aggression," *was* just right for the part.[29] With such seductive lines as the memorable "Do you mind if I slip into something more comfortable?" her career as a Hollywood sex goddess was launched, and Hughes had set a style for sex in the movies that prevailed for years. Ironically, although Hughes was credited with discovering Jean Harlow, he was personally oblivious to her sexual appeal on the screen. After *Hell's Angels,* he failed to exploit his teenage siren even though a national poll ranked her seventeenth in a list of the world's hundred best-known people. Instead, Hughes sold Harlow's contract to Irving Thalberg at MGM for a nominal $60,000 and she went on to become Hollywood's reigning sex symbol until her untimely death in 1937.

When *Hell's Angels* was completed early in 1930, Hollywood was "gossiping, scoffing, laughing up its sleeve," as one observer put it.[30] It had become the movie colony's favorite joke. With 2.5 million feet of film shot for a fifteen-thousand-foot movie, people chuckled about meeting a 105-year-old man who was thought to be "the only living person who could remember when *Hell's Angels* was started."[31] The cost was no joke—$3.8 million—making it the most extravagant piece of filmmaking ever undertaken.[32]

Hughes promoted the movie on an equally extravagant scale, showing for the first time the flair for public relations that would characterize him for the rest of his life. For the California opening, airplanes buzzed Grauman's Chinese Theater in Hollywood and stunt men parachuted onto Hollywood Boulevard. In Manhattan, Hughes took the unprecedented step of scheduling simultaneous openings at two separate Broadway theaters. He was disappointed, though, when the owners of the dirigible *Graf Zeppelin* refused his offer of $100,000 to fly over mid-Manhattan advertising the film. He built up curiosity by banning everyone but himself from a private showing at Grauman's Chinese Theater. Louella Parsons quietly slipped in a side door. When Hughes discovered her inside, he ordered her out. The spunky gossip columnist refused to leave.

At its première on June 30, 1930, *Hell's Angels* dazzled audiences and critics alike. It was, as one later put it, "dramatically commonplace, clumsily strung together and without clear authorship, but the aerial photography is superb, and the scenes with Jean Harlow are startlingly from another, much better picture."[33] Those two ingredients alone combined to make *Hell's Angels* a box-office smash. "Nothing like it has ever happened before," gushed *Photoplay*, "and probably nothing like it will ever happen again."[34] *Hell's Angels* set the theme for all of Hughes's movies—rich in entertainment, low on philosophy and message, packed with sex and action.

It also launched the Hughes legend. As the story of the movie's genesis and production unfolded, Hughes was variously characterized as daring, independent, willing to gamble, and blessed with a Midas touch. One exuberant admirer described him as a "super-individualist . . . whose outstanding characteristic is his ambition and his overwhelming determination to accomplish things."[35] Some of the talk was true. Much was not. But the fact commingled with the myth to form a legend that served Hughes the rest of his life. On its face, *Hell's Angels* had been an extraordinary personal achievement for Hughes. The story of his role in its production, however, began to be embellished to give him more credit than he was due. He had played almost no role in the final script, yet he was pictured not only as having produced and directed the film but as having "written" it as well.[36] Others went further, calling the film a "one-man picture."[37] And then Hughes himself stepped in, with more public relations. As if *Hell's Angels'* critical success were not enough, Hughes manufactured figures showing that the movie was also an "incredible moneymaker," yielding a profit of more than $2 million on his $3.8 million investment.[38] In sober truth, according to Noah Dietrich the movie never recovered its staggering production costs, and Hughes lost $1.5 million.[39] Such a loss had little effect on Hughes's life, since the tool company regularly made ample profits to cover the losses. But to his budding legend as a financial whiz, the story of the *Hell's Angels* monetary success was all-important.

Even Hollywood insiders were enthralled. The British producer Herbert Wilcox wanted to borrow Louis Wolheim, the star of *Two Arabian Knights*, who was still under contract to Hughes, for three days of shooting on a film he was producing. When Wilcox approached Hughes, he found the youthful producer both receptive and charming.

"He will cost you twenty thousand dollars," Hughes said of Wolheim.[40] Although the price was steep, Wilcox was so set on Wolheim that he agreed to pay. When Wilcox's director vetoed his choice of Wolheim, Wilcox hurried back to Hughes's Hollywood office less than an hour later to apologize for "having troubled him" and to let Hughes know the deal was off.

"You made a deal with me for twenty thousand dollars," Hughes answered coldly. "Wolheim will report on your set Monday and be available for three days, and I want that twenty thousand dollars before he starts work!"

Wilcox protested, but in the end he paid. He later reflected that the incident probably illustrated "one of the many reasons Hughes is a multimillionaire—and I am not."[41]

If Hughes exhibited a toughness beyond his years, and unusual for someone so new to the industry, he also spoke with candor and frankness, surprising for Hollywood, a town long accustomed to self-promotion by stars, directors, and producers alike. He refused to claim credit for *Hell's Angels,* and was quick to admit his failures, except for the financial ones.

"Making *Hell's Angels* by myself was my biggest mistake," he confessed in a rare interview in 1932. "It would have been finished sooner and cost less. I had to worry about money, sign checks, hire pilots, get planes, cast everything, direct the whole thing. Trying to do the work of twelve men was just dumbness on my part. I learned by bitter experience that no one man can know everything."[42]

At twenty-six, Hughes had apparently learned the rule of all successful executives: leaders must delegate authority. Yet in the years ahead, he would routinely disregard the lesson, making it a custom to interfere with, second-guess, and deny authority to his managers. If, as he claimed, he "went to school" making *Hell's Angels,* he promptly forgot what he had learned.[43]

CELEBRITIES AND CENSORS

No one embraced Hughes with more enthusiasm after *Hell's Angels* than the charmed circle of stars, directors, and producers who made up the heart of Hollywood's power. They were the beautiful people, written about in movie magazines and gossip columns, and invited to all the right places. Hughes's success with *Hell's Angels* made him an overnight favorite among them— especially with the women. If it was not his power and money they found attractive, it was his dark good looks. The somewhat spindly looking youth who had invaded Hollywood five years earlier had matured into a handsome young man. He was still thin and spare, yet his face had filled out, and he had the look of an older man. With his dark eyes and hair, he was fit for a starring role in one of his own movies.

But even in success, Hughes remained shy, "self-conscious with strangers and reticent with intimates."[44] At parties, he was hopelessly out of place, as one writer noted: "When standing he inclines his head out and down and looks at the ground. Seated, he clasps his hands between his widespread knees and stares at his knuckles."[45] This self-effacing, almost timid public image seemed at odds with the legend that had begun to grow about him—the fearless pilot, the daring driver whizzing through Southern California, the gambler whose stakes were his own fortune. For one who supposedly abounded in courage, Hughes appeared oddly frightened and subdued around others. The contrast only made him more intriguing. To Hollywood, he was a "man of mystery."[46] He never wore a watch, he kept odd hours, he hated to be photographed, and he avoided large parties, preferring small, intimate get-togethers in private homes.

Although Hughes was shy, uncomfortable around strangers, and eccentric, these characteristics, which would become more extreme as the years passed, hardly set him apart in Hollywood. The movie colony had more than its share of eccentrics and misfits. Still, the phobias instilled by his mother, his neurotic fear of illness and disease, were maturing, and they now were compounded by a growing obsession with the details of his work, a compulsive striving for perfection in projects large and small. In the 1920s, these traits were part of Hughes's appeal, part of his growing legend. In time, they would take on a darker meaning.

Although he disliked large parties, Hughes overcame his fears when the host was William Randolph Hearst. The lord of San Simeon gave the most memorable parties of his time, and Hughes was a frequent guest. Invitations were extended shortly before the weekend. Guests were asked to be at the Glendale railroad station at 7:35 P.M. on Friday. There, Hearst's train waited to carry them through the night to his 350,000-acre estate overlooking the Pacific, midway between Los Angeles and San Francisco. There were two sleeping cars and a diner, plentifully stocked with liquor. A strict teetotaler, Hearst forbade his guests to bring liquor into La Casa Grande, although he compromised by serving two cocktails at dinner. On these trips, Hughes found himself in the company of Hollywood's elite: Irving Thalberg, Norma Shearer, Charles Chaplin, Louis Mayer, Mary Pickford, Douglas Fairbanks. Early in the morning the train arrived at San Luis Obispo, where a fleet of limousines waited to chauffeur the guests the final leg to San Simeon. Perched high above the ocean, bathed by soft breezes, Hearst's castle was a make-believe setting for a weekend retreat. Hearst had furnished and adorned the mansion, guest houses, and grounds with priceless antiques collected around the world. On the grounds, zebras, giraffes, emus, camels, and yaks wandered freely, all part of W. R.'s private zoo.

Birthdays meant a lot to Hearst. He always gave a "sultanesque party" to observe his own.[47] He and Marion Davies, his blonde live-in actress, invited scores of people to attend and they were expected to arrive in costumes reflecting a preannounced theme. One year it was the Civil War, and Hollywood's finest turned out dressed in blue or gray and delighted in shoving one another into the outdoor swimming pool graced by the facade of an authentic pre-Christian Greek temple. Hughes observed the rules of the game. For the

A night out with Jean Harlow,
1934.
Bettmann Archive

William Randolph Hearst's Tyrolean Party, 1934. *Left to right*
around table: Eileen Percy, Kay
English, the designer Adrian,
Richard Boleslawsky, Mrs. Boleslawsky, Hughes, Marion Davies,
and Jack Warner.
United Press International

year of a circus theme, he came as a "knobby-kneed lion tamer."[48] At a Tyrolean party, Hughes looked like a bona fide native of that region as he posed, smiling, for photographs with fellow partygoers wearing short pants, an Alpine hat, and a short brocaded jacket.

Hughes got along with Marion Davies. To her, he was a "big, awkward, overgrown country boy" who was polite, nice, and affable.[49] Marion also liked Howard because "he didn't talk too much."[50] They both loved ice cream, and after dinner engaged in spirited "ice cream races" to see who could eat the most.

"Nobody can outdo me," Hughes joked with Marion.[51] From young adulthood on, Hughes had adopted the diet of an unrestrained seven-year-old, and ice cream was near the top of the list of his favorite foods. Still, when he and Marion had finished their "race," he was "green" from overeating and she never seemed to have had enough.[52]

It was Marion who introduced Hughes to Billie Dove, the first in a long line of actresses with whom he would be romantically linked. Billie, an attractive brunette, had excited New York at the age of sixteen as a Ziegfeld Follies girl, and went on to screen stardom in the silent era. After the breakup of his marriage with Ella, Hughes and Billie were frequent companions, although both maintained other relationships. While Hughes engaged in an affair with the promising actress Carole Lombard, Billie renewed a friendship with the dark, handsome George Raft, whom she had dated earlier in New York. The Dove–Raft relationship ended abruptly. After a night on the town, Raft and Billie retreated to a "gorgeous suite" at the Ambassador Hotel.[53] Shortly after, a call came through from one of Raft's lookouts in the lobby, saying that Howard Hughes was down there and that Billie was Hughes's girl. This was news to Raft, who would never have gone near his old flame had he known of her association with the millionaire producer: "The last guy in the world either of us wanted to cross was Howard Hughes."[54] Saying good-bye to Billie, Raft slipped out of the hotel by way of a service elevator. Billie later starred in two Hughes movies, *Cock of the Air* and *The Age for Love.* Hollywood buzzed with rumors of their impending marriage, especially after Hughes financed Billie's divorce from the director Irving Willatt in 1931. But the romance soon fizzled. Hughes once again was unable to forge a lasting relationship.

Hollywood continued to lionize him, but he still kept the movie capital at arm's length. If as a boy he had felt some pangs at not being accepted by his peers, as his mother's letters suggest, he was now a confirmed loner, an outsider by choice who in 1932 told an interviewer asking about the future of motion pictures: "I don't know anything about [it]. . . . Let the big guys do the talking."[55] Sometimes Hughes reveled in this role of maverick, as in the summer of 1931 when he threatened to make a movie exposing Hollywood's sins. To be entitled *Queer People,* the movie's heroines would depict a world "insistently immoral and the scene of their depravities [was] to combine the worst features of Sodom and Gomorrah."[56] Hughes went so far as to hire Ben

Hecht to write a script and Walter Winchell to play the part of a reporter "with a nose for glamorous living" before dropping the project.[57]

After *Hell's Angels,* Hughes returned to his earlier role as producer and let others do the directing. He produced two motion pictures while the aerial epic was under way—*The Mating Call* and *The Racket*—and then five more films in the year following *Hell's Angels: The Age For Love, Cock of the Air, Sky Devils, The Front Page,* and *Scarface.* The last two were the best of the lot, thanks to talented directors. Lewis Milestone directed the screen version of the Ben Hecht – Charles MacArthur play about Chicago newspapermen. Hughes stayed off the set, letting Milestone have a free rein, except for vetoing two relatively unknown actors whom Milestone wanted to use in leading roles. One was James Cagney, whom Hughes called a "little runt."[58] The other was Clark Gable, rejected by Hughes because "his ears make him look like a taxi-cab with both doors open."[59]

In *Scarface,* a thinly veiled story of Al Capone and his Chicago mob, Hughes sought to cash in on a national fascination with gangsters. To direct the film, he turned to one of his adversaries, Howard Hawks. Hughes had filed a lawsuit in July of 1930 in New York charging that portions of Hawks's movie *Dawn Patrol* had been lifted from *Hell's Angels.* The incident marked a further deterioration in relations between Hughes and his uncle Rupert. The script for *Dawn Patrol* was written by John Monk Saunders, who was then married to Rupert's stepdaughter, Avis. Ordinarily, Hughes would never have anything to do with someone he suspected of trying to take advantage of him. Yet this time he put aside those feelings to woo Hawks, a director whose work he admired. It would take all his charm. Hughes selected a golf course for the peace talks. One morning as Hawks was about to tee off at the Lakeside Country Club near Universal Studios, the club's golf pro rushed up with a message.

"Howard Hughes is on the phone and wants to come out and play golf with you."

Hawks was speechless. The man who was suing to stop his film wanted to play golf with him? He bristled.

"Tell him I don't want to play golf with him."

"Why?"

"The son of a bitch is suing me, that's why."[60]

A few minutes later the pro returned with another message—Hughes had agreed to drop the lawsuit and was on his way to the golf course. They played eighteen holes. The story goes that Hawks beat Hughes, who was an excellent golfer, and that before the day was over had agreed to make *Scarface.*

As usual, Hughes spared no expense on the film, which he wanted to be the last word in gang pictures. He gave Hawks a huge budget and stayed out of his way. The director hired Ben Hecht to write a script. He discovered an actor named Paul Muni playing in Yiddish theater in New York and signed him to the lead role. George Raft was to play the part of Scarface's bodyguard. Among the supporting actors was a young Britisher, Boris Karloff.

The finished film pleased everybody who had worked on it but it was so loaded with violence and bloodshed, not to mention overtones of incest between Scarface and his beautiful sister, that when it was submitted to Hollywood's censoring agency, the powerful Motion Picture Producers and Distributors of America, the agency rejected it, demanding substantial cuts and a new ending. By most accounts, the original ending was a brilliant stroke: trapped by police, Scarface degenerates into a blithering coward and is gunned down by police. The new ending demanded by the censors was to show Scarface being tried and executed by the forces of law and order. Hawks was bitterly opposed to the suggested changes, fearing that they would emasculate the film. But Hughes agreed to the revisions. The watered-down version earned the movie a Seal of Approval. Yet when Hughes tried to première the movie in New York, the state's Board of Censors refused to let it be shown. Hughes exploded, issuing a statement that liberal defenders of freedom of expression found heartwarming:

It has become a serious threat to the freedom of honest expression in America when self-styled guardians of the public welfare, as personified by our film censor boards, lend their aid and their influence to the abortive efforts of selfish and vicious interests to suppress a motion picture simply because it depicts the truth about conditions in the United States which have been front page news since the advent of Prohibition.

I am convinced that the determined opposition to *Scarface* is actuated by political motives. The picture, as originally filmed eight months ago, has been enthusiastically praised by foremost authorities on crime and law enforcement and by leading screen reviewers.

It seems to be the unanimous opinion of these authorities that *Scarface* is an honest and powerful indictment of gang rule in America and, as such, will be a tremendous force in compelling our state and Federal governments to take more drastic action to rid the country of gangsterism.[61]

Hughes's fighting stand won him many admirers. The *New York Herald Tribune* praised him for being the "only Hollywood producer who has had the courage to come out and fight this censorship menace in the open. We wish him a smashing success."[62] With six hundred thousand dollars tied up in a production that had not returned a penny, Hughes had little choice but to fight. He filed a series of lawsuits, first in New York and then in other states, for the right to show the movie. After winning the case against the New York censors, he restored the cuts and original ending and released *Scarface* in March of 1932. With so much in its favor, *Scarface* was a splendid success, another jewel in Hughes's crown.*

*Hughes was especially possessive about *Scarface* all his life, and refused to sell rights to the story or to allow other exhibitors to show the 1932 classic. In 1974, Hughes even turned down a $2-million offer from one producer who wanted to buy world rights to the movie, and *Scarface* remained locked up in a basement vault at 7000 Romaine Street in Hollywood, where it had languished more than forty years.

CHAPTER 3

HERO

YOUNG MAN IN A HURRY

Fired by the success of *Scarface,* Hughes toyed with the idea of making another aerial film, one based on the exploits of a First World War German dirigible. The *Hell's Angels* sequence in which a zeppelin bombed London had been most popular, and the huge blimps were still very much in the news; the *Graf Zeppelin* had just set a record, crossing the Atlantic in sixty-seven and a half hours. Hughes gave his projected film the title of *Zeppelin L-27,* but that was as far as it got, for Hughes had a new toy. It would be typical of Hughes throughout his life to focus all his attention and energy in one field only to abandon it suddenly in favor of another. So it was in 1932.

The new obsession was an airplane, a sleek little racer Hughes had bought months before and now housed in an oily, squat hangar in the San Fernando Valley. Through the spring and summer of 1932, Hughes took every opportunity to slip into his Deusenberg roadster and speed toward Burbank to look in on the work of streamlining the plane.

Hughes already owned a small air force. But the racer was special. Built by Boeing for the U.S. Army Air Corps as a military pursuit plane, it was supposedly restricted to air force use, but Hughes had gotten one through "special arrangements" with the Department of Commerce.[1] He was the only civilian in the United States to have that privilege. To remodel it along speedier lines, he leased a corner of a Lockheed Aircraft Corporation hangar and hired a crew of mechanics and designers. As expenses rose, and with them a need for better accounting, Hughes established the Hughes Aircraft Company as a new division of the Hughes Tool Company. In the beginning nothing more than a glorified machine shop and a set of books, in time it would become one of the nation's largest and most powerful defense contractors.

For years, airplanes had provided Hughes with a leisurely escape from pressures on earth. He loved nothing more than rising in the clean air above Los Angeles, flying north over the San Gabriel Mountains, then out across the high deserts toward Palm Springs, and finally back up the coast to the city. At night, he would head far out over the ocean, circle for the return, and watch with growing excitement as the lights of Los Angeles flickered brighter and brighter near land. Hughes was a different man in the air. No longer the shy, tense, highly nervous man people saw on the ground, aloft he was at ease behind a dizzying array of toggle switches and gauges, integrated with the sound of the engine, the feel of the controls, the magnificent view of the earth.

By the summer of 1932, however, aviation was no longer simply a hobby. It had supplanted all the activities he formerly directed from his second-floor office at 7000 Romaine Street, the stucco Hollywood building he had purchased in 1930 as a catchall headquarters for both his motion-picture company and Hughes Tool's West Coast offices. Although he had never kept regular hours, and often did not appear at Romaine for days on end, now he almost never came in. Instead, he could be found in the Lockheed hangar in Burbank, talking to mechanics and experimenting with aircraft engines.

For all his individuality, Hughes was a child of the age. Charles Lindbergh's 1927 flight across the Atlantic had launched a new era in American aviation, and Hughes was caught up in it. Americans were obsessed with conquering time and distance. Pilots and aircraft engineers worked feverishly to make planes go faster. Hardly a month went by but some member of this glamorous fraternity mounted a daring assault on the air, and races were the craze of aviation. With his love of machines, it was natural that Hughes would be drawn into this new frontier. Where once he had flown solely for pleasure, Hughes now flew to learn, jotting down observations on wind velocity, air speed, altitude, engine performance, and fuel consumption. He practiced his skills as a pilot, looping, turning and banking, rolling. Also, as a measure of his ripening ego and concern with status symbols, Hughes badgered the Aeronautic Branch of the Department of Commerce to give his pilot's license a lower number. Charles Lindbergh's license number was 69, Hughes's was 4223. In the fall of 1932, the Commerce Department awarded him number 374, and in the spring of 1933 he received number 80, which he kept for the rest of his flying days. To gain experience as a pilot, he signed on under the name of Charles W. Howard as a copilot for American Airways at a salary of $250 a month. As a junior pilot, he made one trip at the controls of a Fokker F-10 from Los Angeles to New York before his identity was discovered and he resigned from the only outside job he ever held.

When the Boeing was remodeled to his satisfaction, Hughes took it up for a test flight. Powered by a 580-horsepower Wasp engine, the plane performed beautifully, averaging 225 miles an hour, a remarkable speed for the time. Hughes decided to enter a race scheduled for Miami in January of 1934.

On his way to Florida, he stopped off in Houston to visit his aunts, Annette Lummis and Martha Houstoun, whom he had not seen in years. Both

The Boeing pursuit plane obtained from the U.S. Army, 1932.
Philadelphia Inquirer: Charles Bullock

were much involved in raising four children each. Howard stayed with Annette at the family home, now pleasantly revitalized by Annette's two sons and two daughters. Dudley Sharp and his wife Tina, whom Howard had also known while growing up in Houston, dropped over one night for dinner. After they had all finished eating, Hughes whispered to Tina: "I've got something for you."[2] He bounded upstairs to his room and returned shortly with a photograph of Dudley as a boy that he wanted her to have.

Hughes visited with his young cousins, some of whom he was seeing for the first time. He was especially taken with Annette's oldest son, four-year-old William Rice Lummis, or Willie as he was called, who was a carbon copy of Howard at the same age. In a letter to Annette, one of only two letters he ever wrote her, Hughes said he thought Willie was "adorable."[3]

For the All-American Air Meet in Miami, Hughes entered a category called the sportsman pilot free-for-all. On January 14, 1934, the swift Boeing lived up to his hopes. Averaging 185.7 miles per hour over a twenty-mile course, Hughes nearly lapped his nearest competitor to win his first aviation prize. In the closing ceremonies, he was warmly congratulated and given an impressive trophy by General Rafael Trujillo, the Dominican Republic dictator who presided over the meet.

The Miami victory whetted Hughes's appetite. The Boeing had performed well, but already he was thinking beyond it. He quietly studied the technical data flowing out of the aviation industry on proposed mechanical innovations and aircraft designs to improve speed. It only remained for some enterprising airplane manufacturer to put all these ideas together into a single plane. His course seemed clear. Why not build his own plane—and while he was at it, make it the fastest land plane the world had ever seen?

Any airplane builder would have constructed a plane to Hughes's specifications. But Hughes did not want the world to know what he was up to; nor did he want to share any of his ideas with a potential rival. As soon as he returned to Los Angeles, he began pulling together his own team of designers, engineers, and craftsmen.

The young men he selected shared Hughes's enthusiasm for aviation. It was the Depression and many were thankful just to have a job, much less such an interesting one. To head the team, Hughes hired Richard W. Palmer, a recent graduate of California Institute of Technology and a quiet, reflective man who seemed older than he was. Palmer was already known for his radical ideas about aircraft design when he met Hughes in 1934; a group of his fellow Cal Tech colleagues eagerly followed him to the Hughes job.

To supervise construction, Hughes turned to Glenn Odekirk, a cheerful, thoroughly competent mechanic and pilot Hughes had met during the filming of *Hell's Angels*. Hughes gave his team no specific instructions. He just told them in "broad terms" what he wanted: to build a land plane that would fly higher and faster than any other in the world.[4]

Early in 1934, the Palmer–Odekirk team conducted a series of tests with miniature hardwood models in the wind tunnel at Cal Tech's aeronautical lab. As each model was readied for testing, Hughes drove out from Hollywood to take a look. Weeks passed as new models were carved, tested, and rejected or modified, until one day the team called Hughes out to Pasadena for an inspection. Bending down to a small window of the wind tunnel, he saw a futuristic-looking model of a racer and watched approvingly as "swiftly moving vapor flowed smoothly over the highly polished hardwood surfaces."[5]

To build the plane, Hughes leased a corner of the Babb Hangar at Grand Central Airport in Glendale and ordered his section walled off and sealed to inquisitive visitors. With the eighteen men who made up the team laboring daily in the inner sanctum, the outside world grew curious. Soon the undertaking became known as the Hughes mystery ship. Hughes's team had another word for it: the H-1. Under the gifted eye of Dick Palmer, a fascinating airplane was taking shape.

Like most racers, it was a single-seater with an open cockpit. It was small, only twenty-seven feet from nose to tail, and twenty-five feet in wingspan. Beyond those mundane features lay a series of innovations that made the H-1 the most advanced plane of its time. Rivets were placed flush with the fuselage to reduce drag. The wings were shortened to increase speed. The single most revolutionary feature was its unique landing gear which did not remain permanently in place during flight, but retracted neatly after takeoff into a snug compartment under the wings. Some of the aircraft's advanced touches had previously been tested on other planes or written about in technical journals, but no single plane of the time incorporated so many of them.

It was inevitable, as it had been with *Hell's Angels,* that Hughes would get far more credit for the H-1 than he deserved. In truth, Hughes was not an aircraft designer nor an especially seminal thinker in aeronautics. He was, however, an excellent brain-picker. "He knew how to get answers," recalled Robert W. Rummel, an engineer who worked on the H-1 and later worked closely with Hughes at TWA. "He had a habit which I did not really discover until years later. He would call me up and talk about something like wing efficiency. He would want to know my opinion. I'd tell him. Then he would often call back later and say what about this or that, referring to our earlier conversation. Years later I learned he was doing the same thing with five or six guys."[6] By picking brains, Hughes narrowed his options, arrived at the right decision time after time, and wrote aviation history with the H-1. For eighteen months, the work progressed as the plane was assembled, taken apart, then reassembled. Money was no object although the Depression was at its deepest. The old reliable Hughes Tool Company drill bit was still bankrolling Hughes's dreams.

Hughes's growing fame in aviation was in fact making him a folk hero to his workers back in Houston. In the past, they had resented him for squandering the profits generated by their labor in frivolous Hollywood movies. But his entry into aviation was viewed much more positively. Hughes was now spending his money for science and for the advancement of aviation. As Hughes recorded one aerial triumph after another, workers proudly clipped the news stories and pasted the mementos in black-bound notebooks.[7]

As for the tool company's brass, they wished that Howard had stayed with movies. Colonel R. C. Kuldell, the president and general manager of Hughes Tool since Hughes Sr.'s time, was worried that Hughes was going to kill himself flying airplanes and thus destroy the company that Kuldell and his lieutenants had spent a generation building. If Hughes should die without leaving a valid will, the company would be dismembered to pay federal estate taxes.

Early in August of 1935, Kuldell learned that Hughes intended personally to test-fly the H-1. He could no longer keep silent. On August 12, 1935, he wrote Hughes and his Houston lawyer, Frank Andrews, admitting that he was bringing up an "embarrassing subject," but one he felt should be discussed "by those of us interested in the continuity of the institution we know as the Hughes Tool Company."[8] Then he got to the heart of his message:

Two events of immediate and impending importance are before us, which lead me to bring this matter to your attention, at this time. I understand that Howard is about to undertake a most dangerous aviation flight, which may not seem dangerous to him, but certainly in the risks which we know are involved in testing new planes, appear to me to be very considerable. The second event is the pending passage of the new inheritance tax bill, which, if not provided against, would leave the Hughes Tool Company almost entirely to the Federal Government.[9]

Kuldell said he did not know what Howard's "present will contemplates," but suggested that he "immediately rewrite it," leaving a portion of "his estate to his employes and associates." In this way, the company would not be "disintegrated at [Howard's] death" by a 75-percent inheritance tax. "While we all fervently hope Howard will be successful in his airplane endeavors or rather that he will not undertake dangerous flights, still the possibility is there, and we would be negligent if we did not strongly urge him to take the necessary precaution."[10]

Hughes was just twenty-nine, but already he was finding out what a double-edged sword wealth could be. The money that enabled him to indulge himself in motion pictures, women, airplanes—anything he wanted—was also a constant reminder of his own mortality. Noah Dietrich, Hughes's financial adviser in Los Angeles, sent Kuldell a reassuring letter saying that Hughes had revised his will and that it "generously" provided for all his top executives.[11] In fact, there is no evidence that Hughes executed a will at this time. More likely, Hughes told Dietrich he had inserted a provision in his will giving tool company officers a share in his estate when actually he had done no such thing. Over the years, Hughes raised this stratagem to a high art, thinking that the lucky "beneficiaries" would remain loyal.

If Hughes was outwardly making an overture to placate Kuldell, privately he was displeased with the man who was almost a Hughes family fixture. It was Kuldell who had administered his father's estate, negotiated with Howard's relatives to acquire their minority interest in Hughes Tool, and successfully guided the tool company through the Depression's darkest hours. The company was hard hit in the 1930s, but would have been hurt even more had not Kuldell opened a brewery on the tool company grounds at the close of Prohibition. Cashing in on the wet era, the Gulf Brewing Company rushed into business with a product called Grand Prize Beer, and for a time it was the largest-selling beer in Texas. But now Hughes was turning against the colonel.

The reason was Noah Dietrich. Ever since he had gone to work for Hughes in 1925, Dietrich had been skillfully consolidating his power in the Hughes organization. By 1936, he had only one rival—Colonel Kuldell. As Dietrich's influence with Hughes grew—aided by his proximity to the millionaire in California—he became increasingly critical of the Hughes Tool Company management in Houston. Gradually, Hughes paid more attention to Dietrich's persistent complaints. A few months after Kuldell indiscreetly raised the will issue, Hughes sent Dietrich to live in Houston, with orders to keep a close watch over the tool company's balance sheet. Not surprisingly, Dietrich's arrival in Houston set off a corporate power struggle. With Hughes firmly behind Dietrich, the outcome was never in doubt. In less than two years, Kuldell was forced out.

RECORD BREAKER

Even though his concern for Hughes's welfare stemmed in part from self-interest, Kuldell had not exaggerated the danger Hughes would face if he test-flew the H-I. Everyone around him was uneasy about that. For all its safety features, the H-I was an experimental plane. No one knew how it would perform in the air. Palmer and Odekirk pleaded with Hughes to let someone else test it. He ignored them. It was his airplane—he would fly it. To allow otherwise would have "shot his pride."[12]

On August 18, 1935, at Mines Field, Hughes slipped his long frame into the racer's cockpit and started the Wasp engine. Motioning that he was ready, he waited for a ground crewman to remove the wheel chocks, then gunned the engine and gave it full throttle. In a few seconds the H-I was flying. For fifteen minutes it purred over Los Angeles, accelerating up to 300 miles an hour. When word of the flight spread, the aviation world speculated that Hughes would enter the National Air Races over Labor Day and carry off the top prize. Instead, he mysteriously passed up the meet. Ten days later it was clear why.

The racer had performed so well that Hughes was convinced he could easily set a world speed record for a plane flying over land. The existing mark of 314 miles an hour was held by the French pilot Raymond Delmotte. To contest it, a challenger had to fly over an official three-kilometer race course supervised by the National Aeronautic Association. The test was scheduled for September 12, 1935, at Martin Field, a few ramshackle hangars bordering a crude landing strip near Santa Ana, California, now the site of Orange County Airport.

The day was perfect for flying—bright, sunny, and cloudless, with little wind. If Martin Field was an unlikely setting in which to rewrite aviation history, the terrain was at least ideal for the event at hand. All around, the land was monotonously flat with wide-open spaces well suited to the speed runs Hughes had in mind.

Hughes showed up early that morning with his crew and retreated to a hangar to give the H-I a final tuning. Technicians from the NAA measured off the three-kilometer course, running north to south over a bean field next to the airstrip. A chronograph was installed at each end to photograph and clock Hughes's plane as it entered and left the course. He would be required to make four consecutive passes at speeds of more than 314 miles an hour to set a new record.

Hughes shook hands with the judges: Amelia Earhart, fresh from her triumph as the first person to fly solo from Mexico City to Newark; Paul Mantz, a Hollywood pilot who had stunted for Hughes in *Hell's Angels* and also served as Miss Earhart's technical adviser; and Lawrence Therkelson, an official of the NAA. Mantz and Therkelson took off in one plane and Miss Earhart followed in another to observe Hughes's performance from the air. NAA rules required that he could not go higher than 1,500 feet during the record attempt.

Fueled and ready, the H-1 waited for Hughes on the runway, its compact silver body glistening in the sun. Hughes would always be enraptured by the "beautiful little thing"[13] he had created, and clad in an odd flying outfit—a rumpled dark suit, soiled white shirt, and tie—he vaulted into the cockpit, fastened his leather cap, and adjusted his goggles. Gunning the engine, he stirred up a cloud of dust, taxied into position, then gave it full throttle and felt the power take over. As the plane lifted off, he leaned forward, flicked a switch on the sponge-rubber-padded dashboard to retract the landing gear, and headed north toward the mountains.

He flew first across the course from north to south, then circled over the ocean and zoomed back across from the opposite direction. In all, he made four lightning runs and easily topped Delmotte's speed. But by the time of the last run, it was so dark that the cameras could not photograph the H-1 and so Hughes's bid failed. He would try again the next day.

On Friday, September 13, 1935, Hughes posted speeds of 355, 339, 351, 340, 350, 354, and 351 miles an hour. This time, the cameras recorded his triumph. Even so, the victory was almost pyrrhic. After the last run, Hughes flew on, oblivious to his falling gas gauge. North of the course, the H-1's engine suddenly conked out before Hughes could switch to an auxiliary tank. As the ship began to lose altitude fast, Hughes thought of bailing out. But that would have meant the end of the H-1, so he decided to ride it down. The plane drifted into a beet field and bounced to a stop. Hughes climbed out unhurt; the racer suffered only minor damage. When he was told that he had set a land-speed record of 352 miles an hour, he coolly surveyed the H-1's crumpled landing gear and muttered: "It'll go faster."[14]

If Hughes was unimpressed by his first great air record, the aviation world was captivated. No longer just a movie producer who flew as a hobby, Hughes was obviously serious about advancing aviation. Whatever his reasons, no one could deny the superiority of his plane. The H-1 was magnificent, far advanced over all other planes of the time. As usual, Hughes took no credit; he owed it to the plane, he said, and "the boys who worked with me getting the plane ready for the flight. I only flew a perfect machine."[15] But the fame was his.

That fall, Hughes thought about flying the "perfect machine" on to greater glory. The most tempting target was the transcontinental record of ten hours, two minutes, and fifty-seven seconds, then held by Colonel Roscoe Turner, who had worked for Hughes on *Hell's Angels*. A simple calculation showed that the H-1, capable of speeds up to 350 miles an hour, could easily eclipse Turner's time.

While Hughes decided what to do, he spent much of his time in the air, experimenting and testing theories. He was especially interested in high-altitude flying, as a way both to elude bad weather and to increase speed. He had a theory that the instruments used to register speed at high altitudes were inaccurate, and one day he set up an experiment to find out if he was right.

On a map, he laid out a seventy-two-mile-long course from Mount Wilson Observatory, north of Los Angeles, to San Jacinto Peak, to the southeast near

In the beet field near Santa Ana, California, with the damaged H-1, minutes after establishing new world speed record for land planes, September 13, 1935.
Wide World Photos

Palm Springs. Placing several of his Hughes Aircraft workers at specified points along the route, Hughes flew over the course at fifteen thousand feet. Later, by comparing the readings on his airspeed indicator with the timing of his observers posted on land, Hughes discovered that he had been right.[16] His airspeed indicator, calibrated at sea level rather than at high altitude, read fifteen miles an hour slower than he was actually traveling.

This helped him to another conclusion. "I realized," he said later, "that by climbing up to the substratosphere, and taking advantage of the westerly wind created by the motion of the earth, I could reduce the time of crossing the continent."[17]

It followed that airplanes traveling at high altitudes could fly faster and farther on less fuel, and therefore at less cost, than other planes. Clearly, high-altitude flying was going to mean much to aviation. And to Hughes. But first, there was the transcontinental flight. Plans for that were moving forward, but not plans that included the H-1. The racer was not designed to fly long distances. The search for a plane suitable for the cross-country hop soon turned up the perfect candidate at nearby Mines Field in Inglewood, a single-seat, high-powered Northrop Gamma. There was, however, a large hitch. The plane was owned by a pilot who also aspired to break the coast-to-coast record.

Hughes was a wallflower at Hollywood parties, but he knew how to talk to fellow pilots, most of whom were tough-talking, hard-living men used to facing danger. This pilot, however, was nothing like the others. She was a slim, twenty-six-year-old blonde named Jacqueline Cochran, then quietly on her way to becoming one of the great fliers of her era.

If Hughes imagined Miss Cochran to be an easy mark, he soon found out differently. Unlike Hughes, she had come up the hard way. Born in an impoverished Florida sawmill town, she left home at fourteen to become a beautician before being gripped by a passion for flying that would carry her to international fame. Hughes saw her putting the Northrop through a series of fuel-consumption tests at Mines Field, and then called her late one night just before she went to bed.

"Jackie," said a voice on the other end of the telephone, "this is Howard."

"Howard who?" she asked.

"Howard Hughes."[18]

Jackie Cochran was certain the caller was a crank. She had never met Hughes, but like other pilots at Mines she admired his "fabulous" racer, which was guarded by a "great army of police."[19] She had seen Hughes from a distance start up the H-1 and "run it up and down the runways" at Mines to give it a workout.[20] Hughes had a distinctive voice, high-pitched, nasal, with an unmistakable southern accent. But Miss Cochran had never heard him say a word. For fifteen minutes she insisted that the caller was not Hughes while he sought to convince her that he was. Finally, he succeeded.

"I want to buy your airplane," Hughes told her.

"Well, it isn't for sale," she answered. "I'm going to fly it in the Bendix" —a national race.

"I don't want to fly it in the Bendix," Hughes tried to reassure her. "I want to fly it cross-continental."

"So do I," Miss Cochran replied, with a firmness that might well have ended the discussion right there if the caller had been anyone other than Hughes.[21]

But Hughes kept calling—for weeks he pestered Miss Cochran to sell the Northrop. She continued to refuse, but she was short on funds and almost against her will found herself listening to Hughes's tempting monetary offers. During the negotiations, Hughes invited her to the airport and let her sit in the H-1, although he would not let her fly it. Within four weeks, he had won. Jackie Cochran agreed to lease him the Northrop for nearly as much money as she had invested in the plane. Also, with the greatest reluctance, she gave him an option to buy it. Surveying her finances, she had felt that she "just couldn't afford to do otherwise."[22]

Hughes flew the Northrop to Union Air Terminal in Burbank where Hughes Aircraft personnel, now housed in their own hangar at one end of the field, immediately set about converting the plane for its long flight. The most significant change was in the engine. Once again, Hughes received what he called "special permission" from the U.S. Army Air Corps to use equipment that had been developed exclusively for military use.[23] It was a 925-horsepower Wright Cyclone engine capable of generating great power at takeoff and high altitude. By late 1935, the Northrop was refitted and tested, and Hughes waited only for proper weather.

Takeoff was finally set for January 13, 1936. Shortly after noon, with no public announcement, Hughes taxied the heavily fueled Northrop into position on a runway at the Burbank airport. At 12:15 P.M., the plane rolled down the runway, gathered speed, and lifted off for the east. Although the start could not have been smoother, a freak accident—the antenna snapped at liftoff—cost Hughes his radio. He would be out of contact with the ground for the entire trip. Climbing to fifteen thousand feet through "thick" weather, he flew "blind" for two hours.[24] He did not see the ground again until Santa Fe. To test his high-altitude theories, he went up three thousand feet more, inhaling oxygen to ward off drowsiness. At eighteen thousand feet, he throttled back the engine, reducing horsepower, and found, as he had theorized, that his speed was not reduced at that rarified altitude.

North of Wichita, Kansas, Hughes ran into rough weather again, this time in the form of turbulent winds. One gust buffeted the plane so strongly that the needle of his compass was knocked off its point. With neither radio nor compass intact, Hughes was forced to fly by sight, and spreading the map on his knees, he charted the remaining twelve hundred miles visually. Luckily, it was a clear night and he was able to make out the cities by their lights. At 12:42 A.M.—nine hours, twenty-seven minutes, and ten seconds after leaving Burbank—Hughes touched down in the darkness at Newark. His lone welcomer was an official timekeeper.

It was a transcontinental record to be sure, but hardly a spectacular victory. He had shaved only thirty-six minutes off Roscoe Turner's time, and Turner had actually stopped once along the way to refuel. Nevertheless, Hughes's feat depressed Jacqueline Cochran; she said later that it broke her heart.[25] As she had feared when she leased it to Hughes, her plane had enabled him to take her place in breaking the record. Within weeks Hughes set two more records, cutting the flying time from Miami to New York and from Chicago to Los Angeles, and when his lease on Miss Cochran's Northrop expired, he exercised his option to buy and sent her a check. But a few days later, fickle as ever, Hughes abruptly changed his mind, offering to sell it back to her for much less than he paid, and she readily agreed, baffled by the whole affair. Miss Cochran never did understand why Hughes behaved as he did. He had, she later remarked, a "very interesting streak."[26]

As soon as he returned to Los Angeles Hughes set to work remodeling the H-1. The racer was towed into the Hughes Aircraft hangar at Burbank to be made over for long-distance flying so Hughes could try to break his own cross-country record. Larger wings were added, fuel capacity was expanded, a hydraulic mechanism was installed to increase visibility by raising and lowering the pilot's seat at takeoff and landing. A sleek transparent hatch was placed over the once-open cockpit. So many gauges, instruments, and controls were jammed into the tiny cockpit that mechanics could not install the oxygen tank until they found a niche in the right wing above the landing gear, and ran a tube into the cockpit.

As Hughes waited for work on the H-1 to end, he passed the time by playing a familiar role, that of Hollywood's most eligible bachelor. He had not made a movie in five years, yet he was still thought of in Hollywood as a movie producer temporarily pursuing other interests. The romance with Billie Dove had long since cooled, but a string of other attractive actresses followed her: Marian Marsh, Ida Lupino, Lillian Bond, and Mary Rogers, among others.

Hughes had also begun cultivating young socialites, some of whose families would have been appalled had they ever seen their daughters' names in lights. On the night of July 11, 1936, while Hughes was driving one blue-blooded companion home, he struck and killed a fifty-nine-year-old department-store salesman, Gabe Meyer, who was standing in a streetcar safety zone at Third Street and Lorraine Boulevard, a few blocks from Hughes's Hancock Park home. Because he did not want to "drag her name into the affair unnecessarily," Hughes told the girl to flee the scene.[27] She slipped away and boarded a streetcar. After being temporarily held by police, Hughes was forced by a coroner's jury to divulge the girl's name—Nancy Belle Bayly, of a prominent Pasadena family. After hearing Hughes's description of the accident, in which he said he had swerved to avoid striking another car, the jury cleared him of any blame for Meyer's death.

Of all the women linked to Hughes at the time, however, only one, Katherine Hepburn, bridged the worlds of society and film in which he moved. Born into an aristocratic Connecticut family, she was already a great actress, and was having trouble getting parts because many male actors shied away in fear of the competition. Hughes and Miss Hepburn, both lanky and angular, both golfers and pilots, made a handsome pair, and pursued her diligently, even clearing a stretch of beach suitable for landing a plane near the Hepburn family summer home in Old Saybrook, Connecticut. When she flew to the Midwest to star in a road production, Hughes followed in his own plane, and never missed a performance. They were hounded, of course, much to their annoyance, by the press and autograph seekers.

Again, rumors flourished, as they had with Billie Dove, yet like almost all of Hughes's romantic attachments, this one advanced only so far. Although Hughes could be charming, he did not always endear himself to the independent-minded Kate Hepburn. She had, for instance, little taste for luxury, but even so Hughes constantly sent her expensive jewelry, and she in turn, a friend remembered, "was always trying to send it back."[28] When Hughes came to the Hepburn family home in Connecticut, he "was not a very convenient guest, preferring to eat after everyone else had left the table." Miss Hepburn more than once grew exasperated at Hughes's behavior, but eventually despaired of getting angry at him because "he couldn't hear what she was saying anyhow."[29] In time it would end between them because, as one of Miss Hepburn's friends believed, Kate "got very bored."[30]

Anyway, Hughes was concentrating on preparations for his next record-setting effort. In line with its silvery image, he renamed the H-1 the *Winged Bullet,* and he flew back and forth several times between California and New York in another plane, plotting the route he intended to take, occasionally stopping over at the Long Island estate of aircraft builder Sherman Fairchild.

But flying in those days entailed many risks. On November 15, 1936, while attempting to land a seaplane at North Beach Airport on Long Island, Hughes was caught by a tail wind and crashed.[31] It was his third plane accident, but not his last. Hughes escaped uninjured, soon returning to California to begin final planning for the cross-country hop.

On January 18, 1937, the lights in the Hughes Aircraft hangar in Burbank blazed far into the night. Mechanics tested the rebuilt racer while Hughes studied weather reports. He could not have been completely satisfied with what he read. Dense clouds covered most of the country. But the winds were favorable, blowing strongly toward the east. Shortly after 2 A.M., the *Winged Bullet* nosed onto the runway and taxied into position. Weighed down by 280 gallons of aviation fuel, it roared past an official timekeeper at 2:15 A.M. and soared off into the night.

As in 1936, Hughes ran into unfavorable weather from the start. Climbing to fifteen thousand feet, he leveled off above the clouds and throttled back, only to find conditions still choppy and rough. Adjusting his oxygen mask, he accelerated and began a steep climb to twenty thousand feet.

An hour and a half outside Burbank, he caught a fleeting glimpse of Arizona through a hole in the clouds. Cruising at 330 miles an hour, he settled in for the long flight. Then, with no warning, his oxygen mask failed and the grim effects of oxygen deprivation spread through his body. His "arms and legs were practically paralyzed."[32] He could not even raise his hand to his face. Hughes was gripped by a "helpless, hopeless feeling" that within a few minutes he would doze off to sleep.[33] With all his remaining strength, he nosed the ship down, shouting in the cockpit to "equalize the pressure from within his head."[34] It was a solitary performance; his radio had malfunctioned again, but when he dropped down several thousand feet "full consciousness" returned.[35] Hughes had escaped from the only "real jam" he had ever faced as a pilot.[36]

Somewhere over the Midwest, he picked up a lusty tail wind and bolted east into the new day. As he approached the Appalachians, the clouds began to break up and Hughes caught sight of the rolling Pennsylvania countryside as he began the long descent to Newark. At 12:42 P.M., he streaked over Newark Airport for an official coast-to-coast record of seven hours, twenty-eight minutes, and twenty-five seconds. This was an achievement indeed. Averaging 332 miles an hour, Hughes had convincingly beaten his old record and established a time that would hold up for seven years.

"A bit shaky," he climbed out of the cockpit, weary and splattered with oil.[37] This time reporters were waiting, and Hughes smiled as he unbuttoned his flight jacket and jumped to the tarmac. He told of his oxygen problems, then downplayed the flight in his self-deprecating way. The only reason he had made it, he joked, was that he had heard someone was about to try to beat his 1936 record and he wanted to "give them something better than that mark to shoot at."[38] There followed a lot of questions from reporters who knew nothing about airplanes. These Hughes patiently answered, wanting desperately all the while to get away from the crowd. This ambivalence would torment Hughes all his life. He was forever doing things that made him an object of intense public curiosity, only to be repelled by the attention itself.

The 1937 flight made Hughes the undisputed pilot of the year. As winner of the Harmon International Trophy denoting the world's outstanding aviator, the first of many such awards, he was honored by President Franklin D. Roosevelt at the White House. On receiving the trophy, Hughes was his usual shy self in contrast to the president, who effervesced about his First World War days when he had flown in navy planes and blimps over wartorn France. Someday, Roosevelt said, looking wistfully at the lanky honoree, he would like to fly with Hughes.

Hughes was not so shy that he was reluctant to try to capitalize on his fame. He felt the *Winged Bullet* would make an ideal military pursuit plane, and hoped to sell the design to the army air force and begin manufacturing the plane en masse. But the air force declined to buy. Years later, Hughes told a Senate committee that his plane was turned down because of its advanced design, that the air force "did not think that a cantilever monoplane . . . was suitable for a pursuit ship."[39] In fact, cantilever monoplanes (planes whose wings were supported without external metal braces) were already in use by the government when Hughes made his pitch to the air force. The real reason the authorities rejected Hughes's plane was that they did not believe it was suitable for combat.

Nor did Hughes's behavior help matters. After arranging to fly the plane to Wright Field near Dayton, Ohio, where he was to show it off to a delegation of interested air force brass headed by Major General Oliver P. Echols, Hughes failed to keep the appointment. The general and his staff were left fuming on the runway.

RACE AROUND THE WORLD

Whatever his faults, Hughes's achievements at this time were remarkable. In less than two years, he had flown his way into the record books, establishing every land-speed record of consequence. His fame as a pilot and an aircraft builder was firmly set. But he was also finding that he had succumbed to an unwritten rule which drives all achievers: each new triumph only compels another, greater achievement. For Hughes, that meant he now had to fly around the world.

If Hughes raced planes for glory, he concealed the fact well. Yet it was also true that America reserved its wildest acclaim for pilots who hopped over water, not land. Lindbergh's solo flight across the Atlantic had made him a hero for all time. In 1931, Wiley Post and Harold Gatty had electrified America by circling the globe in eight and a half days. Two years later, the amazing Post flew the same route alone and cut a day off the time. In 1935, Post and the comedian Will Rogers were killed in Alaska at the start of yet another attempt to circle the world.

Hughes receives
congratulations
from Dick Palmer
in Newark
after establishing
cross-country
speed record of
seven hours,
twenty-eight minutes
on January 19, 1937.
*United Press
International*

No one admired Wiley Post any more than Hughes. But Hughes had no desire to duplicate the world flight of the colorful, one-eyed Texan. Post had piloted a crude little plane called the *Winnie Mae*. Hughes planned to fly around the world in a sophisticated machine supported by an expert air and ground crew. No longer should ocean hopping be thought of as the province of daredevils. Hughes wanted to dramatize how a well-conceived, thoroughly planned, and carefully executed flight could be carried out without incident.

As usual, the plane was all-important, and for this flight Hughes chose the Sikorsky S-43, a bulky, twin-engine amphibian. When the plane was delivered in the summer of 1937, Hughes quietly applied to the Bureau of Air Commerce in Washington for permission to circumnavigate the globe. Not convinced that there was any scientific merit in the flight, the bureau turned Hughes down.[40]

Hughes, of course, was not easily discouraged, and the following spring he reapplied, citing his already elaborate preparations as a reason why the flight should be approved. This time a more receptive bureau was about to issue a permit when an S-43 crashed. The accident made the agency apprehensive about approving a long flight in a similar airplane, and on May 23, 1938, the bureau informed Hughes that approval was being held up until the Sikorsky accident had been thoroughly investigated.[41]

This threatened to delay Hughes's world flight for another year. His meteorologists had studied weather patterns along the route and had decided that in early July the least amount of bad weather was likely to be encountered. But if the flight was to be made then, Hughes had to prepare now. With the flight in jeopardy, he moved swiftly to keep his hopes alive.

Lockheed Aircraft had just put the finishing touches on a sleek, twin-engine passenger plane—the Lockheed 14—capable of carrying up to twelve people. Hughes conducted hurried talks with Lockheed to acquire one of the new models and in late May requested permission to use the Lockheed for the world flight. While Hughes awaited the government's decision, Glenn Odekirk and his other mechanics worked day and night to ready the ship.

The Lockheed underwent substantial changes at the Hughes Aircraft hangar in Burbank to make it airworthy for the fifteen-thousand-mile flight. Determined to avoid the radio mishaps of earlier flights, Hughes installed three separate transmitters, the largest a 100-watt unit designed and built by his own technicians. To give it more power and range, the Lockheed was also fitted with two specially supercharged Wright G-102 Cyclone engines.

Nothing reflected aviation's advances more than the Lockheed's crowded instrument panel. Lindbergh flew the Atlantic with only a compass to guide him and his two hands to keep the *Spirit of St. Louis* on course. His instruments consisted of an oil-pressure gauge, an oil-temperature gauge, a turn-and-bank indicator, an earth-inductor compass, an airspeed indicator, an engine crankshaft-speed counter, navigation and landing light switches, an altimeter, and an ignition switch—that was all.

Hughes's Lockheed had an automatic pilot that could fly the ship on a predetermined course for hours at a time, oil-pressure and oil-temperature gauges for each engine, cylinder-head-temperature gauges for each engine, four fuel-capacity gauges, an airspeed indicator, dual manifold-pressure gauges, dual artificial horizons, a directional gyrocompass, an engine-exhaust analyzer, two sensitive altimeters, a flap-position indicator, a wheel-position indicator, revolution counters for each engine, oil-pressure gauges for the hydraulic system, light switches for the entire ship and instrument panel, radio-control switches, tuning grinders, volume rheostats, propeller-pitch controls, flap controls, landing-gear switches, fuel-mixture controls, carburetor-heat controls, trim-tab controls, fuel-tank selector switches, dual magneto switches, wobble pumps for the hydraulic system and fuel tanks, fuel-flow meters, dual controls for engine cowling, cooling grills, and throttles.

While Hughes planned, he also indulged his passion for tinkering with his "Last Will and Testament." Except for providing a "pension" of $20 a week to a Houston servant, Lily Adams, and monthly pensions of $150 each to two servants at his Muirfield Road house, Beatrice Donner and a male servant he identified only as "Mr. Henry," this new will was similar to earlier versions.[42] The bulk of the estate was left to medical research. His executors were to establish the Howard R. Hughes Medical Research Laboratories in Houston to combat "the most important and dangerous diseases" afflicting that part of Texas.[43]

The summer before, Amelia Earhart had mysteriously disappeared in the South Pacific near the end of her around-the-world flight. The way she had just vanished made a deep impression on Hughes. He now set down a series of detailed instructions governing the reading of his will "in the event . . . it should be deemed that I may be dead, but not conclusively so proven. . . ."[44] If he were lost, the First National Bank in Houston was to hold his will unopened and not allow his estate to be probated for three years after his "disappearance."[45] Hughes put the instructions in an envelope labeled "No. 1" and the will in another marked "No. 2," and mailed them on March 3, 1938, to the bank.*

Although he had not yet received government approval for the flight, Hughes was confident he would get it, and on the Fourth of July, 1938, he and a four-man crew flew to Floyd Bennett Field in Brooklyn, the traditional jumping-off point for transatlantic flights. The men he selected were seasoned aviators: Edward Lund, a thirty-two-year-old Montana native, was the flight engineer; Richard Stoddart, a thirty-seven-year-old New Yorker who worked for the National Broadcasting Company, would handle the radio; Lieutenant Thomas L. Thurlow, thirty-three, had been borrowed from the army air corps as navigator; and Harry P. M. Connor, thirty-seven, a Department of Commerce employee who had flown the Atlantic once before, was the copilot and backup navigator.

Before flying to New York, Hughes said only that he planned to try to set a record from New York to Paris. Lindbergh's thirty-three and a half hours, set on the memorable 1927 flight, was still the best time between the two cities. But speculation preceded Hughes east that the Paris hop was only the start of an around-the-world flight, and Hughes found his life miserable from the moment he landed in New York.

A crowd of several thousand mobbed him and the crew at Floyd Bennett. For the next few days, Hughes spent most of his time dodging reporters and photographers, holing up in a newly finished pavilion of the upcoming New York World's Fair, reading weather reports, studying the flight plan, and directing last-minute preparations. As a favor to Grover Whalen, the promo-

*The will and instructions were put in safe-deposit box No. 3102 at the First National Bank in Houston. More than thirty-eight years later, after Hughes's death, when frantic efforts were being made to find Hughes's will, the bank reported that it could discover no trace of the 1938 will or related papers. The bank said its records from that period were incomplete. One document found among Hughes's papers was the draft of a telegram ordering the bank to break into the safe-deposit box in 1944 and return the contents to Hughes. But there is no indication whether the telegram was actually sent and, if so, whether Hughes's instructions were carried out.

tion-minded chief of the fair, Hughes agreed to call his flight a goodwill mission promoting the international exposition, and he even named the Lock-heed the *New York World's Fair 1939.* But Hughes's only real concern was the flight itself, and for days it was actually in doubt. A frustrating series of delays kept postponing takeoff. First, government approval did not arrive until July 8. Then there were mechanical problems with the Lockheed. Finally, by late afternoon July 10, 1938, the last repairs had been made and the crew was satisfied that the ship was ready to fly.

When Hughes arrived at hangar No. 7 at about 6 P.M., he was handed the latest weather reports. New York was miserably hot and there was a threat of rain, but over the Atlantic the weather looked good. Everything had led to this moment. There was no more reason for delay.

Grover Whalen drove Hughes out to the runway so he could choose the direction for takeoff. The wind was no problem, blowing softly from the south. But as Hughes looked down the narrow strip of pavement, he felt a twinge of anxiety. Loaded with 1,500 gallons of aviation fuel, 150 gallons of oil, and a laboratory full of equipment, the Lockheed weighed nearly thirteen tons. It was so heavy, in fact, that Goodrich had fashioned special tires to support it. Would Floyd Bennett's short thirty-five-hundred-foot runway be long enough? Hughes guessed that he would need every inch of it. After checking both ends, he decided to take off to the south, where the paved runway gave way to a flat, smooth stretch of earth.

Hughes was ready to go, but Whalen had arranged a brief ceremony. The Lockheed was towed to a spot in front of the administration building where five thousand people were waiting to witness the takeoff. When Whalen lined up Hughes and his crew in a half circle beside the plane facing the crowd, Hughes's companions appeared relaxed and cheerful, as if, one reporter noted, "they were just shoving off for a trip to the beach instead of a flight across the ocean."[46] Hughes, however, looked solemn, nervous, anxious to get under way. Clad in wrinkled gray trousers, a white shirt open at the throat, and a battered brown hat, he stood in silence, hands behind his back, head down, as Whalen's voice boomed out over the public-address system. Christening the Lockheed in the name of the World's Fair, Whalen looked up at the plane and called it a "vivid symbol of the possibilities of international cooperation."[47] Then he turned to the five men beside him, wished them good luck, and praised their courage. Thousands of eyes fastened on Hughes, who grew more uncomfortable, seemingly embarrassed at Whalen's praise.[48]

When Whalen asked him to say a few words, Hughes nervously pulled a piece of paper from the pocket of his gray trousers. To make sure he was not speechless, he had hurriedly scribbled a brief message. As sweat ran down his back in the early evening heat, Hughes bent forward to speak:

"We hope that our flight may prove a contribution to the cause of friendship between nations and that through their outstanding fliers, for whom the common bond of aviation transcends national boundaries, this cause may be furthered."[49]

Putting away his note, Hughes turned to the throng of reporters and photographers who were hanging on his every word and move.

"I want to apologize to the newspapermen and photographers if I seemed rude and impolite last night," he said. "I had received favorable weather reports and had only the thought of hopping on my mind. I did not mean to be rude or impolite and I want to apologize now."[50]

As Hughes turned away, the newsmen applauded.

Just as the ceremonies were breaking up, a young woman slipped through the cordon of police around the plane and pressed a wad of chewing gum to the tail. She was Mrs. Harry Connor, the wife of the copilot, and she told a reporter, "That's for good luck. I told Harry to be sure and bring it back to me."[51]

The tension so evident in Hughes's face when he was standing on the apron vanished the moment he was behind the Lockheed's controls. He slid back the pilot's window and waved to the crowd. Starting first the right engine and then the left, he quickly warmed them up and, with Ed Lund in the seat beside him, and Thurlow, Stoddart, and Connor in the cabin to the rear, Hughes taxied the plane to the northwest end of the runway shortly after 7 P.M. At thirteen seconds past 7:19 P.M., he pulled both throttles wide open. Spectators heard a thunderous roar and watched a cloud of dust billow up behind the plane, silhouetted in the setting sun.

At first sluggish and slow to respond, the Lockheed gradually picked up speed, the runway rumbling underneath. Its enormous bulk finally set in motion, the Lockheed was screaming by the time it passed the halfway point at the administration building. Concentrating on the runway ahead, Hughes felt the ship quicken as he bore down the course. He was rapidly gaining speed, but he was also rapidly nearing the end of the runway. Would he make it? He was almost out of pavement when he felt the tail go up. There was a slight bump as the wheels left the pavement and grazed the hard earth beyond it.

The crowd gasped when it saw the plane leave the pavement and kick up a cloud of dust. For a moment, the Lockheed's roar altered, as if the engines had been throttled back. Then their full thunder came echoing out of the distance. When the dust cleared, the spectators could see the ship just barely aloft. Groaning low over the red clover carpeting the south end of the field, the Lockheed began a slow climb. Hughes banked to the left over Jamaica Bay and started across Long Island. He "dipped the wings" over Katherine Hepburn's Old Saybrook home, pointed the nose toward Boston, and made for the great circle route.

It was 7:20 P.M., July 10, 1938. The world flight had begun.

Hughes's flight was the most thoroughly planned private aviation endeavor of its time. Despite all the aeronautical progress that had been made since Lindbergh's solo jaunt to Paris eleven years before, ocean flying was still hazardous. Hughes and his team had spent months studying weather data, flight plans, and technical material about their plane. They had meticulously gone over each leg of the journey on paper, rehearsing the flight so they would know what to expect along the way. An elaborate radio system had been set up, tying them into ships at sea and ground stations around the world to keep them in constant radio contact the entire trip. Spare parts, including the specially made tires, had been stored at cities and towns where they might have to land. Hughes had tried to envision every conceivable problem. But who knew what would happen over the Atlantic? In a few years flying across the ocean would be commonplace, but in 1938 it was still a daring novelty, full of unknowns.

Like Lindbergh, Hughes had chosen to follow the great circle course, the shortest distance between New York and Paris, 3,641 miles. The route would take them over Boston, Nova Scotia, Cape Breton Island, and Newfoundland. From there it would be eighteen hundred miles of open ocean to Ireland. The flight went smoothly at first, as the East Coast glided by below, but near Newfoundland the Lockheed suffered its first mishap. The automatic trailing antenna broke, and the plane was out of radio contact for an hour and a half while the problem was corrected.

At 1:30 A.M., they were over the ocean. Flying at seventy-five hundred feet, Hughes noted his speed—192 miles per hour—in a logbook that was rapidly filling up with his notations about altitude, wind velocity, and engine performance. Below him was the Atlantic, but he never saw it so dense was the cloud cover that separated them from the sea. Off Newfoundland, Hughes began bucking strong winds, and he was forced to turn the engines up to maintain speed. When the foul weather persisted, Hughes realized that he was burning an alarming amount of fuel. For the first time, it occurred to him that he might not make Paris. At 2:30 A.M., he was so concerned that he radioed back to his ground crew in New York:

"I hope we get to Paris before we run out of gas, but I am not so sure. All I can do is to hope we will get there. I hope that we will have enough gas to reach land. I am throttling back the engines as fast as the reducing load permits."[52]

In time, they flew out of the squally weather and picked up a strong tail wind. Barring further misfortune, he reckoned they would make Paris. As dawn broke, they caught a glimpse of earth through a hole in the clouds, just barely making out Valencia on the southwestern tip of Ireland. Then the clouds closed in again and they were sealed off from the earth once more. As they approached the French coast, Stoddart talked by radio to the French liner *Ile de France* below them at sea. The ship radioed Le Bourget Airfield in Paris that it was calculating Hughes's position and would relay it shortly. But the Lockheed was flying so fast (220 miles an hour on the power dive to the French capital) that by the time the ocean liner reported back, Hughes was already on the ground at Le Bourget.

The speed astonished the French. Sixteen hours and thirty-eight minutes after leaving New York, Hughes was in Paris. No one had thought the trip could be made in less than twenty-four hours. Hughes had cut Lindbergh's record in half. A light drizzle was falling when he landed, about 4 P.M. Even so, thousands of Parisians flocked to the airport to get a glimpse of the marvelous plane and its mysterious pilot. Looking tired and drawn, Hughes was the first out. American Ambassador William C. Bullitt rushed to shake his hand.

"Congratulations," he said. "Did you have a good trip?"

"We had a good flight," was all Hughes could answer.[53]

Bullitt offered to let Hughes and his crew rest at his Paris home. Hughes thanked him and declined. As expected, Paris was only the first stop. Hughes was in a hurry to get under way on the next leg—to Moscow, 1,675 miles east. But suddenly what was to be only a brief stop became an agonizing delay when it was discovered that a rear landing strut had been damaged on the New York takeoff. The French doubted that the part could be fixed, but through the perseverance of Ed Lund, the gritty flight engineer, it was. Even so, the delay lasted eight hours.

At midnight, the Lockheed was towed on the floodlit runway to the spot where Lindbergh had landed in 1927. The rain had stopped, but crosswinds promised to make takeoff tricky. After receiving a warm sendoff from the French and stuffing his pockets full of congratulatory telegrams from home, Hughes buckled himself into the pilot's seat, gave both engines full throttle, and the big ship rolled. Slowly, it rose, climbing to fifty feet. Then it leveled off and actually dipped. The crowd gasped. In the cockpit, Hughes was locked in mortal struggle with the wind, his hands straining at the controls. Gradually, the plane gained altitude, and in a few moments disappeared into the night.

At 11:15 the next morning Hughes reached Moscow. The Russians had gone all out to make him feel at home, and had even rounded up a box of Cornflakes for his breakfast. But Hughes was driven now, oblivious to food, wanting only to refuel and get under way. Well-intentioned though they were, the Russians had interfered with his plans, swarming around the Lockheed and showering him with questions and praise. Hughes was grateful when the noted Soviet pilot Mikhail Gromoff sensed his anxiety and pulled Hughes aside.

"I know what long flights mean," confided Gromoff, who had set a record the previous summer by flying from Moscow to San Jacinto, California, in sixty-two hours, "and so none of us will bother you any more."[54]

The Russians replenished the crew's dwindling stocks of food and water, although Hughes turned down a generous going-away gift of caviar because "every pound counts."[55] After taxiing up and down the runway for fifteen minutes, the five took off for the long haul across Russia.

Back home, the flight was building Hughes into an ever-greater national hero. Americans were eagerly following the flight step by step. It was front-page news every day and the lead story on radio newscasts. Babies were being named after Hughes. Anyone with the courage to challenge the air and win was automatically a hero, yet there was more to Hughes's appeal than that. To millions of Americans, Hughes was a romantic, mysterious figure. Was he movie producer or pilot, aircraft designer or playboy, shrewd capitalist or lucky heir? He defied categorization. Whatever he was, Hughes was leading a highly individualistic life. His achievements were enough to give anyone an oversize ego, yet he appeared to be humble, modest and self-effacing. Of all his qualities, the one that earned him the highest marks was his refusal to rest on his father's money. By putting his fortune to work, Hughes had avoided the most unforgivable sin in work-oriented America: he had "not allowed himself," as *The New Republic* put it, "to be spoiled by inherited wealth."[56]

On through the Russian night the Lockheed flew, deeper into the heart of central Asia. It was the middle of the night when the crew landed at Omsk, an industrial city in western Siberia whose airport reminded Ed Lund of a cabbage patch. They would soon be flying over some of the world's most desolate terrain, so Hughes ordered the Lockheed's fuel tanks filled to capacity for the first time. Loaded with 1,750 gallons of aviation fuel, the plane just barely got off, after struggling down a muddy, slippery, and perilous runway.

Ten and a half hours later, they set down at an even more remote outpost —Yakutsk, in northern Siberia. When an interpreter failed to meet them, the crew luckily found a schoolteacher who could speak English, and with her help the Lockheed was refueled, checked out, and put aloft again, on its way to Fairbanks.

To Lund, every takeoff was a "thrill," but the one at Yakutsk surpassed all that had gone before.[57] First came a magnificent sight: the sun and moon suspended at the same time above the earth, and then the menacing jagged forms of a Siberian mountain range looming up unexpectedly ahead of them. Their maps, supplied by the United States Hydrographic Survey, gave the maximum height of the mountains as sixty-five hundred feet. Hughes's altimeter showed they were flying at seven thousand, yet they were headed right into the side of a cliff. Hughes jerked the Lockheed into a swift ascent, watching nervously as ice began forming on the wings. At ten thousand feet, with the ice growing heavier and the Lockheed straining to gain altitude, Hughes gently slipped the plane over the ninety-seven-hundred-foot crest of the range. "It's a damn good thing I didn't try to fly out of Yakutsk at night," he said.[58]

At 3:01 P.M. on Wednesday, July 13, they landed at Fairbanks. Wiley Post's widow was there and sent them on their way with a tearful farewell. The next morning, they refueled in Minneapolis and chalked up another record of sorts, the shortest pit stop of the flight—thirty-four minutes. They were eager to get going now, hoping for a smooth flight to New York since Hughes had insisted on staying at the Lockheed's controls for the entire three-day trip. Instead, the plane bucked dirty weather all the way. Hughes was bone-tired, yet he held on to the controls, nosing through one volatile cloud bank after another across the Great Lakes.

At 2 P.M., Hughes passed over Scranton, Pennsylvania, and began the descent to New York. A message flashed over the Lockheed's radio from Floyd Bennett Field—an orderly reception was planned for the crew's arrival: "You are in no danger of being mobbed."[59] At 2:33 P.M., the Lockheed broke through a bank of low-hanging clouds west of the airport. Hughes planned to fly over the field, then turn around over Jamaica Bay, come back, and land to the north. As he passed over the administration building, he looked down and shuddered.

A surging mass of people lined streets, sidewalks, and fences bordering the airfield. They were standing on cars, chairs, trucks—anything they could find—waving frantically and cheering as the silver plane swooped by. Police were trying to keep order, but thousands had already spilled over onto the tarmac where Hughes was expected to bring the plane to a stop. By the time he had finally come around and brought the ship in, twenty-five thousand cheering, hysterical people were there to greet him.

It was 2:37 P.M., July 14, 1938. The *New York World's Fair 1939* had set a record for flying around the world—three days, nineteen hours, and seventeen minutes. From now on, Howard Hughes was going to find out what it was like to be one of the most famous men in America.

Grover Whalen had spent a hectic morning putting the finishing touches on the welcoming ceremony. As the man who had welcomed Lindbergh back to New York, Whalen considered himself an experienced hand at the tricky business of controlling the mass hysteria generated by aviation heroes. Hughes was to taxi up to a certain spot on the apron. Then police would cordon off the plane. The flier would step out and place a wreath on the spot where Wiley Post had ended his memorable 1933 world flight. There were to be short speeches by Whalen and Mayor Fiorello H. LaGuardia and a few remarks by Hughes. It was to be a dignified end to the great flight.

But all of Whalen's plans went awry. Hughes taxied to the wrong location. The welcoming committee, the press, and even the police who were to guard the plane were all waiting several hundred yards down the field. When the Lockheed stopped and cut its engines, the throng broke into a mad dash for the plane. Meanwhile, hundreds of spectators began streaming through barriers onto the field. By the time Whalen and LaGuardia arrived puffing at the *New York World's Fair 1939*, there was pandemonium. Connor, Thurlow, and Stoddart were the first to squeeze their way out. Then Hughes, unshaven and smeared with grease, poked his head out, wearing a look that one writer described as midway between a frown and a blush. When he finally clambered down, he was swallowed up by the enthusiastic crowd about evenly made up of those who wanted to snap his picture and those who wanted to snatch a piece of his clothing.

He was borne along to a makeshift reviewing stand at the Lockheed's wing tip, where LaGuardia warmly clasped his hand and threw a momentary hush over the crowd.

"Seven million New Yorkers," said the little mayor, his voice rising emotionally on the scratchy public-address system, "offer congratulations for the greatest record established in the history of aviation. Welcome home."[60]

The mayor motioned Hughes to the microphone and stepped back to let the hero speak. Hughes was so tired, his voice so weak, that his words were inaudible. "Louder, Howard," someone shouted.

"I am ever so much honored," he finally said. "Thank you very much."[61]

With a wedge of police "half dragging them through the galloping crowd," Hughes and his crew were led to a press tent nearby to give interviews.[62] It proved just as chaotic there, with spectators jostling newsmen and departing planes drowning out conversation. Whalen quickly adjourned the session, hustling Hughes into a waiting limousine and whisking him along crowd-lined streets through Brooklyn and Manhattan to Whalen's home, at 48 Washington Mews in Greenwich Village. Sipping a light scotch and soda, Hughes told newsmen of the flight. He was patient, alert, and cooperative. Then, leaving the crew to answer questions, Whalen ushered Hughes upstairs, where the hero "luxuriated in his first bath in a week."[63]

Hughes asked for a clean shirt, and Whalen sent his Filipino valet, Juan, to purchase one. Juan, who was furious the next day when news stories referred to him as "Whalen's Chinese valet," returned shortly with a fresh white shirt, size 15 1/2, and Whalen told Hughes to come down and rejoin the rest of the group when he was dressed.[64]

When half an hour had gone by and Hughes had not returned, LaGuardia became nervous.

"Don't think he fell asleep, do you, Grover?" the mayor asked.[65]

Whalen went to check. Upstairs, the room where he had left Hughes was empty. He searched the other second-floor rooms but found no sign of the guest of honor. He went downstairs and checked the back door, which opened onto a central courtyard that led to Eighth Street. The door was unlocked. When Whalen broke the news to LaGuardia, the mayor flew into a rage, and Whalen feared for a moment that his wife's "treasured antiques would be shattered."[66]

Hughes had indeed quietly slipped out, hailed a cab, and given the driver the address of Katherine Hepburn's Turtle Bay town house. When the cab neared her home, Hughes saw a crowd of reporters and photographers camped out front, and he motioned the driver to go on. Their reunion would have to wait. The driver dropped him off a few minutes later at the Drake Hotel on Park Avenue. Hughes trudged up to his suite, alone, for his first night's sleep in four days.

The next day, New York went wild. More than a million people lined the sidewalks, roaring as Hughes and his crewmen passed by in open cars. More confetti and streamers rained down on them than New York had showered on Lindbergh eleven years before. About three-quarters of a million people were packed into the short stretch of lower Broadway from the Battery to City Hall. As usual, Hughes had trepidations about subjecting himself to such hysterics. While he sat in an open car waiting for the motorcade to begin at the tip of Manhattan, he was nervous and tense. He kept "biting and licking his dry lips" and taking off and putting on his old hat.[67]

"He seemed relieved when the signal came for the procession to start up Broadway," wrote a *New York Times* reporter:

Led by a detachment of mounted police, the motorcade rolled slowly along Battery Place to Broadway, teeming with ticker-tape and sound. At first reluctant to follow Mr. Whalen's example, Hughes finally hoisted himself to the top of the back seat and looked up at the towering buildings with their festoons of papers and myriad eyes all peering down at him. For a time he clutched his hat in one hand and then the other, but before Wall Street was reached, he had let it fall, forgotten, to the floor of the car.

As the procession moved slowly up through the canyon of steel and concrete, the paper snowstorm grew in intensity, long strings of ticker-tape floating in the breeze and festooning itself around cornices and even the spire of Old Trinity. In the brief intervals of silence when cheering died, the paper streamers whispered in the breeze.

Shy and embarrassed at first, Hughes gradually relaxed and seemed to be caught up by the hysteria around him. He waved constantly in response to the cheering and by the time City Hall was reached . . . he was smiling broadly and seemingly enjoying himself.[68]

In contrast to the bedlam the day before at Floyd Bennett Field, the ceremony went smoothly at City Hall, where several hundred perspiring fans were packed into the City Council chamber. The only slipup came when Whalen spoke of the hero as "Edward Hughes." After the usual speechmaking, Jesse H. Jones, chairman of President Roosevelt's Reconstruction Finance Corporation, rose to introduce the aviator. A fellow Houstonian, Jones had known Hughes Sr. and had watched young Howard grow to manhood. He gave a glowing introduction of the young man he had come to admire.

Then Hughes rose, fumbled with some handwritten notes, and slowly began to speak:

I haven't a great deal to say about this, because I am afraid I might get a little nervous and not say just what I want to. However, I haven't it all, because the newspapermen took about half of it away from me. I will just have to do the best I can. At least you may be assured no one has written this for me but myself.

I am not very good at making speeches, and I have consented to make this one only because there is one thing about this flight that I would like everyone to know. It was in no way a stunt. It was the carrying out of a careful plan and it functioned because it was carefully planned.

We who did it are entitled to no particular credit. We are no supermen or anything of that sort. Any one of the airline pilots of this nation, with any of the trained army or navy navigators and competent radio engineers in any one of our modern passenger transports, could have done the same thing. The airline pilots of this country, who in my opinion are the finest fliers in the world, face much worse conditions night after night during every winter of scheduled operations of this country.[69]

If credit was due anyone, Hughes went on, it should go to the men who designed and perfected the "modern American flying machine and its equipment." The speed record he had set, Hughes told them, was secondary to the fact that the flight had been carried out as planned with no unscheduled stops. He was especially proud that the flight had reestablished the United States as a leading force in aviation.

"The airplane was invented and originated in the United States," he said,

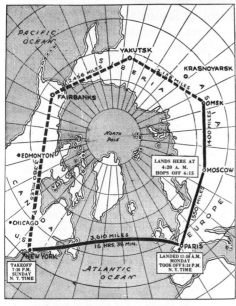

Above: The Lockheed 14 above Manhattan on a test run before the world flight, July 1938. *United Press International*

Below: Hughes talking to reporters in Minneapolis as the Lockheed was being refueled for the final leg to New York, July 14, 1938. *Wide World Photos*

The route of Hughes's 1938 world flight after stops in Paris, Moscow, and Omsk. The Lockheed 14 made additional stops in Yakutsk, Siberia, Fairbanks, Alaska, and Minneapolis, Minnesota (not shown on map) before returning to New York.
United Press International

Hughes and his crew on the steps of City Hall in New York. *Left to right:* Edward Lund, flight engineer; Richard Stoddart, radio engineer; Lt. Thomas L. Thurlow, navigator; Mayor Fiorello H. LaGuardia; Hughes; Harry P. M. Connor, navigator and copilot; and Grover Whalen behind Connor. *Wide World Photos*

Ticker-tape parade on Broadway in New York, July 15, 1938. At left is Al Lodwick, Hughes's press agent, and at right is Grover Whalen. *United Press International*

"yet since then, the countries of Europe have taken from us one by one every record of major importance." The flight demonstrated to Europeans, he continued, that Americans can build airplanes "just as fine and just as efficient . . . as any other country." If the sale of American planes would "increase only a little bit," Hughes said, he would feel "more than ever that the flight was worthwhile."*[70]

In the next few days, Hughes went on to more parades and more celebrations in Washington and Chicago. He was now eager to return to California, but Jesse Jones prevailed on him to make one more appearance. His hometown, Houston, wanted to give Hughes a hero's welcome. Like Lindbergh before him, Hughes was tired of clawing crowds and the mass adulation that accompanied instant fame. Unlike the Lone Eagle, whose disdain for people turned quickly to outright hostility after his epic flight, Hughes hid his feelings, and on July 30, 1938, flew to Houston in the Lockheed for the most tumultuous reception of all.

Ten thousand people had overrun the city's modest airfield, which had been hastily renamed Howard Hughes Airport by the city fathers. And two hundred fifty thousand persons—three-fourths of the city's population—lined downtown streets and showered Hughes and his crew with confetti and cheers. That night, at a banquet at the Rice Hotel, with his aunts Annette Lummis and Martha Houstoun next to him, and the eyes of dozens of childhood friends and longtime associates of his father upon him, Hughes bowed his head when Governor James V. Allred of Texas turned to him and said: "All of Texas is proud of your achievement."[71]

Hughes rose to acknowledge the applause.

Anything which I have done which you may consider worthwhile has been made possible by the genius of my father and the faithfulness, diligence and enterprise of the men who comprise the various parts of the company he created. . . .

Coming from Texas peculiarly fits a person for flying around the world. There's nothing you can see anywhere that you can't see in Texas, and after you've flown across Texas two or three times, the distance around the world doesn't seem so great.

He emphasized that "everyday service" was more important than "spectacular flying." His audience laughed when he told them, in all seriousness, that he could not get a job as a "first pilot" on any airline in the country.

"Don't laugh," he shot back, "for that's really true. I would have to serve a long apprenticeship as a second pilot before I could hold a first pilot's job."[72]

All in all, though, Hughes seemed genuinely moved by the huge outpouring for him.

"Let me tell you one thing," he said, in closing, "this day will never be forgotten by me."[73]

---

*Hughes's flight did indeed spur sales of American-built airplanes, especially those manufactured by Lockheed, which was deluged with orders for the Lockheed 14 from airlines in the Netherlands, Britain, and France.

It was after midnight before Hughes arrived at his family home on Yoakum Boulevard, anxious to get to bed. Much to his surprise, a group of old Houston acquaintances he had not seen in years were waiting on the back porch to say hello. Hughes sat with them for a while, reminiscing and talking about the flight. After they left, he told Annette that he was "shocked" that they had stopped by. "I didn't think any of my friends would speak to me after Ella and I got a divorce," he told her.[74]

He spent the next morning, a Sunday, visiting with more Houstonians and relatives at the Rice Hotel, although there were so many there to see him that he had time to do little more than shake hands and say hello. His tight schedule called for him to fly out around noon for the West Coast. Accompanied by Annette and Martha, he made a quick trip to the sprawling Hughes Tool Company works on Houston's east side to pay a rare personal visit to the institution whose profits had underwritten his rise to fame.

Even though it was a Sunday, the work force had been called together. It was not every day the thirty-five hundred workers got a chance to see their illustrious proprietor. Hughes was reunited with employees he had not seen in years and introduced to others for the first time. He was led around the plant by crusty Louis Enz, the plant superintendent, who had first shown Howard how to operate a lathe as a boy. There was always a soft spot in Hughes for anyone who introduced him to the wonders of machinery, and he had kept in touch with Enz by sending him personal greetings and gifts at Christmas. One year it was a tailor-made camel's-hair coat that Enz treasured.

Later, at the airport, a crowd of several hundred broke through police lines and besieged Hughes's car as it pulled into the hangar where the Lockheed was being readied for takeoff. For twenty minutes, people thrust scraps of paper, dollar bills, and other objects into the car for Hughes to sign. Sitting between Annette and Martha, he appeared in high spirits and patiently signed everything except two-dollar bills.

"No deuce notes," Hughes told one autograph hound who was waving a two-dollar bill in his face. "I'm afraid I'm too superstitious to sign my name to a $2 bill."[75]

Shortly after noon on July 31, 1938, the *New York World's Fair 1939* was refueled and ready. Hughes said good-bye to Annette, Martha, and a host of Gano cousins who were there from Dallas. Roaring down the runway of the airport that now bore his name, Hughes took off at 1:35 P.M. into a nasty cloudbank that quickly blotted out his hometown.

If he still thought of Houston as his father's town, the same could not be said for Houston. It was now Howard's town, and it had gone all out for him. Houston had lavished more honors on him than it ever accorded his father, or any other Houstonian for that matter. Howard might be a rich kid, but he had, as the *Houston Post* put it, "won his own wings."[76] He had "conquered the elements" and returned home "with more glory heaped upon his slim shoulders than a dozen men ever know in a life time."⁷⁷ As Annette and Martha watched the silver Lockheed disappear into the clouds, little did they know that they would never see their nephew again. Hughes would live thirty-eight years longer, but he had just paid his last visit to his hometown.

CHAPTER 4

THE WAR YEARS

BACK in Los Angeles, Hughes was ready to cash in on his fame. With its mild climate and cheap labor, Southern California had become a mecca for the aviation industry in the 1930s. All around him, Hughes saw Douglas, Northrop, Lockheed, Consolidated, and Vultee thriving. Why not Hughes Aircraft, too? So far, he had been thwarted. The blame, as he perceived it, rested squarely with Wright Field, outside Dayton, Ohio, the sprawling complex of hangars, laboratories, quonset huts, supply depots, and runways of the U.S. Army Air Force. The two thousand officers and civilians who worked at Wright touched every phase of military aeronautics, from testing new engines to procuring spare parts to financing experimental research. Of all its duties, though, the most important was the development of aircraft.

By 1939, Wright Field had in fact become the pivot around which American aviation turned. Whatever its future, the industry was still small on the eve of the Second World War, ranking forty-first, or roughly equivalent to what the auto industry had been in 1910. Aviation would have been even smaller and weaker had it not been for Wright Field. When the Depression threatened to end commercial-aircraft production, Wright staved off ruin for plane makers by swiftly awarding millions of dollars in design and manufacturing contracts to struggling companies. It was during this time that Boeing built the B-17; Lockheed, the P-38; Douglas, the A-20; Consolidated, the B-24; Northrop, the A-17; and Martin, the giant Mars transport. On the eve of the war, Wright's action had assured the very survival of the industry, and perhaps even the country itself.

No one was more eager to land a Wright Field contract than Hughes. But he had never succeeded in doing so. In 1937, he had failed to sell the air force the rebuilt H-1 as a fighter. Later that same year, he had submitted a design for a high-speed, twin-engine fighter, but the air force chose Lockheed to build a similar plane. After that, Hughes began imagining that Wright Field's engineers personally disliked him and that a conspiracy was at work to exclude him from government contracts. He began derisively referring to the Materiel Command as the "Hate Hughes Club."[1]

In truth, Hughes's problems with Wright had nothing to do with a conspiracy. Many of the air force's highest officers had great respect for his ability as a pilot and for the design work of his company. But the Materiel Command also had a prescribed way of doing business, and Hughes refused to follow it. With the H-1, Hughes Aircraft had developed its own specifications, mistakenly confident that the plane would prove "so sensational in its performance that the Army would have to accept it."[2] In the case of the Lockheed plane in 1937, Hughes had simply lost out to a superior machine— the high-flying, twin-boomed P-38 fighter so instrumental to the Allied victory in the Second World War.

Wright Field or no, world events seemed to be moving in Hughes's favor by the close of the 1930s. The prospect of war in Europe had created a soaring demand for American airplanes. In 1939, the air force set a goal of 5,500 military planes a year for American manufacturers, then raised it to 10,000. The following spring, President Roosevelt called on the industry to produce 50,000 planes a year. To come anywhere near meeting these demands, the industry had to press every available aircraft engineer, designer, craftsman, and plant into service.

Shortly after the Second World War broke out in Europe in September of 1939, Hughes came up with the design of a medium-range bomber to be manned by a crew of five. The plane would fly at speeds up to 450 miles an hour and have a range of four thousand miles. Hughes Aircraft had never built a plane larger than a single-engine racer, so the new ship would clearly be a drastic departure for the company. Yet its most radical feature was not its size but the material out of which Hughes proposed to build it. The plane was to be constructed almost entirely of plywood, and its construction would involve a newly patented duramold process that bonded thin sheets of wood to a wooden frame. Although the British had experimented with wooden combat planes, Wright Field was adamantly opposed to the material for military aircraft. It considered aluminum superior on all counts. Wood absorbed moisture, developed cracks, and was more likely than metal to shatter under fire. Hughes could not have been unaware of this, yet he pressed forward with his wooden plane, which he called the D-2.

On December 5, 1939, Hughes Aircraft wrote a brief letter to Wright Field, acknowledging that a new plane was in the works. Referring to it variously as a "pursuit airplane" and a "military aircraft," the letter did not identify the type of aircraft under design, but did say the company was confident that it would ultimately be placed in "quantity production."[3] Hughes genuinely loved to shroud his projects in secrecy lest someone might steal an idea. But often, as was probably the case with the D-2, the secrecy was a ploy to arouse curiosity. And often the lure worked.

Not long after Hughes Aircraft had written the letter, an air force staff car pulled onto the road leading to the far end of the runway at the Union Air Terminal in Burbank. Coming to a stop in front of the unimposing hangar of the Hughes Aircraft Company, a group of high-ranking officers piled out. Led by General H. H. (Hap) Arnold, the tall, white-haired commander of the air force, the group had been inspecting aircraft plants in Southern California and had decided to drop by the Hughes hangar for a look at the Hughes mystery ship. To their consternation, the guards refused to admit them. There were strict orders from Hughes that no one was permitted inside without his permission.[4] Arnold's aides were beside themselves. Arnold was chief of the air force, charged with the air defense of the nation, and inside the hangar was an airplane that might contribute to that effort; yet the general was being denied permission to see it. The guards remained adamant. Hughes could not be reached. The officers angrily climbed into their car and sped off.

Whether Hughes's snub was intentional is not clear. It was 1940 and he was juggling various enterprises, including a recently acquired major share in Transcontinental and Western Air (later to be renamed Trans World Airlines). Also, he had returned to movies after an eight-year hiatus, making a film called *The Outlaw,* based on the story of Billy the Kid and a buxom half-breed girl, played by Hughes's most statuesque discovery, Jane Russell.

Hughes had thrown himself into the production of *The Outlaw* with his customary intensity and attention to detail. Howard Hawks had been hired to direct, but Hughes interfered so much the first two weeks the movie was being filmed in Arizona that Hawks quit. Then Hughes took over the direction, giving orders long distance from Los Angeles and having each day's rushes flown to him at night by special plane. If Hughes had one overriding obsession as director of this movie, it was to display Jane Russell's breasts. To that end, the cameras were manipulated at every opportunity, but even so, Hughes was not satisfied. One scene in which Jane, tied between two trees by leather thongs, writhes sensuously in a futile effort to free herself, gave him the idea for a new kind of brassiere. Relying on his knowledge of aerodynamics and stress, so the Hollywood legend goes, Hughes sketched a bra for Russell that would, at the pull of a string, accentuate her already impressive endowments.

Nevertheless, it was the D-2 that embodied his highest hopes in 1940. That spring, he began to buy a tract of land (eventually to total thirteen hundred acres) just west of Culver City, south of Venice, and bordering the Pacific Ocean as the manufacturing site for the D-2. The following spring, the company, still actually a division of the Hughes Tool Company, moved out of its cramped quarters in Burbank into a modern sixty-thousand-square-foot, air-conditioned, humidity-controlled plant.

Hughes had spared no expense. There were new drafting tables, engineering lofts, blueprint and duplicating machines. There was a laboratory for testing glues and resins to be used in building the D-2. There was an emergency power-generating plant. Shops were equipped with the most modern machine tools. Outside, road crews were busily grading a nine-thousand-foot, east-west runway, the longest private airstrip in the world.

Although still small by aviation industry standards, Hughes Aircraft was growing. By the spring of 1941, it had five hundred employees, nearly a hundred of whom were engineers. Hughes's reputation in aviation had often enabled him to attract first-class engineers and draftsmen, yet he had lost Richard Palmer, the man who might have proved their natural leader. After designing the revolutionary H-1, Palmer, disenchanted with the lack of direction at Hughes Aircraft, had moved on to the Vultee Aircraft Company. Hughes could have used him to snare a military contract, but Palmer was busily designing trainers, pursuit planes, and attack bombers that were establishing Vultee as a leading defense contractor.

The D-2 was Hughes Aircraft's only project, and it was plagued by misfortune from the start. Hughes had problems getting the right type of wood, resins, and glues for the duramold process. Then he could not get the engines he needed. The air force, which controlled the flow of strategic aircraft materials such as engines, propellers, and spare parts, had previously assigned the type of engine needed for the D-2 to other manufacturers. This forced him to change the design of the plane from a bomber to a twin-engine fighter. More important, it forced him to face the unpleasant fact that as much as he disliked Wright Field, without its cooperation the D-2 would never be built.

Hughes called Noah Dietrich in Houston and asked him to head a delegation calling on Major General Oliver P. Echols, the air force's top procurement officer, to wheedle a commitment from the government to buy his plane. As the overseer of Hughes's finances, Dietrich was alarmed at the rate Hughes was pouring money into his embryonic aircraft division at Culver City. Hughes had already spent millions on land, buildings, and staff, and there was no prospect of any return on the investment. Still, as usual, Dietrich put his personal reservations about the aircraft company aside and headed for Washington.

On October 3, 1941, Dietrich and a small group of Hughes engineers met with Echols. After acknowledging that the D-2 was in trouble, the Hughes delegation said the problem sprang from a "lack of government interest."[5] Then, getting to the point, Dietrich asked Echols whether the air force would be interested in the plane if it met all military specifications and performed as Hughes hoped.

If Echols, who had once been embarrassed when Hughes failed to keep an appointment at Wright Field to show a group of brass the revolutionary H-1, was enjoying Hughes's predicament, he hid it well. He answered calmly that the air force "knew so little about the [D-2] airplane, due to the secrecy which has been involved around it and the limited number of people allowed to investigate it, that it would be impractical to make any promises or arrangements in regard to this airplane until [the air force] had full information as to what it was."[6] He did assure Dietrich that he would have his staff evaluate the plane and that he would then give an answer.

Within a few days, Wright Field's engineers had concluded that the D-2 was not suitable as a military aircraft. It lacked a bullet-resistant windshield and armor plate, and the landing gear was considered too weak for air force use. Incorporating combat features would make the D-2 so heavy it would be "useless as a military weapon."[7] And Wright objected to the D-2's use of wood.

Disappointed by this latest rebuff, Hughes sent two engineers, Kenneth Ridley and Stanley Bell, to Wright Field in an effort to reverse the decision. But the air force remained firmly opposed to the plane "because of its lack of required military features."[8]

Even after the Japanese bombed Pearl Harbor on December 7, 1941, when every available aircraft-industry resource and plane was being pressed into service, Wright Field saw only one possible role for Hughes Aircraft: to manufacture wooden wings and components for military gliders and other noncombat planes. An internal memo of January 26, 1942, made a stinging assessment of Hughes's fondest enterprise:

It is the opinion of this office that this plant is a hobby of the management and that the present project now being engineered is a waste of time and that the facilities, both in engineering personnel and equipment, are not being used to the full advantage in this emergency. . . . the Air Corps should discontinue any further aircraft projects with this organization.[9]

With a chill wind still blowing out of Wright Field, Hughes gave up trying to woo the Materiel Command. It was time to bypass the Hate Hughes Club.

Hughes seemed to have nothing but enemies in Dayton, but he had a friend in Washington at the highest level. He was Jesse Holman Jones, the "biblically big" white-thatched Houstonian who had saluted Hughes after his around-the-world flight and who was both Roosevelt's secretary of commerce and boss of the Reconstruction Finance Corporation, the recovery agency set up by Herbert Hoover to bail American business out of the Depression.[10] A friend of Hughes's father since the time Howard was a boy, Jones was a holdover from the Hoover years who had come to wield vast power in Roosevelt's Washington. A conservative Democrat, the "Emperor Jones" had adroitly built a "small bureaucratic empire in alien New Deal soil just as he had once built a financial empire in Texas."[11] His open scorn of New Deal social programs might incur the wrath of Roosevelt liberals, but the president had found Jones's shrewd, cautious nature a counterpoint to the effusive exuberance of his closest advisers, and Jones's wide-ranging connections with southern Democrats also proved useful on Capitol Hill. To his enemies, Jones was the second-most-powerful man in Washington.

In an effort to publicize the D-2, Hughes sent an emissary to see Jones in mid-June of 1942. The go-between was Russell Birdwell, a wiry and resourceful Hollywood press agent with a knack for manufacturing "news" out of often outlandish publicity stunts. Birdwell had once charmed the New York press corps by flying the whole town of Zenda, Ontario (population twelve), to New York for the world première of the movie *The Prisoner of Zenda.* While Birdwell was on his way to Washington on the D-2 project, he was also masterminding a nationwide campaign to heighten advance interest in *The Outlaw.* Leasing billboards across the country, Birdwell plastered them with pictures of a seductive Jane Russell reclining in a haystack.

In Washington, Birdwell wasted no time in contacting Jones. When he showed up in a taxi at the Shoreham Hotel where the secretary lived, Jones told him he did not like cabs. Birdwell took the hint and arrived the next time in a limousine with a private chauffeur.[12] Birdwell extolled the virtues of the D-2 and claimed that it might revolutionize warfare. He suggested to Jones that President Roosevelt himself might want to make a public statement about it.

On June 27, 1942, Jones spoke to the president privately at the White House. Exactly what he told Roosevelt is not known, but he apparently explained that Hughes had designed and built a remarkable new military plane that could possibly help win the war. Since the aircraft was about to make its first flight, perhaps the president might want to announce it. Jones left the president with a two-paragraph statement:

Howard Hughes, airplane designer, builder and holder of most of the world's speed records, will send into the sky at an early date his twin-motored plastic bomber which will fly faster than any pursuit ship in the world, 485 miles an hour.

Mr. Hughes has put $6,000,000 of his private funds and several years of intensive work and study into the development of this plane, the Hughes Design No. 2. Hughes Design No. 1, which inspired his fast bomber, was the plane in which seven years ago he flew nonstop from Los Angeles to New York in seven hours, twenty-nine minutes. This record still stands and is by far the fastest cross-country flight ever made. Nowhere in the world has anyone yet approached Hughes' record of 2,500 miles at a sustained speed of 333 miles per hour.*[13]

Roosevelt admired Hughes's aviation feats, but he displayed no special curiosity in this latest venture, and he routinely sent Jones's suggested statement over to General Arnold, commander of the air force, with a one-sentence query: "What is there in this?"[14]

Arnold answered the next day that the air force, fully aware of Hughes's plane, was following work on it and that Hughes was endeavoring to sell it to the government.

Meanwhile, Jones's brief talk with the president had given the fast-moving Birdwell enough ammunition to make a full-scale assault on the White House to coax a statement from the president. If that happened, Hughes must have reasoned, then the air force might be brought around. On July 11, 1942, Birdwell wrote Marvin H. McIntyre, one of three secretaries who controlled access to Roosevelt:

*Hughes had actually established the cross-country record five—not seven—years before. His record-setting time was seven hours and twenty-eight minutes, not seven hours and twenty-nine minutes as given in the memorandum. His average speed was 332—not 333—miles per hour.

On the set of *The Outlaw* with actor Walter Huston, 1941. *Wide World Photos*

One of the infamous billboards of Jane Russell promoting *The Outlaw*, this one in San Francisco in 1942. *Wide World Photos*

A few days ago Mr. Jesse Jones discussed with the President the work Howard Hughes has been quietly doing for the past three and one-half years in developing a twin-motored plastic bomber that will fly faster than any pursuit ship in the world. During all of this time we have kept the project most quiet, but now on the eve of the ship being ready for flight Mr. Jones recommended to the President that he might possibly want to make an announcement to the press concerning Mr. Hughes' plane which will, no doubt, revolutionize all wartime fighting. Mr. Hughes not only designed and built the ship in his own factory but has personally invested some six million dollars into perfecting this design, an evolution of the plane with the plastic wing in which he established his non-stop seven-hour-and-twenty-eight-minute record from Los Angeles to New York seven years ago: a record of sustained flying speed which has not yet been equalled anywhere in the world.

I address this note to you in the hope that I may be able to learn from you what disposition the President intends to make of the statement concerning the Howard Hughes ship which Mr. Jones left with the President.[15]

Two days later, McIntyre read the letter at his desk and was puzzled. Who was this Birdwell and what was the statement he was writing about? McIntyre usually knew of Roosevelt's announcements in advance, yet he had heard nothing about this one. Did one arm of the White House not know what another was doing? He sent the Birdwell letter, along with a note, to Stephen T. Early, another of FDR's White House secretaries. "Do you know anything about the suggested statement referred to?" asked McIntyre. "If not, will you take it up with the Boss?"[16]

Birdwell was no stranger to Early, a former newspaperman who had encountered the high-powered Hollywood press agent during his travels. The moment he saw the Birdwell letter cross his desk, he squelched any talk of Roosevelt's boosting Hughes's plane.

"I would not take this up with the Boss," he wrote McIntyre. "This is a matter that should be called to the attention of the chiefs of air, the Army and Navy. I see no reason whatever to drag the President into it except to publicize the Hughes plane. And that is not the President's job."[17]

Hughes had failed again. The war raged in Europe and Asia, and still he lacked a contract to build military planes.* Douglas and Lockheed were growing into giant corporations employing a hundred thousand people each, while Hughes Aircraft, with its few hundred workers, remained insignificant, nothing more than a "hobby" of Howard Hughes. While others secured multimillion-dollar contracts, Hughes was shelling out millions of his own money. In the summer of 1942, Hughes was a troubled man.

---

*Hughes's companies, like most American corporations during the war, did have contracts to produce equipment and supplies for the war effort. At Culver City, the aircraft company secured a patent on a device called a flexible feed chute that speeded the loading of machine guns on B-17 bombers. The company also manufactured electric booster drives, which made machine guns less likely to jam, and manufactured wing panels and other parts for military training planes. In Houston, the Hughes Tool Company manufactured parts for B-25 and B-26 bombers, and managed, for the army, the Dickson Gun Plant, which manufactured gun barrels.

STRANGE BEDFELLOWS

Four hundred miles north, in Oakland, California, Henry J. Kaiser was also troubled. A large man who exuded confidence and energy, Kaiser had been a builder of roads and dams before turning to shipbuilding at the outbreak of the Second World War. Although he had never constructed a ship before 1940, Kaiser quickly emerged "as a sort of Paul Bunyan of the West," mass-producing steel cargo vessels known as Liberty Ships in his West Coast shipyards.[18] Applying the assembly-line techniques of auto making to shipbuilding, Kaiser made hundreds of desperately needed "ugly ducklings" to bolster the Allied cause. By July of 1942, he had miraculously cut building time for a ten-thousand-ton ship from 355 to 48 days.

But by the summer of 1942, Kaiser feared that it was going to take more than his "miracle" to save Allied shipping. The United States had entered the war supremely confident of victory, only to watch its shipping fleet be devastated by packs of Nazi submarines prowling the Western Atlantic. In January of 1942, seventeen ships had been torpedoed and sunk off the East Coast. In February, thirty-six went down. In March, sixty ships were sunk. In April, it was sixty-eight, and in May, eighty-seven. Like millions of other Americans, Kaiser read these reports with mounting alarm. The German U-boats were sinking ships faster than he and his fellow builders could produce them. Navy convoys might be the answer, but for the moment there were not enough warships to escort cargo vessels to Europe. During the week of July 12, 1942, more than one hundred thousand tons of American shipping went to the bottom of the Atlantic—the largest loss for any week in the war. With the great Allied lifelines in grave jeopardy, "the fate of the war hung in the balance."[19]

The submarine menace weighing heavily on his mind, Kaiser traveled to Portland, Oregon, on July 19, 1942, to launch another Liberty Ship in his bustling shipyard on the banks of the Willamette River. Before sending the *Harvey W. Scott* sliding down the ways, Kaiser spoke to the crowd about "the haunting fear" spreading across America, the fear that German U-boats would eventually cut off the supply of arms and materiel to American troops fighting abroad.[20] To meet this challenge, Kaiser proposed that the nation turn over nine shipyards to construct a fleet of giant flying boats to ferry men and supplies over the oceans where "no submarines could shoot them down."[21] With a fleet of giant cargo planes, Kaiser predicted,

the position of our enemies will be hopeless. We will be able to put down a vast army, anywhere in the world, within a single week. We will be free once and for all of the fear of having our Armies cut off in some place distant from our shores. . . . the whole world will be our front yard. And our enemies will be beaten to their knees.[22]

Overnight, Kaiser's plan caught the imagination of the American people. "To the man in the street," one bureaucrat later lamented, "it was a great idea, a marvelous idea."[23]

If anyone other than Kaiser had made such a fantastic proposal, he might have been laughed at or scorned. But Kaiser's reputation was based on achieving the impossible, and thus the plan had credence from the start. Newspapers readily picked up on the idea and began promoting it as enthusiastically as Kaiser. "An adequate fleet of transports, big ones, could deliver men and munitions safely over great distances, and laugh at the U-boats," the *Philadelphia Inquirer* editorialized.[24] "Flying Freighters—The Ship Of The Future Will Fly Over The Ocean If The Nation Accepts Henry Kaiser's Suggestion" blared a headline in the *Washington Post.*[25] Within days, Kaiser's proposal had generated wide bipartisan support in Congress and lawmakers began pressuring Roosevelt to adopt Kaiser's plan at once.

Enjoying a groundswell of popular support, Kaiser rolled into Washington by train on July 30, 1942, in hope of translating his flying-boat proposal into a firm contract from the Roosevelt administration. An optimist who exuded charm and vitality, Kaiser was successful with almost everyone he met. One high-ranking official who saw him at work rated him with "Diamond Jim Brady and Billy Sunday."[26] Mr. Kaiser, he said, "can sell as very few men can sell."[27] If anything, he was more like Billy Sunday, for there was a messianic fervor to Kaiser's mission, as though he had been divinely inspired to reveal the flying-boat plan to the nation. It was now up to the country to adopt it and get on with the job of building the ships.

When reporters asked Kaiser for specifics on his proposed craft, he invariably sidestepped the questions. When one asked how cargo planes were built, Kaiser told him matter-of-factly, "There's nothing to that."[28] If the president would only give him the green light, Kaiser promised, he would turn out the first flying boat in ten months.

While Kaiser's personal salesmanship was winning converts, powerful opposition was building behind the scenes. The army, the navy, the air force, the Maritime Commission, the War Production Board, and the aircraft industry all had serious doubts. They feared, first, that Kaiser's plan would divert strategic raw materials from other phases of war production, such as the manufacture of combat aircraft, the number-one aviation priority. More significantly, aircraft experts considered Kaiser's plan totally unrealistic. Building airplanes was far more complicated than building Liberty Ships. To design and build a new aircraft usually took years. The idea of doing so in ten months, as Kaiser was proposing, was nonsense.[29]

However potent the opposition, Kaiser still had a powerful ally—public opinion. No one was more aware of that than Donald Marr Nelson, the taciturn, pipe-smoking chief of the War Production Board, the superagency that was now asked to rule on Kaiser's plan. A former chief executive of Sears, Roebuck & Co., Nelson presided over a vast bureaucracy that often allocated $4 billion a month in converting American industry to the war effort. His staff, almost unanimously opposed to Kaiser's plan, had spent many futile hours trying to convince the stubborn industrialist to abandon it. Wisdom dictated that Nelson should veto the flying boat, but Nelson feared the adverse public opinion that was certain to follow. Would such a step not be seen by the country as another case of Washington bureaucrats' being unable to accept a daring new idea? And might the bad publicity not hinder the work of his own agency and make more difficult the already Herculean task of converting industry to war production? Besides, what if the experts were wrong? What if Kaiser, "through some fantastic power," could achieve a "miracle"?[30] Once before, over the objections of experts, Nelson had gambled on Kaiser by lending him money to build a blast furnace to augment his shipbuilding yards. Kaiser had gone on to break all records in shipbuilding. When Kaiser was ushered into Nelson's office in the Social Security Building on August 7, 1942, the bespectacled, austere-looking Nelson had made up his mind. "Henry," he told Kaiser, "I am going to take another chance on you."[31]

Three days later, Nelson sent Kaiser a letter giving him a tentative go-ahead. The letter was a disappointment to Kaiser. Rather than blanket authority to build a fleet of flying boats, Nelson authorized Kaiser only to design and build three of the airships. And before he could even do that Kaiser would have to present plans and drawings in Washington showing the plane in precise detail. It was less than the wholehearted endorsement Kaiser had sought, but it was a start. On August 10, Kaiser left behind a muggy Washington to return to the West Coast.

In proposing the flying boat, Kaiser had said, "our engineers have plans on their drawing boards for gigantic flying ships beyond anything Jules Verne could ever have imagined."[32] It is not clear whose "engineers" Kaiser meant, since his own thirty-thousand-man work force held not one aeronautical engineer. In all likelihood, it was just one of the exaggerations to which Kaiser was prone when promoting an idea. In any event, he was now expected to produce a detailed flying-boat design. Soon after he returned to Oakland, a curious telephone call came into Kaiser's office. Identifying himself as a Portland engineer, the caller had a "tip"—Howard Hughes was just finishing work on an "Army" plane and would have "about 200 aeronautical engineers soon available."[33] If so, Kaiser reasoned, might not Hughes provide him with the technical expertise he needed?

For days, Kaiser sought to talk with Hughes, whom he had never met and knew "only by his fame in aviation."[34] But Hughes's Romaine Street office in Hollywood was consistently vague about his whereabouts. Aides would say only that their boss could not be reached and that Kaiser's message would be relayed as soon as possible. It was not until late August that Kaiser finally got through to Hughes, and when he did, it turned out that Hughes was not in Los Angeles at all, but rather was registered under an assumed name in a suite at the Fairmont Hotel, across the bay in San Francisco, where he was recuperating from a severe bout with pneumonia. On the night of August 21, 1942, Kaiser sped across the San Francisco–Oakland Bay Bridge to meet with him. When Kaiser was ushered into Hughes's suite, he found Hughes stretched out on a bed, looking frail and exhausted.

"Sit up," said the peppery Kaiser, who was twenty-three years older than Hughes. "We want to talk about winning the war."

"I am very tired," Hughes answered weakly. "I haven't had any sleep. . . . Besides, you're crazy."[35]

Hughes was referring to Kaiser's scheme for building giant cargo planes. Kaiser launched into a spirited defense of his plan. He wanted Hughes to join him. Hughes would design the big boats; Kaiser would build them. Hughes listened, no doubt astonished at this bundle of energy that had been unleashed in his suite. Even so, he was bound to be intrigued by any scheme to build an airplane on the scale Kaiser proposed. Nothing was settled. Kaiser told Hughes to think about it, and as he was leaving, offered a bit of advice: "Take a pill and get some sleep."[36]

The next day, as Kaiser was leading Grover Loening, an aircraft consultant for the War Production Board, on an inspection tour of Kaiser's Bay Area shipyards, Kaiser asked casually, "What do you think of Howard Hughes? Is he a good aircraft constructor?"[37] A pilot himself, Loening told Kaiser that he thought Hughes was a brilliant engineer and one of America's greatest flyers, and that his aircraft work "was just about the best that we had in the factories of America."[38]

Loening's praise sent Kaiser racing back across the Bay Bridge the next day to see Hughes, where he turned on all his considerable charm and powers of persuasion. In addition to his aversion to partners, Hughes doubted that the cargo plane could be designed and built in the short time Kaiser was proposing. Pushing hard, Kaiser boasted that he had accomplished the impossible before and that together they would perform the impossible again. Against his better judgment, and swept up by Kaiser's appeal, Hughes began to think that a miracle might in fact be performed.[39] He agreed to the collaboration, but only on the condition that he had complete authority over design. It would be Kaiser's obligation to mass-produce it if that day ever came. The shipbuilder readily agreed. The next day, morning papers across the country carried word of the extraordinary partnership:

Henry J. Kaiser, West Coast shipbuilder, announced tonight he had teamed with Howard Hughes, multi-millionaire Hollywood airplane designer, speed flier and film producer, in a program to build 500 cargo airplanes.

After conferring here several days, Kaiser announced, the two men have reached an agreement "to go forward together and jointly, on an equal basis, in fulfillment of the most ambitious aviation program the world has ever known."[40]

By teaming with Hughes, Kaiser silenced critics who said he lacked the know-how to design airplanes. But in Washington the flying boat still had plenty of opposition. The military and the aircraft industry were convinced that the project was a pipe dream, and the services were worried that it would divert men and materiel from other production. To the press, which kept agitating in the weeks that followed for Washington to support the project, the government's reluctance to approve a final contract was merely a case of bureaucratic red tape.

"We Americans are 'active people,' " said the *New York World-Telegram*.

"We want to get things done. We tolerated red tape in peacetime because we had to, but now, with the fate of the nation at stake, we believe that red tape must be slashed. Who cares where Kaiser gets his steel, his aluminum or his toothpaste as long as he boosts the production of planes?"[41]

Late in August, Kaiser and Hughes submitted the first detailed plans for the flying boat, calling for a gigantic eight-engine seaplane with a wingspan longer than a football field and a hull taller than a three-story building. Because of the shortage of metal, the huge plane was to be built of wood, using the duramold process Hughes had employed for the D-2 fighter. But even so, the most phenomenal aspect was the flying boat's weight—two hundred tons, nearly three times heavier than any airplane in existence.

If Donald Nelson had been a strong-willed administrator, he could have vetoed the flying boat and ridden out whatever public storm ensued. But the chairman of the War Production Board had a reputation as a "weak man," unable to make difficult decisions.[42] Also, as Nelson soon learned, the flying boat, for all its enemies, had its supporters in Washington. One was Jesse Jones. Normally a hard-nosed conservative when it came to underwriting experimental projects, Jones now let it be known that his Reconstruction Finance Corporation would pick up the multimillion-dollar tab to finance the cargo planes.

On September 16, Kaiser dropped by Jones's office at the Department of Commerce. When he asked Jones to evaluate Hughes, the Texan glowed and said, "You are safe in proceeding with Howard Hughes. I have known him since he was a boy—and I knew his able father before him—and I know of no more capable and reliable man than Howard Hughes."[43] Jones then added a word of advice: "Now, whatever you do, Henry, do not interfere with Howard. He is thorough and he is a genius and do not interfere with him."[44]

The next day, the Defense Plant Corporation, a subsidiary of Jones's RFC, notified Kaiser and Hughes "to proceed with the design, engineering and construction of 3 cargo planes (flying boat type) similar to the design you have submitted to the War Production Board."[45] Authorizing an expenditure of up to $18 million, the agency stipulated that the planes should be built at Hughes's Culver City plant and that neither Kaiser nor Hughes would receive a "fee or profit" from the contract.

By the oddest series of events, Hughes at last was on his way to becoming a government plane maker. Yet the long-awaited moment brought him no joy. The more he thought about potential problems, the more he worried and the less he slept. He saw that there was no way to design and build even one flying boat in ten months. When he failed to meet the deadline, the politicians would blame him. The reputation and public image he had spent years building would be severely damaged.

About midnight on September 27, Merrill C. Meigs, the fifty-eight-year-old deputy director of the War Production Board's aircraft division, who had just returned to his Los Angeles hotel room from an exhausting meeting with visiting British aircraft manufacturers, answered a knock on his door. Meigs opened it to find that the visitor was Hughes, looking "very tired and worried."[46] For the next two hours, Hughes poured out his anxieties to the patient Meigs. Hughes was "so tired that it was hard for him even to talk."[47] He told Meigs he knew that he "could not make the big boat in less than two years, and if he failed it would reflect on him."[48]

Agreeing, Meigs assured Hughes that every aircraft expert in the government knew that he could not possibly build the plane in the time allotted by the contract, but that, nevertheless, the public and politicians expected it in ten months and would blame him if he failed to deliver.[49] Meigs then asked Hughes why he had agreed to take part in the project in the first place. Looking sad and exhausted, Hughes admitted that he had been swept up by Kaiser's infectious enthusiasm, and Meigs concluded that the young man had become imbued "with the enthusiasm of an older man."[50] As Meigs listened, he got the distinct impression that Hughes felt he had "bought a bill of goods."[51] Thanking Meigs for listening, Hughes left at 2 A.M., a "very tired, worried, sincere young man," as Meigs noted in his diary, "with every good reason to be worried."[52]

It was still not too late for Hughes to bow out of the deal. The final contract had not been signed. But he went ahead and thereby launched one of the most bizarre events in aviation history.

On November 16, 1942, the contract was signed. In government jargon, the flying boat was known as Plancor 1424, or the HK-1, a designation that stood for Hughes–Kaiser One. To the men who would soon build it, the gigantic airship was known as the Hercules. To the public, for whom the boat later became a symbol of government waste and Hughes's folly, it would collect a host of unflattering nicknames, the best-remembered being the "Spruce Goose"—a name that Hughes despised passionately. But in the fall of 1942 all that lay in the future.

THE FLYING BOAT

Although Hughes had landed the contract largely on his reputation as an aircraft designer and builder, he was woefully unprepared for the task. Aeronautical engineers had never designed a plane of two hundred tons, let alone one to be constructed of wood. Working with wood was much more complicated than working with metal. The skin and structural parts would be composed of thin sheets of spruce plywood, built up layer on layer and bonded together by special waterproof glues that would presumably make the seaplane impervious to water, heat, and fungus. Since every piece of wood has its own density, each would have to be accurately weighed and analyzed before it could be used in the construction.

By industry standards, Hughes Aircraft was a modest company, employing only a few hundred people. Hughes would need far more men. But where would he get them? The aircraft industry had already put every qualified specialist to work, and Hughes was prohibited by the government from raiding other manufacturers to staff his plant. He lacked not only men; there was not even a hangar at Hughes Aircraft large enough to house the flying boat while it was under construction.

If Hughes was to build the ship in a reasonable time, Hughes Aircraft would have to function with uncharacteristic efficiency. New airplanes are built essentially by hand. They require new parts, new molds, new assemblies —even, sometimes, new tools. To succeed, an aircraft plant must be highly coordinated. Hughes Aircraft was anything but that. As a "hobby" of Howard Hughes, it reflected his eccentric style. Departments were independent of one another and tended to report directly to Hughes, when they could find him. Although he was president of the company, he rarely appeared at Culver City, nor did he appoint anyone to run the company in his place. Glenn Odekirk, his pilot buddy and mechanic, was the general manager. But Hughes did not give Odekirk the power to be a true general manager, with authority to hire and fire department heads. Hughes named Neil S. McCarthy, his Los Angeles lawyer, as titular head of the flying-boat project. But McCarthy, a horse-racing enthusiast who had made a fortune representing movie moguls, knew nothing about aviation, and was even afraid to fly. Henry Kaiser, true to his word, had turned the project over to Hughes after the contract was signed and returned to Oakland. Thus, no one was there on the site, in charge of the flying boat on a day-to-day basis.

In the 1930s, when Hughes Aircraft was virtually a cottage industry, this carefree approach had posed few problems. Since the company was small, it was not necessary for Hughes to supervise work. He could show up occasionally, evaluate the work, give new orders, and then disappear again for weeks. Without a deadline, his men usually took their time, and ordinarily their work was good. Hughes was, by universal agreement, a perfectionist who would not tolerate slipshod performance. But by 1942 Hughes Aircraft, while still not large, was no longer tiny either. If the company was actually to build the flying boat, it would require closer direction than Hughes was personally prepared to give. Still, he made no move to appoint anyone in his place. He continued to operate much as he had always done.

By day Hughes's engineers would turn out drawings at Culver City, and at night Ken Ridley, the chief engineer, and Rea Hopper, the chief designer, would drive to Hughes's house and spend hours going over the sketches. (Hughes had moved in 1942 from the house at 211 Muirfield Road, next to the ninth hole of the Wilshire Country Club, to a rented house at 619 Sarbonne Road in Bel Air, behind the tenth green of the Bel Air Country Club.)* Yet even these conferences were irregular, because Hughes was often preoccupied with other interests, such as putting the finishing touches on *The*

---

*Hughes had moved out of 211 Muirfield Road in 1942 to avoid the payment of California income taxes. The state insisted he was a resident because he owned and lived in that house. Hughes maintained that he was a resident of Texas and was in California on business.

Outlaw and rendezvousing with Hollywood's leading ladies.

Indeed, Hughes's amours sometimes led him into unexpected pathways. As reported afterward by the columnist Igor Cassini, when his brother, Oleg Cassini, the designer, came home one afternoon to find that his wife, the actress Gene Tierney, was out with Hughes, Cassini hid in the garage waiting for them to return and then "hit Hughes in the face."[53] Hughes fled, only to bump into Cassini inadvertently shortly afterward at a Hollywood party. Hughes locked himself in an upstairs bedroom and telephoned for help. As Igor Cassini told the story, "twenty minutes later . . . half a dozen gorillas ran into the place yelling, 'Where is he? Where's Mr. Hughes?' " then rushed him to safety.[54]

At Culver City, meanwhile, the only physical evidence of the HK-1 was the construction of a huge hangar north of the existing plant. Because of the steel shortage, the hangar was also built of wood. Measuring 750 feet long, 250 feet wide, and 100 feet high, it covered more than four acres and was believed to be the largest wooden building ever constructed.

But the flying boat itself was off to an unpromising start. Four months after the contract was approved, the government's resident engineer was so concerned about the lack of progress that he wrote his superior in Washington asking for suggestions on how to "jolt" the Hughes company into "better organized activity."[55] He noted:

There does not seem to be any clear understanding in this organization as to who is the boss with authority, driving power, and proper background to coordinate the different departments into an efficiently working unit. Until this is done progress is bound to be slow. I have been trying to help the new organization in every way I can by suggesting and even prodding them along, but I can only go so far, as I cannot run the project for them.[56]

While problems mounted with the flying boat in the spring of 1943, Hughes once again slipped away from the pressure through an energizing and altogether typical diversion. The army Corps of Engineers had laid claim to one of his prized airplanes—the Sikorsky S-43, the twin-engine amphibian that he had once planned to use on his around-the-world flight. Capable of operating off land or water, the S-43 was exactly what the army needed to shuttle engineers back and forth between isolated outposts from Nova Scotia to Iceland, where the corps was building a string of air bases. Most of the time since 1938 the Sikorsky had gathered dust in a Glendale hangar. Even so, Hughes never wanted to sell one of his personal planes, and he especially did not want to part with one as rare as the S-43, on which he had lavished considerable time and money. He stalled as long as he could. But when it became clear that the army was prepared to expropriate the plane if need be, he reluctantly agreed to sell. Since Hughes had modified the S-43 over the years, the corps asked the Civil Aeronautics Administration to check out and approve it "in the normal manner for a civil aircraft."[57]

Nothing was ever that straightforward with Hughes, however. Just when the CAA was ready to start the tests, he suddenly vanished with the plane. No one seemed to know where he had gone or when he might return. Actually, he had flown to Boulder City, a small Nevada town south of Las Vegas, near the shores of newly built Lake Mead. Free from the pressures at Culver City, Hughes spent his nights in Las Vegas, which was just beginning to attract flashy high-rollers, showgirls, and Hollywood types, and his days on the blue waters of Lake Mead, putting the Sikorsky through a series of hull tests. For hours at a stretch, he taxied the plane while speedboats loaded with cameramen trailed alongside shooting hundreds of feet of film of the Sikorsky's hull as it glided through the water. The footage was to be used in the design of the Kaiser–Hughes boat. After a month of these leisurely maneuvers, Hughes flew back to Los Angeles and invited the CAA to test the plane.

The agency assigned an amiable Texan, Charles W. Von Rosenberg, a CAA career man, to conduct the routine flight tests and Hughes insisted on going along on the flights as his own representative. Von Rosenberg was amused at the millionaire's working style since Hughes invariably arrived at the Glendale airport accompanied by an attractive woman and carrying a bag of cookies and milk. After spending hours together in the Sikorsky, however, while Von Rosenberg put the plane through its required tests, the two men developed a mutual respect for each other's abilities as pilots. To the CAA man, Hughes was "just a regular guy" who loved airplanes, although he *was* puzzled as to how Hughes could afford to spend so much time away from his business affairs.[58]

"Howard," he asked one day, "you don't really have time to devote yourself to being a test pilot. Why don't you hire somebody to do that work?"

"Hell," Hughes answered, "why should I pay somebody else to have all the fun?"[59]

By mid-May, Von Rosenberg had completed the tests off land and was ready to put the S-43 in the water for the final three tests before turning it over to the army. Hughes suggested that they run the water tests on Lake Mead, and on May 16, 1943, the two pilots, accompanied by a team of mechanics, engineers, and inspectors, flew to Las Vegas and the next morning drove down to Boulder City, where the Sikorsky awaited them on a little airstrip near Lake Mead. May 17, a Monday, was ideal for the tests. It was bright and clear. Just enough wind blew to create gentle ripples on the lake, which pilots like in order to help them better judge the distance to the water and the velocity of the wind. Shortly after noon, Hughes slipped into the pilot's seat and Von Rosenberg followed, taking the copilot's seat to his right. William M. "Ceco" Cline, a CAA inspector, Gene Blandford, Hughes's flight test engineer, and Richard Felt, Hughes's mechanic, took up positions in the cabin.

Von Rosenberg asked Hughes, since he had previously logged so many hours on the lake, to set the plane down in the water and, once the plane had landed, Von Rosenberg would take the controls for three tests measuring cooling and controllability. Everything set, Hughes gave both engines full throttle and the plane lumbered down the strip, lifted off, and was out over the 1.9-million-acre lake in a few seconds.

"Where do you want me to set it down?" Hughes asked.

"Let's do it over here," Von Rosenberg motioned, pointing to a long, wide part of the lake known as Vegas Gulch.[60]

Hughes began a smooth descent. Von Rosenberg was completely at ease. Hughes had spent so much time recently flying the Sikorsky that the CAA pilot was not "the slightest bit apprehensive" over Hughes's ability to bring it in again. He leaned forward and made sure the landing gear was up, then settled back for the landing. As the lake loomed closer, Von Rosenberg thought Hughes might be coming in somewhat faster than he should have. But he was not worried. "Hell," the CAA pilot told himself, "he's been flying it here off the lake a hundred takeoffs and landings."[61]

A few seconds later, the plane touched down nicely on the placid surface of Lake Mead and for the first few seconds all was well. The Sikorsky started settling in, displacing water, and picking up drag. It pitched forward slightly and became a little unstable, but that was normal during the first few seconds. It started to go left, but Hughes straightened it out. Then, without warning, the Sikorsky lunged forward on its nose and veered sharply right. Before Hughes could react, the plane turned in the water and began skipping sideways on the lake.

"This is it," Von Rosenberg thought to himself. "We have had it now."[62]

Hurtling diagonally at eighty miles an hour, the Sikorsky's ten tons of weight rose and fell on the lake with devastating force, crashing each time in the water with a tremendous impact and roar, as pieces of the wings, engines, hull, and tail ripped off, filling the air with the screech of shredding metal. In a few seconds, it ended. The crippled plane limped to a stop. Von Rosenberg felt an excruciating pain in his back. Two vertebrae had been crushed and all his back muscles had been torn loose. Aware of water "boiling" into the cockpit, he jerked his seatbelt loose.

"Come on, Howard," he shouted. "Let's get the hell out of this thing. It's going to sink."[63]

Still buckled into his seat, Hughes did not move, but sat, "holding the wheel, looking glassy-eyed and looking straight ahead." His head was bleeding from a gash above his forehead. Von Rosenberg reached over, unhooked Hughes's seatbelt, and shook him.

"Get out of here. This thing's going to sink."[64]

The cockpit was now half full of water, and Von Rosenberg looked around nervously for a way out. He reached across Hughes and opened the little pilot's window to his left, then shook Hughes again.

"Get out this window," he told him.[65]

Under Von Rosenberg's prodding, Hughes began to regain his faculties. With the CAA pilot guiding, pushing, and shoving him, Hughes finally started to crawl out the window. By now the water was up to Von Rosenberg's chest, and he was fearful that Hughes would not get out in time for him to follow. Looking around the cockpit, he found the overhead hatch, flicked it open, and then finished pushing Hughes out the window. As the water surged into the cockpit, Von Rosenberg floated up through the hatch.

Outside, he looked down the crippled body of the sinking plane and saw a chilling sight. Hughes's flight engineer, Gene Blandford, was holding Richard Felt, the mechanic, up through a hole in the plane's body. Felt's head had been "cleaved open" as though struck by an ax. He was barely alive.

"Where's Ceco," Von Rosenberg called out, inquiring about his fellow CAA inspector, the fifth crew member.

"I don't know. I don't know," answered a shaken Blandford. "He's gone."[66]

In great pain, Von Rosenberg crawled along the top of the plane to a hatch over the radio operator's compartment where Cline had been sitting, then swam around inside the water-and-gasoline-filled section, but could find no trace of his friend.

A couple who had been fishing nearby took the injured Felt and Blandford aboard their boat and carried them off to a hospital, promising to send help for Hughes and Von Rosenberg, who in the meantime managed to struggle into a rubber life raft as the Sikorsky went down in 165 feet of water.

It was Hughes's fourth plane crash, and although he had cut his head, he came out of it luckier than his companions. Richard Felt died soon after reaching a hospital. Von Rosenberg underwent surgery to repair the smashed vertebrae, wore a full body cast for three months, a back brace for a year after that, and would never be completely free of back problems again. Blandford suffered cuts and bruises. A few days after the crash, the seat in which William Cline had been sitting bobbed to the surface of Lake Mead, but his body was never found.

A federal investigation determined that the crash resulted from a mixup between Hughes and his ground crew. The plane had been incorrectly loaded, altering the ship's center of gravity. The difference was enough to throw the plane off balance when it touched down in the water. Hughes paid all the medical bills and later hired navy divers to raise the wrecked Sikorsky. At great expense, the plane was hauled back to Culver City and painstakingly rebuilt over the next year. Before the war ended, Hughes would fly it again.

By the summer of 1943, Hughes could no longer ignore the growing crisis at Culver City. The lack of leadership was proving catastrophic to the flying boat. Engineering was far behind schedule. None of the major assembly "jigs" for the hull, wings, and tail had been built. Vast sums of money had been wasted on what one disgruntled engineer called "half-baked tooling and engineering ideas."[67] The Defense Plant Corporation had earmarked $9.8 million for the first plane, yet $6 million had already been spent and the project was scarcely one-third complete. The contract called for delivery of the first plane in one month, but at the present rate Hughes would be lucky to finish the ship by 1945.

In June—ten months after obtaining the contract—Hughes at last hired a general manager, Edward G. Bern, a square-jawed, hardened veteran of twenty-six years in aviation. A former vice-president of American Airlines, Bern had served as Hughes Aircraft's Washington representative briefly before being called west. For thirty days, Bern studied the company, and was appalled. The payroll was "padded up with ex-Hollywood people" who never came to work and whose function was unclear.[68] The engineering department, which was designing the ship, and the production department, which was building it, were barely on speaking terms. Engineering was made up of "hometown boys," men who had been with Hughes for years, while production was made up of newer recruits who were looked on by the old guard as outsiders.[69] There was no internal chain of command, no commitment to completing the contract on schedule, no internal controls. Was it any wonder the flying boat was so far behind schedule?

Bern began acting like a general manager, lopping fat off budgets, and attempting to extend his control over the entire work force. This swiftly brought him into conflict with the "hometown boys," headed by Kenneth Ridley, the chief of engineering, Hughes's pet department. To Bern, the engineering department symbolized all that was wrong with Hughes Aircraft: he felt it had failed to meet deadlines, refused to coordinate with other departments, and was constantly giving Huges overly optimistic reports on the flying boat's progress.[70]

By early August, the breach between the two men had widened into all-out war. Work virtually stopped on the flying boat as the battle raged unchecked through the hangars, laboratories, drafting rooms, and tool departments at Culver City. Bern warned Hughes that the flying boat was being "sabotaged, retarded and held up by a clique" at the plant.[71] Had Hughes stepped in and supported his manager, the revolt would have collapsed. But Hughes could never personally perform ugly tasks of that sort, so he ignored the fight and, by doing so, cut the ground out from under the man he had hired less than two months before to save the company. By late August, the situation was hopeless and Bern, gloomy and angry, began to fear that the row would become public, damaging both Hughes Aircraft and his own reputation. On August 27, he called Donald Nelson in Washington:

We have got a terribly chaotic situation out here. It is going to blow right up in your face. . . . I have not gone to the plant for two days. They are running it like a bunch of school kids would do business. . . . I still have to work for a living and I do not want to be tied up with anything that is a lie or anything that involves our Government funds. . . . I have tried to clean up the place. I have so much opposition, and yet I am the responsible party. . . .

The only time we see him [Hughes] is at his home late at night—at 10, 11, 12 or 1 or 2 in the morning. He calls you up and tries to get the picture of that thing. The last man that talks to him of his old bunch is the one who can sell him the idea of doing something.

Bern admitted that he was uncomfortable disclosing such damaging information about his employer to another, but felt that he was not "double-crossing" Hughes:

I feel my first duty is my country. . . . If Howard would turn that over and let them run it—it doesn't matter who, but some one person and kill this dirty lousy politics, we could do something with that flying boat; otherwise it is hopeless. I just cannot stand to see a thing that I believe should be built blown up through politics.[72]

Bern drove over to Hughes's house in Bel Air the next day for a showdown. He told Hughes that unless Ridley was replaced, he was quitting. Hughes protested, saying he could not fire Ridley because the flying boat was "too far" along and Ridley was the man who had brought it that far.[73]

The next day, Bern resigned. With him went several department heads who, with his departure, saw little hope for the flying boat. Bern packed his bags and began the drive back east to his home on Long Island. Hughes Aircraft's first real general manager had lasted a grand total of sixty-one days.

"AN AWFUL SMELL"

Back in Washington, an air force team was setting out on a top-secret mission to the west. Headed by Colonel Elliott Roosevelt, the president's second son, the five-man air force group was surveying aircraft plants in hopes of finding a photo-reconnaissance plane to aid the Allied offensive in Europe. As former head of a reconnaissance unit in Europe, the young Roosevelt was acutely aware of the need. The United States had consistently lacked a plane specially designed to photograph terrain and enemy positions before Allied offensives. Makeshift planes—usually F-4s or P-39s—were pressed into photographic duty, often with tragic results. Higher flying, faster German and Italian fighters gunned down American reconnaissance pilots with ease. As reports of casualties in the North African campaign inundated the air force high command, General Arnold recalled Colonel Roosevelt to Washington. His mission was to fill this photo-reconnaisance gap, and fast.

When the Roosevelt mission reached Los Angeles on August 8, 1943, Hughes assigned his favorite public-relations man, John W. Meyer, a pudgy, fast-talking, fun-loving exponent of the good life, to take the president's son under his wing. A former publicist for Warner Brothers and onetime owner of Hollywood's La Congo nightclub, Meyer was one of Hughes's closest cronies. The two bachelors were often seen together on swings through Hollywood or Las Vegas nightclubs. First working for Hughes Productions* and later, after Pearl Harbor, on the payroll of Hughes Aircraft, Meyer was deferred from the draft six times.

---

*Hughes Productions, also a subsidiary of the Hughes Tool Company, had succeeded Caddo as the motion-picture production arm of Hughes's empire.

Hughes wanted his company to make a favorable impression on Elliott Roosevelt. Although the air force had consistently rejected his wooden D-2 fighter as a military plane, Hughes had never given up on it. He planned to tout it to Roosevelt, who might prove more receptive than Wright Field's "prejudiced" engineers. He had test-flown the D-2 a few weeks earlier, on June 20, 1943, but it had performed so poorly that he had sent it back to the shop for drastic changes. This sale would not be easy. The D-2's latest performance made the Materiel Command more opposed than ever to the plane. An internal memo, written while Roosevelt was heading west, said the air force should abandon all interest in the D-2, which "has not progressed favorably to date and which shows so little promise in the future."[74]

In Los Angeles, Meyer threw parties for Roosevelt and his fellow officers and escorted them on guided tours of the Hollywood studios. During lunch at the Warner Brothers commissary, Meyer introduced Roosevelt to the actress Faye Emerson, a meeting that led to romance and their marriage four months later. Meyer pestered Roosevelt to join him in a spacious house in Beverly Hills and thereby avoid expensive hotel bills. After Roosevelt demurred, Meyer picked up the tab at the hotel where Roosevelt and his men were staying.

On August 11, Hughes personally led them on a tour of Hughes Aircraft at Culver City, then accompanied them on the short flight to Harper Lake, a dry lakebed in the desert a hundred miles north of Los Angeles, where the D-2 was being rebuilt and secretly tested. When Roosevelt walked into the air-conditioned hangar where the plane was housed, the D-2 was partly disassembled and grease-smudged. One engine had been removed from the nacelle and was being repaired. Nevertheless, the essential beauty and sleekness of the wooden duramold fighter was evident.

The officers enthusiastically clustered around the plane, examining its wings, tail, and rear-mounted machine guns, and admiring its smooth lines. Hughes told them it would fly 433 miles per hour at an altitude of twenty-eight thousand feet and had a range of two thousand miles. To the task force, the plane was nothing less than fantastic—the answer to a reconnaissance pilot's prayers. Commander D. W. Stevenson, a much-decorated Royal Air Force ace who was accompanying Roosevelt, told Hughes, "I have never seen anything more magnificent that could do a better job."[75]

When Roosevelt returned to the East Coast, Meyer followed and hosted another round of parties in New York. Faye Emerson joined the group in Manhattan, where Meyer financed a swing through El Morocco, the Copacabana, Monte Carlo, and the Stork Club. Ever the consummate host, Meyer even presented Miss Emerson with $132 worth of nylon stockings, a commodity in short supply all through the war.

On August 20, 1943, Roosevelt submitted a written report to General Arnold recommending that he immediately take steps to acquire the Hughes D-2 for a photo-reconnaissance plane.[76] Wright Field, still recalcitrant, favored a Lockheed plane, but Roosevelt argued that the Lockheed model would require more modification than Hughes's plane. Although the D-2 was made of wood, Hughes had agreed to convert it to metal and saw no difficulty in doing so. Roosevelt contended that Hughes would be a fortunate choice for the air force because "he is primarily a designer of racing aircraft and long-range aircraft and has interested himself in these two fields for the past decade."[77]

No one was more aware of the hazards of doing business with Hughes than General Arnold. Nevertheless, on September 1, 1943, Arnold directed Major General Oliver P. Echols "to get Hughes a contract for photographic planes."[78] Echols, who was thoroughly familiar with the D-2's undistinguished record, tried to change Arnold's mind. He sent him a stack of memos and reports describing the plane's deficiencies and the obstacles to producing it in quantity. But Arnold had made up his mind. He ordered Echols to draw up a contract between the air force and Hughes to acquire 100 photo-reconnaissance planes. The plane was to be redesignated the XF-11. Arnold later explained his action: "At that point it was the Hughes plane or nothing. So, much against my better judgment and against the advice of my staff I gave instructions to buy the famous (X)F-11 airplane."[79]

Behind the scenes, the order caused an uproar. Wright Field was so enraged that Major General Charles E. Bradshaw, the commanding general, took the unusual step of writing to Arnold and suggesting that the Hughes contract was a serious mistake. Bradshaw said Wright felt that the Lockheed P-58 "is much further along engineeringwise and productionwise, and is better in fundamental design and structural integrity, and will fly farther, faster and higher than the [Hughes] plane."[80] "To rush into production with such an undeveloped and unstable article," Bradshaw said, "is an invitation for later severe criticism."[81]

In a telephone conversation on October 21, 1943, Robert Lovett, assistant secretary of war, and Major General Bennett E. Meyers of the Materiel Command agreed that "there's going to be an awful smell" when the background of the Hughes contract ultimately became known.[82] Neither man knew who had exerted influence to secure the contract for Hughes, but they were absolutely certain that pressure had been applied.

"Hughes has got very powerful friends here in Washington," Lovett said.

"Yes sir," Meyers agreed. "Jesse Jones and the President and everyone else seems to be in this. . . ."

"Benny, my own feeling is that I never like any of these projects that are gone into under outside pressure. You can never bring the outside pressure up in your defense."[83]

Even if there was "an awful smell" to it, Hughes at last had an aircraft production contract with the air force—$43 million to build 100 planes. For once he had bucked the "Hate Hughes Club" and won. But he had no time to savor the victory. The XF-11 contract inadvertently further jeopardized the flying boat. The air force viewed the Defense Plant's flying boat as a direct threat to its own contract with Hughes. Hughes Aircraft was too small, in the air force's opinion, to build both the flying boat and the XF-11 simultaneously. One had to go, and in the fall of 1943, the air force began pressuring the Defense Plant Corporation to kill the Hercules. Of course, all the "Queen Elizabeth of the Air," as one government engineer called the plane, needed was more opposition. The flying boat had already lost what little support it had in the federal government. Hughes's failure to meet deadlines, the low quality of much of the work, political infighting at Hughes Aircraft, and a lessening of the submarine menace had combined to override any argument for continuing the plane as a war project. Faced with growing pressure to scuttle it, Donald Nelson called meetings that fall with agencies involved in the project. Without exception, each agreed that the boat would not contribute to the war effort and felt that it should be canceled.

On the afternoon of February 16, 1944, the telephone rang in the office of H. Robert Edwards, the Defense Plant Corporation's resident engineer at the Hughes plant. The caller was W. E. Joyce, the corporation's vice-president in Washington, who told Edwards that telegrams were on their way to Hughes advising him that the contract had been canceled and to stop work. "Keep on with accounting and assemble materials to protect our buildings," Joyce told Edwards, "but all work is to stop today. . . . Stop all work on the plane and engineering work. If you have any problems, do not hestitate to call us up."[84] Edwards walked to the office of Hughes's acting general manager, Gunnar Eriksson, and told him to close down the job at 5 P.M. that day.

Although warning signs had been flashing for months, the cancellation came as a jolt to Hughes. While he had undertaken the project almost reluctantly, he was now wholly caught up in the challenge of building the world's largest airplane. He called Neil McCarthy, his Los Angeles lawyer, and put him to work in an effort to keep the plant running. Meanwhile, Hughes flew east to save the flying boat, as he put it later, "from being burnt up as kindling wood."[85]

For one of the few times in his life, Hughes stepped out of character over the next several weeks. Normally shy, quiet, and ill at ease in official gatherings, he usually let those who worked for him attend meetings and report the outcome. Now he personally shouldered the challenge of saving the flying boat. For five weeks in February and March of 1944, he stayed in Washington, operating out of a suite in the Carlton Hotel, working day and night, calling on officials of the War Department, the War Production Board, the air force —anyone who might assist him. There were not many. If Hughes had always thought of himself as unpopular and beset by enemies in the capital, this time it was true. "It seemed to me that everybody in Washington was against me," he said later. "As far as I could make out, nobody in the War Production Board had anything to do 24 hours a day except to shoot holes at me and my airplane. . . . I thought I was about as unpopular as any country boy who ever came to Washington."[86]

In the eighteen months since he had been awarded the flying-boat contract, Hughes had not demonstrated the slightest ability to build it. Yet when Hughes stormed into Washington that winter, he behaved as though he were the wronged party. To those who heard him argue his case, Hughes was articulate, forceful, and passionate. He felt that the aeronautical knowledge to be gained in itself justified the cost of going forward. To many, he appeared sincere and earnest, a man who believed deeply in what he was doing. Others were disturbed by the extremes to which he was willing to go to win a point. As a government engineer later put it:

The general conclusion and the general feeling of those present who heard Mr. Hughes was that he was adroit in twisting arguments in his favor which did not stand up when analyzed, and unreasonable in his insistence that his estimates were correct, fully to be relied upon, and infallible to such a degree that anyone who questioned them was prejudiced, and he always had some involved excuse as to why he was late in deliveries or why he had used up so much money.[87]

One of the few friends Hughes found in Washington that winter was Bennett E. Meyers, the bald, cigar-smoking air force major general who had earlier opposed the XF-11 contract. After joining the army as a private in the First World War, Meyers had worked his way up to be the number-two man in the Materiel Command. A hard worker who slept on a cot in his office, Meyers was a "go-getter" to fellow officers who respected his undeniable knack for moving large amounts of materiel to the right place at the right time.[88] Unknown to his colleagues, however, Meyers also had a knack for self-enrichment. After the war, it emerged that Meyers had set up an electronics company near Dayton, Ohio, that was selling equipment to the air force.* In any case, Meyers helped Hughes navigate the treacherous bureaucratic waters of Washington. Over dinner at Meyers's apartment, the general would tell Hughes who opposed him and who were his friends. Hughes, in turn, flattered Meyers. One night while they were discussing possible general managers for Hughes Aircraft, Hughes jokingly said he wished Meyers had a "twin brother" he could hire to run Hughes Aircraft.[89] Meyers took a cigar out of his mouth and smiled at Hughes.

"You know," he said, "I might like to have that job myself."[90]

But neither Hughes's salesmanship nor his friends in high places were enough to save the flying boat. For that, Hughes was forced to turn again to Jesse Jones, who quietly intervened for Hughes with President Roosevelt. The full story of what happened between Jones and the president will probably never be known, but according to Jones, this is what occurred:

On February 18, 1944, a Friday, the Cabinet held its weekly meeting at the White House, and afterward Jones asked to see the president. When the two were alone, Jones brought up the flying boat. In a memorandum that Jones wrote later, he portrayed his role that day as little more than a conveyor of

---

*Meyers was later convicted and sent to prison for five years for inducing an associate to lie to a Senate committee about Meyers's involvement in the defense-related company and for evading $61,000 in federal income taxes during the war.

information. He told the president that the Defense Plant Corporation was about to cancel Hughes's flying boat "upon the advice of experts in the aviation field."[91] According to Jones, Roosevelt said he "thought the experience to be gained by completing one plane would be of too much value to throw away the money already expended, and that the contract should not be cancelled."[92] In all likelihood, Jones was much more aggressive than his memo suggests. Given the momentous decisions Roosevelt was then facing (D-Day was just a few weeks away), the flying boat would certainly have ranked low on his list of priorities. Also, FDR liked his Cabinet members to make recommendations on matters they had brought to him for a decision.

In any event, Jones's intervention saved the boat. Just as Donald Nelson was ready to kill it, Jones let him know, as he phrased it later, "the President's thought on it."[93] With no desire to cross either the president or Jones, Nelson backed off, and on March 27, 1944, the Defense Plant Corporation informed Hughes that it was canceling the old Kaiser–Hughes contract to build three cargo planes for $18 million and issuing a new contract to the Hughes Tool Company to build one plane for the same amount. Since more than $13 million had already been spent on a machine that was only about 50 percent complete, Hughes knew that he would end up spending millions of his own funds to finish it. But no matter. For the moment, the Hercules, his obsession, still had life. Late in March, he flew back to California.

The month in Washington had left Hughes drained. Day and night, he had argued and cajoled to sway the doubters to his side, driving himself to exhaustion. High-strung and nervous anyway, he was spent by the pressure and feverish pace he had maintained. If ever he needed a break, it was in the spring of 1944. But the flow of events would not subside. Over the next few months, Hughes was subjected to ever-greater crises and pressures; his frayed nerves were ill-suited to deal with them.

First, his old adversary, Wright Field, held up the final contract on the XF-II. After Hughes had received the tentative go-ahead, he attempted to charge the air force $3.6 million for his costs to design and build the D-2, the forerunner of the XF-II. Since Hughes had embarked on the D-2 venture on his own, and had even kept the plane secret from the air force bureaucracy at first, Wright Field was outraged and called Hughes's contention "ridiculous" and "too far-fetched for further comment."[94] Even so, the air force compromised and awarded Hughes $1.6 million.

Then, in Houston, the ordinarily quiescent Hughes Tool Company became embroiled in a bitter dispute with the United Steelworkers after the union had organized the three-thousand-man plant. When the tool company refused to bargain, the workers struck. Because the company's drill bits and other products were vital to war production, the War Labor Board stepped in, ordered the men back to work, and directed Hughes Tool to negotiate. When the company refused to do so, a squad of army officers took over the plant briefly until the dispute was settled.

But it was Hughes Aircraft, as usual, that posed the biggest problem for Hughes. Lacking leadership, Culver City fell further behind on the XF-11. The air force warned Hughes that unless he hired a competent general manager, the contract to produce the 100 photo-reconnaissance planes would be canceled. With virtually every aircraft executive already gainfully employed, compliance with the air force ultimatum was no simple matter. Fortunately for Hughes, Charles W. Perelle, the able vice-president of production for the Consolidated–Vultee Aircraft Company, had had a falling-out with his bosses and was available. An owlish-looking man who had made a national reputation as the "boy wonder" of aircraft production, Perelle seemed exactly the tonic Hughes Aircraft required.[95]

Hughes offered Perelle a salary of $50,000 a year—$10,000 more than he was then earning—and absolute freedom to manage the aircraft company. Hughes admitted that he very much needed someone to "take complete charge."[96] He appeared sincere, but Perelle was wary. He knew of Hughes's meddlesome ways and of the difficulties at Hughes Aircraft itself. The free-wheeling spirit of the company had earned it an industry nickname—the "Hughes Country Club."[97] Perelle turned down the offer.

Hughes, desperate to get Perelle at any cost, raised the salary offer and put together a package of fringe benefits that Perelle could not resist. The salary was $75,000, far higher than the amount earned by all but a few top Hughes executives. Not only would Perelle head the aircraft company but he was to be a vice-president of the parent Hughes Tool Company as well, with duties throughout the Hughes organization, a move that would almost certainly bring him into conflict with old-line executives in Houston like Noah Dietrich, Hughes's executive vice-president.

Even more indicative of Hughes's desperation was his concession to give Perelle an option to buy, at the current market price, 10,000 shares of Trans World Airlines stock owned by Hughes Tool. The option could be exercised in the future, meaning that if the stock went up Perelle could make a tidy profit. As far as is known, it was the only time Hughes ever granted such an option.

Then, with the Hughes Aircraft problems solved for the moment, Hughes split with his longtime Los Angeles lawyer, Neil S. McCarthy. When Hughes was in Washington in the spring of 1944, Major General Benny Meyers, encouraged by Hughes's extravagant praise, decided that he did in fact want to work for Hughes, and suggested that they draw up a three-year contract that would take effect as soon as Meyers could get out of the air force. But Hughes had no real desire to hire Meyers; he had only buttered him up to assure his support in the XF-11 negotiations. Back in Los Angeles, Hughes asked McCarthy to go to Washington and give Meyers the bad news. Since Hughes already had a flock of enemies in the air force, the matter was to be handled as tactfully as possible.

Traveling cross-country by train, McCarthy arrived on June 2 and had dinner with Meyers in his apartment. When McCarthy explained that Hughes would be unable to enter into the employment agreement during the war, Meyers offered an alternative: Would Hughes loan him $200,000 at low interest to enable him to buy millions of dollars in Liberty Bonds on margin? McCarthy promised to discuss it with Hughes and get back to Meyers with an answer. Before leaving for California, McCarthy phoned Hughes and both agreed that the loan was out of the question. This time Hughes would call Meyers. McCarthy had scarcely reached Los Angeles a few days later when Meyers called to ask about the loan.

"Didn't Howard call you?" McCarthy asked.

"No, he did not call me," Meyers answered, growing irritated.[98]

When McCarthy explained that Hughes had intended to call to say he would be unable to provide the loan, Meyers "exploded," furious that they had "not let him know earlier."[99]

The blowup made Hughes uneasy. Already on shaky ground with air force brass, he feared that Meyers would "find some way to throw a monkey wrench into the XF-11 contract."[100] That never happened, but Hughes spent sleepless nights fretting about the possibility. Hughes blamed McCarthy for the imbroglio, apparently thinking that his lawyer should somehow have been able to handle the volatile situation and enable Hughes to retain Meyers's friendship. All through the summer Hughes kept telephoning McCarthy in the early hours of the morning, badgering him with questions about the Meyers situation and urging him to meet with the general to patch up the relationship. Annoyed by the interruptions and concerned about their effect on his health, McCarthy abruptly resigned in August of 1944. At first, Hughes refused to accept the resignation and pleaded with him to stay on. When McCarthy would not reconsider, the twenty-year association of the two men broke off on what Hughes later described as "very bitter terms."[101]

Prolonged overwork and anxiety—added to his now deeply rooted phobias and neuroses—had left Hughes teetering on the brink of mental collapse. McCarthy's resignation pushed him over the edge. With no immediate family, Hughes was closer to those who worked for him than to anyone else. He could not face the loss of someone like McCarthy, who had been with him so long and whom he had come to trust. Late in August of 1944, Hughes suffered a nervous breakdown and vanished.

In the months preceding his collapse and disappearance, the signs pointing to a mental breakdown were unmistakable. Blessed with an almost photographic memory, Hughes began repeating himself at work and in casual conversations. In a series of memoranda on the importance of letter writing, he dictated, over and over again, "a good letter should be immediately understandable . . . a good letter should be immediately understandable . . . a good letter should be immediately understandable . . . a good letter should be immediately understandable."[102]

When he went on to explain how to make a letter understandable, Hughes again repeated his instructions, the words no sooner spoken than he forgot what he had said. Over and over he dictated, "think your material over in order to determine its limits . . . think your material over in order to determine its limits . . . think your material over. . . ."[103]

Always meticulous, his obsession with trivia reached a zenith. In a memorandum entitled "Notes on Notes," he gave elaborate directions on how a section of his will was to be typed:

A dash, or two, shall be used to denote words preceding, or following a quotation. Two dashes shall be used to denote the deletion of words when a group of words are quoted and one dash shall suffice when only one word is quoted. In either case, there shall be a space between the quotation mark, the dash, or dashes, and the quoted word, or vice-versa: i.e. " -- and will best assure -- ".

The word "shall" shall be used throughout instead of "will" in the third person singular and plural, making all sentences in the imperative rather than the indicative.

The infinitive shall not be used to express a major thought, except as an auxiliary to a main verb.

No changes or marks shall be made on the original pencil version.

The numbering system set forth in the notes shall not be a criterion for any future numbering systems.[104]

Before disappearing, Hughes entrusted the confidential assignment of typing his will to Nadine Henley, his private secretary since late 1943. A year younger than Hughes, the thirty-eight-year-old Miss Henley was now one of his most trusted employees. She had gone to work as an administrative assistant in the engineering department of Hughes Aircraft in 1940. Hughes met her one night at Culver City when she was working late and began calling her occasionally to his house to dictate letters and memoranda. When her immediate boss recommended her promotion, only to be overruled by the conservative tool company management in Houston, which did not approve of female department heads, Miss Henley quit in a huff. When Hughes found out, he hired her back as his personal secretary at Romaine Street.

Although she had studied English and drama in college, it was business that fascinated her. The daughter of a Minneapolis utility executive, she accompanied her father on business trips when she was growing up and later worked for a bank and two securities dealers before joining Hughes. She and Hughes had a formal, businesslike relationship—Hughes called her Miss Henley and she called him Mr. Hughes, even when she was speaking about him to others. To Miss Henley, Hughes was a perfect gentleman, who was courteous and considerate and never lost his temper. They only disagreed on punctuation. Hughes's ideas on that subject often ran counter to established practice. When Miss Henley would object and cite authoritative reference works to support her case, Hughes would ask her how she knew the books were accurate. To further substantiate her argument, she began carrying three or four handbooks on punctuation with her when she took dictation from Hughes.

In the summer of 1944, as Hughes's mental grasp faltered, he continually called Miss Henley to his house on Sarbonne Road in Bel Air to work on his will. In August, shortly before his breakdown, he gave her strict orders to lock up all versions and drafts of the will, along with some other important papers, in a drawer of a safe in Room 216 on the second floor of 7000 Romaine Street. All keys, he said, except one, were to be locked in the drawer itself. "The only key to this drawer not contained in the drawer itself," Hughes noted in one final order, "shall be kept at all times around Miss Henley's neck as long as any part of the above items remained in the drawer."[105]

These aberrations were known to only a handful of people in Hughes's organization. But none of them, including Noah Dietrich, Hughes's top-ranking executive, knew where their disturbed employer had gone. It was not until thirty-one years later that any light was shed on this period of Hughes's life. In an article published posthumously, Joseph Petrali, a onetime mechanic at Hughes Aircraft, wrote that for months he and Hughes had shuttled back and forth by plane from Las Vegas to Palm Springs to Reno, staying in hotel rooms under assumed names and doing no work of any kind.[106] It would not be the last time that Howard Hughes would slip from view, when he felt too much the weight of his world.

CHAPTER 5

THE SENATE
INVESTIGATION

THE XF-11 CRASH

WITH Hughes away nursing his battered psyche, Chuck Perelle took over at Culver City and for the first time the aircraft company had a general manager free of interference from above. Perelle had known the company was in bad shape; he now found out how bad. Both the flying boat and the XF-11 had their own engineering, tooling, purchasing, and industrial-relations departments, as if there were "two separate managements . . . within the same four walls."[1] Relations with Wright Field were at "absolutely the lowest level" Perelle had encountered in his fifteen years of producing military aircraft.[2] The final engineering on the XF-11 was much further behind schedule than he had been led to believe, and some of the completed drawings were so poor they had to be thrown out.[3] To his dismay, Perelle realized soon after his arrival that Hughes Aircraft's problems stemmed mostly from a "complete lack of experience in the design and construction of airplanes in general."[4]

When Perelle attempted to implement reforms, he ran into great resistance. "There was," as he put it later, "a considerable lack of respect for constituted authority."[5] Long accustomed to dealing with Hughes directly, department heads refused to change the habits of years. Also, old-timers doubted that Perelle would last. Hughes Aircraft was too much a part of Howard Hughes for him ever to give up control. In time, they reasoned, Perelle would move on, just as Ed Bern had done. An even greater obstacle was the opposition Perelle encountered from other Hughes executives outside the aircraft company. Never having received a stock option of any kind from Hughes, many seasoned tool company officers in Houston like Noah Dietrich looked on the newcomer Perelle with alarm. Despite Hughes's promise of wide authority throughout the Hughes Tool Company, Perelle found himself frozen out of many corporate decisions by the Houston establishment.

The resistance notwithstanding, Perelle proved to be an able manager at Hughes Aircraft. He merged duplicate departments, streamlined others, and eased strained relations with Wright Field. He even arranged a $1.5-million contract with the Reconstruction Finance Corporation to move the two-hundred-ton flying boat from Culver City to Long Beach harbor and to assemble and flight-test it at that location. Hughes vetoed the agreement because it gave the federal government—not him—the right to select the test pilot, but it was nonetheless a remarkable negotiating coup for Perelle.

In the end, though, Perelle's efforts fell short. Work on the XF-11 was too far behind when he took over for the plane to play a part in the European war. Three weeks after Germany surrendered on May 8, 1945, the air force canceled the production contract for ninety-eight planes. Hughes was to finish the two prototypes, but when they were completed his short-lived career as a military aircraft manufacturer would end. For Perelle, it was the beginning of the end.

By this time, Hughes had returned from his self-imposed retreat and was becoming active again in Hughes Aircraft. With the cancellation of the production contract, he had no need for his high-salaried production chief. Relations between the two men had already deteriorated. Perelle resented the lack of support from Hughes. And Hughes disliked managers as independent and forceful as Perelle had proved to be. Now he began undercutting Perelle's authority. In a blatant case, he financed a fleet of TWA passenger planes without telling Perelle, who was supposedly his chief representative with the airline.

By the fall of 1945, Perelle could no longer postpone a confrontation. On October 29, he reminded Hughes that when he had accepted the job at Hughes Tool he had been promised "complete and unrestricted control" of the aircraft company.[6] Subsequent events made him wonder, Perelle said, if Hughes had acted in good faith. Nevertheless, there was time to repair the damage, Perelle suggested in a memo, if Hughes would clarify his role and authority. If Hughes answered the message, no record of it has come to light.

In December, Hughes routinely called up two men he knew in the engineering department at Hughes Aircraft and told them to report to 7000 Romaine Street for a special assignment. After four years, he was prepared to release *The Outlaw,* the bosomy western starring Jane Russell. By holding up release so long and battling with censors, Hughes had built up enormous interest in the movie. The engineers were to assist in staging a promotion on the eve of the première—the flight over Los Angeles of a huge blimp advertising the film.* When Perelle learned that Hughes had reassigned two employees without going through channels, he exploded and fired off a letter to Hughes:

---

* *The Outlaw* previewed early in 1946 and played to record crowds for years. Leslie Halliwell summed up the movie perfectly in *The Film Goers Companion:* "This notorious censor-baiting western . . . has historical interest as an example of how producer-director Howard Hughes managed to fool all of the people all of the time. The movie is neither sensational nor very entertaining, but by withholding it from release . . . and getting into a lot of arguments with censor boards, Hughes made the world's press believe it was."

As I have previously advised you, this interruption to organization will not be tolerated. The practice of allowing subordinates to advise their superiors as to what their activities are to consist of is the most demoralizing thing that we can possibly do to organization. I am sure you recognize this fact, inasmuch as you have admitted to me previously that you knew it existed. Continuance of such break-down of organization will necessitate my setting up rules and regulations which will undoubtedly be very embarrassing to you and others involved. I trust that you will not make this necessary.[7]

Hughes did not make it necessary. No one had ever dared to address him that way. He called Dietrich and directed him to fire Perelle. The general manager of Hughes Aircraft was guilty, Hughes explained, of "insubordination."[8] Dietrich approached the job with relish. With Perelle's departure, Dietrich was once again without a rival.

Although his time at Culver City was brief, a mere seventeen months, Perelle did leave a mark. By sheer drive, he had managed to push both the flying boat and the XF-11 nearly to completion. Considering the state of both projects when he took over, the achievement was remarkable.

In its wooden hangar, the gigantic flying boat dwarfed the men who were working on it. Its enormous wings, hull, tail, stabilizers, and pontoons lay about on the factory floor like parts of a dismembered dinosaur. Workmen scurried up and down scaffolding and along catwalks applying a final coat of aluminum lacquer to give the great ship's plywood veneer a metallic sheen.

In June of 1946, at a cost of eighty thousand dollars, the parts of the flying boat were loaded onto a fleet of flatbed trucks and carted twenty-eight miles from Culver City to Long Beach harbor, where they would be assembled, tested, and presumably, flown. The mammoth caravan snaked along back roads, down freeways, and across bridges for two days before it arrived at its harborside berth. Along the route, thousands watched as parts of the giant seaplane passed.

Shortly after the Hercules was moved, Hughes put the XF-11 through a series of tests at Culver City in preparation for its first flight. Usually a stranger at the plant, Hughes now showed up almost daily, taxiing the XF-11 up and down the nine-thousand-foot runway, lifting it a few feet off the runway, then setting down gently to let mechanics check out the engines' performance. Testing his own airplanes was one of Hughes's greatest pleasures, and testing the XF-11 was especially gratifying. Hughes had little to do with the actual design and engineering of the flying boat, but the sleek photo-reconnaissance plane was an outgrowth of his beloved D-2, and it embodied many of his concepts, although he had not actually designed it, either.

The XF-11 was indeed a beauty. If Hughes's planes did not always perform as he had predicted, they were at least magnificent looking. Every one of them, including the huge flying boat, had graceful lines, smooth surfaces, streamlined elegance, and the appearance of swiftness. The XF-11 was no exception. Its forty-seven thousand pounds were fitted into a lean design that featured twin booms flanking a short needle-nosed cockpit. The twin-tailed ship was 65 feet long and had a wing span of 101 feet. It was powered by two 3,000-horsepower engines, each equipped with two contrarotating propellers positioned one behind the other. Hughes had promised the air force that the plane would fly at 400 miles an hour, and when it was first towed into the sunlight at Culver City for test runs few people doubted that it would.

Ordinarily, experimental military planes were first test-flown at the Army Test Flight Base (later Edwards Air Force Base) near Muroc, California, in the heart of the Mojave Desert. The sparsely populated region provided an ideal locale for this often dangerous business. Hughes, however, talked the air force into letting him test the XF-11 from his home field at Culver City, and the flight was set for Sunday, July 7, 1946.

Two days before, Hughes drove down to Newport Beach, California, for a Fourth of July weekend party of some Hollywood friends. There, he met the movie colony's hottest new property, nineteen-year-old Elizabeth Jean Peters.[9] A farm girl from East Canton, Ohio, Jean had come to Hollywood that spring after winning a beauty contest at Ohio State University. Twentieth Century Fox was so taken with her screen test that she was signed to a long-term contract and paired with Tyrone Power in the swashbuckling thriller *Captain from Castile.* The forty-year-old Hughes and the teenage actress were enamored of one another from the start, and Hughes invited her to witness the XF-11 test flight on Sunday.

When Hughes arrived at Culver City that day for the flight, he had on a pair of wrinkled slacks, a white sport shirt, and a floppy brown hat, and gave no hint that the day was anything special. Serious and unsmiling as usual, he checked out the plane and talked over the flight plan with Glenn Odekirk, once again the aircraft company's general manager, and Gene Blandford, Hughes's chief flight-test engineer and veteran of the 1943 Lake Mead crash. Then he climbed into the cockpit through an underside hatch and buckled his seatbelt. As Hughes looked across the silvery wings of his plane, adorned with the blue and white air force insignia, he must have felt a surge of pride finally to be flying the plane that had been the target of so much criticism.

Hughes spent the next few hours taxiing the plane at high speeds. It seemed to function perfectly. After each run the right rear propeller required oil, but since there was no evidence of a leak the problem seemed trivial. Shortly before takeoff, Hughes ordered the XF-11 loaded with 1,200 gallons of fuel, even though the air force–approved flight plan limited the load to 600 gallons. The only explanation is that Hughes must have intended from the start to fly the ship longer than the forty-five minutes authorized. By 5 P.M., he was set to go. After taxiing to the end of the runway, Hughes revved the engines and adjusted his parachute. Gene Blandford activated two of the six motion-picture reconnaissance cameras mounted in the plane and slipped out the hatch. Outside, Blandford waved up to Hughes in the cockpit, and Hughes waved back. At precisely 5:20 P.M., Hughes gave both engines full throttle and roared down the grass runway. Three thousand feet later, the plane lifted off into the clear California sky.

As the XF-11 ascended, Hughes retracted the landing gear, apparently to see how it worked. This was another deviation from the air force flight plan, which did not authorize the gear's operation until the second flight.[10] It was standard procedure on test flights to leave the gear down the first time out since the initial flight is simply a test to determine how well a new plane flies. A few minutes later, Hughes noticed that the landing gear warning light was still red.[11] That indicated that the gear had not completely retracted. While he continued to climb, he lowered and raised the gear several times, hoping the light would go off, but it stayed on. By pushing sharply forward on the control wheel as the gear retracted, the light went off, and he "assumed the gear was up and locked."[12]

The XF-11 was flying smoothly at five thousand feet in wide circles around the Hughes field, and the gear light was off, but Hughes still worried. What had caused the malfunction? Why had the light remained on? Had the landing-gear door failed to close? Or was something else amiss underneath? He dipped down over the field to let his men on the ground take a look at the underside. As he was passing over, another of his airplanes, an A-20 attack bomber, took off. Piloted by Odekirk and Blandford, it flew up behind the XF-11 to give the two men a closer look at the ship in flight. Hughes tried to contact them by radio to tell them to observe his landing gear, but their radios were set on different frequencies and he could not reach them. After watching the XF-11's seemingly perfect flight for a few minutes, Odekirk and Blandford returned to the field.

Hughes's concern about the landing gear did not bring him in for a landing. He continued to fly around Culver City well beyond the forty-five-minute limit set by the air force. About 6:35 P.M.—an hour and fifteen minutes into the flight—at an altitude of five thousand feet about two miles east of the Hughes field, the XF-11 suddenly pitched right. Hughes felt a strong drag, "as if someone had tied a barn door broadside onto the right-hand wing."[13] He had two options: he could turn around and land at his home field or he could look for the cause of the drag and possibly correct it. Whichever he chose, he had to act fast—the XF-11 had begun to lose altitude dramatically. Hughes decided to diagnose the trouble. Later, he described what happened next:

I unfastened my seat belt, got up and looked quickly out all windows of the cabin. I wanted to see if any large part of the airplane, such as a section of the wing, tail, or a landing gear door, might possibly have been torn loose and swung by the wind into a broadside position.

With this last thought in mind, I lowered and raised the landing gear, hoping to break completely loose from the airplane any landing gear door which might have jammed into a broadside position. I could not see anything which was holding the plane back, yet it felt as if some giant had the right wing of the airplane in his hand and was pushing it back and down.[14]

Hughes increased power on both engines, cut it back, then increased it only on the right engine. Nothing worked. He was still losing altitude. Looking past the cockpit, he thought of bailing out, but feared he was already too low and also felt he still "might be able to correct the situation."[15] By making major adjustments to ailerons, rudder, and spoilers, he was able to keep the plane level. But nothing slowed the loss of altitude. From five thousand feet just east of Hughes Aircraft, he was at twenty-five hundred feet when he passed over Washington Boulevard, two thousand at Venice Boulevard, and at less than one thousand when he crossed Pico Boulevard on a northwesterly course that was taking him into the heart of Beverly Hills. The plane was making a terrible racket when it crossed Wilshire, and dropped to less than five hundred feet when it groaned over Santa Monica Boulevard. Again, Hughes put the landing gear down, hoping to shake the problem loose. There was no change.

Planting his feet high on the instrument panel, Hughes braced himself for the inevitable. Below were the luxurious grounds, swimming pools, and homes of Beverly Hills, into one of which he was about to crash. Soon he saw the one —a large two-story house with a peaked roof, just a block shy of the grounds of the Los Angeles Country Club. Knowing that he would never clear the roof, Hughes fought to keep the XF-11's nose high to "flare" the ship into the roof and avoid a nose-down crackup.[16]

With a deafening noise, the right engine and landing gear crashed into the second floor of the house, at 803 North Linden Drive. The impact sent the plane yawing to the right, with the right wing slicing into the house and garage next door, at 805 North Linden. As the plane turned sharply right it hurtled sideways through the air, shearing off a utility pole, then bounced and skidded through an alley before finally coming to rest in a heap between two houses at 808 and 810 North Whittier Drive. A fire broke out, engulfing the wreckage and one of the houses.

A few houses away, marine Sergeant William Lloyd Durkin was relaxing with friends after dinner when he heard the whine of a low-flying airplane in distress. Seconds later, after a thunderous crash, he raced outside and saw wreckage down the street. As he ran toward it there was an explosion, and flames shot up in an orange glow. Just as Durkin got to the plane, the pilot crawled out of the cockpit and collapsed on a burning wing. Scrambling into the blaze, Durkin grabbed the man, pulled him from the fire, smothered his burning clothes, and called for help. Several hours later he heard on the radio that the man he had pulled from the wreckage was Howard Hughes.*

No one else was injured. The house at 808 North Whittier burned to the ground, but the owner, Lieutenant Colonel Charles A. Meyer, was in Europe

---

*Hughes rewarded Durkin for saving his life with a $200-a-month stipend. Later, in a lawsuit for damages which he filed against Hamilton-Standard, the manufacturer of the XF-11's propellers, Hughes listed the monthly reward payments to Durkin, as well as the airfare costs of flying Durkin's parents from Pittsburgh to Los Angeles, as among the expenses he wanted to recover from the company as a result of the crash.

Above: Hughes at the controls of the XF-11 in Culver City minutes before the near-fatal crash, July 8, 1946. *United Press International*

Below: The crash scene in Beverly Hills with one of the XF-11's 3,000-horsepower engines twisted in the foreground. *United Press International*

serving as an interpreter at the Nuremberg war trials.

The crash nearly killed Hughes, however. At Good Samaritan Hospital, doctors grimly determined the extent of his injuries. His chest was crushed. He suffered fractures of seven ribs on the left side, two on the right, a fracture of the left clavicle, a possible fracture of the nose, a large laceration of the scalp, extensive second- and third-degree burns on the left hand, a second-degree burn on the lower part of the left chest, a second-degree burn on the left buttock, cuts, bruises, and abrasions on his arms and legs, and many small cuts on his face. His left lung had collapsed and his right was also injured. His heart had been pushed to one side of his chest cavity. He was in severe shock. No one in the emergency room thought he would live through the night.

The two doctors in charge of the medical team attending Hughes were well acquainted with the patient. Verne R. Mason, an internist whose patients included many Hollywood stars, and Lawrence Chaffin, a surgeon for the Santa Fe Railroad's hospital in Los Angeles, had each treated Hughes for about fifteen years. As they inserted a tube in his crushed chest to drain fluid accumulating in the lungs, the doctors told Hughes, who had remained conscious throughout his ordeal, that he might not live. To relieve the pain and make bearable what all of them were certain would be his last few hours, Mason gave him injections of morphine.

Get-well messages, including one from President Harry S Truman, deluged the hospital. Although seemingly on his deathbed, Hughes refused to see most of his friends who hurried to the hospital. The only people he allowed through the armed guard outside his door were several film stars, including Jean Peters, Lana Turner, Errol Flynn, and Cary Grant, and a few employees of Hughes Aircraft. Hughes even refused to see his Houston aunts, Annette Lummis and Martha Houstoun, who had hurried to California to be at his side. Hughes had never indicated any displeasure with his mother's two sisters, and Annette and Martha were mystified, angry, and hurt. Annette lashed out at Noah Dietrich, blaming him, unfairly, for blocking their access to Howard. In truth, Dietrich was as puzzled as they by Hughes's behavior.*

After fighting through the critical hours, weak, disabled, and drugged as he was, Hughes had only one thing on his mind the first few days after the crash: moving quickly to protect his reputation as a pilot. Indeed, he had much to be concerned about. If he had followed the air force–approved flight plan and landed the XF-11 after the authorized forty-five-minute flight, the

---

*In the days following the crash, when Hughes hovered near death, Dietrich had some uneasy moments of his own when it became clear that Hughes had no valid will. For some reason, Hughes had retrieved and presumably destroyed a 1938 will that purportedly left his estate to medical research and his company in the control of longtime executives. He had spent untold hours in the 1940s drafting a new will along similar lines, but had never executed it. The realization that Hughes was near death and had no will caused Dietrich no little amount of alarm. If Hughes died without a will, his estate would go to his relatives, such as Annette Lummis, who no doubt, Dietrich feared, would have fired him as their first order of business and his "life's work," as a lawyer friend called it, "would have terminated."

crash would never have occurred. The night he was wheeled into the emergency room at Good Samaritan, Hughes whispered to Glenn Odekirk and the flight mechanic Joe Petrali to find out what had caused the crash. After he told them about the drag on the right side, they began sifting through the wreckage for a clue. Their investigation showed that the right rear propeller appeared to be in reverse pitch. The forward propeller on the right side had apparently functioned normally, but the rear one had mysteriously begun spinning in the wrong direction—in effect, trying to pull the aircraft backward. Later, it became clear that a seal had broken behind the right rear propeller, allowing oil to seep out. When the oil pressure dropped, the prop reversed pitch.

Four days after the accident, when Hughes was still in critical condition, he called Dr. Mason into his room and asked him to deliver a message to the air force, a prepared statement in which Hughes blamed the accident on the "rear half of the right propeller."[17]

"Tell the Army [Air Force] to look in the wreckage, find the rear half of the right propeller, and find out what went wrong with it. I don't want this to happen to somebody else."[18]

Dr. Mason dutifully conveyed Hughes's message to the military and released the statement to the press as well.

An air force investigating board also found that the right rear propeller had lost oil, reversed pitch, and created a drag on the right side of the airplane. But the board, in a crushing blow to Hughes's ego, concluded that the crash itself was caused by pilot error. It criticized Hughes for not using a special radio frequency that had been assigned to the XF-11 for the test flight, for not being sufficiently acquainted with emergency operating procedures for the propellers, and for retracting the landing gear in violation of the approved flight plan.[19] Criticizing Hughes for failing to consider an emergency landing, the investigating board said it was "of the opinion that this accident was avoidable after propeller trouble was experienced."[20]

After hovering so near death, Hughes slowly began to recover. Dissatisfied with his hospital bed, he called in engineers from Hughes Aircraft and told them to build him a new one, giving them detailed instructions for a sophisticated apparatus that Hughes hoped would relieve some of the pain caused by his injuries.* To the doctors, Hughes's recovery was just short of miraculous. Hughes had a less lofty explanation.

He was convinced, he told a friend later, that his life was saved because he drank great quantities of fresh orange juice daily. Hughes insisted that the oranges be sliced and squeezed in his room. He would not drink juice that came from the hospital's kitchen because he was not certain it was fresh. Hughes maintained that exposing citrus juice to the air for half an hour would rob it of the lifesaving ingredients he needed for recovery.[21]

On August 12, he was released from the hospital. His doctors had advised

---

*The bed was built at Culver City, but according to Dr. Chaffin, Hughes never used it.

him to remain at Good Samaritan, but, eager to leave, he went home to a rented house in Beverly Hills, accompanied by an around-the-clock medical team. During his convalescence, Hughes, who had a low tolerance for pain—owing in part, perhaps, to his exaggerated fear of sickness—demanded increasingly larger doses of morphine,[22] and Dr. Mason unquestioningly supplied it. But as time went by, he prescribed codeine, a weaker narcotic, as a substitute.[23] It was the beginning of a drug addiction that would become Hughes's best-kept secret in a life that overflowed with secrets.

As he grew stronger, Hughes worried that the accident might have made him apprehensive about flying. He need not have. On September 9, photographers snapped pictures of Hughes, sporting a moustache to cover scars on his upper lip, at the controls of his converted B-23 bomber before ascending on his first flight since the crash. For the next few months, to dispel any notion of fear, he flew everywhere—to New York, Kansas City, Dayton, and Mexico, for a much-needed vacation with Cary Grant. Hughes not only had recovered, but had also miraculously suffered no permanent disability. Two fingers on his left hand—the hand that had been burned so badly—did not move as freely as before. Other than that, he complained of no aches, pains, or discomfort. To the world it seemed that Howard Hughes had once again been very lucky.

After the XF-11 crash, Hughes's old antagonist Wright Field imposed what was for him the severest of sanctions. With the second photo-reconnaissance plane ready for flight, Wright asked Hughes Aircraft "to furnish the name of a test pilot, other than Mr. H. R. Hughes."[24] For a man obsessed with flying his own planes and one who jealously guarded his reputation as a pilot, it was an emasculating decision, and Hughes fought back.

On a wintry Sunday early in 1947, Hughes flew to Washington to appeal his case personally to the air force's top command. With the War Department shut down for the day, he headed for the home of Lieutenant General Ira C. Eaker, deputy commanding general of the air force, at Fort Myer, Virginia, the military post across the Potomac River from Washington. Eaker, who once shook hands with Hughes at a reception in 1938 after his around-the-world flight, cordially invited the aviator into his home. Hughes mentioned that Wright Field refused to allow him to test-fly the second XF-11, and said that he thought the decision was a mistake—that it would be "much safer"[25] for him to fly it in view of his familiarity with the plane, and that he would "pay the government" $5 million if the plane crashed with him at the controls.[26]

Eaker listened "very attentively," and then told Hughes that such a decision was for "the boss."[27] He telephoned General Carl Spaatz, the air force's new commanding general, who lived nearby, and asked if he could drop over to discuss a matter with Hughes. When Spaatz arrived and heard the novel proposal, his reaction was unequivocal—he had no objections to Hughes's flying the plane and would issue the "necessary orders to Wright

Field."[28] Elated and "most impressed" with the way Eaker had handled the situation, Hughes thanked the generals and took his leave.*[29]

CIRCUS ON THE POTOMAC

While Hughes was in Virginia defending his honor as a pilot, a more serious challenge to his reputation was shaping up on the other side of the Potomac. The Special Senate Committee Investigating the National Defense Program had quietly opened an investigation of Hughes's flying-boat and photo-reconnaissance-plane contracts. Established by the Senate in 1941 and made famous by Harry S Truman when he was an obscure senator from Missouri, the War Investigating Committee, as it was popularly known, was now in the hands of Republicans, who had won control of Congress in 1946 for the first time in sixteen years. Eager to expose the sins of nearly a generation of Democratic rule, the committee's Republican majority saw Hughes's cozy relationship with the Roosevelt administration as a likely place to start. As best the committee could determine, Hughes had received upward of $40 million in taxpayers' money for two military-aircraft projects, neither of which was anywhere near complete by the war's end. In fact, neither the flying boat nor the XF-11 had even flown successfully. And there was another impetus for the investigation, one not so evident.

The situation was this: In the spring of 1945, Hughes had won a stunning regulatory victory in Washington. Over the heated opposition of Pan American Airways, the Civil Aeronautics Board had awarded Hughes's Trans World Airlines the right to fly the Atlantic. For the first time, Pan American, the nation's premier international carrier, had competition on the lucrative North Atlantic route. Although the CAB victory was a giant step in TWA's drive to become a global airline, Jack Frye, TWA's president, warned Hughes of its possible consequences. "Howard . . . Pan American has the biggest, most complex, and strongest political machine that has ever hit Washington," Hughes later said that Frye told him. "Juan Trippe [Pan American's president] feels you have moved in on his territory . . . and he is going to make your life miserable."[30]

Shortly after TWA inaugurated flights to Europe in 1946, a bill was introduced in Congress that in effect would have taken away those overseas routes. Called the Chosen Instrument Bill, it would have required all United States airlines flying abroad to give up their overseas routes to a new consolidated international airline corporation. Pan American, the largest of the overseas carriers, would hold a controlling interest. Not surprisingly, Pan Am lobbied vigorously for the bill.

The author and guiding spirit of the legislation was a cold, somewhat

---

*Nine months later—on September 16, 1947—Eaker was hired by Hughes as a vice-president of the Hughes Tool Company in Houston.

pompous Republican senator from Maine, Ralph Owen Brewster, whom Drew Pearson once called the "kept senator" of Pan American Airways.[31] A spirited lobbying effort by TWA and other airlines succeeded in blocking the bill's passage in 1946. But no sooner had it died than Brewster drafted and introduced a measure called the Community Airline Bill. To Hughes it was simply "the same baby in a different set of diapers."[32]

As Hughes girded for another attack on TWA, Republican lawmakers gathered in Washington late in 1946 for a rare event, the division of spoils. In Congress, great power is held by committee chairmen, who, through their control over individual bills, direct the flow of legislation. A lawmaker might be arrogant, aloof, even disliked by his colleagues—which was certainly true in Brewster's case—but those personal qualities were secondary when it came to choosing committee chairmen. The only factor that mattered was a lawmaker's years of service. As a senior Republican, Brewster was entitled to head a powerful Senate committee, and in December he was elected chairman of the Special Senate Committee Investigating the National Defense Program. Less than a month later, on January 23, 1947, Brewster announced to the press one of the committee's first investigations—an inquiry into Howard Hughes's multimillion-dollar contract to build the all-plywood flying boat.

Hughes naturally viewed Brewster's probe as another attempt by Pan Am to hurt TWA by embarrassing him. Hughes tried to head off the inquiry. In February, he met with Brewster for lunch in the senator's suite at the Mayflower Hotel in Washington. The two men would later have divergent memories of that lunch. Hughes would charge that Brewster hinted he would call off the investigation if TWA agreed to merge with Pan Am. Brewster would say only that he asked Hughes's support for his new Community Airline Bill. Whatever was said, the luncheon ended amicably.

And Hughes went out of his way the rest of that week to cooperate with Brewster's committee. On February 11, he spent hours testifying in executive session, politely covering his past record in aviation, his partnership with Henry Kaiser, and the way his war contracts were obtained. As far as he could tell, the investigation was still "friendly."[33] But by the time he returned to Los Angeles shortly afterward, he was deeply worried. Always fearful of damage to his reputation, he saw the investigation as a very powerful weapon that could be used against him.[34] Noah Dietrich "did not think the investigation amounted to very much and thought Hughes was unnecessarily excited about it."[35] But Dietrich's efforts to allay Hughes's fears were useless; Hughes was convinced that Pan Am, aided by its senatorial agent Brewster, was out to get him.

If Hughes had any remaining doubts about the seriousness of the investigation, they were soon dispelled. Francis D. Flanagan, the Brewster committee's chief investigator, flew to Los Angeles on March 14 to begin the field investigation of the Hughes Aircraft Company. To appear cooperative, in February Hughes had invited the committee to inspect the aircraft company's books.[36] Now, when Flanagan asked to see the company's expense records, Hughes balked, saying they would only "embarrass a lot of people."[37] That, of course, is exactly what the committee had in mind. It had already picked up a tip that Hughes had paid Elliott Roosevelt's hotel bills and other expenses on several West Coast trips, and that it was Elliott who had recommended the controversial XF-II airplane when virtually the entire air force was united against it. Nothing would have delighted the committee's Republican members more than an opportunity to tarnish the Roosevelt name.

On April 5, 1947, Hughes test-flew the second XF-II for ninety minutes at Culver City, then landed and emerged smiling from the cockpit, to the applause of about five hundred Hughes Aircraft employees. After nearly five years as a government plane maker, one of his government-financed airplanes had flown successfully. But the flight made no impact on the mounting senatorial investigation. Flanagan grew impatient as Hughes stalled. When Hughes stood fast in refusing to turn over his company's expense records, Flanagan threatened to subpoena them. Only then did Hughes open up the records, which quickly proved the bonanza the committee had hoped for.

John Meyer, Hughes's glib, bubbly press agent, had spent $169,661 entertaining air force officers during the war. The money had gone for excursions to the nightclubs and restaurants of Los Angeles and New York, and had paid for private parties where platoons of young Hollywood beauties floated freely among military men. More important to the committee's hope of embarrassing the Democrats, Flanagan turned up dozens of Meyer expense account entries showing charges on behalf of Elliott Roosevelt for hotels, liquor, entertainment, and women. Meyer had even listed as an expense the cost of renting a car and tipping police when he had escorted three of FDR's daughters-in-law into Washington for the president's funeral on April 13, 1945. Moving swiftly, the Senate committee set public hearings for July 28. Clearly, they would be sensational.

Whatever the motivation for Brewster's probe, Hughes was extremely vulnerable to a public inquiry into his role as a war contractor. Perhaps Hughes did not recognize what a mediocre job his company had done during the war. But he did fear that the investigation would ruin him. As the hearings approached, he plotted a counterattack, something to blunt the committee's thrust. He charged that the probe was a "political investigation to smear the Democrats . . . and Elliott Roosevelt," and to smear him and TWA to the "advantage of Pan American Airways."[38] He attacked Brewster's widely known association with Pan American. John Meyer was dispatched on a hurried trip to South America and Europe to document the dates and places where Brewster had accepted Pan Am's hospitality abroad.

The Kaiser–Hughes hearings, as the press labeled them, were called to order at 10:30 A.M. in the ornate, high-ceilinged caucus room of the Senate Office Building on a muggy Washington day, July 28, 1947.* Leaks about Hollywood parties, seductive actresses, and other favors that Hughes had

*The Senate Caucus Room would later host two more famous proceedings—the Army-McCarthy hearings in 1954 and the Senate Watergate hearings in 1973.

supposedly bestowed on the nation's high military chiefs had built up enormous interest. Room 318 was overflowing with fifteen hundred spectators, reporters, and photographers amid a blaze of klieg lights and a forest of motion-picture cameras. In the austere marble hallways outside the hearing room, hundreds more crowded around loudspeakers to follow the testimony and the often acerbic, sometimes comic exchanges that would follow.

The man who rang down the gavel that morning was a little-known Republican senator from Michigan, Homer Ferguson. A former prosecutor and judge from Detroit, Ferguson had been chosen by Brewster to chair a subcommittee of the Senate War Investigating Committee to interrogate and cross-examine witnesses, and although he looked gentle enough, even grandfatherly, he in fact possessed a hair-trigger temper. Long in the shadow of Michigan's senior senator, the nationally known Arthur Vandenberg, Ferguson saw the Kaiser–Hughes hearings as a way to shed his provincial obscurity. The other Republican members were even lesser known: George W. Malone of Nevada, Harry P. Cain of Washington, John J. Williams of Delaware (not yet known as the "conscience of the Senate"), and a newly elected senator from Wisconsin, Joseph R. McCarthy. The Democratic members were Carl A. Hatch of New Mexico, Howard McGrath of Rhode Island, Herbert R. O'Conor of Maryland, and Claude Pepper of Florida.

While the subcommittee was hearing opening testimony the first day from important, though largely colorless witnesses, Hughes unleashed a bombshell on the West Coast. His old friend William Randolph Hearst had turned over the considerable resources of his newspaper empire for a Hughes counterattack. In a series of copyrighted articles appearing under Hughes's byline in Hearst newspapers across the nation, Hughes opened his attack, calling on Senator Brewster to "tell the whole truth" about the investigation.[39] Charging that it was "really born" when TWA began flying the Atlantic in competition with Pan American, Hughes said that Brewster was an odd choice to conduct a probe about favors accepted by government officials. "Why not tell about the two airplane trips you bummed off of me?" Hughes challenged the senator, adding that he had twice provided the Maine senator with a "luxurious private airplane."[40]

Hughes kept up the attack in the days that followed, charging that the probe was instigated by Pan Am and that Brewster had once hinted that he would call it off if Hughes "would agree to merge" TWA with Pan Am.[41] Whether Hughes actually wrote the articles or had one of his public-relations men draft them is not clear. But Hughes did have a flair for publicity, and the articles that appeared under his byline deftly captured the spirit of the sensationalist Hearst press. In one he referred to TWA as the "little dog" and Pan Am as the "big dog."[42] All his trouble began, he said, when the "little dog . . . stepped on the big dog's toes."[43]

While almost juvenile in tone, these Hearst newspaper pieces had the desired effect. By raising the Brewster issue Hughes had deflected attention from himself and onto the chairman of the full committee, who was forced to spend the next few days vigorously denying Hughes's charges at every opportunity. Hughes had both challenged the integrity of the committee and stolen the initiative. Could the committee regain it?

Back in Washington, Ferguson plowed ahead on schedule. One of the first witnesses was John Meyer, Hughes's chubby press agent. Ferguson hoped to show that Meyer was Hughes's diabolical agent of influence peddling. Instead, Meyer, a coiner of amusing one-liners, came off as something less than sinister. To the delight of the audience and the consternation of Ferguson, Meyer spent his three days on the stand wisecracking and generally playing down his wartime duty of entertaining Elliott Roosevelt and other military officers for Hughes. Every time Ferguson tried to trap or embarrass Meyer, the press agent wriggled out of the chairman's grasp. When Ferguson asked Meyer what "good" had resulted from the $169,000 Meyer had spent entertaining government officers during the war, Meyer quipped, "It helped me, did it not? I met a lot of people."[44]

On Monday, August 4, when Elliott Roosevelt took the stand alongside Meyer, the two men put on a show of "high comedy" that had the gallery roaring and Ferguson frantically banging his gavel for order.[45] Roosevelt denied that Meyer had in any way influenced him concerning the XF-II contract, and charged that some of the expenses Meyer had allegedly made on his behalf were actually incurred while Roosevelt was out of the country on active duty. Sitting side by side at the witness table, Meyer and Roosevelt proceeded to ignore the subcommittee and argue over Meyer's expense account:

"Could I ask Mr. Meyer specifically," Roosevelt said, speaking slowly, "were any of these girls that he got and paid money to or that he gave presents to, was it for the purpose of getting in with me, and did any of those girls who were paid, were they procured for my entertainment?"

"I don't like the word 'procured,' " Meyer answered, "because a girl who attends a party and is given a present is not necessarily 'procured.' "

"Use any word you want, but were they for me?"

". . . No," Meyer paused, "but I will say this, that the Colonel well knows that the girls were present."

Ferguson interjected a question. "Were they there to entertain all the people?"

"We were all together," Meyer said. "I would say that the Colonel was almost constantly in the company of Miss [Faye] Emerson."

Roosevelt persisted: "Were any of these girls there specifically to entertain me?"

". . . That is hard to say, because you were quite busy with Miss Emerson."

As Meyer pored over his expense records, he explained that several other air force officers were also in the Roosevelt party under discussion.

"Are you stating that those girls were there to entertain them?" Roosevelt asked.

"They sat around with us and had drinks with us and went to dinner with us, and the girls were probably not with anyone, they just danced with anybody who asked them to."

"That is very interesting," Roosevelt commented. ". . . Must I be my brother's keeper?"

"I cannot answer that," Meyer retorted. "I am not familiar with the Bible if that is what it is."[46]

This circuslike atmosphere went on and on. The hearings were the stuff of great radio drama, and networks regularly preempted scheduled nighttime programs to broadcast long excerpts from the day's events.

The real star, of course, was Hughes. The last witness to be called, he remained secluded in Los Angeles and did not fly to the capital until the very morning of the day he was scheduled to testify. His appearance was set for 2 P.M. on Thursday, August 6, but Hughes kept the senators waiting while the spectators buzzed. At 2:42, klieg lights flashed on, motion-picture cameras rolled, reporters scrambled to the rear of the room, and excitement rippled through the crowd as Homer Ferguson, who had grown increasingly restive during the delay, remarked snidely, "Apparently, the entrance is about to be made."[47]

When Hughes walked into the Senate Caucus Room, accompanied by Noah Dietrich, his attorney Thomas A. Slack, and a group of other aides and lawyers, the audience broke into applause. Wearing a handsome double-breasted gray suit, white shirt, and dark tie, Hughes stood at the witness table exuding contempt for the proceeding and was sworn by Ferguson:

"What is your full name?" the senator asked.

"Howard R. Hughes."

"And what is your address?"

"Business or residence?"

"Give us both."

"I have several business addresses in Houston, in care of the Hughes Tool Company and in California at 7000 Romaine Street."

"Will you speak into the mike so that we can all hear you?"

"In Houston, my address is care of the Hughes Tool Company; in California it is 7000 Romaine Street, Hollywood."

"You are president of the Hughes Tool Company?"

"That is correct."

"And I assume the largest stockholder; is that correct?"

"That's correct, also."

"Is it a closed corporation, or is the stock on the market?"

"The stock is not on the market."

"It is a closed corporation?"

"I do not know what you mean by a closed corporation."

"It is held in a small group; is that correct?"

"I own all of the stock."

"You own all of the stock?"

"Yes."[48]

Hughes's defiant attitude and low opinion of the subcommittee were unmistakable. He told the senators that he thought their investigation was "illegitimate,"[49] and took the pose of an innocent victim outraged at being caught in a political crossfire. Whether feigned or real, Hughes's indignation was a master stroke. By all rights, the hearings should have demolished his reputation. A close look at the war years showed that he was not always an able designer, nor a brilliant pilot, and certainly not a good businessman. He had squandered millions of dollars in government money on two grossly mismanaged projects. Government inspectors told the panel about waste, inefficiency, and bungling at Hughes Aircraft, but their testimony disappeared into the voluminous hearing record, first ignored and then forgotten. Hughes's image remained intact. To the public, he was still an aviation hero who had stormed into Washington to protect his name from being sullied by a group of squabbling politicians.

The first two days Hughes was on the stand, he and Brewster traded charges about Pan Am, and the hearings rapidly degenerated into what one newspaper called a "lie-passing contest."[50] Even so, the bickering worked to Hughes's advantage. By raising the Pan American issue again, Hughes had once more turned the spotlight away from himself and onto his senatorial adversary. As Hughes verbally sparred with Brewster across the witness table, the spectators applauded and cheered the famous pilot, to the annoyance of Homer Ferguson.

The Michigan Republican, picked to chair the hearings because of his courtroom experience as a prosecutor and a judge, was no match for Hughes in the rough and tumble that punctuated Hughes's five days on the stand. Hughes's hostility and refusal to accord the subcommittee the usual measure of respect that senators ordinarily take for granted completely unnerved Ferguson. When John Meyer failed to show up on the morning of August 8 to testify alongside Hughes, an indignant Ferguson tried to force Hughes to tell him where Meyer was:

"Do you know where Mr. Meyers is?" Ferguson demanded.

"Meyers?" asked a puzzled Hughes.

"Yes; John Meyers."

"Oh, Meyer. No; no, I don't."

"Well, he was instructed to be here," said Ferguson, as he fumbled through some papers before him, "and I am just advised by the counsel that he is not here, and they are unable to locate him."

Laughter rippled through the audience, setting off Ferguson's fiery temper.

"He works for you, does he not, Mr. Hughes?" he snapped.

"He works for my company," Hughes said, smiling.

"It may be funny to you that he is not here."

"I didn't laugh, Senator," Hughes smiled. "Somebody laughed back there."

"You also laughed; did you not?"

"Laughing is contagious, Senator."

By now the audience was roaring. Rather than drop the subject, Ferguson plodded ahead.

"Mr. Hughes, Mr. John W. Meyer is your assistant; personal assistant?"

"I have been told that he is so listed."

"Well, is he or is he not?"

"I don't really know, Senator."

"You do not know," Ferguson repeated. "Well, now, you are president of the company?"

"That is correct."

"What is his job?"

"He is director of public relations, and that is one of his jobs anyway."

"He is director of public relations, and that is one of his jobs?"

"I said that is one of his jobs, anyway; it may be his only job."

Ferguson was now so angry he could barely contain his fury. "What is one of his other jobs, whether it is any way or all ways?"

Hughes laughed. "Well, I am not prepared to say if he has any other job, Senator."

"Who would know if the president does not know?"

"Well, there are quite a few other people in the company."

". . . I want to know now whether you know where he is."

"I do not know where he is."

"He is in your employ and you do not know where he is?"

". . . There are a lot of people in my employ. Do I know where everyone is every day?"

"They are not all witnesses here, are they?"

"I have a little work besides this hearing," Hughes shot back. "You may not realize that."

"I do realize that."

"And I don't have time to follow every witness that is at this hearing."

". . . Well, now, will you see that Mr. Meyer comes in at 2 o'clock?"

"What? Today?"

"Yes."

"No. I don't think I will."

"He is in your employ."

"Well, as I say, so are a lot of other people. I don't know where he is; I think my company has been inconvenienced just about enough with respect to Mr. Meyer. I brought him back here twice for you."

"Do you think Mr. Meyer's business at the present time is more important than this committee hearing?"

"Well, it is more important to my company, I can tell you that."

"Who in your company will know the whereabouts of Mr. Meyer at the present time?"

"I don't know that, but you have had him here for unlimited questioning, and I brought him back here twice from abroad. I don't see why I should do any more than that just to accommodate you so you can put him up here beside me on the stand and make a publicity show out of it."

"Well, is that the reason he is not here?"

"That is not the reason," Hughes countered, now angry, "but I think it is the reason you want him back."

"Well, I have some questions that I want to ask him."

"Why didn't you ask him while he was here," Hughes said, raising his voice. "I brought him back here twice from abroad for you."

"Because we wanted to do it as the committee thought they could do it, and that is to go over the matter as we proceeded."

"Yeah," Hughes sneered, "that's what you think."

"That is what I know," protested Ferguson, "not what I think . . . I have asked you whether or not you will produce Meyer and you said you didn't know, as I understand it."

"I don't remember if that was my answer."

"What was your answer?"

"I don't know; get it off the record."

The audience laughed, and Ferguson was beside himself with anger. "Well, now, Mr. Hughes, I am asking you what your answer was."

"I don't remember what it was."

"We will not have this bickering back and forth," insisted Ferguson. "You are before this committee, and you are going to answer the question."

Hughes paused, genuinely amused by Ferguson's mounting frustration. "You asked me just now about a reply that I made. My answer is 'I don't remember.' Now, the man is taking everything down there. Why don't you ask him?"

"I will ask you again."

"What?"

"Will you bring Mr. Meyer in at the 2 o'clock session?"

"No. I don't think I will."

"Will you try to bring him in?"

"No. I don't think I will try."[51]

The exchange was typical of the way Ferguson allowed peripheral issues to dominate the hearings. By focusing on Meyer, a minor character in the drama, and by trying to make more of Elliott Roosevelt's connection with Hughes than existed, the subcommittee failed to exploit Hughes's greatest weakness—his record as a government contractor. Time and again, the senators missed this point. Hours were spent grilling Hughes under oath in a futile effort to establish that he had managed to profit by his two war contracts. In fact, the opposite was true. He had actually lost millions of dollars in trying to become a major aircraft manufacturer. He had lost $7.5 million alone completing the flying boat.

Hughes enjoyed himself throughout his four days at the witness table. The Hughes who emerged at the hearings—outgoing, vocal, almost extroverted—

had never been seen before and would never be seen in public again. He took special delight in rattling Ferguson. At one point, Ferguson asked Hughes if he had certain vital records of the Hughes Aircraft Company in his possession.

"I don't have them on my person, if that is what you mean."

"Now, don't try to get smart with this committee," Ferguson admonished, "you know that was not the question."[52]

When the hearings turned serious, Hughes was an impressive witness. He had a prodigious memory and he put it to good use. Recalling dates, dollar amounts, specific provisions of his war contracts, and other minute details about the operation of Hughes Aircraft, Hughes conveyed the impression of a man who kept his finger on the pulse of his company at all times. He denied that he had used his influence to secure the contracts, and pointed out that many high-ranking air force officers opposed both projects. In defense of the flying boat, he touched on the size of the project and admitted that he had made mistakes:

It was awfully hard to build a ship this big out of wood. None had ever been built before or even dreamed of in a size even as much as one-tenth of this. . . . If I made a mistake on this airplane it was not through neglect. It was through supervising each portion of it in too much detail; in other words, as I look back on it, if I could do the job over, I would have delegated more of the work to other people which might possibly have resulted in a faster job, but I am by nature a perfectionist, and I seem to have trouble allowing anything to go through in a half-perfect condition. So if I made any mistake it was in working too hard and in doing too much of it with my own two hands.[53]

Although he had played only a limited role in the design of the big boat, he nevertheless told the senators, "I carried out the design."[54] And for his labor, Hughes added, he paid a steep price. He was "so completely broken down physically" afterward, he said, that he was sent away for a seven-month rest:[55] "I do not know how anybody could have worked harder than I did."[56]

When the senators criticized the flying boat, taking special note that it had yet to fly, Hughes rallied to the ship's defense. Replying sarcastically that the plane was never meant "to haul excursion passengers from Coney Island to Staten Island," Hughes said the ship could be used only "for testing and research and to provide knowledge which will advance the art of aviation in this country."[57] It had "crossed a barrier in size"[58] and was a "step forward"[59] for American aviation. It must have been a painful admission, but Hughes acknowledged that he was not certain the Hercules would fly. If, however, it were judged a failure, he said he would "probably leave this country and never come back."[60]

On August 11, Ferguson abruptly recessed the hearings for three months, ostensibly because the committee could not find Meyer for more questioning. In fact, Ferguson was under heavy pressure from other Republicans to call the hearings off, at least temporarily, because they were a fiasco.[61]

Outside the Senate Caucus Room, with reporters milling around him, Hughes pounced on Ferguson's announcement, claiming that it was a vindica-

Above, left: Before testifying, Hughes goes over his statement with Thomas A. Slack *(left)*, one of his lawyers, and Noah Dietrich, the executive vice-president of the Hughes Tool Company. *United Press International*

Above, right: Confronting his accusers, Hughes peers down at Senator Homer Ferguson during the Senate War Investigating Committee hearings on August 6, 1947, in Washington. At the end of the table, with his hand on the microphone, is Senator Ralph Owen Brewster, Hughes's principal antagonist. *Wide World Photos*

Right: A pensive mood during the Senate hearings. *United Press International*

Below, left: In the deserted Senate Caucas Room after one day's proceedings. Hughes's attorney, Thomas Slack, is behind him. *Wide World Photos*

Below, right: Waving to admirers at Washington National Airport before flying back to California. *United Press International*

tion of his own position and a rout of his opponent Brewster, who, he charged, was "too cowardly to stay here and face the music."[62] The next day at National Airport, boarding his converted B-23 bomber for the return to California, Hughes told reporters, "I can really say that the people and the press treated me more fairly than I had any right to expect."[63]

Indeed they had. Seizing on Hughes's charges of a smear campaign, they had overlooked all else. He was going home with his reputation intact. The only unsettling aspect of the experience would not surface until later, when it was revealed that a Washington police lieutenant had tapped Hughes's phone and bugged his suite at the Carlton Hotel during the hearings, apparently on orders from Brewster. The incident would feed one of Hughes's growing paranoias—his fear of being overheard or spied upon.

SURPRISE FLIGHT

When Hughes got back to Los Angeles, he had but one thought: to fly the flying boat. The senators had needled him at every opportunity over the fact that the plane had never flown. To take it up, just once, would further undercut their bungled probe. In Long Beach, the job of assembling the Hercules was nearly completed. Its giant wings, tail, and stabilizers were in place, and workers were just finishing the job of hooking up miles of wires, ducts, and tubes. On October 25, Hughes announced that he would conduct taxi tests on the big boat in Long Beach harbor over the weekend of November 1 and 2. No mention was made of any plan actually to fly, but there was little doubt, what with the resumption of the Senate hearings less than two weeks away, that he intended to do just that. So that the event would be properly recorded, he invited reporters from every major newspaper in the country to come to Long Beach at his expense to witness the tests.

In preparation, Hughes put himself through an intensive training period to sharpen his skills flying off and on water. In the Sikorsky S-43, rebuilt after its 1943 crash in Lake Mead, he flew in late October to a remote stretch of the Colorado River near Parker Dam, on the California–Arizona border, to make hundreds of test landings on the river.

On November 1, 1947, when the nation's press people gathered at Terminal Island in Long Beach for their first look at the Hercules in its dry dock adjoining the harbor, they were overwhelmed. None of the press releases had fully conveyed the size of the flying boat. Built to carry seven hundred passengers or a load of sixty tons, the Hercules seemed more a creation of science fiction than the work of flesh and blood men. The tail was as tall as an eight-story building. The wingspan, more than double that of a B-29, was longer than a football field. The propellers were seventeen feet in diameter. The hull stood thirty feet tall. The wings were so thick a man could stand up inside them.*

---

*The Hughes flying boat remains the largest airplane ever built. The Lockheed C-5A Galaxy transport and the Boeing 747 are slightly longer, 230 and 225 feet, respectively, compared to the

As thousands of spectators watched from shore, the dry dock was flooded and the Hercules was afloat for the first time. Although built of plywood—millions of board-feet of plywood—its smooth, aluminum-lacquered hull glistened like metal in the sun. With Hughes at the controls, it was towed carefully into the harbor, but a stiff wind blowing out of the southwest forced him to postpone the taxi tests until the next day. The wind was still blowing hard on November 2, but Hughes decided to execute the taxi runs anyway. With the press eagerly standing by, he had little choice. On the first taxi run, the big plane glided smoothly along the water over a three-mile course at a modest forty-five miles an hour. Reporters were invited aboard for the next test run, and Hughes increased the speed to ninety miles an hour, the big ship once again taxiing smoothly through the choppy waters of Long Beach harbor. Hughes then let the reporters off in a small boat so that they could go ashore to file their stories.

With only his crew and one newsman, Jim McNamara, a reporter for a Los Angeles radio station, aboard, Hughes began what had been billed as the final taxi run of the day. Slowly gathering speed in the face of a blustery wind, the Hercules sliced through the water, then dramatically lifted off. Cruising at seventy feet above the water, the big ship flew for about a mile before Hughes set it down, gently and without incident. The unexpected liftoff caught everyone ashore by surprise. A gasp and then a cheer went up from the thousands lining the harbor. Small pleasure boats, gathered to watch the tests, tooted their horns. In the cockpit, Hughes was like a "little kid," recalled Joe Petrali, one of his crewmen. "He was grinning, and talking a lot, almost jumping up and down in his elation."[64]

A few minutes later when Hughes came ashore, his face revealing nothing more than the trace of a smile, he was his usual serious self. He told reporters he had "sort of hoped to fly" the big boat that day, but had not made any predictions because many things could have prevented it.[65] "I put the flaps down, and that gave so much buoyancy and felt so good, I just pulled it up. I think the airplane is going to be fairly successful."[66] Denying that he had made the flight to impress the Senate War Investigating Committee, Hughes said that he intended to "keep on with the testing, making short flights close to the water."[67] The first major flight would come in the spring.

Three days later, on November 5, the Kaiser–Hughes hearings resumed in Washington, and although there were fresh revelations of influence peddling and incompetence at Hughes Aircraft and of General Benny Meyers's abortive $200,000 loan request from Hughes, the session was anticlimactic. By flying the Hercules, Hughes had stolen the committee's thunder. The Republican members issued a highly critical report, but it made little impact. The hearings closed on November 22, 1947.

---

flying boat's 218 feet. But the Hercules's wingspan is much greater than either of those planes, 320 feet compared to 222 for the Lockheed and 195 for the Boeing. The Hercules is also much heavier —400,000 pounds to the Lockheed's 325,000 and the Boeing's 378,000.

After its one flight, the Hercules was towed to a dry dock on Terminal Island where workmen erected a permanent hangar around it. Within a few months it disappeared from view, not to be seen again by the public in Hughes's lifetime. Years went by without so much as a hint from Hughes that he ever intended to fly it again. His silence was no accident. For all the time, effort, and money expended on the flying boat, the giant craft was woefully underpowered. Something more than piston-driven engines would be required to make it truly an airplane.

Hughes could have turned it over to the federal government, which owned it. But he knew what that would have meant. Too expensive to maintain, the ship would swiftly have been destroyed. Instead, he exercised an option in his agreement with the RFC that gave him the right to lease the flying boat at a rate of $37,500 a month—or $450,000 a year. With additional lease fees to Long Beach for the Terminal Island site and operational costs for maintaining the Hercules year-round in an air-conditioned, humidity-controlled hangar, Hughes spent close to $1 million a year to preserve an airplane that could not fly.

Whatever the amount, it was clearly enormous, and it gradually began to represent to the world one of the clearest signs of Hughes's eccentricity. Even inside his own corporation, the lavish costs required to maintain the ship became a serious problem, and pressure mounted on Hughes to dispose of it.

As for the XF-11, Hughes turned it over to the air force late in 1947, claiming that it was as fast "as any twin-engined propeller-driven plane" in existence.[68] It was used briefly at Wright Field, then went into service at Eglin Air Force Base in Florida, and finally was sent to Shephard Air Force Base in Wichita Falls, Texas, where it was used as a trainer. For all Hughes's hopes, for all the controversy surrounding it, for all the effort that had gone into it, the XF-11, in the words of an authoritative air force history of the war, "did not measure up to specifications."[69] On July 26, 1949, it was "authorized for reclamation"[70]—air force jargon for the decision to cut it up for scrap.

The war years were a period of bitter disappointment and personal trauma for Hughes. He had accomplished nothing of lasting value. His dream of making the Hughes Aircraft Company an aircraft manufacturer was in ruins. His hopes of becoming a major government contractor were shattered. He feared that his reputation had been damaged by the Senate hearings. He had almost killed himself, and suffered a mental breakdown. He had spent millions of dollars in pursuit of an elusive goal, and in the end all he had to show was the great flying boat, propped up in its private, air-conditioned dry dock in Long Beach.

The Hercules did not help win the war, was not a functioning airplane, did very little for aeronautical research, and played little or no part in the march toward bigger and better aircraft. But it was a remarkable achievement just the same. If there was nothing revolutionary about the Hercules, if any number of major aircraft designers and builders could have constructed a plane

Above: The Hercules flying boat—the largest airplane ever built—afloat for the first time at Long Beach, November 1, 1947. *United Press International*

Below, left: Hughes with Senator Claude Pepper of Florida under one of the flying boat's great engines. *Wide World Photos*

Below, right: Hughes checking the controls of the flying boat shortly before he took it up for its one and only flight, November 2, 1947. *Wide World Photos*

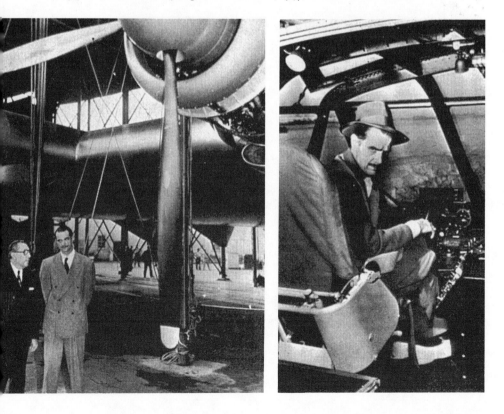

of its scale, the fact remains that it was Hughes who *did* build it, and therein lies a key to understanding the man. Anyone else with the resources to attempt such a feat probably would have been too practical, too concerned for the balance sheet, or too protective of his wealth to have invested a fortune in a project that promised so little return. And Hughes must always have known that the flying boat had a dubious future, no matter how successful the prototype. He was never sure that it would fly, any more than a mountain climber, eyeing the summit above him, knows whether he will reach the top. Although shy and withdrawn, Hughes did have a flair for the grand gesture, a thirst to undertake the new and untried, and periodically to impress the world. Like his 1938 world flight, the flying boat met these criteria. Only this time there were no rewards.

Still, Hughes considered the plane a success. It would remain for him a great triumph. As the years passed and the public's memory of his 1938 world flight faded, Hughes clung more possessively than ever to the flying boat as a reminder of his youth. All through the 1950s, before he slipped into seclusion, the highest honor he could bestow on another was a personal tour of the flying boat, to let a visitor pad around inside its wooden belly, gawking at its enormous size. Hughes had put as much of himself into the Hercules as anything he ever attempted, and he would protect, cherish, and preserve it until the day he died.

CHAPTER 6

MOVIES, MISSILES, AND COMMUNISTS

THE RKO TAKEOVER

THE two long stays in Washington in 1947 convinced Hughes that his personal staff needed reorganization. Over the years, he had come to depend on men at Romaine Street—Lee Murrin, Charles Guest, and Malcolm Smith among others—to take messages, transmit memoranda, make appointments, and otherwise handle paperwork generated by the Hughes empire. It was an ad-hoc system that had grown up in response to the peculiar way Hughes managed his affairs. Rarely operating from an office, he phoned Romaine Street when he needed something done and passed along the order to the man on duty. The system functioned reasonably well up to 1947, but during Hughes's two frenzied sessions before the Brewster committee it had broken down under the deluge of phone calls and the confusion surrounding the hearings. Hughes needed a full-time assistant, someone who could not only supervise at Romaine Street, but also go with him wherever he traveled. When he spoke to Nadine Henley about it, she recommended Frank William Gay, a young man then working for her at Romaine.

Gay, a lanky twenty-seven-year-old, had taken the Romaine job to earn money for a return to college. The son of a Methodist father and a Mormon mother, he had been raised a devout Mormon and enrolled in the church's Brigham Young University. Studying political science, philosophy, and business, Gay had accumulated more than four years of undergraduate credit hours but no degree. He had hoped to go on to Columbia University for graduate work and become a college professor. While he and his wife were visiting her parents in Los Angeles in the summer of 1947, Gay learned about the Romaine Street job from his wife's uncle, Wendell Thain, a close friend of Nadine Henley's, and when he applied, Miss Henley hired him. That fall, he worked with her assembling background materials for the second round of Senate hearings in November. Polite, efficient, and hard-working, Gay quickly earned Miss Henley's respect. She took an almost maternal interest in the welfare of her young protegé. Gay would be ideally suited for the job, she told Hughes, but she doubted he could be persuaded to give up his academic aspirations. "Don't say anything to him," Hughes told her. "Let me handle it personally."[1]

One day in December of 1947, Hughes summoned Gay to his office. Gay had never seen or spoken to Hughes, but like everyone else at Romaine he knew Hughes often worked out of an office at the Goldwyn Studios, two blocks west at Romaine Street and Formosa Avenue. Not knowing what to expect, Gay hurried over to meet his famous employer. When Gay was ushered into Hughes's office, the industrialist introduced himself and began a rambling monologue—he was trying to find someone to work with him and to "put together a staff operation."[2] Would Gay be interested? Surprised by the offer, Gay told Hughes he honestly did not know. His goal was to become a college professor.

"Well, why would you want to do that?" Hughes asked.

"That's a pretty good question," Gay admitted. "I don't know."

"Why don't we try it for three months," Hughes suggested, "and at the end of three months you tell me whether you like me and I'll tell you whether I like you. If we do that, then we can decide whether you can stay permanently. You can afford to take the gamble."[3]

Gay agreed and, following Hughes's instructions, assumed the duties of an administrative assistant, setting up meetings between Hughes and his executives, taking memoranda from him for transmission to lawyers or executives elsewhere, and correlating "the flow of information" to Hughes.[4] To screen his boss's calls, Gay established a message center on the second floor at Romaine Street and hired a group of young men, most of them college students and Mormons like himself, to man it around the clock. As the system went into effect, more experienced workers at Romaine received fewer direct orders from Hughes. Even though Gay went about his duties with reserve, careful not to antagonize older employees, it was clear that Hughes's relationship with Romaine Street had changed and that his trust now lay in the newcomer. Hughes found Gay to be an efficient, obsequious assistant, and Gay in turn sensed that a career with Howard Hughes would be far more rewarding than a college professorship. At the end of the trial period, Gay readily stayed on.

The reorganization of Romaine Street was not the only change Hughes had set in motion by early 1948. The disastrous war years and the Senate investigation had dampened his interest, at least temporarily, in becoming an aircraft manufacturer. But other than airplanes and motion pictures, Hughes had found little in the business world that captured his imagination. And so he decided to try his hand once again at the movie business. Floyd B. Odlum, an old business acquaintance, gave him the opportunity.

As president of the Atlas Corporation, a $70-million investment company, Odlum ruled a conglomerate that controlled properties ranging from aircraft companies to Hollywood studios. A shrewd bargainer, Odlum acquired and discarded properties with the ease of a horse trader, invariably buying weak companies, restoring them to financial health, then selling at a profit. Odlum had bought into RKO (Radio–Keith–Orpheum) in 1935, and had built the once-unprofitable studio into a highly lucrative operation by the mid-1940s. After the war, Odlum, believing that the golden years of Hollywood were past, was ready to move on. For the right price he would gladly sell RKO.

When Hughes learned of Odlum's desire, he became fascinated by the notion of controlling RKO, then one of Hollywood's largest and most prestigious studios. This fascination was, in every way, a curious response. In all his Hollywood years, Hughes had steadfastly avoided any involvement with major studios. He was the most independent of the independent producers. Answerable only to himself, he could take his legendary time in completing films—a luxury no major studio could afford. Nevertheless, Hughes decided to sound out Odlum on a price. To throw the press off the trail, Hughes leaked a tip to reporters early in January of 1948 indicating that he was abandoning motion-picture production temporarily to devote himself to aviation. Then he secretly flew off to Palm Springs and drove the short distance to Odlum's ranch in the Coachella Desert near Indio, California.

Hollywood is no place to keep a secret. Word soon leaked out, and Odlum was forced to confirm that he and Hughes had held preliminary discussions on the sale of Atlas's RKO stock. But Odlum downplayed the importance of the talks. "Under today's almost panicky conditions in the production end of the movie industry," he said on January 15, "it is doubtful if any person or group of substance within the industry has the combined money and nerve to meet the faith of the Atlas Corporation in the industry."' Since Hollywood knew that RKO was for sale, Odlum's disclaimer served only to fuel intense speculation that he and Hughes were about to close a deal.

News of the Hughes–Odlum talks sent shock waves through RKO. Although Hughes had had his successes in the 1930s with *Hell's Angels* and *Scarface,* his reputation had declined in the 1940s. His running feud with censors over Jane Russell's breasts in *The Outlaw* was a far cry from the outspoken defense of free expression in *Scarface.* Since his return to movie-making in the 1940s, Hughes had also adopted practices that struck Hollywood as unbusinesslike, if not bizarre. Hughes Productions routinely placed attractive young women under contract, giving them expensive drama, singing, and dancing lessons, yet few movie roles. RKO was also distressed because of Hughes's reputation as a tireless meddler. In a large studio that produced dozens of films a year, such interference would spell disaster.

Dore Schary was the most concerned. Since being hired as production head in 1947, Schary had generated a sense of enthusiasm at RKO, made good use of the talent on hand, and recruited a promising group of young directors —Joseph Losey, Nick Ray, Mark Robson, Robert Wise, Mel Frank, and

Norman Panama. Fearing that Hughes would interfere with their work and eventually make the studio ineffective, Schary drove out to visit Odlum at his Indio ranch and "urged him not to sell."[6] Schary's contract permitted him to resign if management changed at RKO, and he told Odlum he would do so if Hughes bought control. Odlum replied bluntly, "Look, I'm not a picture man. I bought this company to make some money, and I made some money, and I'm leaving."[7] Odlum also sought to assure Schary, apparently convinced that Hughes planned to devote most of his time to aviation and to leave studio management to the professionals.

All through the spring Hughes and Odlum negotiated. Most of the talks were held at Odlum's ranch, a sprawling 900-acre estate complete with swimming pool, golf course, and guest cottages. On their irrigated land, Odlum and his wife, Jacqueline Cochran, the flier Hughes had known since the 1930s, grew dates, grapes, and grapefruit. Hughes usually arrived about midnight, and he and Odlum would then spend hours haggling, either in Odlum's ranch house or in Hughes's car parked in front. "He must have been to our house sixty times," Miss Cochran recalled. "He just loved to deal. He loved to deal."[8]

In Floyd Bostwick Odlum, however, Hughes had met his match. The son of a midwestern Methodist preacher, Odlum had worked his way through law school before starting Atlas, a New York–based investment company. After riding the crest of the 1920s boom, Odlum got out of the market shortly before the 1929 crash. With the $14 million he realized from the sale, he methodically began to pick up companies at bargain prices during the Depression, then

Floyd B. Odlum, the millionaire financier, negotiating a deal from the swimming pool of his Palm Springs, California, estate. *Wide World Photos*

waited patiently as Atlas ballooned into a $70-million enterprise. Unlike Hughes, who often acted on a hunch or on whimsy in deciding what to buy, Odlum was coldly rational about his investments.

The two were worthy adversaries over the next few months. In addition to their long meetings at the ranch, they talked on the phone for up to four hours at a time—Hughes from the Beverly Hills Hotel, where he was now living most of the time, and Odlum from the heated pool at his ranch. To escape the pain and crippling effects of rheumatoid arthritis, Odlum spent as much as four hours a day in the water with his arms supported by inflated rubber wings and his legs constantly in motion, conducting business on a poolside phone. By late April, they had worked out a deal. On May 1, Hughes, accompanied by Loyd Wright, one of his lawyers, drove to Indio to sign a tentative agreement.

Hughes would buy the Atlas Corporation's 929,020 shares of RKO, about 24 percent of the company's stock, for $9.50 a share—a total of $8,825,690. The offer, about a dollar above the market price, would give Atlas a $17-million profit on its investment and give Hughes working control of RKO's twenty-six sound stages at studios in Hollywood and Culver City, an eighty-nine-acre ranch near Encino where outdoor scenes were filmed, and a chain of 124 movie theaters across the country. On May 10, 1948, the deal was signed. Howard Hughes had added a new branch to his expanding empire.

In an effort to quell anxiety over the Hughes takeover on the RKO lot, N. Peter Rathvon, the studio's president, who had agreed to stay on for Hughes, issued a statement to employees emphasizing stability: "Mr. Hughes has no hungry army of relatives looking for your jobs or substitutes waiting to step into the RKO management. . . . I have had numerous conversations with Mr. Hughes, and we seem to be in agreement in all matters of policy, and there is no reason to assume that it will be otherwise in the future."[9]

A week later, Dore Schary had a long and anxiously anticipated meeting with Hughes at Rathvon's house in Beverly Hills. Schary wrote later, "We met in the garden in late afternoon. Hughes simply touched my hand rather than shook it and then said, 'I hear you want to quit.' I waited a beat and eyed this tall, lean Texan who reminded me of the capable quick gun one saw in westerns, so often played by Gary Cooper."[10]

"Well, I don't think I'll be able to [stay]," Schary answered, "because I know if I had your money and I bought a studio, I'd want to run it myself. I wouldn't want anybody telling me what to do. I have no animus about it. But I believe in being realistic about it."[11]

"No, no," Hughes answered. "I want no part of running the studio. You'll be left alone."[12]

Hughes then asked about the movies that were under way and Schary gave him a rundown on upcoming releases, including one film in particular, *Battleground,* a Second World War epic for which Schary had great expectations. Much to Schary's surprise, Hughes was personable and charming. "He spoke quietly and sincerely," Schary said, "and I agreed to go back to the salt mines."[13]

For the first few weeks, it seemed that Hughes was sincere about keeping his hands off RKO. He occasionally dropped by the studio late at night to view the day's rushes. In early June, he amused the studio by offering Senator Ralph Owen Brewster of Maine, his antagonist at the Senate hearings, a $300-a-week acting job at RKO. "This is twice the usual starting salary," Hughes wrote the senator, "but you are no amateur; your ability as an actor has been well demonstrated."[14] But on a serious level, Hughes made no effort to interfere in the studio's operations.

Then, in late June, he called Schary at his home one night. Hughes wanted to cancel *Battleground.* He did not believe a war picture would be popular at the box office. He also told Schary to fire Barbara Bel Geddes, who was to star in the upcoming film *Bed of Roses,* and to replace her with an actress Hughes would name later. Schary, who had a high regard for Miss Bel Geddes's acting ability, refused, told Hughes to find another "messenger boy," and tendered his resignation.[15] Hughes invited Schary to come and talk it over the following day at Cary Grant's house, where he was staying temporarily. When Schary arrived at Grant's Beverly Hills house, he found "there wasn't a paper, a cigarette, a flower, a match, a picture, a magazine—there was nothing except two chairs and a sofa."[16] The only sign of life, Schary recalled, was Hughes, "who appeared from a side room in which I caught a glimpse of a woman hooking up her bra before the door closed."[17]

When they both sat down on the couch, Schary said,

[Hughes's] head bent forward a bit, his eyes seemingly focused on my shoes. He asked me if I was quitting because I didn't want a boss—didn't want to take orders. No, I said, that wasn't the reason. I added that if I were looking for work in an airplane factory, I would take all the orders because he knew more about planes than I did. However, since I believed I knew more about films than he did, I couldn't stay at RKO and take his instructions. Reasonably and quietly, he pointed out he had to have men to run his enterprises who could take his orders. I understood that—then I realized that I was feeling sorry for him because I was quitting. Recognizing that the feeling was ridiculous and quite conceited, I took hold of myself.

He didn't speak for a moment but kept staring down toward my shoes. Then he asked, "Where did you get those shoes?" I mumbled, "I think they're Johnston and Murphy." "How much were they?" I didn't remember—I guessed $30 or $35. He said they were good-looking shoes. Comfortable? I said they were.[18]

It was clear that Schary and Hughes would part. "What do you want?" Hughes asked. Schary wanted only the right to buy *Battleground,* and Hughes agreed. Was Schary owed any money on his contract? Schary said no. "I told him," Schary explained, "that I simply wanted out before I came into open conflict with him, pointing out that he was tough and too rich for me to fight. He didn't smile. He stood up, ending the meeting, and I left."[19]

Schary resigned from RKO on June 30, 1948, and soon joined MGM, the largest and most glamorous of the big studios, as production head. MGM made sixty-four pictures in Schary's first year. Among them was *Battleground*. Produced for $1.7 million, it grossed $4.5 million and was the number-two box-office success of 1950.

With Schary's resignation, RKO began a downward slide. Hughes had taken the title of managing director – production, but he made no effort to carry out any of the duties associated with it or to fill the void left by Schary's departure. He did not even maintain an office on the RKO lot, but worked at the Goldwyn Studios, about a mile away, summoning underlings there for meetings. Nevertheless, Hughes's presence was felt at RKO.

On July 10–11, about three hundred people, mainly from the writing, publicity, and administrative departments, were fired. Before the summer was over, four hundred more lost their jobs, a 33 percent reduction overall in RKO's work force and more than 50 percent in some departments. Late in July, Rathvon, who had once assured his RKO colleagues that Hughes had no plans to tamper with their jobs, quietly resigned. Floyd Odlum, who had remained on RKO's board after the sale, also resigned. Hughes tried to persuade Harry Cohn, the chief of Columbia Pictures, to manage RKO for him, but Cohn declined—running one major studio at a time was enough. As his stand-in at RKO, Hughes appointed a three-man executive committee headed by the producer Sid Rogell. Nevertheless, within a few months it was clear that RKO had lost the surging momentum that had made it one of Hollywood's greatest studios in the 1940s.

Although he owned only 24 percent of RKO's stock, Hughes was now the studio's undisputed master. In a series of self-dealing transactions, he sold RKO three movies he had personally produced—*The Outlaw, Mad Wednesday,* and *Vendetta*—a volume of old movie scripts, motion-picture equipment, music scripts, and motion-picture titles. Also, at his orders RKO paid the Hughes Tool Company $100,000 for the right to use Jane Russell in a series of RKO films. A lawsuit later filed against Hughes by a disgruntled minority stockholder accused him of "sitting on both sides of the negotiating table" in these transactions.*[20]

By year's end, when Hughes closed the RKO lot for the holidays, he had

*Discontent with Hughes in the industry was not confined to RKO's stockholders. Late in 1948, Hughes surprised and angered other major studios by abruptly bowing to Department of Justice antitrust pressure to separate RKO's production and theater operations. The government had filed suit against the major theater-owning film companies in 1938 to compel them to separate the two main branches of their operations. Over the years, the big five theater-owning companies —Paramount, Loews, Warner Brothers, Twentieth Century Fox, and RKO—had presented a solid front in opposition to the government's case. But on October 30, 1948, the RKO board voted to enter into a consent decree with the Justice Department, agreeing to separate the operations within a year. With RKO's defection, the other companies were compelled to enter similar agreements. RKO's actual reorganization was not carried out until December 31, 1950, when all of its production and distribution assets were transferred to a new company—RKO Pictures Corporation—and all its theater assets were given over to a new company called RKO Theaters Corporation. Hughes was issued 24 percent of the stock in each company.

left an unmistakable mark. RKO still ranked third in total receipts behind MGM and Twentieth Century Fox, but revenue had dropped significantly from the year before Hughes took over—from $39 to $30.6 million—and the studio had lost $5,288,750. Rather than focusing his attention on RKO's deteriorating financial condition, Hughes occupied himself with advance work on a film project of his own for RKO. He had acquired the rights to a story called *Jet Pilot* and he meant to make another spectacular aerial film, a jet-age *Hell's Angels.* Like *Hell's Angels,* the story line of *Jet Pilot* was uninspired. An American test pilot is at first pursued by, then pursues, a female Soviet test pilot (and covert Mata Hari) in a global romance from Alaska to Palm Springs to Russia. But as in *Hell's Angels,* the anemic story was merely an excuse to thrill the world with the sight of jets streaking across the sky.

John Wayne, a Hughes favorite, was to play the American pilot, and Janet Leigh the part of the Soviet spy. The aging Josef von Sternberg was brought in to direct, but he and Hughes soon disagreed and Hughes took over, shooting most of the dramatic scenes in 1949, then turning his attention to the dueling jets. For the aerial footage he wanted, Hughes dispatched film crews to air bases all over the country. As thousands of feet of film poured back to Hollywood, Hughes redoubled efforts. Always the perfectionist, he wanted the same background he had insisted on for *Hell's Angels*—huge, puffy, white cumulus clouds. Before filming was completed in 1951, 150,000 feet of film (about twenty-five hours) had been shot, and the cost of the movie had soared to more than $4 million.

By all accounts, the aerial scenes were indeed spectacular. The moviegoing public, however, would never see most of them, because Hughes so loved every scene he could not make up his mind which to include and which to delete. For six years he struggled mightily with the mountain of celluloid trying to edit *Jet Pilot* down to manageable length. It was 1957 before the film, starring a surprisingly young John Wayne and Janet Leigh, was eventually released, and by then most of the thrilling aerial scenes had been cut because jet-age advances had made the original sequences obsolete. All that remained was an hour-and-forty-minute movie that one critic called a "silly and sorry" film.[21] Hughes lost millions on *Jet Pilot.*

At RKO, as Dore Schary had anticipated, Hughes was not content merely to oversee his own films. He changed the name of a western directed by Fritz Lang from *Chuck-a-Luck* to *Rancho Notorious* because he told Lang he did not believe Europeans would grasp the meaning of chuck-a-luck, a gambling game of the Old West. Lang was furious. The term "chuck-a-luck" appeared all through the movie. It was the name of the ranch where the action was centered and it was the name of the movie's theme song. Nevertheless, Hughes had his way.[22]

Hughes also assigned a new title and demanded a happy ending for one of Bette Davis's films, *The Story of a Divorce.* When Hughes saw the completed film, he decided to call it *Payment on Demand* and summoned Miss Davis and her co-stars to the studio to reshoot the ending. Everybody protested, contending that the original ending was more appropriate. As usual, Hughes stubbornly refused to give in. The scene was reshot and the new ending spliced onto the film.

As time passed, fewer and fewer independent producers chose to do business with RKO. And as the independents shied away, RKO was producing fewer pictures in house as well. Hughes might have been the boss, but he was seldom around to make decisions, and he had not delegated any real authority. Lacking strong day-to-day direction, the studio drifted along. RKO had planned to produce forty-nine pictures in 1949; instead, it made just twelve, and dropped from third to fifth among major studios in gross receipts for the year. With film rentals of $20 million in 1949, the studio had brought in half the film revenue it had the year before Hughes's takeover. Again, there was a substantial deficit—$3,721,415.

Even Hughes's controversial and tawdry advertising techniques were not enough to cut the losses. For years he had relied on a simple formula for success. It went something like this: take a mediocre script, give it a dash of sex and violence, build up advance interest in the film with suggestive advertisements and battles with censors and church groups, then reap a bonanza at the box office. *Stromboli* fit the formula.

Starring Ingrid Bergman and directed by Roberto Rossellini, *Stromboli* began shooting in Italy in 1949. There were immediate rumors of a romance between the captivating Swedish actress, then the image of sweetness and purity to moviegoers in the States, and the fiery Italian director (each was married to someone else). First denied, the rumors were eventually confirmed. Then came other rumors—the two were planning to divorce their spouses and marry. Those, too, were denied, then confirmed. And finally the ultimate rumor: Miss Bergman was pregnant by Rossellini. Also denied. But Louella Parsons broke the story: Miss Bergman was indeed expecting a child. Early in 1950, she bore a son, and following quick divorces, Miss Bergman and Rossellini were married. Miss Parsons never disclosed her source for the story of the *Stromboli* pregnancy, but she did offer an intriguing description: her informant was "a man of great importance, not only in Hollywood, but throughout the United States . . . who had connections in many other parts of the world."[23] No one fit the description better than Howard Hughes, who had long fed tips to Miss Parsons when it suited him. Moreover, *Stromboli* was about to be released by RKO.

Hughes moved swiftly, trying to capitalize on public outrage over the scandal. A series of controversial advertisements portrayed a volcano spurting a plume of lava. To many, the display resembled a phallic symbol, and the ads provoked an uproar among churches and film-industry officials. Eric Johnston, president of the Motion Picture Producers Association of America, ordered Hughes to withdraw the ads or be fined. As he pondered his course, Hughes sought outside advice, turning, curiously, to Dore Schary.

Hughes sent a car with a chauffeur and two bodyguards to drive Schary to the Hughes Aircraft plant at Culver City. Hughes arrived a few minutes later and the two of them climbed into a Chevrolet sedan and drove around the grounds with Hughes at the wheel. Hughes spoke slowly, Schary recalled, saying that "he regretted that he had bought RKO; regretted that he had permitted me to leave; was very busy designing a new helicopter that could lift a freight car, and had so many interests that he now found the operation of the studio an onerous one."[24] Schary still had no idea what Hughes wanted.

They made their way, finally, to a small private dining room somewhere at the plant, where they ate lunch. After a few minutes, Hughes asked Schary, "Do you think I am right or wrong about those ads on *Stromboli?*"

"Howard, I think you are wrong—they're vulgar," Schary replied.[25]

Hughes asked Schary to call Johnston and tell him the ads would be withdrawn. Schary said he would be glad to call Johnston for him, but felt that Hughes should tell him personally.

The ads were withdrawn and the controversy surrounding the film died with them. RKO headed for another bad year, losing $3,471,041. During the three years of Hughes's leadership, RKO had piled up losses of $12.4 million. Even more telling, the company dropped from the ranks of the top five motion-picture companies for the first time in years. Revenue from film rentals plummeted to $9 million, down 77 percent since Hughes acquired control.

TURNABOUT

While RKO was rapidly becoming another of the great business debacles of Hughes's career, nothing less than a miracle was shaping up across town at Culver City. The Hughes Aircraft Company, fledgling defense contractor and perennial money loser of the empire, in constant need of cash transfusions, was by 1950 making a profit for the first time in its eighteen-year history. From a tiny, unimportant defense plant employing fewer than a thousand people manufacturing ammunition belts and reconditioning war transports, Hughes Aircraft had grown into a bustling five-thousand-employee enterprise critical to the nation's defense. To explain this incredible turnaround, it is necessary to go back to 1948.

After the Senate hearings, Hughes had lost all interest in Hughes Aircraft. By then the company, which had never suceeded in putting an airplane into production, was a constant reminder of painful experiences and failed dreams. Moreover, it was a steady drain on the Hughes finances. If the air force had been hostile to doing business with Hughes in the Second World War, it was doubly so after the Brewster hearings. More than the antics of a Johnny Meyer and Elliott Roosevelt would be needed to land another defense contract. Noah Dietrich wanted to close Hughes Aircraft and thereby put an end to the chronic drain on the oil-tool division's earnings. But Hughes, even though he no longer took a personal interest in the company, could not do that. Instead, he recruited yet another team of managers to run it.

All his life, Hughes alternated between enlightened and catastrophic appointments. The men he brought in now to oversee Hughes Aircraft were great choices. Two were retired air force lieutenant generals—Ira C. Eaker and Harold L. George. The third was Charles B. Thornton, a former Ford Motor Company executive. Eaker had been deputy commander of the air force, and George had headed the Air Transport Command during the war. Eaker, a vice-president of Hughes Tool, was to fill the crucial role of liaison between Culver City and the oil-tool division in Houston. George, with the title of vice-president and general manager of Hughes Aircraft, was to be in charge of the company's day-to-day operations. Thornton was to be assistant general manager.

A legend in his own right, George was a man of unquestioned ability and drive. Starting with 78 planes and 1,800 men in 1942, within two years he had built the Air Transport Command into a wartime military airline of 4,000 planes and 330,000 men, ferrying combat aircraft, supplies, and millions of passengers to every part of the globe. George had first met Hughes in 1930 at Kelly Field, Texas, during the filming of *Hell's Angels,* and he accepted the job only after Hughes had promised him complete autonomy. Hughes's reputation for interfering with Hughes Aircraft's general managers was legendary in military circles. Then absorbed in negotiations to acquire control of RKO, Hughes promised George he would have full authority to manage the aircraft company.

When George took over in the spring of 1948, the company was hardly a promising venture, having lost $700,000 on sales of $1.9 million the year before. The only serious work in progress were several low-priority research projects funded by the air force and being carried out by two talented young scientists, Dr. Simon Ramo and Dr. Dean E. Wooldridge. Former classmates at the California Institute of Technology, Ramo and Wooldridge had pursued independent careers in electronics research—Ramo at General Electric and Wooldridge at the Bell Telephone Laboratories—before teaming up at Hughes Aircraft.

The air force had turned to them to undertake several studies aimed at developing "an electronic weapons control system" for air force interceptors, a combination radar set and computer that could find and destroy enemy planes day or night in any weather.[26] The contracts amounted only to several hundred thousand dollars. Nevertheless, they would provide the base for Hughes Aircraft's great leap forward.

By plunging into military electronics—a field the large and established defense contractors were ignoring because of its low priority within the Defense Department and the modest sums set aside for research contracts—Hughes Aircraft got the jump on everyone else. Late in 1948, when the military suddenly became alarmed over the lack of an all-weather interceptor, the only promising electronic weapons system was the one being developed by Ramo and Wooldridge. The air force awarded an $8-million contract to Hughes Aircraft to build and install 200 units in the Lockheed F-94. Building rapidly on this success, Ramo and Wooldridge captured a contract to develop the air force's Falcon air-to-air missile. The six-foot, 110-pound missile was to be part of a complete electronic weapons package that could find an enemy plane, automatically launch the missile, and then assure through radar impulses that the missile would hit its target. Following that, they brought off an even more spectacular coup—winning a design competition for the electronic weapon and navigational control system to be used in the F-102 supersonic interceptor, a revolutionary plane intended to be the backbone of American air-defense strategy for years to come.

If the interceptor business made Hughes Aircraft healthy, the Korean War made it prosperous. When the war broke out in June of 1950, Hughes Aircraft, by virtue of its pioneering work on electronic weapons systems, became the sole source of supply for the entire air force interceptor program, and within two years the work force grew to fifteen thousand. The once-modest research laboratory now bulged with more than a thousand scientists. Revenues of the company—still a division of the Hughes Tool Company—surpassed those of the oil-tool division. And the rise in earnings, after taxes, was remarkable—from $400,000 in 1949 to $5.3 million in 1952.

All the while, Hughes paid it almost no attention. Since General George had taken control of the company in 1948, Hughes had, for once, kept his promise not to interfere. He had retained control over the company's finances —approving the budget, establishing the amount of money the company could borrow, and authorizing all major capital expenditures. George and other executives sometimes had difficulty finding Hughes to get his approval, but it was an inconvenience well worth enduring for the freedom they enjoyed at Hughes Aircraft.

As the company bloomed, there were more financial decisions that only Hughes could make. Conveying their requests to Hughes through Romaine Street, the aircraft company executives were often greeted by days, even weeks of silence. His chronic inaccessibility was threatening to hamstring the company's expansion. Concurrently, Hughes began to grasp the full impact of the technological developments at Culver City. Sensing that Hughes Aircraft might one day rival the fabulously profitable oil-tool division, he began taking a more active role in the company.

Hughes's resurgent interest in Culver City had first made itself felt in the summer of 1950. To fulfill the company's expanding commitments, Ramo and Wooldridge proposed a major expansion of the laboratory and staff. A budget request for the new facilities was routinely passed along to Hughes through Romaine Street. Weeks went by with no word. Finally, Hughes's answer came, through channels, stunning everyone in authority at Hughes Aircraft. Hughes opposed any expansion at Culver City. He wanted the research laboratory built in the desert outside Las Vegas.

Hughes's orders were incomprehensible to the company's executives and scientists. They were opposed to any physical separation of the laboratory staff at such an important stage in the company's growth. Further, Ramo and Wooldridge doubted that first-rate scientists would settle in the neon, honkytonk world of Las Vegas.

But Hughes had a compelling reason, at least in his own mind. While recognizing that Hughes Aircraft needed to expand, any growth at Culver City would eventually force him to pay more California income taxes on the company's earnings. The state's income tax, adopted in 1935, had gradually become an obsession for Hughes. He had sold his house on Muirfield Road in 1945 because state tax officials were pointing to the house as proof that he was a resident of the state and thus subject to the tax. In protest, Hughes had written to California tax authorities the year before, saying that "I am not and have not been a resident of California and will avoid everything that would make the state . . . feel that I should be considered as such."[27] Hughes began living in rented houses or hotel suites in Los Angeles, adopting a transient lifestyle that he hoped would convince California tax agents that he was merely a visitor to the state, not a resident. Unconvinced, California levied the tax on Hughes anyway.

Nevada presented no such problem. The state had no income tax. And unbeknownst to the bewildered executives and scientists at Hughes Aircraft, Hughes had yet another motivation for locating part of his burgeoning defense company in Nevada. As a result of secret negotiations and some powerful Washington lobbying, Hughes was on the verge of concluding an astonishing land deal with the United States government.

As the site for the proposed aircraft company laboratory, Hughes had picked out a 25,000-acre tract just west of Las Vegas. Like most of Nevada, the land was owned by the federal government, but Hughes came up with a scheme, entirely permissible under the Taylor Grazing Act, a little-known federal law, to exchange 73,000 acres he owned in five remote northern Nevada counties for the smaller, but much more valuable acreage outside Las Vegas. On the land adjoining the gambling capital, Hughes planned to build the research laboratory for Hughes Aircraft and whatever additional production facilities might be required in the future. A Hughes subsidiary called the Husite Company was formed, and the formal application for the land exchange was filed with the Department of the Interior on July 19, 1950.

Hughes's petition to the Interior Department said nothing about California income taxes, of course. He contended that he needed the Las Vegas tract to build a plant for "new and improved radar control and guided missile devices for the Armed Services because the West Coast location where the company was then working was considered too vulnerable to attack."[28] According to an Interior study, the land Hughes was offering had an estimated maximum value of $1.25 to $1.50 an acre, while the smaller tract he was seeking had a minimum value of $3 an acre. In other words, it appeared to be a near-even trade. But the appearance was deceptive. The federal lands bordering the Las Vegas Strip were sure to increase in value many times over in coming years. Hughes's acreage, on the other hand, was in a remote area with virtually no prospect for development. After reviewing the proposal, a field examiner for the Interior Department vigorously opposed the exchange, stating that it "would certainly not be to the advantage of the government nor to the general public."[29]

Hughes had no difficulty overcoming this low-level opposition. Over the years, he had retained a growing stable of lawyers in Texas, California, and Washington, D.C., to call on in situations such as this one. He spread his business, financial, and legal affairs among them, thereby assuring that no single individual would be familiar with all his dealings at any one time. In Houston the firm that had represented his father, Andrews, Kurth, Campbell & Jones, continued as legal counsel for the oil-tool division and handled Hughes's federal income-tax returns. In Los Angeles he was represented on movie ventures by Wright, Wright, Goldwater & Wright. Another Los Angeles firm, Waters & Arditto, handled his political liaisons. In addition, there were selected lawyers Hughes turned to for business rather than legal advice —Tom Slack and Raymond Cook of the Andrews, Kurth firm, and Gregson Bautzer in Hollywood. Now, the law firm of Clark M. Clifford, fresh from a tour of duty as one of President Truman's principal aides, was hired to shepherd the land application through the Washington bureaucracy. To further champion his claim for the land, Hughes also persuaded the air force to wage a lobbying campaign on his behalf with the Interior Department. An air force staff officer sent a carefully worded letter to Interior recommending that the exchange be approved in the interests of national defense. The Interior Department subsequently approved the land trade.

Without a doubt, it was a clever deal that Hughes had engineered, but Ramo, Wooldridge, and their colleagues at Culver City were adamantly opposed to the move. Hughes had never been confronted by organized opposition from his own employees, and there was a good deal of stalling and delaying. But when it was clear that his scientists would not relent, he reluctantly gave in and approved the laboratory expansion at Culver City.

The feud over the laboratory site only heightened Hughes's interest in the aircraft company, which was looking a lot like a potential IBM of the space-age weapons and electronics industry. He closed in on it. Demanding approval of all architectural plans for the Culver City addition, Hughes pored over drawings for weeks, debating color schemes, moving a window here, relocating a hallway there. Not even the vending machines escaped his notice. He issued orders for an in-depth study of the sale of candy bars and soft drinks throughout the plant.

These petty directives were regarded by Culver City executives as a vindictive attempt by Hughes to punish them for blocking his Nevada relocation plan. That may have been true in part, but there was also a darker explanation. Hughes's mental collapse in 1944 had left permanent psychological damage and seeds of the phobias planted in childhood now were in full bloom. Hughes's behavior was growing more aberrant, more erratic. Many days he acted in a relatively normal fashion, going through the routines of meeting and dealing with people—politicians, businessmen, and friendly admirers—and expressing lucid thoughts. But these days were now punctuated by periods of marked disturbance in his behavior and thought processes.

Secretive by nature, he imagined that people everywhere were listening to his conversations. To guard against eavesdroppers, he conducted business meetings and legal conferences in cars. He usually did the driving, picking up the appointed person at a prearranged location and driving to an isolated back road in the Los Angeles area. When the talks were held inside buildings, they were likely to take place in the bathroom, where Hughes would turn on the water to thwart listening devices, or in large halls or auditoriums at a conference table placed in the center of the room so that no one could approach without being seen.

Always fearful of germs and disease, Hughes was developing an obsessive avoidance of human contact. He viewed anyone who came near as a potential germ carrier. Those whose movements he could control—his aides, drivers, and message clerks—were required to wash their hands and slip on thin white cotton gloves, the type used in film editing, before handing him documents or other objects.[30] Aides who bought newspapers or magazines were instructed to buy three copies—Hughes took the one in the middle.[31] To escape dust, he ordered unused windows and doors of houses and cars sealed with masking tape. Those who worked near were instructed not to touch him, not to look at him, and not to speak to him directly.[32] Always little concerned about clothing and personal appearance, he began to go for several days at a time without shaving, and his clothes were sometimes soiled and torn. And never a very gregarious person, he now withdrew further, to avoid all those not essential to his work.

Although Hughes had been writing meticulously detailed memoranda for years, now his concerns were often trivial. Form took on a much greater importance than substance. One such memorandum, dictated when he was about to move from a bungalow at the Beverly Hills Hotel, spelled out the care, handling, and disposition of his personal effects and business papers in the bungalow. Nadine Henley, Bill Gay, and Lee Murrin were to sort through and arrange the materials in categories. Business and personal belongings fell into two categories—"dead storage items" and "active items."[33] Dead storage items, mostly old papers, were to be taken to Romaine Street and stored. Active items, or "live items," as Hughes also called them, were toiletries, current business papers, and some of his clothes. In his memorandum, dictated to an aide, Hughes referred to himself throughout in the third person:

He wants all coats that need to be cleaned to be cleaned and hung together some place. He wants the same thing done with the trousers and hung together away from the coats. They may be put in the same closet, but segregated. He wants all shirts and everything else laundered and put in a container of some kind. It is not good to leave these in the laundry boxes because there are other items in there too.

All pockets should be emptied. This means pockets in shirts, coats and overcoats. You may consider that all coats and trousers which were hanging in the closet in the hotel were empty. HRH kept those empty but any coat or trousers that you may have picked up from a chair or anywhere else should be searched. Whatever you take out of the pockets should be placed in the proper category.

Hughes wanted special cardboard boxes in which to transport his clothing. "These should not be prepared for long distance shipment, but they should be so arranged that they will not shake around when transporting them in a car." All of his possessions should be "put away in the manner to protect [them] against deterioration . . . as far as is possible without putting any grease or similar preparation on anything."

"Any metal items of value should be protected against deterioration by putting them in a cabinet or a room that is dehydrated and kept dry. This is the new method of preserving metal articles." His old clothing could be given away, but only after "all identification is removed—any initials, monograms, etc., including laundry marks." Hughes wanted "obsolete" business papers taken to Romaine and "completely destroyed by being burned down to a white ash." Any keys found among his things which could not be identified were to be melted down. Any objects with "no substantial value" were to be destroyed so they would not be left "lying around."[34]

During this period Hughes once again became preoccupied with his will. He had been writing and rewriting the latest version for six years and the draft had swollen to thirty-four pages. Naming eight of his executives as executors and trustees, the will directed, as earlier versions had done, that virtually his entire fortune be used to create a medical institute. In earlier drafts the institute was to develop cures for diseases afflicting the Houston area. Now Hughes had grander plans:

The purpose of Howard Hughes Medical Research Laboratories shall be prosecution of the scientific research necessary to accomplish the discovery and/or development of methods, substances, and/or means for the prevention and/or cure of those diseases and/or maladies (whether caused by bacteria, malignant growth, and/or otherwise) which shall have proven to be the most important and dangerous to the people of the United States and with which a substantial percentage of the population shall have been afflicted. . . . All methods, substances, and/or means, discovered or developed as a result hereof and found to have any appreciable value, shall be made known and available to the people of the United States [and] to the extent practicable . . . the same shall be made known throughout the world.[35]

His medical laboratories, he continued, should be "built up carefully and not wastefully. A large number of technicians hastily thrown together and allowed to tinker aimlessly, each in pursuit of some pet theory, would only expend funds which later might be used to advantage." Another edict, odd for a man who was himself a juggler, was that the laboratories should concentrate on "one basic subject at a time with the aim of really outstanding achievement, rather than dissipation of resources in a number of directions with the likelihood of negligible results in any."[36]

The most curious section of the will, however, was Article 1, in which Hughes bequeathed to his aunt Annette Lummis the Hughes family home on Yoakum Boulevard in Houston. Hughes had apparently forgotten his gift of the house to Annette twenty-two years before. As to his other relatives, his desire was clear:

I have intentionally omitted making provision for all of my heirs who are not specifically mentioned herein and I hereby generally and specifically disinherit each, any, and all persons whomsoever claiming to be or who may lawfully be determined to be my heirs at law, except such as are mentioned in this will."[37]

Early in November of 1950, Hughes told Nadine Henley, who had spent countless hours over the years typing and retyping the will, that he was ready to execute the document. Before doing so, he wanted to know if it should be notarized or have "ribbons and seals" attached to it to make it more authentic.[38] Miss Henley conferred with Tom Slack, Hughes's chief attorney at Romaine Street, who said neither step would add to its validity.[39] It was only necessary that Hughes sign the will on the last page and that the signing be witnessed by two people.

Miss Henley retrieved a copy of the final draft of the will from a safedeposit box at the Security First National Bank in Hollywood to which only she and Hughes held keys. Always security-conscious, Hughes had devised an elaborate procedure to safeguard the will against alteration. When the final draft had been typed, he asked Miss Henley to have it reproduced, using the process by which blueprints are made. Then the photographed pages—Hughes called them "bluelines"—were inserted into a thick binder so that they could not be removed without being torn. In this way, Miss Henley recalled, the will was "impossible to erase or change in any manner."[40]

A few days later, Hughes summoned Miss Henley, Lee Murrin, and Malcolm Smith to his bungalow at the Beverly Hills Hotel for the signing ceremony. In all the time Hughes had been tinkering with his will since the early 1940s, he had never gone so far as to schedule a formal signing ceremony. Whenever a "final" draft had been completed, he had found some reason to insert a new clause or to delete an old one, forcing Miss Henley to retype the complete instrument. Hughes was clearly more reluctant to execute a will as he grew older. He had signed wills in 1925 and 1938, but had then retrieved and apparently destroyed each of them, and for years had not had a valid will. Now, late in 1950, the day had apparently come.

At the bungalow, Miss Henley handed Hughes the bulky bound copy of the final draft. While the three looked on, Hughes studied the document in silence, slowly leafing through the pages, no doubt checking to make sure it had not been tampered with. This went on for a period of time until Hughes, with no explanation, suddenly handed the will back to Miss Henley, unsigned, and asked her to return it to the safe-deposit box.[41] Baffled, Miss Henley dutifully drove back to Hollywood and deposited the draft at the Security Bank where it languished for the next quarter century. Miss Henley, who had been typing and retyping Hughes's draft wills for half a dozen years and who would remain in Hughes's employ until his death, would never again work on a Hughes will. After years of drafting and redrafting the document, Hughes had suddenly and mysteriously had enough. He would talk of his "will" off and on until he died twenty-six years later, but no one ever saw him work on it again.

THE RED MENACE

Early in 1952, RKO released *The Las Vegas Story*, a flashy, Technicolor melodrama about a former nightclub singer who returns to Las Vegas unhappily married and takes up with an old flame. Starring Jane Russell as the singer and Victor Mature as her lover, *The Las Vegas Story* had all the trappings that usually made Jane Russell's movies profitable. The story line was transparent, the action almost nil. Scene after revealing scene showed the 37 1/2"–24"–36" Miss Russell in various attitudes of exposure. One reviewer said that Miss Russell wore so many plunging necklines and strapless gowns that "even the actors have a tough time keeping their minds on their work."[42] Even so, the movie generated only lukewarm interest among the public. After a few weeks of playing to sparsely populated houses, it seemed destined to pass swiftly from public view and be forgotten. Instead, it became the next storm center of Hughes's turbulent reign at RKO.

The reason went back to January of 1951. To write the screenplay for *The Las Vegas Story*, RKO had hired Paul Jarrico, a screenwriter and member of the Screen Writers Guild. Before Jarrico had completed the script, he was subpoenaed to testify before the House Un-American Activities Committee in Washington on the subject of Communist infiltration in the motion-picture industry. First created in 1938 to ferret out alleged subversives in the federal government, HUAC had grown into a potent force. During the war, when the nation was temporarily aligned with the Soviet Union, the committee, under the leadership of the anti-Communist zealot Martin Dies, Jr., had been a small embarrassment to the Roosevelt administration. But afterward, as the Cold War developed, HUAC was no longer merely a gadfly on the American body politic, but a swarm stirring up anti-Communist hysteria and propagating widespread fear that Communists were infiltrating, indeed gaining control of, American institutions. No one was more swept up by this fear of creeping communism than Howard Hughes.

In some ways, this was surprising. As might be expected of a man who distributed millions of dollars to politicians of both major political parties at the local, state, and federal levels, who sought to manipulate officeholders from state legislator to president of the United States, and who attempted to influence the decisions of governmental agencies from city councils to the Internal Revenue Service, Hughes was apolitical. Noah Dietrich worked for Hughes more than thirty years and never knew whether his boss considered himself a Republican or a Democrat. In either case, it would have been an academic exercise, for Hughes never once voted in his entire life. The political issues on which he staked out a position—almost always behind the scenes and without drawing attention to himself—were confined to those that directly affected him or his companies. The one exception, an issue that fanned Hughes's one political passion, was communism.

"He felt that communism versus free enterprise was such an important issue in our time," Bill Gay recalled. "[It was] one of the few issues in his life that he felt that strongly about."[43] HUAC had turned its Red-hunting spotlight on Hollywood in 1947, and Hughes's interest had been engaged ever since. So when Jarrico, one of his studio's writers, was subpoenaed, Hughes responded swiftly. Even though the screenplay for *The Las Vegas Story* was not yet complete, Jarrico was fired immediately, about a week before his HUAC appearance. On April 12, 1951, the writer refused to tell the committee whether he was or ever had been a member of the Communist party.

The matter might have ended there. No one questioned Hughes's right to fire Jarrico, whatever the reason, and no protest was made, not by Jarrico or his union. But Hughes would not let it rest.

A few months later, RKO, which had hired other writers to finish Jarrico's script, informed them that Jarrico's name would be omitted from the picture's screen credits. Knowing that a substantial part of Jarrico's original screenplay had gone into the final version, the writers protested. Under the agreement between the Screen Writers Guild and the Motion Picture Producers Association, the dispute was submitted to a three-member panel of writers for arbitration. Their decision was to be binding on both sides.

After reviewing work papers and film clips, the arbitrators ruled that *The Las Vegas Story* contained at least one-third of the material written by Jarrico and therefore should include his name in the credits. Nevertheless, when the movie premiered in January of 1952, Jarrico's name was conspicuously absent. Hughes had clearly violated the labor agreement between the industry and the guild. More important, he had put the union on the spot. To the union, it was a labor dispute, a clear-cut case in which the employer had openly defied the terms of the contract. But to the public—as Hughes knew and as the Screen Writers Guild no doubt feared—the issue would be viewed in a different light. By arguing the case of a member who had defied a congressional committee investigating communism in Hollywood, the guild would appear to be aiding and abetting the Red cause. Nonetheless, the guild felt that it had no choice but to take a stand against Hughes, lest other studios follow suit. In a move that was widely interpreted as a first step toward a strike, the guild informed RKO that the studio's refusal to credit Jarrico for his work on *The Las Vegas Story* was a clear violation of the contract.

Before the guild could take any action, however, Hughes seized the initiative. On March 17, RKO filed a novel lawsuit in Superior Court in Los Angeles. Asking for a declaratory judgment and to be relieved of any demands for damages that Jarrico might make, RKO contended that the screenwriter had violated the standard morals clause in his contract by refusing to answer questions of the House Un-American Activities Committee and this canceled RKO's contractual obligations to him. The complaint also stated that the final picture did not contain any of Jarrico's material.

Explaining why he filed the lawsuit, Hughes released a statement that endeared him to rabid anti-Communists everywhere. "A great deal of pressure has been brought to bear upon me to pay off and settle Jarrico's demands out of court." Hughes acknowledged that it would be simpler, easier, and cheaper for him to do that: "And maybe it is the sensible thing to do." But Hughes had come to another decision—one that he said was irrevocable, regardless of the consequences. "As long as I am an officer or director of RKO Pictures Corporation, this company will never temporize, conciliate with, or yield to Paul Jarrico or anyone guilty of similar conduct."[44]

A day later, a six-member conciliation committee composed of three members each from the union and industry began an inquiry to determine if RKO had breached its contract with the union. On March 27, Hughes stunned the union and industry alike by announcing that he would not be bound by the arbitration. Maintaining that he was not opposed in general to arbitration as a way of settling labor disputes, Hughes insisted that the Jarrico firing was not a labor issue. The conflict, Hughes said, was solely over Jarrico's refusal to answer government authorities:

The question was whether or not he was a member of the Communist Party. He refused to answer on the ground that his answer might tend to incriminate him. My determination that I will not yield to Jarrico or anyone else guilty of this conduct is based on principle, belief and conscience. These are forces which are not subject to arbitration. My conscience cannot be changed by a committee of arbitrators. Any arbitration of this matter would be without meaning, because regardless of what the outcome of the arbitration might be, R.K.O. will not yield to Jarrico's demands.[45]

Early in April, as the Screen Writers Guild weighed a strike against RKO, Hughes once again took the offensive. On April 6, he dismissed about a hundred employees and announced that he was curtailing production at RKO "until the Communist problem is solved."[46] Hughes stressed that those laid off were in no way "involved in any Communist situation," but were merely "innocent victims of Hollywood's Communist problem."[47] In an interview with Howard Rushmore, a columnist for the Hearst newspapers, Hughes said he was shutting down RKO so he could "clean house" of the Communists.

"During the next two months we are going to set up a screening system as thorough as we can make it," Hughes said. "We are going to screen everyone in a creative position or executive capacity. . . . It is my determination to make RKO one studio where the work of Communist sympathizers will be impossible."[48]

Hughes's crusade and the damaging publicity that went with it were deeply worrisome to Hollywood. But to millions of other Americans, Hughes's staunch anti-Communist stand was heroic. The junior senator from California, Richard M. Nixon, in a speech in Washington, warmly praised Hughes for firing Jarrico. Three Republican members of the House Un-American Activities Committee commended Hughes, calling his action an "important step toward eradication of Communists and Communist influence from the entertainment world."[49] The Hollywood post of the American Legion honored Hughes for anti-Communist vigilance and his efforts to rid the industry of Reds.

Over the next few months, Hughes expanded on his freshly minted image as a savior of the American way of life. The night he accepted the American Legion award, he made a rare public speech, a ringing denunciation of the movie industry: ". . . in spite of all the movement to whitewash the industry, to say that there was no Red influence in Hollywood; to sweep this matter under the carpet and hide it and pretend it doesn't exist, in spite of that, there are a substantial number of people in the motion picture industry who follow the Communist Party line."[50] Although Hughes spent much of his life avoiding courtroom appearances, he eagerly took the stand in court in the Jarrico case to denounce his former screenwriter and to defend his decision.* He further endeared himself to the right wing by taking on the movement's current symbol of subversion, Charlie Chaplin.

Chaplin's latest movie, *Limelight,* had opened to great acclaim in London in October of 1952. Outside the Odeon Theater in Leicester Square, scores of Rolls-Royces lined the curb, and nearly four thousand fans jammed the sidewalk and street chanting "We want Charlie, We want Charlie." Inside the theater, a doting audience that included Princess Margaret gave round after round of applause to the London-born actor who would always be remembered for the character he first created, the little tramp with the soulful eyes and derby hat. The world première of *Limelight* also marked Chaplin's fortieth anniversary on the screen and his first motion picture in five years. The film was all Chaplin—the sixty-three-year-old comedian had written the script, composed the music, and created a special ballet. He was the director, the producer, and, of course, the star.

As a New York film critic observed when *Limelight* opened in Manhattan one week after its London première, "One might as well criticize a rose for having thorns as condemn *Limelight* for its faults."[51] By year's end, the Chaplin film was playing in several large cities around the United States, mostly in the East, and preparing to move into national distribution.

Then, in January of 1953, three Los Angeles area theaters, including Grauman's Chinese in Hollywood, announced that they were canceling the planned showing of *Limelight.* The decision followed a quiet visit to the theaters by Hollywood's most strident and effective critic—the American Legion. Representatives of its Un-American Activities Committee had joined with the Motion Picture Alliance for the Preservation of American Ideals to suggest that the theater owners should postpone showing *Limelight* pending the outcome of a Justice Department investigation of what were described as Chaplin's "subversive tendencies."

Next, the Hollywood Legionnaires fired off a letter to the RKO Pictures

---

*On March 28, 1952, Jarrico filed a $350,000 damage suit in Superior Court in Los Angeles against Hughes and RKO for depriving him of the screen credit for *The Las Vegas Story.* In December of 1952, shortly after Hughes testified in the action, Judge Orlando H. Rhodes dismissed the complaint, contending that Hughes and RKO had done nothing improper.

Corporation urging the company to cancel the showing of Chaplin's picture at its theaters throughout the country. The Legionnaires may not have known that RKO Pictures, which produced and distributed films, by this time was a separate company from the RKO Theaters Corporation. It hardly mattered: the Legionnaires certainly knew they had an old friend in the picture corporation's chief executive.

"I am a director of the distributing unit of RKO and I assure you that this company has not touched . . . *Limelight*," Hughes wrote back to the Legion's Un-American Activities Committee.[52] "I have been making a most concerted effort to persuade the management of the theater corporation to take the necessary legal measures to cancel all bookings of *Limelight*. It is my strongest hope and sincere belief that this will be done."[53] While no official edict on *Limelight* was issued by the theater company, individual RKO theaters around the country heeded Hughes's call: the movie was shown in only a few of them.

Less than eight weeks after throwing his support with the American Legion against *Limelight,* Hughes shifted his attention to a picture called *Salt of the Earth,* which was being made in Silver City, New Mexico. Based on an actual incident, a bitter strike at a New Mexico zinc mine, the film dealt with the desperate plight of Mexican-American miners and the struggle of the miners' wives to gain equality. When news of the film reached Representative Donald L. Jackson of Los Angeles, a member of HUAC, he was quick to act. In a telegram to motion-picture executives and government officials, he asked "what legal steps can be taken . . . toward stopping the export of this picture abroad to the detriment of United States policy and interests abroad."[54]

As before, Hughes had the answer. In this case, he was eager to be even more diligent in his anti-Communist efforts, for *Salt of the Earth* was being produced by none other than Paul Jarrico and directed by Herbert J. Biberman, one of the Hollywood Ten who had gone to jail in 1947 on contempt charges rather than answer questions posed by congressional investigators.

In a letter to Representative Jackson, Hughes pointed out that Jarrico and Biberman could not make a movie in a vacuum. Before the film could be released, they would need the services of a number of editors and laboratory technicians—personnel who might be controlled by the studios. Providing a kind of Hollywood checklist for vigilance against a creeping Red Front, Hughes declared that

[to] prevent this motion picture from being completed and spread all over the world as a representative product of the United States, then the industry . . . needs only to do the following:

Be alert to the situation.

Investigate thoroughly each applicant for the use of services or equipment.

Refuse to assist the Bibermans and Jarricos in the making of this picture.

Be on guard against work submitted by dummy corporations or third parties.

Appeal to the Congress and the State Department to act immediately to prevent the export of this film to Mexico or anywhere else.[55]

After making a ringing denunciation of Communists in the movie industry to the Hollywood post of the American Legion, Hughes receives congratulations from Post Commander John D. Hone, April 2, 1952. *United Press International*

Below: Trying to elude a photographer on November 20, 1952, after testifying in Los Angeles against Paul Jarrico, the screenwriter Hughes fired when he was subpoened to testify before the House Committee on Un-American Activities. *United Press International*

All of this, coupled with the rampant anti-Communist hysteria of the 1950s, was more than enough to censor *Salt of the Earth*. Completed in 1954, the film was shown at several American theaters that year but did not go into general release until eleven years later. Then, movie critics generally agreed that the film was a moving evocation of the plight of poor Mexican-American miners.

While Hughes was working on the Communist menace, RKO continued to decline. The once-bustling studio of more than two thousand people was down to fewer than five hundred employees by the summer of 1952. RKO had begun calling itself "The Showmanship Company," but in fact it was showing very little.[56] With production at a near standstill, the company continued to roll up losses, $3.7 million in the first six months of 1952 alone. Hughes was so disenchanted with RKO that he was ready to sell. Although the company was no longer profitable, it was still a valuable property, mostly because of its lucrative real-estate holdings and a library of more than six hundred feature films. When Hughes quietly put out word that the studio was on the block, he soon had a serious bite.

The prospective buyer was a curious five-man syndicate headed by a little-known Chicago businessman, Ralph E. Stolkin. The other syndicate members were Abraham L. Koolish, Stolkin's father-in-law and also a Chicago businessman; Raymond Ryan and Edward G. Burke, Texas oilmen; and Sherrill C. Corwin, the owner of a chain of Los Angeles movie theaters. Once described by his press agent as one of the country's "top promotional wizards," Stolkin had parlayed a $15,000 stake into a multimillion-dollar mail-order business.[57] Along the way, Stolkin had filled up dossiers in Better Business Bureaus, the Federal Trade Commission, and the Post Office Department on charges ranging from illegal use of the mails to fraudulent business practices. Koolish had been charged with similar offenses and had once been indicted by a grand jury in an Illinois insurance fraud. Ryan had once been a business partner of mobster Frank Costello in a Texas oil deal.

Through intermediaries, Hughes and Stolkin dickered over RKO during the summer of 1952. On the morning of September 23 they came to terms, signing an agreement of sale in Hughes's bungalow at the Beverly Hills Hotel. For $7,345,940, Hughes sold his controlling interest in RKO Radio Pictures. The syndicate was to pay $1,250,000 down, with the remaining $6 million to be paid in installments over the next two years. At the same time, Hughes agreed to lend RKO up to $8 million as a revolving-fund account. In effect, Hughes was lending the syndicate $14 million to take RKO off his hands. Control of the studio was to pass immediately to the Stolkin group. On October 2, Hughes and his directors resigned from the RKO board. Stolkin was elected president, and his partners were named to fill the seats vacated by Hughes's directors. The disastrous Hughes era at RKO was finally at an end.

Or so it seemed. Actually, that era was only entering a new phase. When the sale to the Stolkin syndicate was announced on September 24, Hollywood did not quite know how to describe RKO's new owners, and Louella Parsons mistakenly referred to them as a syndicate of wealthy oil men.[58] By late October, Hollywood had a much clearer fix on the newcomers. When a series of articles in the *Wall Street Journal* exposed the shady pasts and business dealings of Stolkin, Koolish, and Ryan, the revelations sent shock waves through Hollywood. Already reeling from charges of widespread Communist infiltration, the movie industry did not need another scandal. Pressure mounted on Stolkin and his partners to bow out. On October 22, citing a "volume of unfavorable publicity," Stolkin, Koolish, and Ryan's nominee on the RKO board resigned.[59]

RKO was now in complete turmoil. Theoretically, the syndicate still held control, but the Stolkin group had no way to exercise it since giving up its seats on the board. Faced with this impossible situation, the syndicate backed out of the deal with Hughes, who had little choice but to go along. Technically, he no longer had an interest in RKO, yet he had received only $1.2 million of the $7.3-million purchase price. To protect what was left of his dwindling investment, he was forced to take over the studio again. In December he was reelected to the board of directors—this time as chairman—along with a slate of his handpicked directors, including Noah Dietrich.

In February of 1953, the Stolkin syndicate handed back to Hughes his controlling shares in RKO. Hughes kept the $1.2-million down payment, but that was small consolation for the problem the syndicate imbroglio had caused. RKO lost $10,178,003 in 1952, bringing the cumulative losses to a staggering $22,324,583 since Hughes took control in 1948.[60] The abortive syndicate deal had also focused stockholder attention on Hughes's bizarre management of RKO. Shortly after the proposed sale was announced, angry minority stockholders began filing lawsuits against Hughes charging that he had "squandered, wasted, and dissipated" RKO's assets, had engaged in self-dealing transactions to enrich himself, and had not carried out his duties in a "careful, prudent, or businesslike manner."[61]

Worst of all, Hughes was still stuck with RKO. He could not even sell it. Perhaps, he speculated, he could at least free himself from troublesome minority stockholders by another route—buying them all out and gaining 100-percent control. But before he could put this plan into action, he was distracted by renewed rumblings at Culver City.

CHAPTER 7

REVOLT
AT CULVER CITY

"A HELL OF A MESS"

BY 1953, Hughes Aircraft was into its fifth year of phenomenal growth. Its sales to the military were nudging toward $200 million a year. Annual earnings had topped $5 million. The work force totaled more than seventeen thousand. Production efforts of the company had moved beyond fire-control systems for all air force interceptors to similar units for the navy's Banshee fighters and an array of other sophisticated and classified electronic armaments, including the Falcon, the world's first guided air-to-air missile. In addition to the sprawling 1,300-acre Culver City site, the company had built a plant just south of Tucson to manufacture the Falcon missile. The plant in Arizona created a controversy even before it opened.

Hughes had been warmly welcomed to Tucson in 1951 when he announced plans for a multimillion-dollar defense plant that would make the city "the electronics center of the world."[1] Anticipating jobs and increased tax revenue, Tucson accommodated Hughes by spending $459,000 for new streets, sewer and water lines, and a railroad spur. But just as the plant was about to open, Hughes quietly negotiated a deal. He sold the installation to the Defense Department and took back a lease to operate it for the air force. Tucson exploded in indignation. At a stroke, about forty-seven square miles—30,000 acres—had been removed from the Pima County tax rolls. "After going all out to help the Hughes company locate in Tucson by providing every service it requested," complained an angry *Arizona Daily Star*, "the people of Tucson are disappointed to wake up and find that instead of a privately owned industry, they will have another government-owned, tax-exempt installation, operated by private enterprise."[2] There were calls for a congressional investigation and redress from Hughes before the controversy subsided. As in the Nevada land deal, Hughes had once again sought and received preferential treatment from government agencies, then reneged on his end of the bargain.

For General George and his colleagues at Culver City, the decision-making process was not getting any easier. From 1951 on, Hughes was almost always inaccessible in Las Vegas as he rotated among suites at the Desert Inn, the El Rancho Vegas, and the Flamingo. In truth, despite the resistance of Ramo and Wooldridge, Hughes still hoped to move some of his California operations to Nevada. When he told Bill Gay to prepare for a move to Las Vegas, Gay stalled, expecting that his boss's whim would pass.[3] But Hughes kept the pressure on.

Las Vegas held other charms for Hughes aside from a favorable tax structure. He liked the glamor and gaudiness of the town; he enjoyed prowling the city at night, cruising the casinos and hotels in search of attractive young women available for an evening's dalliance. The job of procuring the women usually fell to one of his aides. One former assistant explained the process: "Howard would see a girl he liked. He would motion to one of his men to see if he could get her for him. The aide would approach the girl, and if he succeeded in getting her to agree to join Hughes at his table, he whipped out a disclaimer and asked the girl to sign it before joining them."[4]

So attracted was Hughes to Las Vegas that he leased a modest five-room bungalow adjacent to the Desert Inn. Known as the Green House because of its color, it stood on the grounds of the Sun Villa Motel, now the Bali Hi Blair House Motel, on Desert Inn Road. It had a living room, a screening room, a kitchen, two bedrooms, two bathrooms, and a garage, where aides put the communications equipment. Before he moved in, Hughes had a special crew from Romaine go over the Green House, installing window air conditioners and caulking doors and windows to make the house airtight against dust and pollen.

The Green House was Hughes's main residence for about a year in 1953–54, but eventually, as Gay and everyone else at Romaine Street had anticipated, he abandoned the plan to make Las Vegas the capital of his empire. Even so, he wanted the Green House in a state of readiness, and he gave Gay a detailed set of instructions for "sealing" it against the day of his return. "He wanted everything there beautifully preserved just the way it was, when he came back," recalled Nadine Henley.[5] Gay secured doors and windows with tape, then painted over the tape with a sealer.

Hughes never returned to the Green House, although he did continue to lease and later own it until his death. Two weeks after he died, officials of the Hughes organization opened the house and found a twenty-two-year-old time capsule. In addition to chairs, tables, divans, linen, half-used bars of soap, and other standard household furnishings, the Green House contained an electric Westinghouse refrigerator—still running—two newspapers dated October 13, 1953, and April 4, 1954, keys to Room 186 at the Flamingo Hotel and Room 401 at the Hotel Miramar, twin beds with soiled sheets, some Sahara casino gambling chips, eight telephones in five rooms, a letter from "Jane to Howard"

Right: With Marian Marsh (1934).
Wide World Photos

Above: Billie Dove (early 1930s).

Right: With Ida Lupino in Palm
Springs, California (1935).
United Press International

Left: With Ginger Rogers in New York (1936). *United Press International*

Center, Right: Katherine Hepburn (early 1940s).

Below, Right: With Ava Gardner in New York (1946). *United Press International*

Terry Moore (late 1940s). *United Press International*

dated December 5, 1952, a script titled "Son of Sinbad," two yachting caps, a 1953 appointment diary believed to belong to Jean Peters, a box of Christmas decorations, and a fruit cake.[6]

During the time he lived at the Green House, Hughes often let urgent appeals for action from Culver City go unheeded. Authorization to pave the grass runway, which turned into a quagmire after rain, was two years in coming. But while Hughes was generally unavailable to his executives at the aircraft company, he was talking overtime to certain Hollywood actresses, among them the shapely Terry Moore. As Earl Wilson, the Broadway gossip columnist, disclosed in the fall of 1952, Hughes telephoned Germany almost daily "to talk to beautiful and beautifully stacked Terry Moore, twenty-two, the ex-wife of football hero Glenn Davis. They talked, sometimes for two hours. And friends who overheard her talking to him in a Munich dining room think they might get married after her divorce becomes final in April."[7] Two years earlier, when Miss Moore had left her husband of three months, Glenn Davis, the Los Angeles Rams halfback, rumor had placed Hughes in the rift. Miss Moore had walked out of the couple's Lubbock, Texas, home and returned to her mother's home in Los Angeles, charging, among other offenses, that Davis had ridiculed her acting ability. When Davis arrived to attempt a reconciliation, Hughes also appeared and in a sporting gesture offered to shake hands. But Davis became incensed and slapped the outstretched hand away, sending a startled Hughes stumbling backward over an ottoman and onto the floor. When the former Army All-American approached Hughes as though to kick him, Terry Moore's mother threw herself over the prostrate Hughes, who quickly scrambled to his feet and fled the house.[8]

Such distractions did interfere with the orderly conduct of business required by Culver City. In the past, these eccentricities had been tolerated, but by 1953 Hughes's quirks were threatening important national-defense work. With the Soviet Union on everyone's mind, the fear grew at Hughes Aircraft that production schedules could not be met because of Hughes's antics. Key executives and scientists who had once thrived in an environment that offered maximum freedom for research now faced increasing interference from their erratic employer—an annoyance magnified by two other irritants.

First, in any ordinary company, stock options would have been part of an executive salary package. But Hughes Aircraft was no ordinary company. From the day he took control, Hughes had insisted on 100-percent ownership of his business enterprises. Now, with his key executives pressing hard for a share of ownership in the aircraft company, Hughes stalled for time, dropping hints that stock options would be forthcoming to those who were patient. By 1953, after several years of such reassurances, that patience was wearing thin.

The second irritant was Noah Dietrich, Hughes's stocky, cold-eyed financial vizier, the "iron potentate" of the empire.[9] In the early 1950s, Dietrich, by then executive vice-president of Hughes Tool Company, had moved back to Los Angeles after fifteen years in Houston where he had monitored the operation and consolidated his position as the second-most-powerful man in the organization. Dietrich later said of his authority, "No member of the board of directors of Hughes Tool Company was ever permitted to make, nor did any director ever make any decision other than on routine matters. The members of the board acted as they were instructed to act by me—under direct orders or following a policy set by Howard Hughes, or under my orders on my own initiative. . . ."[10] Dietrich, now in an office at Romaine Street, prepared to confront the Culver City troublemakers.

Dietrich had always scrutinized the books of Hughes Aircraft with special care. At first, in the 1930s, he had viewed the company as an expensive annoyance. To one responsible for preserving and enhancing Hughes's fortune, there was no greater threat. The aircraft company routinely amassed huge deficits made good by the tool company. Twenty years later, of course, everything had changed. Although still a division of the tool company, Culver City was more than paying its own way, and had already passed the oil-tool division in revenues. Dietrich, who should have been pleased by the sudden turnabout, instead saw only a rival, a direct threat to his control over the empire.

To forestall such a turn of events Dietrich began to assert himself in ways that infuriated Hughes Aircraft's executives and scientists. He haggled over the company's financial requests, refused to authorize adequate working capital, withheld annual executive bonuses, and conducted annoying petty internal investigations. When one inquiry disclosed a bit of sloppy paperwork, a Dietrich underling hinted that perhaps some parts were being illegally sold off the assembly line. General George took this as a personal affront and exploded. "What you have just stated is in fact an accusation of fraud, lack of integrity, and deceit on the part of certain principal executives."[11] The charge was withdrawn, but the bitterness remained.

Alarmed over Dietrich's strong-arm tactics, the company's four vice-presidents—George, Thornton, Ramo, and Wooldridge—sent Hughes a memorandum accusing Dietrich of trying to seize personal control of Hughes Aircraft without regard for the consequences. Warning Hughes that deliveries to the air force might be jeopardized, they asked for an immediate meeting with him to resolve the conflict. No answer came. The executives sent Hughes a second urgent communication—they could no longer be responsible for meeting the company's military commitments and they intended to so notify the air force. Faced with this ultimatum, Hughes gave in and agreed to meet his rebellious executives.

On the evening of September 20, 1952, Eaker, George, Thornton, Ramo, and Wooldridge met with Hughes in a bungalow at the Beverly Hills Hotel. Hughes appeared in a conciliatory mood. He told his executives that no real breach existed between him and them. They insisted that Hughes curb Dietrich. The issue was not simply an intracompany squabble; defense work, they argued, was a public trust. Hughes made no response to their appeal for a clarification of authority, contending matter-of-factly that internal fights occurred in all companies. At one point in the discussion, Hughes, alarmed at the united front of disgruntled executives before him, accused them vaguely of "Communistic practices" by challenging him collectively.[12] In the end, nothing was settled.

A few days later, Thornton, Ramo, and Wooldridge flew to Washington to advise the Defense Department of the growing crisis at Culver City. General George later described this as an "early warning" that a blowup was imminent.[13] But still the discontent bubbled just below the surface, held in check by one possible solution.

Late in 1952, the word went out—leaked by Hughes himself—that he might sell his aircraft company if the price was right. The mere rumor was music enough to march a parade of executives from various corporations and banks through the Culver City plant. Representatives of Westinghouse and the Atlas Corporation, Convair, Lockheed, and a New York financial syndicate all expressed interest. The aircraft company's executives and scientists were vastly cheered by this prospect, confident that any new owner would be more responsive to their needs. Everyone should have known better. In the end Hughes rejected all offers. A knowledgeable government official put it succinctly: "I never really thought he was interested in selling. My impression was he was more interested in finding out what it was worth."[14]

With the collapse of this prospect, and in the face of more harassment by Dietrich, the revolt at Culver City broke out. On August 11, 1953, Ramo and Wooldridge, who had together played such a large part in the rise of Hughes Aircraft, resigned. Their loss was a severe blow, for Ramo and Wooldridge soon announced the formation of their own company specializing in military electronics. The Ramo–Wooldridge Corporation, financed by Thompson Products, Inc., of Cleveland, went on to supervise the development of intercontinental ballistic missiles for the air force, and eventually became TRW, Inc., one of the giants of the space and technology industry, with revenues surpassing those of Hughes Aircraft itself.

Meanwhile, in Washington, the air force watched the crisis at Culver City with undisguised alarm. The Pentagon had long anticipated that the differences between Hughes and the aircraft company managers might erupt into a raging internal battle that would jeopardize the company's deliveries to the air force and imperil national defense. The air force could not let that happen. Hughes Aircraft was no longer Howard Hughes's private plaything, but a quasi-public institution, a linchpin in the nation's air defense. In five years, Hughes's empire had been transformed from one totally dependent on private dollars to one increasingly nourished by federal tax dollars. The change was subtle and virtually unnoticed at the time. To most Americans, Hughes still epitomized the rugged individualist, a throwback to the nineteenth-century entrepreneur who had nothing but contempt for big government. In fact, the Hughes empire and the federal government—the Defense Department in particular—had formed a partnership that would last and grow more mutually satisfying for the rest of Hughes's life. If Hughes had failed to grasp that point by 1953, the same could not be said for the Pentagon. A concerned secretary of the air force, Harold E. Talbott, flew to Los Angeles for a showdown with Hughes on September 18, 1953.

Talbott's ties to aviation predated even those of Hughes. In the spring of 1916, Talbott's father and two other men had established the Dayton–Wright Company, taking over what had been the Orville Wright Company. Young Talbott, then only twenty-eight years old, was named president, and Orville Wright became vice-president and engineer. During the First World War, they had employed twelve thousand people and turned out thirty-eight planes a day, providing the Talbotts with a healthy fortune. The energetic Talbott went on to invest in, and exert influence over, a variety of major corporations—he was an original investor in Chrysler—served as director of aircraft production for the War Production Board during the Second World War, and became one of the most effective fundraisers for Thomas E. Dewey and Dwight D. Eisenhower. He was clearly not a man to be trifled with.

Over the years there have been several accounts of Talbott's showdown with Hughes. Some of the details vary, but it is generally agreed that the air force secretary gave Hughes an ultimatum: "You have made a hell of a mess of a great property, and by God, so long as I am Secretary of the Air Force you're not going to get another dollar of new business," Talbott told Hughes.[15]

With the Red menace still on his mind, Hughes responded: "If you mean to tell me that the government is prepared to destroy a business merely on the unfounded charges of a few disgruntled employes, then you are introducing Socialism, if not Communism."[16]

Talbott confirmed that he was pondering cancellation of all Hughes's contracts with the air force—a move that would effectively put the aircraft company out of business—and that he meant to turn the Hughes plant in Tucson over to another contractor. Hughes pleaded for time to straighten out his chaotic management. Talbott relented. He would give Hughes ninety days, and not one day more.

The situation at Hughes Aircraft could not have been worse. A sadder, but wiser General George was convinced that it was impossible to deal with Hughes. Dietrich had fired the comptroller of the company without notifying George beforehand and announced that he was moving his own office to Culver City, presumably to take personal charge. With the last vestige of his authority torn away, George turned in his resignation, paraphrasing Winston Churchill—"I do not intend to preside over the liquidation of the Hughes organization, and so help me God, if present policies are persisted in, the liquidation is inevitable."[17] George's top aide, Charles Thornton, also resigned, and, along with Roy M. Ash, another executive who later left the company, went on to build Litton Industries. These were serious developments, but not so crippling as the news in late September that the aircraft company's entire scientific advisory council, numbering more than two dozen senior scientists, intended to resign. The revolt that the air force had feared was now in full flower.

Hughes could always find a new executive or two to replace George and

Thornton, but if the people responsible for producing the company's products started walking out, he was in serious trouble. "I think Hughes realized that he had a real problem there with those engineers," one government official recalled. "You can lose managers all right, and if the rest of the organization is pretty well functioning, why you can get by. But on the threat that the whole technical management staff was going to pull out, man, that was big news."[18]

The threat brought another anxious visitor to Culver City, Roger Lewis, the assistant secretary of the air force in charge of materiel. Like Talbott, Lewis had spent all of his working life in aviation. After his graduation from Stanford University in 1934, he had worked his way up from a job in the sheet-metal department at Lockheed to vice-president of the Curtiss–Wright Corporation.

On arriving in Los Angeles, Lewis went directly to the Beverly Hills Hotel and found Hughes, dressed casually in a sport coat, slacks, and white shirt open at the neck, hunched over a menu, preparing to order lunch. Lewis recalled years later that Hughes took a long time deciding what to eat. "It took him a hell of a time to order it. He just seemed to be so indecisive about it."[19] After lunch, Lewis and Hughes walked out of the hotel, Hughes carrying his sport coat over his arm, and entered a red Rolls-Royce that Hughes drove to the Culver City plant for a meeting with the scientific staff. Throughout the lunch and short ride, Hughes said nothing about his problems at the aircraft company or the upcoming meeting. Instead, he talked about the engine and propeller business at Curtiss–Wright and Lewis's work there.

At Culver City, an anxious group of scientists was assembled and waiting. The speech that Lewis was about to make to them was probably the most important one he had tackled since becoming an air force executive. "We just had an explosive situation on our hands," he recalled later. Hughes Aircraft was the sole source of a "terribly important weapons system . . . and we had to take all the steps we could to get stability."[20] Looking out at the company's elite scientific corps, the thoughtful and diplomatic Lewis made his appeal, relying on persuasion and patriotism to keep the scientists at Culver City, at least temporarily. "I just told them how important the work was," he said, "and we weren't going to try to demand anything, but that we had to have a little time. You can't tell people what to do in this country, but I just asked them if they would do nothing for ninety days and give us a chance to try and think the thing through."[21]

While Lewis spoke Hughes sat silently nearby. The scientists listened to Lewis's plea for a ninety-day postponement of the resignations, but gave no formal answer. Nevertheless, Lewis left the room with the impression that they would agree to the delay.[22] Hughes had the same feeling, which he passed along to a reporter for *Aviation Week*. "Out of my company of 17,000 men and women only four have left," he said. "According to my best information, which I believe to be more accurate than any other available, no one else intends to leave the company at this time. There has been no effect on the production or output of defense material from this company and there will be no effect."[23]

The statement was carefully phrased: "No one else intends to leave the company *at this time.* . . ." Only Hughes, his employees, and the Defense Department knew that he had ninety days to correct the years of mismanagement.

Hughes was in the position he detested most—circumstances beyond his control were forcing a crucial business decision. The man who took two years to make up his mind whether or not to pave a runway now had only ninety days to satisfy the demands of both the secretary of the air force and the aircraft company's senior scientists. The stakes were not merely financial. In fact, money was not Hughes's main concern. He was quite comfortable making decisions he knew would cost him millions of dollars. Rather, the stake at Hughes Aircraft was the Hughes name itself. A mass walkout by scientists or the wholesale cancellation of government contracts would tarnish forever the carefully cultivated public image of Hughes as a genius of the aviation industry. He could not allow that.

ANOTHER BOSOM BROUHAHA

As usual, not all of Hughes's energy and imagination went into the effort to resolve the dilemma at hand. Some was devoted, in a very personal way, to the promotion of Jane Russell's latest movie, *The French Line,* which RKO had scheduled for release late in 1953. In this 3-D, Technicolor musical, Hughes had cast Miss Russell in the dubious role of a Texas oil heiress who, believing that men were attracted to her only for her money, sails for Paris with a wardrobe of low-cut costumes.

In addition to a script dominated by double entendres and banal dialogue (about to be married, happily and at last, Miss Russell exclaims that she is excited "as a bull mink in mating season"), the film boasted imaginative photography of the scantily clad Miss Russell in a four-minute bump and grind routine labeled "Looking for Trouble." Because of the dance scene, the Motion Picture Producers Association of America, Hollywood's self-censoring body, refused to give *The French Line* its seal of approval. Hughes, in turn, refused to cut the offending number and prepared to release the picture without the industry's seal.

St. Louis was selected as the site for the première. On the surface, it may have seemed an odd choice for the opening of a motion picture about an oil-field debutante seeking true love in Paris. But St. Louis possessed a characteristic that fit quite neatly into Hughes's scenario—65 percent of the city's 857,000 citizens were Catholic.

Advertisements for *The French Line* began appearing in St. Louis newspapers the week before Christmas. On December 18, in the *St. Louis Post-Dispatch,* a two- by four-inch teaser advertisement set the tone for what was to follow. It said simply: "J. R. in 3-D. It'll knock both your eyes out!" For emphasis, the word "both" was underlined.

Two days later, the advertisement grew to six by eleven inches. It now said: "Jane Russell in 3Dimension—and what dimensions! Howard Hughes presents Jane Russell in *The French Line.* "

By Sunday, December 27, the advertisement had swelled to eight by eleven inches and a photograph was added, showing Miss Russell in a bathing suit, standing with her arms spread wide, her long legs rising out of a montage of scenes from the movie. This time the caption read: "J. R. in 3-D. That's all, brother! Howard Hughes presents Jane Russell. *The French Line.* World premier Tuesday."

Response to the advertising campaign immediately justified the site. Throughout the Archdiocese of St. Louis, priests read a "special emergency" letter drafted by the Archdiocesan Council of Catholic Men, urging all Catholics to boycott the film because it violated the motion picture industry's own code as well as the standards of the Legion of Decency.

Readers of the *Post-Dispatch* were appropriately outraged. "Your paper stooped to a new low when it permitted such advertising as that about 'J. R. in 3-D,' " a husband and wife wrote the newspaper's editor. "Your platform states, 'Never tolerate corruption.' This type of advertising surely corrupts the people's minds."[24] Wrote another reader: "The amusement section of your Sunday (God's Day) edition was swiftly utilized at our house as a liner for the garbage can. Exactly where the giant indecent photo of Jane Russell belongs."[25]

When the five-thousand-seat Fox Theater in downtown St. Louis opened its doors at noon on December 29, an overflow audience waited in line. Among the first admitted were officers from the police department's morals squad and crime prevention bureau, adding credence to a rumor that the film would be seized.

As it happened, the film was not seized, and it was left to newspapers and magazines to place Hughes's latest cinematic effort in perspective. A St. Louis film critic concluded that "the only crime I could discern was a dramatic one, the only arrest I would recommend would be for wasting the public's time. The police would not, of course, investigate the fraud being committed—that of continuing to exploit Miss Russell as an actress."[26] *Newsweek* said the film was "more to be pitied than censored."[27] And *Time* described it as "long on notoriety and short on entertainment . . . more notable for poor taste than salaciousness."[28]

Even Miss Russell, a sometime Sunday school teacher who had risen to fame in *The Outlaw* on similar publicity a few years earlier, seemed embarrassed by it all. "There's no reason for those scenes and they ought to be cut," she said. "I don't like the accent on sex and never have. Sex has its place, and I'm no prude, but a thing like this doesn't help anyone's career."[29]

Meanwhile, the churches continued to play into Hughes's hands. On the Sunday following *The French Line* première, a stern warning was issued to parishioners of all St. Louis Catholic churches. This time the message came from the Most Reverend Joseph E. Ritter, archbishop of St. Louis. "Dearly

The provocative poster of Jane Russell from *The French Line* that inflamed St. Louis. *United Press International*

Jane Russell in **3D**
IT'LL KNOCK BOTH YOUR EYES OUT

beloved," the archbishop wrote, "since no Catholic can with a clear conscience attend such an immoral movie, we feel it is our solemn duty to forbid our Catholic people under penalty of mortal sin to attend this presentation."[30]

The Catholic Legion of Decency gave the motion picture its "C," or condemned, rating, and the Better Films Council of Greater St. Louis expressed displeasure with the movie. Far more interesting than all the protests, though, was the lack of any support either for Hughes or for his picture. Even opponents of censorship within the industry maintained a discreet silence on *The French Line.* They recognized that this was not a case of a loner championing free expression, but rather a case of rank opportunism.

As one unidentified industry executive told *Variety,* "The code has been defied before, but for the most part there was some principle involved. In the Hughes matter I fail to see how principle enters into it. I don't quarrel with nonconformists generally, but in this case Hughes is trying to make a buck with his picture at the cost of tremendous industry prestige and at the risk of bringing new censorship upon us far more burdensome than we've ever had before."[31]

THE COUNTERFEIT CHARITY

But *The French Line* was only a sideshow to Hughes's struggle for a solution at Hughes Aircraft. Much as he hated making decisions under pressure, this time Hughes rose to the occasion. As the ninety days ran out at Culver City, Hughes used the crisis to solve the one business problem that had vexed him more, and longer, than any other—his ever-spiraling federal tax bill.

The production of crude oil in the United States reached a high of 6.5 million barrels a day in 1953. Oil-production records were set in twelve states. Forecasts called for a 5.1-percent growth in demand for petroleum products in the coming year. There were 49,279 oil and gas wells that would be completed across the country in the coming year, an increase of 7.5 percent over the previous year. In short, the oil business was booming, carrying the Hughes Tool Company along with it as the chief supplier of oil-drilling bits and equipment.

As profits swelled, more of Hughes's millions went to the Internal Revenue Service. Hughes desperately needed an accounting device to cut his federal income-tax payments. Hughes Tool already had claimed some questionable deductions on its 1952 federal income-tax return, the kind of deductions that might be picked up in a close audit and result both in additional taxes and an interest penalty.

It was against this background of an aircraft company torn by bitter revolt, its top scientists threatening to bolt to competing companies, the military pressuring him to straighten out his business affairs, and a soaring federal income-tax bill, that Howard Hughes devised an intricate and superbly effective scheme: he would go into the charity business.

On December 17, 1953—the ninetieth day of the ninety-day deadline set by Air Force Secretary Talbott—Hughes's attorneys traveled to Delaware, where they filed legal documents with the Delaware secretary of state's office setting up two new corporations. One was the Hughes Aircraft Company, which now would be a separate corporation independent of the Hughes Tool Company. The second company was called the HHMI Corporation. The purpose of HHMI, as stated in its incorporation papers, was "the promotion of human knowledge within the field of the basic sciences and its effective application for the benefit of mankind."[32]

The next day, someone in the Hughes organization, probably Hughes himself, decided that the name—the HHMI Corporation—sounded too much like a business, which it was, rather than a charity, which it was supposed to be. And so the name was changed to the Howard Hughes Medical Institute. Its purpose was also amended by adding that the institute's specialty would be "principally the field of medical research and medical education."[33] Howard

Hughes was the sole trustee of the medical institute—a most unusual arrangement for a legitimate charity, which normally would vest control in a broad-based group of directors.

Once the institute had been founded, Hughes turned his attention to the news release that would properly set forth his emergence as a philanthropist. For several days early in 1954, working on yellow legal tablets in a suite at Las Vegas's Flamingo Hotel, Hughes laboriously drafted and polished the document, then had it typed on hotel stationery. Still not satisfied, he began to write in changes. He had originally intended to put a price tag on the value of his donation, but he now decided against that, writing in a phrase that his initial contribution would consist "of a substantial segment of the Hughes Aircraft Company."[34] Finally he was satisfied. Having drafted a release that was now suitably vague about his gift, Hughes had the statement distributed.

On January 10, 1954, under a Los Angeles dateline, the release announced the creation of a nonprofit charitable institution to "provide millions of dollars for medical research to combat disease and human suffering." The new Hughes foundation represented "years of planning by the famed flyer–industrialist–motion picture producer," who had "for 25 years provided, in the event of his death, for the creation and endowment of a medical research institute, and that five years ago he decided to start it during his lifetime."[35] Although short on detail, the ten-paragraph release generated favorable news stories across the nation. The true intent of the medical institute went unnoticed. Financial transactions at the base of the Hughes "charity" involved one man—Howard Hughes, of course—and three corporations: the Hughes Tool Company (represented by Hughes, its sole stockholder and president), the Hughes Aircraft Company (represented by Hughes, its president), and the Howard Hughes Medical Institute (represented by Hughes, its sole trustee).

On December 31, 1953, the last day on which Hughes and his tool company could take steps to reduce their taxable income for that year, the following took place:

- The Hughes Tool Company gave to the Howard Hughes Medical Institute the patents, trademarks, goodwill of the tool company's aircraft division, and all the stock of the new Hughes Aircraft Company. The declared value of the gift was $36,463.[36]
- The tool company then sold to the medical institute certain assets of its aircraft division—inventories, receivables on government contracts—for $74,618,038.[37]
- The medical institute—the new Hughes "charity"—had no money, so to pay for those assets the institute assumed $56,574,738 in liabilities of the tool company's aircraft division.[38]
- The medical institute then signed a promissory note to the tool company for the $18,043,300 difference between the assets it bought and the liabilities it assumed. The note ran for three years and carried an annual interest rate of 4 percent.[39]

- The tool company also leased to the medical institute certain real estate and fixed assets of the aircraft division—the land and buildings at Culver City. The lease also provided that the medical institute would pay the tool company $26 million over the ten-year, six-month life of the lease.[40]
- The medical institute, in turn, subleased the same Culver City land and buildings to the newly created Hughes Aircraft Company. The sublease provided that the aircraft company would pay $33.6 million to the medical institute during the same ten-year, six-month period.[41]

The net effects of Hughes's creative accounting were these:

Howard Hughes, multimillionaire, had created a charity without donating a single penny in cash or in stock that paid dividends, or any real estate. The charity started life with a debt of $18,043,300 to the man who founded it, meaning that Hughes would collect millions of dollars in interest payments from his own charity. The agreements showed that Hughes had no intention of giving money to his medical-research institute for at least a decade, if ever. Instead, the institute's only source of income would be the payments from the aircraft company for the real estate and fixed assets subleased to the aircraft company.

At the same time, the Hughes Tool Company could deduct its lease payments to the medical institute on its federal income-tax return. Every dollar the tool company saved in taxes was another dollar for Hughes. Even better, the aircraft company's cost of subleasing buildings from the medical institute could be passed along to the American taxpayer. The $33.6 million sublease represented an additional cost of doing business, a cost that Hughes Aircraft could tack on the bill it sent to the United States government for work on military contracts—its only source of income.

In short, Hughes had created the ultimate charity: the American taxpayer was to pick up the entire bill for the Howard Hughes Medical Institute, while Hughes basked in the warm glow of testimonials to his philanthropy and quietly collected money from his own charity.

It was a bold stroke that solved Hughes's many problems. With the organization of the medical institute, the tool company gained an immediate $2-million deduction on its federal tax return, the first of a series of substantial tax benefits over the coming years. The medical institute now owned 100 percent of the stock of the Hughes Aircraft Company and nothing else. Defense officials in Washington would think twice before canceling the contracts of a company owned by a charity devoted to medical research "for the benefit of all mankind." The aircraft company's executives, likewise, could hardly demand stock options from a charity. Finally, over and through it all, Hughes retained complete control. He was the sole trustee of the medical institute and the president of the aircraft company.

There remained only a nagging technicality. In order for this house of cards to stand, Hughes needed a ruling from the Internal Revenue Service designating the Howard Hughes Medical Institute a tax-exempt charitable organization, like the Ford Foundation or the Boy Scouts or the YMCA.

By the fall of 1955, however, the Hughes organization sensed trouble. Rumor had it that the IRS would rule against the medical institute's application for tax exemption. Such a decision not only would have dire consequences for Hughes, but also would reflect unfavorably on his beneficence, exposing the medical institute as something less than a charity.

It was time for another public-relations blitz. In between visits to a Hollywood nightclub and an Arizona dude ranch, about a hundred newspaper and magazine reporters were escorted through Hughes Aircraft plants in Culver City and Tucson, the first time that Hughes had opened those doors. Hughes was not present, but his spokesmen cheerfully trumpeted the message: Hughes, they said, believed that, finally, it was "time for the public to have some information on the electronic systems."[42] The plants had been closed to outsiders in the past because Hughes had "not wanted to talk about . . . the company until he could point to a consistent record of achievement."[43]

The results of the junket were predictable. Newspapers and magazines burst forth in praise of the electronic marvels at Hughes Aircraft. The company's accomplishments were genuine, even if achieved despite Hughes's management. And why dwell on Hughes Aircraft's near collapse two years earlier? It seemed so long ago. As Hughes himself explained, "I know about the important things. What's the measure of this outfit? Our internal problems? Or is it the customer's satisfaction?"[44] The answer to Hughes's rhetorical question was provided by *Time* magazine: "By all signs, the United States Air Force, Howard Hughes' biggest customer, was eminently satisfied."[45] Anyway, *Time* went on, "profits from Hughes Aircraft go into the Howard Hughes Medical Institute for research."[46]

Stories about Hughes Aircraft and the good works of the Howard Hughes Medical Institute notwithstanding, the IRS informed Hughes on November 29, 1955, that it was denying his request to class the medical institute as a tax-exempt organization. IRS agents had concluded that Hughes's self-styled charity was "merely a device for siphoning off otherwise taxable income to an exempt organization, and accumulating that income."[47]

Hughes was furious. He ordered Noah Dietrich to look into the possibility of "revoking the gift to the Institute."[48] Dietrich advised Hughes that that could not be done.[49] In time, Hughes chose a wiser course.

The IRS ruling was a setback, but the decision could be appealed within the agency and then, if necessary, to the federal courts. To handle the delicate negotiations with the IRS, Hughes turned to the well-known and well-connected Washington law firm of Hogan & Hartson. The senior partner, Nelson T. Hartson, had been solicitor for the Internal Revenue Bureau in the early 1920s. Another partner, Seymour S. Mintz, who had first worked in the office of the undersecretary of the Treasury and then as a special attorney in the Internal Revenue Bureau during the late 1930s and early 1940s, was one of Washington's leading tax lawyers.

Hogan & Hartson had just completed a sensitive assignment for Hughes, one unrelated to tax law. The bachelor industrialist wanted information about a man who was dating his sometime girlfriend, Jean Peters. Back in 1947, Hughes had given Jean a diamond and sapphire ring. At the time, the twenty-year-old actress described their relationship as "serious." She allowed, though, that both wanted to wait a year before marriage and that Howard "wants to be very sure that when he does marry, it's for keeps."[50]

Seven years later, Hughes was still trying to decide whether Jean would be for keeps. She was seeing another man, and Hughes suspected that the suitor might be a secret government agent. At Hughes's request, Hogan & Hartson retained the services of a private investigator, a former FBI agent with close ties to both federal law-enforcement authorities and the Washington intelligence community. His name was Robert Aimee Maheu.

The law firm kept the identity of its client a secret in the beginning, and as Maheu remembered some years later, "It was a very insignificant assignment of determining whether a certain individual was engaged in undercover work for the United States government. It pertained to an individual who was then either courting or subsequently married Jean Peters."[51] No doubt the assignment was trivial, but the road it opened to Maheu was a rewarding one.

POLITICAL INSURANCE

While the Hogan & Hartson lawyers were pleading the case for a tax-exempt medical institute, their client was covering his bets by buying some very potent political insurance. He needed all the help he could get. In its first full year of operation, the medical institute reported income of $3,609,785, all from Hughes Aircraft, of course. Of that amount, the purported charity returned $3,024,517, or 84 percent of its total income, to Howard Hughes. Exactly $43,348—or 1 percent of its income—was allocated for medical-research fellowships.*[52]

The physician Hughes had placed in charge of the institute's medical work was Dr. Verne R. Mason, the Hollywood doctor who treated him after his near-fatal 1946 plane crash and who had been supplying him ever since— apparently without any legitimate medical reason—with narcotics. In the beginning, Dr. Mason furnished Hughes with prescriptions for Empirin Compound No. 4, a pain-killing drug that contains codeine. In time, Dr. Mason supplemented the Empirin with pure codeine, one-grain tablets that Hughes consumed in growing quantities, building up a low-level addiction.

In March of 1956, Hogan & Hartson lodged a formal protest with the IRS. Months passed with no word from the agency; in an election year the Washington bureaucracy makes few large decisions. That November, Dwight D. Eisenhower and his running mate, Richard M. Nixon, were swept into office for another term, capturing 57.4 percent of the popular vote—the largest winning margin in twenty years.

*See Appendix A.

For Nixon, a major beneficiary of Eisenhower's broad popular appeal, everything was going just right in Washington. But for the vice-president's brother, Francis Donald Nixon, everything was going wrong in Whittier, California. Donald Nixon was striving to turn Nixon's Inc., his money-losing, mini-conglomerate composed of a supermarket and three restaurants that specialized in Nixonburgers, into a profitable business.

Shortly before the November election, Donald Nixon had tried to raise $300,000 in a public stock offering. To stir up interest, Nixon's broker sent a letter to leaders of sixty-five Young Republican Clubs in the Los Angeles area urging them to "mention the stock offering at your next meeting." The broker's letter concluded with a warm political endorsement: "My best personal wishes to you for what we know will be a very successful campaign."[53] The financial plan collapsed before the election when copies of the letter were sent anonymously to California newsmen who then broke the story.

Three months later, with his brother secure in the vice-president's office for another four years, Donald Nixon arranged a $205,000 loan to rescue his failing business. The date was December 10, 1956, and the lender was Hughes, or more precisely, the Hughes Tool Company.

Hughes hardly ever carried out his own schemes. This time the financial transaction was handled by a Los Angeles attorney, Frank J. Waters, once a registered lobbyist for the Hughes Tool Company and a former member of the California legislature who first went to work for Hughes in 1944. Noah Dietrich made the cash available by transferring $205,000 from a Canadian subsidiary of the Hughes Tool Company, and Waters handled the rest.

The proceeds of the $205,000 loan went first to Mrs. Hannah M. Nixon, the aged mother of the Nixon brothers. She, in turn, loaned $165,000 to Nixon's Inc. and used the remaining $40,000 to pay off an earlier bank loan.

There was no individual responsibility for repayment. If for some reason Nixon's Inc. was unable to repay the loan, no member of the Nixon family would be held responsible for it. Instead, the loan was secured by a mortgage on a lot the Nixons owned at Santa Gertrudis and Whittier Boulevards in Whittier. The lot had been the site of the Nixon family home, purchased back in May of 1923 by Francis A. and Hannah M. Nixon, and then that of a store operated by the vice-president's father, and still later Donald Nixon's first drive-in and gift shop.

Donald Nixon had just signed an agreement with the Union Oil Company to build a service station on the lot and lease the business to the oil company.* But on the date Donald Nixon obtained his loan from Hughes, the Whittier lot had an assessed value for tax purposes of $13,000.[54] Los Angeles County assessments normally equalled about one-fourth of the fair market value. The

---

*The Union Oil lease required the signature of Nixon's mother, who still held title to the property. On October 17, 1956, Mrs. Hannah M. Nixon signed it. Her signature was witnessed and the document notarized by one William A. Ridgely in the District of Columbia. Ridgely was then assistant financial clerk of the United States Senate, over which Mrs. Nixon's son, Richard, presided.

Nixon family had obtained a $205,000 loan from Hughes by pledging as collateral a vacant lot worth no more than $52,000.

But not even the infusion of Hughes's cash could save Nixon's Inc. By February of 1957, concern for the fortunes of Donald Nixon had led to a meeting of Hughes associates at Romaine Street, where it was agreed that an informal management committee would be set up to save the restaurants. In attendance were, among others, Noah Dietrich, Frank Waters, and Phillip Reiner, a certified public accountant who worked for Waters and his law partner, James J. Arditto. After the meeting, Waters called the office of the vice-president and advised a Nixon aide of Hughes's efforts on behalf of the Nixon family.

Less than a month later, the Internal Revenue Service had a change of heart toward the Howard Hughes Medical Institute. The IRS informed Hughes on March 1, 1957, that it was reversing its original decision. The Howard Hughes Medical Institute would now be classified as a tax-exempt charitable organization. At last, Hughes was officially, legally, in a charity business worth tens of millions of dollars to him, both directly and indirectly.

Donald Nixon did not fare nearly so well. Nixon's Inc. collapsed before the year was out and he went to work for the Carnation Milk Company. When he filed for personal bankruptcy in 1960, he listed debts of $206,937.43 and assets of $1,250.[55] His debts came uncannily near to matching the $205,000 loan from Howard Hughes. The Hughes loan was never repaid, but the Whittier lot was secretly signed over to the Hughes organization to avoid the unpleasantries of foreclosure.

Details of the Hughes loan to Donald Nixon were made public in the closing days of the 1960 presidential race between Richard Nixon and John F. Kennedy, and may well have contributed to Nixon's narrow defeat. But the possibility of a connection between the Hughes loan and the IRS's simultaneous about-face on the tax status of the Howard Hughes Medical Institute was never drawn. Nor could it have been, for the IRS carefully kept secret all its dealings with Hughes. To this day, the IRS has refused to make public the rulings and other documents relating to its initial decisions rejecting the medical institute's request for tax exemption, its subsequent reversal of that decision, and other special considerations it subsequently granted to the medical institute. Interestingly, one of the secret rulings Hughes received came directly from the IRS commissioner's office in September of 1959. At the time the commissioner was Dana Latham, who before taking over the top IRS post had been a prominent tax lawyer and a senior partner in the Los Angeles law firm of Latham & Watkins. The law firm eventually represented Hughes Aircraft Company, whose stock was owned by the Howard Hughes Medical Institute. Richard F. Alden, Latham's son-in-law and a partner in the firm, became general counsel for Hughes Aircraft Company.*

*In August of 1975, the *Philadelphia Inquirer* filed a Freedom of Information Act lawsuit against the IRS in United States District Court in Washington, D.C., seeking to compel the agency to make public all its rulings and other documents relating to the tax exemption granted the Howard Hughes Medical Institute. The IRS not only vigorously opposed the *Inquirer* lawsuit, but then Commissioner Donald C. Alexander waged a quiet and intensive lobbying campaign on

If there was one task in which Hughes delighted, it was selecting the site for one of his enterprises. It was a duty that he never delegated. In fact, no Hughes executive could ever on his own acquire land or authorize construction of a building. Hughes reveled in putting advisers to work compiling lists of potential sites, then painstakingly studying each to weigh its advantages and disadvantages. He loved to spend hours analyzing maps and reports and, after making his decisions, he thrived on the opportunity to manipulate politicians, the press, and the public while embellishing his image as a benefactor of mankind. The way he went about announcing the site for his new medical institute was typical.

Once the papers had been signed creating the medical foundation, Hughes advisers recommended locations—cities in California, Texas, and Florida, among other states. Eventually, Hughes selected Florida, but rather than make a straightforward announcement, he decided to build up suspense about his plans and reap some favorable publicity along the way.

While Hughes was visiting Miami early in 1955, rumors began circulating there that he planned to make major investments in southern Florida. Nothing was official, but the news media were led to believe that Hughes was about to move his motion-picture operations, his oil-tool company, or his aircraft plant to Florida. By spring, the media were being cautioned by Hughes's press aides that any premature publicity would jeopardize a "big enterprise."[56] After a series of private conversations with Hughes, Florida governor LeRoy Collins announced that he had a commitment from Hughes to locate "two gigantic industries" in Florida, although the nature of the industries was left to the imagination.[57] Hughes also told Collins he intended to build a magnificent medical-research complex in southern Florida that would have no equal. As Collins recalled:

"He said that he wanted to build something that never had been built in the world. He wanted to build a facility that could attract the finest brains in the world in the whole field of medical science, research, and everything else. He wanted unusual and attractive living accommodations for people who came there. He wanted all the sports facilities. He was going to make it a place that these people wanted to go. They'd have all the best equipment to support them and he was going to pour all his worldly goods into that facility. And it was just going to be something that would be of worldwide

Capitol Hill, urging Congress to enact legislation that would exempt the private IRS rulings from the Freedom of Information Act and forever keep secret the identities of individuals and businesses receiving the rulings. When the legislation was drafted with a grandfather clause allowing any pending FOI lawsuits, notably the *Inquirer*'s, to continue, Alexander wrote a letter to the staff of the Joint Committee on Internal Revenue Taxation urging that the grandfather clause be dropped, specifically singling out the *Inquirer*'s pending lawsuit requesting release of the Hughes documents. Congress eventually passed the legislation keeping secret the names of all persons and businesses receiving private rulings from the IRS, but retained the grandfather clause to which Alexander had objected. Three years after the lawsuit was filed, the IRS was continuing to object to the release of the Hughes documents. Because of this, it is not known whether the ruling issued by Latham's office was favorable or unfavorable to Hughes's interests.

significance and importance and would be a perpetuation of his name on something that he felt was about the most noble thing that could be done. Really a grand concept, in all the ways that grand may be used.[58]

On February 2, 1956, the *Miami Herald* carried a page-one story reporting that the area might become the location of the largest heart-research center in the world, a Hughes project of "more than $100 million."[59] The source of the story was Dr. Louis N. Katz, director of cardiovascular research at Michael Reese Hospital in Chicago and former president of the American Heart Association, who had spoken at a kickoff dinner of the 1956 Greater Miami Heart Fund campaign.

Two months later, a Hughes spokesman made it all official at a press conference in Governor Collins's office in Tallahassee. The spokesman was Delbert E. Webb, co-owner of the New York Yankees, longtime Hughes associate, and multimillionaire head of a construction company that Hughes employed.

Reading from a statement approved by Hughes, Webb announced: "The Howard Hughes Medical Institute has already made its beginning in Florida. It recently acquired by lease a part of the Richmond Naval Air Station south of Miami, and will conduct some of its research there. Officers' quarters will be made into suitable laboratories, administrative offices, lecture hall, conference rooms, library, and dining facilities."[60] And the medical institute, Webb added, was only the start of Hughes's program in Florida. Coming next would be a huge aircraft-manufacturing plant—at a site to be selected—employing thousands of persons.

So there it was, finally. In the year gone by it had been variously rumored that Hughes intended to move his aircraft company, his oil-tool company, and his motion-picture studio to Florida. A noted cardiologist had announced that Hughes would build the world's largest heart-research center in Florida. The governor had announced that he had a commitment from Hughes for two gigantic new industries. And, last, the word from Hughes himself—he was going to locate his medical institute and build an airplane factory in Florida. The image of Hughes—the mystery man who would provide thousands of jobs for Florida residents, the benefactor of the disease-ridden—was firmly etched in the public consciousness.

In the first critical years of the medical institute—when image was all-important in securing favorable action by the Washington bureaucracy—Hughes had devised a scheme to overcome one obstacle that would have proved insurmountable to a less imaginative or resourceful man. That was: how to enlist highly regarded members of the American medical community in his cause and obtain their public endorsements of his good works without personally contributing a penny in cash to his charity. The answer was a subtle blending of the illusion of Hughes money, the aura of the Hughes name, and the inviolate Hughes code of secrecy. There was a Hughes maxim which held that people would give him their time, their talents, and their loyalty in exchange for even the slimmest possibility of financial reward.

Hughes needed only an existing medical organization to give his charity instant credibility. At the University of Miami he found a candidate, a recently established medical school in need of financial support and the public recognition that generates such support. Dr. Homer Marsh, the dean of the medical school at the time, remembers the occasion well. "We wanted a formal affiliation," he said, "because we were all selfish and we wanted to cash in on Hughes' name to attract more support for the medical school. But a formal affiliation was never made. We had visions of large financial support that didn't materialize."[61]

There was no reason for Dr. Marsh to disbelieve Hughes. After all, Hughes had made the medical school much the same promise that he had made the IRS. In a report to the tax agency in 1957, Hughes stated: "Anticipating that the institute's principal facilities will be constructed in the Miami area, the institute has thoroughly studied the potentialities of the area as related to the future programs of the institute. Of particular significance are a more permanent and closer affiliation with the University of Miami School of Medicine."[62]

After the IRS exempted his medical institute from the tax laws, Hughes never built anything in Florida. He did not build the medical institute facilities he described in his report to the IRS, or the sprawling research complex spread over sixty acres pictured by Miami newspapers, or the world-renowned medical institute he described to Governor Collins, or the world's largest heart-research center envisioned by Dr. Katz.

Instead, Hughes rented the top floor and part of the third floor of the four-story Medical Arts Building on the University of Miami campus as the headquarters for the Howard Hughes Medical Institute. There, researchers (the institute called them "medical investigators") conducted their studies using patient data from nearby Jackson Memorial Hospital. The researchers taught occasional classes at the University of Miami School of Medicine and the medical school staff was given access to the institute's library. In addition, each year modest grants were awarded to researchers at half a dozen medical schools around the country. In short, the institute was a nickel-and-dime operation—in 1955, research grants and fellowships totaled $122,611, or $599,120 less than the institute gave Hughes as interest on his loan—and nothing like the wealthy industrialist's grandiose promises.[63] It was a story that went unnoticed. A wall of secrecy had descended around the Howard Hughes Medical Institute and Hughes had moved on to other pursuits.

CHAPTER 8

SEEDS
OF DISASTER

THE RISE OF THE MORMONS

IN October of 1954, Hughes asked a favor of an old acquaintance, Spyros Skouras, the onetime head of Twentieth Century Fox. Confiding that he planned to sell his vast holdings to devote more time and money to medical research, Hughes asked Skouras to find a buyer. The gravel-voiced Greek was soon on the telephone to New York with real-estate promoter William Zeckendorf. Who would have the resources to handle such a transaction, Skouras wondered. Zeckendorf had but one answer: "It sounds like a Rockefeller proposition."[1]

Zeckendorf, who eight years earlier had sold the Rockefellers a seventeen-acre tract of land along the East River in Manhattan that became the United Nations' site, met with Laurance Rockefeller, the family's venture capitalist. Although skeptical about Hughes's intentions, Rockefeller's curiosity was greatly piqued and he flew west with Zeckendorf in anticipation of a meeting with the elusive industrialist.

After lunch in the dining room of the Beverly Hills Hotel, the two found themselves, Zeckendorf later recalled, "programmed into a script" that only a CIA agent would take seriously.[2] At 1:50 P.M., following Hughes's orders, they drove from the hotel to a nearby intersection, parked their car, and were met by a man wearing a red shirt open at the neck. "Follow me," he instructed, walking toward an aged sedan, "something the Okies might have used on the trek west twenty years ago."[3]

The jalopy took them to a "seedy section of town," and stopped in front of a rundown dwelling that looked to the urbane Zeckendorf like a "flop-house."[4] It was patrolled by a silent cadre of Hughes's guards, "neatly dressed, rather good-looking men, all with crew cuts."[5] Zeckendorf and Rockefeller were led to the fourth floor, then down a long hallway, where their guide paused and rapped on a door "with a distinct pattern of knocks."[6] Hughes himself opened the door. His three-day growth of beard, soiled trousers, and dirty canvas shoes were something of a surprise to the impeccably dressed visitors. Inviting Rockefeller and Zeckendorf into his clandestine conference room, Hughes, always slightly nervous around others, slouched on the edge of the couch, sometimes crossing his legs, then leaning forward to shift his weight, but never changing his "facial expression."[7] He directed a hearing aid at the visitors. Zeckendorf recited the inventory of the Hughes holdings, summing up his presentation by offering Hughes $350 million for everything. "You don't know what you're talking about," Hughes answered bluntly, adding that the offer was just "not enough."[8]

"What is enough?" asked Zeckendorf.

"I won't tell you."

"Do you want to sell?"

"Under certain circumstances."

"What circumstances?"

"If the price is right."

"What price?"

"The price you might offer me. If it is enough, I'll sell."

It was obvious to Zeckendorf, a wily negotiator himself, that Hughes was playing the "original coy mistress," yet he persisted.

"I am offering you four hundred and fifty million; will you take it?" demanded Zeckendorf.

"No . . ."

"Howard, just exactly what do you want?"

"I won't tell you."

"Howard, take it or leave it, five hundred million."

"I leave it."[9]

Rockefeller and Zeckendorf had of course been drawn into an old Hughes game. For years, he had amused himself thusly, and eager money men invariably flocked to his door, checkbook in hand. While they got nothing for their trouble other than the rare experience of actually meeting him, Hughes obtained an up-to-date estimate of his empire's worth. Down deep, Hughes shrank from the idea of selling any of his companies, even of diluting his control by giving stock options to top executives. "Howard," one of his former executives said, "was a very possessive man."[10]

By the mid-1950s, Hughes controlled an extraordinary empire. Hardly a corner of the world escaped his touch. There was the Hughes Tool Company in Houston, manufacturing its indispensable drill bits for oilmen around the globe. There was Hughes Aircraft Company in Culver City designing and building sophisticated electronics gear and weaponry, carving out a niche in the nation's growing military-industrial complex. There was Hughes Productions in Hollywood, and although it had not made a movie in years, it was still signing up potential female stars, giving them expensive drama and singing lessons, and looking out for scripts that could bring about Hughes's return to active movie production. Last, there was Trans World Airlines, whose airplanes flew to cities all over the United States and carried the American flag into dozens of capitals in Europe and Asia. The Hughes empire employed nearly fifty thousand people and generated revenues of $1.4 million a day.*

At the heart of this empire was an inconspicuous, two-story, buff-colored building at 7000 Romaine Street in Hollywood. "Romaine," as it was known, looked more like the bakery it had been in the 1920s than the command post for one of America's richest and most powerful men. No sign identified the building. Its exterior did nothing to set it apart from the neighborhood. More or less rectangular in shape, it fronted on Romaine Street and took up the entire block between Orange Drive and Sycamore Avenue. On the Romaine side, the facade was marked by two rows of plain windows on the first and second floors. Except for a touch of art-deco ornamentation above the doorways, Romaine Street blended perfectly with the neighboring film laboratories, motion-picture supply houses, and squat warehouses.

Romaine housed the offices of Noah Dietrich, Nadine Henley, and Hughes's talent scouts, and served as a collecting point for various drivers, male secretaries, messengers, and assorted helpers who made up Hughes's peculiar personal staff. Most of them were fiercely loyal young Mormons hired by Bill Gay, who functioned as Hughes's chief of staff and also worked out of Romaine. Hughes had once kept an office at the building, but now he never came to Romaine. He worked instead from various houses and hotel suites— Marion Davies's Ocean House in Santa Monica, the scene of glittering parties in his youth; Howard Hawks's place in Bel Air; an imposing house on Bellagio Road across from the Bel Air Country Club; a leased house in Palm Springs; and a suite at the Bel Air Hotel. Mostly, however, he lived at the Beverly Hills Hotel, in one of the small, exquisite bungalows that have always given that hotel a special charm. The two bungalows he used most often were 19 and 19A.

Hughes had originally bought Romaine Street in 1930 to house an abortive experiment to produce color films. When the effort failed, the building remained as the site of his motion-picture operations and became a kind of catch-all West Coast headquarters. By the mid-1950s, Romaine had become central to his life in every way. It was the conduit through which he transmitted orders to each branch of his empire, and those who worked there also leased his houses and hotel suites, provided him with drivers and guards, hired his cooks and servants, paid his bills, and answered his personal letters. Centering as it did almost exclusively on Hughes, Romaine Street was tightly controlled, and access to it limited. Locks requiring both a key and a combination

*Hughes still owned the RKO General Corporation, but by the mid-1950s it was nothing more than a holding company and was not producing motion pictures. Hughes sold the company for $25 million on July 18, 1955, to the General Tire and Rubber Company, in what was widely billed at the time as the "largest cash deal in movie history."

7000 Romaine Street, the Hughes command post in
Hollywood. *United Press International*

Frank William (Bill) Gay, Hughes's personal staff
director at Romaine. *Wide World Photos*

secured each outside door. Guards allowed no one inside without prior approval, and very few outsiders were accorded that privilege.

Inside, the building was as drab and spartan as its exterior. The first floor was dark and eerie. Along a concrete hallway running from one end to the other was a series of unused film laboratories and cutting rooms and several walk-in vaults dating from the 1930s. The vaults had come to be used as repositories for Hughes's personal memorabilia. In one air-conditioned, humidity-controlled vault were all the negatives and prints of his movies, as well as thousands of feet of outtakes. In the remaining vaults were Hughes mementos and relics—hundreds of still photographs of him; thousands of feet of newsreel film recording him at historic moments in his career; the flight jacket he had worn the day he flew the flying boat in 1947; models of airplanes used in his motion pictures; pilot logs accounting for his every minute behind the controls of an airplane; aviation trophies, plaques, and medals; some unopened Christmas presents; and even a cache of whiskey and wine dating from the estate of his father, dead more than thirty years.

The only continuing operation on the ground floor was the drivers' room, an around-the-clock motor pool. There were usually about fifteen drivers on the payroll, most of them young Mormons, conservative dressers who drove Chevrolet sedans, which Hughes had chosen as a kind of official Romaine Street vehicle in keeping with the inconspicuous nature of his command post. The drivers picked up visitors at the airport, chauffeured starlets about town, transported Hughes's executives to and from their houses, and ran errands for Hughes.

A flight of metal steps led to the second floor. On both sides of a long, plain hallway running the length of the building were doors opening onto the unpretentious executive offices of Dietrich, Miss Henley, Gay, and the bookkeepers, accountants, talent scouts, and functionaries Hughes had accumulated over thirty years in Southern California. Farther along the hall were a couple of conference rooms and an old screening room with its own projection booth. At the far end of the hall, in a large room overlooking Romaine Street, was the nerve center of the empire itself.

The room was known throughout the Hughes organization as "Operations." If Romaine had a military hue, then Operations was the general staff headquarters—minus, of course, the general. It was largely the creation of Bill Gay, the military-minded chief of staff who had long since given up any idea of pursuing his academic career. Like any good soldier and bureaucrat, Gay had staffed Operations and lesser enclaves at Romaine with men loyal to him, notably fellow members of the Church of Jesus Christ of Latter-day Saints. The nondrinking, nonsmoking Mormons had become so intertwined with Romaine Street that when a job opening occurred notices went up on Mormon church bulletin boards all over Los Angeles.

All decisions, however important or trivial, passed through Operations, from an authorization to spend millions of dollars to a request that a staff assistant awaiting orders from Hughes be allowed to leave his hotel room.

Anyone who wanted to talk to Hughes first called Operations, OL 4–2500. The room was manned twenty-four hours a day, usually by two of Gay's young Mormons. When a call came into Operations from a banker, a Hughes executive, a newspaper reporter, a financier, or anyone else trying to reach the industrialist, one of the polite male message clerks, called "staff men," recorded in shorthand the caller's name, telephone number, and the reason for the call. The message then was typed in a log—referred to as a "call sheet" —kept chronologically by minute, hour, day, and year. Technical messages were taped and transcribed. Each memorandum, no matter how insignificant, was assigned an operating number and filed at day's end. For special people there was a special drill. For example, if Louella Parsons or Hedda Hopper, two of Hollywood's leading gossip columnists, called, there were standing orders for the staff men:

Whenever either of these people call, we are not to hold them on the line while trying to reach HRH. Find out where they are going to be and then make every effort to locate HRH and give him the call.[11]

Under most circumstances, Hughes did not want to be awakened, no matter how important the message, and he did not want to be bothered "during the first two hours of being awake unless a real emergency."[12]

Processing Hughes's telephone calls was therefore a demanding task, requiring staff familiarity with a code of programmed responses. When Hughes himself called in—his telephone had a distinctive ring—the staff man read out his calls and messages.[13] Hughes might dictate a series of replies, return the calls himself, refer them to others, or ignore them. In other cases, he might call and dictate a message for transmittal, either by telephone or written communication. If the message was to be relayed by telephone, Hughes would suggest the "temper" it was to be delivered in. Again, there were standing orders on how to read messages:

The message should be given slowly and clearly with natural pauses. If the insertion of a few of your own words will make it more casual and more natural sounding, don't hesitate to do this. However, all of HRH's points must be covered exactly as instructed.[14]

Written communications were handled in a variety of ways—"the form of a letter for his signature, informal note, memo, or an important communication," known as an "IC."[15]

To assist in keeping track of Hughes's multiple interests, the staff men maintained half a dozen lists of matters pending in his different companies. The lists were assigned designations such as the "priority list," "top priority list," and even "very top priority list." Items that fell into none of those categories were assigned to the "special list."[16] Another was the "alert list," containing the names of people who had been alerted ahead of time that Hughes would call.[17] To receive a call from him was generally no spur-of-the-moment affair. Usually, an aide would first call the person Hughes intended to telephone, explaining that Hughes would call at a specified time, perhaps five minutes or five hours from then. And Hughes would indeed call, although sometimes the procedure was even more complicated, as Governor LeRoy Collins of Florida once found out:

Somebody would call my office and tell them that Mr. Hughes would like to speak to me and wanted to know if I could take a call direct from him at 2:37 that afternoon . . . And so my secretary would check it out with me and I said, "Yes, I'll be right here and I'll talk to him at 2:37." So she would call out there [Los Angeles] and give them that information. And then about 2:30, our office would get another telephone call. And they just wanted to verify the fact that I was actually in the office, and I could actually take the call. And then there'd come a call at 2:37, still from somebody else, wanting me to get on the telephone, wanting to know if I could be on the telephone in one minute, and then he'd call and I'd be there.[18]

To remind Hughes of important deadlines or telephone calls he should make, Operations kept "reminder lists."[19] Even these were subdivided into "master reminder list" and "special reminder list."[20] To keep track of all the lawyers, executives, staff aides, financiers, and others Hughes might want to talk to by phone at any time, Operations kept "locate books," which gave the names, addresses, and current business and home telephone numbers of persons he called most often.[21] All of his executives and lawyers were expected to leave a number with Operations where they could be reached at all times. Operations had also assigned code names to persons Hughes communicated with regularly. Jean Peters's code name was "Major Bertrandez."[22] Another girlfriend, Yvonne Shubert, was known as "The Party."[23]

Finally, there was the classification system that was used to protect the innermost workings and secrets of the Hughes empire, a system more encompassing than that used by the Defense Department. The ultimate authority for classifying Romaine Street files rested with Bill Gay or someone he designated. There were three categories. The highest, or "Secret" classification, was given to that "information and material, the security aspect of which is paramount and the disclosure of which would cause exceptionally grave damage to the interests and prestige of Mr. Hughes or his executive office."[24] Such material, marked "A" and kept in the custody of Gay, was not to be "discussed or referred to except in official meetings of the staff behind closed doors."[25]

The second-highest classification, "Confidential," was given to "information or material the disclosure of which would cause serious injury to the interests and prestige of Mr. Hughes or the executive office and would be of great advantage to competitors."[26] A typical "Confidential" communication—marked "B" and kept in the custody of section heads—was a two-page memorandum on how to arrange transportation on TWA for William Randolph Hearst, Jr., his wife and friends, or others in the Hearst newspaper chain. The memorandum, headed "Special Instruction," directed the Hughes staff to "roll out the super red carpet all the way" on TWA for Hearst, his family and friends.[27] Specifically, "the captain on each leg of their flight should come back and invite the party concerned up front and explain to them those things of interest and importance in the flying of the ship. In this respect the captain should always make certain that he explains he has received instructions from Mr. Hughes to extend every courtesy to the party concerned. The hostesses should be instructed to take very special care of them. The party concerned should be met at the airport by the top man at each point along the route and there should be transportation available at the points of origin and destination."[28]

All communications that did not fall into the "Secret" or "Confidential" categories were classified "Restricted." Such information and material, marked "C," was read and initialed by members of his staff and then returned to a "designated file for safe keeping."[29] A six-page memorandum establishing the security classification system itself was labeled "Restricted." In addition to spelling out the classification of printed matter, the memorandum set forth guidelines on how employees were to conduct themselves:

Do not fraternize with persons outside the office. Do not engage in long, unnecessary conversations with secretaries. Be sure that all confidential and secret material from wastepaper baskets is properly destroyed and burned. Tell your wife as little as possible.[30]

Classified material to be delivered from one office to another had to be placed in an envelope and sealed with wax, "the official seal of the office" imprinted in the wax.[31]

It was a unique, byzantine way of doing business that Hughes had contrived, but one that suited him perfectly. It insulated him from unwanted intrusions, afforded a maximum amount of freedom and flexibility, and cloaked all his activities and movements in absolute secrecy. It enabled him to manipulate his enemies and position his men, even to the point of absurdity, as when an engineer, camped out in a Seattle hotel room awaiting further orders on a pending aircraft deal, was given the following message from Hughes late one night by way of Operations: "I will call you real early in the morning. I hope that you will sleep until I call, that is I hope you will not leave a call with the switchboard girl to awaken you in preparation for my call. I will call you very early and awaken you when I call."[32] Operations also worked to Hughes's advantage by separating the various branches of his empire from one another, allowing him control of each. As a result, one executive rarely knew what another was doing.

THE $400-MILLION ORDER

Of all the companies Hughes controlled through Romaine Street, the most cherished was Trans World Airlines, now one of the world's largest air carriers with more than twenty thousand employees. The tool company produced the profits that made other enterprises possible, but it was TWA on which Hughes lavished his affectionate attention.

In 1939, Hughes began acquiring TWA stock, either on the open market or in exchange for capital he supplied for TWA to acquire passenger planes. By 1944, he owned 45 percent and a controlling interest, although he continued to acquire stock until he owned 78 percent of TWA's outstanding shares. TWA had thousands of other stockholders, but Hughes ignored them and looked on TWA as *his* company. He handpicked most of the directors. He hired and fired presidents. He bypassed the airline's top officers and dealt directly with the staff, whose loyalty he assured by giving them generous retainers from the tool company in addition to their regular TWA salaries. Hughes held no office in TWA, but he was its undisputed boss and dynamic influence.

Of all his properties, it was TWA where Hughes had made his greatest contributions. In 1939, he and TWA president Jack Frye conceived plans for a revolutionary passenger plane. From their rough sketches, Lockheed designed and built the nation's first high-speed, piston-driven passenger plane, the Constellation. The sleek, long-range Connies were the most advanced airplanes of their time when they went into service in 1946. During the war, Hughes's well-placed Washington connections had enabled him to win Civil Aeronautics Board approval, over the opposition of the agency's own staff, for TWA to fly overseas. The decision made TWA unique among American airlines in its substantial mixture of both domestic and foreign routes. The award was made over the bitter opposition of Pan American Airways, which accused the CAB of "gross favoritism to TWA."[33]

Without a doubt, then, Hughes had been instrumental in TWA's growth. But his positive contributions were often offset by a tendency to meddle. Alone in TWA's public-relations office in Kansas City one day, Gordon Molesworth, who had been with TWA less than a week, answered the telephone at lunch hour to find that the caller was Howard Hughes. Explaining that he was new on the job and might not be of much help, Molesworth was stunned when Hughes broke in and told him to fly to Hollywood right away. "I'll have reservations for you, and you are to go to Ciro's [the Hollywood nightclub] where the head waiter will give you further instructions."[34] The bewildered Molesworth flew west and presented himself at Ciro's, where the headwaiter supplied him with a stack of magazines and ice water. At the end of the day, he was told that Hughes could not see him and that he should spend the night at a nearby hotel. The next day, Molesworth learned that Hughes had changed his mind. Molesworth's services were not needed in Hollywood; he was to go back to Kansas City.

Such incidents became almost commonplace at TWA, especially in the public-relations department, one of Hughes's pet divisions. They were part of Hughes's general disregard for standard business practices. He often canceled scheduled TWA flights at the last moment and commandeered an airliner for some personal reason, such as flying a group of Hollywood friends to the East Coast or to Europe. These occurrences created havoc for TWA. Despite Hughes's reputation as a shrewd businessman, he had little regard for TWA's balance sheet. In the first three years after the Second World War, the airline lost a staggering $19 million. That trend was turned around in the early 1950s, but the reversal owed more to the leadership of a new TWA president, Ralph Damon, than to any efforts by Hughes.

As TWA's proprietor, Hughes busied himself primarily with two of the airline's continuing operations—advertising and the purchase of aircraft. As one who had long excelled in Hollywood at extravagant, first-rate promotions for second-rate movies, Hughes naturally took a special interest in extolling TWA's virtues and in bolstering the airline's image. In the fall of 1955, he arranged for TWA to sponsor the weekly radio broadcasts of Walter Winchell. Although the airline's executives were apprehensive about tying TWA's image to Winchell's crusty broadcasts, Hughes was convinced that Winchell would be a valuable ally and insisted that the airline sponsor him. The night TWA debuted as the sponsor, Hughes telephoned Winchell at the Stork Club in New York to congratulate him on the program.[35]

Even more than handing out advertising plums, Hughes delighted in the job of selecting new airplanes for TWA. Of all the airline's operations, it was the one for which he was most qualified. As the man behind the H-1 racer, the Constellation, and the flying boat, Hughes was one of the few airline owners who, in Jack Frye's words, "did have an understanding of the airplane."[36] Since taking over TWA, he had personally selected and helped design the planes that made up TWA's worldwide fleet. Thus, it is the height of irony that aircraft selection would precipitate the next crisis of Hughes's career.

Everybody had known it would happen, but nobody knew when until 1952, when the British, who had pioneered in jet propulsion, inaugurated service on the world's first passenger jetliner, the de Havilland Comet One. The jet age had begun. It was only a matter of time before the world's airlines would convert from groaning, piston-driven machines to powerful, smooth-running jets.

Hughes, who avidly followed each aviation development, was tempted to buy the De Havillands. But he was urged to pass up the opportunity by TWA's chief engineer, Robert W. Rummel, who was convinced that American jets would eventually surpass the British.[37] Hughes had long relied on Rummel's judgment. Their association dated from 1935 when Rummel, then a nineteen-year-old engineering student, had performed the stress analysis on the landing gear and wing skin of the H-1 racer in which Hughes established the land-speed record. Later, Rummel joined TWA at the same time that Hughes was buying control. Their consuming interest in airplanes drew them into a close relationship.

Rummel was an ideal confidant for Hughes, a man to talk with for hours at a time about the most minute and technical aspects of aviation and aircraft design. To review secret plans for proposed aircraft, they often drove into the hills above Los Angeles or met in heavily guarded hotel rooms in Beverly Hills. Mostly, however, they talked on the telephone. Rummel would call Operations and request that Hughes call him. Invariably, one of Bill Gay's polite male secretaries, whom Rummel referred to privately as the "boys in the back room," would ask him to state his business.[38] Knowing Hughes's passion for secrecy in aircraft matters, Rummel would politely refuse to do so. Hughes would always return the call, usually late at night. The tall, mild-mannered Rummel often wound up with no sleep at all.[39] Hughes insisted that a special telephone be installed in Rummel's Kansas City home so that he would not have to compete for the line with the family's five children. Rummel's wife Marjorie grew so tired of the incessant nocturnal chatter that she piled pillows and blankets on the phone one night to muffle the ringing. The next morning, as Rummel passed the stairwell where the phone was housed, he heard a faint ring and reached for the receiver. "Where in the hell were you last night?" Hughes drawled.[40] Working for Hughes was not easy, but for Rummel there was "always excitement about trying to do something new."[41]

Hughes and Rummel sometimes disagreed on what was best for TWA, but Hughes wisely followed his engineer's advice on the de Havilland Comets. Rummel's prediction that American jets would surpass the British soon came true. Early in 1954, Boeing began to design a long-range jet, the 707, and, in a remarkable feat of engineering and production, completed a prototype that spring. It was time to woo the major airlines, including TWA.

Hughes, who prided himself on introducing a number of innovations at TWA, from the Constellation to all-sleeper service to Europe, desperately wanted TWA to be the first airline to introduce jets in the United States.[42] If, however, only Boeing were producing jets, he would not have much leverage in dictating the design features that he felt had long given TWA's planes an individual touch. Further, any features he might suggest would also benefit TWA's competitors. Hughes wanted, as Rummel recalled, to "do the competition one better."[43]

Late in 1954, in nearby San Diego, where a chapter was closing on one of the great success stories in American commercial aviation, Hughes found a solution. At the Convair plant near San Diego Bay, production was winding down on the twin-engine, piston-driven planes of the 240, 340, and 440 series which had made Convair world-famous as a builder of medium-range aircraft. Recently absorbed by the defense conglomerate General Dynamics, Convair was eager to gain a foothold in the emerging jet field. At the suggestion of Hughes, who promised to be the company's first customer, the company began drawing up plans for a long-range jet to rival the Boeing 707.

Convair well knew the risk of doing business with Hughes. Only four years earlier, the company had wasted plenty of time and money trying to sell Hughes a fleet of transports for TWA. Hughes had been so difficult that one Convair executive ruefully joked of negotiations "conducted by flashlight during the small hours of the night, out in the middle of the Palm Springs municipal dump."[44] At the point of contract, Hughes had backed off because TWA's president, Ralph Damon, had committed the airline to another plane. Nevertheless, if Convair wanted a share of the jet field, Hughes appeared to be the company's best hope.

Within a few months, Convair came up with plans for two long-range jets, one a huge plane with six engines, a forerunner of the jumbo jets, and another four-engine model similar to the 707. As the drawings developed in San Diego, they were whisked north to Hughes in Los Angeles. Fascinated by both designs, Hughes succumbed to indecision. He could not make up his mind, and his vacillation proved fatal to the project. In 1955, both Boeing and Douglas Aircraft unveiled mockups of long-range jets, the 707 and the DC-8. That race was over and Convair quickly abandoned its plans for a big jet.

The Boeing and Douglas planes would revolutionize aviation, not only technically, but also financially. With spare parts and engines, each plane cost $4.5 to $6 million. Even so, no airline could afford to stand still while its competitors converted to jets. By the fall of 1955, knowing that TWA had to commit itself to a jet fleet, Rummel recommended to Hughes that TWA order jets so that it would have them at least as soon as its competitors.[45] But Hughes could never be pressured into making a decision. He stolidly refused to act. Fear mounted at TWA that the airline would be outdistanced as commercial air travel entered the jet age.

The fear became reality in October of 1955, when Pan Am ordered a fleet of 707s and DC-8s. Within weeks, United and American followed suit. Now all of Hughes's major rivals would get preferred delivery on the new planes and would therefore introduce jet service months before TWA. As if in a trance, Hughes still did nothing.

Ralph Damon, the airline's president, was under a severe strain, his carefully engineered recovery of TWA jeopardized by Hughes's inaction. Damon warned in December of 1955 that unless the airline moved swiftly to acquire jets it would find itself in "splendid isolation" in the industry, hopelessly "outclassed in speed, comfort, passenger acceptability and economics."[46] A month later, Damon, bitter and frustrated, died of a heart attack.

Damon's death and TWA's obviously worsening competitive position finally moved Hughes to act. In February of 1956, more than three months after other major airlines had ordered jets, he began reserving Boeing 707s, eventually ordering thirty-three planes. Including spare engines and parts, the bill came to $185.9 million, and called for a $39-million down payment. The jets were to be delivered in 1959 and 1960.

Hughes, as usual, was not wholly satisfied with his main solution. In the back of his mind there lurked an old idea, dormant since the Second World War—the design and manufacture of his own planes. A new aircraft plant would require a massive capital expenditure for buildings, land, and equipment —capital which at the moment Hughes lacked. Still, the idea lingered with him, and as a projected site for the new plant, Hughes settled on Florida, a state where he had been spending time the last two years. To those closest to him, Hughes began dropping hints about the new venture.

As usual, Hughes cloaked his scheme in secrecy, advising his trusted confidant Rummel that he did not want anyone at TWA informed.[47] Raymond Cook, a partner in Andrews, Kurth, Campbell & Jones in Houston, who served as an all-around troubleshooter and liaison between Hughes and TWA, dubbed the far-off scheme Project Greenland, a code name that stuck with the few who knew of it.[48] When Rummel, who eagerly followed jet developments worldwide, asked Hughes what type of plane he planned to manufacture, Hughes was vague, saying only that it would be "markedly superior" to those of Boeing and Douglas.[49] Privately, Hughes was stung by the realization that this exciting chapter in aviation was being written without so much as a sentence from him.

On May 10, 1956, Hughes filed an application with the CAB in Washington, seeking permission to build a fleet of jets and to sell twenty-five to TWA and more to other airlines. Special CAB permission was required because the agency's rules prohibit an aircraft manufacturer from owning an airline. As Hughes hoped, his application set the aviation and business world buzzing. "Does Hughes have a design for a plane that will render obsolete the Douglas and Boeing jets?" asked a mystified *Business Week.*[50] Hughes suggested as much in his vaguely worded CAB application. New developments, the application said, "make it possible to design aircraft at this time that are superior in performance, safety and economy to the commercial aircraft now being constructed, the designs for which were laid down four or five years ago."[51]

As one of the seminal forces in aircraft development, Hughes was banking on his reputation to put the planemakers on edge. To some extent he succeeded. There was even speculation that he might be on the road to building a "transonic commercial airliner."[52] With the first generation of jets not yet in production, there was cause for worry by other builders if Hughes had indeed come up with an advanced design.

To those around him, Hughes appeared serious about building his "superior" jet. Options were taken on thousands of acres of land in southern Florida and extensive negotiations were carried on with Governor LeRoy Collins. Early in 1956, Collins, at Hughes's invitation, had flown to California to talk about Hughes's medical institute, then in the planning stage, and another unspecified project. Arriving at the Beverly Hills Hotel, the governor and his staff were treated to a pleasant dinner, during which Hughes asked many questions about Florida and potential industrial sites. The next day, after a tour of the flying boat in Long Beach, Hughes flew Collins to Palm Springs for lunch in one of his private planes. As the party flew back to Los Angeles, a weather report came over the radio proclaiming a smog-free day, and Hughes was ecstatic.

"No smog," he shouted from the pilot's seat, and asked Collins if he had ever seen the lights of Los Angeles at night from the ocean. The governor told him he had not.

"Well," Hughes promised, "you're going to see that."[53]

When Hughes headed the plane out to sea, the governor became slightly uneasy and jokingly asked Hughes if he had enough fuel. Collins also was on edge because the constant chatter over the plane's radio made him feel that the sky was full of airplanes. Only when Hughes steered the plane into an arc above the dark sea and turned back toward land did Collins relax.

"We saw the first lights twinkling and gradually it grew and grew," Collins recalled. "It really was an exciting sort of thing to see. He was so proud of that."[54]

Hughes was at his most charming for Collins. When the governor returned to Florida, he took with him a "tentative commitment" from Hughes to locate two new industries in the state, but he declined to reveal details, saying that a further announcement would come from Hughes.[55] That came three months later. At the same press conference where the location of the Howard Hughes Medical Institute in Florida was announced, the Hughes organization also disclosed that the industrialist intended to "establish in Florida a company which will engage in the design, development and manufacture of airplanes."[56] Hughes spokesmen let it be known that they were searching for a site of up to thirty thousand acres for the aircraft plant, which they predicted would have a work force larger than Hughes Aircraft in Culver City, which then had about twenty thousand employees.

A team of assistants headed by Kay G. Glenn, an assistant to Bill Gay, was dispatched to Miami, presumably as an advance guard for the jet plant. Then, after all the negotiations and the buildup in the press and the grandiose plans, nothing ever came of Project Greenland. At the CAB, the application to build jets languished. Two years later it was withdrawn and Hughes's Miami office was closed. What was one to make of it all? Perhaps the Florida flurry was only a ploy to extract concessions or lower prices from the jet builders. Perhaps it was to remind the world of Hughes's reputation as an aviation pioneer. Or perhaps it was just another in a growing number of business actions that had no rational basis.

Whatever Hughes had in mind for Project Greenland, it was never intended to play any part in TWA's immediate future. While he was toying with Project Greenland, he continued to negotiate for more jets. The Boeing orders had by no means met all of TWA's needs. Unlike Pan Am, whose routes were mostly long-range, TWA had to cover lesser distances also. It needed another jetliner capable of operating off shorter runways and carrying fewer passengers than the 707. Ironically, again Convair seemed to offer a solution. Still eager to manufacture jets, the company came up with a preliminary design that spring of 1956 for a medium-range, four-engine jet capable of seating about eighty passengers.

When Convair passed the rough plans along to Hughes, he was privately enthusiastic and publicly cool. Like anyone else who sought to speak with Hughes, Jack Zevely, the Convair vice-president conducting the negotiations, had to call Operations in Hollywood and leave his name and number. On Monday, May 7, 1956, Hughes gave Operations meticulous orders regarding Zevely:

I do not want anybody to call Zevely unless I specifically tell them to. This is very important as I have a very big deal cooking with him and I don't want to foul it up.

Whenever we talk to him, don't indicate that I'm super anxious to receive the call. Just tell him you'll take the message—be sure and take it very accurately—and then let me know when I ask for my calls. I DO NOT want it volunteered to me at any time. When he calls, just be courteous—don't fall all over yourself so he gets the impression that I'm overly anxious to receive the call—and take the message.[57]

Several days later, Hughes's orders backfired. On Thursday, May 10, Zevely called Operations and asked that Hughes call him. The next day, Hughes spoke to Operations about noon, but apparently did not ask if Zevely had called. And Operations, obeying Hughes's orders, did not volunteer the information. Zevely called back on Friday afternoon and left another message, and on Saturday when Hughes did ask Operations if Zevely had called and learned that the Convair executive had been trying to reach him for two days, he exploded, blaming Operations. Certain that he had asked Operations "several times" if Zevely had called, Hughes demanded to know "the full story on why this call was not given him."[58] It was a side of Hughes familiar to Operations. They let the anger pass. But despite the mixup, Hughes was not about to modify his order. "Do not volunteer anything," he warned Operations again that same night, "just wait until I ask for my list and then tell me."[59]

Despite these delays, Hughes and Convair worked out a contract. In June, Hughes agreed to buy thirty of the new jetliners for $126.4 million. Convair knew that doing business with Hughes would, as one official remarked, probably cost the company "a pile of jack."[60] The company was not even sure whether Hughes would pay for the planes on schedule. But at that late date in jet development, it had no choice but to gamble—Hughes was Convair's only prime customer. And Hughes knew it. He proceeded to extract major concessions from the company, including a provision that after a $26-million down payment, he would not have to pay Convair another cent until the planes were delivered, three years later. Ordinarily, plane builders require progress payments during the manufacturing to defray their enormous capital costs. Such was Convair's desperation that it agreed to dip into its own resources to finance Hughes's jets. Hughes was now publicly enthusiastic about the new plane. He wanted to call it the "Golden Arrow," but Convair eventually decided on a less glamorous name, the Convair 880—in memory, a company executive quipped, of the number of negotiating sessions conducted with Hughes.

With the Convair and Boeing orders and an additional commitment to buy $90 million worth of jet engines from the Pratt & Whitney Aircraft Company, Hughes had committed his tool company to the largest equipment order in aviation history—more than $400 million. Other airlines, equally short of cash at the dawn of the jet age, had turned to banks and insurance companies for long-term financing. This solution had no appeal for Hughes. Lenders usually imposed conditions, and Hughes would not tolerate any restrictions on his freedom to run TWA. In 1946, the Equitable Life Assurance Society had lent TWA $40 million to help finance a postwar fleet of Constellations, and Hughes had come to regret that loan. The Equitable periodically offered advice on managing TWA. Hughes always ignored it, but he was still rankled that any outsider would attempt to intrude. In addition, one feature of TWA's jet program was certain to cause the opposition of lenders. Hughes planned to acquire the jets through the tool company and then lease them to TWA for a fee, rather than allowing TWA to own its planes outright, as was the case with other airlines. In this way, Hughes, always looking for accounting devices to reduce his federal taxes, could charge off the jets' depreciation costs against the profits of the tool company.

WHERE IS THE MONEY?

The question then remained: how would Hughes pay for the jets? He had no clear-cut plan. If he had promptly arranged financing, as other airlines had done, he might have lost some authority at TWA, but he would have retained control. But Hughes could not bear to allow his power to be diluted. Instead, he delayed, hoping that by stalling he would, through his own resources, be able both to raise the capital and to retain complete control of TWA. It was a great miscalculation.

At the Hughes Tool Company in Houston, the fountainhead of Hughes's fortune, the jet orders created a panic among company officers accustomed to disposing of cash rather than having to raise it. Soon after Hughes placed orders for TWA's sixty-three jetliners, the tool company's accountants prepared a "cash forecast" that sent shock waves through the company[61]—the tool company's cash position would become "critical" by early the next year.[62] In Los Angeles, Noah Dietrich, the executive vice-president of the tool company and Hughes's chief financial officer, was equally alarmed. Dietrich was hardened to Hughes's profligate spending on pet projects like the D-2, the flying boat, and various motion pictures, but all past extravagances paled beside the jet orders. Hughes had committed the tool company to a capital program that exceeded the value of the company's assets.

Dietrich was often at odds with other tool company executives in Houston, but in 1956 they were fully united on the threat their leader's latest caper posed to the empire. Both Dietrich and Houston began to press Hughes to arrange financing quickly so as to get the best possible terms. Within the organization, Raymond Cook began a quiet campaign aimed at encouraging Hughes to act. The Houston lawyer suggested to Dietrich that they should "attempt to get Mr. Hughes to focus on this problem so that our bargaining position will not be jeopardized."[63] To make matters worse, as Cook and Dietrich no doubt recognized, Hughes had antagonized many of the eastern money sources he would need to tap for funds. Since Ralph Damon's death in January of that year, Hughes had shown no interest in naming a new president for TWA. The airline was limping along, mismanaged by hostile cliques, and the organizational chaos showed in the balance sheet: TWA lost $2.3 million in 1956. Such casual disregard for the airline was a disquieting note to the financiers, especially the Equitable, one of TWA's creditors.

Within the Hughes empire, there was no way to generate enough cash to pay for the jets. Still, Hughes ignored the pleas of Dietrich and Cook to seek outside financing. In fact, he gave strict orders to Cook that no one was even to discuss financing with potential lenders, for he believed that "a rumor had already started on Wall Street that Hughes Tool Company could not finance this program."[64]

Instead of thinking about money, Hughes concentrated his energies on the color scheme of the Convair 880s. Always intent on giving TWA's aircraft a distinctive appearance, he now was considering having the 880s manufactured in gold-colored aluminum. Hughes asked Jack Zevely to determine the feasibility of gold aluminum. After contacting three aluminum companies and his own experts at Convair, Zevely reported that gold-colored planes could be produced but that no one could guarantee a consistent color match from one section of an airplane's exterior to another.[65] Reluctantly, Hughes gave up on the idea.

Late in 1956, nearly a year after Damon's death, Hughes finally selected another TWA president, Carter L. Burgess, a highly respected thirty-nine-year-old assistant secretary of defense. Known for his hard-driving, aggressive management style, Burgess was an odd choice for Hughes, who liked to bully TWA's presidents. Burgess was as strong-willed as Hughes; he had demonstrated that many times in his Pentagon job. When Defense Secretary Charles E. Wilson was asked how Burgess would get along with Hughes, he turned the question around: "You mean how is Hughes going to get along with Burgess?"[66]

Hughes wasted no time in showing his new president who was boss by embarrassing TWA's chief engineer, Bob Rummel. Shortly before Burgess took office, Rummel had arranged a tour of the Convair plant in San Diego for Burgess to check progress on the 880s. It was to be a ceremonial affair with many Convair and TWA executives in attendance. At 9 A.M., just as Rummel was about to lead Burgess and his delegation into the plant, a messenger rushed up and informed Rummel that Romaine Street had called. Rummel was to go to his motel room and wait. Embarrassed by the untimely interruption, Rummel apologized to Burgess, who was technically his superior, and hurried off to his room. The telephone was ringing when he entered. It was Hughes. When he put down the phone, Rummel's watch read 7 P.M.[67] He had talked nonstop with Hughes for ten hours. The tour was long since over.

At the time Burgess was hired, Hughes and Dietrich were still going "round and round," as Dietrich put it later, over the jet financing.[68] By the end of 1956, tension had built up between them. Hughes's continuing refusal to arrange financing struck Dietrich as irresponsible and potentially catastrophic. Bad feeling had also been mounting between them over an unrelated disagreement. For years, Dietrich had wanted a stock option in one of Hughes's companies. Although he earned a salary of about $500,000 a year, Dietrich paid much of that in federal income taxes. A stock option would be taxed at a lower capital-gains rate. At sixty-seven, Dietrich had done well for himself with Hughes, but he wanted to do better.

As usual, Hughes was not receptive. He was willing to pay almost any salary, grant almost any fringe benefit, but he would not allow anyone the right to acquire stock. Like his father, he disliked partners and minority stockholders. Also, Hughes may very well have felt that he had already provided generously enough for Dietrich over the years. In addition to his substantial salary, Dietrich and his family had free use of tool company houses, cars, and credit cards, and an unlimited expense account. At the time his two sons reached driving age, Dietrich had as many as five Hughes Tool Company Cadillacs assigned to his use.[69] Another source of contention was Dietrich's investments in outside businesses, including some oil leases off Long Beach, despite the fact that Hughes liked all his executives to devote themselves exclusively to him.[70]

With business and financial pressures rising and relations between him and his chief lieutenant increasingly strained, Hughes stepped back and assessed the direction of his life. It was a rare moment of introspection for him. Dispiritedly, he called his boyhood friend, Dudley C. Sharp, whom he had not spoken to in years. Then an assistant secretary of the air force, Sharp was in Tucson inspecting a military plant. To the man who had once been his only friend while growing up in Houston, Hughes poured out his anxieties.

"I've just messed up my life," he told Sharp. "I'm miserable."[71]

Sharp, who was outgoing, optimistic, self-confident—everything Howard had never been—told Hughes there was no reason for his life to continue in the same vein, he could do something about it if he wanted to. But Hughes was in no mood for a pep talk.

"No," he answered, a touch of finality in his voice. "I have just messed it up so much there is nothing I can do about it now."[72] It was the last time Sharp ever heard from his friend.

CHAPTER 9

BREAKDOWN

MYSTERIOUS MARRIAGE

IF any one word might be used to describe Howard Hughes in the years prior to 1960, that word would be *unpredictable*. He hardly ever behaved as others behaved. In late 1956 he proved that once again. With the jet financing still unsettled, the fight with Dietrich at a high boil, and his life turning inward, Hughes married a second time. The choice of partner, Jean Peters, was not as surprising as the event itself. Howard had met Jean in 1946 and they were an off-and-on couple for many years. In one of the off periods Jean had married Stuart W. Cramer III, a wealthy socialite-businessman, and very quickly separated from him, filing for divorce. The relationship with Hughes resumed as before, and about the time the decree became final Hughes asked Jean to marry him.*

Also unexpected was the site of the ceremony—Tonopah, Nevada, an all-but-abandoned silver-mining town two hundred miles northwest of Las Vegas. Jean had never heard of Tonopah and she had "no idea" why the wedding ceremoney was to be held there.[1] Nor, apparently, did she ask. On the morning of January 12, 1957, a curious wedding party gathered for the flight. Years later, Jean could not remember all of their names. "I know Marty Cook was there and [George] Francom, and I think Roy Crawford [and] perhaps Levar Myler," she said, referring to four of Hughes's personal aides.[2] Apparently no women accompanied Jean to her wedding. Most of the aides

---

*After the Cramer–Peters divorce, Cramer married one of Hughes's former girlfriends, the actress Terry Moore. After Hughes died, Miss Moore claimed that she, too, had once married Hughes, aboard a yacht at sea, in a civil ceremony, the records of which, she claimed, were subsequently tossed overboard.

Jean Peters,
Hughes's second
wife.
Bettmann Archive

did not know why the trip was taking place. (George Francom only learned of the marriage on the return flight to Los Angeles.)[3] Boarding one of Hughes's Constellations, piloted by a TWA captain and a copilot, they flew the short distance to Tonopah, landing at an abandoned army air base outside of town, and were met there by James Arditto, a Hughes lawyer from Los Angeles who had made arrangements for the marriage. Howard and Jean sat in the front seat next to Arditto while he drove the thirty minutes or so into town, to a nondescript motel, whose name, too, is lost, and led the couple through the lobby, up a flight of stairs, and into a second-floor room where a justice of the peace was waiting to perform the ceremony. For privacy's sake the couple used assumed names, as is legal in Nevada—G. A. Johnson for Hughes and Marian Evans for Jean.[4] The ceremony over, everybody returned to the abandoned airfield, boarded the Constellation, and flew back to Los Angeles. The entire operation took about three hours.

When the Hughes–Peters marriage was disclosed, Hollywood hailed it as the perfect union. The two were obviously fond of each other, or so it seemed, given the number of times their names had been romantically linked. Also Hughes, so long identified with glamorous actresses, would of course marry one of Hollywood's loveliest women. It also seemed natural that Jean, who still commanded a wholesome, all-American image at the age of thirty, would choose a husband cut from a heroic mold rather than some shallow Hollywood type. Hughes had said he would not remarry until he was fifty; he had just turned fifty-one.

Still, it was in most ways a strange time for Hughes to take such a step. For months he had been absorbed by the TWA and Dietrich dilemmas. Why remarry now after almost thirty years of bachelorhood? Perhaps he had promised Jean. Perhaps he was afraid of losing her again. Perhaps it was only an impulse. Much evidence points, however, not to these apparent and all-too-human possibilities, but to an interpretation that the marriage was one of convenience, prompted by a special set of circumstances.

At the bottom of it was Hughes's already apparent mental instability, a condition Hughes was well aware of. By late 1956, Hughes was fearful that Noah Dietrich was about to have him declared mentally incompetent. The evidence is sketchy as to whether Dietrich was in fact exploring this possibility, but there is no doubt that Hughes's mental condition had become a subject for concern within the empire. A confidential 1958 memorandum written by Raymond Cook, one of Hughes's Houston lawyers, said Dietrich had told Cook that he had been approached by two people—one, a Hughes lawyer otherwise unidentified, and the other, Dr. Verne Mason, Hughes's Hollywood physician—about cooperating in a move to have the industrialist committed.[5] Although it is not clear who actually initiated the discussion, Hughes apparently believed it was Dietrich. Such a move by Dietrich, if successful, would wrest control of his empire from Hughes. What better way to counter the move than to marry? An involuntary commitment, or a court-supervised guardianship, would be difficult if not impossible to arrange without the cooperation of Jean.

In any case, the life of the newlyweds after their return to Los Angeles strongly confirms that the marriage was based on something other than passion. They continued to live separately, Hughes in one bungalow at the Beverly Hills Hotel and Jean in another. They visited occasionally and sometimes traveled together. But it was hardly a close marriage.

In the weeks following the marriage, the feud with Dietrich intensified. Dietrich hardened his demands that Hughes arrange the TWA financing and give him a stock option. Hughes procrastinated. A bitter impasse developed. Then, on the evening of May 12, 1957, a Sunday, Hughes asked Dietrich to stop by the Beverly Hills Hotel. When Dietrich arrived, Hughes refused to see him. Instead, according to Dietrich, Hughes asked him over the telephone to go to Houston at once. His mission: to increase the tool company's profits, a crucial assignment in view of Hughes's need to raise capital for the TWA jets. Reluctantly, Dietrich agreed, but only on condition that Hughes sign an agreement granting the long-sought stock option. "You're holding a gun to my head," Hughes protested.[6] Dietrich said that unless the agreement was signed, he was through. "Starting when?"[7] Hughes countered. "Right now," answered Dietrich.[8] A moment later, both hung up.

Hughes quickly called Bill Gay at home, told him he had just fired Dietrich, and ordered him over to Romaine Street immediately to seize Dietrich's papers and change all the building's locks.[9] At Romaine, Gay and Nadine Henley called together secretaries, accountants, and others who worked under Dietrich and told them that Hughes had fired their boss. They were to pledge their loyalty to Hughes as a condition of staying on the payroll. Thus, with a swift and brutal efficiency was the thirty-two-year-long association of Howard Hughes and Noah Dietrich, an association that dated almost from the day of Hughes's arrival in Los Angeles, brought to an end. As far as is known, the two never saw or spoke to each other again.

Although he had been ruthless in its execution, Hughes was traumatized by the break with Dietrich. He had come to rely heavily on the gruff-talking little man sixteen years his senior. Dietrich had played such a unique role in his life, a combination business manager, restraining hand, and father figure, that over the years he had become almost indispensable, particularly for the most delicate assignments. As Hughes's majordomo, Dietrich had performed a variety of them, as he later acknowledged, from smuggling liquor into California to making a $100,000 payoff to the Democratic party to kill a criminal investigation of one of Hughes's companies. Now, during the gravest business and financial crisis of Hughes's life, Dietrich was suddenly gone; and there was no one to take his place.

Rather than face the impending financial chaos, Hughes decided to get away for a while. Less than two weeks after the break, he flew to Montreal with an entourage of staff men. Although he and Jean had been married only four months, she did not go. Ostensibly, the reason for the trip was to test-fly two turboprop airliners, the Vickers Viscount and the Bristol Britannia, which Hughes was considering for TWA. As a buying trip it made no sense, however, since Hughes had not yet arranged to raise the $400 million for the TWA jets and engines already on order. As usual, Hughes said little to his aides about the purpose of the trip, but he did assure them it would be brief. Once the plane was purring toward Montreal, Hughes stepped out of the cockpit and walked back to the cabin to talk to Bill Gay and two other Romaine Street aides, John Holmes and Charles Woodcock.[10] "You guys are always worried about me hijacking you," he told them. "This trip won't take more than seven to ten days at the most."[11]

In Montreal, at the Ritz-Carlton Hotel, Gay acted as liaison with Romaine while Holmes and Woodcock looked after Hughes's personal needs, serving his carefully prepared food, supplying newspapers and magazines, and attending to other errands. When Woodcock burned himself severely under a sunlamp and had to return to Los Angeles, the job of waiting on Hughes fell exclusively to Holmes, an anonymous-looking little man with a salesman's gift for conversation. This was a good opportunity for Holmes, who was gradually moving into prominence on Hughes's staff. He had lived his entire life in Southern California, graduating from Los Angeles High School in 1935 and then attending Loyola University for a few months before dropping out to become a cigarette salesman for P. Lorillard Company. During the war, Holmes tested guns on Douglas Aircraft's A-20 attack bomber, then became a Johnson's Wax salesman. He went to work for Hughes Productions in 1949, and like most at Romaine Street, began by chaperoning starlets, taking them shopping, to dinner or drama lessons, often accompanied by his wife. In one way, however, Holmes was different from the others at Romaine. He was not a Mormon, but a Catholic. And he smoked. Despite these handicaps, he was a quick student of Hughes's ways and by the time of the Montreal trip, Hughes increasingly liked to have Johnny Holmes around.

In Montreal, Hughes, always fastidious, grew more so, particularly about his food. One day, while eating a dish of French vanilla ice cream, his favorite flavor, he spied a trace of strawberry. Immediately the dish was sent away and a change of brand decreed.[12] To assure that his steaks were prepared on a newly cleaned grill, he instructed waiters to oversee the cooking. The cart on which his dinner would be wheeled into the suite was to remain outside the kitchen while the meal was prepared; Hughes feared it might pick up a sticky substance on the kitchen floor and arrive with a cockroach or some other insect clinging to its wheels.[13]

The "seven- to ten-day" Montreal excursion lengthened into weeks, then months. While Jean remained in Los Angeles, however, Hughes was not without a female companion. Yvonne Shubert, one of the attractive young women Hughes had promised to make a star, flew in for a visit. Finally, in August, after three months, Hughes made plans to leave, not west for Los Angeles, but south to the Bahamas.

In Nassau, where he lived in a suite at the Emerald Beach Hotel, the weeks again slipped by. Ignoring the financing crisis that awaited him back in the States, he weighed the possibility of making real estate investments in the islands. Although the source of the money for any new business venture was not apparent, Hughes nonetheless brought Robert Maheu to Nassau to serve as his envoy to the "Bay Street boys," the bankers, lawyers, and real-estate brokers who controlled the islands, where a real-estate boom was just beginning. Jean Peters even flew in for a time, and she and Hughes went out to look at houses, giving rise to speculation that Hughes might relocate in the Bahamas. But nothing came of the house hunting and Jean returned to California. And nothing came of Hughes's proposed Bahamian investments either. In November, after a six-month absence from California and no nearer to a solution for the jet-financing crunch, Hughes and his crew flew back to Los Angeles.

CRISIS

Once again he lived in the Beverly Hills Hotel, this time in Bungalow 4. Jean was already at the hotel, but in another part of the compound, in Bungalow 19. She thought they should live in the same bungalow, but Hughes told her it was not possible for the moment—he was too preoccupied with TWA and other business matters. Hughes's entourage leased a series of bungalows nearby to house the burgeoning support crew he now required. Bungalow 1-C was for the cooks and waiters. Bungalow 1-A, the storage house, was piled high with cases of Poland water and cartons of Kleenex. Another bungalow was occupied by a crew of messengers, doormen, and assorted helpers—whom Hughes called the "third man" detail.[14] This unit delivered whatever Hughes demanded—newspapers, magazines, Kleenex. When Hughes did not want John Holmes with him, Holmes camped out in Bungalow 1-C. Holmes supervised the preparation of the meals and also began taking dictation, a task performed almost exclusively by Gay until he had become ill in the Bahamas.[15]

The "third man" came under the supervision of Roy E. Crawford, another rising aide. A Mormon, Crawford was in charge of a Romaine Street division called "Special Services," whose duties consisted in good part of sealing Hughes's new residences with masking tape to keep out dust. With a 1937 degree from Wooster College, where he majored in geology, Crawford was one of the few with a college degree on Hughes's personal staff. He had been a navy flight instructor during the Second World War, and a salesman for a refining company in Southern California before going to work at Operations as a telephone operator for seventy dollars a week in 1950.

Hughes rarely left his bungalow now except to fly or to watch movies late at night with Jean at the Goldwyn Studios in Hollywood. While guards kept everyone else out, the couple would watch as many as three films before being driven back to their separate bungalows. On many nights Hughes returned to the studio to "screen" more movies—he always used the Hollywood term "screen"—and sometimes stayed in the studio for several days straight.[16] This continued until Hughes learned that the all-black cast of *Porgy and Bess*, then being filmed at Goldwyn, was using the same screening room. He never went back,[17] but he and Jean began instead to use the private screening room of the producer Martin Nosseck on Sunset Boulevard in West Hollywood.[18]

As pressure mounted on Hughes to solve the TWA financing dilemma, he retreated further from reality. One night, after escorting Jean back to her bungalow, Hughes returned to the Nosseck screening room and told his aides that he planned to live there for a while. And so he did, for several months. Attended around the clock by aides, guards, and projectionists, seated in his own white leather chair, Hughes never left the studio. He spent his time talking on the telephone to lawyers or bankers about TWA, screening movies, rearranging half a dozen Kleenex boxes into various geometric shapes on an end table beside him, or sitting in the bathroom.[19]

His menu remained constant—"fresh whole milk, Hershey bars with almonds, pecan nuts and Poland water," delivered in a brown Kraft paper bag each day by John Holmes, and presented ritually.[20] At a signal, Holmes

would walk into the studio and walk down the right-hand side to the right of Mr. Hughes' chair. He would stand immediately along side of the chair. He would stop there until such time Mr. Hughes looked over and recognized him or said something to him. At that point he would walk over and stand in front of Mr. Hughes and would roll back the outer edges of the bag and would bend over, hold the bag at approximately a 45-degree angle from his body and at that time Mr. Hughes would take Kleenex and reach into the bag and pull out the contents one by one.[21]

For weeks, Hughes wore the same white shirt and brown slacks. Then one day he discarded his clothes and went about naked. He told his small group of retainers that they were not to talk to him; anything to be communicated must be written down.[22] Because he refused to touch doorknobs, when he wanted to leave the studio to go the bathroom in the lobby, he walked to the door and kicked it, a signal for one of the aides in the projection booth to come out and open the door. Suffering from severe bouts of constipation, most likely as a result of his prolonged usage of codeine, Hughes sat in the bathroom for long periods, once for twenty-six hours. He was as likely to urinate on the floor as in the toilet, but he refused to allow the janitors to clean, choosing instead to spread paper towels around and to wrap "all of the porcelain parts of the bathroom fixtures in the paper towels."[23] He also banned his projectionists and guards from the bathroom, suggesting they use milk cartons to relieve themselves.

Hughes did not tell Jean where he was. He called her often, but denied he was living at Nosseck's, and on one occasion told her that he was ill, in a hospital undergoing treatment for an undiagnosed disease.[24] Late in the summer of 1958, Hughes abruptly moved back to the Beverly Hills Hotel.

There, in the seclusion of Bungalow 4, he suffered his second, and most damaging, mental breakdown. In addition to a total disregard for personal hygiene—he now urinated against the bathroom door—Hughes threw tantrums and babbled incoherently, beyond reach until one night, in desperation, Holmes telephoned Jack Real, a Lockheed executive Hughes had known for twelve years and with whom he had hit it off.[25] For hours Hughes and Real discussed over the phone the intricacies of aircraft engines and airplanes. It became a pattern, repeated nightly, as the technical chatter with Real became a form of much-needed therapy.[26] With his second collapse, Hughes ceased virtually all contact with the outside world. He no longer met bankers or businessmen, no longer drove to clandestine negotiating sessions in such remote locations as the city dump or a deserted street in the hills. Even women were shut out of his daily life. He did not see Jean for months. And the only other woman in his life, Yvonne Shubert, came to the bungalow only once, on December 24, 1958, his fifty-third birthday.

The white leather chair had been moved back to the Beverly Hills Hotel, and Hughes spent almost all his time sitting naked in it in the center of the living room—an area he called the "germ-free zone"[27]—his long legs stretched out on the matching ottoman facing a movie screen, watching one motion picture after another. The furniture had been pushed back against the walls and the floor was piled high with stacks of old film cans, magazines, and newspapers. Although he rarely read anything, Hughes insisted on receiving every edition of the Los Angeles dailies. As newspapers accumulated, aides stacked them so as to leave aisles just wide enough for one person, criss-crossing the room. Each day Hughes painstakingly used Kleenex to wipe "dust and germs" from his chair, ottoman, side table, and telephone. Sometimes he spent hours methodically cleaning the telephone, going over the earpiece, mouthpiece, base, and cord with Kleenex, repeating the cleaning procedure again and again, tossing the used tissues onto a pile behind his chair.[28]

By now, Hughes's obsessive-compulsive behavior—his fear of germs and contamination and the rituals he devised to deal with those fears—was dominating his life. He dictated a torrent of memoranda aimed at preventing the "backflow" or "back transmission" of germs to him. In one, three pages long and single-spaced, he explained how he wanted a can of fruit opened: "The equipment used in connection with this operation will consist of the following items: 1 unopened newspaper, 1 sterile can opener; 1 large sterile plate; 1 sterile fork; 1 sterile spoon; 2 sterile brushes; 2 bars of soap; sterile paper towels."[29]

Hughes outlined nine steps for opening the can: preparing a table, procuring of fruit can, washing of can, drying the can, processing the hands, opening the can, removing fruit from can, fallout rules while around can, and conclusion of operation. Hughes detailed how each step was to be accomplished. In Step No. 3, "Washing of Can," he wrote:

The man in charge then turns the valve in the bathtub on, using his bare hands to do so. He also adjusts the water temperature so that it is not too hot nor too cold. He then takes one of the brushes, and, using one of the bars of soap, creates a good lather, and then scrubs the can from a point two inches below the top of the can. He should first soak and remove the label, and then brush the cylindrical part of the can over and over until all particles of dust, pieces of paper label, and, in general, all sources of contamination have been removed. Holding the can in the center at all times, he then processes the bottom of the can in the same manner, being very sure that the bristles of the brush have thoroughly cleaned all the small indentations on the perimeter of the bottom of the can. He then rinses the soap from the cylindrical sides and the bottom of the can.[30]

When the fruit was dished onto the plate, Hughes wanted "fallout rules" in effect: "Be sure that no part of the body, including the hands, be directly over the can or the plate at any time. If possible, keep the head, upper part of the body, arms, etc. at least one foot away from the can of fruit and the sterile plate at all times." During the procedure, there must be "absolutely no talking, coughing, clearing of the throat, or any movement whatsoever of the lips."[31]

To make absolutely certain that, with a few authorized exceptions, no one would come in contact with any of the supplies stored in an adjoining bungalow for his use, Hughes issued explicit orders:

No matter how extreme the emergency, no matter how unusual the circumstances may be, no matter what may have arisen, it is extremely important to me that nobody ever goes into any room, closet, cabinet, drawer, bathroom or any other area used to store any of the things which are for me—either food, equipment, magazines, paper supplies, Kleenex—no matter what. It is equally important to me that nobody ever opens any door or opening to any room, cabinet or closet or anything used to store any of my things, even for one-thousandth of an inch, for one-thousandth of a second. I don't want the possibility of dust or insects or anything of that nature entering.[32]

Anytime an aide, an aide's spouse, or someone close to Romaine Street contracted anything resembling a contagious disease, he or she was immediately placed in "isolation"—off-limits to all Romaine Street personnel. When Hughes learned that Cissy Francombe, a former wardrobe mistress of Jean Peters, had hepatitis, he was terrified.

"Although we have had reason to put into effect a program of isolation before," he wrote Bill Gay,

I want this to be ten times as effective as any we have ever set up before. With the present condition of my business affairs, which in my opinion are in a state of danger and hazard, I am sure if Jean, myself, you, or anyone else important in our organization were to acquire this disease, I just cannot even contemplate the seriousness of what the result might be. I therefore want a system of isolation with respect to Cissy, the doctors attending her, nurses, or anyone in the past or future coming in contact with her, set up that is so effective and complete that anything we have done in the past will be nothing compared to it. I want this to go through the eighth or tenth generation, so to speak. This is one case where incrimination by association is definitely to be recognized. I want this situation to be investigated to see who has been near Cissy in the immediate past and those people are to be included in the program. I consider this the most important item on the agenda, more important than our TWA crisis, our financial crisis or any of our other problems.[33]

Even Bill Gay was placed in isolation in the summer of 1958 after Hughes found out that Gay's wife Mary had a contagious disease. Hughes ordered Gay to work at home so as to avoid passing germs to other staff members and thence to Hughes.[34] But unbeknownst to Hughes, Gay rented offices at 17000 Ventura Boulevard, about six blocks from his Encino home, and with the help of fellow Romaine Street Mormons Richmond Anderson, Rand Clark, Gil Reed, and Hal Tucker, established a satellite operations center, the very existence of which remained a secret to all but a handful of people in the Hughes empire for years to come.[35] Hughes kept Gay in isolation long after Mary Gay had recovered. In fact, it was not until 1973—fifteen years later—that Hughes allowed Gay in his presence again.

Hughes drafted special orders for the drivers and aides to follow that covered almost every conceivable situation. When escorting Jean Peters to the movies, they were instructed, "If [it is] necessary to open the doors entering the theater or closing the doors, do so with the feet, not the hands. If it is necessary or common procedure to enter the theater with her to lower the seat for her, do so with Kleenex."[36] In going to and from assignments, they were directed not to stop for anything—"a package of matches, cigarettes, papers, groceries, drug supplies and so forth."[37] This meant, they were told, "that if they are stopping for a red light and there is a boy selling papers in the street and even though he might have many papers and they feel like they will not waste any time getting the paper by picking one out from the center of the pile, HRH does not want you to do this either."[38] In any houses that were rented for possible future use by Hughes, he warned that "there is to be no meat grinder of any kind either as a separate unit or in connection with a mixing unit in any house. Any such grinders are to be boxed separately and stored in a location away from the premises."[39] There were even special procedures to be followed in removing his hearing-aid cord from the cabinet where it was stored:

First use six or eight thicknesses of Kleenex pulled one at a time from the slot in touching the door-knob to open the door to the bathroom. The door is to be left open so there will be no need to touch anything when leaving the bathroom. The same sheaf of Kleenex may be employed to turn on the spigots so as to obtain a good force of warm water. This Kleenex is to then be disposed of. A sheaf of six to eight Kleenexes is then to be used to open the cabinet containing the soap, and a fresh bar of soap that has never been opened is to be used. All Kleenex used up to this point is to be disposed of. The hands are to be washed with extreme care, far more thoroughly than they have ever been washed before, taking great pains that that the hands do not touch the sides of the bowl, the spigots, or anything in the process. Great care should also be exercised when setting the soap down on the soap dish or whatever it is set on to assure that the hands do not come in contact with anything. A sheaf of fifteen to twenty fresh Kleenexes are next to be used to turn off the spigots and the Kleenex is then to be thrown away. (It is to be understood that while each Kleenex tissue as it is normally pulled from a box consists of a double thickness actually, when one Kleenex is referred to, one of these double Kleenexes is meant). The door to the cabinet is to be opened using a minimum of fifteen Kleenexes. (Great care is to be exercised in opening and closing the doors. They are not to be slammed or swung hastily so as to raise any dust, and yet exceeding care is to be exercised against letting insects in). Nothing inside the cabinet is to be touched—the inside of the doors, the top of the cabinet, the sides—no other objects inside the cabinet are to be touched in any way with the exception of the envelope to be removed. The envelope or package is to be removed using a minimum of fifteen Kleenexes. If it is necessary to use both hands, then fifteen Kleenexes are to be used for each hand. (It is to be understood that these fifteen Kleenexes are to be sterile on both sides of each tissue with the exception of the very outermost edge of the tissue. The center of the tissue only should come in contact with the object being picked up). If something is on top of the package to be removed, a sterile instrument is to be used to lift it off.[40]

ASYLUM

If Howard Hughes had had a friend in the world in 1958, that person would now have encouraged or arranged psychiatric care for him before it was too late. But, always the loner, Hughes had no true friends and no close family ties, no one to say, "Howard, you need help." Instead, those around him did just the opposite. They encouraged his wildest obsessive-compulsive actions and indulged his fantasy that the greatest threat to the empire was indeed an invisible army of death-dealing germs.

Ever so slowly, but ever so surely, Bungalow 4 at the Beverly Hills Hotel had become Howard Hughes's private mental institution—his very own asylum. The aides were attendants, men who came in shifts to bring him chocolate bars, Kleenex, water, newspapers, and movies. They catered to his every demand, no matter how bizarre, no matter how irrational, no matter how degrading, no matter how foolish or injurious to his personal or corporate well-being, and they helped create the make-believe world in which he lived. In the years to come the asylum would change locations. But Hughes would remain very much within its confines for the rest of his life.

Like any mental hospital, the Hughes asylum had its own rigidly enforced rules. But unlike a legitimate institution, where the rules are designed to assist the patient to recognize and overcome his disorders in thought and behavior, the Beverly Hills asylum had rules that served only to move Hughes along on his journey into madness. Romaine Street meticulously developed a "procedures manual" that set down instructions on how, in a "sterile" manner, to set a table, guard an airplane, deliver cans of film. In addition to promulgating its own procedures—every bit as divorced from reality as those of Hughes—Romaine Street recorded, word for word, every directive of Hughes, however irrational, and added it to the ever-expanding operations manual. The patient was writing the rules, and the asylum staff was not only following them to the letter but helping him to make them up.

The practice of codifying Hughes's every thought into a body of corporate law for the empire, begun a few years earlier, grew more precise, more bizarre with each year. It had started innocuously enough. When Hughes expressed an interest in some subject, whether a crowd scene in a film or the food he was eating, Romaine Street immediately produced a memorandum. So it was the day Hughes indicated that he especially liked a grilled cheese sandwich he had just eaten, calling it "the best he'd ever tasted."[41] Under the subject heading "Grilled Cheese Sandwiches," Romaine Street issued this report:

Sandwiches were procured from Huff's, 7920 Sunset Boulevard (HOllywood 7-7324), which is open twenty-four hours a day. Two grilled whole-wheat cheese and tomato sandwiches and one grilled whole-wheat sandwich without tomato were ordered—the tomato slices to be skinned. The waitress and cook were requested to be certain that any knife or cutting board, anything touching the sandwiches, be free from the odor of onion. The bread used looked like the usual bakery wheat bread and may not have been entirely whole-wheat. To make a grilled cheese sandwich, the grill cook followed this procedure: two pieces of heavily buttered bread were placed separately on the grill, buttered sides down and a slice of cheese was placed on each. Then, after sufficient grilling, the two slices were joined to form one sandwich. For a tomato and cheese sandwich, the same process was followed, except that skinned tomato slices were placed on one of the grilling bread slices, on top of the cheese. When grilled enough, the other slice of bread was put on top of the slice with the tomato.[42]

Romaine Street was now matching Hughes bizarre memorandum for bizarre memorandum. When Hughes asked John Holmes to arrange for the delivery of some clothing stored at Romaine Street, Holmes prepared an "operating memorandum"—subsequently "placed in a confidential file for future use"—that spelled out the steps a Romaine deliveryman was to follow in obtaining and bringing three boxes of shirts, trousers, and shoes to the Beverly Hills Hotel. As set forth by Holmes, the operation called for "a brand new knife, never used," a fresh box of Kleenex, and a newspaper to be placed "on a table or a desk as your working area."[43] After slicing open the Kleenex box with the sterile knife, the deliveryman was to build two stacks of fifty Kleenexes each on the newspaper. The twin stacks of tissues, officially designated as "paddles," then were to be used to handle the boxes, thereby ensuring that the deliveryman's skin would not come in contact with the boxes that contained the clothing, let alone the clothing itself. Throughout the procedure, the deliveryman was instructed to hold his head "at a 45-degree angle" so as not to breathe on his "paddles" and other equipment. As Holmes cautioned,

The thing to be careful of during the operation so as not to breathe upon the various items would be things like the knife, the box of Kleenex, the virgin newspaper, the sheets of Kleenex themselves, or the two paddles, the boxes you are to handle and the other boxes you have to handle to get at the boxes you need and also the unopened newspaper which you will be putting in the back seat of your car.

When the deliveryman arrived at Holmes's location, he was instructed: "You are to open the door but we are not to talk. I might do this in two or three operations. I will then use some paddles I have made for taking these up to the boss."[44]

On another occasion, Hughes asked Bill Gay to conduct a survey of grocery stores and devise a germ-free method to buy groceries that would "result in the best sanitation possible."[45] Hughes had laid down some specific guidelines, including the use of a three-man detail—"one man who drives the car and pays for the items, another man who handles the goods, and the third man who would open doors."[46] Hughes directed Gay to exclude from the survey stores that sold meat—he believed meat, especially pork products, was contaminated. If Jean Peters wanted soup, he suggested the grocery detail should not "buy the product of the company which also puts meat products in other cans."[47] And at wholesale stores, he warned, "it is possible that a case of meat might have spilled and the contents spread around by being carried on the feet of the workers and get into the area where no meat products are stored."[48]

Gay responded by producing a memorandum of high concern with supermarket germs. Listing the stores that would best fulfill Hughes's requirements, Gay recommended a market in Loma Linda on the campus of the College of Medical Evangelists:

This market is owned and operated by Seventh Day Adventists. One of the tenets of this faith is to refrain from eating any meat of any kind. The clientele they serve are almost entirely non-meat-eaters, and all food stuffs they handle are carefully screened to eliminate any meat, meat products, meat stocks in soups, pork baked in beans, etc.

No other food or meat stores in close proximity to this market. Their produce is not organically grown.[49]

If canned goods and staples were to be purchased wholesale, Gay recommended Smart & Final:

Their head canned foods buyer states that what few meat products they handle are canned back in the midwest. Their fruits and vegetables are obtained by contract with a number of different canning plants on the west coast, and he knows no cannery where fruits and vegetables are packed that also packs any meat products. With a store room set-up, these cases could be obtained, using all of our procedures, and then individual cans could be taken out and used as needed.[50]

Working with Hughes, Romaine Street compiled hundreds of individual instructions that drivers were required to follow: "When driving special HRH passengers," an operating memorandum directed,

the following driving rules should be religiously followed: The party being driven is to be seated in the back seat (except in cases of car sickness). The party should be properly escorted to the car and from the car at destination and given proper assistance when entering and exiting the car. The speed of the car should not exceed thirty-five miles per hour at any time and then this speed should be governed only by perfectly smooth roads. Ample time should be allowed in order that this speed limit be adhered to at all times. When crossing any bump, dip, swale, ditch, railroad track or any uneven part of any road the speed should be reduced to such a minimum speed that the car can move over the uneven part of the road with no violent motion that would tend to disturb the position of the party. (Two miles per hour has been suggested as such a speed going over rough or uneven roads).[51]

The reduction of speed to two miles an hour on bumpy roads was especially important when the passenger was a woman, usually one of Hughes's erstwhile actresses, because Hughes believed that any jarring motions at a higher speed would damage the breasts.

For a driver delivering film to the bungalow, the rules were equally exacting:

Park one foot from the curb on Crescent near the place where the sidewalk dead-ends into the curb. Get out of the car on the traffic side. Do not at any time be on the side of the car between the car and the curb. When unloading film do so from the traffic side of the car, if the film is in the rear seat. If it is in the trunk, stand as close to the center of the road as possible while unloading. Carry only one can of film at a time. Step over the gutter opposite the place where the sidewalk dead-ends into the curb from a point as far out into the center of the road as possible. Do not ever walk on the grass at all, also do not step into the gutter at all. Walk to the bungalow keeping as near to the center of the sidewalk as possible. Do not sit the film cans down on the sidewalk or the street or anywhere else, except possibly on the porch of the Bungalow area if the third man is not there. While waiting for the third man to arrive, do not lean against any portion of the bungalow or the furniture on the porch, but remain there standing quietly and await his arrival. When the third man clears the door, step inside quickly carrying the can (single) of film, just far enough to be inside. Do not move and do not say anything and do not sit the film down until you receive instructions where to sit it. If possible, stay two feet away from the TV set, the wire on the floor and the walls. When leaving, kick on the door and step outside quickly as soon as the third man opens the door.[52]

As in any mental hospital, there were strict rules at the Hughes asylum governing drugs, but they were quite different from the rules found in a legitimate institution. These rules spelled out how drugs and narcotics, and even medications for legitimate medical reasons, were to be acquired through fraudulent prescriptions. The purpose of the regulations was to insure that Hughes's use of drugs was kept secret from the world at large.

Indeed, only a very few trusted lieutenants within the Hughes organization were aware of Hughes's drug habit, notably Bill Gay, Kay Glenn, John Holmes, and Roy Crawford. Whenever possible, a messenger service was used to deliver a prescription to a specially selected drugstore. The messenger would leave the prescription at the pharmacy—he was paid by the drugstore, which added the the charge to the prescription bill—and one of Hughes's trusted aides would pick it up. Naturally, when the order was placed with the messenger service, there was no mention of Hughes, anyone employed by Hughes, or any address that could be connected to the Hughes organization.

According to the "operating memorandum" on drug acquisition, prepared at Hughes's direction, the following procedure was in force:

If Kay or Bill is masterminding the deal, then have Roy handle the delivering and filling of the prescription (make sure that nobody knows the name or address that is connected with the prescription, or the company's name). When you are talking to the messenger service, tell him: "This is Dr. Hawkin's secretary calling, (Do not use Roy's or any of our people's name) would you please go to such and such address and pick up a prescription and take it to Horton & Converse drug store at such and such address. They will pay you and just put the amount on our bill." Then, Roy should go over and supervise the filling of the prescription. If Roy is out of town, then maybe before he goes he should leave instructions with Kay or Bill, or both, as to the name of drug store and the clerk who does this service for him and also get the name of the messenger service from Roy, as Roy has been doing this for some time now.[53]

There were special orders for Roy Crawford, who had assumed increasing responsibility for the drug buying. Hughes did not want Crawford used indiscriminately. "If the prescription is for Jean, then Roy isn't used at all," the operating memorandum directed, but "if it is for HRH then Roy will do the whole thing, telephoning, supervision and delivery. Do not ever use Roy in a dry-run operation, in other words, if you are trying out a fake operation, do not use Roy in that operation."[54] As for the names placed on the prescriptions, Hughes ordered, "if it is for me, then use the names that Roy has been using. [The name was that of the wife of a low-level Romaine Street functionary.] If it is for Mrs. Hughes, then I would use the name of her aunt. . . ."[55]

The decision to pander to Hughes's phobias and obsessions, and to carry out the unlawful chores he assigned, was a conscious one. It was made by

Romaine Street, most likely by Bill Gay, who had established Operations and hired the men who manned it. No one else had such an intimate knowledge of Hughes's deteriorating mental condition and growing dependence on drugs and narcotics, having waited on him almost daily for ten years before being placed in "isolation." The men Gay hired, first for Operations and then the asylum staff, proved ideal for the task of looking after the inmate. Almost without exception they were cut from the same mold—former truck drivers, construction workers, mechanics, salesmen—men who stood little chance of rising or making big money in a conventional company, but who in Hughes's topsy-turvy world had the opportunity to do both. By becoming willing participants in Hughes's fantasies, they assured themselves of fabulous salaries, lavish expense accounts, the fringe benefits of a corporate executive, and secure financial futures far beyond what their talents would command in the ordinary business world. By going along with Hughes's aberrant behavior, they also made certain that he would never emerge from his asylum. The process now underway would eventually lead to his complete mental deterioration. For the present, Hughes was an inmate in his institution as well as its superintendent, a position that demanded obedience, for he determined who was hired and fired, and how much everyone was paid. In time, he would be only the inmate.

SHOWDOWN WITH WALL STREET

Throughout the time that Hughes was sitting in the bungalow in his white leather chair, naked, unwashed for months, his hair falling down his back, his beard unkempt, his toenails and fingernails grotesquely long, he communicated by telephone with Wall Street investment houses, bankers, and lawyers, sending one and all on a variety of missions he hoped would rescue his failing empire. Hughes's mental illness was such that he could one hour dictate a completely irrational memorandum sealing off Romaine Street from germ-bearing letters and the next hour a rational memorandum on a financing plan for TWA. It was as though half of Hughes's brain cells were functioning, the other half dead or defective. His illness now determined the amount of time he devoted to business affairs. If he was especially preoccupied with one of his continuing skirmishes against contamination, he thought of little else. When the germ fears subsided, he would turn once again to business. It was a pattern that would hold over the years.

By 1958, Hughes's jet-financing problems had been compounded. Carter Burgess, tired of Hughes's erratic conduct, had walked out as TWA's president in December of 1957 after only eleven months on the job. Now TWA was leaderless again. And the bills were coming due: TWA's jets would start rolling off assembly lines in early 1959, each costing about $4.5 to $6 million. The first Boeing plane was scheduled for delivery in March, and TWA would begin receiving one or more a month thereafter.

To make matters worse, Hughes's personal financial condition was grim.

In the more than two years since he had ordered the jets, he had been dipping into his own resources to avoid having to go to East Coast bankers and investors. But he was fast running out of money, and the tool company's profits, which he had been employing to the maximum in a stop-gap effort to pay for the jets, had plunged in the wake of a worldwide downturn in oil drilling that reduced demand for the Hughes bit. For the first time in his life, Howard Hughes would shortly be unable to pay his bills.

So, he finally made a decision: he would try to borrow some money. Using Jack Real as an intermediary, Hughes turned to another business acquaintance, Robert Gross, the chairman of Lockheed, to sound out the eastern financial establishment. It was not the best time for Hughes to be tapping Wall Street for capital. His lackadaisical attitude toward TWA had alienated potential investors. After Carter Burgess resigned in December of 1957, Hughes did not appoint a new president until the following July. In the interim, TWA lost more than $10 million. Burgess's successor was another former Pentagon official, Charles S. Thomas, secretary of the navy under Eisenhower, who before his government service had made a career of rescuing ailing businesses. Although more accommodating than the hard-nosed Burgess, Thomas was still very much his own man and he was excited by the challenge of trying to revive TWA. Hughes agreed to give him free rein in all areas except the jet financing and advertising. Thomas accepted the job on the basis that after two years, if Hughes wanted him to stay, he would be given a stock option in TWA. It all sounded very familiar.

Despite Wall Street's coolness toward Hughes, Gross soon put two investment houses—the First Boston Corporation and Merrill Lynch, Pierce, Fenner & Smith—in touch with Hughes. Under senior executive George Woods, First Boston drafted a proposal to raise capital from Hughes Tool's assets. As Woods's study advanced, he passed word to Hughes that he was prepared to fly west and discuss it in person. Days passed without word. Then one night Hughes called Woods at his home in New York and asked him to put some of his ideas on paper and forward them. "That is not the way I do business, Mr. Hughes," Woods told him. "I am accustomed to dealing with a face, not a voice."[56] That was the end of the First Boston plan.

The Merrill Lynch assignment was no less difficult, but potentially more volatile. The investment firm was to develop a plan for the public sale of the Hughes Aircraft Company, no simple task, since Hughes had already given the company's stock to his Miami-based, tax-exempt medical institute, supposedly "to benefit mankind." A team of Merrill Lynch specialists, headed by William Forrester, Jr., moved into a suite at the Beverly Hills Hotel in December of 1958. There, Forrester never saw Hughes, but he did spend hours on the telephone discussing the plan with Hughes, who was living in his bungalow a hundred yards away. Eventually, the Merrill Lynch plan also fell through.

Hughes had lost more time. It was now February of 1959, just a month before delivery of the first of TWA's thirty-three 707s. There was nothing to do but return to Wall Street. Hughes called an acquaintance, Fred Brandi, a senior partner at Dillon, Read & Company, the investment bankers that represented two consortiums formerly interested in buying the Hughes Tool Company. Would Brandi devise a plan enabling Hughes to raise the capital needed for TWA's jets? Brandi agreed to try.

When not watching movies, Hughes now was constantly on the telephone exploring options from his bungalow at the Beverly Hills Hotel. As usual, Raymond Cook, the intelligent, amiable Houston lawyer, was his main emissary to the financial community in New York. He was also the chief target of Hughes's long-winded calls and soaring paranoia. Hughes believed the only safe telephones in New York were in the Waldorf-Astoria Hotel. When he had orders for Cook, he told Operations, "Get him into a room where he is completely private and with empty rooms on either side with the doors closed on both sides of the empty rooms."[57] Poor Cook was exhausted from shuttling between Wall Street and his hotel rooms.

Two other men Hughes regularly telephoned, usually early in the morning, were Raymond M. Holliday, the vice-president and chief financial officer of the Hughes Tool Company in Houston, and Milton H. (Mickey) West, Jr., his Houston tax lawyer and a partner of Raymond Cook's in Andrews, Kurth, Campbell & Jones. Since Dietrich's departure, the quiet, self-effacing Holliday had inherited the task of advising Hughes on the company's financial picture. A onetime grammar school principal, he had gone to work at the age of twenty-three as a clerk in the tool company's accounting department, just in time to meet Hughes as he toured the Houston plant after his around-the-world flight. Holliday never forgot the thrill: "I thought how lucky I was to be able to work for such an interesting man."[58] Like Holliday, Mickey West also found it stimulating, although sometimes wearing, to work for Hughes. A specialist in income-tax law, West, a big, rawboned product of rural Texas, had become one of Hughes's closest advisers over the years, meeting periodically with his client in old cars or secluded hotel rooms to talk over tax questions in hushed tones. In any complex financial transaction, Hughes was sure to call on West for advice.

By March, two possible financial plans had taken shape in New York. One, the Dillon, Read plan, was a conventional arrangement that called for banks and insurance companies to supply $165 million and Hughes Tool to take subordinated debentures of $100 million to round out a $265-million jet-financing package. The second proposal was mostly Hughes's own brainchild. Known as the lease plan, it envisioned creation of a Hughes Tool subsidiary to acquire the jets and lease them to TWA, enabling Hughes to write off the jets' depreciation costs against the tool company's profits as he had wanted to do all along. As in the case of the Dillon, Read proposal, the banks and insurance companies would supply most of the capital.

Only the lease plan appealed to Hughes because of its obvious tax advantages. Conversely, it was damaging to TWA since it would leave the airline without title to its most vital assets, its airplanes, deprive it of the tax advantages of aircraft ownership, and thus substantially increase the cost of the jets.

Charles Thomas, TWA's new president, vigorously opposed the lease plan, setting in motion a decline in his relations with Hughes. When the plan was formally vetoed by the Equitable Life Assurance Society, TWA's chief creditor, it collapsed. The first serious talks between Hughes and Wall Street had ended on a sour note.

Later that same month, TWA's first Boeing 707 rolled off a Seattle assembly line. Thomas quickly pressed it into service, inaugurating a transcontinental jet flight between New York and San Francisco with spectacular results. Travelers flocked to fill seats on the newly scheduled flight. As more jets arrived, Thomas introduced the faster service on other routes with equal success. Best of all, the planes were not only popular, but also fabulous moneymakers compared to the old piston-driven Connies.

That was the good news. The bad news, at least for Hughes, was that the last of his capital was being used for the jets. The Equitable Life Assurance Society, which insisted that TWA and not the tool company should own the jets, vetoed any TWA lease fees to Hughes. Thus, Hughes was really in a squeeze, paying out millions of dollars and getting back nothing in return.

It was just like Hughes, at such a critical time, to retreat into some unrelated, frivolous subject. Thus, in the midst of his ongoing financial crisis, he fantasized about making movies again, even though he had not produced a motion picture in years. Concluding that he needed some attractive new talent to signal his return to filmmaking, Hughes called Washington and instructed Bob Maheu to go to Atlantic City to sign "ten of the Miss America contestants to movie contracts."[59] Maheu, accustomed to unusual assignments, was becoming a valuable operative for Hughes. He had served as a counterespionage agent for the FBI in the Second World War and as a corporate sleuth thereafter, enmeshed in intrigue from London to the Persian Gulf. For one of his clients, Greek shipping tycoon Stavros Niarchos, Maheu spent several months in the Middle East scuttling a lucrative oil deal negotiated by Niarchos' rival, Aristotle Onassis. A gifted conversationalist, Maheu could be both diplomatic and persuasive, and he was especially skilled in talking the language of politicians. Maheu still owned his own public-relations agency in Washington, but by 1959 his intensifying relationship with Hughes required that he live part of the year in California. Hughes repeatedly urged Maheu to join his staff full time and to become his "alter ego" so that Hughes, as Maheu later explained, would never have to appear before a government agency. Wary of working solely for Hughes, Maheu had always declined, but he was weakening.

The Miss America project was one of Maheu's more curious assignments. The outlook for making any of the beauty queens a movie star for Hughes was certainly not promising. Romaine Street already had under its wing a number of young women who had been promised stardom in a Hughes movie. With visions of the fame that lay ahead, the young women submitted to drama and singing lessons, designed, they were told, to turn them into polished actresses. Some received contracts from Hughes Productions; others, like Gail Ganley, a twenty-year-old singer and dancer, were not so fortunate.

Told by a talent scout that Hughes wanted to "make her a star," she willingly gave up her budding singing career in exchange for a long-term drama-coaching program.[60] The terms were strict—she would refrain from appearing as a singer, dancer, or actress during the training period, she would keep her arrangement with Hughes a secret from all but her immediate family, and "hold herself" ready to meet with Hughes at any time to discuss her career.[61] In return, she was promised a contract paying $450 a week and expenses. A driver from Romaine called for her each day and drove her to the home of a drama coach in Beverly Hills. As months passed and Miss Ganley received neither her contract nor the weekly salary, she began to worry. When she broached the matter to Hughes's aides, they told her not to worry; Hughes had simply been too busy to sign her contract. Miss Ganley was not persuaded. Pressing hard for money and clearly not to be put off, she received instructions finally to drive to Romaine Street and honk her horn three times, whereupon expense money would be provided. Following orders, she pulled up outside Hughes's legendary command post and sounded the horn, at which signal, much to her surprise, a second-floor window opened and a man lowered an envelope on a string.[62] Inside the envelope was money. This ritual was repeated periodically, but in the end, after almost two years of drama lessons, Gail Ganley never did receive a signed contract. She later sued Hughes and accepted an out-of-court settlement.

With this collection of young women waiting for stardom in Hughes's movies, Maheu's Miss America assignment was dubious. Still, he packed his bag, headed for Atlantic City, and even interviewed several contestants. But his heart was not in it. Only one contestant was persuaded to sign a contract with Hughes. Like all of Hughes's other young women of the 1950s lured by dreams of glory, she never played so much as a bit part. By 1959, Hughes's Hollywood days were behind him. He would never produce or direct another film.

If movies were fantasies, TWA's predicament of 1959 was all too real. As much as Hughes may have wanted to ignore or shut it out, events would not let him do so. Paying out millions of dollars a month for newly arriving airplanes and getting nothing back in lease fees from TWA, Hughes was heading for catastrophe. That June, in a desperate move to forestall the inevitable, he sold six of the Boeing 707s that he had ordered for TWA to Pan American, TWA's chief overseas rival. The sale all but crippled TWA on the North Atlantic route, where it competed directly with Pan Am.

Hughes's longtime lawyer Tom Slack once told a friend "Howard's no genius, he's just lucky," but by the fall of 1959 Hughes was fast exhausting his most precious commodity.[63] Only through luck had he managed to avoid ruin, scraping together the last of the resources to pay Boeing, still refusing to negotiate sincerely with lenders, apparently waiting for a miracle to save him from the financiers. Now that he really was running out of time, disquieting word came from San Diego. At Convair, production on TWA's 880s was right on schedule. Each plane would cost Hughes about $3.5 million and delivery would start in a few weeks. To TWA, which needed the jets, it was the best of all possible news. To Hughes, who could not pay for them, it was a disaster.

Hughes reacted to the latest crisis in his own inimitable way. On October 5, he dispatched a force of armed guards to the Convair assembly plant in San Diego. There, the tight-lipped guards surrounded aircraft No. 5, the first 880 scheduled for delivery to Hughes, then in the final stages of assembly, and refused to allow workers to complete it.[64] A few days later, Hughes's army also took up vigil over TWA's next 880 and shut down work on it, too.

The seizure of the second aircraft was particularly frustrating to Convair. Shortly before its capture, Convair had installed in it a seat intended as a prototype for all the 880s. But after the takeover, Hughes's guards would not allow Convair workers even to remove the seat and the company was therefore forced to design and construct another model.[65] Shortly afterward, Hughes's guards seized two more planes and then the four aircraft were towed away from the Convair plant to an apron adjoining the runway.

Convair workers watched in amazement as the uncompleted jets were pulled out of the hangar. But Hughes's desperate act was not without purpose. By preventing Convair from completing the planes, he had postponed the day of reckoning. TWA would be damaged, no doubt. But TWA's financial health was the least of Hughes's concerns; his control of the airline took precedence. Parked outside, exposed to the salt air, the 880s' jet engines began to corrode. J. William Bew, who was overseeing the purchase contract for TWA, pleaded with Bill Gay to preserve the engines.[66] But when technicians approached the aircraft, they were turned back. Although angry, Convair took no action against Hughes. He remained the company's prime customer and it still hoped to sell planes to him once the current unpleasantness passed. Convair responded to the 880s' seizure merely by removing the rest of Hughes's planes from the assembly line. That was another blow to TWA. The airline had been the last major carrier to order jets, and now even those planes would not arrive on schedule.

TWA's loss, however, did not compare to what lay ahead for General Dynamics, Convair's owner. The company's ill-starred venture with Hughes led to what *Fortune* called "the biggest product loss ever sustained by any company anywhere."[67] Due largely to Hughes's interference, Convair rolled up losses of $490 million, more than double what the Ford Motor Company lost in its notorious Edsel fiasco.

By seizing the 880s, Hughes had bought time. But time for what? Despite all his maneuvers, he was still faced with a debt he could not satisfy without the aid of Wall Street. And still he delayed. As TWA's condition worsened for lack of jets, Charles Thomas took matters into his own hands. At a March 1960 TWA board meeting, Thomas persuaded the Hughes-controlled board to approve the long-dormant Dillon, Read plan for conventional financing which would raise a total of $265 million from banks, insurance companies, and the

Hughes Tool Company. To everyone's surprise, Hughes accepted the board's action on March 29. The lenders immediately began to draw up the voluminous loan papers.

From the outset of Hughes's dealings with the financiers, he had harbored dark fears that "unnamed forces" were plotting to take TWA away from him.[68] Now he became convinced of it. Increasingly wary of Hughes's erratic ways, the lenders inserted into the loan documents an undisguised threat to Hughes's rule. As the price for their $165-million loan, they warned Hughes that if he defaulted or forced any change in TWA's management, he would be required to place his airline stock in a ten-year voting trust that gave the lenders the right to select a majority of the trustees. Those trustees then would assume responsibility for management of the airline.[69] Hughes's interference in TWA's internal affairs was legendary. Thomas was the airline's fifth president in a dozen years. The lenders were warning Hughes flatly that if he forced Thomas out, he might lose control of TWA. They set July 28 to close the financing.

It was not the only deadline Hughes faced that month. Thomas had taken over as TWA's president in the summer of 1958 with the understanding that Hughes would give him a stock option in TWA two years later. Now that time was near. Hughes opposed the concept of stock options for his executives and he was not about to change his ways, least of all for Thomas, who had antagonized him by championing the Dillon, Read plan. But if he refused the request, he might lose Thomas and thus control of TWA.

As early as April of 1960, Thomas began trying to reach Hughes by telephone to discuss his future at TWA. Hughes refused to return his calls until July, when he put forth a counterproposal to Thomas's request for a stock option. To Thomas's astonishment, Hughes insisted that he resign as TWA's president and run the airline as "an employee of the Tool company."[70] In all his years of badgering and cajoling TWA's presidents, Hughes had never made such a demand. Thomas knew full well that such an arrangement would place him more than ever under Hughes's thumb, and he refused. The first conversation in months between the two men broke off in acrimony. Rejecting Thomas's demand for a stock option, Hughes voiced a familiar refrain: he refused to negotiate at the "point of a gun."[71]

Once again, Hughes had mishandled a serious personnel situation. Unlike most Hughes executives, Thomas could not be pushed around. With a large private income, he had little need of his $60,000-a-year TWA salary, much of which was eaten up by income taxes. Indeed, he had wanted a stock option as a way to reduce his annual tax bill. As Thomas pondered his future during a vacation at Pebble Beach, an enticing offer arrived—management of the sprawling 93,000-acre Irvine Ranch development outside Los Angeles. At odds with Hughes, Thomas saw no choice but to leave TWA.

More than any other single event, Thomas's resignation on July 23 turned Wall Street firmly against Hughes. TWA's mysterious proprietor had committed the unpardonable sin. The lenders looked upon Thomas as something of a savior for TWA. With him gone, they immediately canceled the closing on the $265-million jet deal and prepared to wait and see what Hughes would do about naming a successor.

If Hughes sensed the enormity of his blunder, he did not confide it, but he certainly felt the financial vise closing around him. Secluded in Room 395 on the third floor of the Beverly Hills Hotel—where he had recently moved temporarily from the bungalow—he was jumpy and ill at ease. Imagining a knock on his door late one afternoon, he picked up the telephone and screamed at Operations: "Did you send somebody up to knock on my door?" Even after the operator protested innocence, Hughes continued to scold him, warning that no one had better knock on his door "unless there is a helluva good reason for it."[72]

For Hughes, in a crisis, there was always something unimportant to worry about—if not someone knocking on his door, then the precise time that one of his executives planned to go to bed. One night he called Operations and gave orders for a memorandum to be sent to Bob Rummel and one of his assistants, who were standing by at a hotel awaiting orders:

If they feel they could go to sleep now or sometime soon, then I would suggest they go right ahead and try to do so and I will call them tomorrow at any hour they would prefer to have me call. On the other hand, if they do not feel they could go to sleep for quite a while yet, in that event I wonder if they could tell you what time they think is the earliest that they will be able to sleep or call [Operation] when they get sufficiently sleepy so that they think they can go to sleep. On the other hand, if they can go to sleep now, fine, I will call them in the morning; but if they think they cannot go to sleep, or if they have no way of knowing this, then why don't they just relax and look at the Tokyo riots on TV so they can tell me about it, and call [Operations] whenever they feel that they are sufficiently sleepy that they could go to sleep. If I had not been able to call them by then, I will call in the morning.[73]

No doubt thoroughly confused, and possibly bemused by Hughes's communication, Rummel opted for an easier course. He told Operations to tell Hughes "he can call any time during the night and not worry about upsetting our sleep too much."[74]

Hughes was not the only one under pressure. Raymond Cook was in New York dealing with TWA's creditors and bankers after Thomas's departure. Cook tried repeatedly, without success, to get through to Hughes, who remained incommunicado in the Beverly Hills Hotel. At 3:30 on the morning of August 3, however, Hughes dictated a rambling memorandum to Operations to be transmitted to Cook.

Apologizing for his failure to return Cook's calls, Hughes said, "I'm extremely sorry, but have been unable to sleep for a combination of reasons for 60 hours now and I'm not going to kill myself and get sick again."[75]

Hughes had good reasons for sleepless nights. On September 1, two earlier loans from the banks and insurance companies totaling $54 million were due, and he did not have the cash to pay them. Sixty days later, he would need $14 million more to retire the principal on a long-standing, although unrelated note from the Irving Trust Company. Hughes had borrowed the money years before to consolidate his hold on RKO. At the time, he routinely pledged his tool company stock as collateral, never dreaming that the great property itself would ever be endangered by such a move.

Hughes had maneuvered himself into an incredibly vulnerable position. If he failed to pay off the notes, the lenders could foreclose and throw him into bankruptcy. Luckily for him, foreclosure was such a mighty weapon that the lenders were fearful of wielding it. To foreclose on Hughes would bring down TWA as well, jeopardizing their own investment in the airline. The September 1 deadline came and went with no action taken.

In the following weeks, Hughes cast about for an alternative to the Dillon, Read plan, vowing to one banker that he would "go into receivership" rather than go through with it.[76] First, he tried to make a deal with a group of banks and General Dynamics. But General Dynamics, weakened by Hughes's own inability to pay for the Convair 880s, was unable to raise the cash. Then Hughes eyed Hughes Aircraft again, claiming that he would "get some money out of [his] charity one way or another."[77] That, too, fell through.

Seemingly trapped, early in October Hughes reluctantly agreed to the Dillon, Read plan once again. Only now the lenders imposed harsher terms. In addition to requiring Hughes to place his TWA stock immediately in a ten-year voting trust—which would remove his control of the airline—they insisted on a stiff prepayment penalty if he paid off the loans before March 31, 1962. When Hughes heard that, he was furious and once more began looking for a way out.[78] He turned to Colonel Henry Crown, a Chicago industrialist, who was General Dynamics's largest stockholder. Through a new scheme backed by a Bank of America loan and the sale of TWA debentures, Hughes hoped to raise the millions he needed. This plan also was aborted when investment bankers warned Hughes that they could not guarantee it would raise the amount he needed.

After the collapse of the Crown deal, Hughes, certain that Wall Street was conspiring to take TWA away from him, telephoned Maheu and ordered him to put all the lenders under "surveillance."[79] Hughes thought, Maheu later recalled, that the financiers had conspired to exert pressure on other bankers with whom Hughes was negotiating, and had succeeded in "scuttling the financing that he was trying to put through."[80] The Dillon, Read plan still looked like the only way Hughes could save himself, but he was as opposed to it as ever. In an October 28, 1960, memorandum to William Forrester, Jr., the Merrill Lynch executive, Hughes poured out his venom against the Dillon, Read plan and the man he considered responsible for it, Charles Thomas, the mild-mannered, conscientious ex-TWA president who had happily washed his hands of the Hughes mess three months before.

"Tell Forrester," Hughes instructed Operations,

that Charlie Thomas negotiated and developed the deal with Dillon Read . . . without my authority or encouragement from me; he forced it down my throat then at a Board meeting at which time he created a coalition of my directors and turned them against me and faced me with a mass resignation of all but one of the TWA directors. I have never liked this plan; I have never been in favor of this plan; I have fought it from the beginning and I am still fighting it and I assure you that if it is employed it will be over my dead body.[81]

By early November, it looked as if Hughes might actually be prepared to "go into receivership" rather than submit to the Dillon, Read plan. The situation was so grave that the CAB's staff in Washington alerted the agency's five-member ruling board that the "crisis stage" had been reached at TWA.[82] Alarmed, a CAB staff attorney warned Cook on November 23 that unless the CAB had "definite assurance" of TWA's financing within a week, he would recommend a full investigation to determine if it was in the public's interest for Hughes to control the airline.[83]

Hemmed in, Hughes capitulated in late November and agreed for the third time to go along with the Dillon, Read proposal. Turning again to Fred Brandi at Dillon, Read, he asked if the plan could be reactivated. Brandi reported back that it could, but on even stiffer terms. The lenders now laid down a series of humiliating conditions aimed at making it virtually impossible for Hughes to back out again. They demanded that Hughes personally, as an indication of good faith, sign letters agreeing to their terms.

A furious Hughes went along reluctantly. But no sooner had he accepted Wall Street's tough conditions than he fired Raymond Cook, his diplomatic Houston lawyer, who had managed to keep relations between his mercurial boss and the staid financiers on an even keel. Why Hughes fired Cook is not clear. Hughes said he was "shocked and amazed" when Cook failed to show up in Los Angeles early the day after Thanksgiving to review certain papers.[84] Cook had flown home to Houston for the holiday. But Hughes's displeasure over that incident was probably only symptomatic of the ill-will he felt toward all who had played an intimate role in this defeat.

With Cook's departure, Hughes seemed resigned to going through with the financing and submitting to the voting trust. He dispatched a replacement to the East, Greg Bautzer, a tall, handsome, Hollywood attorney who had represented Hughes on motion-picture business. Bautzer alarmed the lenders when he briefly made another effort to push for financing without the voting trust. Like all the others, this scheme failed. On December 3, both the TWA and tool company boards approved the $265-million financial package put together by Dillon, Read. Four days later, Bautzer announced that Hughes had personally signed the letters of agreement. On December 15, 1960, Raymond Holliday, acting for the tool company, and the lenders unceremoniously executed the voting trust agreement. After fifteen years as its undisputed master, Howard Hughes had lost control of TWA.

CHAPTER 10

RETREAT

NINE days after the voting-trust agreement was signed, Hughes and Jean moved out of their separate bungalows at the Beverly Hills Hotel and into a rented mansion in the hills of San Diego County a hundred miles south of Los Angeles. Ever since their wedding, Jean had pressed for a house where they could "live together as man and wife."[1] Even though theirs apparently had been a marriage of convenience, Jean had been rankled by Hughes's insistence that they live apart. Now he abruptly gave in. On December 24, 1960—Hughes's fifty-fifth birthday—they took up residence in a $2,000-a-month estate ringed by a fence and patrolled by Hughes's guards near the secluded village of Rancho Santa Fe. For the first time in their four-year marriage, Jean Peters and Howard Hughes were living together under the same roof.

They were not living alone, of course. The usual retinue of aides, cooks, waiters, couriers, and "third men" whom Hughes had come increasingly to depend on at the Beverly Hills Hotel came south, taking up residence at the Inn in the village center of Rancho Santa Fe, a few minutes' drive from the Hughes house. John Holmes and Roy Crawford were the senior aides and spent much of their time in the house itself. Their schedules called for them to alternate every four days, but Hughes often kept one of them on the job for as long as two weeks at a time.

Back in New York, TWA's lenders were luxuriating in the afterglow of the Dillon, Read triumph. The Hughes era at TWA was definitely past, or so it seemed. With the signing of the voting-trust agreement on December 15, only the formalities remained. Even so, Hughes managed to wring the maximum of tension and drama from what should have been a ceremonial affair.

On the morning of December 28, representatives of the lenders assembled at the Farmers Bank, in Wilmington, Delaware, where Raymond Holliday was expected to sign over Hughes's stock to the control of the lender-dominated voting trust. But at the appointed hour, Holliday was not there. Instead, he telephoned, reporting matter-of-factly that he was still in his New York hotel room awaiting authorization to go to Wilmington. The startled lenders warned Greg Bautzer that they would go to court if Hughes backed out this time.[2] Bautzer, mystified, tried to reassure them that Hughes had every intention of completing the deal. All day the lenders waited and by evening, with Holliday still in absentia, they were certain that collapse was imminent.

The next morning Holliday called again. He was on his way to Wilmington, but still without authority to transfer the stock. Bautzer, meanwhile, was having the usual trouble reaching Hughes, and tempers were short all around. If the documents were not signed within thirty-six hours, the end of the last business day of 1960, a new set would have to be drafted and approved by all parties.

On Friday, Bautzer reached Hughes and got his approval for the stock transfer. Executing the documents in Wilmington, Holliday hurried back to New York to sign the loan agreements before the deadline expired. At three o'clock on December 30, Holliday entered the elegant, sea-green conference room of the Chemical Bank. But he refused to sign, protesting that he needed a lawyer to review the voluminous documents. To the lenders, it was clearly another Hughes stall. Bautzer was of no assistance either. Calling his suite at the Hampshire House, the bankers learned that Bautzer had been admitted to Roosevelt Hospital, a possible heart-attack victim.

Left alone to face the lions of Wall Street, Holliday paced the Chemical's conference room as some thirty-five representatives of banks, insurance companies, and investment houses waited. Holliday appealed for a postponement. The financiers stood firm, insisting that he sign the papers. Holliday demurred and slipped into a smaller conference room to place a series of frantic telephone calls to Romaine Street. The hours sped by. Finally, at 7:15, Holliday emerged vastly relieved. Bautzer had recovered sufficiently to call Hughes from the hospital and extract the necessary authority. Dropping into a tangerine-colored leather chair, Holliday signed papers with a flourish.[3] When he had finished, word was flashed to Oklahoma City to register the lenders' names on the mortgages of TWA's new jets. With Holliday's signature, Hughes had averted bankruptcy—and lost something of himself. Always before, his money and power and reputation had forced others to play his game. But the TWA contest had been a banker's game, played out on bankers' turf. While Jean busied herself gardening, swimming in the outdoor pool, building dog runs for her pets, and doing domestic chores around the house, Hughes brooded, shut away in their bedroom. For days he sat propped up in bed, the covers drawn over his bony shoulders, silently mourning his loss and dreaming of ways to recapture his airline.

When control passed to the lenders, TWA's new leader was, for all practical purposes, Ernest R. Breech, a retired executive who had earned a national reputation by rebuilding the Ford Motor Company in the 1940s. Unlike Hughes, whose wealth was inherited, Breech was a self-made man. He agreed to serve without pay as one of the two lender-appointed trustees of Hughes's stock. (The other was Irving S. Olds, a Wall Street lawyer and former chairman of United States Steel.) Breech accepted the TWA assignment "out of a sense of obligation and national duty," believing that TWA had a great future, if only it were allowed "to be like other airlines."[4] Thriving on challenge, Breech set plans in motion to reorganize TWA's board and hire a president. Beyond that lay the enormous task of rebuilding the airline.

Sometimes referred to in the industry as "the largest unscheduled airline in the United States," TWA had suffered grievously under Hughes.[5] The tardily ordered jets had been further delayed by the financial struggle. The impoundment at Convair meant TWA would be a full year late in receiving all the 880s, and the delay had sharply eroded TWA's position as a leading domestic carrier. By late 1960, CAB traffic reports showed that TWA's share of the Big Four domestic passenger market had declined from 23 to 20 percent and that United Airlines was now carrying more passengers than TWA.[6] Last, Hughes's dilatory tactics had forced TWA to pay substantially higher interest for funds than its major competitors.

Even the normally friendly CAB had been alienated. The agency, which had treated Hughes royally since the early 1940s, now viewed him as a menace. Relieved when control of TWA passed out of Hughes's erratic hands, the CAB noted, "No longer will the directors of [the tool company] be free to enforce their dictates or those of [the tool company's] controlling shareholder on TWA."[7] The CAB was so disenchanted with Hughes that it ruled he could not reassume control of TWA without "a searching inquiry" as to whether that would serve the public interest.[8]

Even so, Hughes might one day have regained command. There seems to have been no doubt in his own mind that this would happen. In a memorandum to Holliday on February 20, 1961, concerning additional Convair jets that he had ordered for TWA, Hughes said he did not know how TWA could be compelled to accept the planes, but added confidently: "Most likely HTCo [the tool company] will control TWA when that matter comes up."[9] It was simply a question of conserving his resources, raising additional cash, paying off the loans, and biding his time. But Hughes was not a patient man. Nor was it in his nature to play a passive role. Only a few weeks after the voting trust was imposed, he opened a strident attack on TWA's leaders.

When Breech announced a meeting of TWA's directors on January 26, 1961, Hughes barred his appointees from attending and thus made a quorum impossible, so that Breech was obliged to call off the meeting. Embarrassed by this show of resistance, Breech held a special stockholders' meeting, tossed out the Hughes directors, and replaced them with men independent of Hughes's control. When TWA announced a $100-million debenture offering, Hughes filed a formal complaint with the Securities and

Exchange Commission in an attempt to block the sale, and in March when TWA decided to acquire $187-million worth of additional jets from Boeing, Hughes charged that TWA's management had no authority to do so. Despite Hughes's warning that the projected sale was not binding on TWA, Boeing went through with it.

Waging this phase of the struggle for Hughes was a new advocate, Chester C. Davis, the sharp-tongued head of the trial department of Simpson, Thacher & Bartlett, a prestigious Wall Street law firm. Davis had been recommended by Floyd Odlum, the millionaire financier and husband of Jacqueline Cochran. He was neither as genial as Raymond Cook nor as suave as Greg Bautzer. But he was more aggressive than either. Davis was a graduate of Princeton University and Harvard Law School, but his Ivy League polish was not always evident in the courtroom. He had been born Caesar Simon in Rome in 1910, son of an Italian mother and a French-Algerian father. After his father's death, mother and son immigrated to the United States, where she married Chester Davis Sr. and changed her son's name to conform. After college, Davis married into the socially prominent Ferry family of Detroit and was named a trustee of the family's charitable foundation, only to be removed by disgruntled family members who were alarmed over what they called his "failure and neglect of duties."[10] Davis had spent virtually his entire career on Wall Street, but he was hardly a typical Wall Street lawyer. "He'd fiddle around the office all day then go off to Whyte's [a restaurant] and toss off martinis like glasses of water," recalled a former associate. "Then he'd come back to the office and toss out ideas for his assistants to work up overnight. Nine out of ten were no good, but that tenth one would be a dilly."[11] When the chance to represent Hughes came along, Davis had been associated with Simpson, Thacher for twenty-five years and was a senior partner. Nevertheless, he recognized a great opportunity when it knocked. Resigning, he formed his own Wall Street law firm, and shortly afterward became a vice-president and general counsel of the Hughes Tool Company.

TWA now saw that Hughes, assisted by his lieutenant Davis, was still very much a problem. By questioning the airline's right to sell debentures and to acquire aircraft, Hughes had been more than annoying; he had challenged the very authority of the voting trust itself. No one was more concerned than TWA's latest president, Charles C. Tillinghast, Jr. A native of tiny Saxton's River, Vermont, Tillinghast had been lured away from a secure job with the Bendix Corporation by his old friend Ernie Breech who had given him a lucrative contract and long-term financial security.

Forceful though the Hughes offensive was, Tillinghast was not intimidated. On the contrary, Hughes had gone too far this time, making a final break with the airline inevitable. Everyone now realized that Hughes, in his obsession, would give TWA no peace. As Tillinghast mulled over the situation, he picked up rumors that Hughes was preparing to file a lawsuit against TWA and the lending institutions to formally challenge the validity of the voting trust. Tillinghast and the TWA board had, for their part, authorized the Wall Street law firm of Cahill, Gordon, Reindel & Ohl to determine whether TWA could sue Hughes for having mismanaged the airline. Thus, a climate of litigation had been created. But who would strike first?

On the morning of June 30, 1961, TWA filed a thirty-eight-page complaint in United States District Court in New York, charging Hughes, the tool company, and Raymond Holliday with violating antitrust laws in the sale of aircraft to TWA. It sought damages of $105 million and a court order for Hughes to divest himself of his 78-percent ownership in the airline. Hughes had been outmaneuvered once again.

The legal battle touched off that morning would be one of the most momentous and enduring in American business history. A product of the fertile legal mind of John Sonnett, a partner in the Cahill firm, the TWA complaint was based on a novel view of antitrust law. By compelling TWA to accept aircraft provided by his tool company, the complaint alleged, Hughes had conspired to restrain trade. For all its imaginative thrusts, the complaint also had a practical side. It was aimed squarely at Hughes personally. Sonnett had concluded that Hughes would be vulnerable to a lawsuit that sought to force him to testify in court. Although he had no idea of the extent of Hughes's mental disability, Sonnett had come across bits and pieces of suggestive evidence. There also had been several recent instances in California when Hughes had chosen to defy court orders rather than appear. Clearly, TWA's majority stockholder was, for one reason or another, reluctant to show his face, and Sonnett was prepared to exploit that hesitancy. Hoping to force Hughes into a quick out-of-court settlement, Sonnett asked a federal judge to seal the complaint for a few days so that the parties could quietly try to negotiate a truce. The judge granted the request and the complaint was sealed until July 11, a deadline later extended to August 8.

As Sonnett had expected, the TWA complaint terrified Hughes. He instructed Davis and Bautzer to do everything possible to settle with TWA before the complaint was made public. He told Davis,

One force within me is telling me to stand up like a man and fight this thing through to the finish and prove to the world the utter hypocrisy of these claims and inflict upon the people responsible for this unjust persecution at least some of the punishment they merit. . . . This same voice is telling me that this fight, if it is carried through to completion, could consume the biggest part of the remainder of my productive life and could therefore interfere with the development and furtherance of my medical institution and other important creative things I would like to do before I die. This voice tells me that even though I am completely right and justified I should listen to reason rather than passion and get this thing behind me.[12]

The voice within Hughes that really caused him anxiety was the one telling him that TWA would concentrate all its strategy on forcing him to give

Left: Hollywood attorney Greg Bautzer, who represented Hughes on movie matters and TWA, was often seen in the company of Hollywood actresses, in this case Joan Crawford. *United Press International*

Right: New York attorney Chester C. Davis resigned from a prestigious Wall Street law firm at the start of the *TWA v. Hughes* lawsuit to form his own firm representing Hughes. *United Press International*

a deposition. He viewed that as grossly unfair. The lawsuit would not impose "even so much as an inconvenience" on executives of the "other side," who could "rattle off" depositions in their offices.[13] But as for himself, he knew he could not leave his self-erected asylum or allow anyone from the outside to enter it. Hughes told Davis he was too sick to give a deposition. "I have not been out of bed for more than nine months. My illness is no fiction and my doctor can furnish an affidavit stating that he forbids me to make this deposition on the grounds of further adverse effects to my health and intensification of my illness."[14]

Bautzer and Davis pursued independent strategies. Bautzer was optimistic that a settlement could be negotiated. Davis was concerned that TWA, believing it had Hughes on the ropes, would insist on overly harsh terms. As a precaution, in the event the lawsuit went forward, Davis advised Hughes to retain a prestigious New York law firm immediately. Hughes could not bear to discuss the possibility. "The lawsuit weighs [so] heavily in my considerations," he told Davis on July 16, "that I have decided to submit to settlement terms so heavily favorable to TWA that I feel the directors will be afraid to reject such a settlement for fear of the creation of a very serious liability on [their] part in favor of the TWA minority stockholders."[15]

Worried that Davis was not pushing hard enough for a settlement, Hughes sent him on a purposeless three-day trip to Houston and gave Bautzer full authority to settle the case in Davis's absence. "I want no divided responsibility about these negotiations," he told Bautzer. "I am placing the matter completely in your hands, Greg, with the simple request that you make the best deal you can."[16] Hughes told Bill Gay to keep Davis in Houston for three days. "I don't want any possibility of his leaving there. Do whatever is necessary to accomplish the result."[17]

Davis was kept in Houston for the required three days, but he saw through Hughes's transparent ploy by the end, and when he returned to New York on July 21, he sent Hughes an angry message. "It would have been preferable if you had told me directly and frankly what you wanted to do, even if you anticipated I would express disagreement at the strategy. I have no objection to your efforts at a settlement through Bautzer. However, I thoroughly disagree with the strategy you are currently following. I want no part in it or in its result, whatever it may be. I do not believe that you are following a course designed to achieve your objectives. I believe that you are hampering a settlement so long as you are not prepared to fight them."[18] Davis ended by bluntly offering to leave the case, on any terms Hughes decided. "There will be no disagreement as to proper compensation for my time."[19]

Hughes panicked and, as so often happened when one of his devious maneuvers backfired, he blamed Gay. "Tell Bill this breach with Davis is very likely to cost Bill his job," he fumed to Paul Winn, an aide then taking dictation at Rancho Santa Fe.[20] To smooth ruffled feathers, Hughes instructed Gay to telephone Davis and explain that there had been a communications breakdown, not a strategy change. Gay was to say that he had kept Davis in Houston in the belief that Hughes was planning to call Davis at any moment, but that, unfortunately Hughes's illness had taken a turn for the worse and prevented him from making the call. Davis accepted the olive branch.

Meanwhile, Bautzer was working day and night to negotiate a settlement. By late July, a tentative agreement had been roughed out. If TWA would drop the lawsuit, Hughes would agree to honor the voting trust for its full ten years and to invest $150 million in the airline over the next two years. In turn, the airline agreed to acquire thirteen more Convair jets that Hughes had previously ordered for TWA, a move that would relieve him of a major financial obligation. TWA insisted that Hughes sign the agreement first, a requirement Hughes considered "unwarranted, unjustified, and an insult."[21] Nevertheless, he signed the papers on July 27 and sent them to Bautzer with orders to hold them until several minor changes had been made. To Bautzer, only a few formalities remained before the crisis would be resolved.

But not all of Hughes's attorneys were so eager for him to settle. As soon as he read a copy of the agreement, Chester Davis dictated a memorandum to Rancho Santa Fe on July 28, 1961, urging Hughes to think twice before submitting to TWA's terms. Davis objected in particular to a section which he said amounted to a consent decree. "Irrespective of the legal niceties involved," he said,

it is common knowledge that a consent decree in any trust action means that the defendant recognizes or admits a course of conduct in violation of the antitrust laws without admitting the particulars constituting the alleged violation. . . . The inevitable implication is that the Tool Company must have done something illegal even though there is no admission by the Tool Company or any adjudication by the court as to the particulars which could be a violation of the Federal statutes involved.[22]

Hughes sounded out Robert Campbell, of Andrews, Kurth in Houston, the longtime attorneys of the oil-tool division, and Seymour Mintz of Hogan & Hartson in Washington, the medical institute's lawyers. Both sided with Davis.

Although he was desperately anxious to settle, Hughes found Davis's argument disquieting. As the August 8 date for unsealing the complaint approached, he decided "to fight the TWA lawsuit to the hilt."[23] On August 6, he told Gay to line up an influential New York law firm to assist Davis, but to make sure that Bautzer did not know of his activities. "Bill, I want you to roll up your sleeves and put everything else out of your mind," Hughes told him. "This is far and away the most important assignment you have ever received and please really give it everything you have got. This is going to be an all-out bitter battle and the ramifications of this thing will reach into many, many phases of our operation. These people will be prying around like ferrets looking for something they can use to blackmail us."[24]

Always aware of his public image, Hughes asked Gay to telephone William Randolph Hearst, Jr., and ask him to "issue a general directive" to all Hearst editors "that the Hearst papers are going to be on my side in this controversy. Tell Mr. Hearst I would not make this request at this time except this is of such devastating importance I truly need and must call upon everyone who is willing to stand up and be counted as my friend. These people are going to try their best to destroy me in any way they can."[25] In return, Hughes promised he would provide Hearst with exclusive stories about the TWA controversy, much as he had done in 1947 prior to the Senate hearings. "Tell Mr. Hearst they will be hot enough to curl the paper because I have some information and I am prepared to make some statements which will really shake up some of the better known figures of Wall Street."[26]

The battle lines drawn, TWA's complaint against Howard Hughes was made public on the morning of August 8 in Manhattan, and the lawsuit, destined to be one of the most lengthy and celebrated civil cases of the century, went forward.

Now that the battle was on, Hughes's old combative instincts returned. He and his lawyers were confident. To their way of thinking, TWA had chosen shaky ground in antitrust law on which to make a stand. They believed that although airlines are private corporations, they also serve the public interest and were therefore immunized from the full force of antitrust law by the Civil Aeronautics Board. Until December of 1960, when Hughes lost control, the

CAB had regularly approved his dealings with TWA as in the public interest. Hughes's lawyers reasoned that the federal courts lacked jurisdiction to hear the charges.

Following this logic a step farther, the CAB obviously loomed as crucial to Hughes's fight to turn back the lawsuit and to recapture his airline. He would need the CAB's cooperation. Unfortunately for him, Hughes's standing with the CAB had never been lower. The agency had not forgotten how Hughes had nearly ruined TWA. Even so, shortly after the collapse of the settlement talks late in the summer of 1961, Hughes saw a way to recoup some lost prestige in Washington and at the same time outmaneuver his foes and get back into the airline business. The opportunity came by the oddest of routes.

By the summer of 1961, Northeast Airlines, a small regional carrier based in New England, was verging on collapse. Northeast was controlled by the Atlas Corporation, the investment company still headed by Floyd Odlum, the buoyant financier from whom Hughes had bought RKO back in 1948. Later, through a series of complicated stock deals in the mid-1950s, Hughes acquired 11 percent of Atlas's stock, and thus he owned a piece of the corporation controlling Northeast. Since it is against public policy for a person to control more than one airline, the CAB had forced Hughes to place his Atlas stock in trust.

Hughes was well aware of Northeast's financial distress. A year earlier he had arranged a $9.5-million loan for Northeast in return for its promise to seek a merger with TWA. Nothing came of the proposed merger, and Northeast's financial condition deteriorated. By September of 1961, the airline barely had enough "cash on hand to cover one day's current operating expenditures."[27] Its collapse appeared imminent. The CAB abhors airline failures; they are bad for patrons who are inconvenienced, bad for politicians who hear complaints from outraged constituents, and bad for the CAB itself, which is supposed to prevent such calamities. But how could Northeast be saved? Only through the infusion of millions of dollars in cash. And who would invest such millions in an airline heavily burdened with debt and saddled with an undesirable route structure?

Who other than Howard Hughes? Atlas appealed to Hughes for financial assistance. Early in September Hughes agreed to supply it, but only if the CAB approved. Atlas and Hughes Tool began negotiating a secret memorandum of understanding aimed at providing Northeast with immediate cash and at giving Hughes an option to acquire Atlas's controlling interest in the airline. If the CAB approved, Hughes would lend Northeast $5 million. To help pave the way at the CAB, Hughes rehired Raymond Cook, the Houston lawyer he had fired the year before.* With close ties to

---

*Bringing Cook back on the scene proved difficult. When he had broken with Cook the year before, Hughes had severed nearly all his ties with Cook's law firm, Andrews, Kurth, although the firm did continue to represent the oil-tool division of Hughes's empire. At the time of the break, Hughes had an unpaid legal bill of $386,881. Before Andrews, Kurth would allow Cook to resume work for Hughes, they insisted that Hughes pay his bill. He thought the amount was excessive

the CAB, Cook would be invaluable in the months ahead.

Hughes now had the CAB where he wanted it. If the agency rejected his offer to bail out Northeast, the airline would almost certainly fail. If it approved the loan, the CAB would be handing yet another airline to a man with a demonstrated inability to run one. On September 12, 1961, representatives of Hughes, Atlas, and Northeast assembled at the CAB's headquarters in Washington for a special meeting of the agency's board. The subject was Northeast, and Raymond Cook and Chester Davis made it plain that they expected the board to give Hughes special treatment.

"May I make the observation that quite clearly unusual procedures are required here," Cook told the four CAB board members who were present that afternoon.[28] Davis was more direct: "Let me be very frank. I know for a fact from past experience those who desired to achieve a particular result have always [sought to] examine Mr. Hughes personally. If we are going to get ourselves involved in a hearing where that is likely to develop, I think the conclusion that we would reach is that we are just wasting our time."[29]

Jack Rosenthal, a CAB staff attorney, replied. "In effect, you want a guarantee from the board" that Hughes would not be called as a witness.[30]

"I am not asking for a guarantee of any kind," Davis answered. "I am merely saying that before the Tool Company will once again, and I repeat once more, come to the rescue of an airline in trouble, we want to be satisfied and I don't expect [anyone] to do anything for us they shouldn't do, but we want to be satisfied [that] life [will not be made] more miserable for us than it had already been."[31]

"I think you have made your point," said Robert T. Murphy, vice-chairman of the board.[32]

After listening to the pleas of Hughes's lawyers and representatives of Atlas and Northeast, the CAB adjourned, deciding only that Hughes, like anyone else, would have to file a formal application before it could act. Still, Hughes was optimistic that the CAB would ultimately have no choice but to go along with his masterplan.

In October, when Northeast's cash ran so low that it could not pay its bills, Hughes quietly agreed to guarantee its fuel bills and keep the planes flying. On October 31, 1961, Hughes and Atlas filed a formal request with the CAB seeking permission for Hughes to supply funds to the ailing airline. Disclosing publicly that Hughes had been guaranteeing the airline's fuel bills for two weeks, the application provoked a row. Eastern Airlines, Northeast's competitor on the Florida run, called for the "criminal prosecution of Howard Hughes" for having "illegally acquired control."[33] On November 9, the CAB issued an interim order that was a vague slap at Hughes's dealings. Calling on him and Northeast to file a complete report of all agreements between them, the CAB said it appeared that Hughes Tool had enough

---

and refused. By making a $100,000 good-faith payment, and promising to pay most of the balance, Hughes was able to persuade the Houston firm to reassign Cook to the Hughes account.

power over Northeast to control it.[34] Such control was, of course, illegal without CAB approval. Hughes countered two days later by withdrawing Northeast's fuel guarantee. Five days after that, Northeast made a frantic plea to the CAB to modify the interim order questioning the legality of Hughes's aid lest the airline collapse. Hughes had immensely increased the pressure on the CAB to act in his favor. It was now only a matter of time, he felt, before the CAB would come around.

THE GERM WAR

Hughes directed the TWA and Northeast strategies from his bedroom. His mental condition had deteriorated and his seclusion had deepened at Rancho Santa Fe, where he now rarely left his bed. Hughes summoned aides to the room day and night, where they would kneel beside the bed as Hughes, often with Jean sleeping next to him, dictated memoranda that ran from a few sentences long to several thousand words. The memoranda then were sent to Operations by teletype from the cabana next to the swimming pool. Hughes's compulsive need to send messages at all hours did not disturb his wife nearly so much as his nervous habit of clicking his long toenails while he dictated. To muffle the sound, Jean put Kleenex between her husband's toes.[35]

Next to TWA, the most consuming issue Hughes dealt with in the summer of 1961 was a project to "isolate" five Electras at the Lockheed plant in Burbank. Hughes wanted to purchase three of the planes—apparently for his personal collection—but until he decided which three to buy he wanted all five so well guarded as to be isolated from germs. Two of the planes were parked outside and Hughes worried that the sun, beating down on the fuselages, would make them incubators for microorganisms. He asked Jack Price, a Romaine Street operative, to work out a way to air-condition the planes. Price came up with several ideas—one of which was to purchase window air conditioners, anchor them on stands outside the Electras' cabin doors, and feed cool air inside—before Hughes decided to tow the planes inside a hangar. To preclude the possibility of an aircraft worker's coming in contact with one of the Electras, and thereby spreading germs from human to airplane, Hughes gave Price a detailed memorandum on how to accomplish the move.

Explaining that the project was more important to him "than any you have undertaken before," Hughes beseeched Price to do "an even finer job of moving than you have ever accomplished before."[36] Hughes wanted the planes towed with a precision that surpassed all past efforts:

All I can say is to ask you as urgently and as humbly as I know how—I ask you and implore you, Jack, not to be satisfied with doing it as well or as perfectly or as smoothly or as gently as you have in the past, but please tonight just simply bust a gut striving as you never tried to do anything before in your life not merely to equal the best operation you have achieved in the past, but instead improve upon it and tonight conduct the most careful, the slowest, most perfect, most gentle, the smoothest towing operation ever, ever conducted before and with each acceleration and deceleration so infinitely gradual that it would take a microscope to measure it.[37]

A few days after the Lockheeds were finally moved, Hughes faced an even graver germ crisis. On September 3, 1961, Robert Gross, the chairman of Lockheed and a business associate of Hughes, died of cancer. Gross's wife invited Hughes to a private funeral and asked him to be an honorary pallbearer. Unable to leave Rancho Santa Fe, Hughes, of course, declined. He asked Gay to send a message to Mrs. Gross graciously thanking her for the invitation and explaining that he was unable to attend because of illness. As a sign of friendship for Gross, Hughes instructed Romaine Street to send flowers, telegrams, and messages of condolence to the family, to "really go the limit on this."[38]

Once the formality of sympathetic expressions was in motion, Hughes ordered Romaine Street to put into effect the most far-reaching germ-fighting program ever implemented to make certain that germs from the late Robert Gross did not somehow wend their way to Rancho Santa Fe. As a rule, Hughes feared all germs equally. The one exception, a kind of superbug, was the hepatitis microbe. He had become so terror-stricken of hepatitis that he saw it everywhere, and now for some reason he was convinced that Gross had died of hepatitis, not of cancer. (Ironically, at different times over the years Hughes stood a greater chance of succumbing to hepatitis in his own filthy surroundings, but such was the severity of his disorder that he never recognized this.) Hughes directed Romaine Street to seal off every person and business involved with Gross, his widow, or his funeral, from all contact with the Hughes empire to prevent the "backflow" of germs:

Everything involved in this entire Gross operation, whether it be flowers, telegram, no matter what the hell it is, I want the absolute maximum greatest precaution and even greater precaution than we have ever taken before to close off all return paths. In other words to make the operation truly, literally, absolutely irreversible. This will mean if we are going to use our florist for the flowers then the delivery will again have to be made by some messenger service whom we will never use again, who will not be sending us literature, a bill, who will not be writing to us or sending or mailing us any thing, who will not be calling upon us to try and solicit business, and furthermore, who will not do anything like this with our florist, for soliciting of business, sending literature to our florist, not sending bills or invoices to our florist, and not be used again by our florist in any way. And again I say, the messenger is not to be in a position to attempt to solicit business further from our florist or from us. The message can simply go by telegram. Also I want an absolute blockade for the time being against any pick up at the Lockheed plant. Don't be sending anybody to pick up engineering data, flight manuals from Jack Real concerning Jet Stars, Electras, or anything else. I would like to block off incoming correspondence, data, packages, any incoming items, large or small, even a slip of paper from the Lockheed factory as well as from Gross's office.

Mrs. Gross will undoubtedly write a message of thanks for the flowers and Bill can send me a very complete memo setting forth the scheme for the receipt of this message and Bill Gay can let me know how this will be accomplished. We will have probably 48 hours before we have to worry about that one, but the message telling me how that is to be done will have to be telephoned to Paul [Winn] and I don't want anybody else to know about that.

I want the necessary instructions given to achieve a block off of all return avenues and to make the situation concerning the flowers and the telegram and anything else of that nature which may be required—to make any such transmission completely irreversible so there is absolutely not the slightest possibility of any back flow or return transmission or anything of that kind even of the most indirect nature such as I have described herein.[39]

Now that Hughes and Jean were living in the same house, his phobias sometimes upset even her. Always fearful of dust, he refused to let her clean their bedroom. Jean tried to comply. She kept the rest of the house spotless and ignored their room. As time went by and the film of dust grew into mounds of dirt, she decided to clean—with or without Hughes's blessing. When Holmes, the aide on duty, heard about it, he volunteered to run the vacuum cleaner, but Jean insisted that she wanted to do it herself.

Placing the humming vacuum-cleaner cannister outside the bedroom one night, Jean poked into the room with a long extension hose and began to massage the heavy shag rug that covered the floor. Hughes looked on in silence from his bed as Jean ventured farther into the room, followed by Holmes, who carried a flashlight, shining it into the dark corners that Jean was trying to reach with the nozzle. As they neared Hughes's bed, he said, "Don't touch the TV set," which was covered with dust. Otherwise, he did not interfere. Jean stuck the nozzle under Hughes's bed and began running it back and forth. The task of picking up the dust underneath, however, proved impossible without moving the bed, and eventually Jean, as Holmes remembered, "ran out of steam" and gave up.[40]

Hughes was not insensitive to Jean's own emotional crises. One day her cat wandered away and failed to come home. Jean was distraught. When the aides failed to find the missing animal, and Romaine Street, and in particular Bill Gay, did not respond to the crisis, Hughes became furious. In a heated telephone conversation with Kay Glenn, Gay's assistant, Hughes both spelled out alternative strategies for finding the cat and vented his anger at Gay. He told Glenn:

I want somebody who is an expert in the ways of animals of this type and who would know where to look and how to look and how to go about this line. I mean, for example, directly, dogs get a cat treed up a tree and the cat just stays there, afraid to come down, and the dogs rush around in the vicinity somewhere. . . . If we can find some evidence . . . the cat's body, or somebody who heard the episode. . . . Now, it just seems to me that if Bill gave a goddamn in hell about my predicament down here he would have obtained from somewhere, from some place—I don't know where from—from Los Angeles or some place, he would have got some expert in the ways of animals, cats in particular, and had him come down here and then put about eight or ten of Maheu's men at his disposal and they would have conducted an intelligent search based upon being instructed by somebody who knows the habits and ways of an animal of this kind. But, instead of that, so far as I have been able to make out, not one thing has been done. . . .

Kay, I am not going to run this organization this way any more and now Bill Gay goes cruising around today, having a good time, where nothing is done about looking for this cat down here. Not one goddamned thing except having a few of our guards cruise around in their cars. Maheu is in Los Angeles. You could have had him send a team of men down here. You could have got some experts who knew about cats and know where to look. There are many, many things that could have been done during the entire period of today to try and locate this animal or find out what happened to it today. I am goddamned sure that if some police case depended upon the determination of knowledge of what happened to this animal today, by God, in Heaven, they would have had a team of men scouring the countryside and located the cat or some shred of evidence of what happened to it.

This is not the jungle; this is not the Everglades; this is not New York City with the dense population. It is thinly populated and it is no problem at all to question all the people here and have them questioned by somebody and get at the truth and not permit somebody to conceal the truth just because they are afraid of being sued or something like that. Proper questions by people skilled in questioning could have been had. The animal could have been searched for by a team of people skilled in the ways of animals of this type. I know one thing; if a zoo had lost some valuable animal in this area, there would have been twenty-five or thirty men scouring the countryside, men skilled in the habits and ways of an animal of this kind and would have found it by now.

If there was a dangerous animal escaped from some zoo or circus like a goddamned wildcat or leopard or some animal, you can be goddamned sure they would have found it by now. I consider the loss of this particular animal and the consequences it has had to my wife to be just as important, and in the light of my resources and ability to pursue a matter of this kind, I feel that it is absolutely no reason why a search should not have been instigated for this animal equal in any way to what would have happened if some damn train had broken down here and some leopard or panther or whatnot had escaped. There is absolutely no reason why a man of my resources and having the resources and organization that I have got, there is no goddamned reason in the world why efforts to locate this animal should not have been made equal in every way to what would have occurred if some dangerous animal had escaped in this area. . . .

In this situation here you don't think Bill has done anything wrong, going off today to pursue his social activities, whatever it may be, while this situation of complete tragedy occurs down here and my home is likely to be broken completely assunder [*sic*]. You don't think that at all. You think that is my business and my worry and if Bill wants to go to his social affairs that is OK and I am expecting too much. . . . You repeat this please, if you took this down in shorthand or on the tape. I wish you would repeat it wholly, the whole thing from A to Z and if it is on the tape, I hope you will play it seven times because I never meant anything more sincerely than I mean this and if this is the end of the road for this group then let's wash up the other end of Romaine Street just as we did with Dietrich. . . .[41]

Two days after Hughes's irate telephone conversation, Jean's cat padded quietly out of the trees and into the house.

While waiting for the Civil Aeronautics Board to act on his bid to take over Northeast Airlines, Hughes and Jean moved back to Los Angeles, on Thanksgiving Day of 1961. The plumbing at the Rancho Santa Fe house required major repair, and rather than let plumbers into the house, Hughes decided to move.[42] Romaine Street had several expensive homes under lease in Beverly Hills and Bel Air. Hughes chose a French Regency-style mansion at 1001 Bel Air Road, in a neighborhood of lavish estates. The new house afforded spectacular vistas in all directions—the Santa Monica Mountains to the north and west, the vast Los Angeles basin with its myriad cities and towns to the east, and the gentle coastal ranges rolling out like waves to the Pacific Ocean to the south. But most appealing to Hughes, the house provided extraordinary privacy. A dense growth of foliage and trees shielded all but the very top of the roof from Bel Air Road; a heavy iron—and patrolled—fence barred access to the grounds.

At Bel Air, Hughes and Jean gave up on their brief experiment at cohabitation and moved into separate quarters. Hughes chose a spacious, thickly carpeted bedroom with its own bathroom and dressing room at the southeast corner of the house, far away from the living and dining areas. There was a large window looking south onto far-off hillside estates and beyond them to the mountains bordering the sea. But, as at Rancho Santa Fe, Hughes was oblivious to the beauty around him. Craving only seclusion, he had thick drapes installed to block out the view and shield the room from sunlight. Only the barest essentials surrounded him—a double bed, a small side table, a table-model television set, a contour chair, and two overstuffed chairs. Romaine Street workmen installed a window air conditioner designed to control and purify the air at all times. On arrival, Hughes climbed promptly into bed, as though he had transferred from one hospital to another.

While Hughes cared little where he was living, Holmes and Crawford were glad to be back in Los Angeles. It brought them closer to their families and did away with the weekly two-hundred-mile round trip. Romaine Street sent a third aide to work at Bel Air—George A. Francom, Jr., a quiet, easygoing, devout Mormon and family man. A native of tiny Payson, Utah, the forty-four-year-old Francom had served as a Mormon missionary and attended Brigham Young University before the Second World War. With hopes of becoming a pilot, he enlisted in the air force but "washed out" because of airsickness.[43] For the rest of the war he was a medical technician. He later attended the University of Southern California, planning to become a dentist, but dropped out after two years. He was working in heavy construction in 1954 when a friend told him that Hughes Productions was looking for a driver. Like almost everyone else at Romaine Street, Francom had started by chauffeuring starlets and running errands. With Francom's arrival at Bel Air, the three aides divided up the daily schedule into shifts of eight hours each. They worked every day, seven days a week, covering for each other during emergencies.

Merely having the aides on twenty-four-hour duty at the house was not enough for Hughes. He wanted them in his bedroom. So a small table and two chairs were placed near the door leading to the rest of the house, a telephone was installed for contact with Operations, and the aide on duty sat there for hours at a time, reading or talking to Operations, while Hughes lay propped up in bed at the opposite end of the room. The aides, however, were uncomfortable with the arrangement and soon persuaded Hughes to let them convert a dressing room on the other side of the bathroom into an office. Since it was only a few feet away from the bedroom, the little cubicle was close enough for Hughes's comfort, yet sufficiently removed to give the aides some privacy. Holmes, a smoker, was particularly pleased with the arrangement. Now when he wanted a cigarette he could step into the big walk-in closet and light up. To allay Hughes's fears over not being able to see them, the aides bought him a bell and placed it on the table next to his bed.

Less than two weeks after the move to Bel Air, the CAB handed Hughes his first victory in the grand plan to recapture control of TWA. On December 4, 1961, the board ruled that Northeast could seek emergency aid from the Hughes Tool Company: "We find that Northeast is in such a critical financial condition that it is in need of emergency financial assistance; without such assistance, it is very likely that the carrier will be forced into bankruptcy; and that such a financial collapse will have serious adverse effects on the public interest."[44] For the time being, the CAB sidestepped the delicate questions of whether Hughes had already gained control and whether his return to the airline business was in the public interest. The board promised to make a full inquiry into those questions in the future. "All we decide," it said, "is that the advancement of funds is not adverse to the public interest and meets the approval of the board."[45] Although hardly a warm reception from the CAB, the ruling was nevertheless a victory for Hughes and he gladly accepted it.

Now Hughes moved swiftly to wind up the Northeast deal. He dispatched Raymond Cook to New York to negotiate an agreement with the Atlas Corporation to buy its 55-percent interest. Hughes outlined two proposals. The first was "$3,5000,000 cash for Atlas' interest in Northeast—no strings, no conditions, no option." The appeal of this offer, Hughes said, would be that he was rescuing one of Atlas's major assets from bankruptcy. "I think the absolute, all-out, horror-filled tragedy of Atlas permitting Northeast to go bankrupt to the serious financial destruction of the stockholders is something so serious that it would destroy public confidence in Atlas as a sound investment trust."[46]

His second proposal was the "exchange of my [Atlas] stock plus $1,000,000 cash for Atlas's holdings in NE."[47] Hughes had originally paid slightly more than $6 million for his Atlas stock in the 1950s. If Atlas refused to accept that as the value of the holdings today, Hughes contended, it had only itself to blame: "Atlas management had full control of my $6,000,000 plus and if it is not worth $6,000,000 today, the responsibility lies only one place—Atlas—and it is from this same Atlas that we are contemplating buying Northeast, so I think due adjustment is owing us."[48] Whichever proposal was accepted, Hughes agreed to write off the $10.2

million that Hughes Tool had lent Northeast to keep it flying.

His new orders in hand, Cook returned to the bargaining table and wrapped up the negotiations. Hughes ended up paying $5 million instead of $3.5 million for Atlas's shares in Northeast, and agreed to provide $1 million more to the airline in interim assistance until the CAB approved the sale. With Atlas's 55 percent plus his own holdings, Hughes would own 66 percent of Northeast Airlines. The transaction was completed on December 28, 1961. Almost a year to the day after the eastern financial establishment had forced him to relinquish control of TWA, Hughes was back in the airline business.*

Buoyed by the outcome of the Northeast move, Hughes struck out at his adversaries less than six weeks later. On February 13, 1962, he filed a counter-suit in United States District Court in Manhattan against TWA, Breech, Tillinghast, and the lending institutions that had imposed the voting trust in December of 1960. Charging that the lenders had illegally conspired to seize TWA, Hughes asked the court to dissolve the voting trust, restore him to control of TWA, and award him $366 million in damages. TWA's case against Hughes was now threatening to sink into a swamp of litigation. It was no longer a matter of *TWA v. Hughes.* Now there were the Equitable Life Assurance Society, Metropolitan Life, the Irving Trust Company, and Dillon, Read, as well as Breech and Tillinghast. There would be more briefs, more depositions, more interrogatories. The case had already generated work for a small army of lawyers; it could only get worse.

MANHUNT

On the West Coast, Frederick P. Furth, a young lawyer in Sonnett's firm, was having his own problems. Only three years out of the University of Michigan Law School, Furth had been handed the unenviable assignment of serving Hughes personally with a subpoena. Hughes had not been seen in public for years. He was shielded by a private guard force and an intricate communications network designed specifically to insulate him from the outside world. He had spent years perfecting a reclusive lifestyle. How could any outsider penetrate such a system? Still, TWA was obliged to make the effort, and the energetic Furth set forth.

In Los Angeles, he teamed up with Alfred E. Leckey, a private investigator and former FBI agent. They hired a squad of sleuths to ferret out information on Hughes's homes or whereabouts. Furth and Leckey tried to serve the subpoena at places they suspected Hughes owned or leased and where he might be living. They were barred from the grounds of Rancho Santa Fe. At the gate of the Bel Air mansion they were turned away by the crewcut guards. They got no closer at other houses from Palm Springs to Hollywood where Hughes

---

*Hughes received approval from the CAB on June 19, 1962, to buy controlling interest in Northeast. He formally acquired Atlas's 55-percent interest on December 18, 1962.

was reportedly living. For weeks Furth conducted a vigil at the Beverly Hills Hotel, where Hughes still maintained a bungalow. Hughes, naturally, never appeared.

To help thwart the searchers, Hughes called on Robert Maheu. Using the experience gained in years of counterespionage and corporate intelligence work, Maheu subverted the manhunt. Erroneous tips were passed into the TWA camp that kept Leckey's private sleuths in perpetual motion. At one time or another Hughes was "spotted" in a New York elevator, a Los Angeles drugstore, and a secluded Mexican resort. The press eagerly followed the hunt. On hearing that Hughes strolled through the rose garden at Bel Air in the early morning hours, Thomas Thompson, a writer for *Life*, armed with a photographer, camped overnight outside 1001 Bel Air Road hoping for a glimpse.

All—reporters, detectives, and lawyers alike—were unable to find Hughes. The tips on Hughes's whereabouts, so skillfully planted by Maheu, led nowhere. Frustrated, the TWA investigators staked out the offices and homes of Hughes's top deputies in Los Angeles, hoping one of them might lead to the man. Leckey himself shadowed Maheu, all to no avail. As time went by, the Hughes-hunters developed a grudging admiration for their quarry's security system, and a near mysticism toward the man himself. Hughes seemed by some extraordinary means to be moving secretly around Southern California, shuttling among four or five mansions, always just a step or two ahead. An impressed *Saturday Evening Post* writer called the phantom industrialist a "modern-day Scarlet Pimpernel."[49]

Where high-priced Wall Street lawyers, street-wise investigators, and an army of experienced newsmen failed, however, a child succeeded, slipping through the previously invincible security system to come face to face with Howard Hughes in his bedroom at Bel Air—a bedroom that Hughes never left throughout the manhunt. The incident occurred one day when Jean's sister was visiting the house with her two children. Her son, about five years old, was exploring the long hallway that ran from the living room to Hughes's bedroom at the east end of the house. The door to that room was always kept closed but rarely latched. Jean had become irritated at the sound of Hughes's door opening and closing at all hours of the day and night as aides and cooks passed in and out. To solve the problem, the aides affixed layers of friction tape to the edge of the door and the door frame. This served to keep the door shut tightly and at the same time allowed it to be opened and closed without a sound. But on the day when Jean's nephew started down the hall toward the forbidden room, the system failed. Through constant use the tape had worn down, and although the door was closed, only the slightest nudge was necessary to open it. The little boy, curious to see what was on the other side, grabbed the handle and pushed.

A moment later, Hughes looked up in surprise from his bed to see a small boy staring up at him. "Hi," said the boy. John Holmes, who was then on duty, dashed into the room, picked the boy up, and started to whisk him out.[50] The startled Hughes asked who the boy was.

"That's E.J.," Holmes answered, adding that the child was Hughes's nephew.[51] The boy went by his initials, and Holmes did not know his full name. Holmes was starting out of the room when he met Jean coming down the hall, a big smile on her face. She took her nephew in her arms and carried him back into Hughes's bedroom, where she introduced them. She was amused by the incident and laughed as she took E.J. back with her to another part of the house.

Hughes did not think it was funny.

"Well, how did he get in here?" he asked Holmes when they were alone.[52]

Holmes made a quick examination and explained to Hughes that the boy had been able to simply push the door open. Hughes was skeptical. He thought Holmes had slipped up and left it open, allowing the first uninvited stranger in years inside to see him. He wanted a full report and Holmes obediently prepared one, closing with the fact that fresh tape had been applied to the door and frame and that the bedroom was once again secure.[53]

The more time they spent with Hughes, the more adept the aides became in recognizing his moods. As George Francom put it, "We didn't disturb him with a lot of things which normally a normal person would have liked to know about."[54] They had also perfected their sympathetic responses to Hughes's bizarre demands, handling with equal facility his simultaneous wars on germs and on Wall Street. Romaine Street had sent in another Mormon to ease the staff workload, bringing to four the number of attendants who looked after Hughes's every need around the clock. The extra man was needed because Hughes's withdrawal was continuing. Not only had he shut off all personal contact with his lawyers, the tool company executives, and all other outsiders, but now he used the telephone less and less, relying more on the aides to act as both voice and ears to the world at large. Messages to and from Operations and Hughes executives were transmitted through the aides. The latest addition to the staff was Levar Beebe Myler. Like many of the other Mormons in the organization, the forty-year-old Myler had been born and raised in Utah. After working as an air force mechanic during the Second World War, he took several odd jobs in the West, and entered first Los Angeles City College and then Idaho State College with the intention of becoming a mathematics teacher. In 1950, after one year of college, Myler returned to Los Angeles. When he learned of a job opening at Romaine Street through the Mormon church's employment office, he applied and was hired as a driver. For the first few years, he chauffeured actresses, delivered RKO films, ran other errands, and did "whatever needed to be done."[55] In the late 1950s, he was appointed to the "President's staff," the designation Bill Gay had given to the cadre of helpers who were assigned to Hughes personally.

And for the first time now, the asylum had its own one-man "medical staff"—Dr. Norman F. Crane, a Beverly Hills internist who had once shared offices with Dr. Verne Mason, the physician who treated Hughes following his 1946 plane crash and went on to head the Howard Hughes Medical Institute. Crane's duties were quite unlike those of most doctors. He did not treat

Hughes for his mental disorders. He did not give him thorough physical examinations. He did not treat him for any serious physical ailments. Rather, Crane's practice was limited largely to supplying the prescriptions for Hughes's drugs.[56] In the beginning it was Dr. Mason who furnished the prescriptions, but that responsibility had been taken over gradually by Crane.

During Crane's periodic visits to Bel Air, two changes occurred in Hughes's drug habit. For more than fifteen years he had been taking Empirin Compounds, including one containing codeine. And for more than a decade he had been taking, orally, one-grain codeine tablets. Now Hughes was provided with one-grain codeine tablets that could be dissolved in water and injected by syringe. In addition, he was given Valium, a nonnarcotic, but habit-forming tranquilizer. The prescriptions were written in the names of the aides—especially Holmes, Crawford, and Francom—and filled at designated pharmacies. The Horton & Converse drugstore on Wilshire Boulevard, where Crawford began filling prescriptions in the 1950s, remained a favorite.[57] Another was the Roxbury Pharmacy on Olympic Boulevard in Beverly Hills.[58]

Hughes himself had fallen into a fixed routine. He usually slept until midafternoon, waking at two or three o'clock and receiving a glass of fruit juice for breakfast. His reading had picked back up, and he read then or watched an afternoon movie on television. If he decided to read, it was a weekly newsmagazine, *Time* or *Newsweek,* a recent newspaper, or more often, bulky manuals of aircraft specifications. Using a powerful, black-handled magnifying glass, he scanned the columns of type and specifications like a detective in search of a clue. He was farsighted and very much needed eyeglasses, but he refused to wear them, or even submit to an eye examination. In the early evening he watched the news and then studied *TV Guide,* selecting a series of television shows and late movies to watch until dawn. He rarely screened movies at Bel Air. Los Angeles television stations were serving up a steady diet of the films he liked—adventure movies with a lot of action and little romance. When the last movie ended, Hughes ate his one meal of the day, usually a steak and a vegetable, topped off with his favorite dessert, French vanilla ice cream. He ate slowly, sometimes taking as long as two and a half hours to finish a meal. Then he turned to business, reading memoranda from the field and dictating replies. In the early-morning hours, when many Americans were arriving at work, he dropped off to sleep.

Except for visits to the bathroom, Hughes remained in his double bed, which he later exchanged for a metal hospital bed he ordered specially. He seldom washed. His hair fell down his back. His beard trailed onto his chest. And he was naked most of the time. His sealed chamber was barred to all but a few authorized people: the aides, the cooks, his doctors, a few trusted functionaries from Romaine Street like Oran Deal—who dutifully picked up and disposed of Hughes's trash each day—and Jean Peters. Jean usually visited twice a day, once in the late afternoon and again for twenty or thirty minutes late at night. Her visits were arranged through the aide on duty. Hughes did not like to be interrupted during a television show or while occupied in one of his rituals. When ready to see his wife, he summoned the aide: "Would you ask Mrs. Hughes if she could visit now?"[59] Jean would make her way from the other side of the house, draw one of the overstuffed chairs up close to his bed, and tell him about her day and her plans for the next. Hughes would respond by telling her about his day. To win her sympathy, he often complained of a "very bad day, didn't eat as much as he wanted to, didn't feel good."[60] If Jean had enjoyed a good day, the aides recalled, then Hughes invariably reported the opposite.

The secrecy that cloaked Hughes's life was so complete that no word leaked out indicating the true state of the marriage. What little did appear in print suggested that the two were—in their own eccentric way—happily married. A September 1962 article in *Life* said that "according to one of the few friends who still see Jean Hughes, life with Howard is a 'lonely one,' but she has apparently adjusted to it. She genuinely loves Howard, and despite his strange ways, theirs is a good marriage."[61]

THE VICTOR AND THE SPOILS

Despite the failure of the TWA manhunt, John Sonnett, the architect of TWA's case, was determined to keep the pressure on Howard Hughes. By ducking the subpoena, Hughes had both complicated and delayed TWA's case and convinced Sonnett of the wisdom of his course. Clearly, Hughes was deeply afraid of being forced into the open. In the spring of 1962, Sonnett hit on a new avenue of attack.

If TWA could not find Hughes, perhaps the tool company could be forced to disclose his whereabouts. Sonnett drew up interrogatories—a series of formal written questions requiring written answers under oath—focusing on Hughes's residency and applied to the court for an order compelling the tool company to respond. Judge Charles M. Metzner had appointed a special master, J. Lee Rankin, former solicitor-general of the United States under Eisenhower, to represent him at pretrial proceedings and depositions, and it was to Rankin that Sonnett appealed. If Rankin approved, Hughes's wholly owned company would have to reply or risk a contempt citation. Sonnett's timing could not have been better. By avoiding the subpoena, Hughes had impressed the court as one who held himself above the law. While TWA executives were submitting to months of questioning by Hughes's attorneys, Hughes was beyond the reach of his opponents. On April 17, 1962, Rankin granted Sonnett's motion and gave TWA the right to question the tool company about Hughes's whereabouts. July 1 was the deadline for a reply.

The next day, April 18, Sonnett filed a second TWA lawsuit against Hughes and the tool company, this one a $35-million damage claim in the New Castle County Chancery Court in Wilmington, Delaware, the state where both the tool company and TWA were incorporated. In going to Wilmington, Sonnett sought to apply pressure on Hughes by taking advantage of an unusual provision in Delaware law. In Delaware civil cases, the stock of a defendant can be seized and sequestered by the court while the lawsuit is being heard. Thus, if Hughes failed to appear, the court could order his stock sold to satisfy any judgment. The day the complaint was filed, TWA obtained an order seizing Hughes's 25,000 shares of Hughes Tool Company stock. The stock could not be voted or sold without approval of the court. For the first time, Hughes's ultrasecret corporate umbrella was technically under the control of an outsider.

Of TWA's two legal maneuvers, the court order requiring the tool company to divulge Hughes's location posed the gravest immediate threat to Hughes. Unlike the manhunt, which could be foiled, the residency questions had to be answered or Hughes would run the risk of inviting a default judgment. As he would so often, Chester Davis appealed to the special master for an extension, and when that was denied, appealed once again to Judge Metzner for more time. On July 27, the judge extended the tool company's deadline until August 27.

Hughes was running out of time. Would he answer? When August 27 came and went, Sonnett thought not. But the next day, Davis surprised him. He had in his possession, Davis said, a letter from Hughes authorizing acceptance of the long-delayed subpoena calling for Hughes's appearance for a deposition. Rather than respond to the court order to disclose Hughes's residence, Davis had chosen a lesser evil, and one that would buy him more time. Davis asked that the document not be made part of the court record. Sonnett was intrigued. A few days later, when he got a look at it, Sonnett was puzzled by Hughes's so-called authorization. On a standard eight-by-eleven sheet of white paper, bearing no letterhead or any other identifying mark, was a simple declaration: "Mr. Chester C. Davis. You are hereby authorized to accept service on my behalf." The paper was signed: "Howard R. Hughes."[62] There was no date, no address, no mention of the case, nothing at all to bear out the authenticity of the document.

On September 6, 1962, Sonnett rocked Judge Metzner's courtroom in Foley Square by charging that the Hughes authorization was a fraud. Sonnett had called in Charles A. Appel, Jr., a handwriting expert, who concluded that the signature on the paper was not Hughes's. Sonnett told the judge: "It is beyond doubt that somebody in the Hughes Tool Company willfully, knowingly, purposefully, in order to mislead counsel for TWA and this court, submitted a forged document. I think on that ground alone your Honor should strike the answer and give us a default judgment."[63] Although Sonnett did not know it, Hughes's signature had been forged by a Romaine Street lieutenant. Whether it was the first time his signature had been forged, is uncertain, but it would not be the last. Still, Judge Metzner was in no hurry. Earlier that morning, he had learned that the subpoena calling for Hughes's court appearance had finally been served. Davis had accepted it for his client in Los Angeles. "If Mr. Hughes appears on September 24th," the judge asked, "then hasn't all of this been moot?"[64] He took no action on TWA's forgery charges.

The stage was set for Hughes's deposition.

It is unclear whether Davis was aware of Hughes's mental state and that he was totally incapable of appearing in a courtroom. Davis had never met Hughes, had only talked to him a few times on the telephone. Whatever the case, Davis initiated a series of evasive actions and counterattacks to keep Hughes out of court. By deluging the court with motions, he won two postponements. But on October 29, Rankin, the special master, set a mid-February appearance date and warned that there would be no more extensions.

Davis then appealed to the United States Court of Appeals, claiming, as he had all along, that the CAB, not a federal court, was the proper forum to hear antitrust charges. The motion was denied. Ten days later, Davis hurriedly filed a similar motion before Judge Metzner. This was also denied. Time was running out again. Hughes was to appear at 10 A.M. on February 11, 1963, in the United States Courthouse in Los Angeles to give his testimony. In deference to his hearing problem, special amplifying equipment and a set of foam-rubber padded earphones were provided in the courtroom. To almost no one's surprise on February 11, Hughes did not appear.

Sonnett had been been right. Now he moved swiftly in New York for a default judgment. It seemed certain that the lawsuit would never even advance to a hearing on its merits. By defaulting, Hughes had given TWA a victory without a contest.

On May 3, 1963, Judge Metzner awarded a default judgment to TWA and dismissed Hughes's $366-million countersuit. Contending that Hughes's deposition was essential to the case, the judge said his failure to appear was "deliberate and willful and justifies the court entering a default judgment."[65] Metzner referred the case back to the special master to establish the amount of the damages, which TWA said could run as high as $145 million. The only ray of hope for Hughes in the otherwise crushing defeat was Judge Metzner's inaction on TWA's motion for a court order forcing Hughes to sell his 78-percent stock interest in TWA: "The propriety of granting this prayer for relief will be determined [later] by the court."[66] Chester Davis took the only option he had—he appealed the decision to the United States Court of Appeals.

Admirers and critics of Howard Hughes might disagree in their evaluations of his intelligence and business acumen, but on one point there is no argument. He was exceptionally strong-willed and stubborn. Once he engaged in a fight, he stayed to the end, and so it was in the TWA struggle. In the spring of 1964, as he awaited the decision of the Court of Appeals, Hughes launched a legal counterattack against TWA.

On April 29, 1964, Hughes Tool applied to the CAB for permission to acquire $92.8 million in notes outstanding from the loan agreements executed at the time the voting trust was imposed. It was a bold stroke. If the CAB approved, Hughes could buy out the lenders, dissolve the voting trust, and regain control of TWA. The securities were 6.5-percent sinking-fund notes held by the Equitable Life Assurance Society and the Metropolitan Life Insurance Company. In addition to serving notice on TWA that the battle still raged, this latest move also proved that Hughes, close to bankruptcy in 1960, had weathered the storm. The tool company was once again producing profits to underwrite the rest of his empire.

But before the CAB could act, the United States Court of Appeals on June 2 affirmed Judge Metzner's default judgement and, if anything, came down even harder on Hughes for his "intolerable" conduct in the case.[67] The three-judge panel ruled that Hughes's "deposition was absolutely essential to the proper conduct of the litigation. Yet he and [the tool company] seized upon every opportunity to forestall this event. Hughes and [the tool company] seemed to look upon the entire discovery proceedings as some sort of a game, rather than as a means of securing the just and expeditious settlement of the important matters in dispute."[68] Last, the court dismissed Hughes's claim that his conduct at TWA had been "immunized" from antitrust law by the CAB, ruling that the CAB's approval of his control of TWA "did not carry with it approval of every transaction which [the tool company] might choose to effect in the exercise of its control."[69] Hughes had lost the second round. Davis began preparing an appeal to the United States Supreme Court.

Five weeks later, the CAB handed Hughes a stunning, if temporary, victory. Acting on his April 29 application with extraordinary speed, the board voted to allow Hughes Tool Company to reassume control of TWA by acquiring the $92.8 million in notes from Equitable and Metropolitan. The board's only condition was that Hughes would first have to offer a plan divesting himself of control in Northeast Airlines, since one person could not control two airlines. The CAB order was Hughes's greatest coup. That the decision was made without a full-scale CAB investigation, and despite the pending TWA lawsuit, and in violation of the CAB's own 1960 dictum that said Hughes would not be permitted to run TWA ever again without a "searching inquiry" by the agency, was a measure of Hughes's restored political influence at the CAB. TWA was enraged. Tillinghast found the CAB order "deeply disturbing."[70] In view of the lawsuit, he was "astonished" that the agency could issue an order "without any hearing."[71] TWA appealed.

The CAB maneuver was brilliant, but in the end not enough to reverse the tide of battle. On December 7, 1964, the United States Court of Appeals in New York set aside the CAB order, claiming that the agency had acted improperly. In March of 1965, the Supreme Court refused to hear an appeal in *TWA v. Hughes*, meaning that the judgment against Hughes was left to stand. One by one, the avenues of appeal were sealed off. Now only one remained—appealing to the Supreme Court the decision setting aside the CAB order. But Hughes could not have been hopeful. Rejected consistently by the courts, he was beginning to worry about what the case might eventually cost. After more than four years, his goal of recapturing TWA was even more distant.

In October of 1965, the Supreme Court, confirming Hughes's worst fears, announced that it would not review the Court of Appeals decision which overturned the CAB order. The battle was virtually over. Still to come were only hearings before the special master to establish the amount of damages he would have to pay TWA. More important, it now seemed impossible for him ever to control TWA again. Faced with that prospect, he decided early in 1966 to sell out.

With airline stocks booming, the timing was perfect. A group of brokerage firms headed by Merrill Lynch, Pierce, Fenner & Smith was organized to handle the sale. Documents were forwarded to Romaine Street, which sent them on to Bel Air, where Hughes signed them, authorizing the sale of his TWA shares. On the morning of May 3, 1966, the Hughes era at TWA ended. His 6,584,937 shares were snapped up at $86 a share in little more than an hour. After brokers' fees, Hughes received a check for $546,549,171, making the sale one of the largest stock transactions in history. By a curious irony, Hughes owed this great good fortune to his enemies—the men who had forced him to put his stock in trust back in 1960. Under new management, TWA had rolled up record profits, more than $215 million in the last five years, or more than double the profits the airline earned in Hughes's fifteen-year reign.* The airline's stock was selling at near its all-time high. Had Hughes sold out in December of 1960, when the lenders forced his hand, and when TWA stock was going for about $13 a share, he would have come away with a check for about $85 million. His enemies had given him a $460-million windfall. Even so, there was no rejoicing at Bel Air. There were still the two TWA lawsuits —in federal court in New York, where a special master was conducting hearings to assess damages against Hughes, and in the state court in Wilmington. In addition, the incredible profit from the stock sale created a special problem for Hughes. Not only would he have to pay a substantial federal capital-gains tax on his more than half-billion dollars, he also faced a stiff California income tax.

For years, Hughes had been feuding with California tax authorities, who insisted that he should pay the state income tax. Even though he had lived almost continuously in Los Angeles since 1925, Hughes always maintained that he was a resident of Texas and not subject to the California tax. "I am a Texan and always will be," he had protested in 1944 to one California tax man.[72] Not buying the argument, California levied the tax, and Hughes, under protest, paid. But now, if he remained in the state he would face a tax bill running into the millions of dollars. As he often did when he was anxious about taxes, Hughes turned for advice to Mickey West, his tax lawyer in Houston. West prepared a list of states and foreign countries with favorable tax structures, and while West did not "presume" to tell Hughes where he should live, he did stress that it was "highly advisable that he physically depart from California."[73]

*See Appendix B.

And why not? There were no compelling reasons to remain in California, certainly no business reasons. Hughes no longer met anyone from the outside world; his own men communicated to him by memoranda, which, of course, he could receive anywhere. Hughes considered a number of potential locations —the Bahamas, the Mediterranean, England, Las Vegas—finally settling, incredibly, on Boston, a city he had known only slightly as a student in the Fessenden School forty-six years ago. Equally surprising, he did not want to fly. He wanted to go by train.

Hughes had George Francom call Robert Maheu to work out the security and transportation. Maheu lined up two private Pullman cars and began the complicated negotiations with several railroads for transporting the cars cross-country. The aides began to worry. Hughes had not told them why he was leaving California or what his plans were. He told the newest aide at Bel Air, Howard L. Eckersley, only that he wanted to move. The thirty-nine-year-old Eckersley, another Mormon, had joined the aide corps in 1964 after Levar Myler suffered a serious heart attack. Eckersley required no orientation: he was very familar with how to attend to Hughes. He had once operated the movie projector in Bungalow 4. Like his co-workers, Eckersley had a lackluster record before going to work for Hughes. Raised in Utah, he had attended Brigham Young University, the University of Washington, UCLA, and the University of Utah twice, accumulating credits in industrial psychology but no degree. Afterward, he worked for a finance company and then spent three years as an industrial psychologist for the state of Utah. Feeling "dead-ended," he talked to a friend who worked for Hughes Productions in Hollywood and in 1957 went to work in Operations as a message clerk. Like Holmes, Crawford, and Francom, Eckersley could talk about aviation with Hughes. He was an amateur pilot.

None of the aides wanted to leave California. They were unsettled by the idea of traveling three thousand miles to a new place of work for an indeterminate length of time, without their families. As usual, there was no way of knowing how long Hughes might stay in Boston, but they feared the worst. Several remembered Holmes's unhappy Montreal–Bahamas experience in 1957, when Hughes had stretched a trip of "seven to ten days" into six months. By mid-July, Maheu had completed arrangements for the journey. The two private railroad cars, under tight security, sat ready at the Union Pacific terminal in Pomona, a suburb in eastern Los Angeles County. Not a word had leaked that the reclusive industrialist was about to make a cross-continent journey. On the night of July 16, 1966, Maheu passed word to Bel Air that everything was set.

The next night, Hughes, Holmes, Crawford, Francom, and Eckersley drove the fifty miles from Bel Air to Pomona to board the train. It was the first time Hughes had been outside in four and a half years.

CHAPTER 11

A NEW CAREER

THE GUEST WHO OVERSTAYED

WHEN Hughes and his staff arrived in Boston after an uneventful three-day train trip, they took over the entire fifth floor of the fashionable Ritz-Carlton Hotel. Although never formally acknowledged, Hughes's presence was quickly confirmed when the fifth-floor waiter was assigned to other duties, the brass knob was removed from a fire door on the stairs, the flower-scented elevators no longer stopped on five, and anyone who still managed to reach the floor was confronted by guards.

When the news media discovered that Hughes had quietly slipped into Boston, it was widely speculated that he was ill and required the attention of medical specialists. A three-room suite, it was said, was reserved for him in Peter Bent Brigham Hospital. The rumor made sense because Dr. George W. Thorn, physician-in-chief at the hospital, also happened to be director of medical research for the Howard Hughes Medical Institute. Half a dozen physicians or medical specialists in Boston-area hospitals and medical schools had also worked for or were then receiving grants from the institute.

The train trip itself was considered evidence that Hughes was too sick to fly. His legend, after all, had been built in airplanes. It was reported variously that he was in Boston to undergo treatment for emphysema, to correct his chronic deafness, or to cure a heart defect. One newspaper disclosed that "word has leaked out that he's suffering 'eye trouble,' but some sources suspect the ailment is more serious than that."[1]

But as was so often the case in Hughes's life, the public view and the private reality were greatly at odds. It was just as well, for few would have believed the truth.

Ever since 1925 when he had moved to Hollywood and begun making movies, Hughes had lived in the Los Angeles area. There were brief interludes in Las Vegas, Miami, Montreal, or Nassau, but he always returned to California. Now he had left permanently. And in a decision befitting the "eccentric" label he had so richly earned, Hughes traveled three thousand miles to Boston and spent a quarter of a million dollars to ponder the weighty question of where he would make his next home.

Hughes talked to Holmes about going to the Bahamas or to Montreal. As he considered his options, his staff kept planes and trains in readiness to leave the minute the world's wealthiest procrastinator made up his mind. The weeks turned to months. Running true to form, Hughes could not make a decision. Jean flew to Boston and spent "two or three weeks" with her husband at the Ritz-Carlton.[2] They looked over maps of the Boston area and Hughes told her he was considering buying a summer house there and planned to go yachting, but Jean "did not feel that [he] was serious."[3] When she returned to the Bel Air house, Jean continued to talk with Hughes by telephone, discussing where they would live next. On one occasion, Hughes told her he was calling from Florida, but in truth he was still in Boston. Finally, after four months of deliberations, Montreal, Nassau, Boston, and Miami all were rejected for a more nostalgic setting—Las Vegas.

With his customary attention to detail and secrecy, Hughes turned to planning the actual move, which once again was to be made by train. The trip, he ordered,

must be through Chicago. Must be 20th Century and Union Pacific streamliner City of Los Angeles. Maximum security should be possible. Ready now [to] definitely leave very earliest departure possible by train consistent with maximum security. Will leave present local men here, but in a room not visible to public or hotel employes. Expect bring them west and make a part of permanent group, but not until I give signal. This location will be permanent for foreseeable future, but don't disclose that. This should make a practical and happy arrangement.[4]

During Thanksgiving week, Hughes left Boston as quietly as he had arrived, in a pair of private railroad cars. The journey was uneventful until the Union Pacific's *City of Los Angeles* suffered an equipment breakdown in Ogden, Utah. Hughes was greatly distressed. He might reach Las Vegas now in the middle of the day, under the bright desert sun, rather than at night as he had planned. If that happened, he might be seen and recognized or, worse, photographed. The dilemma was resolved when Jack Hooper, a former Los Angeles police officer who was assisting Maheu with security, rented a locomotive that pulled the Hughes cars to the gambling capital during the early morning hours of Sunday, November 27. About 4 A.M., the abbreviated passenger train stopped at a crossing just north of the city and a waiting motorcade whisked Hughes and his aides to their new home—the top floor of the Desert Inn Hotel and Casino.

For Hughes, the man who set airplane speed records, who was more comfortable alone in the air than with people on the ground, the cross-country railroad trips symbolized a complete break with the past. For the time being at least, Romaine Street, which had been such a crucial part of his daily existence for the past two decades, and which had been so instrumental in the creation and maintenance of the asylum, had been shoved into the background. Hughes had maintained a love–hate relationship with Romaine Street's anonymous chief of staff, Bill Gay, for years. When he was waging one of his intense campaigns against germs, Hughes treated Gay deferentially, showering him with praise, insisting that he was the only man capable of guarding the empire against contamination. But when it came to business or other personal affairs, Hughes often berated Gay for the most trivial, if not imagined, failings. When he once asked for some aviation magazines to read in his bedroom and they were not delivered promptly, Hughes bitterly denounced Gay and his Romaine Street crew:

I want these aviation magazines and I requested them four days ago and it is just ludicrous that I have not received them. There is *Aviation Week, Aviation, Aero Digest, Flying*—the one that I got—there is *American Aviation,* there are countless aviation magazines in this country and an equal number in England and France and for me to sit here for four days and have two issues of one British magazine and one issue of one American magazine, this just absolutely is ludicrous. They didn't even get me a copy of *Flight*—they didn't get me any copy of any U.S. magazine until after forty-eight hours, whereas during that time a simple trip to one of the airports would have obtained at least *Flying.* This is just absolutely appalling to me. . . . This is typical of our whole slovenly indifferent way this entire operation of mine is handled and I can name so many more parallels I would be here the whole stinking day doing it. . . . It just saps at my guts and my ailing constitution. The damage it does to my system physiologically is beyond imagination. I am telling you I would be better off if I did not have the assistance of that Romaine Street office than to have it go on in this very disappointing fashion. I want to know why my office has to be so completely inefficient, inadequate, careless, indifferent, ineffective, slovenly, and Christ almighty it is now four days since my request. I want to know what Bill intends to do about that office at Romaine Street.[5]

But a far more serious dereliction than the undelivered aviation magazines was Gay's failure—at least in Hughes's view—to make Hughes's marriage to Jean Peters prosper. Even Hughes sensed that his relationship with Jean—no matter how odd it had been—was nearing an end, and he placed the blame squarely on his chief Mormon aide. "Bill's total indifference and laxity to my pleas for help in my domestic area, voiced urgently to him, week by week throughout the past seven to eight years, have resulted in a complete, I am afraid irrevocable loss of my wife," Hughes said later. "I blame Bill completely for this unnecessary debacle. I feel he let me down—utterly, totally, completely."[6]

Against this background, Hughes, who had been gradually coming out of his severe depression of the past several years, decided to cut the ties to Romaine Street, and especially to Bill Gay. He was provided with the perfect opportunity to do so by Robert Maheu, who had so efficiently managed the moves from Los Angeles to Boston and from Boston to Las Vegas, and who always seemed to succeed where Romaine Street failed.

Hughes instructed Maheu "in no uncertain terms that he wanted a complete severance from the Hollywood group; that he did not want [Maheu] to bring any of the Romaine people to Las Vegas."[7] He went so far as to insist that "he did not want Mr. Gay even to visit Las Vegas."[8] In addition, "he did not want any communications devices set up between the penthouse and the Hollywood offices."[9] Not long after, when Hughes learned that Kay Glenn, Gay's chief assistant, was in Las Vegas to install a teletype system linking the Desert Inn and Romaine Street, "he advised that this should be discontinued immediately."[10]

A few days after Hughes came to Las Vegas, he was warmly welcomed by the *Las Vegas Sun,* one of the gambling city's two daily newspapers. Sounding a theme congenial to the recluse, Herman M. (Hank) Greenspun, the newspaper's owner, criticized members of the news media who over the years had "hounded" and forced Hughes "into a life of seclusion."[11]

Now, Greenspun wrote, "news media locally and around the country are speculating as to Mr. Hughes' whereabouts, his purposes and state of health. Frankly, it is none of their business unless he wishes to make it so. Such is the nature of our democratic form of government with its guaranteed right of privacy and dignity for the individual." Assuring Hughes that the *Las Vegas Sun* stood apart from all the other prying newsmen, Greenspun said his newspaper had "camped" on the story of Hughes's move to Las Vegas "for over a month," adding that "standing instructions were issued to the staff that no news stories appear for we believed the contributions made by this man entitle him to the privacy he seeks." Hughes's "self-effacement and humility," Greenspun said, "entitles him to a little private space here on his own earth. We hope he finds it in Nevada."[12]

But at least one Las Vegas citizen was unmoved by Greenspun's plea to allow Hughes a little "private space" in Nevada—or at least the particular private space which Hughes was then calling home. The citizen was Morris Barney (Moe) Dalitz, one of the four principal owners of the Desert Inn.

Back in the 1930s, Dalitz had been Cleveland manager of the national crime syndicate operated from New York by Charles (Lucky) Luciano, Benjamin (Bugsy) Siegel, and Meyer Lansky.[13] During the years of Prohibition, Dalitz was credited with building "a pretty good little nest egg out of rum running."[14]

But gambling was Dalitz's first love. One of his Cleveland enterprises back in the 1930's had been the Prospect Advertising Company, a front for a gambling operation. The company had achieved some prominence following the gangland-style murder of a Cleveland city councilman who was about to disclose some awkward details. Over the years Dalitz had also maintained an interest in such assorted illegal gambling enterprises as the Lookout Club in Covington, Kentucky, the Beverly Country Club in Newport, Kentucky, the

Pettibone Club in suburban Cleveland, the Jungle Inn near Youngstown, the Frolics Club in Miami, and a dog track at Dayton, Kentucky.[15] Once asked the secret of his ability to run gambling clubs in cities and states where gambling was unlawful, Dalitz observed, "Well, I don't know. I don't know if I can answer that intelligently."[16]

Dalitz and three of his Cleveland colleagues were among the original investors in the Desert Inn, which opened in April of 1950. With the affable Wilbur I. Clark, a former San Diego bellboy and riverboat gambler, serving as the front man, few took notice—or at least were impolite enough to mention —that the Desert Inn had been built largely with ill-gotten gains. In time, Dalitz became a respected member of the Las Vegas business community and an elder statesman of Nevada gambling.

A hard-nosed businessman noted for the profitability of his casinos, Dalitz had grudgingly rented Desert Inn rooms to Hughes only after extracting a promise that he would be out by Christmas.[17] As December wore on and the busy New Year holiday approached, Dalitz grew increasingly unhappy about his most affluent guest. All the Desert Inn's ninth-floor rooms were rented to Hughes. All the rooms on a lower floor were rented to members of his staff. Dalitz needed the rooms for people who would gamble.

Christmas came and went, and Hughes and his aides stood fast, showing no inclination to leave. Meanwhile, all along the glittering Strip the NO VA-CANCY sign appeared. Western Air Lines, a major carrier serving the gambling mecca, had every piece of its equipment in operation, ferrying twenty-four hundred passengers a day in and out of Las Vegas. At United Air Lines, passenger traffic was up 25 percent over the previous year and there was not one seat available out of Las Vegas until well into January.[18]

As New Year's Eve approached, Dalitz's apprehension turned to distress. "We had already confirmed many reservations for those two floors," he said, "in anticipation of Mr. Hughes moving, as he had promised."[19] The rooms had been set aside for in Dalitz's words, "very desirable patrons, who use the casino extensively."[20] These were the high-rollers, "the kind of people who do bet high, and who are responsible, and whose credit is good," Dalitz explained.[21] By this definition, Dalitz could not regard either Hughes or his aides as desirable patrons. Hughes, naturally, never left his room. His Mormon aides never gambled. Their mere presence was eroding Moe Dalitz's profits. And so, when it became clear that Hughes had no intention of voluntarily giving up his two floors, the Desert Inn management ordered him out of the hotel.[22]

This confrontation between one of the country's shrewdest gamblers and its wealthiest eccentric presented Maheu with his first critical test since arriving in Las Vegas. With other veteran Hughes lieutenants isolated in Los Angeles or Houston, Maheu was the man closest to Hughes, and he rose to the occasion. Hughes had an option generally unavailable to a tenant facing eviction: he could buy the building. It was an option he quickly decided to exercise, and he gave the assignment to Maheu.

MAHEU'S OLD FRIEND

As Maheu was wont to do when thrust into unfamiliar situations, he turned to an old friend for assistance, a man he had worked with in earlier days and other places. He was John Rosselli, a dapper, silver-haired, sixty-one-year-old Italian immigrant who wielded a certain influence along the Las Vegas Strip, where he was often found in the company of starlets, showgirls, or entertainers like Frank Sinatra and Dean Martin.

For both personal and professional reasons, Rosselli had early discarded his family name, Filippo Sacco. Skimming through an encyclopedia one day, he settled on the name Rosselli in memory of Cosimo Rosselli, a fifteenth-century Florentine painter, one of several artists summoned to Rome by Pope Sixtus IV to decorate the Sistine Chapel. The switch from Sacco to Rosselli was accomplished without benefit of legal formality, owing at least in part to the cloudy circumstances surrounding his arrival in the United States.

In the late fall of 1966, when Hughes settled into the Desert Inn, Rosselli was the Chicago crime syndicate's accredited representative in both Las Vegas and Hollywood, a dual position in which he had distinguished himself for more than a decade, earning the unwavering support of crime chieftain Salvatore (Sam) Giancana. Rosselli's credentials were indeed impeccable. His business career had begun at the age of eighteen when he attempted to burn down the family homestead in Somerville, Massachusetts, to collect the insurance. For a brief time he served as a courier in a narcotics ring, and then he moved on to the Capone gang in Chicago. With his profits from bootlegging he acquired an interest in Nationwide News, a wire service for bookmakers.

By the late 1930s, Rosselli had moved on to be the Chicago crime syndicate's labor-relations specialist in Los Angeles, where he lived with his wife, the actress June Lang. It was a job that came to an untimely end in 1943 when Rosselli, Charles (Cherry Nose) Gioe, Francis (The Immune) Maritote, three other members of the old Capone gang, and a union business manager were convicted in a multimillion-dollar motion-picture-industry extortion plot.[23] For his part in the shakedown, Rosselli spent more than three years in prison.

Throughout Rosselli's career, the list of his friends, associates, and co-workers—"You either click with people or you don't," he maintained—read like a "Who's Who of Organized Crime."[24] They included Al Capone, Frank Costello, Charles (Lucky) Luciano, Charlie Fischetti, Louis (Little New York) Campagna, Benjamin (Bugsy) Siegel, Anthony (Big Tuna) Accardo, Paul (The Waiter) Ricca, Frank (The Enforcer) Nitti, and Meyer Lansky.

It was precisely these associations that led Rosselli and the ex-FBI agent Maheu to form an alliance back in 1960. At the time, Maheu was on a leave of absence from Hughes, freelancing for the Central Intelligence Agency, as he occasionally did whenever the CIA had an especially sensitive mission in which it "didn't want to have an agency person or a government person get caught."[25] In this case, the mission was the assassination of Cuban premier Fidel Castro.

Morris B. "Moe" Dalitz, the dean
of Las Vegas's gambling entrepreneurs.
United Press International

Above: Robert A. Maheu, chief of
Hughes Nevada Operations.
United Press International

Right: John Rosselli, the Chicago
crime syndicate's man in Las Vegas.
Wide World Photos

The CIA had retained Maheu to serve as a go-between, and early in September of 1960 he met with Rosselli in the Brown Derby Restaurant in Beverly Hills and offered him a $150,000 contract to kill Castro. Rosselli accepted, and later that month the two men flew to Miami to lay the ground-work for Castro's removal. Rosselli, using the cover name John Rawlston, started screening Cuban candidates to carry out the work. Not long after, Rosselli introduced Maheu to two of his associates, a "Sam Gold," who he said would serve as a "backup man," and "Joe," who would "serve as a courier to Cuba and make arrangements there."[26] Sam Gold turned out to be Salvatore Giancana, of the Chicago crime syndicate. Joe was Santo Trafficante, the organized-crime boss in Cuba before Fidel Castro came to power.

From the very beginning Maheu had trouble with Giancana, whose mind was not on his work. The mobster was obsessed with a notion that his girl-friend, Phyllis McGuire of the singing McGuire Sisters, was having an affair with comedian Dan Rowan in Las Vegas. To allay Giancana's suspicions and keep him in Miami, Maheu arranged to have an electronic eavesdropping device installed in Rowan's room.

With the CIA's blessing, Maheu gave $1,000 of the agency's money to a Florida private detective to plant the bug. But after doing so, the detective unwisely left his monitoring equipment unattended in a nearby hotel room where it was discovered by a maid. The maid reported her find to local authorities. The detective was arrested, and he implicated Maheu before Ros-selli could post bond.

The FBI, completely unaware of the Castro assassination plot, launched an investigation. When FBI agents questioned Maheu, he was vague, telling them only that the wiretap was placed in connection with a project "on behalf of the CIA relative to anti-Castro activities."[27] At the same time, Sheffield Edwards, the CIA's director of security, sought "to persuade the Justice Department, via communications to the FBI, not to prosecute" Maheu and the others involved in the bugging.[28]

With the CIA applying pressure to kill the investigation, and with the FBI unsure of what Maheu, the syndicate, and the CIA were doing, the probe dragged on for more than a year. Finally, on March 23, 1962, FBI director J. Edgar Hoover wrote to the CIA's Edwards asking that the "CIA specifically advise whether it would or would not object to the initiation of criminal prosecution" against Maheu and the others on charges of conspiracy to violate the wiretapping statutes.[29] A few days later, Edwards advised the FBI that "any prosecution in the matter would endanger sensitive sources and methods used in a duly authorized intelligence project and would not be in the national interest."[30]

To further emphasize the need to protect Maheu and his crime-syndicate operatives, Lawrence Houston, the CIA's general counsel, asked the Justice Department not to prosecute "on grounds of security."[31] As the situation later was explained to FBI director Hoover by Attorney-General Robert F. Kennedy, the "CIA admitted that they had assisted Maheu in making this installation and for these reasons CIA was in a position where it could not afford to have any action taken against Giancana and Maheu."[32] For his part, a dismayed Hoover "expressed great astonishment at this in view of the bad reputation of Maheu and the horrible judgment in using a man of Giancana's background."[33]

Even after the wiretapping incident, the CIA zealously shielded Giancana from any annoying interference by the FBI so that the syndicate hoodlum could focus on Castro's assassination. Both Rosselli and Giancana carefully weighed the advantages and disadvantages of the various methods of fulfilling their contract. Giancana rejected the more traditional gangland approach of simply gunning Castro down "because it would be difficult to recruit someone for such a dangerous operation."[34]

Instead, he opted for poison, which the CIA agreed to produce. The first batch of pills was rejected "because they would not dissolve in water." A second batch, containing botulin toxin, was tested successfully on monkeys.[35] The pills were delivered to Rosselli in February of 1961. He in turn passed them on "to an official close to Castro who may have received kickbacks from the gambling interests." The official returned the pills a few weeks later, apparently because "he had lost his position in the Cuban government, and thus access to Castro."[36]

A second Cuban selected for the mission was given a $10,000 advance and the lethal pills by Maheu at a meeting at the Fontainebleau Hotel in Miami, according to Rosselli. With Trafficante and himself looking on, Rosselli recalled, Maheu "opened his briefcase and dumped a whole lot of money on his lap and also came up with the capsules and he explained how they were going to be used. As far as I remember, they couldn't be used in boiling soups and things like that, but they could be used in water or otherwise, but they couldn't last forever. It had to be done as quickly as possible."*[37] For whatever reason, this attempt to eliminate Castro, and several later efforts, ended in failure.

Throughout the period, as if Maheu did not have enough on his mind in trying to manage Castro's murder, keep Giancana on the case in Miami, and avoid a criminal indictment on wiretapping charges, he also had to placate Howard Hughes. The industrialist was greatly annoyed by Maheu's extended absence from the West Coast. At one point, Hughes called Maheu in Miami and demanded that he return to Los Angeles immediately. Because Hughes was becoming an important client and Maheu did not want to lose him, he explained the nature of the top-secret intelligence assignment, telling Hughes that "it included plans to dispose of Mr. Castro in connection with a pending invasion."[38] It was a piece of information that had not even been given to the president of the United States, John F. Kennedy.

When it became clear that Giancana could not deliver on the contract— the only such recorded failure in a career littered with corpses—Maheu headed

---

*Maheu denies that such a meeting took place, and he says he cannot recall being present when the pills were passed.

back to Los Angeles and the CIA began to work directly with Rosselli. A CIA official instructed Rosselli to maintain his Cuban contacts, according to testimony before a congressional committee, "but not to deal with Maheu or Giancana," whom he described as "untrustworthy" and "surplus."[39] As a result, in 1962, Rosselli delivered another batch of poison capsules and an arms shipment to his Cuban associates. Castro, however, was proving an elusive target. Once again the mission was unsuccessful, and with only failure to show for all its work, the CIA finally abandoned the assassination scheme.*

Their previous dealings made it only natural that Maheu should seek Rosselli's assistance when Hughes decided to buy the Desert Inn. Hughes himself approved of this approach, for he, too, had known Rosselli "for many years," although the nature of their relationship remains a mystery.[40] Rosselli had no direct financial interest in the Desert Inn, but Maheu had observed that his former CIA colleague "was able to accomplish things in Las Vegas."[41]

Maheu held his first talks about the Desert Inn with Rosselli and one of his friends, Ruby Kolod, another graduate of the Cleveland mob who was a part-owner. A compelling reason had recently developed for Kolod to sell his share of the Desert Inn and to encourage his partners to do the same. He had been convicted on federal conspiracy charges growing out of an extortion case, and the Nevada Gaming Control Board was determined to force him out of the gambling business.

Kolod's troubles had begun several years earlier when Robert Sunshine, a Denver lawyer and business promoter who was a frequent patron of the Desert Inn and an especially heavy loser, offered to sell him some shares in a Nebraska oil venture. Kolod accepted, walked over to the cashier's cage in the Desert Inn casino, and "instructed the woman in the cashier's cage to give Sunshine $68,000. The entire amount was handed to him in bills of $1,000, $500, $100 and $50 denominations."[42] Later, Willie Israel (Ice Pick Willie) Alderman, a gambling supervisor in another Las Vegas casino (who, it was said, had earned his nickname by developing the art of inserting an ice pick into the skulls of recalcitrants), acquired a half-interest in Kolod's investment. When Sunshine eventually informed Kolod that the $68,000 "was lost in dry wells and drilling expenses," the news was not well received.[43] Kolod told Sunshine that he could expect a visit from Kolod's "lawyers."

*Shortly before midnight on June 19, 1975, a visitor to Giancana's fortress-like home in Oak Park, a quiet suburb west of Chicago, pumped half a dozen .22-caliber bullets into the face and neck of the sixty-seven-year-old syndicate boss. Five days later, on June 24, Rosselli testified secretly before a United States Senate Select Committee investigating CIA efforts to assassinate foreign leaders, recounting the roles he and Giancana had played in the CIA's unsuccessful attempt to dispose of Castro. One year later, on July 28, 1976, Rosselli was stuffed into a fifty-five-gallon oil drum in Miami. Holes were punched in the drum, and it was weighted with chains and dropped into Biscayne Bay. Ten days later, two fishermen discovered the drum floating in Dumfoundling Bay, between North Miami and Miami Beach. Gases from Rosselli's decomposing body had brought the oil drum to the surface. The murders of both Giancana and Rosselli remain unsolved. For the record, the CIA announced that it was not involved in either slaying.

On a July afternoon in 1961, the "lawyers" dropped by Sunshine's Denver office. One of them was Felix (Milwaukee Phil) Alderisio, a Kolod associate from the Chicago crime syndicate whose expertise lay in the enforcement area. Alderisio was a suspect in more than a dozen unsolved murders. The other "lawyer" was Americo (Pete) DePietto, a syndicate hoodlum whose interests included bombings, strongarm robberies, hijackings, arson, and narcotics. Alderisio dispensed with the subtleties and forthrightly explained to Sunshine the purpose of the visit. "We're here to kill you," he said.[44]

For the next ninety minutes Sunshine frantically went through his books and records, trying to explain to the visitors what had happened to the $68,000. Alderisio listened. Then he told Sunshine that "only one man could save his life—Ruby Kolod."[45] After a hurried telephone call to a resort in the Catskill Mountains where Kolod was vacationing, the Desert Inn owner "consented to lift the death penalty" if Sunshine "agreed to repay the $68,000 at the rate of $2,000 a month."[46] Kolod warned Sunshine, however, that "if he failed to live up to his contract, Alderisio would be sent back to Denver and would take care of the job without even bothering to talk with him first."[47]

Sunshine heeded the warning and began to embezzle funds from his law clients to repay Kolod and Alderman. When the extortion conspiracy was uncovered, Kolod, Alderisio, and Alderman were indicted, and in April of 1965 were convicted in United States District Court in Denver. All three were sentenced to prison, but they remained free on bail while appealing their convictions.

When Maheu sat down with Ruby Kolod and John Rosselli in December of 1966, the initial discussions centered on securing a stay of Hughes's threatened eviction. Help for Hughes in that quarter came from an unexpected source. James Riddle Hoffa, president of the teamsters union, called his old friend Moe Dalitz and urged him to allow Hughes to remain at the Desert Inn. Dalitz and Hoffa "were practically raised in the same neighborhood" in Detroit, and teamsters pension funds had built and expanded several Las Vegas hotels and casinos, including the Stardust, in which Dalitz was also a major invester.[48]

Hoffa's call had been engineered by Maheu, via Edward P. Morgan, one of the union president's Washington attorneys and a personal friend of Maheu's from their FBI days. The call did not bring much more time—only until early January of 1967, but that was all the time Maheu needed. By now, Dalitz was very upset by all the pressure to permit Hughes to stay. When he encountered Hank Greenspun, the *Las Vegas Sun* editor and publisher, at the Desert Inn Country Club, he vented his feelings.

"Boy, if ever a man was ready to sell something, I am ready to sell this place," Dalitz snapped.

"Why don't you call Ed Morgan in Washington. He may be able to help you find a buyer," suggested Greenspun, who was a friend and client of Morgan's.

"Good idea," Dalitz said. "You call him."[49]

Greenspun obliged, and Morgan flew to Las Vegas to see if he could find a buyer for the Desert Inn. Maheu was waiting for him.

APRIL FOOL'S DAY

Thus, in January of 1967 the negotiations began in earnest. Maheu collected financial data on the Desert Inn and forwarded it to Hughes. Every day, Hughes had a dozen questions for which he wanted immediate answers. As the talks progressed, Maheu became concerned. He was negotiating a multi-million-dollar deal on behalf of a man he had never met and from whom he had no written authority. What's more, the purchase would be handled through the Hughes Tool Company in Houston, and Maheu had no authorization from the company to act in its name. He was also unsure of his ability to evaluate the complex financial statements of the Desert Inn and he therefore suggested to Hughes that Raymond Holliday or Calvin J. Collier, Jr., the tool company's two top officers, come to Las Vegas to assist in analyzing the Desert Inn proposal. But Hughes told Maheu that the tool company had nothing to do with the negotiations and that he alone would make the final decision on price.

When Maheu asked Hughes to provide a resolution from the tool company board of directors authorizing the purchase "in the event some misunderstanding should occur sometime in the future," Hughes refused, and when Maheu pressed, Hughes exploded: "Bob, I own 100 percent of the stock and the board of directors has nothing to say about any of my decisions."[50]

Hughes, of course, was absolutely correct on that point: he and he alone would decide what to pay for the Desert Inn. In reaching that price, Hughes was engaging in his most pleasurable pastime, now that his flying years were over. For an average businessman, negotiations leading to an acquisition are little more than the means to an end. To gain control of the company or the product is gratification enough. For Hughes, however, the thrill lay in the negotiation itself; the rest was mere dénouement. Haggling for weeks on end, shaving $5,000 here, adding a liability stipulation there, he sought not so much to exact favorable terms as to prolong the game. In fact, his interminable negotiations often produced agreements that were financially unfavorable. In the early years, Hughes had negotiated face to face, in the back seats of Chevrolets, on street corners, and in hotel rooms. Now, the negotiations were carried on by telephone or through messages relayed by the aides, as Hughes gradually wore down the unseen opponent at the other end of the long-distance bargaining table. Few businessmen had his stomach for marathon wrangling. Moe Dalitz was no exception.

"This deal kept changing daily," Dalitz later said of the Desert Inn negotiations. "We agreed on a price at one time and he [Maheu] says, 'I think that will conclude the sale; if you will do such-and-such and such-and-such, I think we can get that through.'

"All right, we'll do it," Dalitz would tell Maheu.

When Maheu "tried to complete the deal that way, he was told that it wasn't good enough."

The next session, Maheu would say "he was authorized to close and accept this price. Then when we agreed to the price, he called up [Hughes] and said, 'I've got a deal'; and then he came back and said, 'I'm told that I can't make this deal.'"[51]

As he called each move made by Maheu in the daily haggling, Hughes continued to collect financial information from other sources. When he ran across figures that puzzled him—like the dollar value of markers, the outstanding IOUs of creditworthy gamblers—he sought advice from knowledgeable associates.

One such was Delbert E. Webb, the multimillionaire Arizona contractor and former co-owner of the New York Yankees. Del Webb's company had worked on various projects for the Hughes organization, including construction at the Hughes Aircraft Company plant in Culver City. On occasion, Webb served as a front man for Hughes, as he had in 1956 during the Florida airplane-manufacturing boondoggle.

This time, Hughes had a more practical reason for going to Webb: the Del E. Webb Corporation was the single largest operater of hotels and gambling casinos in Nevada, owning the Sahara along the Strip, the Mint in downtown Las Vegas, and the Sahara–Tahoe at Lake Tahoe. Hughes wanted to know if Webb "had anyone in his organization who could make an analysis of the operating figures which had been submitted by the sellers of the Desert Inn."[52] Webb said he had just the right candidate for the task, a prominent Las Vegas businessman, E. Parry Thomas, chairman of the board and chief executive officer of the Bank of Las Vegas, vice-chairman of the board of the Valley Bank of Nevada at Reno, and a director of Webb's company. More important, the forty-five-year-old Thomas was the banker for many of the large Las Vegas hotels and casinos. He was regarded as a power not only in Nevada financial circles but in the political community as well.

Depending on who did the talking, Thomas was pictured as a man who "has done more for the development of Las Vegas in the last half dozen years than any other single individual," or as "the hoodlum banker" and the "front man for Jimmy Hoffa," whose teamsters union pension funds seemed to flow so freely into Thomas's Las Vegas construction projects.[53] Thomas viewed his teamsters association with equanimity. "The Teamsters are good people to work with," he maintained. And he took a proprietary interest in the growth of Las Vegas. "I've got to see that this community stays healthy," he said. "I'll take dollars from the devil himself if it's legal—and I don't mean anything disparaging toward the Teamsters by that."[54]

Thomas also had ties to Dalitz and his Desert Inn. He was a director of the Desert Inn Country Club, and two years earlier Dalitz had served as chairman of the Anti-Defamation League of B'nai B'rith's annual banquet, when the organization presented Thomas with its "Man of the Year" award.

With the addition of Thomas, the number of people involved in the Desert Inn negotiations, or in bringing the negotiators together, had swelled to more than a dozen. All the key participants, with one exception, formed a network. Robert Maheu, representing Hughes, was a close personal friend of Edward Morgan, representing Moe Dalitz. Parry Thomas, who had business dealings with Dalitz, was evaluating Dalitz's financial statements for Hughes. Jimmy Hoffa, who had persuaded Dalitz to allow Hughes to remain at the Desert Inn, was well known to Thomas and Morgan. And Hank Greenspun, the editor and publisher of the *Las Vegas Sun*, was a friend of all. The odd man out was Howard Hughes.

In March of 1967, bargaining moved into its third month. J. Richard Gray, a Houston lawyer Hughes brought in to assist Maheu with the legal aspects of the transaction, wondered how long he would have to stay in Las Vegas. Gray, a partner in Andrews, Kurth, Campbell & Jones, had other legal business in Houston, as well as a family, and he had not counted on a change of address. Hughes assured him that all would be concluded in two weeks. In a classic display of Hughes's casual regard for the clock and calendar, the two weeks eventually grew into more than three years.

But as questions from the Desert Inn penthouse grew fewer in number and it became apparent that an agreement was near, Gray, like Maheu, sought reassurance about his authority. Unlike Maheu, however, who never did have a face-to-face meeting with Hughes, Gray insisted on one. His initial request received a chilly reception, but he persisted. When Hughes finally relented, Gray one day took the elevator to the Desert Inn's ninth floor, where he was greeted by one of the around-the-clock security guards in the hallway outside Hughes's rooms. As Gray was ushered into the three-room suite, Hughes appeared in his bedroom doorway, dressed in a robe.

"Well," snapped Hughes, "I exist, damn it. Are you satisfied?"[55]

With that, Hughes turned and closed the bedroom door, and Gray left the way he had come. The meeting—Hughes's first with one of his lawyers in half a dozen years—had lasted about five seconds, and Gray had uttered not one word.

Gray now began drawing up the complex legal and financial papers for the Desert Inn acquisition, based on the understanding reached by Hughes and Dalitz. Hughes had agreed to pay $6.2 million in cash and to assume $7 million in liabilities, for a total investment of $13.2 million. But he was not acquiring either the land or the buildings that made up the 450-room Desert Inn Hotel and Casino complex. In effect, he was buying only the right to operate the hotel and casino until the year 2022.

The grounds and buildings, the physical property, were owned by Desert Inn Associates, a partnership that included Dalitz and a number of other investors. Desert Inn Associates, in turn, leased the land and buildings to the Desert Inn Operating Company, a Nevada corporation that actually ran the hotel and casino. A majority of the stock in the Desert Inn Operating Company was owned by Dalitz and his three Cleveland colleagues.* For his $13.2 million, Hughes would only acquire this lease the Desert Inn Operating Company had with Desert Inn Associates.

The terms of the lease called for payment, on top of the $13.2 million, of $1,115,000 a year to Desert Inn Associates until 1981, and $940,000 annually thereafter. In addition, Hughes would pay all taxes, water and sewer charges, insurance premiums, repair and maintenance bills, and other operating expenses.[56]

On Friday, March 24, Hughes signed a power of attorney authorizing Gray to act on his behalf before "the Nevada Gaming Commission, the Nevada Gaming Control Board and any and all governmental or regulatory agencies or authorities of the State of Nevada." The power of attorney was witnessed by Howard Eckersley and George Francom, two of his personal aides.[57]

Gray moved with dispatch, filing that day with the Nevada Gaming Control Board, seeking to have Hughes approved as the sole licensee of the Desert Inn. A spokesman for the board, which investigates all gaming license applicants, was optimistic that Hughes's request could be considered at its next meeting the following week.

A gaming-license application in Nevada demands much detailed financial and personal information: "In essence, Nevada law requires every applicant or holder of a gaming license to fully disclose all aspects of his personal and business life."[58] This is a routine affair for most who seek the license. They complete the applications, provide the necessary financial information, furnish photographs and fingerprints, make a personal appearance before gaming authorities, and undergo a routine background investigation. If they meet all the tests, a license is issued.

This information was not supplied by Gray, nor did Hughes have the slightest intention of disclosing "all aspects of his personal and business life." He never did that, even when ordered to do so by a federal court, as in his battle with TWA. And, of course, a personal appearance was out of the question. Hughes was certain that with the proper attention to detail he could avoid complying with those onerous, supposedly mandatory licensing requirements imposed on others. He had done it for years at all levels of government—local, state, and federal—through the judicious use of money and political influence, the magic of the Hughes name, and masterful public relations. Nevada politicians and licensing authorities should prove no tougher than the CAB and the Congress of the United States.

Some local assistance was, however, advisable, so Maheu opened a talent search for an attorney with the appropriate political connections to represent Hughes in Nevada. He settled on Thomas G. Bell, a hometown boy with a law degree from George Washington University. From 1955 to 1958, Bell had

*The partnership and lease agreements are accounting devices designed to enable investors in Las Vegas hotels and casinos substantially to reduce their federal income taxes.

worked in Washington as an administrative assistant to Senator Alan Bible of Nevada before returning to Las Vegas to establish a law practice.

The forty-year-old Bell had been warmly recommended for the Hughes post not only by Senator Bible, who looked on him as "one of his proteges," but also by the state's other Democratic senator, Howard W. Cannon, and its Republican governor, Paul D. Laxalt.[59] Bell also just happened to be the brother of Lloyd Bell, the undersheriff of Clark County. The sheriff, in turn, was chairman of the Clark County Liquor and Gaming Licensing Board, which had to approve Hughes's takeover of the Desert Inn.

But Bell was no more important to Hughes's plan than Governor Laxalt. Laxalt was one of six children of an immigrant sheepherder from the French Pyrénées. Although he spoke better Basque than English when he entered first grade in Carson City, Laxalt went on to compile an enviable academic record in high school and college, graduating at the top of his class at the Denver University Law School. Beginning his political career in 1950 as district attorney of Ormsby County, Laxalt step by step moved up the political ladder, finally capturing the governorship in November of 1966, shortly before Hughes arrived in Las Vegas. At age forty-four, Laxalt was pictured as a consummate politician, "a thorough, methodical man who tackles situations one at a time and dislikes disorder and confusion."[60] Happily for both Laxalt and Hughes, Nevada's disorder and confusion were of a kind that Nevada's wealthiest citizen could handily dispel.

For nearly a year, the state had been withering under a barrage of unfavorable publicity that gambling profits in Las Vegas were being funneled into organized crime. It had begun in the summer of 1966 when the *Chicago Sun-Times* disclosed that millions of dollars were being skimmed off the top of casino revenues each year before the earnings were reported to state and federal tax collectors. The untaxed millions were then invested, as FBI director J. Edgar Hoover put it, in a "multitude of nefarious purposes."[61] Among those sharing in the skim and holding secret interests in Las Vegas casinos, the Chicago newspaper asserted, was Sam Giancana, Maheu's partner in the CIA assassination plot.

The *Sun-Times* disclosures were based on an FBI investigation of Las Vegas skimming in the early 1960s. For months, eavesdropping FBI agents meticulously recorded conversations among the gamblers, from the business offices of the Desert Inn Hotel to the bedroom of the casino manager at the Sands. Federal agents had even set up a front, the Henderson Novelty Company, that leased twenty-five telephone lines to monitor hotel and casino calls. In May of 1963, the FBI had sent to the Justice Department a "two-volume document called 'The Skimming Report,'" that laid it all out.[62]

The skimming charges had undermined a carefully nurtured Nevada myth—that through rigid licensing standards and zealous enforcement the state had freed its gaming industry of any criminal element. Within Nevada, there was, to be sure, a far more relaxed and casual attitude toward the people running the state's largest industry.

"As far as I know," Clark County Sheriff Ralph Lamb once observed, "everyone in the gambling business out here always has been a gentleman. Maybe they got caught elsewhere doing the same thing they do here legitimately, but that don't make them wrong, just the laws where they come from."[63] Or as Governor Grant Sawyer once put it, "Our attitude toward life, save under the most urgent provocation, is relaxed, tolerant, and mindful that if others are allowed to go on their way unmolested, a man stands a chance of getting through the world with a minimum of irritation."[64]

Unfortunately for Nevada, the rest of the country did not see it that way. Skimming allegations were still very much in the news when Governor Laxalt took office in January of 1967. He needed a way to repair his state's tarnished image. The hostile publicity was discouraging tourism, the state's economic heart. The freshman governor realized early that Hughes could only be good for Las Vegas's image. The mere presence of the powerful industrialist might well discourage further investigations by federal agents, whose forays into the gambling capital were making everyone nervous.

Governor Laxalt's backing for Hughes's Desert Inn gaming application was assured. The governor held sway over the State Gaming Control Board and the Nevada Gaming Commission, which would make the decision. A highly influential local attorney was on a Hughes retainer. Even so, Hughes could not be certain that his Desert Inn gaming license was a sure thing. And Howard Hughes liked a sure thing. In one final move to cover all his bets, he seized on a dispute in the state legislature, turned it to his own advantage, and overnight made himself a hero to the state's citizens.

Nevada legislators and educators had been squabbling for weeks over the merits of establishing a medical school and the site for it. The problem was money, for medical schools initially run heavily in the red. On Monday, March 27, three days before the State Gaming Control Board was to consider his application, Hughes wrote a personal letter to Laxalt and had it delivered by hand:

Last Thursday, March 23, in the *Las Vegas Review Journal,* there appeared large headlines covering five columns as follows: "Medical School to Die?" The *Las Vegas Sun,* on the same day, headlined: "Senate Action Could Be Kiss of Death for Medical School." In the *Review Journal* this morning, Monday, March 27, there was given the sum of money required each year to make possible the medical school—between two hundred thousand dollars and three hundred thousand dollars.

If it meets with the approval of those responsible for this project, I would like to instruct my attorneys to prepare a document, in language and form satisfactory to the state's attorneys, which will be legally binding and enforceable upon me and upon my estate after my death. This document will consist of a written agreement to make a gift to the university of the sum mentioned above, each year for twenty years, commencing whenever the university requires the money. I attach no strings or conditions to this proposal. The medical school need not be located in southern Nevada. The state is free to locate the school wherever it may desire.[65]

Always the master politician, Hughes allowed Laxalt to release details of his offer and reap the political benefits. At a hurried news conference forty-eight hours before the State Gaming Control Board meeting, the governor announced Hughes's pledge and read the letter. Across the state that afternoon and the following day, newspapers blossomed with page-one accounts of Hughes's beneficent gesture:

"Billionaire Howard Hughes today offered to finance a big share of the cost of operating the proposed University of Nevada medical school," began a story in the *Reno Evening Gazette.* [66] "The industrialist, famed for his mysterious living habits, offered to support a proposed University of Nevada medical school for 20 years to the tune of $200,000 to $300,000 annually," reported the *Las Vegas Sun,* under the headline "Howard Hughes Offers $6 Million for Medical School." [67]

As Hughes fully expected, a divided Nevada legislature suddenly joined ranks in gratitude. "I would say this is marvelous news," said Charles Armstrong, the president of the University of Nevada. "For a certain number of years the state could operate the school at no cost at all—for a good many years," he added. [68] "I think it's wonderful that he made this offer," said Dr. Fred M. Anderson, chairman of the university's board of regents. [69]

When Hughes's letter was read to the Nevada Assembly by Speaker Melvin D. Close, Jr., a Las Vegas Democrat, the legislators broke into applause. Senator Floyd Lamb, a Las Vegas Democrat who had opposed the medical school—and whose brother was the sheriff of Clark County—allowed that Hughes's offer put an entirely different light on the situation. James Wood, a Reno Republican who was the Senate minority leader, told the Assembly that "I knew there was something special about this day." [70]

The only discordant note in the state capital was sounded by a reporter who wondered whether there might be some connection between the Hughes gift and his pending application for a gaming license. The question was airily dismissed by Laxalt. "The announcement speaks for itself," the governor said. [71]

On Thursday, March 30, two days after Hughes's gesture toward the new medical school, the State Gaming Control Board met in Carson City, reviewed the incomplete application—which contained neither a photograph nor the required financial information—and promptly recommended to the State Gaming Commission that it approve the Desert Inn sale. "Hughes's life and background are well known to this board and he is considered highly qualified," explained Alan Abner, the board chairman. [72] The following day, the State Gaming Commission, in a 5 to 0 vote, swiftly rubber-stamped the Gaming Control Board's decision and awarded a license to Hughes to operate the Desert Inn Hotel and Casino. "The commission was satisfied as to the investigation conducted into Mr. Hughes' background and recommended approval without qualification of any kind," explained Donald W. Winne, counsel for the commission. [73]

With the last of the legal and regulatory requirements fulfilled, the way was clear for the new proprietor to take control of the Desert Inn, a Las Vegas Institution— a gathering place for the statesmen of organized crime; a hotel that had housed Chief Justice Earl Warren, the king and queen of Nepal, and two American presidents, John F. Kennedy and Lyndon B. Johnson; an innovating force in Las Vegas entertainment, where Noel Coward made his only appearance in the gambling capital, where Johnny Weissmuller and a troupe of singers, dancers, and swimmers staged a twice-nightly Tarzanic water ballet and aquatic extravaganza in the hotel pool.

At midnight that Friday, March 31, the Desert Inn changed administrations. The Cleveland mob that had run it so profitably for seventeen years moved out. The Hughes organization moved in. On April Fool's Day, 1967, Howard Robard Hughes, Jr., at age sixty-one, assumed a new role—the hermit gambling entrepreneur of Las Vegas.

With his entry into the highly specialized world of gambling, whose rituals and practices are as inscrutable to the layman as a physicist's equations, Hughes broke a forty-year pattern. Since settling in Hollywood in 1925, he had concentrated his energies in just two areas—movies and airplanes. In both businesses he had a consuming personal interest, whether it was directing a scene, cutting film, selecting a location, designing aircraft, tinkering with engines, or picking color schemes for his planes. In short, he loved movies and he loved flying, and he understood both. But he had no such fascination for gambling and no understanding of the business. Neither did any of his executives.

"None of us knew snake eyes from box cars," admitted Raymond Holliday, the top officer of Hughes Tool Company in Houston and number-two man in the empire. "We didn't know a thing about it [gambling] and nobody here was interested in learning."[74]

Nevertheless, Holliday sent Calvin Collier, the tool company's vice-president and treasurer, to Las Vegas to assist temporarily in managing the new property. For the next three months, Collier, Maheu, and Dick Gray "formed somewhat of a circle of management."[75] By accepted business standards it was an odd management team. "I certainly had no expertise in the hotel and casino management," Collier said. "As a matter of fact, that was my first good baptism to all of that gambling. I don't think Dick Gray had been exposed to that type of operation or had any experience in it. Mr. Maheu indicated that he had no expertise in it. The fact of the matter is: We were all looking for somebody to run the place."[76] Because of their general unfamiliarity with gaming operations and hotels, Collier said, "there was some discussion of the possibility, perhaps, of hiring or engaging under contract some hotel management firm to operate the thing for the company, and I believe Hilton was mentioned—one of the big chains was mentioned. This was pursued for a time and then it was dropped."[77]

Faced with the responsibility for managing a business in which he had no particular skills, Maheu decided to seek the assistance of a local gambling expert. At no cost to either Hughes or himself, he retained the services of a consultant to advise him on the intricacies of gaming policies and the management of a successful casino. The consultant was Moe Dalitz.

"I was asked to be available for any assistance I could give them pertaining to casino policy and so forth," Dalitz said, "and I volunteered this on a no-pay basis."[78]

Why would Moe Dalitz, the former Cleveland bootlegger and one of the country's most successful gambling entrepreneurs, offer his services free of charge to a competing Strip casino? "I felt they were an asset to Las Vegas," Dalitz said. "I felt it was a good thing for Las Vegas when they moved here, and I was glad to be on their team, so to speak."[79]

Perhaps so, but Dalitz also no doubt saw what a lot of others saw: a mark with an unlimited bankroll. After the Desert Inn sale, Dalitz gave a $150,000 finder's fee to Edward Morgan, Maheu's friend. Morgan, in turn, shared the proceeds, giving $50,000 to Rosselli, the syndicate representative, and $25,000 to Greenspun, the *Las Vegas Sun* owner. As Dalitz summed up the future when he asked Morgan if he would like to represent him again soon, "I explained to him that other deals would materialize and that if I had an opportunity I would like to have him involve himself as my legal adviser in some other deals that I'd been contemplating."[80]

Over the next three years, Dalitz, Morgan, Greenspun, Maheu, Parry Thomas, and many others would profit handsomely by Hughes's presence in Las Vegas. The only loser in the lot would be Hughes himself, and he would count his losses in the millions of dollars.

CHAPTER 12

LORD OF THE DESERT

A $13.2-million outlay was but a petty-cash expenditure when measured against the billions of dollars that had passed through the Hughes empire over four decades. Yet acquisition of the Desert Inn in 1967 had a special significance that transcended any dollars-and-cents assessment. It revitalized Hughes and finally brought him out of the deep depression he had been in ever since the TWA jet-financing battle in the late 1950s.

Perhaps the negotiations with Moe Dalitz had awakened memories of more tolerable times. Perhaps it was the realization that at age sixty-one he had little time to achieve some new success, to offset, in the history book of American business, all his failures—TWA, RKO, the D-2, the Hughes Tool Company Aircraft Division. Or perhaps he was just feeling a bit better, physically and mentally. Whatever the reason, the purchase of the Desert Inn marked the beginning of a new phase in Hughes's life, a renewal of his spirits, a return if not to the way he had lived twenty years before, at least to an active business career, or as active as the geography of a hotel bedroom would permit, for he would never again live outside its protective environment. In his own fashion, Howard Hughes was ready to go back to work.

Now that he had severed his ties to Romaine Street, Hughes leaned more than ever on the four aides who lived with him twenty-four hours a day. Indeed, the aides had replaced Romaine Street and established a new Operations in the room next to his. There they processed the tide of paperwork to and from the various outposts in the empire, screened his telephone calls, recorded and transmitted any messages he had for others, and, of course, saw to his personal needs.

Hughes's first priority was a personal one—to get his wife to Las Vegas.

He had not seen Jean since the stay in Boston in 1966. Although they never exchanged letters, they did talk on the telephone almost daily.[1] Hughes knew that Jean detested hotel rooms, that she intensely disliked their life in separate bungalows at the Beverly Hills Hotel. If he could offer her a home, he reasoned, she would move to Las Vegas. And so he directed Parry Thomas, his principal banker in Nevada, secretly to buy the estate of Major A. Riddle, an old-time gambler and part-owner of the Dunes Hotel and Casino. The palatial Riddle estate—its master bedroom and dressing area were several times larger than Hughes's bedroom in the Desert Inn—was in an exclusive section of Las Vegas where entertainers like Phyllis McGuire and Buddy Hackett maintained homes. Because Hughes demanded immediate possession of the property, "Thomas allowed Riddle to move into his [Thomas's] home"—the Thomas family was spending the summer in California—and the banker moved into the Desert Inn.

For insurance, Hughes decided to buy a second place, the 518-acre ranch owned by Vera Krupp, who had been married to Alfried Krupp, the German arms merchant. The two properties cost Hughes nearly $1 million. Now Jean could have a choice: she could live in the lavish Riddle house near the Strip or at the ranch a half-hour drive from Las Vegas, or both.

Hughes sent Jean "a scrapbook, with photographs and floor plans" of the ranch.[2] When they chatted on the telephone, he told her what he wanted at the ranch—"his own landing strip, a really good projection room, a really modern up-to-date kitchen, bath, a stable with horses."[3] Every time Hughes called, Jean said, "the question before the house was what we were going to do about our living arrangements, and we spent a great deal of time at first discussing a house in Las Vegas and we discussed the ranch and we discussed how he was going to set up his offices there and when he was going to move out of the hotel into the house."[4] Each time Jean pressed Hughes about leaving the Desert Inn and settling in the ranch, he stalled. For her part, she told him that she would move to the ranch "if he would be there first."[5] He could not do that, at least not then. And so the husband and wife stalemated over who would move first.

While Hughes was trying to persuade Jean to come to Las Vegas, he sent Bob Maheu out scouting for additional investments. Maheu's old friend Edward P. Morgan, the Washington lawyer and power broker, thought the Sands Hotel and Casino could be bought for the right price. Moe Dalitz, Maheu's consultant on casinos, heartily endorsed the suggestion, saying he thought the Sands "would be a good acquisition" and would be most profitable if Hughes "could continue to maintain the array of talent that had been presented there."[6] When Maheu passed the proposal along to the Desert Inn penthouse, Hughes instructed him to begin the negotiations at once.

The Sands, which opened in 1952, had long attracted the highest of the high-rollers and all the big names in entertainment. It was owned by a syndicate of more than a dozen investors headed by Jack Entratter, who held 16 percent of the stock. A onetime bouncer at the Stork Club and part-owner of the Copacabana in New York, Entratter more than anyone else had created the superstar image for Las Vegas. Opening night at the Sands in 1952 featured Danny Thomas. By 1960, the power and excitement of the Sands had grown to extravagant proportions, when the celebrated clan—Frank Sinatra, Dean Martin, Joey Bishop, Sammy Davis Jr., and Peter Lawford—played to standing-room-only audiences. Sinatra himself had owned 9 percent of the Sands until 1963, when the State Gaming Commission forced him out because of his continued association with Chicago mob boss Sam Giancana.

Maheu had little difficulty reaching a quick agreement to acquire the Sands. Conveniently, the negotiators on the other side of the bargaining table, representing the owners, were his friend Edward Morgan and Parry Thomas, who now wore different hats at different times—one when he acted as Hughes's banker and personal agent, and another when he represented those doing business with Hughes. After the talks were completed, Maheu invited Dick Gray, the Houston lawyer, and Calvin Collier, the chief financial officer of the Hughes Tool Company, to his home on the edge of the Desert Inn golf course, where he told them he had negotiated the Sands acquisition.[7] It was Maheu's way of letting the old-timers in the Hughes empire know that someone else was running things, at least in Las Vegas. Gray in particular was annoyed by Maheu's brashness, but he said nothing. He just "assumed" that that was the way Hughes wanted it.[8]

Maheu, Morgan, and Thomas had agreed on a $14.6-million purchase price for the 777-room Sands and the 183 acres of prime real estate on which it was situated. Oddly, Hughes decided that rather than use any of the proceeds from his TWA stock sale to pay for the property, he would borrow. He directed Raymond Holliday, the chief executive officer of the Hughes Tool Company, to make the financial arrangements. Holliday, in turn, called E. O. Buck, an officer at the Texas Bank of Commerce. "Raymond asked me to arrange a $15 million unsecured note for Howard Hughes," Buck said, "and I asked him if he wanted Houston funds, Houston banks, or could I have an election of partners, because my loan limit at the bank was six and a half million dollars, and Hughes already owed me three, so obviously I was going to have to have a partner, and Raymond said that he would prefer that we kept the loan local."[9] On July 25, 1967, the $15 million was deposited in Hughes's account in the Texas Commerce Bank and transferred to his bank account in Las Vegas.

At settlement a week later, when Hughes took possession of the Sands, Parry Thomas and Edward Morgan received, respectively, $275,000 and $225,000 for representing the sellers of the hotel. As he had done after the Desert Inn sale, Morgan shared his fee with, among others, the ubiquitous John Rosselli, who received $45,000. In the eight months since Hughes's arrival in Las Vegas, Morgan had gotten $375,000 in fees for representing the owners of two hotels and casinos sold to Hughes, and he had passed along $95,000 to Rosselli. In addition to his $275,000 fee for representing the Sands's former owners, Thomas had received additional fees and commissions for

Herman M. "Hank" Greenspun, editor and publisher of the *Las Vegas Sun*. *United Press International*

representing Hughes in other transactions. But Morgan, Rosselli, and Thomas were not the only ones benefitting from Hughes's arrival in Las Vegas.

The financial future of Hank Greenspun, the publisher of the *Las Vegas Sun,* for example, had brightened considerably since Hughes moved into the Desert Inn. Through the efforts of Maheu, the *Las Vegas Sun* had received an unusual $500,000 prepaid advertising contract from the Hughes Tool Company. The agreement contained two unique features. First, the tool company paid to Greenspun the full $500,000 in advance. Then, instead of deducting the cost of each advertisement from the advance as it was published, the tool company simply paid again. Greenspun thus was blessed with half a million dollars to use as he pleased. Sometime later, Greenspun insisted that "it was just supposed to be a contract for advertising, the money came as a surprise."*[10]

Then in September of 1967, Greenspun, whose newspaper had so warmly

---

*From 1967 until 1971, the Hughes organization placed $487,994.99 worth of advertising in the *Las Vegas Sun*. Hughes paid for all the advertising on a current basis, using none of the prepaid $500,000 credit.

welcomed Hughes to Nevada, received a $4-million loan from the Hughes Tool Company. When the loan papers were being drawn up, Hughes's conservative lawyer, Dick Gray, suggested an interest rate of 6 percent. Greenspun balked. He told Gray he "didn't think it was a proper rate because I didn't think Mr. Hughes wanted that much interest from me. In fact, I told him Mr. Hughes didn't want any interest from me."[11] Greenspun later said he based that statement on his understanding that Hughes was in a "peculiar tax position" and was "making too much interest on his money as it was."[12] In any event, Greenspun said, his attorney and Gray finally decided "that a legal rate that the Internal Revenue would accept would be about I think 3 or 4 percent or something, so I said, 'Okay, make it 3 percent.' "*[13]

Greenspun banked a check for the $4 million on September 20, 1967. The following day, his friend and lawyer, Edward Morgan, called to say that Bob Maheu "needs money pretty badly.

"Is it possible for you to make arrangements at a bank for him to get some money?" Morgan asked Greenspun.[14]

"Ed, I'm leaving town, but if Maheu needs any money, I'm flushed," Greenspun said. "I don't have the time to go to a bank, but if it's an urgent thing, I'll stop at his house on the way to the airport and ask him how dire the need is, and if it can wait 'til I come back. I can get any bank to loan him the money. But if it's just a question of for a short time, I'll be glad to let him have it myself."[15]

A short time later, as he prepared to leave for a speaking engagement in San Francisco, Greenspun dropped by Maheu's house.

"I understand you need money," Greenspun said. "I don't have any time to go to the banks, if you can wait 'til I come back from out of town, why, I'll be very happy to explore with banks or maybe even help get you a loan."[16]

Indeed, Maheu could not wait. Despite a $520,000-a-year retainer from Hughes, a generous expense account, and other miscellaneous perquisites, Maheu was in financial difficulty, mainly with the Internal Revenue Service, which contended that he had failed to report all his income. "It is kind of urgent," he told Greenspun.[17]

"Well, I'll let you have the money. When do I get it back?" Greenspun asked.[18]

"Well, at the end of the year," Maheu said. "Will that be all right?"[19]

"How much do you need?" Greenspun asked.

"$150,000," Maheu said.[20]

"If that's all that's involved," Greenspun said, I'll be glad to let you have it."[21] Greenspun wrote out a check for $150,000 on the account that he and

*Greenspun said that one of Hughes's personal aides, Roy E. Crawford, told him that "the man wants you to get your money right away, and he doesn't want any interest from you." Both Greenspun and Maheu had a closer relationship with Crawford than with any of the other aides who saw Hughes daily.

his wife Barbara maintained at the Bank of Las Vegas, and handed it to Maheu.

As for interest on the loan, Greenspun never considered it. "I thought it was just a question of a couple of months," he said.* "I didn't even discuss any interest or anything else with him."[22]

It was not at all unusual that Morgan had interceded with Greenspun on behalf of Maheu. Morgan had known both for years. Morgan and Maheu had met during their days in the FBI in the 1940s. After leaving the bureau, they saw each other occasionally over the years, and about 1959 or 1960 Maheu asked Morgan to do some legal work for him—" prepare a will and a partnership agreement."[23] Morgan had met Greenspun in 1954, shortly after Greenspun was indicted by a federal grand jury for using the United States mail for "inciting the murder of United States Senator Joseph McCarthy."[24] The Justice Department had used an obscure federal statute to bring the indictment against Greenspun, whose newspaper routinely denounced the Wisconsin senator for his anti-Communist tactics. Copies of the *Las Vegas Sun* carrying Greenspun's outspoken comments, mailed to subscribers, were used as the basis for the charge. Morgan represented Greenspun and subsequently won an acquittal. "That was the beginning of my representation," Morgan said, "and, I should say, very close friendship, because I regared myself as a very close friend of Mr. Greenspun."[25] Morgan, who continued to represent Greenspun in other matters, did not submit a bill. As Morgan explained it, "To be very honest and frank about it, Mr. Greenspun's financial problems were quite acute for a long, long while and I didn't even charge him for defending him on the criminal case."[26]

So it was, then, that even before Hughes arrived in Las Vegas the Morgan–Maheu–Greenspun connection was invoked. While Hughes was on the train from Boston to Las Vegas, Morgan called Maheu and told him that Greenspun was about to publish a story disclosing that Hughes was en route to the gaming capital. Maheu said he begged Morgan "to put pressure on Greenspun to kill the story, with the hope that maximum security could be maintained." Morgan talked to Greenspun and, according to Maheu, "he did kill the story."[27] Once Hughes established residence at the Desert Inn, Maheu called Morgan innumerable times to "solicit his help with Mr. Greenspun so as to secure from him favorable stories pertaining to Mr. Hughes and the Hughes interests."[28]

In addition to the advertising agreement and the loan, Greenspun was negotiating with Maheu for the sale of his television station, KLAS–TV, to Hughes. He had agreed to sell the station, a CBS affiliate, for much the same reason that Dalitz parted with the Desert Inn—exasperation. On moving to Las Vegas, Hughes gave up his practice of renting and screening motion pictures. Instead, he watched the late-night movies on television. But Hughes liked to look at films around the clock, and it annoyed him that KLAS ended

---

*Six years later, according to Greenspun, Maheu still had not repaid the loan.

its telecasting day while he was still in a watching mood.

"The man wanted the station open all night long, and he wanted certain pictures to be shown," Greenspun said. "Every night it was a call at my home or a call some place else, 'Can't you keep it open an extra hour?' and things like that. If Mr. Maheu wasn't calling me to put a certain picture on, then Mr. Gray was asking me to do it. And then they had asked me to put somebody to work who would be helpful in ascertaining what kind of pictures Mr. Hughes liked." Finally, Greenspun asked one of Hughes's lieutenants, "Why don't you buy the station, and run it any damn way you please?"[29]

When Hughes decided to do just that, he asked Maheu to recommend a Washington attorney who could persuade the Federal Communications Commission to grant him a license without the customary personal appearance and submission of detailed financial statements.

Maheu, naturally, had a candidate at hand—Edward P. Morgan. Not only did Morgan's law firm, Welch & Morgan, specialize in communications law and practice before the FCC—Vincent B. Welch was a former FCC attorney—it was already representing Maheu and Bill Gay in their bid to obtain a license to operate a Fullerton, California, radio station. Maheu and Gay each owned 15 percent of Orange Radio Inc., a California corporation that was seeking the license. Orange Radio Inc. was typical of the many sideline business ventures engaged in by Hughes executives, most often without Hughes's knowledge.

Morgan proved to be a fine choice for the licensing chore. Transfer of the KLAS–TV license was arranged with no inconvenience whatsoever to Hughes. Only one concession was required—that the application papers identify Raymond Holliday, rather than Hughes, as the person with the "authority and responsibility" for managing the station.[30] Everyone knew that Hughes, not Holliday, would exercise final control, but the FCC went along with the charade. Its records gave no indicationt that Howard Hughes had the slightest influence in running KLAS–TV. Therefore, the agency rationalized, no special favors had been granted to the reclusive industrialist by the failure to require his appearance in Washington.

The television station cost Hughes $3.6 million. With its acquisition in 1967, a substantial cross-section of Las Vegas business and real estate now resided in his investment portfolio. Besides the Desert Inn, the Sands, the Krupp ranch, the Riddle estate, and KLAS–TV, Hughes had acquired the Castaways Hotel and Casino, a 229-room hotel and thirty-one acres across the Strip from the Sands; the Frontier Hotel and Casino, 571-rooms, opposite the Desert Inn; Alamo Airways, a small charter service and its fixed base operations at McCarran Airport; North Las Vegas Airport and a motel and restaurant on the 225-acre airport grounds; some hundred residential lots in a subdivision adjoining the Desert Inn Country Club; and assorted tracts of land in and around the Strip. Within one year, Hughes had spent some $65 million in Las Vegas, an average of more than than $178,000 a day. His hotels, the sixth-, eighth-, twelfth-, and fourteenth-largest on the Strip, with a total of about two thousand rooms, represented "20 percent of all resort hotel accommodations on the Strip."[31] No longer was Hughes just another Nevada curiosity, like bare breasts and all-night wedding chapels. He was one of the state's largest private landowners and employers.

THE PUBLIC-RELATIONS BLITZ

Such an unprecedented buying spree prompted many to wonder whether Hughes had embarked on some grand plan. Johnny Carson greeted audiences at Del Webb's Sahara by saying, "Welcome to Las Vegas, Howard Hughes' monopoly set. You ever get the feeling he's going to buy the whole damned place and shut it down?"[32] But Carson's remark was only half a jest. From the seclusion of his Desert Inn penthouse, Hughes's finely tuned political ear could detect faint rumblings of discontent within the state's power structure. And if there was unease in Carson City, what about Washington?

For instance, what possible violation of federal antitrust guidelines might ensue from a continuation of the hotel- and casino-buying binge? Hughes asked Dick Gray to consult with Robert F. Campbell, a senior partner in Andrews, Kurth, Campbell & Jones in Houston about the antitrust implications of additional acquisitions.

He was not pleased with the answer he received. Gray, who seldom got back to Houston these days—for more than eight months he had worked out of a room in the Desert Inn—told Hughes to forget about buying any more hotels or casinos along the Strip. "Mr. Campbell is quite concerned," Gray said, "over the extent of acquisitions in the Strip area, which is a relatively small 'market area.' Therefore, he feels that any additional acquisitions of property of the same nature would be exceedingly dangerous."[33] The lawyers even rejected a Hughes plan to buy a pair of motels and a restaurant near the Sands and the Desert Inn. "Mr. Campbell is of the opinion that the acquisition of any additional motel, hotel, or restaurant property would 'add fuel to the fire' of what we have already acquired in your behalf."[34]

Closing the otherwise gloomy news on an optomistic note, Gray reported Campbell's opinion that Hughes could buy a hotel and casino far removed from Las Vegas, perhaps in the Reno or Lake Tahoe area, without encountering antitrust difficulties. Even so, neither lawyer was enthusiastic about Hughes's investing more money in Nevada's most important industry. If Hughes wanted to increase his cash flow, as he claimed, then he should consider, they said, investing in businesses "outside the hotel-casino area."[35] Hughes ignored the advice. At that particular moment he was interested only in casinos. He did, however, agree to look to northern Nevada.

Hughes had already cast a covetous eye on the Reno and Lake Tahoe properties of William Fisk Harrah. Even though northern Nevada ranked a distant second to Las Vegas in volume of tourists and gamblers attracted each year, Harrah methodically piled up the largest profit margins of any casino operator in the state. At his Lake Tahoe casino, the take from the gaming tables ran upward of $20 million a year, the only casino in the state to reach that heady level. Unlike some Las Vegas casino operators, who had clearly traceable ties to organized crime or who came from questionable backgrounds, Harrah was regarded by state and federal law-enforcement officials alike as a model citizen. Some federal authorities pointed to Harrah's profits as proof that money was being skimmed from Las Vegas casinos controlled by the crime syndicate. Wallace F. Turner, a *New York Times* reporter who had conducted an extensive investigation of the Nevada gambling industry in the early 1960s, found Harrah to be the most widely respected gaming figure in the state. "The people with foresight in Nevada, those who sit and think about the future of the state's gambling business, look on Bill Harrah as a shining example," Turner wrote a year before Hughes's arrival. "If more gambling houses were in the hands of men like him, one is told over and over, then the future of Nevada gambling would be completely safe. In short, Bill Harrah is what they wish they had everywhere in Nevada."[36]

No wonder Hughes wanted to add the Harrah properties to his empire. He dispatched Maheu to northern Nevada to open talks. Whether Harrah actually considered selling his hotels and casinos or whether he was simply stringing Hughes along, as Hughes had done in the past with suitors for his tool company, is unclear. What is perfectly clear, however, is that Hughes believed every man has his price, Harrah included. It was a belief that Maheu shared and he began to spend more time in Reno, seeking to make the belief come true.

With Maheu negotiating with Harrah, Hughes rejected the legal advice of Gray and Campbell and secretly pushed ahead with schemes to buy two more hotels and three more casinos on the Las Vegas Strip. Two properties he eyed were established money-losers—the Bonanza, then in receivership, and the Silver Slipper, a casino that drew small-stakes gamblers and featured a burlesque show and a sixty-nine-cent breakfast served around the clock. But the third, the Stardust Hotel and Casino, was one of the most profitable in Las Vegas, and the largest—1,500 rooms. The principal owner of the Stardust was a now-familiar figure, Maheu's gaming adviser Moe Dalitz.

While Hughes quietly sought nearly to double his Las Vegas holdings, a small group of state legislators, alarmed over the growing concentration of ownership in the gaming industry, called for an investigation of state licensing practices. The legislators—of course unaware of Hughes's ambitious expansion plans—were concerned not only about his ownership of four hotels and casinos, but also about the mysterious circumstances under which the gaming license was issued for the Frontier Casino.

Back on November 27, Las Vegas members of the State Gaming Control Board, accompanied by Hughes's lawyer Dick Gray, had gathered in the agency's Las Vegas office to work out the Frontier takeover. Of special note was the time of the meeting—midnight. To gain the necessary votes to approve the license, a telephone conference call was placed to board members in northern Nevada, rousing them from their beds. By 1:30 A.M., the board had approved Hughes's fourth casino, although two board members were not notified of the meeting.

George Dickerson, the chairman of the Nevada Gaming Commission, insisted that the board had acted under standard "emergency participation" regulations, but the extraordinary midnight meeting aroused the curiosity of legislators suspicious of Hughes's motives and of his unusual relationship with state gaming officials. The legislators also were interested in the gaming licenses held by Del Webb because rumors were rife that Hughes was buying up blocks of stock in the publicly owned Webb corporation. Early in January, Melvin D. Close, Jr., a Las Vegas Democrat who was the State Assembly speaker, announced that he and eighteen other lawmakers were prepared to conduct an investigation of the holding of multiple casino licenses at a special session of the legislature in February.

Undaunted by his lawyers' warnings of potential antitrust problems on the federal level and the proposed investigation by state legislators, Hughes plunged ahead with plans to buy the Silver Slipper, the Stardust, the Bonanza, the Silver Nugget, and Harrah's hotels and casinos. To ease the expected opposition to his next round of acquisitions, Hughes did what he had always done—he initiated a public-relations campaign.

Governor Laxalt was the key. Hughes placed a telephone call to the governor, chatting at length about his future plans for the state. The conversation immediately became a major news event because, for the first time since his arrival in Las Vegas, Hughes had talked with someone outside his inner circle of aides and executives. Laxalt reacted predictably. "It was one of the most interesting conversations of my life," the governor declared, marveling at Hughes's knowledge of Nevada.[37] "It's like he lived here 20 years," the governor said. And his praise of the invisible casino owner was effusive. Hughes's presence, the governor declared, "has added a degree of credibility to the state that it would have taken years of advertising to secure. Let's face it, Nevada has an image problem—the typical feeling is that sin is rampant here. Anything this man does, from the gaming industry all the way down the line, will be good for Nevada."*[38]

---

*Governor Laxalt neglected to mention those parts of the conversation which underscored Hughes's erratic behavior and eccentricities, in particular his germ phobia. One of the subjects Hughes discussed with Laxalt was a proposed water-treatment project he feared would provide the resort community with little more than treated effluent. Laxalt humored Hughes; he said he was aqually concerned about water quality and would see what action could be taken to halt the project. After the telephone call, the governor forgot Hughes's apprehensions. But Hughes did not. On January 17, he wrote Maheu: "When I spoke to Governor Laxalt, I told him I was truly and urgently alarmed at the way the authorities were rushing ahead into the so-called 'Southern Nevada Water Project.' I told him I felt the entire plan simply was not palatable. That the water might be treated with sufficient chlorine so that it would meet the minimum test requirements and be technically drinkable—just as they boast that you can drink the effluent of the Los Angeles

After reaping the goodwill that flowed from the accolades bestowed upon him by the governor, Hughes staged a second public-relations coup of equal brilliance. Nevadans had long talked about diversifying the state's economy beyond gambling, but had made little headway. Now, working with Laxalt, Hughes arranged to provide land he owned near McCarran Airport as the site for a plant of a New York–based electronics company—Solitron Devices Inc. On January 19, when Laxalt unveiled the development at a press conference, appropriately enough at Hughes's Desert Inn, the governor gave Hughes most of the credit for Solitron's decision to locate in Nevada. The company's president, Benjamin Friedman, agreed, adding that Solitron enjoyed "excellent relations" with the Hughes organization. "We believe these people plan the future," he said. More important, promised Friedman, "a lot of companies will follow us into this area."[39]

For twenty years, Nevada had tried unsuccessfully to encourage an industrial development boom, and now, overnight, Howard Hughes seemed to have accomplished the impossible. "We have managed to acquire a super salesman as a resident, and the results will undoubtedly be exciting and profitable," said the *Las Vegas Review–Journal*.[40] Pointing out that Hughes had achieved what three state administrations had failed to do, the newspaper observed that "most southern Nevadans have long been convinced that this area offers a host of advantages to industry. They have not been very successful in selling the idea to easterners, however. It takes someone of the stature and reputation of Howard Hughes in the world of industry to make the point." If he had done nothing else, the *Review–Journal* continued, "Hughes has made a major contribution to the state by forcing other industrialists to take an objective look at Nevada's potential. This, along with the nationwide publicity Hughes has generated since his arrival, promises to give our economy a giant boost."[41]

Hardly had Nevadans counted their new industrial blessings than Hughes put forward plans for a truly spectacular project—the world's largest hotel, a $150-million, 4,000-room addition to the Sands. Hughes envisioned "a complete city within itself," a resort complex so magnificently planned "that any guest will simply have to make a supreme effort if he wants to be bored, whether he is a sophisticated VIP or jet set type, or one of the children of a family spending their vacation with us."[42] One floor of the ultramodern hotel would house stores and shops open twenty-four hours a day. Another would be devoted entirely to family recreation—an ice-skating rink; rooms for chess, bridge, skeeball, and table tennis; a theater showing only first-run motion pictures; and "the largest bowling alley and billiard and pool facility in any hotel in the world."[43] The theater would utilize "projection equipment and

sewage disposal plant. But that is not the point. We are in competition with other resorts and if it becomes known that our new water system is nothing but a closed circuit loop, leading in and then out of a cesspool, our competitive resorts will find this out and they will start a word of mouth and publicity campaign that will murder us. The governor said he was aware of this situation and 'sick about it.' I urged him to see what could be done to hold it up temporarily while he and I try to find some solution. I have not heard a word in reply."

sound equipment so modern it has not even been shown yet to the public in literature or trade publications, and the same is true of the bowling and billiard equipment."[44] Another innovation would be an indoor computerized golf course "so carefully designed that the shots will feel just like outdoors, and the spin of the ball in a slice or hook is even measured electronically and indicated to the player."[45]

The picture of this $150-million, 4,000-room pleasure palace painted by Hughes was breathtaking, but not greatly more so than a project he had announced four months earlier—construction of an airport in the Nevada desert that would be the West Coast terminus for supersonic transports. The press release was rhapsodic about an airport serving "the entirety of southern Nevada, California and Arizona. "From this terminus," Hughes said, "passengers may be flown by regular jet aircraft to any normally located present-day airport. Also, from this same SST terminus, they may be flown by new and thoroughly proven helicopters and other VTOL [vertical takeoff and landing] designs, to many landing terminals which will be closer to the passenger's ultimate destination—on top of buildings downtown, on top of hotels and in residential areas."[46] High-speed trains, Hughes suggested, could whisk passengers from the airport to downtown Las Vegas on a "micrometer-laid track down the present freeway right-of-way."[47]

Keeping up a steady beat of the publicity drums, Hughes, in another special message to Governor Laxalt, revived his offer of financial help to the proposed University of Nevada Medical School. Nearly a year had gone by since Hughes first volunteered to endow it, but there had been no binding commitment. Several legislators were contending that the state's failure to pin Hughes down to a formal contract was reason to scrap the medical school. Now, confronted by a small group of potentially hostile lawmakers intent on looking into his ownership of casinos, Hughes dusted off his pledge and renewed the offer in a February 9, 1968, letter to Laxalt.

In what he described as an attempt to clarify his earlier offer, Hughes told Laxalt that "when the medical school has been constructed and opened for academic session, and to insure its successful operation, I hereby commit to furnish . . . from $200,000 to $300,000 per year for 20 years to make up any deficit in annual operating funds." Hughes added that "I sincerely hope my commitment will enable you to obtain commitments from others who are interested in the welfare of the state to the end that the medical school may soon be a reality."[48]

In truth, the letter was no more than a restatement of the original pledge, but it attracted the same favorable publicity when the governor delivered copies to the news media, pointing to Hughes's signature on the letter as an affirmation of the industrialist's sincerity.

Two more weeks went by and then Governor Laxalt disclosed that Hughes was establishing a unique tax-exempt, nonprofit foundation to assist a newly proposed state agency in developing a comprehensive masterplan for Nevada's orderly development. The foundation was to be known as Nevada

Essential Development Surveys (NEEDS). The state agency was to be called the Comprehensive Environmental Development Agency (CEDA). Together, they would work toward improving the quality of life for Nevada residents. NEEDS and CEDA, a state official explained, would conduct in-depth studies on a cross section of community problems and needs in such areas as mental health, crime, higher education, libraries, preventive medicine, poverty, welfare, industrial development, and care and treatment of the elderly. "Studies would be conducted in areas where nothing is being done or where the present work is insufficient," Laxalt said.[49]

It was reported that Hughes would establish the foundation with a $5-million grant, but an aide to the governor allowed that the figure was exaggerated and that besides Hughes's undisclosed gift, it was hoped that "contributions would come from private industry, foundations and maybe even the federal government."[50] Hughes had assigned one of his executives to the project, John H. Meier, a computer specialist. Everybody was enthusiastic about the foundation.

In the first eight weeks of 1968, Nevada citizens were showered with promise of an unprecedented number of good works by Howard Hughes. He was credited with restoring the luster to Nevada's tarnished image around the rest of the country, and bringing new industry to the state. He would change Nevada's physical, economic, social, and educational landscape by building the world's largest hotel and one of the world's grandest airports, underwriting a medical school, and creating a foundation to provide for the state's orderly growth and make life more pleasant for everyone. With each fortnight bringing a fresh report of some new Hughes contribution to the public welfare, it was none too surprising that the state legislature lost interest in conducting a serious investigation of concentrated ownership in the gaming industry. Once again, public relations triumphed.*

MASTERPLAN

Unfortunately, Hughes's bid to buy more hotels and casinos was not faring nearly as well. The negotiations with Harrah were proceeding aimlessly. No agreement was in sight. Hughes was irritated not only by the failure to conclude the deal but also by Maheu's increasingly negative attitude. He had never been especially eager about expanding to Reno or Lake Tahoe. Even so, for some weeks, Maheu had dutifully bargained with Harrah. As the talks dragged on, however, Maheu began to sense that Harrah would probably not sell at any price, and that, for the first time since he began serving as Hughes's front man in Nevada, he would fall short of Hughes's wishes. He began to downplay the importance of the acquisitions in his reports to Hughes, dwelling at length on all the reasons that he, and others, believed it

---

*The results seldom measured up to Hughes's press releases. Solitron never moved to Las Vegas, and Hughes never built his new Sands hotel or jetport.

would be a mistake to buy the Harrah hotels and casinos.

Despite years in isolation, Hughes could read human behavioral patterns as well as he had once read an instrument panel. Hughes and Maheu had never met, but Hughes knew Maheu better than Maheu knew Hughes. He knew immediately that Maheu's deprecating remarks simply meant that Harrah most likely would not sell. He was angered by Maheu's pretense and he let him know it.

"Regarding your rationalization of why Harrah's is not for us," he wrote Maheu, "please don't give me any further report on this subject unless Harrah indicates he wants to sell. You know, Bob, sometimes I think you have an idea that I am about 12 years on this world instead of 62." Posing a series of rhetorical questions etched in sarcasm, Hughes asked Maheu, "Just answer one simple question: If this project is so far beneath my national standing, etc., just why did the governor tell you, on your return from Washington, 'Okay, Bob, I'll do this one for you. It will require a little time. I want to see some of the influential men in northern Nevada, and pave the way, etc.' Why would he do something harmful to me, as he now claims this is, if he was our friend? And why would you permit me to invest nine months of my time thinking about this deal, writing messages about it, etc., if it is so God damned bad?"[51]

Hughes reminded Maheu that "the reason I have been so insistent about Harrah's facilities has been the fact that they are *now, at present,* laying off the profits we need. The Stardust–Slipper combination can only be fully productive with a lot of work."[52] Even though he was quite correct in his judgment that the Reno and Lake Tahoe properties were sounder financially than the Stardust and the Silver Slipper, Hughes by mid-February had resigned himself to life without them and yielded to Maheu's pressure to concentrate on the Las Vegas market.

To reconcile their personal differences, for the relationship between the two men had grown more tense with each passing week, Hughes dashed off a memorandum to Maheu lamenting their estrangement. It is important, he wrote, "that you and I find a way to lay aside any differences and attempt a return to the atmosphere of complete harmony and unity and, most important, enthusiasm that prevailed between us in the beginning of our Nevada activity. . . . I am only content to give up all my plans in the north and focus right here next door if you will revert to your old attitude of enthusiasm and accord that we had in the early stages of this operation. Please do this, Bob."[53]

Sounding at times like the rueful partner in an unhappy marriage—a marriage conducted by telephone and letter—Hughes wrote, "I used to be able to communicate with you and not be frightened for fear each word I spoke or wrote might be the one that would cause you to get angry with me and wind up with my stomach tied up in knots. Please, Bob, let us go back to the environment of friendship that used to exist between us. That is all I ask. And if our differences are due to something I have said or failed to say in the past, or any other mistake I have made, I apologize most sincerely and I hope you will accept this apology and let us put it all behind us."[54]

As usual, Hughes needed Maheu for a reason. He had the rough outline of a plan of action, which he sketched for Maheu, accompanied by the obligatory admonition on the need for secrecy. Only three weeks had gone by since he announced his intention to turn the Sands into the world's largest hotel, but Hughes confided that he would put off that venture in favor of a more expedient project involving the Stardust and the Silver Slipper. From his Desert Inn penthouse, Hughes could look across Las Vegas Boulevard to his Frontier Hotel. A few yards to the north of the Frontier was the Silver Slipper and, just beyond it, the Stardust. What Hughes had in mind was the quick construction of an inexpensive hotel that would serve as a source of additional patrons for the Silver Slipper and the Stardust casinos.

To scrap the Sands expansion, which had produced so much favorable publicity, was, however, fraught with danger. "I am willing to postpone the building of the new Sands hotel," he said to Maheu, "but only if you will absolutely give me your most solemn word of honor that this postponement will not leak out to anybody. And, Bob, I mean any body *whomsoever!* Not to Hooper, Thomas, Moe, Laxalt, Bill Gay, any of my men, or anybody at all." Delaying the Sands construction, Hughes explained, "will mean that the funds (not the entire amount *by any means*), I should say that portion of the funds which was intended to be expended upon the Sands this year, will be available to build a single hotel building upon the Stardust property. Just a simple building out of simple materials, but one that can go up real fast and contain a lot of rooms. Then if the Stardust and Slipper casinos are enlarged to accommodate the people presumably sleeping in those new rooms, there should result a complex capable of those real large profits that Mr. Harrah achieves in the north."[55]

Maheu needed no further encouragement. His once cheerless reports took on a new optimism. The two men still had their differences, but Maheu's querulous reservations and sulking questions about the things Hughes wanted done now gave way to glowing accounts of progress on all fronts. The new mood ran throughout a dozen projects that Maheu was managing, from a continuing Hughes battle to force the Atomic Energy Commission to discontinue its nuclear testing program in Nevada to a still-secret plan to begin mining gold and silver. Even the desultory negotiations with Harrah turned upbeat. "As undemonstrative as this man is I am convinced that he feels that we have a deal subject to mutual agreement on the numbers," Maheu reported following a meeting with Harrah.[56]

There were, to be sure, the usual stumbling blocks. Dalitz once again was bargaining stubbornly about the Stardust price. A group from Texas made an offer to the Silver Slipper owners in an effort to buy the casino out from under Hughes. Another group of investors was trying to reopen the Bonanza. Governor Laxalt was advising Maheu privately that approval of Hughes's new casino acquisitions by state gaming authorities would require some concession, perhaps a public announcement that these would be his last purchases. The governor even suggested the phrasing of a statement, but it received a chilly reception from Hughes.

"I still want to leave the door open regarding the Nugget in North Las

Vegas," Hughes told Maheu. "Also, I am concerned about the Bonanza. The people trying to reopen this affair seem just unwilling to give up. If we make the kind of a statement the governor wants we will be forbidden from going near either."[57]

Hughes drafted a step-by-step masterplan for Maheu. Everything was to be accomplished in its proper order. First, he wanted to buy the Bonanza, close the casino, and operate the place solely as a hotel, avoiding the need for a gaming license. The Bonanza transaction would be followed immediately by the purchase of the Stardust and the Silver Slipper. In the interim, an option to buy the Silver Nugget would be continued. Until public opinion could be effectively manipulated, the option was not to be exercised. Simultaneously, Hughes suggested issuing a public statement declaring that the Stardust and the Silver Slipper would be his last acquisitions in Las Vegas, thereby complying with the governor's wishes in word if not in fact.

"If you will go to work on the Bonanza buyout," Hughes said to Maheu, "then I would favor this kind of approach to the governor: Provided the commission will take a long look at any new gaming application for the strip, and not rush into any precipitously, I will be happy to agree that the request for licensing of the Slipper–Stardust will be our last for a long time in the strip area. The above avoids saying anything about Bonanza as I expect you to move quickly and try to close that deal before the meeting." As for the Silver Nugget, Hughes said, "we just say nothing at all plus or minus —hoping that we can extend that option until we have the groundbreaking for the airport. Once this takes place (I mean the big airport), I feel the opinion of the entire community concerning us will be different. So, I am relying upon you to obtain a longer option on the Nugget in North Las Vegas and say nothing whatsoever concerning this at this time."[58] To conceal his interest in the bankrupt Bonanza, Hughes wanted Maheu "to handle this affair from behind a third party, so that we are at no time in a position publicly of having any interest in the place."[59]

WARNING FROM WASHINGTON

Although Hughes was managing nicely to keep his interest in the Bonanza a secret, there had been a security breach in the Stardust talks. On March 10, the *Nevada State Journal* in Reno proclaimed in a page-one headline: "Hughes Moves to Add Stardust to Holdings." The publicity annoyed Hughes. He had wanted no announcement until a day or two before the state gaming authorities met to consider his applications for the Stardust and the Silver Slipper. The opposition would now have several weeks to prepare its case. Once again it was public relations to the rescue, via the support of one of the state's heretofore leading critics of concentrated hotel and casino ownership.

On March 15, Hank Greenspun, the *Las Vegas Sun* editor and publisher —once described as "a sort of Robin Hood of the gambling community, attacking the wealthy and corrupt and taking up for the underdogs who were sometimes equally corrupt"—traveled to Carson City to lobby before the State Gaming Policy Board on behalf of Hughes's takeover of the Stardust and the Silver Slipper.[60] For Greenspun—who in the past year had collected some $8 million from Hughes in assorted business transactions—his appearance, to champion Hughes's bid for his fifth and sixth casino licenses represented a complete about-face. Eight years earlier, Greenspun had vigorously and successfully argued against the award of a third gambling license to Moe Dalitz and his associates, who were attempting to buy the Riviera Hotel and Casino.

But now, drawing on a theme expressed by Governor Laxalt, Greenspun stressed the positive effect that Hughes's presence in Nevada was having on the state's image. In a speech accented by Greenspun hyperbole, he recounted his role as a goodwill ambassador and volunteer fireman, criss-crossing the country to quench rumor and accusation about Nevada, and especially Las Vegas. "The past three years in particular have brought me into practically every principal city of this nation as well as Canada, and I have been subjected to the most searching and penetrating questions, most of them dealing with rumors, suspicions and outright distortions of our area by the outside press," Greenspun asserted. "It was my purpose to defend the state of Nevada and the city of Las Vegas in particular for many reasons. Foremost among them being that my children were born here and I felt it a duty—an over-riding responsibility—to insure they would never have cause for misgivings or even hesitation when the need arose for them to disclose their place of birth. It was my desire to make them proud of their home, and in making it possible for my children, all children born in Nevada would be equally benefitted."[61]

Howard Hughes had already performed miracles for Las Vegas's image, Greenspun told gaming officials, and "it is within our grasp now to look the world straight in their national magazines and law enforcement and say, 'We have achieved a clean, decent society.'" As for Hughes himself, Greenspun said,

he is a modest, self-effacing person whose contributions to the betterment of mankind are unmatched by any group or man in contemporary history. He has never throughout his career displayed any tendencies of control or monopoly. To the contrary, he is a lone operator and seeks not to impose his will on others nor to permit others to impose their will upon him. His fertile mind is too occupied with exploration and discovery far beyond the scope of ordinary men to concern himself with smaller problems which appear here present.[62]

Meanwhile, as had happened in the Desert Inn negotiations, the Stardust talks had reached a standoff. This time Hughes could not understand Dalitz's intransigence. The United States and other Western nations had been plunged into the worst financial crisis in forty years; economic forecasts were unanimously gloomy. Hughes was distressed that Dalitz had failed to take note and lower his Stardust asking price accordingly. Dalitz was asking $34 million and Hughes was offering $5 million less.

"We have received no adjustment for a worldwide financial crisis, which has thrown the financial community of the nation into a panic," Hughes wrote to Maheu. "It has canceled innumerable plans for the public distribution of securities, common stocks, convertible debentures, etc., one issue after another, which had been announced, have now been canceled. Merrill Lynch tells me there just is no money around. It is like 1929. Moe is welcome to check this through his contacts on Wall Street. Or I will be glad to have Merrill Lynch call him."[63]

Still, Hughes felt confident that he would settle his $5-million difference with Dalitz. He had already reached an agreement with the Silver Slipper owners* to lease the casino, with an option to buy for $5,360,000. The casino would change hands on midnight on April 30. He hoped to assume control of the Stardust about the same time, and so he directed Maheu to begin filing all the required applications for county and state gaming licenses, for both properties.

With the strong support of Greenspun already on the public record, and with Hughes's other powerful public-relations gimmickry continuing to pay off, Hughes and Maheu were reasonably certain that the state gaming authorities would approve the two license applications. It was a feeling emphatically not shared by Dick Gray, who believed that Laxalt would not be able to deliver the necessary votes on the Nevada Gaming Commission for both the Silver Slipper and the Stardust. Gray's pessimism finally moved Hughes to entertain an incredible plan. He asked Maheu what might happen if he went to see the governor,

and if I agreed *and did* join with Laxalt and you in a statement to the press that we are bringing Hughes Tool Company to Nevada (with a long recitation of the company's many accomplishments), and if we supplement this with a board meeting by Hughes Tool Company (certified copy to Laxalt) passing a resolution *instructing* and authorizing Holliday, as secretary, to do the necessary to accomplish the change in the corporate setup from Delaware to Nevada.[64]

Hughes was ready to do this within the week.

It was, to say the least, one of Hughes's more bizarre plans. The Hughes Tool Company, registered as a Delaware corporation for three decades, and headquartered in Texas for more than half a century, made its many millions by servicing oil companies. Why would it move from Houston—the heartland of the American oil industry—to Las Vegas, where the oil industry was nonex-

---

*In December 1967, six persons were indicted by a federal grand jury in Los Angeles on charges that they conspired to cheat card players at the Friars Club, a fraternal organization whose members include prominent show-business personalities. Three of those indicted were Maurice H. Friedman and T. Warner Richardson (who had interests in both the Frontier, before Hughes bought it, and the Silver Slipper), and John Rosselli. It was charged that card players at the club —including Tony Martin, Zeppo Marx, and Harry Karl, the shoe-store magnate and husband of the actress Debbie Reynolds—were cheated of some $400,000 in rigged gin-rummy games. A conspirator on the floor above the game room watched through peepholes in the ceiling and electronically signaled his colleagues in the game what cards the players were holding. Freidman, Richardson, Rosselli, and two others were convicted of the charges.

istent? Why should anyone expect its personnel to be willing to uproot their families to move from conservative Houston to gaudy Las Vegas? In any event, the relocation of Hughes Tool was not actively pursued, although the proposal was later dusted off as a bargaining ploy. Maheu, who had in any case been supremely confident that the licenses would be granted, and without any commitment to move Hughes Tool, told Hughes, after a conversation with Laxalt, that the governor said "he has no reason to believe it will not be approved."[65]

Hughes, however, saw conspiracies all about him—an outgrowth no doubt of his own conspiratorial nature. These optimistic reports from Maheu and others might be made to have a dark side, and Hughes found it. Now it became a question not of whether the commission would grant the licenses but of how many licenses would be given to competitors. "I am informed that, since the word has gotten out that our applications will be approved," he wrote to Maheu,

everybody and his little dog is filing for a gaming license because they all reason that if the commission passes ours they cannot very well refuse somebody else. I am sure my reports are exaggerated but there must be some truth. So what I want is a report on those applications which are nearest to being considered favorably, in order that we can see just how far this movement has gone, and in order that we may take whatever preventive measures may be indicated by the report. Please let me know when you can give me something on this subject. Also, please let me have meanwhile whatever inputs or rumors you may have heard along this line.[66]

For his part, Maheu worked diligently, tending to the licensing formalities. He exuded his usual air of self-confidence, advising Hughes that even the United States Department of Justice had sanctioned the action. This last bit of news was especially heartening to Hughes in light of the dire warnings some months earlier from his attorneys Dick Gray and Robert Campbell, who had vetoed further acquisitions on the Las Vegas Strip because of potential antitrust problems. "Thank you most, most deeply for your message," a grateful Hughes wrote to Maheu. "I am truly impressed with what you tell me about Justice. That makes me feel better for the first time in some while." Hughes was so impressed that he said to Maheu, "I will continue to leave everything completely in your hands. If I did not have the most unlimited confidence in you, I would not say that."[67]

But Maheu had promised Hughes more than he could deliver. On April 24, 1968, six days before Hughes was to take control of the Silver Slipper, James J. Coyle, an assistant United States attorney in the San Francisco field office of the Justice Department's Antitrust Division, visited Dick Gray in Las Vegas to talk about the pending acquisitions. For several hours, Coyle questioned Gray about Hughes's business interests in Las Vegas in general and his hotel and casino properties in particular. Gray related that Hughes planned "to bring some of the manufacturing activities of Hughes Tool Company to Las Vegas" and that he also had "offered to construct a true jet age airport in Las

Vegas and is already committed to underwrite a feasibility study on such an airport."[68] If the study shows that such an airport would be feasible, Gray said, "Hughes will then build the airport and sell it to the city at cost." As for the industrialist's hotel and casino purchases, Gray pointed out to the Justice Department attorney that "the FBI, Internal Revenue and law enforcement agents generally are very glad to see Hughes come in and acquire gambling interests from less desirable owners."[69]

Gray's dutiful recitation went on. The Frontier Hotel was losing money when Hughes bought it and had just now "come around to a break even point." The Castaways was in even worse shape, Gray said, and he dismissed it as "a bad investment." While he seemed to be advocating Hughes's right to buy more hotels and casinos, Gray's choice of words conveyed to Coyle the unmistakable feeling that he was not an eager supporter of that policy. "I got the impression," Coyle said later, "that he would not be too unhappy if we took action to curtail future investments by Hughes in hotels and casinos and that he might recommend cancellation on the Stardust if we moved against it."[70]

Coyle, in turn, gave Gray the impression, without actually saying so, that the Justice Department would allow the Silver Slipper deal to go through if Hughes would cancel the Stardust purchase. The meeting between the two lawyers ended on a friendly note, with Gray promising to pull together for Coyle some reports and documents on Hughes's holdings in Las Vegas.

Back in San Francisco two days later, Coyle prepared a twelve-page memorandum on the interview, recommending to the chief of the Justice Department's San Francisco office that antitrust proceedings be instituted against Hughes to block his purchase of the Stardust:

If we are to follow the mandate of Congress and the recent victories we have won in the courts, I do not see any good reason for not proceeding in this matter. . . . It is contrary to our basic concept to permit one individual or one firm to control one-fifth of the economic activities of a city of 250,000 people. Already columnists such as Art Buchwald are commenting upon the Hughes acquisitions and implying, with some justification, that he is in the process of acquiring the entire state of Nevada.[71]

Rejecting the now-familiar contention that Hughes was ridding Las Vegas of an undesirable element, Coyle observed that "most monopolists have used such an argument but the law does not favor vigilante or 'extra-legal' enforcement. I do not believe," he concluded, "we should abdicate enforcement of the antitrust laws on the theory that duly constituted law enforcement agencies are incapable of enforcing the law without assistance from Hughes."[72] Coyle's memorandum and a draft lawsuit to be filed against Hughes were forwarded to Justice Department officials in Washington for review and approval.

Gray had meanwhile relayed to Hughes the substance of his interview with the Justice Department lawyer and recommended that he pull out of the Stardust negotiations. Hughes reacted defensively, mindful that it was Gray who had earlier warned him of the potential antitrust consequences of buying more Strip properties. Never willing to concede a mistake, Hughes asked Gray if it would not be "more prudent to go ahead and close both [the Silver Slipper and the Stardust] and then negotiate with the Justice Department, enlisting the help of the governor and the legislators, who, I feel want me here." Hughes added that "if we cancel the Stardust now, it certainly puts us in a position of admitting that we have done something wrong."[73]

Gray acquiesced and on April 30 went before the Nevada Gaming Commission to testify on behalf of Hughes's two license applications. He told the commission that Hughes wanted to take over the Silver Slipper at midnight that day and that "we have provided for a closing on June 30 of the Stardust, but this really has not yet been fully decided."[74] Gray reported that Hughes's investment in the Silver Slipper would amount to $5,360,000, and his investment in the Stardust would total $30.5 million. He assured the commission that Hughes had no desire to obtain a monopoly position in the gaming industry, but he stopped short of promising that the industrialist would make no further investments in Las Vegas. He acknowledged that Hughes also owned a valuable tract of land along the Strip once occupied by the El Rancho Vegas, which had been destroyed in a fire, but he insisted that the property had been bought for investment purposes and that there were no plans to erect another resort complex on the site. Commission members questioned Gray for nearly two hours on the consequences that concentrated ownership might have on everything from wages to the purchase of supplies. In the end, the commission voted 3 to 2 to grant both licenses. Later in the day, at a hastily called meeting of the Clark County Liquor and Gaming Board in Las Vegas, that board also approved Hughes's takeover of the Silver Slipper and announced that it would approve the Stardust transfer in the near future. With the addition of the two hotels and casinos, Hughes would become Nevada's biggest gambler, surpassing William Harrah in casino revenue. His casinos would account for 28 percent of all gaming revenue in Clark County; his hotels, with their thirty-five hundred rooms, would account for 35 percent of all rooms on the Strip, and 17.5 percent of all rooms in Las Vegas.

When Hughes asked Gray to push ahead with the Stardust licensing despite signals from the Justice Department that it would intervene, he explained that this approach would enable him to use the Dalitz hotel and casino as a bargaining tool with the federal government if the threatened antitrust action materialized. "If we come to a real impasse," Hughes said, "we could offer to divert the Stardust in settlement of the claim. If we cancel the Stardust now, we have nothing to offer in settlement."[75]

Hughes's legal theory made little sense to Gray, especially since the Justice Department had indicated that no lawsuit would be filed unless he went through with the Stardust purchase. But in Hughes's logic it made a great deal of sense. He wanted the Stardust as a bargaining chip in a bigger game—one that he knew full well would vex his Houston lawyer. It involved a scheme to eliminate, or at least neutralize, his most feared competitor—the Fresno-born son of an Armenian fruit peddler who, like Hughes, was a recent arrival in Las Vegas.

CHAPTER 13

OUT OF CONTROL

A RIVAL

KIRK KERKORIAN was an eighth-grade dropout. While Howard Hughes tinkered with his racer and perfected his flying skills, Kerkorian cut logs in a Civilian Conservation Corps camp. Most of the $25 a month he earned went home to help carry his family through the Depression. A succession of jobs followed—he steam-cleaned automobile engines, he bought and sold used cars. And all the while, he put every extra dollar into flying lessons. In 1941, he obtained a commercial pilot's license—three years after Hughes, who was thirteen years older, acquired his.

After the Second World War, in which Kerkorian was a flight instructor and a ferry pilot, he bought a used C-47, and with his sister Rose keeping the books, started the Los Angeles Air Service. Aided by lucrative military contracts during the Korean War, the tiny air service grew into a worldwide nonscheduled air carrier, renamed Trans International Airlines. By the time he moved to Las Vegas in 1967, Kerkorian was a brilliantly successful but largely unknown businessman who had amassed a personal fortune of well over $100 million.

Kerkorian's first significant Las Vegas transaction was the purchase of Bugsy Siegel's Flamingo Hotel and Casino, which had fallen on hard times. Neither Hughes nor the rest of Las Vegas paid much attention at first. The Flamingo was a loser. That attitude quickly changed when it became apparent that Kerkorian, a former Golden Gloves boxer (thirty-three wins, four losses), saw the Flamingo only as a preliminary to the main event, the construction and operation of the largest high-rise resort hotel in Nevada. To be called the International, the hotel was announced with Hughes-like superlatives. In addition to more than fifteen hundred rooms, it would contain the world's largest casino, a swimming pool to be the biggest man-made body of water in Nevada, after Lake Mead, and a showroom more spacious than the stage in Radio City Music Hall.

Kerkorian's publicity angered Hughes. It threatened to overshadow his own bid to become Nevada's premier gambler, it bruised his fragile ego, and it meant more competition for the tourist dollar. Hughes was so fearful, in fact, that during the early months of 1968 he explored ways to block construction of the International. The announced conversion of the Sands into the world's largest hotel was timed in part to do that. "The disclosure of my new $100 million establishment will make it much harder for K-I to get financed," Hughes wrote Maheu, reasoning that if Kerkorian continued to receive "a lot of publicity about [his] new hotel, he could generate so much desire among local citizens who stand to profit that it would be very difficult for anyone to stop."[1]

The Sands announcement, however, failed to deter Kerkorian. With financing for the International in hand and construction under way, Hughes settled on a new approach. Maheu was to confide to Kerkorian that the Sands expansion was being scrapped because the Atomic Energy Commission intended to step up its underground nuclear-testing program in the desert not far from Las Vegas:

Please tell Kerkorian the reason I postponed the new Sands is because I learned of the possibility that the testing would be resumed in this area on a heavier than ever basis, and that my architectural and geological experts advised me it will be utterly impossible to get a foothold in this sandy soil, solid and predictable enough to build a really tall building with any assurance that it will not be seriously damaged by these continuing tests plus the earthquakes generated by them.[2]

Warming to his story, Hughes went on,

please further tell him that the high-rise of our Desert Inn, only nine stories, has been very definitely damaged in a number of places. That we firmly believe the Mint and the Sahara and the Riviera have also been damaged very seriously, but the owners of those hotels, like ourselves, have decided that the likelihood of recovering damages from the government is not good enough to justify the long arduous effort, and the owners of the other hotels, like ourselves, are reluctant to file a claim for damages. . . . We are convinced the public is already staying away from Las Vegas because of distaste for everything connected with atomic bombs, and if we admitted damage, the public would surely be frightened for fear the hotel, already damaged and weakened, might come piling down on top of them if it receives another good shake.[3]

Whether Maheu actually relayed the message to Kerkorian is not known. If he did, it had no effect, and Hughes continued to plot. Could Kerkorian, who was becoming known as the Avis of Las Vegas, be lured into some joint and no doubt lucrative undertaking? He assumed that Kerkorian, like every other businessman with whom he had ever dealt, would be enamored of the intrigue and secrecy surrounding any dealing with Howard Hughes:

Below: Kirk Kerkorian, the self-made millionaire whom Hughes feared might overshadow him in Las Vegas. *Wide World Photos*

Penthouse aides Levar B. Myler, *above,* and John M. Holmes, Jr. *below, right. Wide World Photos*

I urge you to tell him that there may be many things that will come up from time to time and if I could believe, truly and completely, that I can discuss these matters with him without even a small chance of an inadvertent or accidental leak, I would do so without hesitance and that any one of these matters could turn out to be a multimillion dollar blockbuster. Once you feel he is really impressed with the urgency of secrecy, why not tell him that I am at this moment negotiating with Terry Drinkwater to acquire control of Western Airlines, and that we might be able to work out something jointly.[4]

But what Hughes really wanted was to be rid of the International, and to that end he concocted a scheme that would halt its construction, enable him to acquire yet another Las Vegas hotel and casino, and relieve him of his extravagant offer to build a jetport. As Hughes told Maheu, with great exaggeration, "I have invested $200 million in this strip region, and I simply cannot see Kerkorian stand between the airport and our area, and that is where he will be if the traffic flows in Paradise Road and thence to the strip."[5]

The site of the International Hotel was on Paradise Road which began at McCarran Airport and ran alongside Las Vegas Boulevard for the entire length of the Strip before intersecting with it. Thus, inbound traffic from the airport could pass Kerkorian's International Hotel rather than any of Hughes's hotels on the Strip. For the most part, Paradise Road had remained undeveloped commercially. On its west side, just across from the International site, stood the empty, unfinished, thirty-one-story Landmark Hotel and Casino, then the tallest structure in Nevada, a monument to cost overruns and disastrous planning. Around Las Vegas it was called the haunted house.

"Suppose," Hughes said,

we offer to Kerkorian that we will turn the Stardust over to him, on whatever kind of deal it takes, and we will buy from him his International Hotel property plus the building in progress at his cost, agreeing not to complete it. Then, I had in mind as follows: I think it logical to assume that somebody is going to finance that damned Landmark Tower. . . . So, we must assume that entity will be fed into the competitive picture one way or another. Now, if we sell Stardust to Kerkorian and if we agree not to attempt to license International Hotel, I thought we might take over the tower to avoid it falling into somebody else's hands. I am sure that if we build some more rooms on one of several locations I have in mind, and if we then operate the tower as a sort of a glorified Top of the Mark, kind of like the little Skyroom used to be here at the Desert Inn, when it was very popular, I am certain it will be successful. And mainly we will keep somebody else from operating it as competition.[6]

Only Hughes knew why he believed that Kerkorian would surrender his International. But he correctly sensed that his attorney, Dick Gray, "will have a fit about stopping the International Hotel in progress." As a result, he said, "we will probably have to persuade Kerkorian to stop it gradually before he delivers it to us."[7]

Hughes never had an opportunity to pursue this plan, not because of its folly but because he lost his trading card. Just as he was preparing to assume control of the Stardust, the Justice Department advised Gray that it would sue

Hughes if he attempted to go through with the acquisition. Hughes was furious —at the Justice Department for meddling, at Maheu for saying that the government would not intervene, and at Gray and Campbell for having been right all along.

"I thought for practical purposes that we had nothing to worry about if we got board and commission approval," he whined to Gray. "If this is not true, I better get right through to the White House and find out if the administration wants me to pull out of Nevada. Because I am not going into a contest with the Justice Department. And if this is where we are headed, I prefer to sell to Hilton or Sheraton or one of the companies who are set up to go through a hassle with the Justice Department."[8]

Maheu was equally bitter. He had suffered a humiliating defeat in the area of his special abilities—arranging political favors. "You can bet your life that the antitrust division will live to regret their contemplated action," he told Hughes.[9] Maheu demanded a conference with the antitrust lawyers in San Francisco, and on July 2, he and Dick Gray met with James J. Coyle, the government attorney who had recommended the legal action; Lyle L. Jones, chief of the Justice Department's antitrust office in San Francisco; and James E. Figenshaw, another attorney in that office. Maheu emphasized that "Hughes was cleaning out various undesirable elements connected with gaming operations in Las Vegas, thereby improving the image of the city and the state." Any legal action by the Justice Department might result in unfavorable newspaper articles that would "rehash stories of 'skimming' in the past that the Hughes' interests have taken steps to insure against in the future."[10]

Further, Gray argued that other divisions of the Justice Department had given the Stardust acquisition "unofficial approval."[11] Fred M. Vinson, Jr., the assistant attorney-general in charge of the Criminal Division and son of the former Chief Justice of the United States, had accepted the contention that Hughes was driving undesirables out of the Las Vegas casinos. In a memorandum for Attorney-General Ramsey Clark, Vinson recommended "against taking action" in the Stardust transaction, implying that J. Edgar Hoover himself looked favorably upon the Hughes purchase. "With respect to Las Vegas operators," he said, "I have heard Mr. Hoover say that Del Webb and Hughes were far preferable."[12]

But Gray and Maheu could not turn the Antitrust Division around. Somewhat a maverick within the Justice Department, the division had persuaded Attorney-General Clark to oppose Hughes on the Stardust purchase. Antitrust lawyers heard a hollow ring in Maheu's argument that Hughes was driving "undesirable elements" out of Las Vegas. During the Stardust licensing hearing, Gray had testified that there would be no changes in hotel and casino management: "The people are there and that's one reason we were interested in it."[13] Justice was prepared to go through with the lawsuit, so Gray asked to see a copy of the complaint. The antitrust lawyers refused to show it to him, saying it would be filed as soon as possible unless Hughes abandoned the

Stardust acquisition.* They did agree, however, to give Hughes three weeks, until July 27, to decide what to do.

Maheu refused to give up. He applied pressure on the Justice Department, first through Nevada's two senators and then through Governor Laxalt. In a letter to Attorney-General Clark, the governor charged that the Antitrust Division had "jeopardized the employment of 2,000 people in the Stardust enterprise" and threatened "permanent damage" to Nevada's economy. He warned Clark that if legal action were taken against Hughes, Nevada "would be faced with no alternative other than to intervene and oppose the action with all the resources of the state."[14] It was to no avail. Clark stood firm. When Hughes realized that the federal government fully intended to sue him, he caved in and withdrew his offer for the Stardust.

It was Moe Dalitz's turn to be vexed. He had a signed commitment from Hughes to buy the Stardust, but now the industrialist wanted to walk away from the deal. Dalitz consulted his lawyer, Edward Morgan, who was also Maheu's friend and Hughes's lawyer in the KLAS–TV licensing case before the FCC. Dalitz said Morgan told him, "We're in a great position for a big damage suit."[15] Sensing a potentially more rewarding course of action, though, Dalitz rejected the proposal. "You see if you can't get us a deal that we can live with," he told Morgan, "that we can straighten out the obligations that we've incurred, and we'll settle it that way."[16]

The "obligations" Dalitz referred to involved a multimillion-dollar renovation of the Stardust. During the negotiations, Hughes's representatives had told Dalitz to go ahead and let contracts on a long-planned refurbishing of the hotel and casino. Now that the deal had fallen through, Dalitz felt the "Hughes people should do something about sharing this damage with us in some way."[17] Hughes's withdrawal, coming in the midst of the actual reconstruction, had left the Stardust in a "very shaky financial position."[18] When Dalitz and Morgan expressed their concern to Maheu and Gray, the Hughes lieutenants asked what could be done. "I want to get enough money to pay off these construction costs," Dalitz told them. Gray and Maheu readily agreed "to make that available."[19]

The resolution turned out to be a $3-million loan. As with the $4-million loan to Hank Greenspun, Gray wanted to charge the prevailing rate of interest.

---

*The antitrust lawyers were holding an eight-page complaint ready for filing the moment Hughes tried to go through with the Stardust purchase. The complaint, which already had been signed by Attorney-General Clark, charged that the acquisition "will violate Section 7 of the Clayton Act, in that the effect of said acquisition may be substantially to lessen competition or to tend to create a monopoly." In addition to asking the court to rule the Stardust acquisition a violation of the Clayton Act and to bar the sale, the complaint went a step further. Had Hughes known the contents of the lawsuit, he truly would have panicked, for the government sought to make all future Hughes acquisitions of hotels and motels in Las Vegas subject to court approval. The complaint requested "that the defendant Hughes Tool Co., and all employes, agents, and other persons acting on its behalf be enjoined from directly or indirectly acquiring the stock or assets of any other corporation engaged in the operation of a resort hotel or motel in the greater Las Vegas area without the prior approval of the court."

Dalitz, possibly mindful of Greenspun's deal, thought "we should get the very lowest possible rate of interest, which is what we felt we were entitled to get because of this unfortunate thing."[20] And Gray gave in again, setting the rate at 3 percent.

"It was all very, very pleasant," Dalitz said. "There was no argument about it, nobody tried to gouge, nor did anybody try to welch out."[21]

No doubt, it was pleasant for Dalitz, who was known to some as "the underworld's Metternich," responsible "for the supervising of underworld investments in Las Vegas" and rumored to be "one of the architects of the skimming process."[22]

The pleasantries extended to Edward Morgan who had conducted the negotiations. To show his gratitude Dalitz offered Morgan a choice—he could buy an interest in the Stardust or accept a $500,000 fee. "He was very solicitous of getting as good a deal as he could for us," Dalitz said, "and I felt that we should be liberal with him, and I thought we were."[23] Less than a year later, the Stardust was sold to the Parvin–Dohrmann Company. Rather than exercise the option, Morgan took the $500,000 fee and once again graciously shared it, giving $150,000 to his friend Bob Maheu. By then, Maheu had placed Morgan on a $100,000-a-year retainer from the Hughes Tool Company, and Morgan, representing Dalitz, had collected an additional $100,000 from the elder stateman of gaming in yet another multimillion-dollar sale of Strip real estate to Hughes.

How much did Hughes know of this fee splitting? Would it have occurred to him that while Hughes Tool was paying Morgan for certain services, Morgan was collecting fees from Dalitz to represent him in transactions with Hughes, or that Morgan shared one fee with Maheu, whose annual retainer from Hughes ran well above half a million dollars? Could Hughes have known that $150,000 of a low-interest loan to Greenspun went to Maheu? Was it likely that Hughes knew that Parry Thomas collected fees for representing people dealing with Hughes in one transaction while collecting fees from Hughes for representing him in another? There is no evidence that Hughes was aware of most extracurricular business dealings of his aides, executives, and longtime associates. They quite often traded on their relationship with him, using the power of his name, and occasionally even his money, to further their own interests. If he ever learned that Hughes Aircraft funds were used to bankroll stock deals for certain company executives, or that a Hughes foreign subsidiary's funds had bailed out a financially distressed company in which Maheu was a stockholder, it was by chance. No one in the empire volunteered such information to Hughes. It had always been that way. But now it was worse. Hughes's problems were magnified, on the one hand by his resumption of an active—and far more varied—business life, and on the other by his total isolation and dependence on others, including many men he had never met.

Almost all his life, Hughes had focused his energies on motion pictures and aviation, two businesses he understood. Until the late 1950s, he was both mobile and, to certain people, accessible. He was as likely to involve himself with the phrasing of a publicity release as with complex financial negotiations involving hundreds of millions of dollars. He was reasonably aware of much that was going on throughout his organization, which he ruled with unquestioned authority. Individual initiative was not encouraged. Those who worked for him during that period would have had serious reservations about making any significant business decision without his approval.

But by the time Hughes moved to Las Vegas in 1966, he had been isolated from the daily workings of his organization for almost ten years. Where once he kept in constant touch with key executives and associates, sometimes in person, more often by telephone, now there was no personal contact whatsoever, and few telephone conversations except with Maheu. All calls and information were received and transmitted through the hands of one of his five personal aides—Roy Crawford, Howard Eckersley, George Francom, John Holmes, and Levar Myler, who had rejoined the aide corps in 1968 after recovering from a heart attack. It mattered not whether the communication was a call from his wife, a legal analysis of his federal income taxes, or a corporate report on bids for a government contract.

The aides—they preferred to be called "staff executives" or "staff executive assistants"—had completely replaced Operations at Romaine Street as the conduit to Howard Hughes. Although Operations was still manned around the clock, this was out of tradition rather than necessity. The telephone with a distinctive ring signaling a call from Hughes was silent. No one could "speak directly" with him.[24] Nevertheless, the Desert Inn system functioned much as the one at Romaine Street had. Callers were asked by the aides to give their name, telephone number, and the nature of their business. If the aides felt that Hughes ought to know of the call, he was told. Hughes then would decide whether to reply. Later, telecopiers were installed in the penthouse, the tool company's offices in Houston, and Chester Davis's New York law office for transmission of memoranda, and calls to the penthouse were reduced even more. Hughes saw only seven people besides the aides—three doctors, his cook, his waiter, his barber, and one of his lawyers.

During this Las Vegas period, Maheu was the only executive in the empire, as well as the only outsider, with whom Hughes maintained any consistent contact, and that was always by telephone or memorandum, never in person. Since his move to Las Vegas two years earlier, in 1966, Hughes had not even seen his wife. He and Jean spent the eleventh and twelfth years of their marriage in separate states. The purchase of the Krupp ranch and the Riddle mansion, where he thought they might live together once again, had not brought Jean from California. Although they spoke on the telephone almost daily, Hughes treated Jean as he would any other caller, sometimes refusing to speak to her, sometimes insisting that they speak at a stated hour. When he did not feel like talking, he would instruct one of the aides to tell her he was too ill:

(To Mrs.) Dearest, I am very ill but confident I will feel better by 10:30. You will hear from me the minute I feel just a little bit better. My very most love.[25]

The aides worked out of a room adjoining Hughes's bedroom, at the southeastern corner of the Desert Inn's ninth floor, opposite the elevator. The elevator required a special key to operate it. An armed guard sat in front of it twenty-four hours a day. No door led from the hallway into Hughes's bedroom. The only entrance was through the aides' room. The remaining two suites and four bedrooms on the ninth floor were vacant. The fire doors were bolted.

Because Romaine Street was no longer the central repository for Hughes's working files, the aides established a makeshift office in their room, equipping it with a desk, an IBM typewriter, a Xerox machine, a telecopier, a pair of four-drawer file cabinets, and a paper shredder. To staff the office around the clock, the aides worked eight-hour shifts, "four days on one schedule, followed by four days on a different schedule, followed by four days on a third schedule, and then four days off."[26] Ordinarily, only one aide would be on duty at a time, although when Hughes was especially active, a second might be pressed into service.

It was a curious crew that served as Hughes's link with a billion-dollar empire. Myler had been a former burr- and milling-machine operator, Holmes a wax salesman, Francom a heavy construction worker, Eckersley a finance company employee, and Crawford a manufacturer's representative for an oil refiner. They had no special business abilities or secretarial skills. Nor did they owe their position to an intimate knowledge of high finance or corporate procedure, but rather to their decision to cater to Hughes's every wish and to make sure that his private asylum remained impenetrable to outsiders. By the time they reached Las Vegas, all the aides were seasoned veterans who fully understood Hughes's fickle, sometimes infantile moods. They knew when to bring him a message, when to stay away. They knew exactly how he wanted his food prepared, his bed made, his "insulation"—the layers of paper towels —spread on his bed and chair.

By virtue of their access to Hughes, the aides were a powerful clique in the empire. Hughes executives and lawyers were wholly dependent on them to pass along their messages promptly and accurately to Hughes, and to take him news that he very often did not want to hear. "If you had something you just had to get his attention on, and you could explain to them why it was, then they would go to bat at the risk of his wrath," explained Mickey West, Hughes's tax lawyer who spent much time over the years talking to the aides.[27] Theoretically, the aides were answerable only to Hughes, but all of them were still politically tied to Romaine Street and Bill Gay, who had hired them. Although Hughes had cut all ties with Romaine, and Gay was *persona non grata,* the aides quietly communicated with Gay or his deputy Kay Glenn, passing along information about Hughes's physical or mental state, his financial deals, his current whims.

Although Holmes was considered the senior aide because he had worked for Hughes longer than the others, he exercised no supervisory control. "We never had anybody in charge," Eckersley said. "Everybody was his own guy, and he worked with Hughes, and that was the way Hughes liked it. So that we never had really hard-and-fast policies. We'd decide what to do together, and some would do things, and some wouldn't."[28]

As a result of this casual management style, messages sent to Hughes from throughout his organization were processed according to the individual disposition of the aide on duty. Eckersley, for example, typed each incoming telephone message that he delivered to Hughes. "They could all type," he said, "but some didn't like to, and they would prefer not to do it if they could do it some other way. Some would prefer to write it in longhand. Mr. Hughes didn't care, as long as he knew what the message was."[29] Before the messages were given to Hughes, they were sometimes copied and filed, sometimes not. "Everybody didn't do it," Eckersley said, "but I filed things by subject and by the author."[30] In contrast, Myler recalled that several factors determined whether he would copy and file an incoming communication for future reference. One was "the availability of the [Xerox] machine. Sometimes it would be out of order." Another, he said, was time: "Sometimes I just wouldn't have time to make a copy." Then, too, he said, "some messages I just didn't think were important enough to copy."[31] If Myler thought a message was important enough to copy, and if he had enough time to do so, and if the Xerox machine was working—then he would make two copies and file them. But there was no master index to the files and no filing system. As for the original messages, Hughes would stack them up beside his bed. Sometimes he would read them, sometimes not. When he read and returned a message, it was filed. Occasionally, he would return a message to the aides with instructions to "destroy" it.[32]

Hughes either wrote out his messages in longhand with a blue ballpoint pen on a yellow legal tablet or dictated them to an aide. He seldom rewrote or tinkered with the language in any of his handwritten communications. "He might change a word here and there, or add a phrase, but not generally," Crawford said. "Usually when he wrote something out, that's the way it was. That's the way it remained."[33] When Hughes dictated a message, the aides made no attempt to take down his words verbatim—whether it involved a multimillion-dollar financial transaction or a business decision affecting the livelihood of hundreds of workers. "We would listen to what he said," Myler recalled, "then you would repeat as well as you remembered."[34]

Because Hughes had never lived by the clock, and was as likely to conduct business at 3 A.M. as at 3 P.M., the aides maintained a twenty-four-hour log. The log began shortly after Hughes arrived in Las Vegas and was a detailed accounting of his daily activities—they called it an "information sheet"—and it enabled an aide coming on duty to know what had taken place in the preceding shifts and to respond promptly to Hughes's requests. In addition to noting occasionally Hughes's business transactions, the aides duly recorded in the log when he went to the bathroom, how long he remained there, when he received an enema, when he fell asleep in his chair, when he went to sleep in his bed, and when and what drugs he took. "We'd just write down everything that happened during the day," Eckersley said. "We'd put the day and the time, and we wrote down when he would eat, what he ate. If he signed a document or if he authorized somebody else to sign it, we'd make a note of what he said so we'd have some kind of record of that."[35] There was a reason for the systematic cataloging of Hughes's menu and various bodily functions. Quite often, Hughes would want to know what time he had gone to sleep, when he had last eaten, what it was he ate, what time he had taken his tranquilizers. Without Hughes's knowledge, the aides sent copies of the daily logs to Kay Glenn at Romaine Street so that he and Bill Gay would be kept apprised of Hughes's routine. The practice was discontinued after three months, however, for fear the embarrassing material might inadvertently fall into the wrong hands in transit. From then on, the logs remained in the penthouse.

If the aide system that had evolved on the ninth floor of the Desert Inn was unorthodox for a worldwide conglomerate, the Hughes organization outside the penthouse was equally strange. Bob Maheu had been working for Hughes for more than a decade. His salary had soared to more than fourteen hundred dollars a day, plus expenses. But Maheu had no employment contract and he held no position in the Hughes Tool Company or any other Hughes corporation. Yet with the move to Las Vegas he had assumed a growing responsibility for Hughes's affairs. He needed a title to point to, a position of authority, to help him in representing Hughes in the world at large.

So Maheu created his own organization. He called it Hughes Nevada Operations and he appointed himself chief executive officer. Hughes Nevada Operations was not a formal legal entity. It did not have authority to enter into contracts on Hughes's behalf. It could not disburse Hughes's money—only tool company executives in Houston had that authority. But it did oversee the management of Hughes's Nevada properties. It was an organization that existed largely on paper, but it fitted Maheu's needs nicely. He ordered stationery printed with the organization's name and his title. Announcements were released to the news media in the name of Hughes Nevada Operations. Both the organization and Maheu's impressive title were accepted without question by everyone with whom Hughes—and Maheu—did business. Even many veterans in the Hughes organization assumed that Hughes had set up Hughes Nevada Operations. As Richard Hannah, a vice-president of Carl Byoir & Associates, Hughes's principal public-relations agency, put it, "I'm sure this cumbersome title was designed not to offend others in key positions, the aircraft people, the helicopter people, the oil tool people, not to offend them by suddenly putting Maheu into a title that would sound to be something higher than they have. His present title aptly describes what he does in Nevada, but he does in fact do more than that."[36] In due time, Hughes Nevada Operations would do just what Hannah said it was intended to avoid—offend long-time Hughes executives.

To run his new organization, Maheu recruited relatives, friends, and former government agents, and placed them on the Hughes payroll at handsome salaries. When Nadine Henley offered to enroll Maheu's son Peter in the Hughes Tool Company training program, the idea was flatly rejected because "the rate of pay" for trainees "did not interest Mr. Maheu nor Peter."[37] Instead, Maheu hired his son as an administrative assistant, at a much higher salary, to work for Hughes Nevada Operations. Maheu's nephew, Frank L. Doyon, also came on board to handle incoming telephone calls, correspondence, mail, and special projects. Doyon was placed on the payroll of Hughes's Sands Hotel. Maheu took on retired air force Major General Edward H. Nigro, a Holy Cross classmate, as deputy chief executive of Hughes Nevada Operations. He hired Dean Elson, the special agent in charge of the Las Vegas FBI office, to deal with sensitive security matters. Walter Fitzpatrick and Henry Schwind, two former IRS agents, were to monitor hotel and casino operations. He hired Jack Hooper, a retired Los Angeles Police Department detective he had used on special assignments since the late 1950s, to supervise overall security. Demetrios Synodinos, better known as Jimmy the Greek, the Las Vegas oddsmaker, became a public-relations consultant.

When Maheu formed Hughes Nevada Operations, he took a page from Hughes's textbook on organizational structure and internal secrecy. It was "very secret," recalled Richard Ellis, who was Maheu's accountant at the time.

It operated very similar to that of the Hughes organization, wherein one individual never particularly knew what the other individual was doing. One individual would never know, therefore, why a bill was made, or what expense was involved, what particular operation was being conducted and, in all likelihood, wouldn't ask, under most circumstances, except possibly in a periodic summarization of activities.[38]

There were similarities also in the way money was spent. The free-spending practices of executives were, if not actually encouraged, never seriously questioned. Inadequate internal controls and careless investments were followed by multimillion-dollar losses. The prices paid for many properties from real estate to silver mines were substantially higher than their fair-market values.

Hughes Nevada Operations was also at the personal beck and call of Maheu and other top executives. The duties of Frank Doyon at the Sands, included supervising the "construction of a mountain cabin in the Mount Charleston area" for his uncle.[39] The construction took about forty-five days, and Doyon spent a "good part of the time" at the site. "I sometimes made as many as two or three trips a day up there from Las Vegas," he said.[40] Another time, Doyon supervised the refurbishing of Maheu's thirty-five-foot yacht *Alouette,* at Newport Beach, California. Work crews from Hughes's Frontier Hotel in Las Vegas assisted not only in refitting the sailboat but also in remodeling Maheu's penthouse apartment at the Balboa Bay Club at Newport Beach. As for why Frontier workmen were sent to California to service Maheu's yacht and remodel his apartment, Edwin L. Daniel, the hotel's engineering director, said, "Mr. Maheu was always pleased with the quality of work that was done and so was Peter, so evidently they wanted my crew to do the work."[41]

When Peter Maheu wanted a doghouse custom-made, he used Frontier Hotel workmen. Daniel himself watched over construction. Made of redwood, the doghouse had a "peaked shake-type roof" and measured about four feet by six feet by four feet in height. Designed to match young Maheu's home, the doghouse was built at a cost of four to five hundred dollars.[42] Another time, cabinetmakers and a plumber from the Frontier spent two to three weeks building a wet bar in Peter Maheu's home, at a cost of more than eleven hundred dollars. On still another occasion, Daniel remodeled the apartment of a Frontier Hotel executive. The cost of the renovations, including papering, painting, and the reupholstering of furniture, came to "around $7,000."[43] On a grander scale, Maheu built a mansion that he and his family lived in, with Hughes's money, at a cost of more than half a million dollars.

Not everyone approved of this casual outlay of money. Henry Schwind, the former IRS agent who audited the Frontier Hotel's expenditures, complained that Peter Maheu especially took advantage "of his relationship with his father in getting people from the hotel to do things for him in his house."[44] He also complained about abuses of complimentary privileges and requests for favors from executives throughout the Hughes empire—from Howard Eckersley and John Holmes on Hughes's personal staff to Nadine Henley and Bill Gay in Los Angeles, and Raymond Holliday and Calvin Collier in the tool company's corporate headquarters in Houston. Schwind's vigilance was not much appreciated. In June of 1968, he said, "General Nigro and Jack Hooper visited my office at the Frontier and told me there was a general dissatisfaction with the way I was conducting myself at the Frontier in that I was rocking the boat; I was causing dissatisfaction with influential people . . . I was bearing down too hard; that I didn't spend enough time playing golf and going to cocktail parties."[45]

Schwind asked General Nigro and Hooper exactly what they wanted. "Stop being a cop and a Hitler," he was told. When Schwind questioned how he would be able to show a profit at the Frontier if the wasteful practices were not ended, he was told that no one had asked him to show a profit. Finally, General Nigro and Hooper agreed to give Schwind six months to "shape up" and show a "better attitude." After that meeting, Schwind said, "I never questioned anything that took place or happened or I was asked to do."[46]

So it was that on the outside of the Desert Inn there was Hughes Nevada Operations created by Maheu, a casually-run organization staffed by many persons without experience in gambling or corporate finance, which handled the millions of dollars a day that flowed through five hotels and casinos, and oversaw investments of more than $100 million. Inside the Desert Inn penthouse, there was the staff of "executive assistants," equally inexperienced in business, lacking even in secretarial skills, who were responsible for processing every scrap of information that entered or left the penthouse command post. Presiding over it all was Howard Hughes—or rather, two Howard Hugheses.

There was the Hughes who for limited periods could conduct himself in a rational and seemingly intelligent manner, who could chat at length over the telephone with a Paul Laxalt, conveying the image of a well-informed and perceptive—if possibly eccentric—business genius. Then there was the other Hughes, the drug-ridden and psychologically crippled man who saw conspiracies all around him. Foremost among his fears in the spring of 1968 was the conviction that his enemies were about to destroy him by means of an Easter egg hunt and a revue playing at the Desert Inn.

A GRAVE CONSPIRACY

The annual Desert Inn Easter egg hunt was a famous Las Vegas affair. Most people, even those who cared little for children or Easter, would have accepted it at face value—as an Easter egg hunt. But for Hughes it boded darker, even violent activity. Children searching for brightly colored eggs, he feared, would suddenly run amok, rampage through his hotel and casino, destroy his property. Some of them might even slip through his security system, rush to the ninth floor, and crash into his room. Even if the hotel security agents were able to contain the rioting egg hunters, the resultant publicity would be devastating, and at the very least, Hughes believed, this was what his enemies were plotting.

Hughes decided that the event had to be moved from the Desert Inn. It was, obviously, a delicate assignment, one that he entrusted to Maheu in a six-page memorandum that alluded to the devious schemes of his enemies:

I have a most important request. Not a directive or anything like it, merely a request. I am well aware that this is not anything that is important to you, but merely something you were pressured into doing by certain groups here. I am speaking of the Easter Egg Hunt. I have been told, however, that although there are a number of people in Las Vegas who favor this event, there is a more powerful group who are dedicated to discrediting me and that this second group will stop at nothing.[47]

Describing his fears and offering several alternative ways to deal with the situation, Hughes wrote:

This Easter Egg Hunt is something else. I am not eager to have a repetition, in the Desert Inn, of what happened at Juvenile Hall when the ever-lovin' little darlings tore the place apart. I am sure your reply to that will be that with our better-trained security force, such a thing just could not happen. However, my information is to the effect that our opponents hope we do set this riot down because they feel they can get more publicity if we do. I suppose you saw what Paul Price* had to say about the use of riot sticks and even a modified teargas on juveniles. And these were duly authorized law enforcement officers. What do you think the press would say about the use of a private security force for such an operation.

Anyway, Bob, I am not asking you to consent to do something about the Easter party, I am only asking that you quietly explore alternate possibilities such as: moving it to the Sunrise Hospital and making it a charity event involving donations. We could start the ball rolling by donating $25,000 or even $50,000. Another possibility would be to say we feel it has gotten so big that with our other increased activity and traffic here, it just loads us up too much. So we feel we must transfer it to the Convention Center or some civic owned facility. In other words, I don't think they would stage the riot if we made it a city-sponsored or county sponsored, or in some way remove it from the private sponsorship of the Desert Inn. Or, even if we move it to a facility that is publicly owned or controlled. I am completely willing, in such event, for you (in my name if you wish) to assume full responsibility for the management and funding of the entire event. This means I am perfectly willing for us to pick up the tab to the full extent as in the past. I just want to see it moved to a place where, if something goes wrong, it will be a black mark against Las Vegas—not a black mark against us. I feel that, once this is the case, there will be no riot. And, at least, if there is, it will be up to the city or county police to suppress it—not up to us.[48]

For Hughes, the impending Easter egg riot was linked to another enemy plot involving *Pzazz '68,* a revue that had been playing in the Desert Inn since the fall of the previous year. By the community standards prevailing in Las Vegas, *Pzazz '68* was pristine family entertainment, "a strait-laced variety show" in the words of one reviewer.[49] Since he entered the gambling business, Hughes's public-relations staff had portrayed him as determined to clean up Las Vegas. Hookers and gamblers, it was loudly proclaimed, were banned from all Hughes hotels. That was not the case, but it was part of the image which Hughes had sought to project. Now, Hughes confided to Maheu, his enemies intended to build a gossip campaign out of the show *Pzazz,* timed to coincide with the Easter riot:

The substance of this story (and it has already been fed to certain Hollywood columnists, who very fortunately are friends of mine from my motion picture days) the substance is that: I am ashamed for my sinful past (adventures with females, etc.) and I am having a backlash here, manifest in my extreme isolation from social contact, presumably for the purpose of putting temptation out of reach, and an intensive and very expensive campaign to reform the morals of Las Vegas. According to the rumor, *Pzazz* was just the beginning. I am supposedly waiting until we have the two additional clubs to start a real all-out war against the normal customs of Las Vegas—such as: topless show girls, etc., etc., dirty jokes, dirty advertisements, etc.

Now, I am further informed, and this is what really has me worried, that this militant group plans to stage a really vicious all-out juvenile riot at our Easter party.[50]

In asking Maheu to move the Easter egg hunt, Hughes pointed out that he had given Maheu a free hand to manage the Las Vegas properties:

*A *Las Vegas Sun* columnist.

Please bear in mind, Bob, that outside of the golf tournament, this will be the only time, in almost two years, that I have sought to interpose my judgment on one smallest detail of the operation of the four hotels.*

I call attention to my long experience in motion pictures. Under this circumstance, it would not have been the least bit surprising if I had asked for schedules for all of the theaters and bars providing entertainment throughout all of our holdings. I might, quite properly, have asked a number of changes—substituting performers I know and in whom I have confidence in place of others tentatively penciled in. You are well aware that I have done nothing like this. I have not even asked for you to change one item of food in one of your restaurants. And, I certainly have not saddled you with a lot of requests for employment of relatives, which is par for the course. So, I don't really feel you should consider it unreasonable that I make these two requests—the golf tournament and the Easter Egg Hunt in a period of almost two years. Anyway, I certainly hope you do not feel it to be unreasonable.[51]

Maheu got the message. If Hughes began to take an interest in restaurant menus and entertainers, life at Hughes Nevada Operations would be a very different thing. So Maheu took care of the Easter egg hunt, and Hughes was delighted. Easter of 1968 passed uneventfully in Las Vegas.

Hughes expended as much energy trying to eliminate what he perceived as threats as he did managing his business affairs—perhaps more. Any item that came to his attention, usually by way of one of the Las Vegas newspapers or television stations, might set him off. When he heard that Governor Laxalt was leaning toward the enactment of an open-housing bill, he became incensed. He thought that one of his local lawyers, Thomas G. Bell, had made it clear to the governor that he considered such legislation objectionable. "Bob, what is this about Laxalt's open housing bill?" he demanded of Maheu. "I thought he was a friend and I thought Bell had told him how I felt about that issue."[52]

The riots that followed the assassination of the Reverend Martin Luther King, Jr., on April 4 intensified Hughes's fears and strengthened his opposition to any campaign mounted by the civil rights movement. "I have just finished watching CBS news on TV," he wrote Maheu:

The riots, looting, etc. in Washington, Chicago and other cities was [sic] terrible. I wonder how close we are to something like that here? I know that is your responsibility and also your specialty but I also know there is tremendous pressure upon the strip owners to adopt a more liberal attitude toward integration, open housing, and employment of more negroes. Now, Bob, I have never made my views known on this subject. And I certainly would not say these things in public. However, I can summarize my attitude about employing more negroes very simply—I think it is a wonderful idea for somebody else, somewhere else. I know this is not a very praiseworthy point of view,

---

*One of Hughes's first directives to Maheu after buying the Desert Inn was to unload the Tournament of Champions, the popular golf tournament sponsored by the hotel. The match subsequently was moved to Moe Dalitz's growing West Coast investment, Rancho La Costa, a $100-million resort complex not far from San Clemente. At the time Hughes ordered the golf tournament off the Desert Inn grounds, the most popular explanation for his action, one only whispered, was that he feared the germs that tournament crowds would carry into his hotel.

but I feel the negroes have already made enough progress to last the next 100 years, and there is such a thing as overdoing it. Also, I was born and lived my first 20 years in Houston, Texas. I lived right in the middle of one race riot in which the negroes committed atrocities to equal any in Vietnam. I just don't want to see you badgered into some concession, because once you do consent to some such concession, you can never cancel it and put things back the way they were.

I know this is a hot potatoe, and I am not asking you to form a new chapter of the K.K.K. Just let's try to do what you can without too many people getting upset about it. I don't want to become known as a negro-hater or anything like that. But I am not running for election and therefore we don't have to curry favor with the NAACP either. I thought I better get this to you before somebody (probably John Meier) commits you to head up some pro-negro committee.[53]

Whenever Hughes shifted attention from imagined personal threats to financial matters, he concentrated not on the properties he already owned but on acquiring new ones. At any one time he might have Bob Maheu, Dick Gray, Raymond Cook, Greg Bautzer, Jack Real, Del Webb, any number of other specially selected representatives—or a combination of them all—collecting information about something he was planning to buy and relaying the material to his aides. Yet the result was almost always the same. The deal fell through. More often than not, the goal had not been attainable in the first place. Hughes never recognized the failing. And hardly anyone sought to divert him from these ventures so clearly destined to fail. In fact, as in 1968 he was often encouraged to pursue illusory acquisitions.

Although Nevada law barred casino license holders in that state from investing in gambling operations elsewhere, Hughes viewed the restriction as applicable to others, not him. Thus, as he sought to buy more hotels and casinos in Las Vegas or Reno, he also was negotiating through Greg Bautzer, his Hollywood confidant and lawyer, to buy the new Paradise Island Casino, the 503-room Paradise Island Hotel, and the 52-room Ocean Club, all on a four-mile-long islet across the harbor from Nassau. Improbably, the properties were owned by the Mary Carter Paint Company. Mary Carter's business was indeed paint, but the company's prized possession was the expanding resort complex on Paradise Island, which before its conversion to a tourist and gaming mecca was known as Hog Island. The chief executive of the company was James F. Crosby, a Miami businessman who numbered among his friends and associates Richard M. Nixon and a Key Biscayne banker, Charles G. (Bebe) Rebozo.

Hughes's feelings toward the Paradise Island property were paradoxical. He had spent some time in the Bahamas in the 1950s. While in Boston in 1966, trying to decide where to establish his next home, he had vacillated between Las Vegas and the Bahamas. Because taxes were almost nonexistent there, the islands appealed strongly to Hughes. At the same time, though, he feared and distrusted the area. The political stability of the islands, a British colony granted limited self-government in 1964, was in doubt. The long-term economic outlook for American investment was bleak. And more important to

Hughes, considering his racism, the islands were 84 percent black and under the control of a black government for the first time in history. That government had just begun its second year in power with the announced intention to seek "full and complete independence" from Great Britain.[54] And there was talk of sharply restricting the number of jobs that foreigners could hold in the casinos and other businesses.

Despite his reservations, Hughes decided to make a bid for the Mary Carter hotels and casino. He peppered Bautzer with questions. He wanted to know the monthly take from the casino and the projected earnings for the coming year. What was the cost of security, utilities, water, road maintenance, and insurance? He wanted to know the adequacy of existing firefighting facilities, whether water for the island came from wells or the sea, and how it was treated. What was the quality of television reception? He wanted to know about the sewage-disposal system. And most of all, he wanted to know about the rats:

When I was there last they had a very serious rat infestation, which was publicized to the hilt in Florida. These rats had dug in in a section of the embankment between the road and the beach, extending from Emerald Beach Hotel to the west to the airport, the most desirable and expensive residential area at that time.[55]

Hughes recalled from a decade earlier a low embankment, about seven feet high,

honey-combed with tiny little caves, and the rats lived in these caves. There was a tremendous amount of unfavorable publicity from it. Even the Nassau newspaper (negro-published) printed pictures of these caves and the thousands of occupants thereof. Even played up the humorous side showing one photo I remember that hit the wire photo service in the U.S. This was a photo by a real genius. The camera was down very low (rat's eye view) showing a rat (very much enlarged due to it being so close) . . . chewing away at some garbage. In the background was a group of playboys and playgirls around a swimming pool, and a magnificent millionaire's mansion in the background.

Now, Greg, when this infestation broke out, I questioned some of the natives about how long this colony of rats had been there. I was told that the rats had been there near as long as anyone could remember. That there was a tremendous population of them down on the docks and all through the food market areas. Then I remember one of the prominent white citizens said to me, "If you think there are rats here, you should look along the north coast of Hog Island."[56]

Displaying a bit of his dry humor, Hughes asked Bautzer how the rat problem had been solved, if it had been. "Did they have to bomb them with napalm, or did they take a hint, when the name of the island was changed to 'Paradise,' and decide they were no longer wanted. Seriously, I would like to know the present status of the rat situation—both on Paradise Island and on New Providence Island."[57]

If the suave Bautzer, who was Hollywood casting's image of a lawyer, got an answer to the Bahamian rat question, it remains filed away in the Hughes archives. Bautzer's talks with a Mary Carter representative proceeded aimlessly for several weeks and when their negotiator grew weary of the pace, Hughes instructed Bautzer to assure him that "I have a very detailed and firm proposal all prepared and awaiting transmission. I only need the answers to a few specific questions before I can send it out."[58] Eventually, the talks were abandoned, later revived briefly, and then abandoned again. Shortly thereafter, Mary Carter sold its paint business and took a new name—Resorts International, Inc. In time, a Resorts International subsidiary—Intertel—would figure prominently in a power play for control of the Hughes empire.

A NOSE FOR NEWS

Just as Hughes's acquisition of the Desert Inn had whetted his appetite for more hotels and casinos, his purchase of Hank Greenspun's television station had spurred his interest in buying not only more television stations but radio stations and newspapers as well. He had failed some months earlier in an attempt to buy the *Las Vegas Review–Journal,* the largest and oldest of the city's two newspapers. Now he envisioned a mini-communications conglomerate across Nevada, blanketing the state with Hughes-owned newspapers and television and radio stations. He wrote Maheu, "I want to start immediately a program designed to result in acquisition of *all* the additional media with Nevada penetration that you can dredge up at any fair and reasonable price."[59]

This was an extraordinarily ambitious plan, especially considering that all of Nevada held fewer residents than Columbus, Ohio, and they were spread over a land area larger than New Jersey, Delaware, Maryland, Pennsylvania, and Ohio combined. To anyone else, the geography of Nevada would have posed an insurmountable obstacle to the creation of a network of television stations. To Hughes, it was an asset:

Each of the small communities in Nevada presents a really good potential prospect for conventional TV for this reason: Due to long distances and low population, Nevada offers probably the only territory remaining for expansion of VHF TV. In other words, any other state, due to more favorable terrain and larger population probably already has a saturation coverage. And any place we might select would most likely have a station or lie in the pattern of existing nearby stations. However, Nevada, with its long distances and mountains to cut off transmissions from one city reaching another, offers the perfect territory for expansion of VHF TV. . . . Every small town would prefer its own TV station as a matter of civic pride over being fed the programs of some Reno station by cable. So, we will have everybody going with us if we do this.[60]

Hughes had given some thought to his acquisition strategy:

The clear path as I see it is to buy a Reno TV station, and then to build a small station in every small town in Nevada big enough to support it. In that way we would have spectacular coverage of the whole state while we are going through this conversion to

CATV which is not coming as fast as some people expect. Anyway, if we gain strength we can wind up with the CATV franchise for the whole state except Reno and Vegas, and at those cities, we will have powerful and prominent TV stations.[61]

Hughes wanted to follow much the same strategy in developing a chain of radio stations across Nevada's 110,540 square miles, and a station outside Las Vegas so powerful that it could serve the entire state. Such a station, he believed, would have broad listener appeal. "This being a sparsely settled state," he explained to Maheu, "such a facility is at its best. People living on ranches, small towns, and motoring on long lonely trips across these deserted roads, they all love to tune in a very distant radio station; they get a charge out of it."[62]

As was his custom, Hughes mentally constructed his radio station on a grand scale. He told Maheu,

My idea is that such a huge station—tremendous towers and a gigantic transmitter could be the first truly large transmitter erected in many years, and you know how these Nevadans love to set records. I can see the publicity now. They would make a big thing about stringing the special line in carrying God knows how many KWs. And the erecting of the towers—and then the climax when the transmitter arrives from some outfit in the east—the biggest in the last 20 years—etc., etc.[63]

Hughes recognized that the Federal Communications Commission would probably oppose his communications network. He intended to counter opposition by favorable publicity: "We could jazz that deal up until I think the local and the Carson City politicians would put some real pressure on Washington," he said. "We have noted here in this entire region they seem to go absolutely crazy when anybody announces intention to build anything." Since it was a national election year, Hughes was certain the FCC would heed "popular feelings far removed from Washington." Not wanting to take any chances, though, he asked Maheu "to hire the very best FCC specialist in Washington."*[64] Whomever Maheu retained, Hughes suggested "one of the first things he ought to do is to persuade the FCC that we will provide a really much-needed service in all of these smaller cities, and that, in return for this probably unprofitable effort, we ought to be allowed to own radio stations also in those locations."[65]

As for potential newspaper acquisitions, Hughes urged Maheu to reopen negotiations with Donald W. Reynolds, whose Nevada holdings included, in addition to the *Review–Journal,* the *Nevada Appeal* in Carson City and the *Times* in Ely. "If we make strong enough fuss about building a chain of media," Hughes said, "Mr. Reynolds may change his mind."[66]

When his newspaper, radio, and television schemes all failed, Hughes merely broadened his horizon to include the financially troubled American

---

*Oddly, Hughes seemed to have forgotten that the law firm of Maheu's friend Edward P. Morgan specialized in practice before the FCC and had represented him in the KLAS–TV licensing.

Broadcasting Companies, Inc. What had eluded him in Nevada perhaps could be achieved across the entire country in one bold stroke.

Certain aspects of national broadcasting held no appeal for Hughes. Entertainment was one of them. Either his years in Hollywood had soured him or he had simply tired of it. "I have no desire to produce a long line of 'Batmen,' etc.," he confided to Greg Bautzer. "I have no desire to be associated with a lot of artistic crap. I have no desire to remake the entertainment policy of TV, as many people want to do."[67] What did interest him was the thought of revamping, from his Desert Inn bedroom, the network's nightly news program, carried by 143 television affiliates. "My only real interest," he said to Bautzer, "is in the very areas in which I understand ABC is really hopeless, News and Public Events and the technical side of the business in which field I am equipped to do a really outstanding job."[68]

It is unclear who first suggested the acquisition of ABC, but Bautzer at least encouraged it. At one point, after Bautzer remarked about the lack of progress in negotiations, Hughes told him, "If you really want action on ABC, please get me the information I have requested, or as much of it as possible."[69]

On Monday, July 1, 1968, the Hughes Tool Company made a public offering "to purchase up to two million shares, or approximately 43 percent of the outstanding common stock" of ABC.[70] The offer was $74.25 a share, or $148.5 million—a hefty markup over the $58.87 the stock had posted on the New York Stock Exchange the previous Friday. By the end of business on the first day of Hughes's tender, ABC's stock had shot up eleven points.

ABC's management both resented the takeover bid and was skeptical of Hughes's goodwill. On Wednesday, July 3, Bautzer met with Leonard H. Goldenson, the president of the network, and two other network executives. Simon B. Siegel, executive vice-president of ABC, recalled Bautzer's saying that "Mr. Hughes would like to work this out on a friendly basis, had no ulterior motive against management, would be a source of financing for us just by request."[71] Bautzer went on to say that Hughes "had no great interest in profits," Siegel remembered, and that "you fellows had said that you needed $90 million and Mr. Hughes is prepared to give it to you. You said you needed new facilities and he's prepared to build them for you and we see no reason why you shouldn't accept Mr. Hughes."[72]

The ABC executives were unmoved by Bautzer's presentation. They wanted no part of Hughes. To stall the takeover, ABC filed a lawsuit in United States District Court in New York requesting an injunction against the offering, charging that it would violate FCC rules and federal antitrust law. Although Hughes won that legal skirmish and the appeals that followed over the next few days, he was confronted with more pressing problems . If the tender succeeded, he would have to come up with $148.5 million to pay the selling shareholders. On top of that, Bautzer had committed $90 million more to ABC for working capital and had agreed to build new facilities for the network at a cost of many more millions. Although *Fortune* magazine had lately labeled Hughes the country's richest man—giving him a slight edge over J. Paul Getty, the oil tycoon, with $1.373 billion to Getty's $1.338 billion—the value of Hughes's holdings was much less.

Hughes could not make good his $148.5 million offer along with all the extras Bautzer had promised unless he drained his bank accounts and sold one or two investments. For a while, he considered selling all his newly acquired Las Vegas properties, but then discarded that idea. Finally, he poured out his problems, not to Bautzer, who had handled most of the ABC transaction, but to Maheu.

"We have got to dig up some money from somewhere," he wrote. "I am opposed to selling the hotels. After vacillating back and forth for quite a while, I have finally reached a definite decision against selling and I hope we can truly forget this one. . . . So, therefore, where does the money come from for ABC?"[73] Hughes answered his own question with a series of ill-conceived proposals, including one involving TWA. The legal battle with the airline was entering its eighth year, and indications were that TWA would win a hefty damage award from its former owner. Hughes wanted Maheu to work out a settlement under which TWA would agree to accept only a fraction of the amount the court would likely grant. Such a feat would obviously free many millions of dollars. "I am counting on you to effect a settlement by one means or another," he told Maheu.

The other problem confronting Hughes was the Federal Communications Commission. A day after the ABC offer the FCC, in a unanimous decision, ordered Hughes not to try in any way "to influence the policies or operation of ABC" until the commission had an opportunity to hold public hearings.[75]

By July 15, the day Hughes had set as the deadline for ABC to respond to his offer, he had received 1.6 million shares of ABC stock, 400,000 shares short of his goal. He had several options. He could extend the offering for an additional week in an effort to reach two million, a possibility that had been spelled out in the original offering circular. He could keep the stock and resell it later, possibly at a profit. Or he could simply await the outcome of the FCC hearings. At 5:15 the next morning, Hughes sent Bautzer an urgent message:

I am in a real predicament. Holliday and Maheu are absolutely twisting my arm off at the shoulder to persuade me to walk away from this tender. I am resistant to doing this for a number of reasons, the principle is that I feel some of the stockholders will be very disappointed if this happens. I am confident that dumping this much stock upon the market could cause a real break. Holliday and Maheu have as their major argument the claim that the Justice Department Antitrust Division will descend upon us and drive us crazy. You have often said several buyers were available. I don't really want a buyer. What I mainly want is somebody with whom I could trustee this stock in one way or another, just until we could have a few meetings with Justice and the FCC. In other words, I just don't want to have the stock transferred directly to me or Hughes Tool Company for fear this will be the signal for the Justice Department to light on us like a swarm of bees.[76]

Only two weeks earlier, the Justice Department's Antitrust Division had threatened to sue him over the Stardust acquisition. While Hughes fretted in his Desert Inn bedroom about the ABC dilemma during the morning hours that Tuesday, all trading in ABC stock was halted on the frenzied floor of the New York Stock Exchange as officials awaited word of his intentions. At noon he made his decision, and it was flashed to Wall Street. He would abandon the ABC takeover.

Hughes's official statement attributed the withdrawal to "inordinate opposition" by ABC's management.[77] A more likely explanation was another FCC demand: if he wanted to take control of the network, he would have to testify in Washington. Hughes was trapped again. He had been confined to a bedroom twenty-four hours a day for almost ten years. A public appearance was impossible.

BOXCAR

Although Hughes never ventured beyond his bedroom, he now tried harder to control the world outside it. Nevada proved an ideal place to exercise his power. Ranking forty-seventh in population, it had one of the smallest state governments (fewer than ten thousand employees) and one of the smallest legislatures (sixty members) in the nation. A healthy infusion of cash would make a big splash in such a small pond. Hughes had always given money to politicians, but in Nevada the money flowed with a new freedom as he sought to make officeholders beholden to him.

The job of handing it out went to Thomas G. Bell, the Las Vegas lawyer with the right connections whom Maheu had brought into the organization during the Desert Inn acquisition. Bell advised Hughes on the background and qualifications of "everyone" running for political office in Nevada and made recommendations on who to support.[78] He was also the liaison with Governor Laxalt, who periodically passed along the names of worthy Republican candidates. Bell would send a memorandum to Hughes through one of the penthouse aides and invariably word would come back to "comply with Paul Laxalt's wishes."[79] Bell handed out substantial sums to Democrats as well. Hughes's overriding interest was not ideology, but in backing winners. In many races, he gave liberally to both Democratic and Republican contenders. Hughes did not establish the amount of the donation; that was left to Bell who, after weighing the importance of the race and the candidate's chances, would dispense from $500 to $15,000, almost always in cash.*

*The cash came from the cashier's cage of the Silver Slipper, the only Las Vegas casino held in Hughes's own name, rather than through the Hughes Tool Company. The Silver Slipper was designated as the funnel for cash contributions to politicians, because there would be no restriction on the amount of money Hughes as an individual could give to political campaigns. The tool company, as a corporation, was barred from such activity for federal races.

Bell's office on the ground floor of the Frontier Hotel became a fixture of Nevada political life as candidates paraded through to pick up the money of Howard Hughes. Bell would welcome the office seeker, hand over an envelope stuffed with bills, then send the candidate on his way. The routine was open and informal, as on one occasion when an aide of Democratic gubernatorial candidate Mike Donal N. O'Callaghan left the motor of his car running outside the Frontier, bolted into the hotel's executive offices, picked up an envelope containing $10,000 in cash from Bell, and hurried back to his idling car.[80] In this manner, several hundred thousand dollars entered the Nevada political process.

When he was not handing out money, Bell was to keep track of state and local officials in Nevada to make sure they did not take any action contrary to Hughes's wishes. Not surprisingly, as the state's largest private employer and the premier power on the Las Vegas Strip, Hughes wanted Bell to monitor measures in which Hughes had a clear and obvious interest—such as bills enacting new taxes, amendments to gaming laws, or zoning changes on the Strip. But that was not all Hughes asked of Bell. As the tide of memoranda rose from the Desert Inn penthouse, so too did Hughes's ambitions. As Bell later explained, Hughes sent him messages asking him to:

advise him on every single bill introduced in the Nevada legislature. . . . to encourage members of the legislature to adopt his views on what bills should and should not be passed. . . . to defeat bills authorizing dog racing in Henderson, Nevada, at a proposed race track there. . . . to do everything possible to prevent the calling of a special session of the Nevada legislature in 1970. . . . to stop the legislature from increasing the sales tax, the gasoline tax and the cigarette tax in Nevada. . . . [to] stop the Clark County School District integration plan . . . to resist the passage of legislation making gambling debts legally collectable. . . . to prohibit the appropriate governmental agencies from realigning any streets in Clark County without his personal views being first given to those particular governmental agencies. . . . to deter any further expansion of the Las Vegas Convention facility. . . . [to] take whatever steps necessary to prohibit any annual sessions of the Nevada legislature and to limit the length of the Nevada legislative sessions. . . . [to] stop any legislation involving censorship and/or antipornography obscenity laws. . . . to slow down the further expansion of McCarran International Airport until he personally determined the feasibility of a regional airport. . . . [to] take whatever efforts are necessary to prohibit rock festivals in Clark County. . . . to prohibit any further annexation by the city of North Las Vegas.[81]

These instructions added up to something very near a program to control the entire state of Nevada.

But the one local issue that obsessed Hughes above all others was his campaign to end underground nuclear testing. Hughes was not philosophically opposed to the atomic bomb, or even to nuclear tests. Rather, he objected to the tests being conducted near him or his hotels and casinos. He had begun a low-key campaign in 1967, and by the spring of 1968 it had escalated into an undeclared war against the Atomic Energy Commission. The turning point had come in April with the AEC's announcement that the largest atomic device in history—more than fifty times as powerful as the bomb exploded over Hiroshima—was about to be detonated at the bottom of a thirty-eight-hundred-foot shaft at Pahute Mesa, a barren stretch of desert one hundred fifty miles northwest of Las Vegas. Code-named Boxcar, the nuclear device was to have a yield at least equal to a million tons of TNT.

When Hughes heard that, he marshalled his forces for a showdown with the AEC. To assist in developing strategy and to execute battle plans, Hughes relied on Maheu and a computer technician by the name of John H. Meier, who was to play a much larger part in Hughes's life. In most of Hughes's Nevada endeavors, he had had little difficulty lining up media support. The *Las Vegas Sun* especially had treated him with great reverence. But he was unable to recruit the *Sun* as an ally in his war with the AEC. Hank Greenspun recognized that the AEC was a major employer in Nevada and that it would be a severe blow to the state's economy if the agency pulled out. So Greenspun refused to join Hughes's cause. As a last resort, Hughes decided to try to buy Greenspun with promises. He prepared a script for Maheu to follow in his conversations with the editor and publisher. First, Maheu should suggest to Greenspun that the nuclear-testing program had hidden costs:

Has anyone ever tried to estimate the number of people who might have come here, but who went to Hawaii or some place else, because they are afraid of nuclear bombs or because they find nuclear bombs and the poisonous polluted devastation they leave behind to be too gruesome and incompatible with the spirit of a vacation?

Furthermore, to be a little more specific about it, has anybody tried to compute the price paid . . . for the privilege of laying waste, mutilating, and contaminating for all the days to come millions of acres of good, fertile, vegetated Nevada earth, has anybody tried to compute this price . . . [for the privilege to desecrate, ravage and lay waste], has anybody balanced this price against all the many sums being lost to this area through the damage wrought by these explosions?[82]

Maheu should follow this argument with a pair of proposals designed to convince Greenspun that any loss in government jobs would be offset by new jobs created by Hughes.

Given any kind of a settlement of the bomb dispute, not necessarily a victory, just a settlement on some reasonable basis, Howard is all set to break ground on the new Sands Hotel the very next day. And the $150 million to build plus the cost to staff and operate this hotel would not only equal, but exceed by many, many times any possible loss to this area from the kind of settlement Howard would gladly accept in the bomb dispute. Also, at this point you could tell Hank that I am all set to buy the Sunrise Hospital and to move my huge medical foundation here to Las Vegas without a moment's delay. In other words, Bob, I think there is a possibility—I know it is not easy—but I think there is a chance to convince Hank that this area is losing more by keeping the explosions, many times more, than it would by making the compromise necessary to satisfy me which is not very much.[83]

Of course, Hughes had not the slightest intention of building the new Sands Hotel or of buying the Sunrise Hospital or of moving the Howard

Hughes Medical Institute from Miami to Las Vegas, but he would employ any tactic to end the nuclear tests. Although he was politically conservative, Hughes was even prepared to join forces with the emerging new left and the ban-the-bomb movement. "I prefer that we not be classified as peaceniks," he said to Maheu, "that is why I am reluctant to go the anti-war, anti-bomb route in the conventional sense. However, if that is the only way we can gather support for our cause, I will go to bed with the devil himself."[84]

Hughes also sought relief from Boxcar through the channels he knew best —Washington politicians and the government bureaucracy. First, he asked the AEC to delay Boxcar for ninety days so that an independent study could be made of the explosion's possible effects. If the AEC would agree, Hughes personally would "pay all overtime and all other expenses required to achieve a completion of any weapons program based on this test at the original target date for completion, should the Defense Department decide they need those weapons."[85]

The AEC rejected the proposal, informing Hughes that all requisite studies had been made, and that the nation's defenses would be seriously weakened by any delay. Hughes was furious: "We must be careful not to place ourselves in the position of disclosing military secrets," he confided to Maheu, "but I can tell you, based upon actual Defense Department technical information legally in my hands, that this last AEC statement is pure 99 proof, unadulterated shit. . . . Any statement that this test could, even possibly, affect the final combat-readiness of this country on a future battlefield is a pure undiluted lie."[86]

Persuasion having failed, Hughes concluded that stronger measures were needed. He would pressure the AEC. Hughes suggested that Maheu begin a secret negotiation with the commission and deliver this ultimatum: if the AEC refused to make any concessions, Hughes would use his fortune to finance an all-out war against nuclear tests, not only in Nevada but anywhere in the world. To put further pressure on the AEC, Hughes decided to step up his antitest campaign in the national news media, which had already carried articles contending that the scheduled explosion might cause a crack in Hoover Dam and trigger a series of earthquakes. "Anything the AEC can do in brain washing, we can do better," Hughes told Maheu. "The advantage always favors the one who is trying to create fear, over the one who is trying to erase it."[87]

In this off-the-record negotiation, I urge we point out to the AEC that, after this uproar and public exposure and after the fears and curiosity of the public have been aroused, the entire situation, not only in Nevada, but throughout the nation is going to prove highly explosive. It will only require a leader. I could easily be that leader. Therefore, in one way or another, I think the AEC must be made to understand that if they want to continue their tests in continental United States, Hawaii, Alaska, Puerto Rico, Virgin Islands, any of the United States Pacific islands, or the Philippines, they damned well better get down off their high autocratic horse and start talking a compromise with us.[88]

As time ticked down toward the Boxcar explosion without any sign that the AEC might relent, Hughes pulled out all the stops. First, he urged Maheu to arrange a strike at the test site through Walter Reuther, the president of the United Auto Workers and a strong labor supporter of liberal causes. Then he proposed that a large political contribution be delivered to Vice-President Hubert H. Humphrey, who was thought to be considering another campaign for the Democratic presidential nomination. As Hughes wrote to Maheu:

I understand the union that is striking the Bell Telephone System (200,000 men out) has jurisdiction over the Test Site. Maybe Reuther can persuade the head of the Communication Workers to strike that Test Site operation as I am informed all our troubles will be over. The phone operation, unhampered by a strike, is absolutely necessary.

Now, one other thing, I read an article in the paper saying H.H.H. is sore-pressed for solvency at the moment. Are we marching through this obvious opening? I mean in a really big and definite way?[89]

Finally, the day before the bomb was scheduled to go off, Hughes summoned Roy Crawford, the aide on duty, to his bedside and gave him a letter that he wanted typed and hand-delivered to President Johnson. Crawford took the letter back to the aides' office and read it over. He noticed that Hughes erroneously referred to Johnson as having served as vice-president under Harry S Truman. If there was a single unwritten rule that all the aides followed religiously, it was never to question anything Hughes said or did, no matter how flagrant the error, how outrageous the action. Crawford worried about sending a letter to the president that misstated his background. He called Maheu and discussed the letter with him. Then he went into Hughes's bedroom and pointed out the mistake. Hughes told Crawford to correct it, but when he learned that the aide had conferred with Maheu, he flew into a rage. As he later explained to Maheu, after he had calmed down, "I asked him [Crawford] what the hell he was doing reading my letter to you, or even telling you it existed, without my consent. I was angry because he had startled me and I don't like to be startled and I told him he should have corrected the obvious mistake without coming back to me or consulting you."[90]

The letter to Johnson read, in part:

Based upon my personal promise that independent scientists and technicians have definite evidence, and can obtain more, demonstrating the risk and uncertainty to the health of the citizens of southern Nevada, if the megaton-plus nuclear explosion is detonated tomorrow morning, will you grant even a brief postponement of this explosion to permit my representatives to come to Washington and lay before whomever you designate the urgent, impelling reasons why we feel a 90 day postponement is needed?

Hughes went on to explain:

I have tryed [sic] every conceivable way to avoid bothering you with this. I appeal to you only as a last resort.

The independent scientists and technicians to whom I refer are not a part of any of the groups who have historically championed the anti-bomb cause.

I am certainly no peacenik. My feelings have been well known through the years to be far to the right of center.

It is not my purpose to impede the defense program in any way, and I can positively prove that if my appeal is heeded, the nuclear test program will proceed *more rapidly* than at present.

It is not my wish to plead the case in this document. But, if you doubt any of my statements, please ask yourself the following questions:

1. If the AEC technicians did not consider the nuclear explosion at the Las Vegas Test Site to be of marginal safety, then why did they make a firm agreement with me eleven months ago, to move the large explosions to central Nevada or to some more remote place? And why did they, in fact, move to central Nevada and build a test site there and detonate one explosion there, and also why did they move to the Aleutian Islands and build a test site and detonate one or more explosions there, which brought objections from Russia?

It just does not seem to me that the citizens of southern Nevada should be forced to swallow something that the citizens of central Nevada would not tolerate and something that was removed from the Aleutian Islands because the Russians objected. I think Nevada has become a fully accredited state now and should no longer be treated like a barren wasteland that is only useful as a dumping place for poisonous, contaminated nuclear waste material, such as normally is carefully sealed up and dumped in the deepest part of the ocean.

2. The AEC technicians assure that there will be no harmful consequences, but I wonder where those technicians will be ten or 20 years from now.

There are some sheep lying dead in nearby Utah.

Surely the technicians in charge of that experiment were equally certain that there would be no harmful consequences. In that instance, it did not take 10 or 20 years for the effects to be felt.[91]

It was an incredible letter that one of the nation's two wealthiest citizens —and its largest private defense contractor—was sending to the president. He talked about "definite evidence" demonstrating the risks of Boxcar when in fact he had none. He spoke of a "firm agreement" he had with the AEC to move the test site when no such agreement existed. His statement that the nuclear testing program would "proceed more rapidly" if Johnson would just delay this particular explosion was nonsensical. The letter was clearly hysterical, and Johnson ignored it.

At 7 A.M. (Pacific Time) on Friday, April 26, Boxcar exploded on schedule, carving out a desert cavern more than seven hundred feet in diameter with such force that it jiggled seismographs on the East Coast. Although chandeliers swayed over the gaming tables and the carpeted floors vibrated in Las Vegas hotels, there was no damage to buildings, no earthquake, and Hoover Dam remained intact. But Howard Hughes was near collapse. The feverish race against the clock that week had taken its toll. "I was physically very ill and emotionally reduced to a nervous wreck by the end of the week," he said, "and life is too short for that."[92] When he learned that further AEC tests were imminent, he told Maheu, "Everything indicates that if we don't start a program and push it for hell and high water, we will go through last week all over again, and Bob, I just don't think I can sit still through that."[93] Hughes decided to use his most powerful weapon—money.

The day after Boxcar, Vice-President Humphrey formally announced that he would seek the Democratic presidential nomination. It was the perfect time for Hughes to implement his earlier plan. "There is one man who can accomplish our objective thru Johnson—and that man is H.H.H.," Hughes wrote to Maheu. "Why don't we get word to him on a basis of secrecy that is *really, really reliable* that we will give him immediately *full, unlimited* support for his campaign to enter the White House if he will just take this one on for us?"[94]

On July 29, Maheu checked into the Century Plaza Hotel in Beverly Hills carrying an envelope containing $25,000 in cash. That same day, back in Las Vegas, Maheu's son Peter, who like his father had once worked for the CIA, handed a locked briefcase to Gordon Judd, a Hughes employee. He instructed Judd to deliver it to his father at the Century Plaza. Without elaborating, young Maheu said the briefcase "had important contents."[95] It contained $25,000 in $100 bills, wrapped in five bundles inside an unsealed envelope.

After Judd arrived at the Century Plaza and turned the briefcase over to Bob Maheu, the two men had dinner in Maheu's suite. When they finished eating, Maheu added his $25,000 envelope to the one in the suitcase. He then left the suite, saying he would return shortly, and Judd stepped out onto the balcony. As he recalled the scene:

The hotel had been the scene of a lot of activity. There were police helicopters hovering in the area, a lot of police motorcycles in the area. It was dark out, except that those helicopters had spotlights on them and the whole scene was quite light. I was observing the action of the helicopters, and I also noticed some increased activity on the part of the police, motorcycle units, some of their red lights were turned on, and it looked as though there was going to be some type of a motorcade, and I recall that somewhere between the curb and the hotel grounds area, that I noticed Mr. Maheu, who had just left me, walking towards the curb. A black Cadillac or Lincoln limousine—at any rate a limousine—pulled up to the curb. Mr. Maheu got in with the briefcase. I watched then and saw that the car, the limousine pulled away from the curb and proceeded southbound on the Avenue of the Stars and drove what could have been 500 feet or less and stopped, and Mr. Maheu got out of the car without the briefcase.[96]

Maheu returned to his suite. "Mission accomplished," he told Judd.[97] Maheu offered no further explanation, and Judd did not ask, but the "mission" was the delivery of $50,000 in cash to presidential candidate Hubert H. Humphrey.

The next day, Maheu met with Nadine Henley and Bill Gay at the hotel. He told the two longtime Hughes lieutenants that Hughes "had approved some unusual contributions." On a piece of Century Plaza notepaper, he jotted down several figures: "$25,000, which he explained was for deficiencies in Robert Kennedy's committees; $50,000, Humphrey; and $50,000, Nixon."[98]

Miss Henley provided the $25,000 for the Kennedy committees that same day. She did not bother to "double-check Mr. Maheu's request for a total of

$125,000 with Mr. Hughes," even though the figure equalled Hughes's combined political contributions for the preceding five years. Maheu, she said, "was a trusted member of our team, and I always accepted his word. I had no reason not to."[99]

Later that summer, in August or early September, Maheu called Miss Henley and said that "Mr. Hughes had approved a $100,000 for each presidential candidate, a $100,000 for Mr. Humphrey and a $100,000 for Mr. Nixon, rather than the $50,000 discussed at the hotel."[100] On September 9, Miss Henley said, Maheu called again and asked her to write out a check for $100,000 for the Humphrey campaign and a check for $50,000 for Nixon. "He said he would get the other $50,000 later for Nixon."[101] That day, Miss Henley wrote out the checks on Hughes's bank account, making them payable to Robert A. Maheu Associates.

Hughes believed he had bought a decision to end nuclear tests in Nevada from the next president of the United States—whoever that might be. However, he still wanted to make one last approach to Lyndon Johnson before his fellow Texan left office. Without explaining why, he ordered Maheu to arrange a meeting with the president.

Maheu called a contact in Washington, D.C., who told him that the president was resting at the LBJ Ranch in Texas. Maheu recalled that his contact placed him in touch with one of the "president's assistants from whom I received a telephone call, and he requested that I have the pilots contact their people at the ranch for landing instructions on a certain date within a matter of a few days."[102]

When all the plans for the trip were completed, Maheu asked Hughes what he wanted him to discuss with the president. "I am not ready to tell you yet," Hughes replied.[103] Because of poor weather conditions, Maheu left Las Vegas in a Hughes executive jet the day before his appointment. After landing at Dallas and checking into a motel, Maheu called Hughes.

"I have an appointment with the president of the United States tomorrow morning," Maheu said. "I wish you would tell me what it is that you want me to discuss with him so that I could be thinking about it, at least during the night." Hughes demurred. "Call me in the morning just before you leave," Hughes said, "and in the meantime just sleep comfortably."[104]

"It is kind of difficult . . . to sleep comfortably when you have an appointment with the president of the United States tomorrow morning and I still don't know what it's all about," Maheu replied.[105] Hughes remained silent.

The next morning Hughes gave Maheu his instructions. Maheu was to take up two matters with the president. First, he said, he wanted Johnson's views on when the war in Vietnam might end. Second, he wanted Maheu to tell the president that he "was prepared to give him a million dollars, after he left the office of the presidency, if he would stop the atomic testing before he left office."[106]

When Maheu arrived at the LBJ Ranch, he was greeted by Mrs. Johnson, who told him the president had become ill during the night and had been taken to the hospital, but would return shortly. She gave Maheu a tour of the ranch and afterward they settled on the terrace. The president arrived about II A.M. They chatted for a while—"We discussed various affairs," Maheu recalled— and had lunch, and then the president drove him around the ranch. When they returned to the house, Maheu told Johnson, without mentioning the $1 million or nuclear testing, that "Mr. Hughes was very interested in his future and how could we be of help to him." The president, according to Maheu, said "that he was very dedicated to the Johnson Library, which was either under construction or—I do not recall—or was to be built in Austin, Texas, and that the only thing that he wanted was a very small contribution for the library and this would make him very, very happy if Mr. Hughes or the Hughes interests could make such a contribution."[107]

Maheu said he did not mention the Atomic Energy Commission's nuclear-testing program in Nevada because he was convinced that Johnson believed it was a "very important project insofar as national security was concerned."[108]

If Maheu had had any hesitation about ignoring Hughes's wishes on that subject, it was dispelled by a remark Johnson made early in their conversation. It was the only reference to nuclear tests that day, and as Maheu recalled it, the president "mentioned that he had received a note from Mr. Hughes relative to atomic energy testing. He mentioned that the note had been delivered by an attorney in Washington, D.C.; that it contained inaccuracies; and he said this was one document that he would not place in the Johnson Library, because it would prove to be embarrassing to Mr. Hughes if he did."[109]

CHAPTER 14

THE $90-MILLION MISTAKE

HELICOPTERS

THE 1968 letter from Hughes to Lyndon Johnson about Boxcar contained a long and revealing preamble designed to stir the president's sympathies:

You may not remember it, but years ago when you were in the Senate, you and I were acquainted, not intimately, but enough so that you would have recognized my name.

So, when you became President, I was strongly tempted to communicate with you, as one occasion after another developed in which I urgently needed your help.

The last of these was last year when I undertook the manufacture of a small 5-place helicopter for use in Viet Nam. I lost in excess of 1/5 of everything I possess in the world on this one project, purely because the price was miscalculated.

I was beseiged by my people to seek a renegotiation of the contract, and I was sorely influenced to contact you.

However, in this case, as in the past, I decided you were too busy for me to disturb you for anything with a purely selfish purpose.

So, we went ahead, spending more and more for overtime with only one objective: to build the 700 helicopters in shortest possible time. The loss was far greater than I have ever suffered in my lifetime. The price we collected for these machines was less than the bill of material alone.[1]

It was Howard Hughes at his best, or worst. True, the loss on the helicopter contract was greater than he had sustained on any other single business venture. The loss, however, had not come about because some anonymous Hughes executive had simply "miscalculated." In fact, it was the direct result of a scheme devised by Hughes to corner the market on one model of a military helicopter and simultaneously become a major aircraft manufacturer. Hughes had appealed to the wrong man, for President Johnson was well aware of the circumstances surrounding the helicopter debacle.

The story begins in 1953. That year, after establishing a new Hughes Aircraft Company, Hughes gave its stock to the Howard Hughes Medical Institute and transferred to that company almost all the operations of the original Hughes Aircraft Company that had been formed in 1932. Of more than seventeen thousand employees in the original Hughes Aircraft Company, all but a few dozen went to work for the new Hughes Aircraft and its new owner, the medical institute. Similarly, of more than $200 million in defense contracts, all but a few million dollars' worth also were turned over to the new Hughes Aircraft. What was left of the original Hughes Aircraft—several dozen workers and several million dollars in military contracts—became the Hughes Tool Company Aircraft Division.

Although Hughes was the sole trustee of the medical institute, and therefore in control of Hughes Aircraft Company operations, the company was no longer a part of his personal portfolio. This distinction made the aircraft division of the Hughes Tool Company—his wholly owned holding company —all the more important to Hughes. In essence, the aircraft division was the lineal descendant of the first Hughes Aircraft Company which Hughes formed to build his racer and the D-2. The aircraft division, some of whose employees had worked for him on the flying boat, was Hughes's tie to his halcyon flying days and it also represented the vehicle through which he might achieve the goal that had always eluded him—the mass production of commercial and military aircraft.

Once the medical institute gained responsibility for the Hughes Aircraft Company, Hughes severed all ties with the company. He never again interfered with its management. He never insisted on being consulted on major decisions. He seldom even communicated with the aircraft company's general manager, Lawrence A. (Pat) Hyland. In short, he allowed the company to go its own way, and he granted Hyland the autonomy that he had denied to all Hyland's predecessors. In the process, the Hughes Aircraft Company flourished, winning more and more defense contracts and rolling up multimillion-dollar profits. By fiscal 1960, its military prime contracts totaled $349.1 million, making it the country's eleventh-largest defense contractor.[2]

In contrast, the aircraft division of Hughes Tool Company, directly under Hughes's hand, did not flourish. Described as "a lousy, inept operation," it sputtered along on a few modest army contracts worth less than 5 percent of the aircraft company's volume.[3] As aircraft division workers tinkered with experimental projects and rolled up substantial deficits, the division became a reminder of the days when the first Hughes Aircraft Company was little more than a hobby to its owner. Even the aircraft division's modest gross-revenue figures were inflated, because the division received subcontracting work from the Hughes Aircraft Company in a self-dealing relationship that the Defense Department's auditors chose to overlook. Conveniently, though, all work was performed at the same location, since the Hughes Aircraft Company and the aircraft division of Hughes Tool both occupied buildings centered on 1,317 acres in Culver City. The aircraft company occupied 96 percent of the more than one million square feet of plant space, the aircraft division the remainder.

James A. Carmack, a former vice-president of the aircraft division, testified that Hughes had insisted, when the flying-boat project was abandoned, that Rea E. Hopper, one of the engineers, and other members of the work force be kept on, prepared to undertake some new aviation venture:

It was my understanding that Hopper was left in charge of that group of artisans and told to keep them together, that Howard had plans for them. He never told them what the plans were. So Hopper kept them together and it got sort of boring to play cribbage and acey-deucey and poker, and so on, in that plant, so they began to look for a little work to try to keep them busy. I don't mean to be facetious. This is my understanding of what actually took place. And they got into the subcontracting business. . . . They got to fiddling around with one thing and another, and one thing and another didn't work, but in any event they were carrying out Howard's directive to keep the crew together. . . . Howard told Raymond Holliday and Monty Montrose and the crew . . . "We're going to become a major aircraft contractor." Somewhere along the way they got into the helicopter business.[4]

In 1955, Hopper and his men at the aircraft division began design work on a two-seat helicopter, concentrating on simplicity and easy maintenance. The army bought five preproduction models and after extensive testing expressed an interest in the machine, but placed no orders. The aircraft division, meanwhile, set up an assembly line to manufacture the helicopter, Model 269A, for commercial sale. Production began in 1960, with the first deliveries

Lawrence A. (Pat) Hyland, vice-president and general manager of Hughes Aircraft Company, the man generally credited with building the company into one of the nation's leading defense contractors.
Wide World Photos

in October 1961.[5] It was a low-volume production line, and the sales were unprofitable. Nevertheless, for the first time in three decades Hughes was actually manufacturing aircraft.* His interest sufficiently whetted, he prepared to enter the helicopter business in a big way. He meant to win what could be the largest military helicopter contract ever awarded.

This period—from the 1950s to the 1960s—was one of transition for the military. Needing the capability to wage a limited conventional or guerrilla war as well as a global nuclear conflict, military planners began to reorganize American ground forces. Strategists foresaw an army division that would be a self-contained, highly mobile fighting unit. It would operate independently and without regard for forests, mountains, and other obstacles that had dictated battlefield tactics so long as divisions moved on wheels. The new army division would move by air—specifically, by helicopter. It was a logical extension of the technology of warfare. The truck had replaced the horse. The helicopter would replace the truck.

Helicopters had come of age during the Korean War. While their most impressive achievements were recorded on medical-evacuation missions—in Korea the number of deaths from battlefield injuries dropped to the lowest level in the history of warfare—helicopters also were used to ferry troops and supplies. Now planners hoped to integrate helicopters into infantry combat operations. Helicopters would move artillery—a critical requirement in battles that had no clearly defined front lines. They would reconnoiter and serve as aerial command posts, and supply food, fuel, ammunition, and other equipment. Some helicopters would be the equivalent of flying tanks, armed with missiles and rockets and machine guns, able to go where no tank could go. The helicopter would, in effect, become a partner of the foot soldier, its pilot a member of the same division.

Such a division required helicopters not then in the army inventory, or even on the drawing boards. Chief among these was a light observation model that could maneuver better and fly faster than any existing machine. The army, however, lacked authority to deal directly with industry for the design and development of new aircraft. When the armed forces were realigned in 1947, the army's very limited aircraft development program was given to the air force. In 1956, the navy was also authorized to buy aircraft for the army. While army personnel might be active in decision making—setting specifications and the like—all else was handled by another branch of the Pentagon. It was a system that rankled the army and one it wanted to end.

In October of 1960, the Bureau of Naval Weapons, acting on specifications prepared by army planners, invited design proposals for the light observation

---

*The army eventually selected the machine for use as a light helicopter primary trainer and in 1964 awarded the first of several contracts to the Hughes Tool Company Aircraft Division. In all, Hughes produced for the army 793 of the helicopters, designated the TH-55A, from 1964 through 1969.

helicopter. Rumors abounded in the military-industrial community that the army would eventually buy upward of four thousand of the helicopters, and if that were true, the contract would be the largest ever granted by the government.

THE LOBBYING COUP

Everything about this contract appealed to Hughes. It would be the easiest and surest route to establish himself as a major manufacturer of aircraft. American demand for helicopters would surely be accompanied by a similar need among foreign military forces. More important, the civilian helicopter market had gone virtually untapped. With minor modification, a light observation helicopter built to military specifications could be converted to a commercial model that would fetch a fancy price from American business. The army contract would, of course, pay for the tooling and the assembly line that would turn out the commercial helicopters.

At the end of January 1961, Hughes and eleven other aircraft manufacturers—including some that had built only airplanes—submitted seventeen different design concepts for the competition. Because of the intense rivalry, the navy issued an order barring any lobbying by the manufacturers while the designs were being evaluated. "The interests of both industry and the government," the navy declared, "will best be served by strict observance of this moratorium on sales efforts relating to this design."[6]

Over the next several weeks, a team of navy officers made a technical evaluation of the seventeen proposals while the army evaluated them operationally. At conclusion, the navy team recommended a single manufacturer, the Hiller Aircraft Company, whose "design was the only one acceptable from a technical viewpoint."[7] The army team recommended two awards for the building of prototypes, one to Hiller and one to the Bell Helicopter Company. A Light Observation Helicopter Design Selection Board established by the army chief of staff would make the decision, but it was expected that the board would follow the recommendations of the evaluators. Hughes was out of the running.

On May 3, 1961, the selection board began a formal review of all seventeen proposals. The board was comprised of six army generals and a colonel, two navy admirals, and a marine corps general. Headed by Lieutenant General Gordon B. Rogers, deputy commanding general of the Continental Army Command, it became known as the Rogers Board. As the board listened to the reports of the army and navy evaluation teams, it eliminated the design entries one by one. There was no serious disagreement among the officers until the following day, when the proposed Hughes helicopter was rejected. After putting up a spirited defense of the Hughes machine, Brigadier General Clifton F. von Kann, director of army aviation in the office of the deputy chief of staff for military operations, bitterly denounced the competence of the navy evaluators. Captain Samuel R. Boyer, the army liaison officer who worked with the Bureau of Naval Weapons in drawing up the helicopter specifications, recalled that General von Kann "stood up and made some very strong accusations about the technical competence of the bureau, and that he did not believe some of the data that was being presented."[8] But General von Kann found little support among other board members. Even his fellow army generals dismissed the Hughes design, and one, Major General Richard D. Meyer, the army's deputy chief of transportation, defended the work of the evaluators.

On May 6, 1961, the Rogers Board, accepting the advice of the army and navy evaluation teams, recommended to Lieutenant General Arthur G. Trudeau, army chief of research and development, that "the army develop the Bell D-250 design and the Hiller 1100 design for further competitive evaluation."[9] Because the light observation helicopter would become an integral part of the army equipment inventory, it was decided to have the two companies build prototypes, with the production contract to be awarded for the more effective machine. There was one dissenting opinion. In a minority report, General von Kann recommended the decision be revised "to provide for a competition between the Bell and Hughes entries, rather than Bell and Hiller."[10] His immediate superior, Lieutenant General Barksdale Hamlett, army deputy chief of staff for military operations, endorsed General von Kann's recommendation and sent a memorandum to General Trudeau urging a "separate action to procure and test the Hughes helicopter."[11] That same day, General Trudeau informed the army chief of staff that he, too, preferred to include the Hughes helicopter design in the final competition.

General Clyde D. Eddleman, then acting chief of staff, ordered the design selection board to meet again. On May 17—twenty-four hours after General Eddleman issued his directive—the board was reconvened. General Rogers announced that he had been instructed "to have the board reconsider its findings and accept the Hughes machine as a third entry in the race. The chairman then moved that the board add Hughes, requesting that all those in favor say 'aye.' All said 'aye' and the meeting was adjourned."[12] The board wrote a second recommendation to the chief of staff, urging that Bell, Hiller, and Hughes all be given contracts to build prototypes. The amended decision was reached, it was said, after "a careful review" that lasted "about ten minutes."[13] The minutes of the meeting, if any were kept, were either "lost or destroyed."[14] And only the army board members attended. The navy and marine officers were not invited, even though the navy was ostensibly responsible for issuing the contract. Now Hughes was back in the running.

Some weeks after the Rogers Board reversed itself, Captain Boyer, the army liaison officer to the Bureau of Naval Weapons, was visiting the Hughes Tool Company Aircraft Division's plant in Culver City when he happened to meet Albert W. Bayer, a Hughes vice-president.

"How in the devil did you people get in this competition?" the army officer asked Bayer.

"Well, I will tell you," the Hughes executive said. "I was a house guest of General Eddleman during the Rogers Board review, and I was instrumental in getting this aircraft into competition."

"Well, I guess that is a way of winning the competition," the army captain replied.*[15]

Whatever the merit of this particular claim, Albert Bayer was more than a casual name dropper. He had many close friends in the upper echelons of the army. One of the closest was General von Kann. While the evaluation was underway, General von Kann, despite the navy ban on discussions of design proposals with industry representatives, attended "a number of briefings" arranged by Bayer, who, the general remembered, "was very effective in telling the Hughes story."[16]

Bayer's official title was vice-president for marketing of the Hughes Tool Company Aircraft Division. Unofficially, he was the aircraft division's chief Washington lobbyist. And in that, except for differences in style, his role was not unlike that of John W. Meyer, the affable Hughes Aircraft Company lobbyist of the 1940s. It was Meyer's lavish entertainment and political connections that had helped Hughes win the contract in 1943 for 100 photo-reconnaissance planes. His lobbying efforts were documented in his expense accounts. Entry: "Entertainment by John W. Meyer: Beverly Hills Hotel—room and miscellaneous charges for Colonel Elliott Roosevelt, $576.83." Entry: "Presents for four girls, $200." Entry: "Dinner—Mocambo, $58.00; Ciro's (late), $33.75 (Also in attendance, Lieutenant Colonel John W. Hoover)." Entry: "Girls at hotel (late), $50."[17]

All that was back in the days of the Second World War. For the 1960s, Bayer altered the format and added new dimensions. Now there were coyote hunts by helicopter across the Texas prairies for Pentagon brass "and pretty nice parties afterward or before," a former Hughes executive recalled. There was a moonlight barge trip "on the old canal up beside the Potomac River" in Washington that became "quite the talk of aviation circles."[18] In addition, expense accounts were processed with a new sophistication, for Meyer's scrupulously detailed and itemized records had provided the most embarrassing and damaging moments of the Senate War Investigating Committee hearings in 1947 on Hughes's flying-boat contract.

Hughes executives issued a standing order: the names of military personnel entertained were to be omitted from all expense accounts. Thus, when Bayer's assistant, Carl Perry, whose "old friends" included Lieutenant Gen-

*Shortly after General Eddleman retired in the spring of 1962, he became a member of the Military Advisory Board of Hughes Aircraft Company. He attended Hughes Aircraft board meetings, at $200 a day plus expenses, and later traveled around the country, visiting military installations, chatting with senior army officers—many of them old friends—sounding them out on army projects of interest to Hughes, and picking up the latest intelligence on weapons development. In time, General Eddleman would be just one of scores of retired air force, army, marine corps, and navy officers recruited by Hughes not only for their expertise in scientific and military affairs, but also for their critical connections in Washington and throughout the military establishment.

eral Barksdale Hamlett—the superior officer who seconded General von Kann's recommendation on the Hughes helicopter—had a "breakfast conference" in his hotel room on November 29, 1962, his guest or guests were not identified on his Hughes expense account.[19] "That was company procedure," Perry explained.[20]

There were other differences in style between Johnny Meyer and Albert Bayer. Whereas Meyer could be found at 21 or the Stork Club, with a starlet at his side, extending his ritualistic greetings to all who passed his table, "Hi, loveboat" or "Love ya," Bayer was more likely to be found in the company of his scrapbook, wandering the corridors of the Washington bureaucracy, looking for just the right door to open.[21] The scrapbook was an impressive catalog in words and pictures of Bayer's contacts with official Washington. There were letters from high-level army officers thanking him for his assistance on some matter. There were photographs of senior officers with their arms around him. There was even a picture of Bayer playing golf with Major General Chester V. Clifton, the military aide to President John F. Kennedy.

Bayer once showed the scrapbook to William D. Rollnick, who at the time was in charge of military marketing at the Hiller Aircraft Company. It was "a very fancy letter-photo album," Rollnick said. "It opened up, had celluloid pages and you inserted the letters and he went through this and showed letters and an invitation to the White House, and pictures of he and General Clifton on the golf course and letters from army generals, some social and some not, telling what a wonderful guy he was and how much they needed him. And it was impressive. There was one that I recall, and I cannot remember the man who wrote it, except I believe he was a vice chief of staff, and the reason I remember it is that he said, 'Fanny and I send our regards.' "[22] Among the letters pressed into the pages of Bayer's scrapbook, Rollnick remembered, was one written by Brigadier General Clifton F. von Kann.

Bayer's performance in the helicopter competition pleased the Hughes corporate hierarchy. Rea Hopper, the aircraft division's general manager, raised Bayer's salary from $29,000 to $35,000 a year, increased his yearly bonus to $15,000, and boosted his flight pay to $5,000, giving the lobbyist an annual income of $55,000. The tool company arranged a $17,300 no-interest loan for Bayer when he purchased a house. The loan was given with the understanding that it would some day be forgiven.

Even though the aircraft division was back in the helicopter design sweepstakes, much remained to be done. Hughes had to win the approval of other levels in the army bureaucracy. There was the troublesome stricture against direct dealing between the army and the aviation industry and the irksome fact that the navy still supported the Hiller and Bell machines.

But the Hughes people need not have worried. The army had simply decided to ignore the fourteen-year-old directive. On May 25, the army advised Dr. Harold Brown, the newly appointed director of research and engineering for the Department of Defense, that "development contracts for the light observation helicopter aircraft would be awarded directly to industry by the

Army."[23] Dr. Brown, the czar of Pentagon weaponry, was prepared to give the army its way. He was also prepared to approve the awarding of contracts to Bell and Hiller. But he questioned the third contract to Hughes. Why spend so many millions for the simultaneous development of three versions of the same helicopter? The army, however, continued to lobby on Hughes's behalf, and in June Dr. Brown gave his approval. "I still have reservations regarding taking a course which results in three parallel developments to meet a single requirement," he said. "However, if the Army is sincerely convinced that this is necessary for satisfactory fulfillment of its requirements, I withdraw the restrictions on the third approach."[24]

On November 13, 1961, the army awarded contracts in varying amounts for the production of five helicopters of each design. Bell received $5.78 million; Hiller, $6.54 million; and Hughes, $6.35 million. All three models were to be powered by the "T-63 engine which had been under development as a routine Army research project at the Allison Division of General Motors Corporation." The contracts required the three aircraft manufacturers to deliver the helicopters "at a rate of one per month beginning November 1963."[25]

Building the prototype, however, was not so easy. Bell, Hiller, and Hughes all encountered technical problems and missed the first delivery deadline. Bell finally produced one helicopter and Hiller two in January of 1964, two months behind schedule. In February, Bell and Hiller each delivered two more, while Hughes turned out its first. In March, Bell delivered two more and Hiller one, thereby fulfilling their commitments. Hughes delivered two that month, and one each in April and May. From January until mid-July, army pilots logged nearly five thousand hours flight-testing the helicopters at Fort Rucker, Alabama, and Edwards Air Force Base, California. Afterward, weeks more were devoted to analyzing the performance data and making economic comparisons. Based on confidential financial information supplied by the three companies, army and independent analysts developed estimates of the cost of producing each model in lots of 714, 3,000, and 4,000.

Throughout these months, the Hughes Tool Company Aircraft Division mounted a coordinated lobbying and corporate espionage campaign to sell the army its helicopter, to find out what Bell's and Hiller's would cost, and generally to monitor the progress of the competition. An intelligence manual was prepared, spelling out procedures to safeguard the data collected and to protect the identity of the sources who furnished it. Nothing was left to chance. Section three of the Hughes intelligence field-report system directed: "At your discretion, instead of naming names when this may be more than a normal necessity, use instead 'reliable source.' "[26]

Intelligence reports flowed into Culver City from Hughes operatives across the country. In St. Louis, Robert P. Pettengill, Hughes's representative to the Army Aviation Materiel Command, had lunch at the Playboy Club with his close friend William Leathwood, a materiel command official, on the same day that Leathwood returned from a conference at Fort Meade, Maryland, on the secret pricing data submitted by Bell, Hiller, and Hughes. Afterwards,

Pettengill sent a memorandum to headquarters advising that: "Hiller's end item price was lower than Hughes' up through the 714th unit. As we surmised, Hiller has a slight edge."[27]

In October of 1964, the army chief of staff appointed a second design selection board with different members, this one made up of seven army generals, headed by Lieutenant General Charles G. Dodge, to select the winner of the helicopter competition. For two weeks the board deliberated secretly. Accepting the recommendation of the army's flight-test evaluators, the board rejected the Bell helicopter because it had more armament and therefore was slightly heavier and slower than the two other prototypes. The board found the Hiller and Hughes helicopters about equal in performance and cost. A financial analysis showed that the Hiller machine would be slightly cheaper on a contract for 714, the Hughes machine slightly cheaper on a contract for 3,000 or 4,000. Because the two helicopters were so evenly matched, the board "recommended to the chief of staff that a fixed price contract be awarded for at least 1,000 aircraft to be delivered over a three-year period" to the company that submitted the lowest bid.[28]

Hughes's light observation helicopter on a test flight in 1963.
United Press International

On October 14—after the selection board had reached its decision, but before the still-secret decision had been delivered to the secretary of the army —General von Kann, Eugene L. Vidal (a highly respected aviation pioneer friendly to Hughes), and Albert Bayer met for a leisurely dinner at the Madison Hotel in Washington, where they talked about light observation helicopters. Bayer was no longer employed by the Hughes Tool Company Aircraft Division, having lost his job in the wake of an unsuccessful struggle with Hopper. But he remained on friendly terms with other Hughes executives, and was still very much interested in the outcome of the helicopter competition.*

The following day, Bayer dropped by the Washington office of the Hiller Aircraft Company to talk with Stanley Hiller, Jr., the company's president, about possible employment. The meeting between the two men lasted thirty to forty-five minutes, and when Bayer left, Hiller emerged from his office "visibly shaken, actually white," according to Warren T. Rockwell, the company's Washington representative, who had been working in an adjoining room. "You just won't believe it, but I have just been told what the army is going to do," Hiller said.[29] Rockwell recalled that Hiller then related what Bayer had told him about the selection board's decision. "Number one, of course, that it would be a three-year cost competition between Hiller and Hughes. Number two, that this competition on a three-year basis would be for a total quantity of 1,000 aircraft."[30] The quantity particularly shook Hiller and Rockewell. They had assumed all along that the contract would be for fewer than a thousand aircraft, most likely 714, and had compiled their financial estimates accordingly. "We had never heard that before," Rockwell said, "because the cost data we had already submitted to the Fort Meade evaluation group were on lower quantities."[31] Even more startling, Bayer had told Hiller that the costs of the Hiller helicopter were "lower than Hughes," a piece of information which indicated that confidential financial reports Hiller had given to the army had been leaked to Hughes.[32]

Hiller immediately lodged a complaint with the army and an investigation was ordered. But it came to nothing. "An analysis of all the evidence," Secretary of the Army Stephen Ailes reported three months later, "fails to substantiate the contention that Hughes has received information concerning your costs from army sources directly, or through a third party."[33] The army had cleared itself of any wrongdoing even though Bayer knew to the smallest detail the results of the selection board's confidential decision and the army's secret pricing comparisons of the Hiller and Hughes helicopters. Hiller and Hughes were invited to submit bids for the building of 1,071 helicopters.†

---

*It was some indication of the depth of the intrigue in the Hughes empire that after Bayer lost his job in a management dispute with Rea Hopper, the general manager of the aircraft division, the lobbyist was placed on another Hughes payroll without Hopper's knowledge. Bill Gay, the veteran Hughes executive who was senior vice-president of the parent Hughes Tool Company, arranged a $3,000 monthly retainer for Bayer for five months.

†The contract actually called for the production of 714 helicopters, but it contained an option clause allowing the army to buy an additional 357 machines, for a total of 1,071, at the same price.

THE "BUY-IN"

At the Hughes Tool Company Aircraft Division offices executives agonized over the final price. They knew that the army had calculated the cost of the Hiller model to be somewhat below theirs. But how much lower might Hiller go in the final bidding? Having made it to the last round, Howard Hughes had no intention of losing—no matter what the cost. With Hughes's personal blessing, the aircraft division prepared a bid that would yield a $10-million loss on a $30-million project, but assure the contract and gain a foothold in the helicopter-manufacturing business.

In technical terms, Hughes planned a "buy-in," a practice forbidden under Department of Defense procurement regulations because "its long term effects may diminish competition and it may result in poor contract performance."[34] Experience had established that after a buy-in, manufacturers often raised prices during the life of the contract through change orders or an inflated follow-on contract.

Hughes had estimated the unit cost of building the helicopters at $30,200. If he absorbed a $10,000 loss on each, he could submit a bid of $20,200. But Hopper wanted to drop the price "a little under the $20,000," and so the bid was fixed at $19,860. It was not "really a very good figure," Hopper said later, with some understatement. "That is not the way people are supposed to price things, I don't think."[35] When the bid arrived at the Army Aviation Materiel Command in St. Louis, a contract officer there, assuming that a stenographic error had been made, wired Hughes asking for confirmation of the numbers. The answer came back: the $19,860 figure was accurate. The Hiller bid, tied to actual production costs, was $29,415—nearly 50 percent higher.* On May 26, 1965, the army awarded the contract to Hughes. After two unsuccessful attempts at building airplanes for the military during the Second World War, Howard Hughes was going to get a third chance to become an aircraft manufacturer.

Hughes executives were jubilant. They forecast "orders over the next ten years for up to 7,000 aircraft from the army and other United States military services," and expected "a commercial and foreign military market for an additional several thousand aircraft." The result would be "one of the largest helicopter production efforts ever undertaken."†[36]

---

*The production cost included manufacturing the airframe and assembling the helicopter. The army provided the engines, communications equipment, weapons system, armor kit, and navigation system under other contracts. The fly-away cost of the helicopter was estimated at more than $75,000.

†As was the case in so many of Hughes's business dealings, the public perception of his helicopter contract, shaped by the industrialist's artful publicists, bore little resemblance to the truth. In an article describing the contract and the helicopter, *Aviation Week* reported on June 28, 1965, that "Hughes officials said the company definitely expects to make a good profit from commercial and military sales of the OH-6A but will not break down the profit potential from military and civilian sales separately." Hughes officials knew, of course, that the contract would result in at least a $10-million loss.

Stanley Hiller summed it up bitterly. "We were not in a competition. We were in an auction," he said. "I have been in many, many competitions over a long period of time with the government, none like this. I suspect that because the Hughes company had never been successful in the aviation business, that they looked upon this as a good possibility to get in."[37] William Rollnick, Hiller's military marketing chief, viewed the Hughes bid philosophically. "They were totally out of their minds," he said. "They used the old adage: 'Use a sledgehammer to kill a fly. They really kill them.' "[38]

The army contract called for Hughes to produce eighty-eight of the helicopters, designated the OH-6A—a two-seat machine with room in the cabin for cargo or four fully equipped soldiers—in fiscal year 1967, with the first to be delivered in June of 1966. Until the awarding of the contract, the army's planners had assumed there would be no significant need for the helicopters in the immediate future. But 1965 marked a turning point for the United States in the Vietnam War.

The year started with 23,000 American noncombat troops in South Vietnam serving in an advice-and-support capacity. In March, more than a hundred American jets carried out the largest air strike of the war—and the first nonretaliatory raid—bombing a North Vietnamese munitions depot. In June, the first army combat forces landed, more than doubling American troop strength. In July, President Johnson announced that he was stepping up the United States commitment to South Vietnam from 75,000 to 125,000 troops —a 443-percent increase since January. The American mission had changed from advice and support to search and destroy. In September, the army's First Cavalry Division (Airmobile) arrived—the division that would test on the battlefield the air-mobility strategy so painstakingly drawn on paper as the decade began. The division's arrival brought the number of helicopters in South Vietnam from about four hundred fifty to nearly a thousand. Vietnam had become an American war. By December, the full impact of the escalating conflict reached the United States.

For the first time since Korea, newspapers and magazines routinely published photographs of American soldiers in battle, wounded and dead GIs. For the first time ever, a war came into American homes in living color on television's nightly news. In Columbus, Georgia, and nearby Fort Benning, where more than twenty-two hundred families of First Cavalry Division soldiers lived, the anonymous Western Union messenger, delivering formal notification of death, was becoming a familiar figure. In Culver City, the Hughes Tool Company Aircraft Division received a special request from the army for 121 additional light observation helicopters to meet the urgent demand in Vietnam. The army wanted the helicopters concurrently with the eighty-eight scheduled for production between July of 1966 and June of 1967.

The third week in January 1966, Hughes advised the army that he would be willing to manufacture 121 more helicopters, but for rather more money. The price tag on each helicopter would be $55,927—a 182-percent increase over the contract signed seven months earlier. Now that he was the army's sole supplier of light observation helicopters, Hughes intended to recover, as quickly as possible, the loss he had deliberately taken to win the contract, and reap in addition a windfall profit. Colonel A. M. Steinkrauss, a contracting officer at the Army Materiel Command in St. Louis, was stunned when he received news of the increase. He fired off a letter to the commanding general of the Army Materiel Command in Washington. "There appears to be no foundation or rational basis for the dramatic increase in price," Steinkrauss wrote. "The variance is so great between the contractor's bid and his current proposal that the issue is not only money but has also become a matter of principle."[39] In Washington, the army high command, which desperately wanted the helicopters, ordered Steinkrauss to negotiate a more realistic price. Over the next several months, Hughes and the army bargained while American troops continued to stream into South Vietnam. Hughes lowered his selling price to $49,500—still a 149-percent price increase—and then refused to negotiate further.

In Washington, the army bureaucracy, too desperate for aircraft to be concerned about price or principle, was prepared to pay the price. But late in April the generals had a change of heart. As the cost of the war spiraled, Congress scrutinized military expenditures more closely. When the Defense Department submitted a request for a $15-billion supplemental appropriation —part of it earmarked for the 121 additional helicopters—members of the House Armed Services Committee seized upon the astronomical price increase for the Hughes machines. L. Mendel Rivers, the South Carolina Democrat who chaired the committee, ordered an inquiry by the Subcommittee for Special Investigations. Confronted with a potentially damaging congressional investigation, the army quietly withdrew its request for the 121 additional helicopters late in April. The subcommittee, however, now curious about this strange contract, pushed ahead with the probe. In the field in South Vietnam, commanders eventually substituted the older Bell Iroquois helicopter, a larger, heavier, slower, less maneuverable machine. It was not a satisfactory solution. The Hughes helicopter was a multiple-mission aircraft. The Iroquois was not.

Even if the army and Hughes had agreed on a price, the extra helicopters could not have been delivered on schedule. Hughes was already having trouble delivering the eighty-eight machines called for in the first year of the contract, an embarrassment that no one spoke of publicly. The company of Howard Hughes, the man who set aviation records, whose name was synonymous with the development of the aviation industry, had engineered a production nightmare. In fact, there was precious little production. And it looked as though the war might well be over before Hughes got his helicopters off the assembly line. The first machine was owed to the army in June of 1966. It arrived in August. When House investigators visited the Hughes plant in September and October, they were appalled at what they found. "There wasn't a blessed thing going on when we sent our people out there," Porter Hardy, the chairman of the Subcommittee for Special Investigations, recalled later. "They took pictures of the production line, or what should have been a production [line]. And anybody with two grains of sense examining those pictures would have known it was impossible for this delivery schedule to be met."[40]

Feeling the pressure of the congressional investigation, the army asked the Defense Department to conduct its own survey of the Hughes plant. Carried out by an air force contract specialist, the study concluded that Hughes's problems stemmed from "a lack of experience" and "a lack of proper and timely planning."[41] In addition, it was found that space at the Culver City plant was "poorly utilized."[42] There was inadequate tooling and a shortage of skilled workers. There was difficulty molding the sheet metal. All of this was eerily reminiscent of Hughes's performance two decades earlier, when he failed to put into production either his flying boat or photo-reconnaissance airplane. His inability to deliver on those projects was attributed to a "complete lack of experience in the design and construction of airplanes," "poor planning and insufficient supervision," and "unsatisfactory tooling."[43] In twenty years, Howard Hughes had learned nothing about aircraft manufacturing.

By January of 1967, Hughes was to have delivered sixty-six helicopters to the army; only twelve had made it off the assembly line. In March 1967, the month the army meant to have over a hundred light observation helicopters in Vietnam by accelerating production, not one arrived.[44] By July, with the war raging more furiously than ever in South Vietnam, the army prepared to place an order for 2,200 more light observation helicopters. Under normal circumstances, this would have simply been a follow-on contract. The price would be negotiated, a new contract drawn up and signed. It was unofficial Defense Department policy that once a manufacturer became the supplier of a piece of military equipment—whether a rifle, a tank, or an airplane—it normally remained the supplier as long as that equipment was in service. But these were not normal circumstances.

The House Subcommittee for Special Investigations, after a series of largely closed hearings, had issued a blistering report on the army's handling of the original helicopter contract. The subcommittee had recommended that "the secretary of defense strictly enforce his directive that research and development of army aircraft be the responsibility of the air force or navy until the competence of the army in this area has been firmly established" and that contractors be required to pay damages "for failure to meet delivery schedules."[45] More to the point, the subcommittee urged that "consideration be given to alternate sources for the light observation helicopter."[46]

The army preferred to give the 2,200-helicopter order to Hughes, no matter what the cost, rather than operate and maintain two separate models of aircraft to serve the same purpose. Not wanting to antagonize the House Armed Services Committee again, however, it announced a request for new competitive bids.[47]

For some months, it looked as though Hughes would be the only bidder. Amid industry charges that the army had "structured the competition to favor Hughes," little interest was expressed by other manufacturers.[48] The most logical contender, Hiller, now the Fairchild–Hiller Corporation, declined to compete. Only Bell was a serious contender. After the army had rejected Bell's model the first time around, Bell had successfully converted its military proto-type to a business helicopter. Called the Bell JetRanger, the helicopter had proved both a commercial and a technical success. With modifications, the JetRanger could be reconverted to a light observation helicopter.

Howard Hughes was in serious trouble. He had assumed that the army would give him the follow-on contract and that he would negotiate a price enabling him to recover his losses under the original agreement. Now he was back where he had started. In fact, he was considerably farther back. The Hughes Tool Company Aircraft Division had lost $23.2 million in 1967, more than double the $10-million loss projected over the life of the helicopter con-tract.[49] It was predicted that the loss for 1968 would approximate $41.2 million, a deficit so large as to create a net loss for the parent Hughes Tool Company.[50] Not even the profits of the oil-tool division, which had sustained Hughes's extravagances for four decades, could offset the anticipated deficit. To cover the loss and provide additional working capital, Hughes had to dip into his personal bank accounts to pump $45.7 million in cash into the aircraft division in 1967. Another $44.1 million would be needed in 1968. Hughes Tool Company executives issued orders to other divisions "to reduce expenses or attempt to defer until 1969 any expenses that can be deferred."[51]

Incredibly, Hughes was losing more than $62,000 on every helicopter he produced. To make matters worse, the army had exercised its option and ordered the 357 additional helicopters at the $19,860 price. Thus, these huge losses would continue through 1969. If he lost the follow-on contract, he would never recoup his millions. Yet he could not afford to submit another bid below cost. His bid had to be both profitable and less than Bell's bid—no easy task. Bell was the military's largest supplier of helicopters, manufacturing twelve different helicopter models, ranging from two-place to fifteen-place aircraft.[52] Bell had far more production experience than the Hughes Tool Company Aircraft Division, and a more efficient and reliable plant. It had compiled a record ten consecutive years of on-time deliveries. Bell was sure to have an edge in a pricing competition.

To make certain that nothing went wrong this time, Hughes took charge of the bidding for the second contract. He solicited financial information and proposed bids not only from Rea Hopper at the aircraft division's plant but also from Raymond Cook, his lawyer, and Jack Real, the Lockheed executive and longtime business confidant. As Hughes lay in his Desert Inn bedroom pondering what to charge, he was gripped by the mental paralysis that so often afflicted him in times of decision. Cook had suggested a bid of $66,000. Hopper had proposed $58,500. Real had recommended $57,500. Cook, mindful of the enormous losses Hughes was running up in the helicopter business and of the steady erosion of his bank accounts, wanted to insure that a second army contract would not be as financially devastating as the first. He was wary of the calculations of both Hopper and Real. "I have talked to Jack Real and tried to reconcile his cost breakdown and ours," Cook said to Hughes. "My conclusion, and I believe Jack's, is that his $57,500 is a highly optimistic one which is remotely achievable, but with low probability under normal pricing tests."[53]

Hughes, always casting about for the loophole in his contracts when doing so fitted his needs, began to think of bailing out of the existing contract if Bell won the competition. By halting production, he could at least cut his losses.[54] Cook pointed out the flaw in Hughes's logic. "The Army needs your helicopters substantially on the schedule contracted for," he wrote. "It may be that in 1969 and following the Army will have a preference for the ship which is acquired in this follow-on competition, but I am certain that win or lose we cannot avoid performance under the existing contract. Furthermore, the Army could never justify with Congress a decision to cancel 700 helicopters at $20,000 each in order to buy at a price several times that."[55]

After further sparring with Cook, Hughes settled on a bid amount of $59,700. As the hours to the bid deadline ticked away, the tension on him mounted. At one point, an aide walked into the bedroom and handed Hughes an urgent message: "Our man is waiting at the phone now, and the time is critical. Shall we send him out to look for a closer phone and have him out of touch, or could we get word to him by half past. It will take him about half an hour to fill out the forms and go to the bid opening."[56] It was TWA all over again as a frantic Hughes agent waited, one eye on the clock, for the indecisive industrialist to flash instructions. Once it was done, Hughes, reflecting the strain, told Howard Eckersley, the aide on duty, that he did not want to be disturbed any more. "I don't want any messages or upsetment on this deal either way," he said.[57]

Exactly when Hughes received the bad news, or whose lot it was to deliver it, is uncertain. But on March 10, the army announced that the Bell Helicopter Company had won the contract, worth $123 million. Bell's bid of $53,450 per helicopter was $6,250 below Hughes's offer. Hughes faced two more years of huge deficits at the aircraft division, and no chance of recovering his losses after that. When the last Hughes helicopter came off the assembly line, the company's loss on that one contract would total a monumental $90 million.[58] Someone, as Hughes opined to President Johnson in 1968, had indeed "miscalculated," and that someone was Howard Hughes himself.

CHAPTER 15

THE BILLION-DOLLAR DEAL

MERELY A MILLIONAIRE

ONE day in 1968, as Howard Hughes rested abed in his Desert Inn penthouse reading the Las Vegas newspapers, he came across an article that irritated him. It was not the subject of the article that he found offensive, but rather, a single word. The article had described him as a "millionaire." Hughes reached for a yellow legal tablet and began to jot a message to Bob Maheu:

At the present time when I am having a little trouble making both ends meet, I am sure there is a large army of people waiting in expectant, hushed silence for the first indication of a slide backward in my financial resources, no matter how small. There is only one thing worse than being broke, and that is to have everybody know that you are broke. In most cases, and at normal times, I am quite content to be referred to merely as an industrialist without a price tag. However, at present, in my highly critical situation with the TWA judgment hanging over me, I think it is a bad time for us to put out publicity referring to me as a mere millionaire. There are several hundred millionaires on the horizon now, and since I have been referred to as a Billionaire ever since we became established in Las Vegas, I am fearful that some enemy of mine will pick up this small deviation and make a story about it—you know, something like: "Well, well, has he finally gotten to the bottom of his bankroll, etc., etc."[1]

Noting that it was one of his own publicists who had issued the offending press release, Hughes asked Maheu,

Without letting *anyone* know that this displeased me, would you most carefully try to find out who of our people put this out? Then possibly you can work out a most carefully planned means of discontinuing the use of the millionaire reference without *anybody* at all knowing that any instruction whatsoever was issued. . . . This has been handled most skillfully in the past with the result that I have been always referred to as "billionaire" yet we were never accused of putting out this publicity. I was very pleased with the result with respect to this particular point, until Kerkorian was likewise billed as a billionaire. If you could find some way of obtaining the result which you formerly achieved, prior to Kerkorian's ascendancy into the ranks and at the same time, without our being held responsible for the origin of the publicity, I would be very grateful indeed.[2]

The memorandum reflected two of Hughes's personality quirks which often seemed at odds. Despite his mania for privacy, he was consumingly concerned with what the world thought of him—so much so that the most innocuous news report, such as a favorable recounting of Kirk Kerkorian's career, would trigger a tantrum. More to the point, the message to Maheu demonstrated once again Hughes's singular ability to focus on the trivial when confronted with a serious business dilemma. The dilemma in 1968 was that the Hughes fortune was in fact beginning to disappear.

The Hughes Tool Company, which for all practical purposes was Howard Hughes, had entered 1967 with $607.7 million in the bank, about 10 percent of it in cash, 90 percent in United States government securities.[3] Throughout the year and into 1968, Hughes had been spending money at the rate of $367,579 a day. Some of the money was going for the acquisition of hotels, casinos, gold and silver mines, and other properties in Nevada. Some had been employed to shore up the Hughes Tool Company Aircraft Division. Other millions were simply being wasted. By December 31, 1968, Hughes would run through $268.7 million, leaving his cash and government securities bank balance at $339 million.[4] All that money was coming out of what was in effect Hughes's savings. Unless the spending stopped, sometime during the summer of 1971 Hughes would exhaust his savings.

Even so, in 1967 and 1968 Hughes was involved in more different business undertakings than at any other time in his life, a situation owing in some part to his failing mental health. If Hughes's lifetime involvement in business and financial transactions were to be charted, the curve would peak in 1967 and 1968. If the same graph measured productivity—a return on his investment of time and money—the curve would reach its lowest point in those same two years. The Hughes empire had become a sort of Rube Goldberg machine run amok. It was as if Hughes sat atop it, feeding millions into this contraption that funneled the money along circuitous routes and spewed it out to executives who underwrote dozens of ill-starred business ventures.

In 1968, Hughes tried and failed to buy William Harrah's hotels and casinos in Reno and at Lake Tahoe, and the Bonanza, the Stardust, and the Silver Nugget hotels and casinos in Las Vegas. He tried and failed to block construction of Kerkorian's International Hotel and Casino. He lost a bid to buy Western Air Lines and National Airlines. He tried and failed to buy the Mary Carter Paint Company's hotels and casino in the Bahamas, the American Broadcasting Companies, and the *Las Vegas Review-Journal.* He was unable to establish a radio–television–newspaper conglomerate in Nevada. He thought of buying several luxury liners and fitting them out as cruising casinos, but discarded the idea. He looked into the purchase of MCA Inc., the entertainment conglomerate, but did not go through with it. He explored the possibility of buying Four Star Productions, a producer and distributor of television shows and motion pictures, but the deal collapsed.

Hughes's only accomplishments during these years were hollow. He did manage to buy Sports Network Inc., a New York company that telecast sporting events, but it was losing money and would continue to do so. He did open negotiations leading to the acquisition of the Landmark Hotel and Casino, but it would lose money every year for the rest of his life.[5] He bought scores of gold and silver mines across Nevada, but they never yielded a return on his investment. He did begin negotiations in 1968 to acquire Air West, but that transaction resulted in civil lawsuits and, worse, his indictment by a federal grand jury.

His Castaways Hotel and Casino consistently lost money, as did the Frontier Hotel and Casino. His fixed base operations at McCarran Airport and Alamo Airlines were unprofitable. So was his Warm Springs Ranch.[6] Of all his 1967 acquisitions in Las Vegas, only the Desert Inn and the Sands were in the black. And their lofty profits of earlier years had melted away. Indeed, the combined profits of the Desert Inn and the Sands for 1967 and 1968 totaled less than $5 million—a fraction of what the Sands alone had formerly earned in a single year.[7]

If Hughes took note of these dismal business facts or of his alarming cash flow, he made no effort to reverse the trend. Instead, he pursued one costly venture after another. The life he adopted in his darkened Desert Inn bedroom foreshadowed these outcomes.

The room itself hardly suggested the work space of one who ran a worldwide, billion-dollar empire. Tightly closed drapes shut out the desert sun during the day and the neon lights of the Strip at night. They were never opened. Spartan furnishings were dominated by a hospital bed, a reclining chair, and a television set. The room was never visited by a vacuum cleaner.

The wardrobe of one of America's richest citizens was equally simple, consisting of two sport shirts, two pairs of slacks, and one pair of shoes. Hughes never put on any of these. There was one bathrobe, two pairs of pajamas, and one pair of sandals. These he wore occasionally. A television addict, Hughes stared at the screen for hours at a stretch, watching movies into the early-morning hours. He spent most of his time lying in bed, surrounded by piles of newspapers; a collection of old *TV Guide* magazines that he hoarded with a numismatic fervor; used Kleenex and paper towels, empty boxes, and medicine bottles—"He never liked to throw anything away," an aide explained —and stacks of memoranda and reports from his corporate executives and lawyers.[8]

Hughes was forever losing important documents in the mountain of papers. On one occasion, Raymond Holliday beseeched Hughes to sign a note to renew one of his multimillion-dollar Houston bank loans that was due.

Hughes procrastinated. Finally, one Thursday afternoon he picked up a yellow legal tablet and wrote a note to Holliday in Houston:

Dear Raymond,

I will positively have the signed note in your hands by Monday. Please convey my very deepest thanks to the bank and my most humble apologies.[9]

Hughes then began rooting through the chaos of papers strewn about his bed, looking for the bank note. After an unfruitful search, he picked up the legal pad and added a postscript to Holliday:

P.S.
Raymond—
Will you send me as quickly as convenient a new note, correctly made out, because I have "filed" the other one accidently [sic] some place among my stacks of papers, and it might take me all day to find it. My very most extreme thanks.[10]

For the most part, everything Hughes needed was in easy reach of his bed, including the metal box where he kept his tranquilizers and narcotics and the syringe he used to inject himself with the drugs. From time to time he would have one of the aides lay what they called a "foundation" of paper towels on the bed, thereby extending, at least to Hughes's satisfaction, the life expectancy of the soiled sheets, which were changed, it seems, no more often than once a season. "He hated the inconvenience of changing the linen, so he would make his sheets last as long as he could," an aide said.[11] The only time that Hughes left his bed was to rest, often naked, on his reclining chair, or to go to the bathroom, where he sometimes would sit so long that he fell asleep. Occasionally, "on the way to the bathroom, or on the way back," a stark-naked Hughes would pause by the door to the adjoining room where the aides maintained their office and dictate instructions to be forwarded to one of his lieutenants.[12]

CORNERING A MARKET

This, then, was the Hughes who early in 1968 began laying the groundwork for the largest business deal of his life, one that he hoped would enable him to unload his debt-plagued Hughes Tool Company Aircraft Division and at the same time propel him back into dominance in the American airline industry. The customary Hughes secrecy was more intense than ever—so intense that the planned transaction never leaked out at the time, and the details have never before been made public.

Hughes's plan required the cooperation of one company—the Lockheed Aircraft Corporation, with which he had enjoyed an amiable relationship for thirty years. His record 1938 around-the-world flight had been in a Lockheed 14 and he had contributed to the design of Lockheed's Constellation. Friendship alone, however, would not be inducement enough for Lockheed to buy his money-losing helicopter company. To make the deal attractive, Hughes decided to throw in the Hughes Aircraft Company, which had received $419.5 million in prime military contracts in the preceding fiscal year. Although Hughes Aircraft Company stock was owned by the Howard Hughes Medical Institute, Hughes, as sole trustee of the institute, could sell the stock.

Hughes believed that his old friends at Lockheed would receive the offer favorably. He had made a similar pitch back in the early 1950s to Robert and Courtlandt Gross, the brothers who had built Lockheed into one of the giants of aviation and defense. Although the Gross brothers had rejected the proposal then—it was a time when the Hughes Aircraft Company plant in Culver City was in turmoil as a result of Hughes's mismanagement—Hughes learned much later that they regretted the decision. By 1968, Robert Gross was dead and Courtlandt Gross was no longer active in the company, but Hughes still had friends at Lockheed. He passed word that he would like to sell both the Hughes Aircraft Company and the aircraft division of the Hughes Tool Company. To his chagrin, Lockheed replied with a polite brushoff. Miffed, Hughes sent a special message to his longtime acquaintance Jack Real, a Lockheed vice-president, intended to stir some action:

I must get down to short strokes on an immediate sale of both the Hopper and the Hyland properties. If your people are not interested, I will have to talk to North American and Douglas. I have held this package exclusively available to you and have not talked to anyone else. I have reached the end of the line. Your people told me (both Courtlandt and Robert Gross) that their failure to purchase the entire package, when I offered it on a bargain basis to Bob at Las Vegas, was the biggest single mistake he had ever made. Now do you mean to tell me they are going to do the same thing over again?[13]

When Hughes's threat to take his business elsewhere brought no serious response, he countered with a startling new proposal: Lockheed would buy the Hughes Aircraft Company and the aircraft division of the Hughes Tool Company. Hughes, in turn, would sign an order for 100 of Lockheed's newest jets —the L-1011 TriStar—at a cost of more than $1 billion.

From any standpoint the proposal was mindless. Hughes did not own an airline. Even if he had owned one, no airline could economically use 100 widebody jets. Moreover, there was not the remotest possibility that he could raise $1 billion to pay for the planes. The scheme had a familiar ring. Twelve years earlier he had ordered sixty-three jets and engines for TWA at a cost of more than $400 million—the largest single commitment in airline history. The order included thirty 880 jets from Convair, a subsidiary of the General Dynamics Corporation, under an unusual financing plan that was especially favorable to Hughes. What happened next was a matter of record. Hughes could not raise the money to pay for the planes. Convair was ruined, and Hughes lost control of TWA.

Now Hughes was about to repeat his mistake on a scale nearly three times grander. Further, his jet-buying plan would surely have a disastrous effect on the outcome of his seven-year-old legal battle with TWA. Herbert Brownell,

Jr., the former United States attorney-general, was about to complete nearly two years of hearings as special master to fix damages in the case. Within months Brownell would set the amount of money that TWA was entitled to collect from Hughes. Brownell's predecessor as special master, J. Lee Rankin, had tentatively ruled in favor of Hughes on one crucial point in the complex litigation: that the Hughes Tool Company was not a manufacturer of airplanes. TWA had maintained that because Hughes had ordered the planes through his tool company, he was in the business of producing planes and therefore had violated the antitrust statutes under which the legal action was initiated. It was a critical part of TWA's case, and Hughes seemed to have won the point. But if the Hughes Tool Company announced that it intended to buy 100 jets, and Hughes no longer had an airline, then the courts would no doubt accept TWA's argument. In short, Hughes's Lockheed jet order would result in a whopping judgment.

Nonetheless, Hughes pushed ahead. This time, Lockheed listened with interest. Lockheed had once been a major supplier of planes with its Constellation, but the commercial jet age had passed the company by, just as it had Hughes. In the late 1950s, the Boeing Company cornered about half the commercial market and the McDonnell Douglas Corporation picked up most of the rest. At first there was little concern at Lockheed. Lucrative military and aerospace contracts made the company America's third-largest aircraft manufacturer and a respectable profitmaker. But by the mid-1960s, its growth had slowed. The company's new management team concluded that if there was to be a resurgence in the years ahead, Lockheed had to regain a share of the commercial-airplane market.

Ordinarily, aircraft manufacturers have at least one airline signed up before they undertake to develop a new plane. Lockheed, though, in a desperate gamble, struck out on its own to make the L-1011 TriStar, a three-engine, 250-passenger, multipurpose luxury plane designed for use on short, medium, and long routes. In September of 1967, Lockheed announced that it would soon begin taking orders for the L-1011. While the airlines took a wait-and-see attitude, McDonnell Douglas rushed ahead with its own design of a similar plane, the DC-10. By January of 1968, the two companies were locked in a fierce sales battle. In February, McDonnell Douglas rang up the first sale. American Airlines agreed to buy twenty-five DC-10s and took an option for twenty-five more. In March, Eastern Airlines and a British holding company each agreed to buy from Lockheed fifty L-1011s, and TWA ordered forty-four. At the same time, Hughes spoke of buying 100 L-1011s—double the largest individual order pending. Lockheed was in no position to dismiss Hughes's overtures out of hand. In the beginning, talks were carried on directly between Hughes and Lockheed executives by either telephone or letter. Then, early in April, Lockheed told Hughes that it wanted to bargain face to face with one of his representatives—specifically Raymond Cook.

Cook was by now a veteran representative of his quirky, reclusive employer. A Phi Beta Kappa graduate of the University of Texas Law School, the fifty-four-year-old Cook had developed a reputation for the kind of practical business sense and financial responsibility that Hughes so often lacked. He even managed to gain the respect of the Wall Street bankers during the difficult TWA financing negotiations—a respect enhanced when Hughes fired him and replaced him with the flamboyant Greg Bautzer. Hughes later rehired Cook, but relations between the two men were never the same. Now Lockheed's desire to deal with Cook posed a serious problem. So far, Hughes had told few people of his scheme. Bob Maheu was unaware of the Lockheed negotiations. So, too, were Pat Hyland, general manager of the Hughes Aircraft Company, and Rea Hopper, vice-president in charge of the aircraft division of the Hughes Tool Company. Not even the top tool company officers in Houston knew of it. To bring Cook in, Hughes not only had to gain the lawyer's promise of secrecy, but also to sell him the Lockheed plan. And he knew that Cook would try to talk him out of it.

Cook was one of the few persons who often pointed out to Hughes the error of his business ways. It was a thankless task. Other high-level executives and lawyers surrounding the industrialist assured the permanency of their positions by never questioning his judgment. As a result, Cook had earned Hughes's lasting enmity. Further, Hughes believed that Cook always treated him condescendingly. A recent report from Cook to the Desert Inn penthouse on some relatively unimportant subject had provoked a testy retort from Hughes:

Raymond! If you would treat me as something other than a cross-breed between an escaped lunatic and a child, you would be surprised how much better we would get along! . . . I think it is some kind of a game with you, Raymond. I think that when you see an opportunity to embarass [sic] me, you leap at the opportunity, without really knowing why—just because it is part of the contest. I wish you would think about it and give me your viewpoint. I think it is important for us to get along.[14]

Of course, what Hughes meant by it being "important for us to get along" was that Cook should stop telling him things he did not want to hear, and he knew full well what Cook would say about the jet transaction. Yet Lockheed had insisted on Cook's presence in the negotiations. On April 3, Hughes dictated a four-page letter to Cook setting forth his plan:

Hughes Tool Company will sell to Lockheed for Lockheed's stock or debentures, cash or notes, all of the assets involved in the Hughes Tool Company Aircraft Division and simultaneously either Howard Hughes Medical Institute will sell Hughes Aircraft Company or Hughes Aircraft Company will sell its assets to Lockheed, likewise for stock, etc., etc. The next part of the transaction is as follows: Hughes Tool Company will purchase from Lockheed on standard sales contract 100 of Lockheed's new type 1011 aircraft.[15]

It took Hughes just ten lines to describe an acquisition that called for a cash outlay equal to ten times his investment in Las Vegas. The remaining eighty-five lines were devoted to arguments that might bring Cook around:

Regardless of how totally you may be opposed to our becoming involved in this transaction, I want you to realize that I have had a great deal more time to think about it. At first reaction I am sure you will feel this transaction is beyond our capabilities. I want to assure you, Raymond, that this is not the case. You will gradually appreciate, as you become more and more familiar with all the details, that staggering as this deal is, it is well within our capabilities to accomplish it. In any event, I must have this gentlemen's agreement with you, Raymond, regardless of how convinced you may be that we should not and cannot enter into this transaction, I do not want a hint of this [feeling] to penetrate through to the Lockheed people—not a hint from you to any of the people you may find necessary to bring into this matter.[16]

Hughes made it clear that the jet order would be carried out, and that he intended to return to the airline business:

I want you to know that it is my firm decision that Hughes Tool Company will go back to the air carrier business. Naturally, I do not want this known to Hopper or any of his people yet. I am sure your reaction will be that even though I am determined to go back to the air carrier business, this order is far larger than we can safely undertake. However, Raymond, I repeat, I have had a great deal more time to consider the risks and the potential benefits to be derived from this transaction. I have made a firm, irrevocable decision that we will go ahead with this. So if you do not make an all out effort to accomplish this objective you will only serve to embarrass and humiliate me.[17]

An excerpt from one of Hughes's handwritten memoranda taking Raymond Cook to task.

As for his ability to finance such a huge acquisition, Hughes foresaw no difficulty. His plan, calling for payment of each plane as it came off the production line, was a carbon copy of his disastrous TWA arrangement. But Hughes had continued to believe that if the banks had supported him "TWA would have achieved the equipment breakthrough of the century with the respect of its competitors."[18] He had even convinced himself that the banks deliberately sabotaged his jet plan because "the consequences to United and American would have been literally devastating." Now, Hughes reasoned, "I am betting the banks will not be so short sighted this time."[19]

Although Hughes had insisted in his talks with Lockheed that his order for 100 L-1011s was firm and the number of planes not negotiable, to Cook he confided differently. "Lockheed has already made an all out effort to persuade me to reduce the number of aircraft to fifty."* Admitting that he might be willing to accept fewer planes for other concessions, Hughes cautioned Cook not to let Lockheed know this. "When Lockheed insisted upon you personally to be here for these negotiations, I knew instinctively that they felt they could persuade you to prevail upon me to reduce the number involved in this order. If we should decide later on that we want to reduce the number, we can obtain important concessions for this sacrifice. If events should so transpire, I know what concessions I want in exchange and you do not. That is why I implore you not to yield even the slightest iota toward reducing the commitment and not under any circumstances to give Lockheed the slightest hint that you are afraid of this transaction."[20]

With a last exhortation, Hughes sent Cook off on his important assignment: "So, Raymond, I pass the ball to you and I hope you will give this matter your full time and the most intense effort you have given anything in your life. It is the biggest and most important transaction we have ever undertaken."[21]

Cook recognized at once that Hughes's proposal was devoid of business logic and financially impossible. In the past, he might have responded with an itemized demurrer. This time, for whatever reason, he raised no strong objection. Perhaps weary of saving Hughes from himself, Cook thought it high time for the sixty-two-year-old industrialist to learn a hard lesson. In any case, he plunged into negotiations with Lockheed, following Hughes's instructions to the letter, except for an occasional lapse, such as when he confided to Lockheed executives that he was not personally aware of any specific plan of Hughes's to return to the airline business. If that was true, Hughes's purpose in buying the L-1011s must be to resell them at a profit. It was a prospect that chilled Lockheed officials. Their interest in the negotiations cooled.

*It is unclear why Lockheed tried to persuade Hughes to reduce his order for L-1011s from 100 to 50 planes. Because Hughes commonly mixed fiction with fact in his messages, perhaps he simply was not being truthful with Cook. If his assertion was correct, then possibly Lockheed recognized what Hughes chose to ignore—that he did not have the financial resources to buy 100 planes. Another, more likely explanation, is that Lockheed feared that Hughes—who as an early customer would get a bargain price on the L-1011s—would resell the planes at a profit, thereby undercutting future Lockheed sales.

But Hughes never relied on a single individual when he was negotiating. He had continued to deal directly with Lockheed through his old associate at the company, Jack Real, and when he learned of Cook's bargaining error, he immediately called it to his lawyer's attention. "You will recall that I originally asked you to be most careful not to imply that we were buying these aircraft for a resale program and to take every opportunity to confirm that we have extensive air carrier plans," Hughes reminded Cook. "Instead of following this request, you permitted Lockheed, as the result of meetings last week with you, to reach the conclusion that there was no such air carrier program. This is what caused Lockheed to lose interest in the deal."[22]

By telephone and by letter, Hughes repaired Cook's damage, persuading Lockheed that he would indeed procure an airline that would fly the fleet of L-1011s. Whatever Hughes's failings as a business executive, he was a consummate salesman—even by long distance. He was soon able to inform Cook that Lockheed's top officers "have now accepted the fact that some way or other Hughes will be an air carrier, or will be directly or indirectly involved with a major carrier."[23]

By April 9, just five days after Cook had come into the negotiations, Hughes himself had worked out a tentative agreement through Jack Real that called for the purchase of seventy-five aircraft. Real then came under pressure from his superiors to conclude the transaction. He called the Desert Inn penthouse and dictated a message to Hughes. "Now that we've got this agreed to," Real said, "please do everything in your power to expedite the formalization of this agreement. As I've told you in previous messages we must have some kind of formal agreement by the close of work April 10. My management is relying that I will be able to make this date. Please don't disappoint me."[24]

Now they were playing Hughes's game, and Hughes was not to be rushed. He sent a memorandum to Cook relating Real's plea to sign an agreement by April 10, but cautioned that "this does not mean I want you to drop any stitches in your haste. No matter how trivial they may appear at this time, these things have a way of becoming important later on. So, please give this deal the most intense care and microscopic scrutiny that you can possibly give it, regardless of how long it takes. However, if you can formalize it by the night of the 10th, no matter if it runs into the morning of the 11th, and if you can do this without any slightest possibility of any slightest omission or undesirable commission, then please do so."[25]

Negotiations were in progress around the clock. At 4:45 A.M. on April 10, Hughes dispatched an updated directive to Cook: "Work on 1011, but do not make even the slightest concession. If we get bogged down, work on Hughes Aircraft Company."[26]

But Cook was pessimistic about Hughes's suggestion to tie the Hughes Aircraft Company sale to Lockheed with the purchase of the jets. Lockheed officials had refused to consider the Hughes Aircraft proposal until the L-1011 contract was "firm, with the money paid." And, because the aircraft company was owned by Hughes's tax-exempt charitable foundation, linking its sale to the jet deal could have serious tax consequences. Cook pointed out that "we are playing with dynamite even to mention Hughes Aircraft Company while the 1011 deal is cooking."[27]

At four in the afternoon on April 10, Cook told Hughes that an agreement on the L-1011s was near and that he hoped to avoid a Lockheed demand that the contract contain a clause prohibiting resale of the jets. Two hours later, Cook advised, "I received Lockheed's official assurance that our agreement is firm notwithstanding that the letter agreement will not be signed and the money delivered until tomorrow."[28]

A HUGHES LESSON

Cook had wrapped up the negotiations for the L-1011s that Hughes had sought so desperately. Hughes, who should have been pleased, was angry. While he wanted to close the deal, Hughes wanted to close it on his own time schedule. Cook had violated that whimsical time table by agreeing to deliver the required deposit. Hughes was ready to sign the order for the jets, but he was not prepared, mentally, to part with any cash.

"You must not have heard me in our last conversation," he scolded Cook. "I said we would sign tomorrow and pay in not over two–three days thereafter. Just tell them it takes that long for us to handle that much money with due regard for interest, etc."[29]

But Cook had been working against another deadline. Lockheed had advised the nation's airlines that the initial $14.8 million price tag on the L-1011 was about to be raised sharply. The company's long association with Hughes notwithstanding, there was no way for Lockheed to allow Hughes to buy the planes at the original price while it was charging the airlines substantially more. To save Hughes millions of dollars, Cook had rushed the deal to completion before the price increase, arranging to deliver the deposit the following day, April 11. "Today before leaving Lockheed," he told Hughes, "Holliday reviewed with Frain [F. L. Frain, Lockheed's treasurer] the procedure for transferring the cash tomorrow, and I know of no easy excuse for Holliday to delay payment."[30]

As was so often the case, though, Hughes got his way. The agreement was signed, but no money changed hands. Now Hughes could disclose a few details to Bob Maheu, who for some weeks had been pressing to go forward with new Las Vegas business deals. Getting no decision had angered Maheu, and Hughes sought to use the Lockheed agreement both to explain his actions and to stroke Maheu's ego. On one of his yellow legal tablets, Hughes wrote a euphoric message to the chief of his Nevada operations, placed it in a sealed envelope, and gave it to one of the aides to deliver. The message began:

Bob—

I know you think I am over cautious, but I will prove my confidence in you by disclosing a piece of information known only to seven men altogether—three in Hughes Tool Company and four at another company. It must be kept in deepest confidence.

I am telling you because it may explain why I do not enter quite as quickly into some of the investments that we consider as you might expect. We can publicize this later, but for now it must be kept tightly secret.

I just tore off the rest of the last page, because I stated the exact amount and the number of aircraft involved and, upon hindsight, I decided those figures should not be floating around, even in a sealed envelope.

So, suficeth [sic] to say that the contract I just signed is an agreement with the Lockheed Aircraft Corp. for substantially more than one billion dollars, in purchase of a fleet of the very latest (far more than anything flying) design of jumbo-jet. There is nothing like this airplane in process of design or construction anywhere else in the world. Needless to say I intend to get back in the air-carrier business. And, hopefully, with headquarters and main offices in Nevada. This also is known to nobody, and I must ask your all-out pledge of secrecy. . . .

Now this does not mean that I want to sacrifice *any* of the favorable or important opportunities that we have developed and that are awaiting action. I am ready now to move on all of these and make a decision without further delay. I am merely explaining the past delay. Please don't tell me later we lost some deal because you thought I had no further interest in view of the air-carrier program. Actually, I am hopeful that the cash requirements will not be as great as I had anticipated. I just wanted an opportunity to evaluate carefully the cash requirements of this program.

Thank you for your patience. Incidentally, it is my belief that this is the largest commercial transaction ever consumated—either for airplanes, automobiles, washing machines, or what the hell have you. . . .[31]

Hughes's euphoria was short-lived. At 5:15 P.M. on April 11—after the Lockheed commitment had been signed—Cook advised Hughes that the purchase of the jets could injure his "chances for successful termination of the TWA lawsuit."[32] Hughes exploded:

If you really had my best interest at heart and if this past trip to California has not been some gigantic chess game, wherein the real motive was to lead me into making some kind of mistake, in order that I would be personally chastised and cured from ever again daring to think that I could handle something as important as this Lockheed deal without you leading me by the hand from the very outset, if you really had my best interest at heart, please just tell me in a few words why you waited the entire week (during which we have been in communication every single day) to tell me this simple and vital and frightening bit of information.[33]

Hughes had conveniently forgotten his strictures to Cook a week earlier, when he had admonished his lawyer not to question the transaction. It was typical of him to ignore advice, or insist he did not want any, and later complain bitterly about the lack of it. And, as was his custom, Hughes had not been candid with Cook. Cook's statement to Lockheed officials had been true. He was not aware of any specific Hughes plan to return to the airline business. But there was one. Hughes had not told Cook that Keath Carver, a vice-president of the Bank of America, had been conducting preliminary talks on his behalf aimed at acquiring Western Air Lines.

Having told Maheu about the Lockheed deal, it might now be time to advise Cook of negotiations for Western Air Lines. This he did in a brief message, adding that Western Air Lines would fit in "with our Nevada plans and would involve the addition of two Mexican airlines. I would plan to move its offices to Nevada and to have Carver full time to run the operation."[34]

Cook replied by warning Hughes that "even an attempt to acquire control of a trunk carrier would be adverse. It would suggest, both before the Civil Aeronautics Board and in the New York courts, that you are planning on using the carrier as a captive market in violation of the antitrust laws."[35] In other words, it would suggest to them that Hughes planned to take advantage of Western Air Lines by forcing it to buy planes from Hughes Tool Company to the latter's profit—exactly what he had tried to do with TWA.

For the next week, relations between Hughes and Cook went from bad to worse. For whatever reason, it had become increasingly apparent to Hughes that the L-1011 deal was not feasible, but rather than admit his mistake, he blamed Cook, directing a stream of biting memoranda toward his Houston lawyer. He took Cook to task again for not warning him about the deal's effect on the TWA lawsuit, and he made a vague reference to having gotten out of the L-1011 contract, although he gave no details. "I had great trouble in extricating us," he wrote, "and what I had to tell Lockheed is my business. So I would appreciate it very much indeed if you would stay off the 1011 subject with Lockheed and with everybody else, whomsoever."[36]

Over the years, Hughes seldom repeated the same story to any two of his executives or lawyers. He often had three or more operatives negotiating some phase of a particular deal, each ignorant of what the others were doing and working under conflicting instructions. Thus, Hughes would play one off against another while truth faded into the background.

So it was that one hour and twenty minutes after Hughes complained to Cook that he had "had great difficulty extricating" himself from the Lockheed contract, he assured Real that "I don't want to lose the airplane deal, you must realize this."[37] Still intent on acquiring an airline to go along with his fleet of L-1011s, Hughes shifted bargaining strategy, assigning Real and Keath Carver at the Bank of America to act as his front-line negotiators. In the meantime, he kept Cook standing by, withholding the details of his latest maneuvers. In fact, he directed his two new negotiators to keep their talks secret: "I urge you not to mention my air carrier hopes to Cook," Hughes said to Real. "He has approved from a legal standpoint but is still trying to discourage me. I would hate to have him say anything in opposition while in the presence of any of your people."[38] Hughes's reference to Cook's legal position was partly accurate. Cook had raised no "legal" obstacle to the acquisition of an airline, but he had pointed out that such a purchase could result in the loss of the TWA lawsuit.

Western Air Lines, the focus of Hughes's takeover efforts, was controlled by Terrell C. Drinkwater, a sixty-year-old Denver-born lawyer who had assumed management of the airline in 1947—a time when it was selling surplus airplane tires to meet its payroll—and built it into a successful regional carrier serving cities from Calgary, Canada, to Acapulco, Mexico, and in more than a dozen western states, including Nevada. "My best hope is Western," Hughes told Real. "Since it has so much service in and out of here [Las Vegas], it would fit into my plans just right."[39] But Hughes did not want to foreclose other opportunities. When it was suggested that National Airlines also might be available, he asked both Real and Carver to pursue that carrier as well. "I am anxious to make one of these deals," he said to Real, "because we can then go right ahead with a deal [on the L-1011s] with no resistance from my attorneys."[40]

To keep Cook occupied, Hughes tossed out another proposal for him to study: the possibility of merging the Hughes Tool Company Aircraft Division into the Hughes Aircraft Company and at the same time making a public offering of the aircraft company's stock owned by the Howard Hughes Medical Institute. If Cook agreed that the plan had some merit, then Julius Sedlmayr, the Wall Street broker he consulted on occasion at Merrill Lynch, Pierce, Fenner & Smith, "could be induced to go to Culver City with no difficulty at all" to work out the financial arrangements.[41] When Cook responded dourly, expressing the view that the aircraft division, a money loser for three decades, was next to worthless, Hughes bristled. "I don't agree with you," he chided Cook.[42]

But Hughes could come up with proposals as fast as his lawyer could knock them down:

I have what I think is a really good idea and I don't want you putting the chill on it just because it happens to be my concept. Here is my idea: Hughes Tool Company sells [the] Aircraft Division to Hughes Aircraft Company on the following terms: Hughes Aircraft Company pays no price for [the] Aircraft Division at this time (except possibly picking up the cost of some categories of material, tooling, work in progress, inventories, etc.). Hughes Aircraft Company agrees to absorb any and all losses incurred through the operation. Hughes Tool Company agrees to hold Hughes Aircraft Company harmless against any cumulative losses remaining after five years, and to make payments against such losses whenever the accounting department of Hughes Aircraft Company may estimate that, in fact, such losses appear to be inevitable and can make any kind of an estimate as to the amount thereof.

This, of course, is all just very rough. The term perhaps should be six years. The obvious purpose is to take advantage of Hughes Aircraft Company's normal carry-over privilege and to make an all out effort to recoup any losses in an efficiently run operation, devoid of the handicap of being the unwanted small brother in the Culver City plant, and benefitted by any economies of the merger. Then, any losses remaining would be paid by Hughes Tool Company and the Aircraft Division would be a part of Hughes Aircraft Company, where it belongs.[43]

As usual, Hughes insisted on absolute secrecy. He especially did not want Cook to inform other partners at Andrews, Kurth, Campbell & Jones. "This is in the most all-out secrecy," he declared. "I don't want one single soul in your office to know one blessed thing about it. You will just have to give me your own personal opinion, based upon your present knowledge—no help from anybody."[44]

Here was yet another indication that the Howard Hughes Medical Institute—so often portrayed as a symbol of Hughes's philanthropy—was simply a sophisticated tax gimmick. Hughes proposed, in essence, to take the millions of dollars the aircraft division was losing each year and offset those losses, for tax purposes, against the profits of the Hughes Aircraft Company. His stipulation that the Hughes Tool Company would pay the Hughes Aircraft Company for any losses the aircraft division incurred after five years was a sham. The contract for manufacturing light observation helicopters would run out in less than three years. The aircraft division then could be dismantled and there would be no further losses. In one of those financial sleight-of-hand schemes at which Hughes excelled, he was promising to underwrite any future deficits when it could be guaranteed there would be no deficits. In the interim, he would profit handsomely. The losses of the aircraft division, which he now was absorbing personally, would be picked up, in effect, by his tax-exempt charity. The medical institute, of course, would never miss the money, because it got almost nothing from the Hughes Aircraft Company. And the institute was still paying interest to Hughes on the debt it incurred when he created it.

From its founding in 1953 through 1967, the medical institute had collected $2 million in contributions or dividends from the Hughes Aircraft Company, whose operating profits through those years ran a hundred times that amount. During the same period, the medical institute—sanctioned as a charitable organization by the Internal Revenue Service—had given $22.9 million to Hughes in the form of interest and lease payments. This was made possible by the ingenious lease and sublease arrangement that Hughes had devised, in which his Hughes Tool Company, owner of the land and buildings at the Hughes Aircraft Company plant site in Culver City, had leased the plant to the medical institute, which in turn subleased the property—for more money, thus generating income—to the aircraft company, which in turn tacked the lease payments onto its government contracts as a cost of doing business.

Cook ignored Hughes's warning against "putting the chill" on his latest concept and did just that. Undaunted, Hughes countered with yet another variation, urging Cook to push ahead with talks on the sale of both the aircraft division and the aircraft company to Lockheed. At one point, Cook was to attend a dinner party with Carl Kotchian, the president of Lockheed. Learning of this, Hughes lectured his lawyer on conduct. "I prefer you not discuss business at all," Hughes directed. "If he insists just tell him you hope he will accelerate the progress of his men in negotiating the Hughes Aircraft Company, Hughes Tool Company Aircraft Division transaction as much as he can conveniently."[45] Hughes instructed Cook to "Give my very best regards to Kotchian. I want him to know you have spoken to me today and that the decision not to try to engage him in business discussion was my decision, in consideration of Mr. Kotchian's having an enjoyable evening, instead of being plagued with business talk. I don't want him to think your failure to mention our business affairs was an accident."[46]

For a while it seemed that Hughes might pull it off—that he would be able to unload his helicopter company and also get back in the airline business. He told Real at one point that Carver was "confident we are near an offer from Drinkwater" for Western Air Lines. But as the weeks went by, first the bid for Western and then for National collapsed.* So, too, did his plan to buy 100 L-1011s, and to sell to Lockheed the Hughes Aircraft Company and the Hughes Tool Company Aircraft Division. Hughes had not accomplished any of his objectives.

Howard Hughes, however, never learned the ordinary and obvious lessons of life. From his fruitless negotiations he concluded not that his scheme to buy 100 L-1011s was ill-conceived, or that buying an airline while the TWA lawsuit was pending was bad timing, or that his proposal to sell the assets of his tax-exempt charity was an invitation to a federal investigation. Rather, he concluded that the next time he wanted to buy an airline—and there would be a next time—negotiations would best be entrusted to someone other than Raymond A. Cook.

*Seven months later, Hughes's Las Vegas nemesis, Kirk Kerkorian, made a public offer to purchase, at $45 a share, up to 1.5 million shares, or about 31 percent, of Western Air Line's outstanding stock. The offer was successful and soon allowed Kerkarian to place his own slate of directors on Western's board.

CHAPTER 16

THE HIJACKING
OF AIR WEST

"AIR WORST"

THE weekend of July 4, 1968, promised to be another high-roller for Las Vegas. The desert gambling spa had always prospered on long weekends which gave tourists time to shuttle in for at least three uninterrupted days of profligacy. As usual, on the eve of the holiday there was hardly a room to be found anywhere in town.

But not all the gamblers made it to Las Vegas that weekend. Some were left stranded at airport gates because their flights were overbooked. Others had been sold tickets on flights that no longer existed. Still others arrived at the airport well in advance of departure time only to learn that the plane had already left.

The culprit was not some fly-by-night travel agent but Air West, a new airline that had stumbled into business just four days earlier. Air West had been formed by the merger of three small airlines—Bonanza Air Lines in Phoenix, Pacific Air Lines in San Francisco, and West Coast Airlines in Seattle. On paper, the merger created an impressive regional air carrier. Employing thirty-eight hundred persons and generating revenues of $70 million a year, the Air West system spanned eight thousand miles in the western United States, Canada, and Mexico. But whatever its potential, the airline had, in fact, started life hopelessly undercapitalized and virtually unmanaged.

One bit of poor planning was Air West's management's refusal to spend $35,000 to test a newly installed computer that was supposed to schedule departures and arrivals at seventy-five airports. As a result, when the system was placed in operation on that busy Fourth of July weekend, it broke down. Confusion was so complete that it was not uncommon for Air West agents to rush toward an arriving flight, open the plane's door, and ask: "What flight are you and where are you from?"[1]

In many cities, faulty airline service might have gone unnoticed to all but its unfortunate passengers. But not in Las Vegas. Hundreds of miles from the nearest large city, it relies on airplanes to bring the tourists in. Any break in service means a break in the flow of money. To make matters worse, Air West was the only airline certified to fly from Las Vegas to northern Nevada, to Carson City, the state capital, and the only one to Phoenix, long a steady supplier of weekend gamblers. As it became apparent that the July 4 breakdown was no isolated lapse, but was symptomatic of a fatal flaw in the young airline, Las Vegas city officials prepared a formal complaint to the Civil Aeronautics Board urging federal action. Newspaper articles castigated Air West for the threat it posed to Las Vegas's economic health. Even Strip comedians began to work jokes into their acts about "Air Worst." Concurrently, Air West's dismal performance led immediately to huge operating losses.

In the chaotic birth of Air West, Howard Hughes saw a chance to try again to return to the airline business. Of course, Air West was not TWA. It consisted largely of twin-engine, propeller-driven airplanes shuttling in and out of such obscure hamlets as Chico, California, and Moscow, Idaho. But Air West was nevertheless an airline, and Hughes wanted very much to own one again. Moreover, Air West's haphazard service was interfering with the flow of gamblers to his hotels and casinos. By acquiring it he could once again play his role as the savior of Las Vegas. The opportunity was too good to pass up. Bob Maheu was instructed to find out if Air West could be acquired.

As Maheu investigated the struggling airline he found among its twenty-four directors only one familiar name—Patrick J. Hillings, a former Republican congressman from California who was then practicing law in Washington, D.C. Hillings was in Miami, shortly to attend the Republican National Convention in Miami Beach that would nominate Richard M. Nixon for president. When Maheu asked Hillings whom to contact about Air West's availability, Hillings suggested Nick Bez, the airline's board chairman, chief executive officer, and largest stockholder, who lived in Seattle.[2] Hillings cordially arranged a meeting between Bez and Maheu on July 30 at the Century Plaza Hotel in Los Angeles.

A tall, powerfully built man, Bez was, in his seventy-third year, the premier Horatio Alger figure of the Pacific Northwest. He had come to the United States from Yugoslavia in 1910, at age fourteen, with eleven dollars in his pocket. Borrowing a skiff to fish for smelt, he soon caught enough to buy his own boat, and by the time Maheu met him Bez presided over a multimillion-dollar fishing fleet and canning empire stretching from Alaska to Seattle. For the "Sultan of Salmon," commercial aviation was a sideline that started when Bez founded West Coast Airlines in 1941. When that line merged to become Air West, Bez was elected chairman of the board and chief executive officer. Although he possessed obvious business ability, Bez was nonetheless a prime reason for Air West's problems. He rarely set foot in the airline's headquarters near San Francisco International Airport, preferring to run it by remote control from Seattle. Not one to mince words, Bez made it clear to Maheu that he was both interested in selling and flattered that Hughes was interested in buying.

After the meeting, Maheu quickly dictated a summary memorandum to one of Hughes's aides in the Desert Inn penthouse, describing Bez as a "diamond in the rough."[3] Bez "does not have too good a command of the English language," Maheu said, but he warned Hughes not to underestimate Bez's shrewdness: "I can assure you that his mother did not bring up a stupid boy."[4]

In situations like this, Maheu never knew what Hughes would do next. Burning issues quickly cooled. But Maheu soon knew where Hughes stood on Air West. He telephoned Maheu within hours and sent him frequent memoranda outlining strategy. He wanted a full report on Air West, including the price of its common stock "high, low and recent" since the merger.[5]

By early August, Hughes had formulated an Air West masterplan, not as Bez advised involving purchase of stock, but rather through purchase of the carrier's assets, a complicated move dictated by Hughes's special tax needs. He urged Maheu to proceed with the acquisition of the airline, whose stock was traded on the American Stock Exchange. His plan hinged on one simple fundamental force—bad news. "This plan," he wrote Maheu, "necessitates that the stock edge downward with the existing continuous bad news, and then that we come along with a spectacular offer to pay the stockholders in liquidation a price substantially above the market. Any rise in the market before our offer will adversely affect the plan."[6]

The plan was meant to appeal to Air West's thirteen thousand stockholders, many of whom lived in the West, where they could view firsthand the abysmal performance of their investment. Over the years, the three airlines that formed Air West had attracted a diverse group of investors, including movie mogul Darryl F. Zanuck, actor Henry Fonda, and erstwhile businessman F. Donald Nixon, brother of the newly nominated Republican presidential candidate. Hughes was depending on stockholder fears to carry the deal for him. Remembering what he termed his "God-forsaken TWA experiences," he was confident the plan would work, mainly because of the rate at which Air West was losing money. "Believe me," he confided knowingly to Maheu, "when an airline starts losing money, you simply have no idea how fast they can lose it."[7]

As Hughes plotted strategy in the penthouse, Maheu was active on other fronts. If an agreement to purchase Air West was negotiated, the Civil Aeronautics Board would have to approve it. Maheu began lining up Washington contacts. He alerted his friend James N. Juliana, a former staff director of the CAB who still had close ties with the board's staff, that his help might be needed.[8] And, he touched base with his old friend Edward P. Morgan, who had an entree with the CAB itself. One of Morgan's classmates at Georgetown University Law School had been Robert T. Murphy, CAB vice-chairman and one of the five board members who would pass on the Hughes offer. Maheu assured Hughes on August 2 that Morgan was already at work trying to "run down Bob Murphy for a preliminary conference."[9]

On August 8, Maheu flew to Seattle to open informal talks with Bez and his allies on the Air West board in an effort to reach a tentative understanding with them on the selling price of Air West. If that were achieved, Maheu hoped Bez would then use his influence to persuade the full Air West board to approve the Hughes offer. When the talks got under way at the Olympic Hotel, Maheu was "very bullish" about an agreement.[10] Hughes told him to offer up to $20 a share for Air West's 3.9 million shares, meaning he was prepared to pay about $80 million. When Maheu actually got down to numbers with Bez and his associates, his optimism faded. With the stock selling for $16 on the American Exchange, the Air West group wanted $25 a share from Hughes. "I think they have lost their marbles," Maheu opined.[11]

Maheu went back to the bargaining table, but made no progress. The talks were complicated by disunity in Air West's ranks. If he had had any doubts beforehand, Maheu now saw that it was a merged airline in name only. Behind the name was a jumble of petty jealousies, conflicting management philosophies, separate stockholder constituencies, and personal antagonisms. "A mixed-up bunch of kids" is how Maheu described them to Hughes.[12] He wondered if the smart move might not be to pass up the deal, at least for the time being.

"Who in the hell needs it?" Maheu asked Hughes. "I think we are in a perfect posture of having evidenced good faith and to call these negotiations off on a very friendly basis. Unless I miss my guess, I think we can come back in six months to a year hence and make ourselves one hell of a lot better deal."[13]

But Hughes could not wait. He sent Maheu back to the bargaining table and finally, after compromises on both sides, a price of $22 a share was reached. On August 11, Bez signed an agreement pledging his "best efforts" to achieve the sale of Air West to Hughes. The agreement also provided that Bez would use his influence to allow the Hughes Tool Company to examine Air West's books and to provide Hughes a current balance sheet. The press release announcing Hughes's proposal said the purchase price would provide "approximately $22 per share for the stock of Air West."[14]

Having secured Bez's support, Maheu set out to win over the rest of the airline's directors. He hoped the agreement would create a bandwagon effect for Hughes's offer. Instead, it produced the opposite, galvanizing the already bitter opposition to Bez. The Seattle talks aroused the suspicions of Bez's enemies. The meeting with Maheu had been conducted in secret and without authorization from the full Air West board. Bez had pledged to try to sell the airline without even polling the board to determine if it favored the sale. The day after the Hughes offer was made public, three powerful officers of the airline—G. Robert Henry, president; David R. Grace, executive committee chairman; and Edmund Converse, board vice-chairman—announced their opposition to the sale.

Of the three, the most important was Converse, who headed the Bonanza faction on the Air West board. A former intelligence officer in the Second

World War, Converse had founded Bonanza in 1946 and was instrumental in building it into a $10-million enterprise by the time of the Air West merger. Like other Bonanza stockholders, he was sold on the merger because he believed Air West's extensive sunbelt route system would eventually yield handsome returns. Thus, his opposition to Hughes was mostly economic.

On August 20, Maheu flew to Phoenix to woo Converse. Once captain of the Holy Cross debate team, Maheu was a gifted speaker who ordinarily could be quite persuasive. But Converse, after listening politely to Maheu extol the virtues of the Hughes Tool Company and Howard Hughes, still opposed the sale. His only concession was that if stockholders voted to accept Hughes's bid, he would support the Hughes application before the CAB. In a memorandum to Hughes that night, Maheu made the best of it, assuring Hughes "it is not the end of the road. There is still time to do a lot of work on Converse."[15]

By late August it was clear that the Hughes organization was faced with a lot of work—first on Air West's divided directors and then on the airline's stockholders—if the acquisition were to go through. Hughes fretted. "I have no taste for a proxy fight," he wrote Maheu. "I do not let anybody know this, but I tell you. I think the delay would be devastating in a hundred of our other projects. We need this Air West deal settled off or on now!"[16] It was vintage Hughes, displaying nerves in the heat of the battle, one day urging his executives forward, the next day full of doubt.

Ignoring Hughes's fears, Maheu pressed on. The most potent force working in Hughes's favor was Air West's slipshod service. News stories about the airline's performance frightened patrons away and plunged it deeper into the red. Maheu still lacked reliable figures, but Air West was clearly losing millions. As time went on, stockholders were bound to look favorably on the Hughes proposal.

Now that the Air West issue was joined, every branch of Hughes's empire, including Romaine Street, was mobilized to campaign for the acquisition. Publicity was a key. Maheu reached outside the organization and hired Jimmy (The Greek) Snyder, the Las Vegas oddsmaker and public-relations man. Snyder was delighted to land the $7,500-a-month Hughes account. Convinced, as an associate recalled, that the Hughes retainer would "insure financial success for him forever," Snyder drafted a series of news releases praising the Hughes offer and criticizing Air West directors who opposed it.[17]

"Directors of Air West who think the Howard Hughes offer of $22 a share isn't enough are barking up the wrong tree," said one typical release. "Hughes usually makes one offer for properties he wants to buy and it's usually above market value. After that—no quibbling."[18]

To create an illusion of widespread support for Hughes, Snyder released statements to the news media in the name of a fictitious group of Air West stockholders he said had hired him to support the sale.[19] Even the respected *Wall Street Journal* was taken in, reporting on September 19, 1968: "One group of Nevada stockholders has banded together and hired Jimmy (The Greek)

Snyder, Las Vegas sports figure and publicity man, to push acceptance of the Hughes offer."[20]

Snyder also tapped his political friends in Nevada for public statements on behalf of the Hughes campaign. Among those who eagerly complied was Alan Bible, Nevada's popular Democratic senator, who was then seeking reelection. Bible issued a statement criticizing Air West's service and saying Hughes's offer "represents an excellent solution to what has become a deplorable situation."[21] At the time of Bible's warm endorsement, his office received at least $30,000 in cash from Hughes to support his reelection drive.*

Hughes also received his customary support from the *Las Vegas Sun,* especially from Hank Greenspun, who continued to write glowingly: "When an airline goofs off and discourages the flow of tourism, it does give a town a feeling of well-being to have a fellow around to purchase the whole doggone airline just to improve service."[22] As it happened, Greenspun had a financial interest in the Air West outcome. The day after the Hughes offer was announced, Greenspun bought 15,000 shares of Air West stock for roughly $19 a share.[23] At $22 a share, Greenspun would make a $45,000 profit.

SQUEEZE PLAY

Despite Hughes's pressure tactics and Air West's mounting losses, the opposition did not collapse. Converse had proven to be an able and stubborn adversary. Bez, on the other hand, had not rallied the expected support, in part because of an illness which forced him to play a much reduced role. Early in September, doctors at the Mayo Clinic diagnosed Bez's disease as terminal liver cancer. Although not yet hospitalized, he was unable to leave Seattle for extended periods.

When the Air West board met on September 20 in San Francisco, Chester Davis, Hughes's New York lawyer, presented the Hughes case. Speaking to the full twenty-four-member board, Davis told the directors that Hughes would acquire Air West's assets, assume all liabilities, and pay each stockholder "approximately $22 a share for his stock."[24] The stock was selling for about $18 that day. Nonetheless, some directors were still opposed to the sale. They believed in Air West's long-range profitability or were concerned by what they described as "large holes" in the Hughes offer.[25]

The largest hole was the so-called net-worth provision, a clause Davis had drafted in Seattle and slipped into the "best efforts" agreement with Bez. It provided that on the day Hughes actually acquired Air West, the airline would have to have a net worth equal to 75 percent of its worth on July 31, 1968, when

---

*The amount Bible actually received is in dispute. An aide of the senator's told the Internal Revenue Service that in September of 1968 he received a "cash payment of $30,000–$80,000 from Tom Bell [Hughes's attorney]," according to documents of the Securities and Exchange Commission.

the negotiations with Hughes had begun. With Air West rapidly accumulating losses, there was no way the airline could meet that provision. Thus, when the time came for Hughes to acquire Air West, he could either back out of the deal or renegotiate it on lower terms. In either case, Air West stockholders would lose. At the Desert Inn penthouse, Hughes awaited the outcome. After hours of bitter debate, the board voted 13 to 11 to recommend stockholder acceptance of the Hughes offer, "subject to a better proposal from another source."[26] It was a precarious victory, but other developments, fast coming to a head, would enable Hughes to make up ground.

The bitter fight that Hughes had spawned began to work in his favor. With the energies of every high-ranking Air West official consumed by the political battle, no one was in charge at Air West. Losses soared to more than $1 million a month, alarming the airline's major creditor, the Bank of America. On September 19, the bank informed Air West that it was in default on a loan, and three weeks later shut off the airline's credit, warning that it would supply no more money until Air West established a "satisfactory management climate."[27]

Next to the Hughes offer, the chief obstacle to management stability at Air West was Nick Bez. The old fisherman was obviously ill, but few knew that he was dying. Hughes was one of the few. Maheu told Hughes that Bez was receiving "treatment for a condition which is much worse than he or any member of his family has been informed. Through our confidential sources we were able to ascertain that he has terminal cancer of the liver and one lung has been badly affected."[28]

Even though Bez had little of his old drive, he worked out an agreement to turn over the reins of Air West to Converse if stockholders approved the sale to Hughes at a meeting on November 26. By doing that, Bez hoped to preserve Air West's assets until the Hughes takeover. The Bank of America endorsed the idea and promised to restore Air West's line of credit as soon as the airline's board approved the change.

But on November 18, when the board met, Chester Davis vetoed the Bez–Converse agreement. Davis insisted that Bez remain as Air West's chairman until the CAB ruled on Hughes's application.[29] Worn out and desperately ill, Bez was not the least bit eager to stay on. But he felt that his commitment to the Hughes offer gave him no choice. The refusal to allow Bez to step down was a momentous decision. Bez would be dead in three months and the failure to shore up the airline's management would by then have led to greater losses. The Hughes forces did go along with an Air West request to postpone the stockholders' meeting until December 27 and to extend the option to acquire Air West until December 31. Although Hughes virtually controlled the airline, Air West's stubborn board now deadlocked 12 to 12 on whether to recommend shareholder approval of the Hughes bid. Clearly, the fate of the Hughes offer would be decided by the stockholders.

The Hughes team lavished great care on a proxy statement mailed to every stockholder prior to the meeting. The statement stressed that they would receive $22 a share. It also touched superficially on the net-worth stipulation. Buried in the fine print of this proxy statement was a clause hinting that stockholders might receive less than $22 if Air West failed to meet its "obligations."[30] The point was not explained. The document made no mention at all that Air West's net worth was already below the 75-percent requirement and that continuing losses made it unlikely that the airline could ever comply with the net-worth agreement. In other words, stockholders were sure to receive far less than $22 a share. Many did not understand this.

On December 27, 1968, at a meeting at the Thunderbolt Hotel just south of San Francisco International Airport, the Hughes offer was approved, despite a spirited last-ditch effort by opponents. (Actor Jimmy Stewart, once a Hughes supporter, had his 11,890 shares cast against the purchase.) Of the 3.8 million shares outstanding, 1,987,397, just over 52 percent, were cast for Hughes. Two last-minute proposals—one from the Mallory–Randall Corporation, a Brooklyn-based mini-conglomerate, and one from Northwest Airlines —momentarily threatened to upset the Hughes campaign, but Bez refused to allow those offers to be considered. Jubilation reigned in the Hughes ranks that night. All that remained was for Air West's board to approve the purchase contract with Hughes. Then it was on to the CAB.

Late the following morning, Davis and Maheu lounged in the Thunderbolt's bar awaiting the outcome of the Air West board meeting upstairs. What was expected to be a mere formality turned out to be a bombshell. Shortly before noon, word came down that the board had voted 13 to 11 against Hughes. The dissident directors had decided instead to pursue the Northwest offer. A Hughes ally on the board argued incredulously: "Can we trade a bird in the hand for a bunch of nebulous birds out in the bush?"[31] Apparently, the stubborn Air West board wanted to try.

Maheu reported the bad news to Hughes and said he doubted that the deal could be salvaged: "I do not think these selfish bastards are about ready to change their position."[32] Time was running out. Only three and a half days remained before Hughes's option expired at midnight Tuesday. But Davis was not as pessimistic. Long years of legal maneuvering in the TWA case had taught him that a cause was never truly lost. Now a plan began to take shape to crush the Hughes opposition once and for all.

It was simple enough: Air West stockholders would file a lawsuit against the opposing directors seeking to make them personally liable for any damages the airline might sustain because of their refusal to honor the stockholders' mandate to sell to Hughes. If the lawsuit were filed in Delaware, the Hughes forces could resort to a technique used in the TWA case. They could ask the courts to seize the stock of dissident directors until the case was resolved. Many of the directors had a large portion of their net worth tied up in Air West stock. Hughes lieutenants were convinced that the directors would swing over to Hughes if their assets were placed in jeopardy. Davis discussed these plans briefly with Hughes over the telephone and Hughes approved.[33] The greatest obstacle was time. The lawsuit would have to be filed Monday and the directors capitulate on Tuesday if the plan was to work before the midnight expiration of Hughes's option.

Before returning to Las Vegas, Davis and Maheu called on Bez in his suite at the Thunderbolt. Physically exhausted and crushed by his inability to swing the deal, Bez broke down and cried, confessing his distressed opinion that another director and longtime friend had "betrayed him personally" by voting against the Hughes offer.[34] All was not lost, Davis assured him; stockholders might file lawsuits against the dissident directors.

Peter Maheu, Robert's son, picked the party up in a new Mercedes after they landed in Las Vegas and whisked them off to his father's house on the Desert Inn grounds for cocktails, dinner, and strategy sessions. That evening, Hughes called and spoke to Maheu about progress on the lawsuit. Davis in turn asked a Delaware lawyer who was accompanying him, George Tyler Coulson, if he would draft a complaint which could be filed in Wilmington on Monday. Coulson readily agreed.[35]

Arising at 4:30 the next morning in his suite at the Frontier, Coulson roughed out a draft along the lines discussed the previous day. Convinced that the complaint would "call the directors' bluff," Coulson showed it to Davis, who agreed.[36] Coulson then made contact with a Seattle lawyer and friend of Bez's, who was able to supply the names of Air West stockholders to serve as plaintiffs.

As Sunday wore on, feverish activity emanated from various command posts of the organization: the executive offices of Hughes Nevada Operations at the Frontier Hotel, Maheu's home, and, of course, Hughes's penthouse atop the Desert Inn. Couriers were dispatched to pick up and drop off legal materials from one end of the country to the other. As soon as Coulson's complaint was complete, he forwarded it to his law firm in Wilmington—Morris, Nichols, Arscht & Tunnell—to be put in final form. Davis had a copy delivered to an attorney in New York where he had decided to file another stockholders' lawsuit Monday to generate even more pressure on the dissident directors. Hughes's public-relations men were alerted to see that major news media got word of the stockholders' actions as soon as they were filed. Telegrams were readied to be sent to the opposing directors giving them specific details about the complaints and their possible liability. The Hughes camp even made plans to place anonymous telephone calls to opposing directors urging them to change their vote. By midnight Sunday, the Hughes organization was poised to strike what it hoped would be a fatal blow at the opposition that had nagged it for nearly five months. The next forty-eight hours would tell the tale.

Meanwhile, a delegation of opposing Air West directors headed by Converse and Joseph Martin, Jr., had flown to New York to meet with Northwest officials concerning that airline's bid for Air West. The Northwest proposal would have yielded roughly the same dollar amount per share as Hughes's $22 offer. Some directors considered Northwest's offer more attractive than Hughes's because Northwest would acquire Air West's stock but not its assets, as Hughes planned to do, and that would have meant special tax advantages to shareholders that would not be possible under Hughes's plan. On Monday morning, the dissident directors met with Northwest officials in Manhattan. The meeting went "smoothly," one director recalled, until a telephone call informed them of the filing of the stockholders' lawsuit in Delaware.[37]

From that moment, serious negotiations with Northwest ended. Acting like "frightened rabbits," as one director described them, the Air West directors began to make impossible demands, seeking a guarantee from Northwest to supply interim financial aid while awaiting CAB approval to acquire Air West, a practice specifically forbidden by CAB rules.[38] In the afternoon, they received word that another stockholders' lawsuit had been filed against them in New York. By four o'clock, when the Northwest meeting adjourned, even Edmund Converse, the most ardent Hughes opponent among the Air West directors, was shaken.

The next morning, pressure rose as the price of Air West's stock fell in a frenzy of trading. The directors, already jittery over the stockholder suits, now feared that investors were panicking because Hughes's offer had not been accepted. In truth, there was no panic—only the Hughes organization manipulating the stock market.

Three days earlier, Hank Greenspun, the publisher of the *Las Vegas Sun,* had called Maheu in San Francisco to learn the outcome of the Air West board meeting. While talking to Maheu, Greenspun said he heard someone else come on the line and tell him: "I think you better sell your stock."

Greenspun owned 15,000 shares of Air West. Because of noise at the other end and confusion in his own office, Greenspun said, it was not clear to him who was speaking, but he heard the voice say of the Hughes offer: "It looks like it isn't going to go through."

When Greenspun pointed out that he might lose a lot of money if he sold then and Hughes later acquired the carrier at $22, the voice reassured him:

"Well, you know that the man will make you whole. He wouldn't let you lose on it."[39]

Although the identity of the voice was uncertain, its authority was not and Greenspun had no reason to doubt "the man." He gave his broker orders to sell his entire Air West portfolio. The 15,000 shares were sold on Tuesday morning.

Similar guarantees were made to two other men, David Charnay and George Crockett. Like Greenspun, both had previously dealt with Hughes or his organization. Charnay was an independent Hollywood producer who had once produced a documentary on Hughes's life, only to sell the film to the mysterious recluse because Hughes did not want it aired. Hughes had known Crockett for years. A longtime Las Vegas businessman with interests ranging from real estate to aviation, Crockett performed many assignments for Hughes and was one of the few who could ring through to the penthouse.

On Tuesday, Charnay placed orders to sell 59,100 shares, of which 19,100 were sold. Crockett sold 12,000 shares. The sell orders of Greenspun, Charnay, and Crockett accounted for 92 percent of all trading in Air West's stock that

Tuesday morning. Not surprisingly, Air West's stock fell from 18 3/4 at closing Monday to 15 3/4 by noon the next day.[40]

When the Converse directors resumed negotiations with Northwest on Tuesday, there was little enthusiasm, especially after the demoralizing drop in Air West's stock. At 2:30 that afternoon, Converse called fellow director John Parker in Washington, D.C., and told him that the Northwest offer had "fallen through."[41] Parker, one of the opposing directors at the December 28 meeting, then called Nick Bez in Seattle to change his vote in favor of the Hughes offer. Bez immediately relayed the news to Maheu and Davis in Las Vegas, and one by one that afternoon five other dissident directors changed their votes. "Well, Howard," Maheu reported to the penthouse, "the opposition has capitulated. Chester and I are on our way to Seattle as soon as possible to have Air West execute the agreement."[42]

Only Nick Bez's signature on the purchase contract was required to complete the deal. But that signature had to be affixed before midnight. It was late afternoon. The flight from Las Vegas to Seattle took only two and a half hours. Savoring their victory, Maheu and Davis boarded a de Havilland 125, a private jet belonging to Hughes Nevada Operations, for the routine flight. As they neared Seattle, they learned that a severe snowstorm had crippled the area. The airport was closed. But not to Howard Hughes's men. Francis Fox, Hughes's director of aviation, who had arrived before the storm on a commercial jet from Los Angeles, came to the rescue. An airport manager by trade, Fox helped mobilize ground crews to clear a landing strip for the de Havilland, a rugged craft that could operate off unpaved runways. It was the only plane to land that night in Seattle. Shortly before midnight, Maheu and Davis arrived at Bez's apartment overlooking Shilshole Bay.

It was New Year's Eve, and with the signing of the purchase contract there was a genuine reason to celebrate. The Hughes party joined with a handful of Bez's friends to ring in the New Year. Maheu called Hughes to tell him the agreement had been signed and to encourage him to thank Bez personally.

"Do it now," Maheu urged. "Don't wait. Do it now."[43]

When Hughes failed to call, Maheu again urged the gesture.

"This guy would be the proudest man in the world if you would just say hello to him this evening. Howard, I have seen evidence of hero-worshipism before, but never the likes of which this man holds you in his esteem."[44]

Maheu reminded Hughes that the deal could never have been closed without Bez, who may have "60 or 90 more days to go. Howard, will you please reconsider and just say good night to this great guy?"[45]

At 12:15, to everyone's surprise, he did. For fifteen minutes, the old fisherman and the old aviator talked. It was a social conversation. Hughes thanked Bez for his support and aid, and then, becoming quite chatty, invited Bez to Las Vegas for a visit. Every Hughes executive in the room was flabbergasted by this outpouring of charm from the penthouse. When Bez finally put the phone down, he walked away "nine feet tall."[46]

With the signing of the purchase contract, there remained only one hurdle to the Air West takeover—CAB approval. The agency was required by law to pass on all airline mergers and acquisitions. After five months of trying to harness Air West's stubborn directors, the Hughes camp looked forward to the CAB proceedings almost with pleasure. Hughes had clout with the CAB and plenty of influential friends in Washington. James Juliana, the former CAB staff director, was still around to serve as liaison with the CAB. Claude Desautels, an associate of Democratic power Lawrence F. O'Brien, then a private public-relations consultant on a retainer from Hughes, was expected to generate pressure on Capitol Hill. And there was, of course, the sympathetic ear of Robert Murphy, the CAB vice-chairman. Murphy had supported Hughes in an earlier, even more controversial acquisition case. In 1962, he had cast a deciding vote on the five-member board enabling Hughes to acquire Northeast Airlines.* Murphy's friend Edward Morgan would be a leading member of the Hughes legal team in proceedings before the CAB.[47]

Also working in Hughes's favor with the CAB was Air West's financial condition. Unless someone rescued the airline it was likely to fold, and that was the one eventuality the CAB dreaded above all else. Clearly, Hughes was dealing from strength with the CAB. "The monkey's squarely on the board's back," Maheu told him, "and we should damn well leave it right there."[48]

Thus, on the eve of the CAB hearings, Hughes stood on the last step of a triumphant ascent. Yet he was unhappy, worrying that he could not "afford" Air West.[49] The losses now frightened him. They had reached $100,000 on some days, and while that was higher than before, it should have come as no surprise to him, given the quality of Air West's service. Indeed, the airline's finances had worked in Hughes's favor in the takeover. And Hughes had not helped matters by refusing to replace Bez. But he seemed to have forgotten all that as he whined to Maheu what a "lousy deal for me financially" Air West had become.[50]

Hughes did have substantial commitments. There were continuing losses from his Las Vegas operations and the Hughes Tool Company Aircraft Division, plus the prospect of a multimillion-dollar judgment in the TWA case. But these were not new. They predated Air West. Still, Hughes's financial anxieties were so strong that the day before Maheu was to leave for Washington and the CAB hearings he thought of pulling out of the deal. "I will give you my final conclusions concerning our acquisition of A.W. in the A.M.," he wrote Maheu shortly before midnight on January 14. "Most likely I will recommend going ahead. I just don't like being forced to do so."[51] But who was forcing him to go ahead? Certainly not Maheu, who had long been against it.

Still, complain though Hughes might, the acquisition went forward. Once

---

*Hughes owned controlling interest in Northeast only two and a half years, selling his holdings on July 30, 1965.

set in motion, a Hughes project tended to assume a life of its own. While Hughes wallowed in doubt, Maheu and Davis simply went on with the task of gaining CAB approval.

On January 17, 1969, Hughes and Air West filed a joint application with the CAB seeking approval of the purchase. Northwest Airlines and Western Airlines, which flew into many of the same sunbelt communities as Air West, speedily opposed it. This commercial opposition worried the Hughes camp less than the lengthy regulatory process in which the CAB would decide whether Hughes was "fit, willing, and able," as the Federal Aviation Act of 1958 put it, to own an airline.

That was no rhetorical question. Although the CAB had no knowledge of Hughes's mental state by 1969, it was well aware that his mismanagement of TWA in the late 1950s had nearly ruined the airline. And if that were not inducement enough for the board to proceed cautiously, there was a peculiarity in the Hughes application. Ordinarily, the agency requires voluminous reports from an applicant detailing how the airline would be financed, managed, and operated. But Hughes refused to spell out his plans for Air West. Other than that it would be a division of the Hughes Tool Company with "separate books and accounts," the Hughes application said nothing about the amount of money he would invest, the cities he intended to serve, or even the personnel who would manage the airline.[52]

Yet his arrogance drew no reprimands from the CAB. The board not only went along with Hughes's pathological love of secrecy, but bent over backward to accommodate him. When Western Airlines issued a subpoena for Hughes to testify at the proceeding, a CAB hearing examiner quashed it summarily. When Hughes asked that the tool company's financial reports be sealed from public scrutiny, the CAB complied. When Hughes's attorneys refused to provide the tool company's operating statistics to CAB staffers, a CAB hearing examiner did not press the point. The CAB, in fact, was curious about only one aspect of the transaction—why an "astute businessman" such as Howard Hughes would want to acquire a company that had lost $25 million in its first year?[53] Hughes's lawyers gave no answer to that question either.

Some essential information did have to be given to the CAB, such as the identity of Air West's operating head, and Chester Davis was nearly beside himself in Washington trying to get an answer out of Hughes in Las Vegas. It was a question that had persisted in the hearings. Davis was wary that Hughes's opponents might make capital of it. Finally, picking up a telephone at the Madison Hotel in Washington, Davis spoke to one of the penthouse aides and demanded a name. At last, one issued forth—that of Edward Nigro, the retired air force general who was Maheu's chief assistant. General Nigro's lack of commercial airline experience did not trouble the CAB.

Indeed, little seemed to trouble the CAB, and in the end the board gave Hughes almost everything he wanted. It ruled that the acquisition was "consistent with the public interest" and upheld a finding of the CAB hearing examiner that the amount Hughes intended to pay, $22 a share, "is fair and reasonable to all stockholders of Air West."[54] The CAB even awarded Hughes a federal subsidy amounting to as much as $10 million a year to finance air service into small towns—a move hotly opposed by Western, Northwest, and part of the CAB staff.

All had gone as Hughes hoped, with one exception. He had asked the CAB to designate the "Air West Division" of the Hughes Tool Company as the official corporate entity to operate Air West.[55] But the CAB said the law required that it name the tool company. Hughes did not like that prospect at all. If Hughes Tool were considered the carrier, it meant that his supersecret holding company would be exposed to scrutiny by the CAB, which routinely audits the affairs of airlines it regulates. The CAB pointed out that Hughes could avoid this problem by forming a subsidiary. So on October 23, 1969, Hughes established the Hughes Air Corporation in Delaware. The tool company would own 78 percent of the stock of Hughes Air and Hughes personally would own the rest. In December, the CAB approved the sale of Air West to the new Hughes subsidiary. The delay had been costly. Hughes had originally planned to take possession of the airline in November. But creating Hughes Air Corporation had forced him to postpone the closing date to March 31, 1970. During the four-and-a-half-month period, Air West lost several more million dollars.

The airline's losses once again plunged Hughes into depression. Financial aspects of the Air West deal were looking worse all the time. Hughes would be paying $90 million for an airline that recorded $25 million in losses its first year, and he would have to assume those losses. Worse, Hughes saw his financial outlook clouded by an event he could not have foreseen a year before—the downturn in the national economy. If he were forced to liquidate assets to raise cash for the Air West purchase and the TWA judgment, it would be at the worst possible time, when the economy was depressed.

To make the Air West deal more financially attractive for Hughes, someone in the organization or an ally on the Air West board came up with the idea of putting the net-worth clause of the purchase contract to a use that had not been envisioned by the company's stockholders when they approved the sale. In its simplest terms, the scheme called for Air West to feed back to Hughes, subtracting from his $90-million purchase price, an amount equal to the carrier's losses. At the time the concept was first discussed the losses totaled about $16 million.

When Maheu explained the proposal, Hughes was enthusiastic, calling it "the key to the entire situation."[56] He asked Maheu to call Davis and have him dictate to one of the penthouse aides a step-by-step "foolproof plan of action to accomplish consummation of the Air West purchase including the feedback of the 16+ million."[57] Davis opened talks to put the rebate plan into action, and on September 11 reported to the penthouse: "They [Air West management] recognize and accept the principle that the purchasing price is to be reduced by the operating losses prior to our takeover."[58]

Only Bob Maheu saw trouble ahead. Once again, he recommended to Hughes that they "bail out" and explained why:

I have very serious compunctions as to our position vis-a-vis the individual stockholders when they grasp the full realization that they will be paid considerably less than $22 per share. We must remember that at the stockholders meeting in December, 1968, only 51% of the outstanding shares were voted in favor of the acquisition, when they *believed* they would receive $22 per share. Howard, this may be a long way of telling you that in my humble opinion, the time has come to fish or cut bait. I truly believe that this is the most propitious time in which to indulge in *OPERATION EXTRICATE.*[59]

But Hughes felt he could not turn back now. If Air West was a loser, backing out would be worse. He would lose "standing" in Nevada, California, and "even in some degree in Washington."[60] When Maheu continued to urge him to drop the deal, Hughes answered:

Hughes periodically worried about "financial insecurity," as in this August 2, 1969, memorandum to Bob Maheu weighing the pros and cons of the Air West acquisition.

"Frankly, I was surprised by the extent to which your thinking seems to have progressed toward abortion of the Air West purchase. I understand fully the disadvantages of the Air West deal from the economic standpoint, but I am concerned about the general underlying attitude of people in this community toward everyone associated with me if the Air West company collapses."[61]

Early in 1970, Air West officials and Hughes's lieutenants met in Chester Davis's New York law office to work out the final details of the sale. In two day-long sessions, the question of Air West's worth was hotly debated. In preparation for the March 31 closing, Air West's accountants had prepared a balance sheet of the airline's assets and liabilities. This was a most important list since Hughes was buying not Air West's stock, but its assets. An Air West director recalled that Davis "loudly and clearly" told the airline's representatives that the figures "shown on the books of Air West were not acceptable and that Hughes Air Corporation would not 'pay for' certain of the assets shown on those books."[62] Haskins & Sells, the accounting firm that had long represented Hughes and his business interests, supported Davis's assertions.

Among the Air West assets dismissed out of hand by Davis were its route structure—generally considered a valuable asset by any airline—and its pilot training operation.[63] Davis also contended that the value of air frames, engines, and spare parts had been overestimated. By the time he finished subtracting what Hughes accountants considered all the nonassets and overcharges, Davis had come up with a net-worth figure about $20 million under the airline's own estimate. Davis was adamant. Unless Air West accepted the lower figure, Hughes would not go through with the sale.

It seemed obvious to Air West's directors, as later testimony indicated, that Davis was attempting to reduce even further the price Hughes would pay. Milton W. Odom, an Air West director from Seattle, who was one of the earliest supporters of the Hughes offer, figured that Davis's suggested revisions would reduce the overall purchase price from roughly $22 a share to about $10. He stepped into Davis's private office at one point during the meeting for a word with Hughes's chief lawyer.

"I can see that you are not going to go by the Air West statements, and that you have a certain figure in mind which you want to pay," Odom told Davis. "Why don't you tell us what it is?"

"No," Davis answered, "we're going to go strictly by the contract."[64]

Air West was cornered. Late in 1968, when it had flirted with Northwest, Air West still had bargaining power. By early 1970, burdened with debts, it had none. So its directors acceded to Hughes's demands, many, if not all, knowing that stockholders would receive only half, or less, of the money they expected.

But Hughes had also gotten boxed in by events. If he decided to abandon the acquisition—a move almost certain to plunge Air West into bankruptcy —he might make himself liable to a stockholders' lawsuit for breach of contract. If he did go through with the transaction, and shareholders received much less than they had been promised, he might also be sued. Neither course was inviting, but the momentum of nearly two years of negotiations pushed Hughes onward.

On April 3, 1970, the long Air West campaign drew to a close. On that day in San Francisco, Hughes formally made the purchase. A check for $89,398,091 was delivered to Air West. The airline placed $48 million of that in a special account to make up for the decline in its net worth and conveyed the account to Hughes as an asset at closing.[65] That left $41 million for Air West's stockholders. After contingency fees, only $33 million was distributed to them. The shareholders who had been lured into voting for the Hughes offer with the expectation of receiving $22 a share in the end received only $8.75.

Even so, there was no joy in the penthouse. Hughes no longer had the emotional or physical stamina for protracted negotiations. He still fretted over the deal and was ill at ease acknowledging that he had played any role in consummating it. His way of distancing himself was to blame everything on Maheu who, of course, had long been against the purchase. Hughes was innocence itself: "I did nothing really in the entire affair but follow your recommendation, step by step."[66] Only a man remote from reality could have made that statement. And yet Hughes's desire for a scapegoat foreshadowed a bitter truth: the Air West takeover would spark a legal battle that would outlast his lifetime.

Still, in 1970 Hughes had acquired Air West for what appeared to be a bargain-basement price. Ironically, during these same long months when he sought, in a sense, to take again to the air, he was also probing for the oldest of Hughes obsessions—wealth beneath the earth.

CHAPTER 17

GOLD FEVER

"COMSTOCK SHARES SHOWED MODERATE GAINS"

THE economic warnings were unmistakable: a steadily rising worldwide demand, a static supply, and government policies that favored both conditions. After three decades of monetary stability, the United States was running out of the two precious metals long used as the basis for American currency—gold and silver. The great gold and silver rush of 1967–68 was under way, and the United States and the rest of the free world were headed into the worst international monetary crunch since the Great Depression.

Through 1967 and into 1968, record quantities of gold and silver flowed out of the United States Treasury as speculators, hoarders, businessmen, and wary bankers inundated the government and money markets with buy orders for both metals. By March of 1968, the London gold market was in a frenzy. One-day sales totaled as much as $180 million—more than thirty-six times the average. When $1.1 billion more in gold left the Treasury, Congress rescinded its requirement that Federal Reserve notes be backed by gold. The price of the metal soared on international markets.

The surging gold and silver prices triggered a renewed interest in mining around the world. In London, gold-mining stocks more than doubled their 1967 lows. In Toronto, an index of thirteen gold-mining stocks rose nearly one hundred points. In Leadville, Colorado, there was talk of reopening silver mines that had been idle since the turn of the century. And in Las Vegas, Robert Maheu sent a one-paragraph memorandum to Howard Hughes:

Because of the gold situation and since we know where the proven gold deposits and reserves are in the State of Nevada, what do you think of the possibility of our moving expeditiously and tying them up forthwith.[1]

The response was swift:

This sounds good, why don't you find out specifically what we can tie up and upon what terms. However, why don't you let me know first from your own knowledge—before you make any inquiries. I would hate to attract somebody else to these gold properties before we are ready to move in any substantial degree.[2]

The gold fever that was sweeping the world had gripped the world's best-known recluse. There was a touch of irony to this. After more than half a century, the Hughes family had come full circle. Unable to discipline himself to a law career in Iowa, Hughes Sr. had set out in 1896 to seek a fortune "under the surface of the earth."[3] Two years of mining for low-grade silver in Colorado and two more years seeking zinc in what is now Oklahoma had been followed by a stint in lead mining near Joplin, Missouri. Although Hughes Sr. did not strike it rich as a miner, he came away with something as valuable as the mother lode—knowledge of drilling techniques which he later put to use in developing the Hughes drill bit. Now it was the son's turn.

Less than two weeks after Hughes's directive to Maheu, paperwork on his initial mining transaction was quietly begun. On March 27, 1968, two deeds to a string of mining properties were signed over to the Hughes Tool Company by their joint owners, Eldon L. (Jack) Cleveland and George Von Tobel. The sale price of $225,000 was a mere suggestion of what the future held.

Jack Cleveland, a collector of Jim Beam whisky bottles and ornamental mining rocks, was a promoter, stock dealer, and claim trader with three decades of experience in mining, and a millionaire in his own right. Cleveland's investments ranged from mining claims to California real estate to a Las Vegas casino. He bought and stored silver at the Chase Manhattan Bank in New York, and dabbled in stocks until the late 1960s when "he got disgruntled with the market and just quit."[4] More often than not, a large bundle of cash accompanied Cleveland wherever he went, at least five or ten thousand dollars which he carried "in his pocket, or in a zipper belt or zipper neck tie."[5]

Von Tobel was a former Republican state legislator, onetime president of both the Las Vegas and Nevada Junior Chambers of Commerce, and a member of a pioneering Las Vegas family. Although he was a member of the five-man Nevada Gaming Commission, the agency charged with issuing licenses and approving the sale of casinos, Von Tobel saw no conflict of interest in selling mines to Hughes while regulating Hughes's gambling operations. "It was a bona fide sale of a mining investment," he explained. "It has nothing to do with Hughes' interest in the future or in the past on gaming transactions."[6]

The Von Tobel and Cleveland claims were near the historic Comstock Lode at Virginia City, an area that from 1860 to 1880 was "the most important and productive mining camp in the world," yielding upward of $300 million worth of gold and silver.[7] Untouched by serious prospectors for fifty years, the Cleveland and Von Tobel claims carried names like the Fort Knox Placers, the Delaware Lode, the Red Jacket Lode, and the Santiago Lode.[8]

Five days went by from the time Cleveland and Von Tobel signed the deeds until their signatures were notarized. The date proved to be an omen for Hughes. It was April Fool's Day.

When the deeds were filed on April 3, 1968, at the Storey County Recorder's Office in the old courthouse at Virginia City, Howard Hughes's secret mining project was no longer a secret. An eight-column headline in the *Las Vegas Sun* announced "Hughes Buys N. Nevada Mines."[9] The *Reno Evening Gazette* noted that "Nevada mining officials have predicted a rebirth of the Comstock area because of rising gold and silver prices."[10] But it was left to the *Virginia City Territorial Enterprise,* a newspaper whose tradition of tongue-in-cheek prose traced back to Samuel L. Clemens, to place the Hughes purchase in perspective. Under the simple one-line, one-column headline "Vegan Buying Area Land," the newspaper reported:

Comstock shares showed moderate gains on Virginia City brokers boards on Thursday when it was learned that a Las Vegas businessman named Howard Hughes had, through his Hughes Tool Company, exercised options on 260 acres of land and four mining claims at the Lyon County end of American Flat, about 4.5 miles south of here. . . . When the *Enterprise* phoned Hughes' office on Thursday for further information, the girl said he was out for coffee. Since we were on deadline we couldn't await his return.[11]

In keeping with tradition, Hughes Tool Company officials declined to comment on their chief executive's latest undertaking, leaving Nevadans to guess Hughes's intentions. Even so, optimism bloomed in Virginia City. Gold and silver dug out of the Comstock had helped to finance the Civil War for the North, lifted California out of a severe depression, provided capital for the building of San Francisco, and seeded family fortunes for men like George Hearst, the father of newspaper publisher William Randolph Hearst. But little of the wealth had remained in Virginia City, and few of the people. Where once more than thirty thousand had lived in the 1800s, there was now a town of only two thousand people, many of them engaged in the tourist business. A revival of the mining industry would mean a revival of Virginia City.

There were, to be sure, skeptics. A state mine inspector questioned whether Hughes could ever profitably mine gold and silver claims. Other mining engineers doubted that "any commercially practical breakthrough in mining" could be applied in the area.[12] It was naturally assumed that the eccentric industrialist had a masterplan for reopening the state's long-abandoned gold and silver mines, a plan based on inside information and unique expertise not available to anyone else. That was the way Hughes did business. Everyone knew it.

Hughes had assigned full responsibility for securing gold and silver claims to John Herbert Meier, a thirty-four-year-old Long Island native and former life insurance company manager. A big, genial man who was six-foot three and weighed 205 pounds, Meier had an engaging manner and shared Maheu's facility for moving comfortably within political, business, and social circles. But he was an odd choice to head a multimillion-dollar mining program. Most recently he had worked in electronic data processing. His mining experience was nil and, moreover, Maheu had just recommended to Hughes that Meier be fired for continuing indiscretions, the latest being his premature release of information to the media about Hughes's mining plans. Instead, Hughes told Maheu not to fire "this bastard Meier,"[13] and two weeks later, Hughes, curiously, placed Meier in charge of mining.

Meier had come to Las Vegas on a strong recommendation from Bill Gay. Before Nevada, he had worked as a $17,500-a-year assistant in marketing management at Hughes Dynamics, an obscure subsidiary of the Hughes Tool Company in Los Angeles. Hughes Dynamics, which sold a computerized management-information service and later branched out into computerized credit reporting, had been "formed without [Hughes's] knowledge" by Gay.[14] When Hughes subsequently learned that $9.5 million of his money had flowed into the struggling company, he ordered it closed.* It was at that point, according to Maheu, that Gay took a keen interest in Meier's future welfare, asking Maheu if he could find a place for the young man on Maheu's payroll. Gay spoke highly of Meier's background, averring that he "had been employed by Hughes Aircraft, that he had two doctorates, that he [Gay] had brought him over to Hughes Dynamics."[15] There had been some suggestion, by Gay or one of his associates, that "Meier's wife was dying of cancer and that he was in dire financial straits."[16]

Maheu obliged, and Meier's first assignment was to evaluate investment opportunities for Maheu himself. Soon thereafter, Meier went to work full time persuading the Atomic Energy Commission to abandon its underground nuclear tests in Nevada. With the new job came a new title—"scientific adviser to the Hughes Tool Company," and frequent trips to Washington, where he met with government officials and politicians.[17] It was Meier's behavior on these trips that first provoked Maheu's displeasure. Wherever he went, it seemed, Meier regaled politicians and even fellow Hughes employees with stories about his intimate relationship with his boss. When he described himself as the "right-hand man" of Howard Hughes, everyone was impressed.[18] Not many visitors to Washington could tell of personal experiences with Hughes.

In an organization where the only constant was secrecy, no executive could be sure with whom Hughes was, or was not, meeting or talking. It was safest to assume that anyone who claimed to have had lunch with Hughes really had—or at the very least that he had had, say, a telephone conversation and was embroidering it. After all, what other Hughes lieutenant would question the assertion and thereby admit that he himself was not so favored in the

---

*Robert Maheu has testified that Hughes learned about the existence of Hughes Dynamics quite by accident. The company was making arrangements to share the top floor of a Los Angeles office building with a fashionable restaurant. "Jean [Peters] had gone there for lunch" one day, Maheu said, and the maitre d' or one of the captains "happened to mention how pleased they were . . . that her husband was going to occupy the balance of the top floor, whereupon she went home and told him about it and he blew his top. . . . That is what he told me."

Desert Inn penthouse? Least of all Maheu, who never once met his employer.

Meier's stories, however, eventually proved embarrassing to Maheu. After Nixon entered the White House, Maheu, working through his own political channels, secured a promise that the president would either call Hughes or send Secretary of State Henry A. Kissinger to meet with Hughes to explain the administration's position on underground testing. But then he was thwarted by Hughes's reclusiveness. Despite the urgency of the subject, Hughes was not prepared to deal with any strangers, whether in person or on the telephone, whether the president or the secretary of state. So Maheu could not follow through on the White House promise. But with Meier running around Washington recounting tales of his luncheons with "the old man," Maheu found "it very difficult for us to explain to Dr. Kissinger and the President of the United States that they could not talk to Mr. Hughes."[19]

Meier, of course, had never lunched with Hughes. He had never met Hughes. He had never talked with Hughes on the telephone. All his reports to Hughes were channeled through Maheu or one of the five aides in the Desert Inn penthouse. Finally, "Dr. Meier," as he had been known at Hughes Dynamics, had apparently never earned one doctorate, let alone two. According to a loan application Meier submitted to a bank, he had a high school diploma and some technical training in the United States Army. Nonetheless, Meier began 1968 as the Hughes organization's ambassador without portfolio to Nevada's mining towns, seeking out gold and silver claims.

A PARADE OF PROSPECTORS

The Virginia City properties were just the beginning. Two weeks after the quarter-million-dollar purchase of the Comstock claims, Maheu forwarded a memorandum to Hughes touting another acquisition: "We obtained an option from Mr. and Mrs. Denny Hill last month on 240 acres of mining property including seven patented mines for $240,000. The estimated value of this property is $2 million. It is primarily composed of zinc, lead and silver at Goodsprings in Clark County. . . ."[20]

To convince Hughes of the true value of the Hill claims, if such convincing was necessary, Maheu noted that two wealthy Texans, the Murchison brothers (John Dabney and Clinton William, Jr., whose fortunes also flowed out of their father's oil business) were ready to pounce on the property if Hughes did not exercise his option. "The man representing the Murchison interests from Texas is in town waiting to give them a firm offer if we turn this down," Maheu reported. "The Murchison people do not know that we have an option on this property."[21]

Three months later, on July 18, 1968, Maheu sent along to the Desert Inn command post two more memoranda enthusiastically summarizing the potential of more mining properties on offer to Hughes: "Approximately $150 million worth of silver, lead, zinc, gold and copper can be produced from mining properties available to us in Nevada. Many of these are eligible for exploratory funds from the federal government. . . . John Meier has estimated the approximate net profit after development would be $50 million. We can acquire this group of diversified mining properties for $2.5 million."[22]

And further, Maheu reported, "there are 900 acres of mining land available in Mineral County, Nevada, near Mina. . . . The gross value of ore according to engineering reports is anywhere from $3 million to $30 million worth of gold and silver. This property is available for $276,500, which includes title to the land plus water rights. . . ."[23]

Word of Hughes's approval was flashed from the penthouse. On August 26, the Hughes Tool Company bought eleven claims in Clark County from Mr. and Mrs. Dennis C. Hill at a cost of $240,000, and on October 16, thirty-six claims in Mineral County from a company called Basic Industries, Inc. The sale price was $276,500.

That was only the beginning. From August until the end of the year, Hughes acquired mining claims with the same facility that he acquired movie starlets when he was in Hollywood. In August, Hughes gave Jack Cleveland $146,000 for five claims in Churchill County. In October, a big month, he paid $35,000 to Atlas International for two claims in Clark County, $340,000 to Henry Eddy for thirteen claims in Mineral County, $220,000 to the Arivaca Mining Company for six claims in Mineral County, $250,000 to Leonard F. and Josephine Traynor for sixty claims in Nye County, and $240,000 to Harry Vonderheide for four claims in Lyon County.

In November, $220,000 went to Arivaca Mining Company for nine claims in Esmeralda County, $262,000 to Mr. and Mrs. Dennis Hill for five claims in Nye County, and $375,000 to Clarence Hall for four claims in Humboldt County. In December, a handsome $752,000 was paid to the same Clarence Hall for fifteen claims in Nye County.

Nevada had seen nothing like it in a hundred years. By spreading more money around the state than had been spent by any single individual since the great gold and silver rushes of the nineteenth century, Hughes had collected nearly two hundred claims and hundreds of acres of land at a cost of about $4 million. The claims were scattered across the 110,540 square miles of Nevada, and if, when viewed on a map, the Hughes acquisitions appeared to follow no order, no masterplan, that is because there was none. But there was a master plan of a different sort at work in the claims that John Meier selected for Howard Hughes to purchase.

There were, for example, the mining claims owned by Mr. and Mrs. Dennis Hill, claims that Meier had advised Maheu that Hughes should buy. Hill, a lifelong resident of Nevada, happened to be well acquainted with Jack Cleveland, the wily prospector who sold the first Virginia City properties to Hughes. In fact, Hill and Cleveland had engaged in joint business ventures, including ownership of mining claims, for some three decades. It was Cleveland who suggested to Hill that he could arrange for Hughes to buy the Hill claims. In return, though, Cleveland insisted that a substantial percentage of the sale price be paid to him. When Hill sold his properties for the $240,000 recommended by Maheu, he retained only $55,000. After paying federal income taxes, he turned over the balance to Cleveland, who had suggested that Hill report the entire proceeds of the transaction on Hill's federal income-tax return. This would allow Cleveland to receive his share of the Hughes money without reporting it on his own tax return.

Hill, in turn, was a lifelong friend of Harry Vonderheide, and they, too, had done business together since the Second World War. One of those ventures had ended badly, and as a result, Vonderheide owed Hill somewhere between $35,000 and $50,000. The precise amount was a matter of dispute between the two men. Sensing an opportunity to recover at least a part of his loss, Hill—who knew that Vonderheide also owned some mining properties—passed the information along to Cleveland. In turn, Cleveland, arranged with Meier for Hughes to buy Vonderheide's claims for $240,000. Out of the $240,000, Vonderheide received $55,000, Hill picked up $20,000 for his services as an intermediary, and the rest of the money went to Cleveland.

Bennie Ball was yet another Hill acquaintance who owned mining claims. Once again acting as the middleman, following instructions from Cleveland, Hill informed Ball that if he sold the mining properties both men could make $25,000. Ball immediately suggested that he and Hill should go into the deal as partners. Hill demurred. Ball recalled: "I asked him [Hill], 'Why don't we go in partners on this?' and he said that he didn't care to have his name appear on it, that he had been on other mining ventures at that time, and didn't want his name on the sale."[24] When the transaction was completed on February 9, 1969, Hill and Ball each received $10,000 instead of the $25,000 originally mentioned, and the rest of the $180,000 went to Cleveland. Hill characterized the money he received in the various Hughes mining deals like this: "Well, I would get a piece of it, of any of them [mining properties] that were sold . . . kind of like a commission."[25]

Leonard Traynor, a deputy state mine inspector, was another close friend of Cleveland and an acquaintance of Hill. Cleveland arranged for Traynor to sell Hughes sixty mining claims for $250,000. It is unclear how much, if any, of Traynor's $250,000 found its way back to Cleveland. Both men have since died. But on November 4, 1968, Traynor and Dennis Hill opened a joint savings account at the First National Bank in Las Vegas and deposited a cashier's check for $77,539. The check represented part of the proceeds from the sale of Traynor's claims to Hughes.

Then there were the thirty-six mining properties in Mineral County that Hughes purchased on Maheu's recommendation for $276,500 from Basic Industries, Inc. According to a stock-ownership certificate for Basic Industries, dated February 21, 1968, "all of the issued and outstanding stock" of the company was owned by Jack Cleveland.[26]

As for the two claims that Hughes bought for $35,000 from the Atlas International Corporation, the president of the company and a major stockholder was Hill. Another substantial stockholder was Cleveland.

All in all, 1968 was a good year for prospector Cleveland. Of the nearly $4 million paid by Howard Hughes for one series of mining properties, Cleveland owned, had an interest in, or received "commissions" on the sale of more than half. And 1969 started out every bit as well.

Cleveland and his company, Basic Industries, now became something more than just sellers of gold and silver mines. Cleveland, in fact, was serving as a mining consultant to John Meier, who was serving as a mining consultant to Hughes. There was even talk that Basic Industries would act as a managing agent for Hughes's growing inventory of claims. During May and June of 1969, Cleveland's company established an office in the central Nevada mining town of Tonopah and collected $99,186.33 more from Hughes for miscellaneous services.

By this time, Basic Industries had taken on a new employee and stockholder, John Herbert Meier.

Mrs. Jean Beckers, who worked as Cleveland's private secretary in 1968 and part of 1969, was unable to remember precisely how much Cleveland and his company paid Meier. But she did recall that Meier was paid by check. Sometimes the checks were drawn on an account in a northern Nevada bank, and sometimes Mrs. Beckers wrote the checks at Cleveland's office in Las Vegas. Her memory was hazy on amounts, although she "would guess they would be more in the thousands than in the hundreds."[27]

And what services was Meier performing for Basic Industries in exchange for the payments?

"I really don't know what you would call his services," mused Mrs. Beckers. "I really don't know."[28]

Whatever his services, "Dr. Meier" was being paid by Hughes to buy mining properties at the same time he was being paid by a company that was selling mining properties to Hughes.

A PIG IN A POKE?

As 1968 gave way to 1969, Meier continued to press for the acquisition of additional mining claims. On January 9, 1969, he put together a three-page report for Maheu outlining proposals to develop Hughes's properties:

Hughes Nevada Operations has now acquired approximately one-half of the area of Tonopah mining, some in Nye County and some in Esmeralda. This consists of approximately 80 percent of the known silver reserves in this area.

I am recommending the establishment of an exploration headquarters for a milling facility to mill on a custom basis and for a metallurgical testing program. This would include a modern assay office. . . . This program would be a preliminary to a larger milling facility established in the center of the known reserves as determined by the exploration program. . . .[29]

The one-year price tag on the milling operation was $950,000, but there were complications. Remembering Hughes's pathological concern about federal income taxes, Meier pointed out,

One of the prime advantages of mining for silver is that the mined silver can be stored without having to pay income tax on it as a profit. Continuous mining expenses can be incurred and until the silver is actually disposed of, no credit need be taken for the silver mined. It should be stored in the mines. Thus a considerable loss can be sustained prior to having to pay income taxes on the silver mined.[30]

And last, but not least, the Hughes mining chief proposed that "during 1969 we acquire additional mining properties, after we have carefully evaluated them, as we have done in the past four months."[31]

By now, there seemed no need to wait for an answer from either Maheu or Hughes. In the time before and after the report to Maheu, Meier continued to negotiate for more gold and silver mines. In one of those transactions, Traynor, the deputy state mine inspector, sold seven more claims to Hughes for $200,000. The sale was noteworthy for two reasons: first, deeds filed in the Virginia City courthouse showed that Traynor had bought the claims just one day before he sold them; second, the claims were situated on rocky sagebrush land surrounding the old Occidental Mine outside Virginia City. The Occidental was one of those mines which even during the great gold rush of 1860–1880 was most unprofitable. Miners and investors had poured a lot more money into it than they had taken out.

Once again, the natives speculated as to Hughes's plan. One perplexed Storey County official observed, "Old timers here can't figure out what the deal is. There's other property might be more productive he could've gotten."[32] When Traynor was asked whether he had sold any other properties to Las Vegas's biggest gambler, he declined to discuss the matter, but said he saw no conflict between his position as a state mine inspector responsible for enforcing Nevada mining laws and his position as a private investor selling mines to Hughes. "I wanted to make some money for myself and help mining in the state," Traynor said. "I read up on the history of Virginia City and checked out the mine some time back. Hughes might do some good for mining in this state. They are a good legitimate operation. Look what they did for gambling. . . . Hughes might be the best thing this state has ever had for mining."[33]

Traynor also took exception to the criticism leveled at Hughes by some miners who contended that he could not be serious about mining because of the scattered location of his claims and who charged that his free spending was driving up prices on all properties. These people, said Traynor, "can't see the forest for the trees. The Hughes people are serious about this. They are not just playing around. They didn't just buy a pig in a poke. They studied this."[34]

Jack Cleveland, who had already sold Hughes more than $1 million in mining properties, was equally enthusiastic. "The theory is that a major part of the silver is still there in those mines," Cleveland maintained. "We have 400–500 percent better methods of mining than they had in the boom days of those mines. The only advantage they had was cheaper labor."³⁵

For one who once said too much, Meier now said very little; he just continued to buy claims. In January, Cleveland's Basic Industries sold sixty-eight claims in Churchill County to Hughes for $340,000; Dennis Hill sold four more claims in Esmeralda County for $280,000; and Hill and Cleveland's Atlas International sold twelve claims in Nye County for $120,000. Maheu later maintained that all the mining transactions were handled exclusively by Meier. The payments for all the claims were made directly from the executive offices of the Hughes Tool Company in Houston, after authorization was received from one of the penthouse aides.

After merrily spending $1 million more of Hughes's money without having received a response to his January 9 memorandum, Meier sent along a second memorandum, labeled a "Mining Status Report." Alluding to the intense rivalry for choice mining properties, he confided to Maheu:

"We have assiduously cultivated [an official] of the Department of the Interior on trips to Washington on other matters. He has supplied to us the advance sheets on new mining possibilities long before they have been released to the general public. On the basis of these specific studies we have been able to obtain choice mining properties. We have moved quickly but with the very best advice on these matters."³⁶

Maheu was either impressed by Meier's presentation or simply was not taking any chances. On February 5, he submitted a report to the Desert Inn penthouse advising Hughes that "we still have a few more options outstanding that we are going to close within the next few days. Under the properties we have bought there is an estimated $200 million worth of silver and gold at present prices."³⁷ Repeating in an abbreviated version the information Meier had given to him, Maheu focused on the potential for avoiding federal income taxes by mining and then holding the processed gold and silver. Without mentioning Meier by name, Maheu concluded that "our expert mining consultants recommend that we budget $950,000 on an exploration, evaluation, drilling and comprehensive assay program. At the same time we will establish a custom mill. . . ."³⁸

The command post apparently did not hesitate. Maheu and Meier were authorized to proceed with the mining program. But even as Hughes was spending millions in a mining venture that had not returned a single penny, and that gave no indication it would ever do so, he was deeply concerned about his personal finances. In a handwritten memorandum to Maheu dated February 12, 1969, he complained about the seemingly endless flow of cash from his bank accounts:

"I don't hold you responsible for all of the expenditures and losses we have encountered since coming here [Nevada]. Cook is responsible for the helicopter losses, and I share with you the responsibility for the Las Vegas expenditures. However, that does not make the financial horizon any brighter. I am concerned about Air West because I don't think I can afford this acquisition at this time."³⁹

Two days before Hughes wrote those words, Meier had completed the purchase of nearly $1 million in mining properties in two separate deals. The sellers were both familiar figures. Jack Cleveland's Basic Industries received $490,000 for nineteen claims in Nye County and Clarence Hall received $430,000 for seventeen claims in White Pine County.

The news media were intrigued more than ever by Hughes's plans. In a story about his Nevada mining operation, the *Los Angeles Times* reported:

One Hughes aide, who declined to be identified, said plans are underway to reopen many of the mines, using a new mining process developed by the Hughes–Nevada Operations.

No timetable on the reopenings was given and Hughes aides refused to give the details of the new process. They said, however, that it involved new methods of finding ore bodies, new methods of mining and of crushing and separating worthless minerals from valuable metals, and new cost-saving methods of making finished products at the mines.[40]

The anonymous aide was vague about the "new mining process developed by the Hughes–Nevada Operations," but the newspaper noted that "there is talk about atomic blasting, laser-beam mining, and computerized systems."[41]

It was that kind of talk that conjured up visions of a new Tonopah, Nevada, where Hughes had pulled together a substantial collection of gold and silver properties. Tonopah, like Virginia City, was once a miner's Mecca. Legend had it that Jim Butler, a forty-five-year-old prospector, was wandering about the desert in the spring of 1900, drifting from water hole to water hole, when his burro ambled off toward one of the six-thousand-foot peaks on the southern end of the San Antonio range. While seeking the animal, Butler noticed some outcroppings on the mountain. He took a few samples, acquired a partner to finance the assaying, and shipped the rocks off to Austin, the county seat.

The rocks contained high-grade silver, and in the boom that followed, Tonopah was founded. From 1900 to about 1930 a hundred miles of mining tunnels were carved out beneath the town and in the surrounding mountains. The mines produced $150-million worth of silver and other precious metals, and Tonopah came to be known as the Silver Queen of the West. With the onset of the Depression, however, the mines were shut down and the miners and the townspeople drifted away. By 1969, Tonopah's population was seventeen hundred, the town little more than a rest stop along the 450 miles from Las Vegas to Reno. The mountains around the town were a graveyard of weathered head frames, abandoned mine buildings, and the skeletal remains of mills.

But when Howard Hughes's money began arriving in Tonopah, it brought the hope of instant renewal. Hughes, after all, was no stranger. Tonopah had been the site of his marriage to Jean Peters. At the Mizpah Hotel, one of Tonopah's genuine landmarks—the saloon opened in 1901 and rooms were added two years later to make it a hotel—local citizens gathered to discuss

Hughes and the future. Pat Naylor, a waitress, reflected an optimism tempered by experience:

I've seen this town when you had to fight your way to cross the street. I've seen it when you could throw a ball down the street and never hit a dog, let alone a human. People have come through here off and on through the years talking about opening the mines. But nothing has ever come of it. This time I don't know. With a man like Howard Hughes—this could be the brass ring.[42]

Others were more certain of the brass ring. Like Traynor, the deputy state mine inspector who sold claims to Hughes, who also lived in Tonopah: "This is one of the biggest things to happen to this state in its history. It sure as hell will give this part of the country a boost—improve it 500 percent."[43]

The belief in the rebirth of Tonopah was so strong among some people that in the weeks preceding Hughes's actual purchase of the claims, residents who knew about the negotiations kept it to themselves, fearing that if word leaked out, prices would rise steeply and Hughes would pull out. Instead, the pace of purchasing quickened.

It was a peculiar parade of mining entrepreneurs that "Dr. Meier" led across Nevada and even parts of California, marching them up to bank windows to exchange the Hughes millions for their titles to gold and silver believed buried in the deserts and mountains of the two states. There was, for example, the Arivaca Mining Corporation, an Arizona company established by Thomas J. Garrity, a 1954 Yale Law School graduate and onetime attorney in the New York City law firm of Donovan, Leisure, Newton & Irvine. When it came to adding up the dollar value of minerals mined by Arivaca, the company was less than a spectacular success. From the time it was organized in 1963 until 1970, Arivaca spent $334,829 "in exploration for lead, zinc, silver, and copper without developing commercially mineable ore bodies."[44] In 1968, Arivaca began negotiations to secure a lease on thirty-one copper claims, known as the Courtland property, in Cochise County, Arizona.

On August 27 that year, Arivaca awarded 20,000 shares of stock in the company to one J. E. Cravotta as a "finder's fee" for the Courtland claims.[45] John Meier's wife was named Jennie Elizabeth Cravotta. In October and November of 1968, two months after J. E. Cravotta received 20,000 shares of stock in Arivaca Mining Corporation, Arivaca sold fifteen mining properties in Mineral and Esmeralda Counties, Nevada, to Howard Hughes, for $440,-000. By the spring of 1970, stock in Arivaca was trading at $5 a share.

Then there was the Georgetown Research and Development Corporation, which maintained an office in a Washington, D.C., apartment building. The company was formed by Thomas E. Murray, Jr., whose father was a member of the Atomic Energy Commission from 1950 to 1957 and later served as a consultant to the Joint Congressional Committee on Atomic Energy. Meier placed the younger Murray on the Hughes payroll as a $3,000-a-month consultant, and in April of 1969 Georgetown Research and Development Corporation sold six mining properties to Hughes for $250,000. The claims were in

Mono County, California, along the California–Nevada border. Later, Murray and Meier went into business together, setting up a motion-picture company called Meier–Murray Productions.

There was Alan E. Jarlson, a Las Vegas newsman, who was first approached by Meier and later by both Meier and Cleveland and invited to enter the mining business. Jarlson agreed, and in December of 1968 he acquired an option to buy certain mining properties. Two months later the properties were transferred to Jarlson, although he still had no financial interest in them. Then late in February of 1969, Jarlson sold the properties to Howard Hughes for $243,000. Jarlson received a check from the Nevada Title Guaranty Company for $85,895.17. Where the rest of the money went is unclear, but later Jarlson, acting on "instructions from John H. Meier, delivered to Eldon L. Cleveland the sum of $45,000 in currency."[46]

Such was the way of the mining business of Howard Hughes. But if Hughes and his staff showed little concern about the way Meier was parceling out the Hughes millions, someone else was very concerned about John Meier. That someone was the president of the United States.

THE PRESIDENT'S BROTHER

Shortly after Meier went to work for the Hughes organization in Nevada, he began to cultivate an association with Francis Donald Nixon, the younger brother of President Richard M. Nixon. It was Donald Nixon who had obtained a $205,000 loan from Hughes back in 1956 in an unsuccessful effort to save one of his failing businesses. The loan, never repaid, became a large political liability for Richard Nixon when it was disclosed during the 1960 presidential campaign. Eight years later, with Nixon finally in the White House, the president, his aides and friends all were uneasy about the possibility of another embarrassing Hughes–Nixon family relationship. It was not that anyone questioned the integrity of Donald Nixon. Rather, it was, as Charles G. (Bebe) Rebozo, the Florida banker who was the president's friend and confidant, expressed it:

"I don't think Don Nixon is dishonest; I think he's very naive. And I was concerned, again, about the possibility of some more embarrassment, such as he had showered on the president in 1960 and 1962. . . . Many families have relatives they would like to keep in the closet for awhile now and then, but I'm not saying—I don't mean to say this derogatorily about Don, because I want to repeat, I really just feel that he's overly endowed with naivete."[47]

John Meier was not the only person connected with the Hughes organization who had developed a fondness for the president's brother. So too had Meier's personal mining consultant, Jack Cleveland. The three men sometimes exchanged telephone calls and met in Nevada and California to review prospective business ventures. Cleveland once invested in some real estate for himself and Donald Nixon, as the president's brother recalled:

Jack Cleveland, I have known him for many years, and in discussing with him I often mentioned to him—he was telling me about all the properties he was buying out there in Nevada. He was going in the farming business. He was going to raise four crops of alfalfa a year on this Nevada property, and he said that there are some real good buys out there.

And he says, "Don, you ought to buy a piece of one of these properties out there with me."

And I said, "Well," I says, "I haven't got any money to buy property with." And I said, "If you come across a real good buy, why just let me know and I will think about it." But I said, "It has to be nothing over $5,000 as far as my investment is concerned.". . .

The guy went ahead and bought this property without me even seeing the property, told me, "Don, you own a half interest in a 300-acre piece of property out in Nevada."

And that is how it came about. Then I told him, "Well, Jack, goddam it, I don't have $5,000 right now."

He said, "Well, we will work out something on this." He says, "You can pay me when you have the five later on or work it out in some way."[48]

Then there were Donald Nixon's efforts to secure financing for a new Cleveland-backed company called Separation and Recovery Systems, Inc., which had developed a process to separate oil and water. The president's brother was to receive 25,000 shares of stock in the company if he could raise the money needed to get it started. Donald Nixon, whose efforts to market Nixonburgers a decade earlier had ended in insolvency, offered this accounting of his duties:

My responsibility was to try to find them a buyer, an investor that would—or say a big daddy here with the money to come in here to take over this company and give it performance. . . . I don't mind telling you I took this to Mr. [Aristotle] Onassis, and Mr. Onassis made them an over $3 million [offer]. . . . They turned it down.[49]

As for Donald Nixon's association with Meier, two weeks after Richard Nixon won the 1968 presidential election, Meier and his wife were on their way to Washington with Donald Nixon and his wife for a meeting with the president-elect, followed by a New York meeting with the other Nixon brother, Edward C., "for purposes of laying out suggested programs with the Nixon administration."[50]

By January of 1969, stories like this were appearing in newspapers:

John H. Meier, executive aide, Hughes–Nevada Operations, met recently in New York with President-elect Richard Nixon, Secretary of Interior-designate Walter J. Hickel, and the Task Force on Resources and Environment, headed by Russell Train, president of the Conservation Foundation. . . .

Also attending the top-level session were Dr. Lee Dubridge, Nixon scientific adviser, and Dr. John W. Tukey, chairman of President Johnson's Environmental Pollution Panel.

"After meeting with members of this distinguished committee—all of whom are concerned about preserving the quality of our natural environment from continued pollution—I am confident that conservation of our natural resources as well as their profitable development will be a major goal for the future good of America," said Meier.[51]

By the spring of 1969 the president was concerned about his brother's blooming relationship with Meier. He asked his friend Bebe Rebozo to use his influence with the Hughes organization to put an end to Meier's association with Donald Nixon. Rebozo promptly called an old personal friend, Richard G. Danner, a former FBI agent who was managing director of Hughes's Frontier Hotel in Las Vegas.

"Mr. Rebozo called me and told me that it had come to the administration's attention that Donald Nixon was spending quite a bit of time in Nevada with John Meier," Danner recalled.[52] "He [Rebozo] . . . wanted to know first of all what he was doing, if I knew what connection he had with any of the Hughes organizations. They felt it was bad judgment, it could lead to bad consequences, both from the administration's standpoint, and from our standpoint, being the Hughes standpoint."[53]

Danner took up the matter with his boss, Major General Edward H. Nigro, and together they questioned Meier about his association with the president's brother. "Meier at the time assured us it was a personal friendship," Danner recalled. "He visited Donald Nixon's home, and vice versa. They were not involved in any business deals. Don Nixon had his own interests in Nevada and Utah, which necessitated his visiting the state. When he came up, he would usually call on Meier, and that was the extent of it."[54] Both Danner and Nigro warned Meier about doing business with Donald Nixon. At the same time, Robert Maheu assigned Dean W. Elson, another FBI agent who had joined the Hughes organization after retiring from the bureau, to keep an eye on Meier and generally supervise the mining project.

Still, the worried president took additional measures. Herbert W. Kalmbach, the president's personal attorney and a Newport Beach, California, neighbor of Donald Nixon, began dropping by Donald's home to discuss his investments and his recurring money problems and tax troubles. After each meeting, Kalmbach reported back to H. R. Haldeman, the White House chief of staff, and John D. Ehrlichman, the assistant to the president for domestic affairs. Both Haldeman and Ehrlichman sought to separate Donald Nixon and John Meier. But Donald Nixon, who was then an executive in the food-service division of the Ogden Corporation, had his own reasons for cultivating Meier —he was trying to get the food concession at the Hughes Aircraft Company plants. He put it this way:

"Keep this in mind, I am still working for a company who is still pursuing the business of Hughes Aircraft Company see, the food service business. That is the business we were in. And I am not about to, you know, slap John Meier down when he is No. 2 man with Hughes."[55]

Although Hughes executives had promised Rebozo that Meier would break off his relationship with Donald Nixon, and Rebozo, Kalmbach, Ehr-

Left:
F. Donald Nixon, the president's brother, whose budding relationship with Meier created alarm at the White House.
United Press International

Right:
John H. Meier, who oversaw the acquisition of millions of dollars in worthless mining claims for Hughes and later fled to Canada.
United Press International

lichman, and Haldeman were all watching over the president's fifty-five-year-old brother, Richard Nixon took one last precaution: He ordered government agents to place a twenty-four-hour-a-day wiretap on his brother's telephones. The wiretap was installed on June 1, 1969, discontinued on June 19, and reinstituted on June 26. According to logs maintained by government agents, Donald Nixon called Meier on July 6, and agents prepared this summary of the conversation:

On July 6, 1969, subject was in touch with Meier. At this time it was learned that Jack Cleveland might also be involved in this deal. Meier indicated to the subject that he would be at the Orange County Airport at 11 A.M. on Tuesday, July 8, 1969. The subject suggested that Jack Cleveland and Carl Lans could pick Meier up at the airport and that they could then go to San Diego. The subject indicated that he did not want to go. Meier said that this would only complicate things and that things were already complicated enough. He indicated that the subject should meet him. Meier said that he would not even be using his own name on the flight from Las Vegas.[56]

When the president's brother arrived at the Orange County Airport to greet Meier on July 8, government agents were on hand secretly photographing the meeting. The information was quickly passed to the White House, which notified Rebozo, who in turn conveyed the White House displeasure to Maheu. Once again, Maheu asked Hughes for permission to fire Meier, and once again word shot back from one of the aides in the Desert Inn penthouse "that Meier should not be fired under any circumstances."[57]

Whatever the reason, it was clear that Hughes, or someone in the Desert Inn command post acting on Hughes's behalf—for not every message got through to Hughes—was a firm believer in Meier. By now, the White House was concerned with more than John Meier's association with Donald Nixon. Meier had brought a third party into the relationship, one "Tony," who was mentioned during the tape-recorded telephone conversation Meier had with Donald Nixon on July 6.

"Tony" was Anthony G. Hatsis, a Salt Lake City businessman, owner of a wholesale liquor distributorship, operator of mining companies, friend to politicians and judges, and as described in a confidential report circulating among high-level government officials—and made public during Senate Watergate hearings—an "unsavory character."[58]

Despite the White House's concern, the president's brother was soon flying off to Europe and South America with Meier and Hatsis. On a trip to Geneva, Donald Nixon was impressed by the Meier–Hatsis bankroll, a stack of $100 bills about an inch and a half thick which "never seemed to go any lower than that all the time they were over there."[59] The president's brother was along with Meier and Hatsis because "I was supposed to have met a couple of gentlemen who had a lot of money to invest in hotels. But I never met anyone."[60] Meier "spent most of his time, a great deal of his time, in fact, away from us. . . . In fact, I spent more time relaxing by myself, and these guys were on the go. They had some business to take care of."[61]

Donald Nixon was never quite sure who paid for the stay in Switzerland, but he believed that it was Hatsis. "It was charged to some travel service in Utah. So I surmised it must have . . . come from him, and I thought it was John Meier who was supposed to have been picking up the tab. . . . I will say this for John Meier, that fellow had a lot of money."[62]

On another occasion, Meier, Hatsis, and Donald Nixon visited the Dominican Republic. Nixon went looking for oceanfront property on which to build an apartment complex. Meier and Hatsis went in search of mining concessions. An agreeable President Joaquin Balaguer received the trio warmly. Like his American visitors, Balaguer had a special interest: he hoped to persuade the United States to increase its sugar quota for the Dominican Republic, and being nice to the brother of the president of the United States ought not to hurt his cause. Meier and Hatsis eventually got their mining concessions, while Donald Nixon abandoned his apartment project.

THE STING

Hatsis and Meier had only recently become friends, having met in 1968 when Hatsis was vacationing at Hughes's Sands Hotel in Las Vegas. On learning that the Salt Lake City visitor also was in the mining business, Meier suggested that Hatsis prepare a brief summary of his mining interests. The Hughes organization, Meier explained, was still in the market for gold and silver mines. Hatsis was president of the Toledo Mining Company in Salt Lake City, which had been formed in July of 1968 by the merger of West Toledo Mines Company and the American Mining Company, two other companies in which Hatsis had an interest.*

Hatsis delivered the mining information requested by Meier in August of 1968, and sometime thereafter the two talked by telephone. An ebullient Meier, saying that he had discussed Hatsis and his Toledo Mining Company "with Howard Hughes personally," reported that Hughes not only was interested but was "greatly impressed with [Hatsis] because he was a man from a modest background and a small coal-mining town in the State of Utah, who had made it on his own."[63]

A series of conferences followed, often late at night, during which Meier would refer to some approval from the "penthouse" or "the old man." He said Hughes wanted to buy from Hatsis, but only if Hatsis would deal with an intermediary, one Everd B. Van Walsum, an accountant and representative of a Netherlands company known as Maatschappij–Intermovie N.V. The Dutchman, confided Meier, "was internationally connected with Howard Hughes personally" and it was "the personal desire and direction of Howard Hughes" that Hatsis should work only with him.[64]

Hatsis was ready. He advised Meier that his Toledo Mining Company already owned a number of claims in Nevada and Utah that "might be sold to the Hughes organization."[65] Meier responded that Hughes was most interested. This intense interest by Hughes ignored a report filed just weeks before with the Securities and Exchange Commission in Washington, listing the various Toledo Mining Company claims and offering this assessment of them:

There are no known commercially mineable ore bodies on any of the claims in which [the company] has an interest or which [the company] owns, and [the company] has no present plans for exploration on these properties.[66]

No one in the Hughes organization seemed concerned that a lot of money might soon be laid out for worthless claims. The game went on. In December of 1968, Meier told Hatsis that Hughes was ready to buy mining properties known as the Rattler group for $300,000. That transaction and the sale of other Toledo Mining Company claims for $330,000 were completed within two months. In April of 1969, Meier interrupted Hatsis's game on a Salt Lake City golf course with an urgent telephone message—Hughes wanted to buy a group of mining properties called the Battle Mountain claims.

Hatsis, in a negotiating mood, replied that another person who had an interest in the claims quite probably "would not be willing to make a deal unless [he] could net approximately $3 million to himself."[67] Impossible, said Meier. Hughes would pay only $2.9 million, and $900,000 of that had to go to the Dutch money man, Van Walsum, because "Howard Hughes had his

---

*The vice-president of the new Toledo Mining Company was J. Bracken Lee, the mayor of Salt Lake City and a former Republican governor of Utah, who gained some notoriety in the mid-1950s when, to demonstrate his opposition to the American foreign aid program, he refused to pay his federal income taxes.

reasons for wanting to get money out of the country through a foreign corporation."[68] The deal was struck. But Toledo Mining could not be involved in the sale in any way, Meier stressed. That, too, was the way Hughes wanted it. When the sale was completed and the money changed hands in June, Meier had Hatsis give the $900,000, not to Van Walsum, but to a Los Angeles attorney representing Van Walsum and his Dutch company.

By now, Hatsis clearly had developed a feeling for the way Hughes conducted his mining business—or at least for the way Meier conducted the business for Hughes. He became more active, purchasing a group of claims for $25,000 and 30,000 shares of stock in another Salt Lake City company, Globe Mining Company, and immediately negotiating with Meier the sale of the same claims to Hughes for $850,000. In a personal letter dated June 18, 1969, Hatsis wrote to Van Walsum, then operating out of an office in Toronto:

"I have contacted Hughes Tool Company, and made arrangements to acquire the Huper claims. I believe we will have a deal and make a quick bundle. As per our understanding, $500,000 will go to your people, if we make the deal. No sense having our lawyers prepare a document—the deal will close before they get through a first draft."[69]

Van Walsum also saw no need for attorneys. He wrote his approval of the transaction on June 30: "I had my attorney draft up some kind of memorandum but it seemed to be a bit too stuffy for the Huper matter. I thought I would simply summarize the matter in this letter, and if it meets with your approval, please sign and return a copy to me. . . ."[70]

It was now well established that if you wanted to sell a gold or silver mine to Hughes, the man to see was "Dr. Meier," who had such a close relationship with the recluse. What other explanation could there be for the White House's failure to break up Meier's relationship with Donald Nixon or for Maheu's inability to fire a man who was on Maheu's very own payroll?

As always, Meier made much of his Hughes connection. Maheu had been hearing these stories for a year now, although never from Meier. Indeed, Meier always denied them when confronted. Usually, the tales filtered back to Las Vegas from Washington, New York, or other cities. For example, the letter Maheu received from his old friend, the Washington attorney Edward Morgan, dated August 15, 1969:

This one will give you a boot! I had lunch today with Steve McNichols, former governor of Colorado. After two or three "swacks" he told me of his great deal for the sale of a silver mine near Tonopah, Nevada. He had the top man, so he said, in the Hughes organization lined up to make the purchase—the only man who sits at Hughes' right arm. I inquired as to who this man of influence might be and learned, to my great surprise, that it was your Mr. Meyer [sic]. I suggested to Steve that I understood that a fellow named Maheu was Mr. Hughes' top man. He seemed undismayed in the certain knowledge that Mr. Meyer was *the* man who truly had Mr. Hughes' ear. According to advice from Mr. Meyer, the only thing holding up the purchase of the mine was Mr. Hughes' absorption with the Air West deal. I did not disillusion him. Where ignorance is bliss, 'tis folly to be wise. So sayeth the bard.[71]

If Maheu found this news disconcerting, he made no outward sign. The mining business proceeded apace. On September 2, Meier wrote Maheu that "the next of our options which we have outstanding expires September 20 midnight. We have an option on 69 claims in White Pine County, Nevada, near other properties we own. This particular property has silver, lead, copper, and gold on it. From 1920–40, the shipping records show that over $20 million of ore was taken out during that time; 95 percent of which was high grade silver. . . . In one area alone there was approximately 400,000 tons of ore which can be put into production immediately and have an ore value of from $12–$17 a tone. . . . The option is for $1.9 million."[72]

The option was exercised, and the acquisition completed in December. Of the $1.9 million that Hughes paid for the claims, the two owners of the properties received about $165,000. It was not an unreasonable return on their investment, considering that they had bought the claims earlier in the year for $25,000.

What happened to the remaining $1,735,000 of Hughes's money? A total of $585,000 is unaccounted for. But on December 19, two checks totaling $1,150,000 were issued by the First Security State Bank in Salt Lake City to Everd B. Van Walsum, who promptly moved the money into foreign bank accounts.

Was anyone in the Hughes organization auditing the mining expenditures? In the year and a half since the purchase of the first gold and silver claims, the Hughes treasury had been disbursing mining money at the rate of more than $1 million a month with no questions asked. This free-spending policy was in marked contrast to the negotiations over the purchase of Air West, where Hughes executives scrutinized every line on the financial statements and even considered scrapping the deal because of the cost. No one apparently ever considered turning down a mining deal. On October 28, 1969, Meier recommended to Maheu the purchase of claims "on a major piece of gold and silver property, adjacent to and surrounding the recent acquisition we made in the Golconda Mining District. . . . We find that this acquisition, added to the one we already have, will give us all of the known copper and gold properties in the area, and would assure us that no other mining company would be able to touch the additional grounds around us without going through our property."[73]

To pique Maheu's interest further, Meier confided that he had been "approached by two separate mining companies who have recently done extensive exploration, adjacent to us, to find out if we had this option. . . . The option is for 38 major mining claims for a price of $1.4 million. Please advise."[74]

Six days later, a memorandum went to Hughes bearing Maheu's typewritten initials. It was almost identical to Meier's memorandum, except that Maheu did not attribute the information to Meier. Instead, Hughes was simply advised that acquisition of the claims, "added to the ones we already have, will give us all of the known copper and gold properties in the area and would assure us that no other mining company would be able to touch the additional grounds around us without going through our property. . . . The option is for 38 mining claims for a price of $1.4 million and will expire at 6 P.M., Nov. 15, 1969. Please advise. In sincere friendship."[75]

Several years later Maheu would testify that he could not recall ever having seen that particular memorandum or several other memoranda concerning mining properties that bore his initials and were addressed to Hughes. Furthermore, he doubted that he had written them. The implication, of course, was that Meier or someone else in the Hughes organization sent reports to the Desert Inn penthouse under Maheu's name and without his knowledge. If true, it was an alarming breach in the Hughes security system. It meant that Howard Hughes was making business decisions based on bogus documents— if it was Hughes making the decisions to begin with.

On the day the memorandum bearing Maheu's initials was delivered to the Hughes suite at the Desert Inn, the *Las Vegas Sun* published a story that began:

John Meier, executive aide to Hughes Nevada Operations, has resigned, effective immediately, to form a research foundation, he has announced.

Meier, thirty-six, said his resignation from the Hughes organization was based upon a desire to apply system analysis and practical research to a solution of ecological problems in and around Nevada. . . .

"This foundation," Meier commented, "will give me the opportunity to use what I have learned as an executive in the Hughes organization to analyze problems as diverse as the regeneration of natural resources to school dropout rates and causes."

Robert A. Maheu, chief executive of Hughes Nevada Operations, in a statement following Meier's announcement, said, "John Meier has made a significant contribution to the Nevada Division of the Hughes Tool Company."[76]

There had always been an air of mystery about John Meier's relationship with Hughes and the Hughes empire. He had been placed on Maheu's payroll at the request of Bill Gay, who exercised stringent control over access to Hughes, and he had stayed on, unassailable, until the day of his resignation. Even the resignation was not exactly a resignation, if Maheu was to be believed. Maheu insisted later that Meier resigned only under duress after he had demanded the resignation, ignoring orders from the Desert Inn command post to keep Meier on the payroll.

"Mr. Hughes requested that I go back to Mr. Meier and ask him to come back aboard forthwith," said Maheu. "I explained to Mr. Hughes that I would not do that, that under no circumstances would Mr. Meier ever again be on the payroll of Robert A. Maheu Associates, and that if he, Mr. Hughes, was really serious about having him come back that he should work out whatever arrangements he wants with Mr. Meier."[77]

So Meier was gone, but his influence lingered on. Negotiations continued for the purchase of the last group of mining properties he had recommended. These had until recently been owned by the Jackson Mountain Mining Company. But Jackson Mountain had sold the claims to Globe Mineral, Inc., in

Salt Lake City for $57,000. Globe Mineral, another company in which Hatsis had an interest, then sold the claims to Howard Hughes for $1.4 million. The transaction was completed on March 3, 1970, when the Hughes Tool Company deposited $1.4 million into the Globe Mineral escrow account at the Continental Bank and Trust Company in Salt Lake City. Escrow and attorney's fees amounting to $13,023.98 were paid by the bank, which then issued a check for the balance of $1,386,976.02 made payable to Globe Mineral.

The president of Globe Mineral endorsed the check back to Continental Bank, and the bank in turn issued a cashier's check in the amount of $1,386,976.02. The check was made payable to none other than Maatschappij–Intermovie N.V., the Netherlands company represented by Everd B. Van Walsum.

This was the last of a series of deals in which nearly $5 million from the sale of mining claims to Hughes was moved through a string of foreign corporations and trusts and bank accounts in the Bahamas and Liechtenstein, and finally to a secret numbered account in Switzerland.

Everd B. Van Walsum, of course, had never met Hughes. He had never spoken with him, and he most assuredly was not "internationally connected" with Hughes, as Meier had assured Anthony Hatsis.

Rather, Everd B. Van Walsum was working for John Herbert Meier.

In a little less than two years, Meier had overseen a Hughes payout of $20 million for more than two thousand mining claims scattered across the deserts and mountains of Nevada and California. What were they worth?

Meier had estimated to Maheu, and Maheu had reported to Hughes, figures adding up to hundreds of millions of dollars. But a consulting geologist who studied the Hughes properties in the Belmont Mining District in Nye County, Nevada, concluded that "105 of the 112 claims involved had no value in terms of recognizable mineral deposits." He recommended that "they be dropped from ownership rolls."[78] In the Morey Mining District in Nye County, a geologic study "found that no metallic mineralization occurs anywhere on the property." The 104 Hughes claims were described as "worthless as mining prospects."[79] In the Red Hills Mining District in White Pine County, a geologic examination disclosed that sixty-five of eighty-five Hughes mining claims "lack metallic mineralization and can be considered worthless as mining properties."[80]

Not only had Hughes paid dearly for gold and silver properties that contained no gold or silver, some of the claims he paid for were not even owned by the sellers. In one instance, Hughes was obliged to pull up his claim stakes when the real owners of the property complained. Some claims, to be sure, did have recoverable mineral deposits. A modest mill was constructed at Tonopah, but the mining operation never made any money and the mill was closed several months after Hughes died in an effort to conserve the assets of his estate.

And what of "Dr. Meier"? In December of 1969, a month after leaving the Hughes organization, Meier was hired by Anthony Hatsis in Salt Lake City to serve "as a special adviser and consultant" to the president of the Toledo Mining Company.[81] His fee was fixed at $6,000 a month and he was granted an option to buy 300,000 shares of stock in the Toledo Mining Company.

That same month, Meier, true to his press release, created his Nevada Environmental Foundation, a tax-exempt, nonprofit organization "to provide research, education, information, publications, conferences and scientific knowledge for the practical solution to problems encountered in a comprehensive inventory of the degradation of our ecological environment in the United States."[82] It was an imposing charter, but the foundation eventually became best known for an incident involving a prominent California ecologist who was invited to deliver a speech in Reno at the foundation's expense. Believing that the Nevada Environmental Foundation was supported by Hughes, the ecologist was perplexed when the check he received from the foundation bounced. Meier then drifted on to New Mexico, where in 1972 he mounted a desultory and unsuccessful campaign for the Democratic party's nomination for the United States Senate.

At that time Meier still owned his home in Las Vegas. But in July of 1972, he sold it, moved his family to Vancouver, and applied for permanent residence in Canada.[83] Later in the year, Meier also sold two apartments he owned in Hermosa Beach, California, apparently liquidating the last of his holdings in the United States.

His decision to relocate and sell off his properties was a fortunate one, for in 1973 and 1974 Meier was indicted by a federal grand jury in Las Vegas for income-tax evasion. He was accused of failing to report some $2.5 million in income, mostly money that IRS agents said he had pocketed in the Hughes mining transactions.

Meier subsequently was arrested while visiting Point Roberts, just inside the United States border and not far from his suburban Vancouver home. Government attorneys, sensing that he would not show up for trial, requested bail of $100,000, which Meier promptly posted in cash. He then returned to his home in Canada. As feared, Meier did not appear for trial; his bail was forfeited and a bench warrant was issued for his arrest, with new bail to be set at $500,000.* Through it all, Meier maintained his innocence, claiming to be the victim of a conspiracy by the Internal Revenue Service, the Central Intelligence Agency, the Justice Department, and the White House.

After he left the United States, Meier continued to wheel and deal, working on a complex series of financial transactions involving stock transfers and, once again, mining claims, this time in New Mexico. Sometimes using aliases, Meier was connected to a string of corporations, mostly dummy companies,

---

*Because income-tax evasion is not an extraditable offense, Meier cannot be brought to trial unless he returns voluntarily to the United States. He continues to live comfortably in Delta, British Columbia. Jack Cleveland, who sold the first mining claims to Hughes and who worked closely with Meier in the mining venture, also was indicted on federal income-tax evasion charges and also fled to Canada. He died on November 9, 1973, at Vancouver, British Columbia, at the age of sixty-four.

but the real business action centered around a company called Transcontinental Video Corporation, a New Mexico corporation.

Late in 1974, Alfred Netter of Vancouver, an associate of Meier's in Transcontinental Video, flew to Los Angeles. On Tuesday, November 26, Netter, forty-four years old, Israeli-born, who stood five feet, seven inches, weighed 155 pounds, and wore a black toupee, checked into the Beverly Hilton Hotel in Beverly Hills. What happened during the next few days is uncertain. But on Friday, November 29, Netter called Meier and the two discussed "business."[84] About eleven o'clock that night, a waiter brought dinner for two to Netter's room. At 2:25 P.M. the following day, when a hotel maid entered the room, she found Netter, wearing only a pair of shorts, lying on the floor. There was blood on the twin beds, blood on the floor between the beds, blood on the lamp, blood on the clothes closet, and blood on the bathroom sink. There was a stab wound on Netter's head, four stab wounds in his chest, two in his back, two on the right forearm, and multiple perforations of the heart, liver, and lungs.[85] Someone had carved up John Meier's partner. After Netter was murdered, the London Life Insurance Company paid $400,000 on a "key-man" life insurance policy that had been issued to Netter as an officer of Transcontinental. In time, according to law-enforcement authorities, the $400,000 found its way to a Meier account in Switzerland.[86] The murder remains unsolved.

By 1978, Meier, still carefully avoiding the United States, was deeply involved in a business deal with the king of Tonga, a string of some one hundred fifty Polynesian islands about two thousand miles northeast of Australia. With the backing of King Taufa'ahua Tupou IV—also commander-in-chief of Tonga's 50-member navy and 251-member army—an ordinance had sailed through Tonga's parliament a year earlier granting Meier authority to establish the Bank of the South Pacific and giving him "a 99-year monopoly on merchant banking in the kingdom."[87] The rising expectations of the islands' 100,000 natives soared with Meier's arrival and subsequent forecasts of an unprecedented economic development boom. There was talk of "aircraft assembly plants, pharmaceutical factories, and shipbuilding companies. Tonga would launch its own satellite. It would build a 250-unit condominium complex with a 550-room luxury hotel. There would be an industrial park and a national airline. And the airfield on the main island of Tongatapu would be expanded into a top-class airport."[88] Indeed, the king announced that Meier's fledgling bank would join the Tonga government and a Taiwanese group to "establish an airline to link Tonga with Australia, New Zealand, the United States and other Pacific Islands."[89]

There were, to be sure, a few setbacks along the way. In March of 1978, a United States district court judge in Utah ordered Meier to pay $7.9 million to the Hughes organization. The court entered the judgment against Meier in a lawsuit brought by Hughes in which the company charged that the onetime "scientific adviser" had defrauded Hughes of more than $8 million through the acquisition of worthless mining properties. Even when Tongans eventually learned about Meier's past misdeeds, they still welcomed him in May of 1978 when he showed up with a man he identified as a contractor and four slightly worn bulldozers, to begin work on Tonga's new airport. At a ribbon-cutting ceremony, the king announced that "this airport will put Tonga at the crossroads of the southwest and the northeast."[90] While his colleague the contractor knocked down a few coconut trees, Meier moved into the International Dateline Hotel, where he handed out "$100 tips to the headwaiter in the restaurant."[91] When he finally left the islands, Meier took with him a special Tongan diplomatic passport bestowed on him by the king.

Meier put the passport to good use in the summer of 1978 in Australia. He was arrested in Sydney in July at the request of United States authorities, who wanted to extradite him on yet another criminal charge that had been lodged against him in the states. Meier had been indicted for obstructing justice as a result of filing forged Hughes documents with the United States district court in Salt Lake City in connection with the civil lawsuit brought by the Hughes organization against him. But when Meier was brought before an Australian magistrate, he was promptly released after he produced his passport identifying him as a Tongan diplomat.

As one Tongan official philosophically lamented, "If he did it to Howard Hughes he could do it to us. The world is full of stupid people."[92]

One question, however, persists: How was it possible for Hughes, the businessman always so suspicious of others, to spend $20 million for gold and silver mines that, for the most part, had no value?

Perhaps the most likely explanation, and one never pursued by either the Hughes organization or by any law-enforcement agency, was the most obvious. It also was the most embarrassing, and far-reaching in its legal ramifications. Simply stated, it was this: the great gold- and silver-mining swindle could not have been carried out without the cooperation of someone in the Hughes hierarchy, someone in a key position until the day Howard Hughes died.

CHAPTER 18

TURNING POINT

RUMBLINGS

IF any year in the life of Howard Robard Hughes can be labeled different from all the others, a point from which there was no turning back, it was 1970. The year began with an announcement from Jean Peters Hughes, in Beverly Hills, that their "marriage has endured for 13 years, which is long by present standards," and that she would obtain a divorce.[1] Perhaps the oddest feature of this odd marriage was that it had lasted at all. The tone of the marriage had been set a few weeks after the ceremony when Hughes flew off without her to Montreal. Months later, when he returned to California, he had insisted that they live apart. He had also compelled Jean to adopt the ritualistic procedures practiced by everyone else around him. She was to telephone Operations when she awoke, when she went to bed, when she wanted something to eat, and even when she wanted to talk to him. Like everyone else, Jean could not call Hughes direct. From the Romaine Street logs:

6:55 P.M., December 4, 1958—"Any messages?" Jean asked an Operations clerk. "Tell Mr. Hughes I am up."

8 P.M., December 4, 1958—"Ordered NY steak, stewed tomatoes, hash browns, hearts of lettuce salad w/ roquefort, large orange juice, coffee, 4 bottles water and rolls."

3:50 P.M., December 18, 1958—"Have you heard from HRH? Tell him I'll be asleep in about 1 hour."

8:45 A.M., December 9, 1958—"Ordered 6 milk, sweet rolls, toast, 2 baked eggs, 3 raw eggs, cheddar cheese, large orange juice, coffee, papers, and 6 Poland water."

7:40 P.M., December 18, 1958—"I would like to talk to HRH within the next half hour."

8 A.M., December 16, 1958—"Ordered a minute steak, hash browns, hearts of lettuce salad with roquefort, V-8 juice, orange juice, milk, coffee, ½ loaf of sour dough French bread, vanilla ice cream."

10:20 A.M., Christmas Day, 1958—"Have you any messages?" Jean asked.
"No."
"Have you heard from Mr. Hughes?"
"No."
"Please tell him I'm up."[2]

Also, early on Hughes had sought to deceive Jean about his health, using it as an excuse to avoid her and to account for his growing seclusion. And he had often used Operations to make her think he was especially solicitous of her well-being. The logs of Operations are filled with instructions such as: "When [Jean] calls in, tell her that I have been working diligently all morning and that I have called a number of times to see if we have heard from her and that I will [be] calling back shortly."[3] Or another time: ". . . tell her that I have been calling constantly since midnight. Then say, 'Actually the last time he called couldn't have been more than 3 or 4 minutes ago.' "[4]

Hughes had tried to control Jean's life, as though she were another Romaine Street operative. Without her knowledge, he set down procedures to be followed by the aides to assist her in an emergency if he were asleep or "otherwise unavailable"[5] (they were never allowed to awaken him). One memorandum covered what to do if Jean became ill. Under no circumstances, Hughes warned, were the aides to allow Jean to see a doctor until he had been consulted:

If the situation is critical enough, then it is permissible to let a doctor call her on the telephone. Under no circumstances should she be allowed to go see a doctor either at an office, a hospital or any place else, until HRH has talked to her first. The doctor will be cautioned to give her only such information that might be required for immediate relief of the pain, or immediate medication, if required. This is only to be done if the immediate effect on the disease would be impaired by a delay. It is assumed that there will be some conversation had over the telephone if all other efforts to delay EVERYTHING until HRH is either awake or available fail and you have to put a doctor in touch with her, . . . the doctor must be instructed, not told but instructed, to tell her nothing more than what desired medicine she should take at the particular time in order to prevent further expansion of the ailment. This doesn't mean that this doesn't have top priority because of the way I want this handled. It should be the absolute first and number one project. We should hear her story in complete detail and chat with her a little bit if she wants to. The doctor should also get a most complete history of the ailment and chat with her, but the doctor should avoid giving her a diagnosis of any kind or indicate the treatment required on an extended basis. Only the very immediate treatment should be offered and it should not be indicated whether the treatment is the last one, the first one or whether there is to be more following. . . .
In other words, HRH could use the fact that there is to be further treatment, or the fact that she doesn't know what the specific ailment is, as the basis of telling her something which might break her of the smoking habit, get her to eat more regularly, or any number of things that would be for her own good.[6]

At Rancho Santa Fe, in 1961, living with Hughes in the same house, Jean had been free of the Operations bureaucracy, free to approach and talk with her husband. It was small consolation. Hughes was slipping ever deeper into seclusion and increasing his use of drugs. Nevertheless, he still made obsessional demands of her, refusing to let her register to vote or to receive mail at Rancho Santa Fe.[7] After the move to Bel Air, some older patterns had returned. Jean once again had to go through the aides to see Hughes, and after he went to Las Vegas and Jean stayed behind at 1001 Bel Air Road, even the fiction of the marriage crumbled. By early 1970 neither of them was pretending any longer. They had not seen each other in three and a half years. The marriage was over.*

For Hughes, the year that began with the announcement of a divorce from his wife ended with a permanent separation from his country, as the industrialist, a six-foot, three-and-three-quarters-inch skeleton weighing less than a hundred pounds, was lifted onto a Lockheed Aircraft Corporation plane and flown to the Bahamas, there to become a citizen of the world, to drift from hotel to hotel, from nation to nation, never again to live in America.

It was also the year that Hughes irrevocably lost control of his empire, the year that his executives began to use his name and freely assert the power of his organization without his will or knowledge. It was the year that he ceased to be both superintendent and inmate of his twelve-year-old asylum, and became only the inmate.

And who would know the difference? Hughes was now sixty-four years old. He had not seen half a dozen new faces in the last decade and now saw no one but his aides. The transfer of power would, of course, come gradually, the pace dictated by Hughes's failing health and the subtle influence exerted on him by faceless executives within the empire. It was the kind of suggestive influence to which all aging and infirm people are susceptible, but Hughes was especially so because of his complete isolation and the disorders of his mind.

Enormous pressures lay upon him. The intense Air West negotiations had taken their toll, both physically and mentally. As feared, the airline's operating losses continued unchecked. After a decade of litigation and legal bills running into the millions of dollars, a final judgment of $145,448,141.07 was recorded against him in favor of TWA. His Las Vegas hotels, gambling casinos, and other Nevada properties were losing money. His helicopter division was losing money. He had been swindled out of $20 million in a mining scheme. And all of this at a time when the earnings from the oil-tool division of the Hughes Tool Company, the original source of all his wealth, had fallen sharply from their high levels in the 1950s and showed no sign of recovery.

*The divorce became final on June 18, 1971, in Hawthorne, Nevada. Under the settlement terms, Hughes agreed to pay Jean from $70,000 to $140,000 a year for twenty years. The actual amount was determined by the cost of living index each year. He also conveyed to her a house at 507 North Palm Drive in Beverly Hills. Two months after the divorce, Jean married Stanley Hough, vice-president in charge of production for Twentieth Century Fox.

Physically, Hughes was in terrible shape. His kidneys were deteriorating and shrinking, the left one slightly faster than the right as a result of two decades of abuse of Empirin Compound No. 4, an analgesic that contains both codeine and phenacetin whose prolonged and heavy usage is known to damage the kidneys.[8] He was anemic. His increasing use of codeine and Valium often left him confused and depressed. His red corpuscle index indicated a brain starved for oxygen. A tumor was forming on his head. His gums were receding. His teeth were rotting away. His bones were becoming brittle. His chronic constipation was so severe that he had to call a physician "to administer a local anesthetic in the area of his rectum, so that he wouldn't have the severe pain when he did have his bowel movement."[9] He had a peptic ulcer. He had suffered a severe bout of pneumonia. By year's end, Hughes's days of lucidity were growing fewer in number as his smouldering psychological afflictions flared anew. He continued, as always, to insist on the use of "insulation," the Kleenex and paper towels that protected him from germs. Now he demanded that his urine be preserved. After he urinated into a bottle, it was capped and placed on a shelf in his closet, alongside dozens of other specimens. Unable to grapple with daily business affairs, Hughes concentrated on merely existing. On most days his largest achievement was to walk the distance from his bed to the bathroom.

His aides and the few executives who were in contact with him insisted nonetheless that Hughes still controlled his business organization. That was to be expected. Family fortunes, the future of many businesses, entire careers were built on maintaining that illusion. To shatter the illusion would have led to a legal and financial nightmare without precedent in American business history.

Within the empire, the decline of Hughes was accompanied by the rise of Bill Gay. When Hughes had left Los Angeles in 1966, Gay had been isolated, cut off from direct involvement in Hughes's affairs. After more than a decade of growth in influence over Hughes's daily life, Gay's Romaine Street communications center had suddenly become a very quiet place. Hughes began to deal directly with Gay's rival Bob Maheu, and when he moved to Las Vegas in November of 1966, he "instructed [Maheu] not to have Mr. Frank W. Gay come to Las Vegas and not to deal with him or the 'Hollywood people.' "[10] The Hollywood people were the Gay loyalists at Romaine Street.

But it was only a matter of time before Gay reasserted himself. He waited until the summer of 1970 to make his move, but there had been tremors of intent long before that.

It was at a party in Santa Monica around 1968, Maheu has testified, that Gay—nearly as secretive as his employer—raised the question of having Hughes declared mentally unfit in order to assume control of the empire. Maheu said that Gay made the proposal in a conversation with Dr. Robert Buckley, a Santa Monica physician who was attending several persons associated with the Hughes organization:

He [Gay] specifically asked Dr. Buckley whether Buckley felt he was qualified to file a statement in the event it were decided to have a guardian appointed, with the hope that Mr. Hughes might be declared mentally incompetent. Dr. Buckley asked Mr. Gay to describe mental deficiencies to which he might be referring, and after a brief discussion in terminology which I personally did not comprehend, Dr. Buckley stated that he would have to pace Mr. Hughes for some period of time before he could answer Mr. Gay's question. . . . The conversation came to a screeching halt when both Dr. Buckley and I told Mr. Gay that we were not the least bit interested in participating.[11]

That evening in Santa Monica, Maheu has testified, was actually the second time that Gay had approached him on the matter of orderly succession.[12] Several months earlier, Gay had pushed much the same plan during a meeting with Maheu and Edward Morgan at the Bel Air Hotel in Los Angeles. At that time, Maheu said, Gay talked about "initiating a plan whereby effectual control of the Hughes Tool Company might be worked out by a very selective group of a few individuals in the event certain physical or mental problems should arise insofar as Mr. Hughes was concerned. . . . He indicated that he was constantly afraid that Mr. Hughes because of physiological problems might suddenly die, at which time he felt that the 'Houston group' would move in and attempt to control the empire. He further stated that he feared that Mr. Hughes' mental condition might cause him to crack up at any moment, and he wanted to be in a position so as to take advantage of such an eventuality."[13] According to Maheu, Gay said the "selective group" that would assume control of the empire should include, in addition to himself and Maheu, Edward Morgan, Chester Davis, Nadine Henley, and "a few of his selected and trusted aides."[14]

For his part, Gay denied ever suggesting that Hughes be placed under the care of a guardian. Indeed, he maintained that he had only heard "general talk" by others of Hughes's mental competency, and that the talk was all positive—"he's brilliant, he's a genius, he has a fantastic memory, never forgets anything, logical."[15]

Whatever the case, Hughes himself had long feared that he would be labeled mentally incompetent, his fortune placed under the administrative control of a court, his life regulated by a guardian. The fear of being found unfit to a large extent underlay Hughes's marriage, his retreat from public view, and the pathological measures he adopted to avoid an appearance in any legal proceeding.

Friends and associates of Hughes offered quite a different reason for his seclusion. Hughes, they said, simply wanted to be left free to run his businesses without interruption by subpoena servers. It was an explanation Hughes encouraged. "I don't want to spend the rest of my life in some courtroom being harassed and interrogated," he once said.[16]

But that explanation did not square with events. True, Hughes and his companies were named as defendants in dozens of civil lawsuits filed in the 1950s and 1960s. During his first decade of isolation, however, the cases, with a single exception, turned on issues that would have been resolved through routine legal procedures and negotiated settlements—as many were—without requiring Hughes ever to set foot in a courtroom. The lone exception was TWA, a lawsuit that Hughes brought on himself.

Hughes's fear that a court would take control of his empire made him wary about meeting anybody new, as Dr. Buckley, the Santa Monica physician, was to learn. Like others in the Hughes organization, Dr. Buckley had been called on to perform some unusual services. Sometime back about 1966, according to Maheu, a friend of Jean Peters "had a son with some mental disorder and had tried to kill his wife. Mr. Hughes wanted the young man cleared without any charges. . . . And it became necessary to get a psychiatrist in whom we had implicit faith and confidence. . . . I recommended Dr. Buckley and, if I recall correctly, Mr. Hughes did not want any of the payments made to Buckley at that time to come through any Hughes accounts and some arrangements were made to pay him in cash."[17]

By 1968, Dr. Buckley, "after being assured Howard Hughes had offered to retain [him] for lifetime employment," closed his Santa Monica office and moved to Las Vegas.[18] He was to become the medical director of Hughes Nevada Operations and "personal physician" to Hughes at an annual salary of $50,000, plus the usual Hughes smorgasbord of fringe benefits.[19] "I was to be allowed to have a private medical practice in Las Vegas," Dr. Buckley said. "The Hughes organization would give me a fully equipped and staffed medical office as well as pay the premiums on my disability, hospital, life, and malpractice insurances. The Hughes organization would pay annually certain licensing fees and association dues on my behalf. I would receive fringe benefits similar to other high-ranking Hughes officials—an automobile, including upkeep and maintenance—a specially equipped radio, and the privilege and ability to charge at all facilities operated by the Hughes organization in Nevada, as well as a participation in the Hughes Tool Company retirement program."[20]

But Dr. Buckley never treated Hughes. In fact, he never saw him. Shortly after arriving in Las Vegas, he was asked to obtain blood for transfusions that Hughes required. When he asked to examine Hughes, not an unreasonable request from a physician who has never met his patient, Buckley was informed by Maheu that it would not be possible. "Because of my psychiatric residency," Buckley said, "Mr. Hughes would not allow me to personally examine him."[21]

Maheu's refusal to join in an alliance with Gay was not an entirely unselfish decision. In 1968, Maheu was firmly in power not only in Las Vegas, but in the Hughes empire at large. By virtue of his own public-relations machine, he had become identified in the public eye as Howard Hughes's chief executive. Maheu did not need Bill Gay. But like Gay, Maheu feared the so-called Houston crowd, notably Raymond Holliday, who controlled the purse strings, and Raymond Cook at Andrews, Kurth, Campbell & Jones. Indeed, as Maheu once confided to Hughes, "it is unfortunate but true that the Houston crowd is trying to get me."[22]

While "the Houston crowd" may have been out to get Maheu, as he feared, Maheu had been out to get the Houston crowd. Early in 1968, Hughes had been urged by one of his Houston or Washington lawyers to create an executive committee to manage the affairs of the Howard Hughes Medical Institute. Hughes appointed Holliday, Cook, and James R. Drury, another partner in Andrews, Kurth. Within months, the newly formed executive committee quietly and without Hughes's knowledge moved to gain long-term control of the medical institute, and, thereby, the Hughes Aircraft Company.

When he established the medical institute in 1953, Hughes had made certain that he would exercise full control for the rest of his life. The institute's charter called for the appointment of a single trustee, Hughes himself, and provided that any successor trustee could be named only by "the original trustee [Hughes] or in such manner as the original trustee may designate."[23] But the executive committee enacted a set of bylaws allowing the committee not only to designate a successor trustee, but also to fill any vacancies on the committee or appoint new members if the committee were expanded.

Maheu called Cook's maneuver to Hughes's attention in May of 1969 and Hughes fired off a memorandum to Maheu and Davis: "If these actions were taken, as Bob says they were, out of motives of personal enmity and disloyalty against Maheu, Davis, and me, then it certainly seems to me that the Campbell firm has violated their pledge of relationship of fiduciary trust and loyalty toward the Hughes Tool Company and me."[24]

For whatever reason, Hughes took no immediate action and Maheu continued to chip away at Cook and the medical institute. By May of 1970, he had found an ally on Hughes's personal staff. On May 13, Howard Eckersley typed and handed this memorandum to Hughes:

While taking Bob's memo this morning on Cook, I couldn't help thinking that he was, perhaps, too restrained in his comments. Cook is, indeed, reorganizing HHMI—and I don't think it is for tax considerations only. In fact, I understand that the reworked bylaws are strong enough that he could fire you as trustee. It is demoralizing to have a guy like Cook in a top executive position. Everybody knows how bad his track record has been. And how dangerous and expensive has been the course he plotted. In addition he had been disloyal and dishonest. To my knowledge he has lied to you deliberately. I hope you don't mind my bringing this up again but I think it would be in your best interest to take a good hard look at this situation once more. I would certainly feel more secure with Cook gone, and so would every other executive and close employee, with the possible exception of Holliday.[25]

A week after Eckersley gave the memorandum to Hughes, the executive committee of the Howard Hughes Medical Institute met in Holliday's office in Houston and Cook and Drury submitted their resignations.[26] Not long thereafter, Hughes named Chester Davis and Bill Gay to replace the two Houston lawyers on the committee.

And so the stage was set for a bitter and secret power play. Because the penthouse aides owed their loyalty to Romaine Street, they kept Gay informed of what was happening in Las Vegas. In time, Gay began quietly reasserting his authority, exercising control over the flow of information to Hughes—without Hughes's knowledge—and limiting the access of other executives to the industrialist. During the protracted Air West talks, for example, Pat Hyland, general manager of the Hughes Aircraft Company, had an urgent message that he wanted delivered to Hughes. Maheu suggested that Hyland "dispatch the message forthwith to the penthouse at the Desert Inn."[27]

Later, while Maheu and Gay were in Washington for an Air West hearing before the Civil Aeronautics Board, Maheu overheard a telephone conversation between Gay and Howard Eckersley. Gay was issuing specific instructions to Eckersley that "under no circumstances was he to deliver the message from Mr. Hyland to Mr. Hughes."[28] Thus, not even the chief executive officer of Hughes Aircraft, one of the nation's largest defense contractors, a company engaged in all kinds of highly classified work, could get a message through to his president without Gay's approval.

Eventually, as Maheu later testified, even his own reports were short-circuited by Gay. During legal work on the appeal of the TWA judgment, Maheu said he "sent urgent messages through the aides begging Mr. Hughes to communicate with Mr. Clark Clifford."[29] A prominent Washington lawyer who had served as secretary of defense under President Johnson and as adviser to three presidents, Clifford was one of a battery of attorneys assisting in Hughes's appeal of the TWA decision. The aides received Maheu's messages, but acting "upon the specific instructions of Gay," they did not deliver them to Hughes.[30]

OUSTER

If Hughes's decline and Gay's rise were gradual and hard to pinpoint, Maheu's fate may be fixed in time and place. For some months Maheu had been working on a deal in which Hughes would purchase a financially distressed helicopter commuter service, Los Angeles Airways, Inc. Maheu's chief assistant in Las Vegas, retired air force general Edward H. Nigro, had signed a letter on Sands Hotel stationery in the summer of 1969 indicating that the Hughes organization would guarantee payment of a multimillion-dollar bank loan to Los Angeles Airways. By May of 1970, the commuter service had what it considered a firm commitment: the Hughes Tool Company and the Hughes Air Corporation would buy Los Angeles Airways from its owners for eight dollars a share. As part of the agreement, the Hughes companies "acknowledged that they were aware of the deteriorating financial condition of [Los Angeles Airways] due to reduced air traffic and . . . agreed that they would provide financial assistance."[31]

Maheu passed news of the pending acquisition to Donovan, Leisure, Newton & Irvine, the New York law firm which, with Chester Davis, was representing Hughes in the TWA lawsuit. Donovan, Leisure in turn sent a letter on May 22, 1970, to United States District Court judge Charles M.

Metzner, who had presided over the TWA case, advising him that the Hughes Tool Company planned to buy the helicopter commuter service and yet another hotel and gambling casino in Las Vegas. Donovan, Leisure was most anxious to notify Judge Metzner of the transactions before he learned of them from another source, and with good reason. Just two days before, the judge had opened hearings to determine the "appropriate means" of requiring the Hughes organization to guarantee payment of the $145-million TWA judgment during its appeal.[32] Hughes's attorneys were contending that "there was no need to post any bond" to secure payment of the judgment, as required by court rules.[33] TWA, on the other hand, was "demanding either full payment of the judgment or the posting of a bond."[34] Thus, Donovan, Leisure prudently wrote a letter calling Metzner's attention to the acquisitions.

They informed the judge that Los Angeles Airways was "of great importance as a feeder line to Air West and to all other airlines operating into and out of Los Angeles. It is presently planned, assuming Civil Aeronautics Board approval, that the company [Hughes Tool] will lend Los Angeles Airways $4 million and that, some six to eight months in the future, it will acquire Los Angeles Airways." The letter concluded that Chester Davis, who had coordinated Hughes's legal defense ever since the TWA action was started, "is presently out of the city, but he will be available beginning next Wednesday to meet with you and plaintiff's counsel to answer questions and to supply any needed information."[35]

As the letter was delivered to Judge Metzner in New York, a copy of a proposed press release announcing the Los Angeles Airways transaction was delivered to Hughes in Las Vegas. The press release began:

Clarence M. Belinn, president of Los Angeles Airways, Inc., pioneer southland helicopter operation, disclosed today than an agreement in principle has been reached whereby the Howard Hughes interests will purchase the company. Tentative plans provide for Hughes to acquire Los Angeles Airways for $3,116,640 which is estimated to net $8.00 per share to the stockholders.[36]

When Hughes read the planned announcement, he exploded. He had not approved the acquisition—indeed, had not even authorized any financial commitments to Los Angeles Airways. He ordered the press release killed and told Maheu to call off the purchase. The Los Angeles Airways deal had always been a Maheu project. Negotiations had actually started back in 1968, and at that time Hughes was at least generally aware of the talks. But once negotiations for Air West began in earnest, Hughes forgot all about Los Angeles Airways. Maheu, however, continued to bargain. When the commuter service experienced serious financial problems, Maheu and Nigro came to the rescue. Late in 1969, the Hughes-owned Sands Hotel guaranteed a $1.8-million loan to Los Angeles Airways, and in January 1970 guaranteed another loan for $750,000.[37] With these financial commitments, Maheu pushed ahead and negotiated the acquisition. But Hughes, now that he had Air West, a monumental money loser, was not the least bit interested in acquiring another sick air carrier, especially with the TWA judgment—and its interest charges running at nearly three-quarters of a million dollars a month—hanging over his head.

Chester Davis was not much better informed about the Los Angeles Airways purchase, despite Donovan, Leisure's assurances to Judge Metzner that Davis would be able "to supply any needed information."[38] A few weeks after the letter went to Judge Metzner, Davis summoned Hughes executives to a meeting in the Presidential Suite at the Century Plaza Hotel in Beverly Hills. Holliday and Calvin Collier came from the tool company's offices in Houston. Maheu and an associate, Francis T. Fox, head of aviation for the Hughes Tool Company, came from Las Vegas. Gay came from Encino. The purpose of the meeting, at least as far as Davis, Gay, Holliday, and Collier were concerned, was to determine what commitments Maheu had made to Los Angeles Airways. Gay later described the session as "the donnybrook meeting," a conversation punctuated by shouting matches:

"Now, Bob, can you or Fran tell me what the facts are with respect to Los Angeles Airways?" Davis asked Maheu.

"Chester, we have a commitment with respect to Los Angeles Airways," Maheu answered.

"Fine, what is the commitment?" Davis pressed.

"Chester, are you doubting my word?" Maheu demanded. "I tell you we have a commitment. If I tell you we have a commitment, we have a commitment."

"Bob, no one is doubting your word. Just tell me what the commitment is," Davis persisted.[39]

Maheu refused to spell out the commitment, and Davis kept asking the question. As Gay remembered, the more the two men went around and around, "the shorter tempers became. And at the time I went, it was still in that status. Everybody was aware by that time there was a problem. It was adjourned into futility."[40]

Even Gay, the Mormon church leader who was usually a model of self-control, got into an argument. He clashed with Holliday on a subject unrelated to Los Angeles Airways, finally telling the tool company's executive vice-president to "shove it" and walking out of the room. "I try not to lose control," Gay said.[41]

Later, Maheu and Fox finally revealed to Davis that the commitments involved two guarantees of bank loans to Los Angeles Airways. One guarantee was verbal, the other written, but both made the Hughes-owned Sands Hotel liable for the loans. Maheu had made a disastrous mistake. He had entered into a business deal and pledged Hughes's money without the authority to do either. And there were two other problems, one related to Los Angeles Airways, that further aggravated Maheu's position.

Davis learned that the helicopter commuter service had obtained some of its equipment from the Systems Capital Corporation, a Phoenix-based company in which Maheu had a personal financial interest. More serious, however, was another financial commitment made by Maheu in Hughes's name without

Hughes's knowledge. Maheu was then also negotiating for the purchase of the Dunes Hotel and Casino, an acquisition that had Hughes's approval. During the negotiations, Maheu had made "a personal commitment to loan some $4 million" of Hughes's money to Sidney Wyman, a part-owner of the Dunes and a onetime member of a St. Louis bookmaking syndicate that dealt with friendly Western Union employees around the country in placing illegal bets.[42]

But Hughes had no more interest in loaning $4 million to Sidney Wyman than he had in buying Los Angeles Airways, and for the same very good reason. Now Maheu was angry. His reputation in Las Vegas was built on the illusion that the word of Robert Maheu was the word of Howard Hughes.

"Mr. Maheu was extremely upset," Davis recalled, and "in effect said that if need be, he would mortgage his wife, his children, sell his boat and by God, come hell or high water, somebody was going to lend Wyman $4 million. And [he] complained to me bitterly about what he felt was an obligation which he thought Mr. Hughes owed to him. His credibility in Las Vegas would be gone if this thing didn't go through."[43]

As the days dragged by and Hughes stood firmly negative, another meeting of Hughes executives was arranged. This time Maheu extended the invitation, but he asked just Davis and Gay to join him for an afternoon at the Balboa Bay Club in Newport Beach, California. After a leisurely lunch, a few sets of tennis, and a brief excursion on Maheu's boat, the chief of Hughes Nevada Operations made his pitch.

"Chester," he said, "if you will help me to put through the Los Angeles Airways deal and the Wyman loan and help me to convince Hughes to authorize and direct it to take place, I give you my solemn word that I will not commit myself to anybody any more without written authorization."[44]

"Bob, you don't need to give me such solemn promises," replied Davis.[45]

All in all, "it was a very friendly, warm meeting in contrast to the earlier meeting at the Century Plaza."[46] Gay and Davis could well afford to be gracious and sympathetic to Maheu's predicament. They knew that Maheu was on his way out of the Hughes empire.

"Chester, let me tell you something that I know," Maheu confided to Davis. "Mr. Hughes will never fire me, and he'll never fire Bill Gay."[47]

The remark illustrated a fundamental and ultimately decisive difference between the ebullient Maheu and the reserved Gay. Maheu was a corporate architect without credentials. He had never had any general authority to conduct Hughes's business affairs. He held no corporate position in the tool company, the holding company that controlled the empire. He could not spend the tool company's money, even on the Las Vegas properties, without permission. To compensate for his lack of formal authority, he had created a castle in the air, called it Hughes Nevada Operations, and bestowed on himself the title of chief executive. He freely invoked Hughes's name. He made himself conspicuous, from his diamond cufflinks to the lavish parties at his half-million-dollar mansion to which Hughes held title. Maheu had no sense of his own vulnerability. He was not a realist—and Bill Gay was.

Gay was also a splendid corporate designer whose political structure inside the Hughes empire had withstood the lances of corporate rivals. His power rested on a solid foundation, built one block at a time with favors and the appointment of people loyal to him. He kept meticulous records on the moves of his rivals. He was inconspicuous, never insistent about his authority and responsibility. He never made corporate commitments he could not keep, and he made no lasting important enemies.

Maheu had incurred the displeasure of virtually all the Hughes executives at one time or another. An illustration was his break in 1967 with Nadine Henley, Hughes's private secretary before she became manager of the West Coast office of the Hughes Tool Company. After Hughes established his residence in Las Vegas, Maheu submitted bills for expenditures made by Hughes Nevada Operations to Miss Henley. Maheu's financial recordkeeping system was casual, and the gimlet-eyed Miss Henley took exception to his procedures and his large expense accounts. Relations between the two deteriorated until Collier, the vice-president and treasurer of the tool company in Houston, was forced to intervene. Collier "talked individually, back and forth, in person, on the phone," with Maheu and Miss Henley, resolving the dispute by setting a fixed fee for Maheu's services and shifting responsibility for monitoring Maheu's expenditures from Romaine Street to Houston.[48]

Relations between Maheu and Holliday, the executive vice-president of the tool company and the top official on the corporate organization chart, were even worse. Holliday primarily managed the oil-tool division, the empire's money-making machine. But he also watched over other divisions, and had authority to write checks on Hughes's bank accounts. Maheu resented Holliday and generally refused to deal with him directly. During the Air West negotiations, it was suggested that Maheu should become an officer and director of the Hughes Tool Company. He rejected that and made "it clear that under no circumstances would he be, or would he consider assuming the position that would make him subservient to or junior to Mr. Holliday."[49]

Holliday quietly returned Maheu's disdain. He resented Maheu's carefree spending habits, annoyed that profits generated by his oil-tool division were subsidizing the Hughes Nevada Operations. Equally disturbing were Maheu's flamboyant lifestyle, his gilded expense account, his unauthorized purchase of an executive jet, and his French Regency mansion on the grounds of the Desert Inn known affectionately as "Little Caesar's Palace."

So there was the empire in the summer of 1970, with its three power centers, each hostile toward the other. The man at the top, Howard Hughes, was gravely ill. His physical and mental conditions worsened with each passing day. Very often he lay in a trancelike state, detached from his surroundings. Maheu was at odds with just about every influential executive in the empire. He antagonized them, he embarrassed them, he ignored them. And he flaunted the Hughes power. When he committed the cardinal sin of pledging Hughes's money without Hughes's authority, he signed his own pink slip.

In Houston, Raymond Holliday prepared a report for Hughes outlining the tool company's bleak financial condition in the wake of the TWA judgment. The company, Holliday said, had "a total of about $111 million" in cash and certificates of deposit.[50] Of that $111 million, $75 million had to be kept on deposit as a bond for the TWA judgment, and another $16.5 million was pledged as collateral for a bank loan. This left Hughes with $19.5 million in working funds for the year. Holliday estimated the needs of the various divisions would total about $30.1 million—including $10.2 million for Hughes Nevada Operations—leaving Hughes with a cash deficit of $10.6 million.[51] After laying out the stark figures, Holliday, in a memorandum tinged with sarcasm and hyperbole, made it clear who he believed was responsible:

You will note that no provision is made for a dividend to you and you will certainly require at least $2 million by year-end. However, provision is made for payment to Maheu of his $10,000 per week basic compensation, but without provision for expenses that will be considerable. In other words, no provision is made for the purchase or use and the personnel that might be required of a right hand or left hand ass wiping machine that he may require. But provision is made for Ed Morgan's fees and costs and other reasonably contemplated hijacking costs. The long and short of our position is that we are in trouble, and very serious trouble.[52]

Some weeks later, Holliday forwarded another financial report to Hughes. This one dealt with Nevada. The report showed that Hughes's Nevada properties lost $3.2 million in 1968 and $8.4 million in 1969. For the first seven months of 1970, the losses amounted to $6.8 million. "If the 1970 losses continue at the present rate," Holliday said, "it appears that the overall loss for 1970 will be on the order of $13–$14 million."[53] Considering that Hughes had invested more than $150 million in Nevada since 1967, the figures were most depressing.

Against this background, a whispering campaign began in Las Vegas. Someone whispered to Hughes that Hughes Tool and Romaine Street had given hundreds of thousands of dollars to Maheu that he was unable to account for, that Maheu was stealing. Hughes believed the whispers.

Clearly, Hughes had been swindled out of millions, and clearly, many an executive on the Hughes payroll, including Maheu, was doing quite nicely for himself at Hughes's expense. Some segments of his empire—and not only those in Las Vegas—were outrageously mismanaged.

Maheu was certainly not a financial wizard, or an especially talented business executive. Back in 1948, about a year after he resigned from the FBI, he became president and major stockholder of a company called Dairy Dream Farms, which had obtained a franchise on "a new process for canning pure cream without additives."[54] Supported by "unlimited credit," the product was on sale in twenty-two states when a company chemist determined "there was a problem with the lining of the can which caused oxidation."[55] The Food and Drug Administration was notified, and the Dairy Dream Cream recalled, plunging the company into a financial crisis. Maheu "had made so many personal loans to try to keep the [company] viable" that it was suggested he should "go through bankruptcy."[56] Rejecting the advice, he said, he eventually "paid every creditor one hundred cents on the dollar," although it took him some time.[57] Twenty years later, while directing Hughes Nevada Operations, Maheu was "almost always overdrawn at the bank," displaying "little concern for cash deficits."[58]

This fumbling in business administration or finance, however, could hardly be equated with thievery. Nor could Maheu be held accountable for the financial performance of all Hughes's Nevada properties. But he had created a potential monster in Hughes Nevada Operations, and in his imperious attitude toward it.

The whispering campaign and Holliday's financial report were followed by a breakdown in communications between Maheu and Hughes. The telephone in Maheu's home, once so active at all hours of the day and night, fell silent. When Maheu called the Desert Inn penthouse, he was told that Hughes could not come to the telephone. At least some of the messages he left at the penthouse were not delivered to Hughes.

There was a touch of irony in Hughes's succumbing to the whispering campaign against Maheu. He had fallen victim to his own management philosophy. Over the years, Hughes had run his empire by pitting one executive against another. He deliberately provoked corporate rivalries and encouraged petty jealousies. It was his way of keeping the people around him unsure of themselves so that they would do exactly as he wanted. He constantly criticized or ridiculed one executive to another, often without justification.

About the middle of August, the plan for Maheu's removal began to take shape. Levar Beebe Myler, one of Hughes's five aides, met privately with Bill Gay. The portly, bespectacled Myler, who had celebrated his forty-seventh birthday a few days earlier, had an urgent message for his fellow Mormon and friend of twenty years. He told Gay that "Mr. Hughes was going to prepare a form of proxy," turning over authority for all Nevada operations to Gay, Chester Davis, and Raymond Holliday.[59] The significance of the proxy was obvious: it would be a license to fire Maheu.

Myler next notified Davis, and Kay Glenn, the administrative assistant to Gay, was soon on a plane from Los Angeles to Washington where he visited the offices of a private security firm called International Intelligence, Inc., for a meeting with its president, Robert D. Peloquin. The firm, better known as Intertel, was run by Peloquin and William G. Hundley, both former attorneys in the Justice Department's Criminal Division. Peloquin had headed the first Justice Department Organized Crime Strike Force in Buffalo in 1966. Intertel's staff was made up largely of former government agents and lawyers from the FBI, the IRS, the CIA, and the Justice Department, and its clients ranged from the National Football League to Wall Street investment houses. More important, at least to Bill Gay and Chester Davis, Intertel was a subsidiary of Resorts International, Inc., formerly the Mary Carter Paint Company, which owned and operated a casino and several hotels in the Bahamas.

Glenn told Peloquin that Hughes wanted to retain the services of Intertel for an especially sensitive assignment, work that would include auditing the operations of Hughes's gambling casinos and hotels in Las Vegas and Reno. "The decision had been made to get rid of Maheu," an Intertel operative recalled, and "they brought in Intertel to make the case against Maheu."[60]

By September, Maheu had learned of the campaign against him and he sent a flurry of memoranda to Hughes, defending himself and imploring Hughes to go through with the acquisition of Los Angeles Airways, which could no longer pay its bills and was headed for bankruptcy. On September 16, he wrote:

Howard, things are truly falling apart. We have now been formally advised by the three banks holding the Nigro guarantee that they want immediate payment from us. The attorneys for Belinn [Los Angeles Airways] now have completed their complaint in order to file a lawsuit [against Hughes]. Howard, I don't know what else I can tell you about this entire situation except to repeat that this is going to be one hell of a mess.[61]

Maheu no longer received any answers to his messages. The Desert Inn penthouse was silent. In October, Intertel's Peloquin flew to Los Angeles to attend a meeting in Chester Davis's West Coast law office in Century City. The meeting was arranged by the Gay and Davis forces to discuss in more detail the "use of Intertel as advisers to the board of directors of Hughes Tool Company as to security of casinos in Nevada."[61] Peloquin said he consulted with Hughes executives about "a plan for a change of management in Nevada" and that he gave "recommendations as to the security of the properties involved during whatever interim period would exist until the new management was brought in."[63]

While the campaign for his banishment quickened, and his isolation grew, Maheu made some plans of his own. Having excelled at back-room political deals, and even once negotiated an assassination contract with the Mafia, he thought he could manage a coup. He meant to remove Davis from the TWA case and personally direct Hughes's appeal of the $145-million judgment to the United States Supreme Court. Thus, while Gay and Davis were preparing to dump Maheu, Maheu was preparing to dump Davis.

Realizing that his position within the organization was in jeopardy, he decided to strike out in a bold bid to restore himself to Hughes's good graces. Maheu had the written authorization of both Hughes and the Hughes Tool Company Board of Directors to act in the TWA case. Should Maheu win the case that Davis had so far lost at every turn, he would earn Hughes's undying gratitude. It would also be fit retribution for Davis's failure to help bail Maheu out of his commitments to Los Angeles Airways and Sidney Wyman.

Maheu's authorization in the TWA matter dated back to October 16, 1968, when the Hughes Tool Company Board of Directors gave him carte blanche to conduct the Hughes defense. The board had adopted a resolution providing that "Robert Maheu be, and he hereby is, appointed the company's agent and attorney-in-fact and delegated executive authority to represent the company in any and all phases of the lawsuit brought by Trans World Airlines."[64]

With a "Dear Bob" letter written the following day, Holliday sent a copy of the resolution to Maheu and solicitously inquired whether it reflected the broad authority he wanted. "If the language of the resolution doesn't seem to you to be adequate," Holliday wrote, "it can be easily changed since it was the intent to grant full and broad authority."[65]

Whatever the reason for the two-year delay in invoking this resolution, Maheu made his move on November 6, 1970, firing off a telegram to Davis:

For good and sufficient reasons in the best interests of an effective appeal you and your firm are hereby advised that you are not to be officially identified with the appeal of the TWA judgment and that neither your name nor that of the firm is to appear on the appeals brief.

This action is being taken upon the specific authority given me in this case by Mr. Hughes and by resolution of the Board of Directors of Hughes Tool Company.

Nothing herein is intended to relieve you of responsibility to cooperate fully with other counsel in the preparation of the appeal. . . .[66]

At the same time, Maheu sent a copy of the telegram and a letter to James V. Hayes, a partner in Donovan, Leisure, advising him "to take whatever action is necessary to make certain that the name of Chester Davis and/or his law firm do not appear on the brief." He concluded the letter, "this action is taken in my sincere belief that it facilitates the likelihood of an effective appeal."[67]

Four days passed before Davis replied to Maheu's telegram. Considering his reputation for an acid tongue, Davis's response was filled with the sweet reason and good taste of a man in control:

I have consulted Messrs. Irvine and Hayes of the Donovan firm, who assure me that there is no reason for not proceeding in a normal manner insofar as names appearing on the brief. I have also consulted the Clifford firm, who feel that my failure to appear on the brief could raise unnecessary questions in the mind of the court with a possible adverse effect.

Under the circumstances, I must ask you to reveal the good and sufficient reasons you refer to so that the matter may be properly evaluated.

Your present activities in connection with this lawsuit are not in the best interests of the client and I must ask you to cease interfering with counsel in charge of and responsible for the case.[68]

Maheu shot back an angry reply two days later. He was dismissing Davis because of "the firm conviction that a successful appeal will be more likely if you are not officially associated with it. To date you have lost this case at every level with catastrophically adverse financial and other injury to the defendants. This consideration alone dictates that responsibilities for the appeal should be placed in other hands. Furthermore, I have no confidence in view of your unfortunate record thus far that your presence will contribute to a successful appeal and that, to the contrary, it may prejudice a favorable result."[69]

Again ordering Davis to withdraw, Maheu reminded him that it is "important that you appreciate that I have been placed in full authority and responsibility for the handling of the TWA case, including the selection of counsel."[70]

On the very day that Maheu sought to remove Davis from the TWA litigation, the Hughes Tool Company Board of Directors adopted a resolution revoking his authority in the TWA case. The directors declared that Chester Davis "shall continue to act and have full authority with respect to any and all phases" of the TWA lawsuit.[71]

On Friday, November 13, Calvin Collier, the Hughes Tool Company vice-president and treasurer, wrote Maheu informing him of these actions and directing him to return "all copies of the October 16, 1968, resolution as well as all copies of other authorizations relating to the same subject matter which you have in your possession."[72] There remained only one piece of business for Gay and Davis before Maheu could be fired.

Levar Myler reported to work about 10:30 on Saturday morning, November 14. Shortly before eleven o'clock, the telecopier machine in the office next to Hughes's bedroom was turned on to receive a transmission from some outpost of the Hughes empire. Howard Eckersley watched the document chatter off the machine. A proxy prepared by Davis was being transmitted from his law office. Eckersley showed the proxy to Myler, then took it into the adjoining bedroom and gave it to Hughes. Myler, meanwhile, waited at the telecopier while two more proxies came off the machine. Eckersley called and Myler took the two other proxies into Hughes's room. When Hughes saw Myler, he turned to Eckersley and asked what he was doing there. Eckersley replied that Myler was going to witness the signing of the proxy and "that he was going to notarize the signature."[73]

The frail Hughes reached up from his reclining chair, selected one of the three proxies, placed it on a yellow legal pad on his lap, and began to write his name. "But it was too flimsy. He requested that [Myler] go get a number of other pads."[74] Myler brought Hughes three more pads and, using them as a table, he signed the proxy. Hughes handed the document to Myler, and he and Eckersley returned to the office, where they both signed it. Myler then destroyed the two other proxies.

The proxy and power of attorney signed by Hughes was a sweeping document. It designated "Chester C. Davis, Raymond M. Holliday, and Frank W. Gay, or a majority of them, my true and lawful attorneys" and authorized the three "to vote and to otherwise exercise all rights" Hughes had as the sole stockholder and proprietor in the companies that owned his Nevada hotels, casinos, and other properties. The three men were authorized to carry out "any and all actions with respect to management" of the Nevada holdings. The document's only restrictions prohibited them from selling the stock or changing the names of the various businesses.[75]

The proxy amounted to an undated order for the elimination of Maheu. With the proxy in hand, Myler notified just two persons that the task begun three months earlier had been finished. The first telephone call went to Bill Gay at his Encino office, a clear indication, if any was needed, of Gay's ranking in the Hughes organization as well as his role in the overthrow of Maheu. The second call was to Davis.

Although the proxy effectively conveyed control of $150-million worth of

Hughes properties, it was handled in a most casual way. Myler carried the document around in his briefcase for a few days and then placed it in his personal safe-deposit box in the Bank of Nevada. Neither Holliday nor Davis nor any other officer of Hughes Tool Company had access to it. Myler, who was paid $45,000 a year to answer the telephone and deliver messages to and from Hughes, held the key to Hughes Nevada Operations.

THE EMPIRE CHANGES HANDS

Around this time, workmen arrived at the Britannia Beach Hotel in the Bahamas to install a special long-distance telephone system. The 270-room Britannia Beach, located on Paradise Island, about twelve hundred feet across the harbor from Nassau and the main island of New Providence, was one of the resort hotels owned by the parent company of Intertel, the security firm collecting information for the firing of Maheu. When completed, the hotel's new telephone system would allow its penthouse occupants to place calls directly to any city in the United States without going through the Bahamian telephone network. Rent for the hotel's top floor was already being paid by the Hughes organization.

Concurrently with the signing of the proxy and the installation of the telephone system at the Britannia Beach, one of the aides called Jack Real, Hughes's longtime acquaintance at Lockheed. The aide's message was brief—Hughes would be needing a plane for a trip to Nassau; could Real oblige?

All that remained was to assure a steady supply of narcotics for Hughes after he left the country. At one point, an aide urged a delay in the departure date in order to obtain "2 more small items." The "items" were the packages of Hughes's codeine. "We only have one (1) left and it has been lasting for 5 days," the aide wrote Hughes. "I cannot ask for any more tomorrow or Friday because we are behind on Norman's paperwork to my man (covering what he gave me the other day). Norman in turn cannot supply the paperwork any closer in dates than he is doing already."[76]

On Thanksgiving Eve, four years after his arrival in Las Vegas, Howard Hughes—just recovering from an attack of pneumonia—was placed on a stretcher, carried out of the Desert Inn unnoticed to a waiting van, and driven to Nellis Air Force Base where a Lockheed JetStar was waiting, courtesy of Jack Real, to fly him to the Bahamas. Nobody noticed. On Thanksgiving Day, the drapes remained tightly drawn across the Desert Inn penthouse windows and life in Las Vegas went on as it had when the state's largest private employer and landowner was in residence. Robert Maheu, the former FBI agent, and Jack Hooper, the former Los Angeles police officer responsible for protecting Hughes and his casinos, were unaware of the successful evasion of their security system by Hughes himself.

It took almost a week for Maheu and his associates to piece together Hughes's disappearance. On December 2, the *Las Vegas Sun,* whose owner

Hank Greenspun was close to Maheu, published an extra edition with a copyrighted article written personally by Greenspun under two bold headlines screaming across the front page: "Howard Hughes Vanishes! Mystery Baffles Close Associates." Greenspun's story began: "Howard Hughes, often called the phantom financier since he established permanent residence in Las Vegas in 1966, is involved in a disappearance from Nevada under circumstance even more mysterious than his secrecy-shrouded arrival. He was spirited away from the Desert Inn the evening of November 25 and even his top aides profess no knowledge of his whereabouts."[77]

Newspaper, radio, and television reporters descended on the Hughes organization and Las Vegas. Carl Byoir and Associates, the public-relations firm that had represented Hughes for more than a quarter century, issued a cryptic and deceptive press release declaring that "a spokesman for the Hughes Tool Company acknowledged today that Howard Hughes left Las Vegas last week on a business trip. He is retaining his living quarters at the Desert Inn."[78]

That same day, Myler informed Holliday that Hughes wanted Maheu fired. Holliday, Gay, Davis, and Collier caucused in Los Angeles to map strategy.

On the following day, Thursday, December 3, the executive committee of the Hughes Tool Company—whose three members were Gay, Holliday, and James R. Lesch—enacted a resolution calling for the immediate firing of Maheu and Hooper and the termination of "any and all authority heretofore conferred" on Maheu and his associates. The resolution authorized Gay and Collier to "notify appropriate company personnel, governmental agencies, banking institutions, and others."[79]

Meanwhile, at the Britannia Beach Hotel, the *Las Vegas Sun* story about his mysterious disappearance had reached Hughes, and when he saw the headline he told Myler that "Bob [Maheu] had to be behind this, because Greenspun would not have dared print any such thing without Bob encouraging him."[80] Hughes instructed Myler to release the proxy.

No one in the Gay and Davis faction wanted to confront Maheu. Instead, they summoned Richard Danner, the managing director of the Frontier Hotel, and Edward Morgan, the Washington attorney who was a personal friend of Maheu's—and on retainer from the Hughes organization as a result of that friendship—to an afternoon meeting at the Century Plaza Hotel in Beverly Hills.

Without ceremony, Davis told Morgan that Hughes wanted Maheu to resign or he would be fired. He asked Morgan "as a close personal friend" of Maheu to convince him to "gracefully bow out and clear the way" for the new management.[81] How much time did Maheu have? Morgan wondered. "It's been delayed too long," Davis said. "It will have to be done by sundown tonight. He'll be off the payroll by close of business today."[82] But why? asked a stunned Morgan. "Mr. Hughes had become quite dissatisfied with Robert Maheu's administration of his affairs and as a result he had issued orders that Maheu, Jack Hooper, and all the Maheu crowd be summarily fired," Davis snapped. Being the sole stockholder, Hughes "did not have to give reasons."[83]

On receiving the bad news, Maheu, who believed that neither Gay nor Davis had any authority to fire him, gathered his troops in the Frontier Hotel to plan his defense. Meanwhile, Gay and Davis had followed Morgan and Danner back to Las Vegas and had taken over the top floor of the Hughes-owned Sands Hotel, just down the Strip from the Frontier and the Maheu faction. The lines of battle were drawn.

Late that night, teams of Haskins and Sells auditors escorted by Intertel agents swooped down on the Hughes casinos and attempted to seize control of the cashier's cages where the money and chips were kept. Under Nevada's gambling laws, only authorized representatives of the holder of a gambling license are permitted in the cage areas. In some casinos the Gay and Davis auditing teams were prevented from entering the cages. In other casinos they gained access only to be expelled.

Maheu immediately informed hotel and casino employees that "an effort has been made to effect an unauthorized takeover of the operations of Mr. Howard Hughes' properties" and that he would "continue to be responsible for such operations."[84] Later in a busy day, he went into Nevada District Court and secured a temporary restraining order barring the Gay and Davis forces from interfering in casino operations. Meanwhile, Carl Byoir and Associates distributed a press release stating that Hughes had severed "all relations" with Maheu and that Intertel had been hired as "consultants" to the Hughes Nevada Operations.[85] And a letter written by Collier was delivered to Maheu confirming that he had been fired and ordering him "to turn over immediately to me or my representative all property, files, and documents in your possession, custody or control."[86]

During the first forty-eight hours of this bitter corporate struggle, Nevada authorities threw their support to Maheu. Governor Laxalt and two members of the State Gaming Commission announced that "for changes in management, a high degree of proof will be demanded by the state, including possibly a personal appearance by Mr. Hughes himself."[87] The response was a natural one. After all, Maheu had always been the chief spokesman for Hughes in Nevada. Gay, Davis, and Holliday were virtually unknown, and it was not clear what authority they had for the takeover. Oddly, Gay and Davis had not disclosed the existence of the proxy. But early Monday morning, the confusion was quickly dispelled for state officials, if not for Maheu.

About 1 A.M., Governor Laxalt, Clark County district attorney George E. Franklin, Jr., and gaming commission chairman Frank Johnson were asked by Gay to come to the eighteenth floor of the Sands Hotel. Hughes, he explained, wanted to talk with them on the telephone. The conversations lasted more than an hour, Hughes speaking with Laxalt, Franklin, and Gay, in that order. Afterward, the governor announced that Hughes had said that he was greatly disturbed by press reports that he had been taken from Las Vegas against his will and that the industrialist wanted to make it clear that "he left freely and that his trip was arranged by executives of the Hughes Tool Company."[88]

Hughes told Franklin that "I'll be home shortly" and that he intended to "spend the rest of my life" in Las Vegas.[89] "He's merely firing a couple of people who were working for him," said Franklin.[90] Later, the district attorney airily dismissed the corporate battle, observing that "a guy fires two employees and goes on a vacation and all of a sudden it's news."[91]

After speaking with Hughes, Laxalt took on "as tough an assignment as I've ever had," the task of telling Maheu, his old friend and tennis partner, that he was indeed no longer employed by Hughes.[92] Maheu had steadfastly maintained that he would not step down unless he heard from Hughes himself. Once again, Maheu's perception of Hughes was faulty. Hughes had never personally performed unpleasant tasks. As it turned out, Maheu had been at least partly correct in predicting five months earlier that Hughes would never fire him or Bill Gay. The firing was carried out by Gay and Davis, and confirmed by the governor of Nevada. Maheu never heard from Hughes.

On that Monday, despite the message from Laxalt, Maheu refused to give in. So later in the day, attorneys for the Hughes Tool Company went to the Nevada District Court and obtained a temporary restraining order barring Maheu from Hughes's properties. With each faction now in possession of its own restraining order, and each side seeking a permanent injunction against the other, the action shifted from the Las Vegas Strip to the Clark County Courthouse.

A series of stormy hearings followed. Maheu argued that his authority to run the Nevada hotels and gambling casinos grew out of "his personal relationship with Mr. Hughes," and that Hughes's signature on the proxy had been forged.[93] Gay and Davis maintained that the proxy was signed by Hughes and that Maheu's "authority to manage the Nevada properties was terminated by appropriate corporate resolutions" enacted by the Hughes Tool Company Board of Directors.[94]

During the proceedings, a handwritten Hughes memorandum was produced in which Hughes chided Gay and Davis for their failure to resolve the dispute with Maheu. "I do not understand why the problem of Maheu is not yet fully settled and why this bad publicity seems to continue," wrote Hughes in a "Dear Chester and Bill" message. "It could hurt our company's valuable properties in Nevada and also the entire state [sic]. . . . You told me that, if I called Governor Laxalt and District Attorney George Franklin, it would put an end to this problem. I made these calls, and I do not understand why this very damaging publicity should continue. I ask you to do everything in your power to put an end to these problems, and further I ask you to obtain immediately a full accounting of any and all funds and/or property to which Mr. Maheu may have had access."[95]

After hearing two weeks of testimony and legal arguments, Nevada District Court judge Howard Babcock upheld the Hughes Tool Company's position and rejected Maheu's request for an injunction. In a Christmas Eve ruling,

Judge Babcock found that the proxy was valid and not a forgery as Maheu contended. He ruled that Maheu's authority over Hughes Nevada Operations had been "duly and lawfully terminated by action of the executive committee of the board of directors of Hughes Tool Company."[96] Furthermore, the judge said, Maheu's continuing interference in hotel and casino operations "has caused and is continuing to cause irreparable injury to Hughes Tool Company and the public interest."[97] Robert Maheu was now legally as well as officially fired.

And so the Hughes empire changed hands. However obscure the motivation for Hughes's flight to the Bahamas, the practical results were clear. While in Las Vegas and dealing through Maheu, Hughes maintained at least some control over his business interests. Now, thousands of miles from the center of his business world, isolated from its day-to-day affairs, dependent on an

Hughes was upset over the continuing uproar about him after his flight from Las Vegas. This is an excerpt from a memorandum to Chester Davis and Bill Gay urging them to quell speculation about him.

internal communications network that censored his flow of information, Hughes was a captive of his own system. The asylum might as well have had bars on the windows and locks on the door. As if to underscore the depth of this new isolation, at the Britannia Beach Hotel the Hughes staff system underwent further refinement. Next to the bedroom, the aides set up their office, and next to it a second, so-called outer office was established. It was manned by aides who waited on the aides who were looking after Hughes. Outside the outer office, the guards were stationed.

Shortly after the move, Roy Crawford, second in seniority to John Holmes among the penthouse aides, was taken off Hughes's staff and reassigned to Los Angeles. The most likely of several explanations is that Bill Gay questioned Crawford's loyalty. In the Las Vegas years, Crawford had worked much more closely with Maheu than the other aides. To replace him, Romaine Street sent Clarence A. (Chuck) Waldron, thirty-five, another Mormon with longstanding ties to Gay and his staff. A cabinetmaker by trade, Waldron had gone to work as a driver in 1957 and moved up quickly, thanks to promotions from his cousin Kay Glenn, Gay's chief lieutenant. Within months, Glenn had named Waldron his assistant and soon placed him in charge of the Romaine Street building, a "big job" as Waldron recalled.[98] Over the years Glenn and Waldron were "very close friends."[99] So Waldron was a logical choice for penthouse duty when Gay began considering staff men who would be unswervingly loyal to him.

The principal beneficiary of Hughes's departure from the United States and the subsequent routing of Maheu was Gay. He was now number two in the Hughes hierarchy. Only Raymond Holliday, head of the oil-tool division, stood between Gay and the top.

With Hughes and Maheu gone, Gay moved in his quiet and efficient way to fill the vacuum and enlarge his organization. He began by annexing the Nevada properties. He fired those employees who might be loyal to Maheu. He shifted his own men into key positions. He added new responsibilities to an already swollen inventory of functions that he controlled. Not even the smallest division within Hughes Nevada Operations failed to escape his attention. Hughes's modest corporate air service is a case in point.

Its equipment included a twin-jet de Havilland 125 and two Cessnas.[100] Until December of 1970, the half a dozen pilots and mechanics on the payroll received their orders through Maheu's office. By the spring of 1971, Chief Pilot Robert F. Wearley, a retired air force major, was reporting directly to Kay Glenn, the Gay underling at Romaine Street.[101]

In addition to carrying out the routine assignments of any other corporate air fleet, the planes were used for assorted services peculiar to the Hughes empire. One such service represented a fringe benefit for favored executives. When Maheu was running the Nevada properties, Hughes planes flew him to Acapulco where he vacationed; to Waterville, Maine, where he visited relatives in his hometown; and to Newport Beach, California, where he maintained an oceanside apartment and yacht.

A far more sensitive service, however, involved free air transportation for politicians, congressional staff members, and their influential friends. A Hughes plane ferried Nevada governor Laxalt between Las Vegas and Reno, and to Washington for a meeting with President Nixon when the governor was considering running for the United States Senate, a race he later made successfully with Hughes's support. A Hughes plane carried Bebe Rebozo, President Nixon's confidant, to such places as Nassau and Washington when Rebozo was accepting secret campaign contributions from Hughes. The Hughes planes were at the disposal of any government official in a position to aid the Hughes organization, from a lawyer on the staff of the Senate Select Committee on Small Business, whose chairman was Senator Alan Bible of Nevada, to a member of the staff of Senator Richard B. Russell of Georgia, then the chairman of the Senate Armed Services Committee.

Under Maheu, the flight operations were a model of discretion. No potentially embarrassing lists of passengers were kept. Quite often even the pilots were unaware of the identity of their passengers. There were exceptions. Wearley, the chief pilot, recalled "picking Mr. Rebozo up at Carlsbad, California, Palomar Airport, and transporting him to Las Vegas. It was the first time that we had carried him. I wasn't sure who the individual was until after the flight, and I was told that his name was Bebe Rebozo, a friend of Mr. Nixon's."[102]

Wearley remembered a later flight on which Rebozo was one of several passengers. "We left Las Vegas on February 2, 1970. We flew to Dallas, Texas, made a passenger drop at Melbourne, Florida, proceeded to Miami. The 4th of February we went from Miami to Nassau, on the 5th from Nassau to Miami and Miami to Washington, D.C." The passenger who got off the plane at Melbourne was one of those anonymous Hughes guests, but Wearley believed he "possibly was an astronaut. Rebozo got off in Washington."[103]

The pilots maintained detailed records of their flights and the aircraft, entering all kinds of information into logs, except, of course, the names of passengers. The information recorded included "the departure point to the arrival point, the destination, takeoff time, the landing time, the pilots' names, a breakdown of the flying time that each pilot logged, a maintenance record, a discrepancy record. In the event there was some malfunction, the pilot would write it up, the mechanic would take corrective action, also write it into the log. The total time on the aircraft, the total time for that flight or that day, and the total time at the end of the day which was carried forward to the next log."[104]

With the change in administrations in Hughes Nevada Operations, the practice of omitting the names of passengers from flight log books was quickly ended. "After I reported to Kay Glenn," Wearley said, "he asked that we put the passengers' names on one copy of the log that would go to accounting."[105] The accounting office was Romaine Street.

Listing the names of passengers on Hughes's private planes may have been a sound business decision, but it also served another purpose. The new information was an important piece of internal political intelligence. In the four years he ran Hughes's properties in Nevada, Maheu operated independently —except when he needed to spend Hughes's money—seldom confiding in Gay or anybody else. The seemingly inocuous practice of compiling passenger lists would go a long way toward curbing ambitious executives.* For Gay, control of the corporate aircraft represented just one more small addition to a corporate insurance policy designed to protect him against the rise of another Robert Maheu, as well as assure his own succession to the top in the Hughes empire.

*In time, the passenger lists would serve as a testimonial to the fact that while there had been a change in the Hughes executive ranks, there had been no change in the way corporate aircraft were used. Where once there was no record that a Hughes plane flew Bebe Rebozo from Las Vegas to the Bahamas, now it was duly noted when a Hughes plane flew United States Senator Howard W. Cannon from Reno to San Francisco. Where once there was no record of Maheu's personal use of the corporate aircraft, now the flights of the husbands, wives, and children of Hughes executives were entered into the record: "N. Henley, S. Marshall [Snowden Marshall, Miss Henley's husband] and party" from Las Vegas to the Grand Canyon. Even the names of prominent entertainers who were passengers on Hughes planes were jotted down: Robert Goulet and party of seven from Las Vegas to Philadelphia, Juliet Prowse from Van Nuys to Acapulco. So, too, were the names of personal business associates or friends of Hughes executives and aides, like "F. Bleak" who flew about Arizona and Utah with Howard Eckersley. (Eckersley was president, and Floyd R. Bleak was vice-president, of Pan American Mines, a mining company whose press releases claimed greater assets than it possessed and which became embroiled in a stock fraud scandal in Canada.)

CHAPTER 19

THE POLITICAL CONNECTION

"I CAN BUY ANY MAN IN THE WORLD"

BY the late 1960s, the Hughes empire had crafted perhaps the most powerful private political machine in the country. Other corporations, other business-men, engaged in some of the same practices, lobbied as vigorously as the Hughes organization, and rang up important victories. But none could match Hughes's long Washington record. For more than two decades the IRS had granted it one special favor after another. So, too, had the Department of Justice, the Civil Aeronautics Board, the Department of the Interior, the army, the navy, the air force, and any number of lesser agencies and departments. The empire spent billions of American tax dollars without public accountabil-ity, received billions of dollars in government contracts without competitive bidding, and received millions of dollars in subsidies. It submitted to federal courts fraudulent or forged documents. It ignored federal court orders with impunity. It was exempted from the myriad laws and regulations binding on others.

The empire thrived on shadowy alliances, intricate deals, quiet under-standings, secret political contributions. The beauty of it all was that the machine was apolitical. By 1970 it had become so potent that the identity of the man in charge did not matter. It could be Bob Maheu one day, Bill Gay the next. The changing faces mattered not at all in the nation's capital. The power rested in the magic of the Hughes name. Whoever chose to invoke the name, and exercise the influence that went with it, could do so. After all, everyone—from the man in the White House to the man in the street—believed it was Howard Hughes making the decisions and issuing the orders. Thus the political machine never once sputtered when the empire changed hands in 1970.

On January 23, 1970, Richard G. Danner, the empire's liaison officer to the Nixon administration, was in Attorney-General John Mitchell's office to discuss a sensitive subject. His employer, preparing to buy another Las Vegas hotel and gambling casino, wanted a sign from Mitchell that the Justice Department would not block the acquisition or file an antitrust lawsuit.

Two years earlier, under another administration, Attorney-General Ramsey Clark had threatened an antitrust proceeding if Hughes carried out his purchase of the Stardust Hotel and Casino. Clark had gone so far as to draft the complaint, but had never had to file it because Hughes, bowing to Justice Department pressure, backed out of the deal. It was one of the very few times in a career distinguished by harmonious relations with government agencies that Howard Hughes had been thwarted.

With the inauguration of Richard Nixon, however, harmony between Hughes and the federal government had returned. When Hughes let it be known late in 1968 that he intended to buy the Landmark Hotel and Casino, Clark was still in office and the Justice Department had reacted in the same hostile way, advising Hughes's lawyers that "the Department of Justice cannot undertake to refrain from taking action with respect to the proposed acquisition. It appears that Hughes' acquisition of the Landmark would violate Section 7 of the Clayton [Antitrust] Act."[1] Four weeks later, as Richard Nixon moved into the White House, the Justice Department had a change of personnel and a change of heart. Hughes's lawyers were advised that the Department of Justice "does not presently intend to take action with respect to the proposed acquisition."[2] And the Landmark deal went through.

Hughes hoped now for another Landmark-like accommodation. This time he wanted to buy the Dunes Hotel and Casino, which would boost his Las Vegas holdings to six hotels—24 percent of the hotel rooms in the city—and seven casinos. Danner spelled out the proposal to Attorney-General Mitchell, who asked Danner to supply a statistical summary of Hughes's Las Vegas hotel and casino investments. The meeting lasted fifteen minutes.

A month later, Danner returned to the attorney-general's office with the report. After glancing at it, Mitchell told Danner, "Let my people look at this, and we will let you know."[3] Mitchell's "people" included Richard McLaren, the hard-nosed assistant attorney-general in charge of the Antitrust Division. Mitchell did his best to coach McLaren. He told him that the governor of Nevada was "trying to drive out hoodlum elements influential in various Las Vegas hotels and casinos, including the Dunes," and that he was "inclined to go along with Hughes' purchase of the Dunes if it could be approved without doing too much violence to established antitrust policies."[4] McLaren was not inclined to go along. He reported to Mitchell on March 12 that the acquisition would definitely violate antitrust guidelines and "that approval would appear inconsistent with the Justice Department's earlier refusal to approve Hughes' proposed purchase of the Stardust."[5]

Such positions on McLaren's part often incurred the wrath of the White House. That anger was reflected in a telephone conversation later between

President Nixon and Deputy Attorney-General Richard G. Kleindienst concerning McLaren's handling of another antitrust issue—the ITT–Hartford Fire Insurance Company case. "I want something clearly understood," the president raged, "and, if it is not understood, McLaren's ass is to be out within one hour. I do not want McLaren to run around prosecuting people, raising hell about conglomerates."[6]

In the Hughes case, however, the attorney-general simply ignored the advice of his antitrust chief. He called Danner and told him to stop by the next time he was in Washington. On March 19, Mitchell gave Danner an opinion the Hughes organization wanted to hear: "From our review of the figures, we see no problem. Why don't you go ahead with the negotiations."[7]

There were no written accounts of the understanding. It was just a gentleman's agreement between the nation's chief law-enforcement officer and the special emissary of Howard Hughes. "Insofar as getting a ruling, anything in writing from the attorney general, it was very informal," Danner explained.[8] He reported on the conference to Robert Maheu and flew to Florida to meet with President Nixon's friend and financial adviser, Charles G. (Bebe) Rebozo. It did not take long for the story to move along the Las Vegas Strip that John Mitchell had told Howard Hughes he could buy the Dunes. On March 23, four days after the Danner–Mitchell meeting, FBI director J. Edgar Hoover sent a memorandum to McLaren.

"Information was received by the Las Vegas, Nevada, office of this Bureau that on March 19, 1970, a representative of Howard Hughes contacted officials of the Dunes Hotel, Las Vegas, Nevada, and stated that Hughes had received assurance from the Antitrust Division of the Department of Justice that no objection would be interposed to Hughes' purchasing the Dunes Hotel," Hoover wrote. "The above is furnished for your information."[9]

The memorandum was a classic Hoover communication. It was the FBI director's way of telling Justice that he knew it had reached a private understanding with an influential citizen. Should the matter later become public knowledge, or improper conduct be shown on the part of a government official, Hoover's record was clear.

McLaren puzzled over Hoover's memorandum. Surely there had been some misunderstanding. He wrote to Mitchell reiterating his objections to Hughes's purchase of the Dunes. "I trust," he said, "that the attached FBI report inaccurately records the understanding received from the Department."[10] Again the attorney-general ignored McLaren. Negotiations for the sale continued.*

This quiet understanding between the attorney-general and the Hughes organization was not unusual. For years, Hughes had cultivated politicians, making a campaign contribution here, dispensing a favor there, encouraging

---

*The Dunes deal later fell through, not because the attorney-general failed to keep his word but because someone in the Hughes organization made a multimillion-dollar accounting error in calculating the value of the Dunes. Hughes was unwilling to pay the higher price.

an aspiring government official by lending him the magic of the Hughes name. His political equation was quite elementary—the right amount of money made available to the right people would produce the right result. There were sometimes variations. Personal favors—a sinecure in a Hughes company, a Hughes plane for business or pleasure, an all-expense-paid trip—could be substituted for cash. Also, fear of losing a job or a contract.

Mostly, though, it was hard cash that Hughes used to work his political will, such as in the summer of 1968 when he dispatched Maheu to deliver personally the $50,000 campaign contribution to Vice-President Humphrey in an effort to persuade him to end nuclear testing if he were elected president. Covering his bets, Hughes instructed Maheu later to go "see Nixon as my special emissary. I feel there is a really valid possibility of a Republican victory this year. If that could be realized under our sponsorship and supervision every inch of the way, then we would be ready to follow with [Nevada Governor Paul] Laxalt as our next candidate."[11]

Spelling it out in the crudest possible terms, Hughes advised Maheu on another occasion, "You just remember that every man—I can buy—I, Howard Hughes, can buy any man in the world, or I can destroy him."[12]

The Hughes equation contained a built-in multiplier. The formation of one relationship led to a second and a third until scores of government officials and congressmen and congressional staff members and influential associates of politicians and lawyers were involved.

The maze of intertwining relationships—always shrouded in Hughes's secrecy—made it difficult, if not impossible, to pin down responsibility for governmental favors accorded to the Hughes empire. The only certain thing was that the relationships existed and that their presence defied coincidence.

The political power of Howard Hughes took on a new significance in 1970. Even as he lost his grip on the empire, his influence reached to the highest level of the United States government.

Richard Danner—onetime special agent in charge of the Miami FBI office, Lincoln–Mercury car dealer, campaign manager for Representative and later Senator George A. Smathers of Florida, Washington lawyer, campaign worker for Richard M. Nixon, and now an executive in the Nevada operations of the Hughes organization—sat one July afternoon in 1970 on the patio of the Western White House at San Clemente, chatting with his friend Bebe Rebozo.

Rebozo—a former filling-station attendant, chauffeur, airline flight attendant, owner of a tire-recapping business, operator of a self-service laundry chain, real-estate speculator, campaign worker for Smathers, and now bank president, millionaire, and confidant of the president of the United States—was drinking coffee.

After Rebozo had finished his cup, he and Danner strolled across to the guest cottage where Rebozo was staying at the San Clemente compound. Once inside, Danner handed his friend a bulky, unmarked manila envelope. It contained ten bundles of $100 bills—$50,000 in all—each bundle secured by a Las Vegas bank wrapper. Rebozo "laid the bundles out on the bed and counted them, but he didn't fan them or break down the amounts, he put them back in the envelope and put them in his handbag."[13] There were no formalities. Danner did not ask for a receipt. Rebozo did not offer to write one. The two men had been friends for thirty years. They had a quarter century of mutual experience in political fundraising, dating back to George Smathers's first campaign for Congress. This was a private matter, the first installment of a previously arranged $100,000 contribution to the president from the Hughes empire.*

The transaction completed, Danner and Rebozo walked about the San Clemente estate, inspected the golf course, and then dropped in on the president in his office. Danner and the president were also well acquainted. Danner had introduced Rebozo to then Senator-elect Nixon in Florida in 1950. Since then, Rebozo had become a fifth member of the Nixon family, sharing holidays and vacations and attending church services with them. The president asked Danner how he liked working in Las Vegas, and lamented his "problems at the White House in getting entertainment that [was] suitable for a young audience, a mixed audience, and so on. How difficult it was to get movies that were not a little too raw."[14] Which Las Vegas entertainers, Nixon wondered, "would be suitable for the White House?"[15] No mention was made of the money, Danner said, for "Rebozo had always made it clear that he didn't want any discussion with the President having to do with contributions, receiving them, or soliciting them."†[16]

---

*The Hughes organization had actually pledged to make the $100,000 secret campaign contribution the year before, when Hughes was anxious to secure, among other things, Nixon administration approval of the Air West acquisition. President Nixon signed a Civil Aeronautics Board order on July 23, 1969, giving Hughes the go-ahead to purchase the airline. When Richard Danner was first questioned by IRS agents in May of 1972, he said that the first $50,000 was delivered to Rebozo late in the summer of 1969 at the Key Biscayne Bank, and that Robert Maheu was present when the money was handed over. In November of 1972, Danner told IRS agents that he delivered the second $50,000 to Rebozo on July 3, 1970, at San Clemente. Robert Maheu told the Senate Watergate Committee staff that "he was present when an envelope filled with cash was passed to Rebozo in Key Biscayne." Rebozo originally told IRS agents that the first $50,000 delivery took place in "late 1968 or early 1969 and that there were two or three months between each delivery." He said one delivery occurred at San Clemente and one at Key Biscayne, but he was unsure of the sequence. In July of 1973, Danner submitted an affidavit to IRS correcting his earlier statements. He said that the first delivery took place on July 3, 1970, at San Clemente, and the second at the Key Biscayne Bank in August 1970 with only Rebozo and himself—not Maheu —present. When Rebozo testified before the Senate Watergate Committee, he said he had concluded after checking his hotel and airline records that the first delivery took place on July 3, 1970, at San Clemente, the second delivery a few weeks later in Key Biscayne, and that Maheu was not present for either.

†This was sharply at odds with a White House memorandum that H. R. Haldeman, the White House chief of staff, wrote to John D. Ehrlichman, the president's domestic-affairs adviser, in February of 1969: "Bebe Rebozo has been asked by the President to contact J. Paul Getty in London regarding major contributions," wrote Haldeman. "Bebe would like advice from you or someone as to how this can legally and technically be handled. The funds should go to some operating entity other than the National Committee so that we retain full control of their use."

Left: Richard G. Danner, the Hughes agent who delivered the mysterious contribution.
United Press International

Right: Charles G. "Bebe" Rebozo, the president's friend and custodian of the $100,000 secret campaign contribution from Hughes.
United Press International

Rebozo maintained later that, without discussing it with anyone, he placed the $50,000 in his suitcase and on returning to his Florida home, stopped by his Key Biscayne Bank, took the manila envelope, wrote "HH" on the corner, and placed it in safe-deposit box 224.

In August, Danner flew to Miami to visit Rebozo at his bank office—where photographs of Nixon and Smathers adorned the walls—and handed over a second manila envelope containing $50,000. Once again, the money was gathered in ten bundles of $100 bills held in place by Las Vegas bank wrappers. Rebozo later removed the wrappers "because of the stigma that is applied to anything from Las Vegas."[17] His action had nothing to do with Hughes personally, whom Rebozo admired. Hughes had earned his respect long ago when, after inheriting a fortune, he "went ahead and did a lot on his own, without living off of it or becoming a bum."[18] Rebozo removed the wrappers also because he recalled "vividly" the scandal over Hughes's 1958 loan to Donald Nixon. This time, Rebozo wanted to make certain that no one found out about the $100,000 Hughes gift.

Exactly what happened to the Hughes cash after Rebozo placed it in his safe-deposit box may never be known. It was said later, and vehemently denied, that Rebozo "had disbursed part of the funds to Rose Woods, to Don Nixon, to Ed Nixon [the president's two brothers] and to unnamed others."[19]

Rebozo steadfastly insisted that the entire $100,000 remained intact in the safe-deposit box. He said he intended to use the money in Nixon's 1972 reelection campaign, but changed his plans because of the furor that erupted with Maheu's ouster from the Hughes organization. After the firing, "Maheu got mad at Danner," who remained on the Hughes payroll, Rebozo recalled.

"When you get family squabbles sometimes they shoot from the hip in every direction and I thought that I just didn't want anything, even remotely, to reflect on the campaign. I didn't want to risk even the remotest embarrassment about any Hughes connection with Nixon."[20]

The "stigma" of Hughes and Las Vegas notwithstanding, Nixon's money managers did put to use $150,000 more in Hughes contributions that were delivered through other channels for the 1972 election. Still, the secret $100,000 gift languished, held in waiting, Rebozo said, for use in 1974 or 1976. But then, he said, "matters went from bad to worse with the Hughes organization and I could just see one talking about the other, and I felt that sooner or later, this matter would come up and be misunderstood."[21] So in the spring of 1973, in the midst of the spreading Watergate scandal, Rebozo "decided to return" the $100,000.[22] He called on the special agent in charge of the Miami FBI office to witness the opening of his safe-deposit box and the counting of the money that "had been in the box all these years."[23] Subsequently, the cash—there turned out to be an extra $100 bill—was returned to the Hughes organization. It was, Rebozo reaffirmed, the very same money that he had received in 1970 from his friend Danner.

Rebozo's otherwise very tidy story held, however, a fatal flaw. The bundles of $100 bills inventoried under FBI supervision included some whose serial numbers showed that they "were not available for commercial distribution until after August 1970," the month of Danner's second delivery to Rebozo.[24]

THE SECRET INVESTMENT

Herbert W. Kalmbach and Frank DeMarco Jr., his partner in the Los Angeles and Newport Beach, California, law firm of Kalmbach, DeMarco, Knapp & Chillingworth, arrived at the White House about noon on Friday, April 10, 1970.

The two lawyers were soon ushered into the Oval Office for a private meeting with the president.[25] They had coffee and discussed the upcoming California elections, and then DeMarco, turning to the purpose of the visit, told the president that he had some good news. He had just completed work on Nixon's 1969 federal income-tax return, and the president would receive a large refund. DeMarco "went through the pages of the return," showing that Nixon's income for the year totaled $328,161.52.[26] Taxes withheld on his salary as president, combined with a previous payment of estimated taxes, amounted to $107,983.26. But owing to a variety of deductions, the president's taxes were only $72,682.09, and therefore he was entitled to a refund of $35,301.17. With an income of $328,161.52, his effective tax rate was 22 percent, slightly above that applied to families earning $30,000 a year.*

---

*The tax refund was based on the president's failure to report all his income, such as the $75,924 he made on the sale of his New York apartment, and improper deductions, such as the $95,298 he claimed for the gift of certain prepresidential papers and other memorabilia. The errors

Nixon was pleased with the work of DeMarco and Kalmbach.[27] "That's fine," the president told his two lawyers. He signed the return and called Mrs. Nixon, on the second floor of the White House, to tell her that DeMarco would bring the return up for her to sign. After Mrs. Nixon signed, DeMarco personally took the president's tax return to IRS officials.

The Kalmbach and DeMarco law firm had represented Nixon since shortly after his inauguration in 1969. The relationship seemed to be working well for all parties. In addition to looking after the president's taxes, the firm was responsible for establishing the Richard Nixon Foundation and acquiring Nixon's San Clemente estate. And Kalmbach was the president's most effective fundraiser.

Everyone knew that the Kalmbach law firm represented the president. What only a very few knew was that the firm also handled a secret investment scheme financed by the assets of a tax-exempt charity for some of the top executives in the Hughes empire.

Five months after the president's tax return was filed, DeMarco and Arthur Blech, a Los Angeles accountant retained by the law firm "to maintain the president's financial books and records and to assist in the preparation of his tax returns," were named general partners in Del Rey Investors, a California limited partnership.[28] Del Rey Investors was one of a number of partnerships and companies created to build and operate a large luxury apartment project at Marina del Rey, just south of Los Angeles.

Today, Marina del Rey is a deluxe collection of high-rise apartments and hotels, fashionable shops, three dozen restaurants, and exclusive clubs spread over four hundred acres around the country's largest man-made small-craft harbor. Located along the Pacific Ocean midway between Santa Monica and Los Angeles International Airport, it houses nine thousand residents and six thousand yachts.

At the center of Marina del Rey is the luxurious Marina City Club, six curved apartment towers containing 671 garden, ocean-view, and penthouse units renting for as much as $2,300 a month. There are swimming pools and tennis courts, a computerized golf course, handball courts, health-spa facilities, three dining rooms, and the Wine Tasting Cellar, an intimate setting for twelve oenophiles. There are facilities for more than four hundred boats, a twenty-four-hour switchboard, and a private security service to screen every person seeking to enter the thirty-acre compound. A staff of more than two hundred provides maid and porter services and parks cars. The residents are "affluent men and women from a wide variety of fields. Financiers, doctors, lawyers, entertainment-industry personnel, publishers, corporate executives, and management consultants."[29]

The Marina City Club is the heart of Marina del Rey, "the unchallenged pacesetter of singles hanky-panky," as one writer described the area. With

in the return were later uncovered by the Joint Congressional Committee on Internal Revenue Taxation and confirmed by the IRS, which had previously approved the tax return.

singles accounting for 70 percent of the area's population and nearly half of them divorced at least once, the Marina, it is said, represents "a sort of sexual supermarket—chock-full of glittering new goodies to help obliterate painful old memories."[30] As one resident, a divorced anesthesiologist, described it, "This place is paradise. I mean, I love living here 'cause everyone looks so pretty. Matter of fact, you could say it's the home of the Pretty People. Not the Beautiful People. The Beautiful People are phonies, tinseled stuck-ups. The Pretty People, on the other hand, are just—well, naturally pretty."[31]

Back in 1970, when all this was still only a gleam in a hedonist's eye, rumors abounded that the Marina City Club was being financed by Howard Hughes. That was to be expected. Hughes had owned part of the land on which Marina del Rey was built. He still owned land adjoining it. And the main plant of his Hughes Aircraft Company in Culver City was just a few minutes away. But the rumors were laid to rest by a story published in the Los Angeles Times which asserted that "contrary to some reports, neither industrialist Howard Hughes nor the Hughes Tool Company has a financial interest in this $70 million development."[32]

That was true. Howard Hughes did not have a penny of his money invested in the Marina City Club. Neither did the Hughes Tool Company. But the Howard Hughes Medical Institute, the alleged charity created by Hughes "for the benefit of mankind," was deeply involved. Its investment had been made through the Hughes Aircraft Company, all of whose stock was owned by the medical institute.

In the beginning, the aircraft company merely guaranteed millions of dollars in loans for the Marina City Club. It did so not for itself or the medical institute, but for the personal benefit of various Hughes executives.

The Marina City Club project was in fact conceived as an investment device and tax shelter for key people at the aircraft company. "In the late 1960s, competitors were raiding Hughes Aircraft Company of its executive and technical talent by offering stock options," explained a high-level company official. "Hughes Aircraft pays reasonably good salaries, but offers no stock options. That's why we were losing some very fine people. Pat Hyland [the general manager of the company] and [another officer] decided we had to do something. That is how Marina City evolved."[33]

In keeping with Hughes's own business practices, his executives established a maze of interlocking partnerships and companies to build and run Marina City. These partnerships were linked to President Nixon's law firm, Kalmbach, DeMarco, Knapp & Chillingworth. Del Rey Investors, of which DeMarco and Blech were general partners, was only one of half a dozen.

The limited partner of Del Rey Investors, for example, was another partnership called Executive Investors Limited, made up of some sixty individuals, mostly Hughes Aircraft executives. Then there was Horizons West, another limited partnership. Alan R. Wolen, an attorney in the Kalmbach and DeMarco law firm, was a general partner of Horizons West. The other was Arthur Blech, who before he handled Nixon's tax returns had assisted the president's brother Donald, "in serious tax trouble" himself at the time.[34] The limited partner of Horizons West was yet another partnership, Management Investors Limited. It, too, was made up of some sixty Hughes Aircraft executives.

Under the terms of the partnerships, the financial obligations of the Hughes executives were substantial. The commitments of John D. Couturie, then the treasurer of the aircraft company, totaled $381,256 in both Executive Investors Limited and Management Investors Limited. Executive Vice-President Allen E. Puckett's commitments amounted to $330,414, and those of John H. Richardson, the senior vice-president, were $268,278.

Long before Marina City opened it got caught in a severe financial squeeze. Construction costs far exceeded estimates. Interest charges soared. When the first apartment towers opened, rental income fell far below original projections as more than half the apartments remained empty. Other apartments, including expensive penthouse suites, were occupied by Marina City Company officers who lived there rent free. "As of August 1, 1972, Marina City Company reported to Aetna Life Insurance Company [a mortgage holder] occupancy of 48 percent—140 apartments rented, 151 apartments vacant."[35]

Losses for an eight-month period ending June 30, 1972, totaled $1,458,-593.[36] By 1974, the annual loss had spiraled to $9,165,228. On its federal income-tax return for the fiscal year ending October 31, 1974, Marina City Company reported income of $2,382,921 against expenditures of $11,548,149. Interest payments for the year amounted to $3,117,972, while income from apartment rentals totaled just $2,179,243, according to its federal tax return prepared by Arthur Blech, the president's accountant.

And that's when Hughes Aircraft intervened in a big way. To avoid the embarrassment of having many of its top executives caught in a financial disaster, the company did more than guarantee loans—it invested millions of dollars to bail the development out. Every dollar invested was an asset of the tax-exempt Howard Hughes Medical Institute. The law firm and the accountant handling the legal and financial details were the same ones representing the president of the United States in his tax affairs. And all the while the Internal Revenue Service looked the other way.

THE SECRET MISSION AND SECRET ALLIANCE

In the fall of 1970 *Glomar II,* a 5,500-ton, 268-foot-long ship able to drill nearly five miles into the ocean floor, began conducting tests at undisclosed locations in the Pacific Ocean. The *Glomar II* was one of a fleet of vessels owned and operated by Global Marine, Inc., a Los Angeles–based company specializing in offshore drilling and related services for the oil and gas industry. But on this particular voyage, the *Glomar II* was not looking for undersea oil and gas deposits. The ship, which had just undergone modifications, was said to be testing a prototype mining system, the results of which would "determine the economic feasibility of deepsea mining operations."[37]

Global Marine was conducting the tests under a contract with the Hughes Tool Company. The work was to signal a new era in mining for metals, in which specially designed ships would scoop up from the ocean floor nodules containing manganese, copper, cobalt, nickel, and other ores. Enthusiastic about its new venture, Global Marine explained to stockholders that "growing interest in deep-ocean mining is prompted by accelerated demand for various strategic ores, many of which will become increasingly scarce in the years ahead."[38]

That was the beginning of the cover story for a top-secret United States intelligence operation. For five years it would have everyone believing that Howard Hughes was preparing to mine the ocean floor for minerals. In truth, the voyage of the *Glomar II* that fall, and the Hughes Tool Company contract with Global Marine, were part of one of the most expensive and bizarre intelligence projects in American history: the effort to retrieve a sunken Russian submarine.

Code-named Project Jennifer by the Central Intelligence Agency, the mission's goal was to raise a vessel that had exploded and sunk in 1968 between Hawaii and Midway and was resting at a depth of more than three miles. By almost any assessment it was an odd intelligence target. The submarine was a conventional diesel-powered model, 320 feet long, which had carried a crew of eighty-six. It was already twelve years old, an outdated submarine carrying outdated equipment. Nevertheless, the CIA wanted it, or so it said, and the agency settled on Howard Hughes to provide the cover story.

There were sound reasons for selecting Hughes. He was a zealous patriot. The Hughes payroll was studded with former intelligence operatives, government agents, and retired army, navy, and air force officers. The Hughes Aircraft Company was deeply involved in the intelligence community's spy-satellite program. And because the project called for construction of a unique salvage vessel at a cost of a quarter of a billion dollars, who better than the notoriously eccentric industrialist could build and operate such a ship without attracting undue public attention? Lending further credence to the ocean-mining cover story was the fact that Hughes had already spent a fortune buying up mining claims across Nevada, where it was rumored that he would soon introduce new computerized mining techniques.

As the CIA was negotiating with the Hughes Tool Company to act as a cover for Project Jennifer, a veteran CIA agent and a CIA front man were preparing to retire from the intelligence business. The spy was fifty-two-year-old Everette Howard Hunt, Jr. Born at Hamburg, New York, the son of a state court judge, Hunt had spent twenty-one years in the CIA working on clandestine assignments from Montevideo to Tokyo. But by 1970, he was bored with his desk job at CIA headquarters, where he had gone following his role in the agency's Bay of Pigs fiasco.

So Hunt went job hunting. There are conflicting versions of his departure from the agency. Some say that CIA Director Richard M. Helms had arranged for Hunt's new job, and others that the agency merely gave Hunt the same good recommendation it gives any loyal spy. Whatever the case, on April 30, 1970, Hunt retired from the CIA and on May 1 he went to work for Robert R. Mullen and Company, a Washington, D.C., public-relations firm. In a city abounding in public-relations offices, one characteristic set the Mullen Company apart. It was a CIA front.

The CIA's alliance with the Mullen Company dated back to 1959 when it was founded by Robert R. Mullen. A longtime Republican party stalwart, Mullen was a former editorial executive at *Life* and the *Christian Science Monitor* and director of information for the Economic Cooperation Administration. In the 1960s, the Mullen Company began to establish foreign branch offices from Mexico City to Amsterdam and Singapore. Each office was staffed by a CIA agent posing as a Mullen Company publicist. Even the company's bookkeeper was a retired CIA finance officer, and Mullen himself had helped to set up the Cuban Freedom Committee in the days before the Bay of Pigs.

In addition to its CIA business, the Mullen Company had contracts with other government agencies. When Hunt joined the firm, at a salary of $24,000 a year, his first public-relations efforts were on behalf of a project that the Department of Health, Education and Welfare was conducting on behalf of handicapped children. Later, he moved on to assignments more in keeping with his previous experience—surreptitious interviews, the bugging of offices, burglaries, forging government documents, and the like.

During this period, Mullen was planning his own retirement, and he began looking for someone to take over his agency. Because of the firm's relationship with the CIA, he needed just the right person, someone of unquestioned loyalty who would follow CIA orders and ask few questions, someone with a measure of influence in political circles and who could deal expertly with the media. After considering and then rejecting the idea of allowing Hunt and another employee to buy the company, Mullen settled on an obscure Washington bureaucrat who then was the director of the Office of Congressional Relations in the Department of Transportation.

He was Robert Foster Bennett. The youngest of the five children of Wallace F. Bennett, the conservative Republican senator from Utah and one-time president of the National Association of Manufacturers, Robert Bennett possessed every credential for the presidency of the Mullen Company. He was a conservative and fiercely loyal American. By virtue of his father's twenty years in the Senate, he had solid political connections, yet he remained in the background, the model of anonymity. Perhaps best of all was his uncanny ability to manipulate the news media.

But Mullen was not alone in his interest in Bennett's future. Bill Gay was also interested. After the overthrow of Robert Maheu in December of 1970, Gay wanted to install his own man as Hughes's Washington representative. What better person for the job than another Utah Mormon, whose father, like Gay, was prominent in the church?

So it was that as Mullen negotiated with Bennett to take over his CIA front, the CIA was arranging for the Hughes organization to manage its secret Russian submarine project, and the Hughes organization was hiring Bennett to become its official Washington representative. By January of 1971, the alliance was forged.

Bennett's political connections were already working for him when he moved into the Mullen offices just down the street from the White House. On January 15, 1971, Charles W. Colson, special counsel to the president, sent a confidential memorandum on White House stationery to a staff aide concerning Bennett and his new job:

Bob Bennett, son of Senator Wallace Bennett of Utah, has just left the Department of Transportation to take over the Mullen Public Relations firm here in Washington. Bob is a trusted loyalist and a good friend. We intend to use him on a variety of outside projects. One of Bob's new clients is Howard Hughes. I'm sure I need not explain the political implications of having Hughes' affairs handled here in Washington by a close friend. As you know, Larry O'Brien has been the principal Hughes man in Washington. This move could signal quite a shift in terms of the politics and money that Hughes represents.

Bennett tells me that one of the yardsticks by which Hughes measures the effectiveness of his Washington lobbyist is the important people he knows; that's how O'Brien got on board. Bob Bennett tells me that he has never met the Vice President and that it would enhance his position greatly if we could find an appropriate occasion for him to come in and spend a little time talking with the Vice President. Maybe you can think of a better way to do this than a meeting in the office; maybe there is a social occasion that Bennett could be included in on. The important thing from our standpoint is to enhance Bennett's position with Hughes because Bennett gives us real access to a source of power that can be valuable, and it's in our interest to build him up.[39]

At that moment the White House and the Hughes organization had special concerns that each believed the other could resolve. President Nixon was worried about Lawrence F. O'Brien, the chairman of the Democratic National Committee. The Hughes organization was worried about Robert Maheu and the lawsuit that he was pressing against Hughes.

For some months the White House had been obssessed with O'Brien's position on the Hughes payroll in Washington. The president and his aides wanted to know the current status of O'Brien's relationship with the Hughes Tool Company, the financial details of the arrangement, and exactly what services the Democratic official was performing, all with an eye to leaking the information to the news media as a major political scandal. The day before Colson wrote about the need to build up Bennett, the president himself had expressed a strong interest in the Hughes–O'Brien connection.

"It would seem that the time is approaching when Larry O'Brien is held accountable for his retainer with Hughes," Nixon wrote to his chief of staff, H. R. Haldeman. "Bebe [Rebozo] has some information on this, although it is, of course, not solid. But there is no question that one of Hughes' people did have O'Brien on a very heavy retainer for 'services rendered' in the past. Perhaps Colson should check on this."[40]

With Nixon's approval, Haldeman gave the assignment to John W. Dean III, the president's counsel, instead of Colson. But Dean discussed the problem with Colson, who told him about Bennett and his new position. A meeting with Bennett was promptly set up, and on January 26 Dean relayed the results to Haldeman:

Bennett informs me that there is no doubt about the fact that Larry O'Brien was retained by Howard Hughes and the contract is still in existence. The arrangements were made by Maheu and Bennett believes that O'Brien, through his associate [Claude] Desautels, is going to seek to have Hughes follow through on the alleged retainer contract even though Maheu has been removed. Bennett also indicates that he will be going to the West Coast to talk about the specifics of his Hughes relationship with Mr. Gay (the man who is responsible for releasing Maheu). Bennett also indicated that he felt confident that if it was necessary to document the retainer with O'Brien that he could get the necessary information through the Hughes people, but it would be with the understanding that the documentation would not be used in a manner that might embarrass Hughes.[41]

Haldeman responded two days later, telling Dean that he "should continue to keep in contact with Bob Bennett, as well as looking for other sources of information on this subject. Once Bennett gets back to you with his final report, you and Chuck Colson should get together and come up with a way to leak the appropriate information. Frankly, I can't see anyway to handle this without involving Hughes so the problem of 'embarrassing' him seems to be a matter of degrees." Confirming the importance of Bennett's relationship with the White House, Haldeman concluded that "we should keep Bob Bennett and Bebe out of it at all costs."[42]

When Bennett flew west for his meeting with Bill Gay, the shrewd Hughes executive advised him that he could not provide information relating to the O'Brien contract, even for the White House. Perhaps Gay sensed, as Haldeman had told Dean, that any use made of the information would be embarrassing to Hughes. Or perhaps Gay just adhered to the policy that helped him rise from telephone message clerk to top executive in the Hughes empire—never to discuss Howard Hughes or his business affairs with any outsider.

On his return to Washington, Bennett had few specific details and no documentary evidence on the O'Brien contract to offer Dean. Instead, during his meeting with the president's counsel, Bennett described the bitter struggle taking place between his superiors in the Hughes Tool Company and the ousted Maheu. The two sides, he said, were "trying to destroy each other."[43] He pointed out that since O'Brien had been hired by Maheu, his services were no longer needed and negotiations were proceeding toward an amicable parting of the ways.

Bennett also had a warning to convey to the White House. Dean recalled his explaining that "Maheu had handled all Hughes' political activity for the last 15 years," that he had information relating to the association between the president's brother and the Hughes organization, and "since O'Brien was close to Maheu, there was a presumption that he knew a great deal. He had to be handled delicately." But Maheu himself might be dealt with more aggressively; Bennett asserted that Maheu had been fired because of "his involvement with notorious gangsters and suggested that the administration pursue a criminal investigation." As Dean remembered later, "I recoiled at the rat's nest he was revealing. I admired how carefully he phrased his sentences, and I wondered about the things he was not telling me."[44]

The White House took heed of Bennett's subtle suggestion about the need to handle O'Brien "delicately." O'Brien certainly had knowledge of Donald Nixon's dealings with the Hughes organization. Perhaps he also knew of the $100,000 locked away in Rebozo's bank. Any political gain to be achieved by leaking some O'Brien story would surely be more than offset by potential revelations about the tie between Hughes and the Nixon administration.

So the first dealings between the two parties ended pretty much where they began. The White House did not get from Bennett documentary evidence of O'Brien's work for Hughes. Bennett did not get from the White House the federal investigation of Maheu that the Hughes organization wanted. It mattered little, though, for soon the Hughes empire would be rid of Maheu entirely, and the White House found another way to deal with O'Brien.

Of far more importance were the new relationships that had been formed, the new doors opened. The White House and Bennett each had a keen awareness of what one could do for the other. In fact, the White House was so pleased with the new alliance that Colson immediately lined up another project for Hughes's Washington representative.

The Associated Milk Producers, Inc., seeking higher price supports for milk, had offered to contribute $2 million to Nixon's reelection campaign. But rather than making the contribution in one lump sum—a move that would attract undue attention and require the payment of federal gift taxes—the decision was made to break up the contribution into amounts of $2,500, each coming through a separate campaign committee. To create the hundreds of committees that would be necessary, the White House turned to Robert Bennett.

It was no easy task, coming up with enough people who would serve as chairmen and treasurers, people who would be discreet about heading dummy committees. Even so, Bennett rose to the occasion, finding faithful party workers, friends, and associates, and their husbands or wives. Displaying a fine flair for the ironic, he gave the committees names like the League of Dedicated Voters, Organization of Moderate Americans, Americans for Sound Ecological Policy, and Americans United for Decent Government. Bennett appointed himself chairman of Americans United for Economic Stability. He named Dorothy L. Hunt, the wife of his Mullen Company colleague, as chairman of Americans United for Political Moderation. Soon the money was rolling in from the dairy industry.

For its part, the Hughes empire also needed something special—preferential treatment in a critical tax case. And Bennett, with all his freshly minted

White House contacts, appeared to be just the man to get it.

The problem had started back in 1969, when Congress enacted the most sweeping tax-reform legislation in history. The new code cut the long-sacred oil-depletion allowance from 27.5 to 22 percent, raised capital-gains taxes to a maximum of 35 percent, repealed the investment tax credit for businesses buying machinery and equipment, extended the income-tax surcharge, ended unlimited deductions for charitable contributions, and imposed a minimum tax on certain income. These and a number of other changes in the code were designed generally to make the tax system more just. In time, the various provisions of the 1969 Tax Reform Act were applied to every working American family, business, corporation, and tax-exempt organization, with only a few exceptions. The most notable exception was the Hughes empire.

Among the principal targets of tax reformers were the tax-exempt foundations and charitable trusts. By 1969, their number had swelled to more than thirty thousand. For the most part, they were seldom audited by the Internal Revenue Service, and their operations almost never monitored, despite the fact that they were accumulating billions of untaxed dollars. The not-too-surprising result of the IRS' inattention and years of congressional neglect was a tax-exempt system riddled with abuse and corruption. Self-styled charities were being used as devices by the rich to increase their holdings and reduce their tax bills; often the purported beneficiaries saw little of the charities' money.

Some years earlier, a congressional committee had established that "foundations have engaged in business operations in competition with private companies which lack the enormous advantage of a tax-exemption certificate. Foundations have loaned money to their creators, traded stock and property with them, paid for insurance policies on the life of the donor, financed benefit programs for a contributor's employes and engaged in many other activities whose relevance to charity and social welfare seems remote."[45]

To end such abuse, the 1969 act contained a series of tax-reform measures aimed specifically at foundations and other tax-exempt organizations. The reform act divided all tax-exempt organizations into two categories: private foundations, such as the Ford and Rockefeller Foundations, and public charities, such as the United Fund and Red Cross.

The toughest restrictions applied to the private foundations. They were required to spend an amount equal to 6 percent of their assets each year, in order to prove they were truly charitable and not just interested in accumulating money. A 4-percent tax was imposed on their investment income. They were barred from owning more than 35 percent of the stock in any one company; in some cases they could own no more than 20 percent. Foundations that existed before 1969 were given up to twenty years to sell off their stock in excess of the 20- or 35-percent limitations. They were barred from engaging in transactions with their founders, managers, or anyone who had a substantial interest in businesses that were major contributors. Failure to abide by the new tax laws could result in stiff penalty taxes and even loss of tax-exempt status.

By 1971, most tax-exempt organizations had been designated either private foundations or public charities. The few not designated were awaiting the Treasury Department's publication of regulations implementing the tax code in their categories. Among those waiting were medical-research organizations, and most prominently the Howard Hughes Medical Institute. In May of 1971, the Treasury Department finally published a set of proposed regulations under which a medical-research organization could be classed as either a private foundation or a public charity. To qualify as a public charity like the American Cancer Society, a medical-research organization was required to spend an amount of money equal to 4 percent of its assets on research each year. Thus, an organization of $100 million in assets would have to spend $4 million a year on medical research. The penalty for noncompliance was designation as a private foundation, and more stringent regulation.

Hughes executives panicked on learning of the new regulations, and with good reason. From its inception in December of 1953 through 1970, the Howard Hughes Medical Institute had spent an average of only 0.6 percent of its assets each year on medical research. Even that figure was inflated because it was based on the medical institute's own estimate of the value of its sole asset, the stock of the Hughes Aircraft Company, and that estimate was a false one. The medical institute had grossly understated the company's value by anywhere from 200 to 300 percent. When the aircraft company's real worth was taken into account, the institute's expenditures for medical research averaged between 0.2 and 0.3 percent of its assets, less than a tenth of the amount required by Treasury Department regulations.

To make matters worse, the Howard Hughes Medical Institute had spent substantial sums of money unrelated to medical research. In seventeen years, the institute had given $10.3 million directly to research—for salaries of research workers, fellowships, laboratory supplies and equipment, and a medical library. During that same period, it gave $25.6 million to Howard Hughes's wholly owned Hughes Tool Company in interest payments on an outstanding loan and lease payments on real estate. In other words, for every $1 million the institute gave to medical research, it gave $2.5 million to its founder, Howard Hughes.*

It was little wonder, then, that Hughes executives were distressed. If the regulations became final, the medical institute would be designated a private foundation. That would mean it would have to spend an amount equal to 6 percent of its assets on medical research, and if it failed to do so, penalties would be imposed. Even worse, the medical institute would have to begin selling its stock in the Hughes Aircraft Company to meet the limitations set on stock ownership in a single company. Howard Hughes, sole trustee of the institute, and Howard Hughes, president of Hughes Aircraft Company, would be obliged to surrender the control he exercised over the aircraft company.

It was a foregone conclusion that the medical institute would not go to

*See Appendices C and D

its own funeral. On June 21, 1971, a month after disclosure of the proposed Treasury regulations, the Washington law firm of Hogan & Hartson, which had represented Hughes and his medical institute ever since it was established, sent off a nine-page letter to the Internal Revenue Commissioner. Basically, the letter insisted that the provision requiring a minimum yearly expenditure for medical research "should be eliminated in its entirety."[46] Two weeks later, Hogan & Hartson attorneys met privately with Treasury Department officials to present their case.

That was one level of Washington activity. In another part of town, Hughes's Washington lobbyist was at work on a different level. On July 30, Robert Bennett took time off from creating phony campaign committees for the White House to write a "Dear John" letter to White House counsel John Dean, calling his "attention to a situation with which I think you should become familiar."[47] Bennett explained the consequences of the Treasury Department regulations for Hughes's self-styled charity, asserting, quite incorrectly, that "Hughes Aircraft is operated like any other business, with all of its dividends going to Howard Hughes Medical Institute for expenditure on medical research."[48] Bennett warned that if the aircraft company, whose annual sales to the United States government were nearly $1 billion, had to increase its annual contribution of $2.5 million to the medical institute, it would be severely pressed:

It seems to me incongruous for the Treasury Department to be spending so much of its time and expertise on an effort to aid the Lockheed Corporation, a company with cash flow problems, while at the same time embarking on a course of dubious statutory legitimacy which will create similar if not more serious cash flow problems for Hughes Aircraft. I don't want to challenge for a moment the wisdom of the decision to try to save Lockheed; instead, I want to put the Hughes Aircraft problem in the same perspective and urge the Administration to think long and hard about whether or not it wishes to precipitate a crisis for another contractor.[49]

Bennett added that certain material had been passed along to the Treasury Department, including the "text of a proposed grandfather clause" that would exempt the Howard Hughes Medical Institute from the onerous spending requirement. "If you wish further information from me," Bennett concluded, "I would be more than happy to supply it."[50]

John Dean touched base at the Treasury Department and responded to Bennett's plea for assistance with a reassuring "Dear Bob" letter—"the proposed regulations are being reconsidered in light of this particular situation, but that no final decisions have been reached. I appreciate your bringing this matter to my attention."[51]

What happened next was a textbook demonstration of assent by silence and of the political influence wielded throughout the United States government by the Hughes empire. The Treasury Department did not amend its regulations as Bennett and Hogan & Hartson had hoped. But it did the next-best thing: nothing. It simply did not enforce the 1969 Tax Reform Act on the

Howard Hughes Medical Institute. The months slipped by and 1971 turned to 1972. Then 1973 came and went, and 1974 and 1975 and 1976 and 1977. As of this writing, the IRS has yet to make a final ruling.

Nothing changed at the Howard Hughes Medical Institute. It continued to spend only a token amount on medical research. In 1974, when Hughes Aircraft Company sales to the Defense Department totaled $813.2 million, the company gave just $3.5 million to the medical institute, 0.4 percent of its revenue from United States military contracts alone. Of the $3.5 million, the medical institute returned almost $1 million to Hughes's holding company in interest on the outstanding loan.

During this same period, the Internal Revenue Service was rigorously enforcing various provisions of the 1969 Tax Reform Act as they applied to the more than thirty thousand other tax-exempt organizations. Large, legitimate foundations like Ford and Rockefeller and Mott were all paying the new taxes and adhering to the regulations governing the amount of money they had to distribute each year for charitable purposes.

The failure of the government to enforce its tax laws fairly saved the Hughes empire tens of millions of dollars. It also enabled the Hughes Aircraft Company to divert to other ventures money that should have gone to taxes or to medical research. Not the least of those ventures was the sultry singles ghetto built and operated for the enrichment of Hughes executives at Marina del Rey.

CHAPTER 20

LIFE IN EXILE

TUESDAY, December 7, 1971, was like any other day in the penthouse suite at the Britannia Beach Hotel on Paradise Island. At 6:45 A.M., Hughes ate a piece of chicken and began watching an Agatha Christie whodunit, *Ten Little Indians*. An hour and twenty minutes later he counted out eight one-grain codeine tablets, put them in his syringe, added a few drops of water, and injected the solution into his arm. That afternoon he finished watching *Ten Little Indians*, went on to a western, *Tension at Table Rock*, took twenty-five milligrams of Valium, and fell asleep.[1]

In New York City that day, at the offices of McGraw-Hill, Inc., Albert R. Leventhal, a vice-president, announced a publishing coup: McGraw-Hill had acquired "world publishing rights to a 230,000-word transcript of taped reminiscences of Howard R. Hughes."[2] Leventhal said the autobiography of the reclusive industrialist—based on almost one hundred taping sessions—would be published March 27, 1972, and that *Life* magazine would serialize the book in three installments of ten thousand words each, beginning March 10. Hughes had spent the past year, Leventhal said, working on his memoirs with Clifford Michael Irving, an American novelist living on the Spanish island of Ibiza. The surprise disclosure was accompanied by a press release that McGraw-Hill said had been prepared by Hughes himself to explain his decision to write the book. It stated, in part, "I believe that more lies have been printed and told about me than about any living man—therefore it was my purpose to write a book which would set the record straight."[3]

Within hours of the McGraw-Hill announcement, a Hughes Tool Company spokesman branded the autobiography a hoax. Clifford Irving, with eight books to his credit, charitably brushed aside the tool company charge, observing that it "was not malice on their part, it was ignorance. They didn't know a damn thing about it."[4] McGraw-Hill and *Life,* among the most respected publishers in the country, stood firmly behind the book. "We never dealt with the Hughes Tool Company," Donald M. Wilson, vice-president for corporate and public affairs at *Life,* told reporters. "It doesn't surprise us that they know nothing of this since Mr. Hughes was totally secretive about the project. We are absolutely certain of the authenticity of this autobiography and we wouldn't put McGraw-Hill's and *Life*'s name behind it if we weren't."[5] To further authenticate the book, Irving delivered to McGraw-Hill a handwritten memorandum from Hughes affirming the validity of the work, and Osborn Associates, a nationally recognized firm of handwriting experts, concluded that the memorandum was indeed written by Howard Hughes.

Throughout the controversy, an oblivious Hughes continued to watch his films—*Deadlier than the Male, The Wrecking Crew, No Highway in the Sky, Bullet for a Badman,* and *Gunfight in Abilene* among others—inject himself with narcotics, and gulp tranquilizers. There were occasional other concerns and instructions dutifully entered in the logs by an aide so that the next shift would be current. On December 12, the subject was pills: "Have Carl or Gordon count out the medicinals so we do not touch bottles. They can be prepared in advance and left in cup in refrigerator."[6] On December 21, pajamas: "He wants his P.J. top neatly folded and placed on his table to the left of the chair."[7] On December 23, it was his pillow: "His head pillow is to be inserted with the hard blue-green pillow next to his back and the open end of the pillow case on his right (not the left as before). Also, carry the pillow by the bottom seam."[8] On Christmas Day came desserts: "Wants to start orange tarts again. Also wants to change the Napoleons so there is cake between custard rather than the flaky pie crust material they now have. The custard and frosting should remain as is."[9] And on January 2, the movies: "HRH says not to get any more Italian westerns."[10]

The McGraw-Hill announcement of the autobiography had meanwhile thrown the Hughes organization into turmoil. Those in control knew the book was an elaborate hoax. But how to prove it? There was no way that Hughes could even briefly leave his institutional surroundings and make a public appearance to deny authorship. Although tool company officials continued to insist that Hughes had not written any book, they failed to produce the hard evidence that would discredit Irving. The resulting stalemate would require some dramatic act to convince a skeptical public. The vehicle finally settled on was a telephone interview to be conducted by seven reporters who had known Hughes before he went into isolation and thus could identify his voice and ask questions designed to trip up an impostor. The reporters selected to question the industrialist over a three-thousand-mile telephone hookup between the Britannia Beach Hotel in the Bahamas and a makeshift studio at the Sheraton–Universal Hotel in Hollywood were James Bacon of the Hearst newspapers, Gene Handsaker of the Associated Press, Gladwin Hill of the *New York Times,* Marvin Miles of the *Los Angeles Times,* Roy Neal of NBC (who was to act as moderator), Vernon Scott of United Press International, and Wayne Thomis of the *Chicago Tribune*.

The interview posed certain risks. Hughes might display a telltale sign of his mental state. Yet if the questions were none too probing or hostile, he probably could make it through without any unfortunate disclosures. It was reasonable to expect that the questions would not be searching. The reporters had known Hughes in happier days, before he went into seclusion. Then, too, there was Hughes's memory. Neither age nor his psychological disorders had affected his remarkable powers of recall, especially about airplanes, a subject the newsmen were sure to focus on since all had known him when he was an active pilot.

The date set for Howard Hughes's first meeting with the press in more than fifteen years was Friday, January 7, 1972. At 3:15 A.M. that day, Hughes began watching the Len Deighton spy thriller *Funeral in Berlin*. He watched the first reel of the film, the second reel, the third reel, and then all three once again. At 12:45 P.M. he picked up his cache of narcotics, counted out eight one-grain codeine tablets, dissolved the tablets in water in his syringe, and injected himself. He looked at *Funeral in Berlin* one more time and then at 6:45 P.M.—exactly six hours after he had shot up—Howard Hughes picked up the telephone and met the press.[11]

"Good afternoon, Mr. Hughes," said Roy Neal.

"Good afternoon to you," Hughes replied.

"One question all of us have at the outset is, where are you speaking from right now, sir?" Neal asked.

"Paradise Island," Hughes said. "Nassau seems to be a more widely known name. I notice accoutrements here at the hotel [say it] is called Paradise Island, Nassau. That must be because Nassau is a more widely known name than New Providence. But in truth, New Providence is the main island here in this group, and Paradise Island, which used to be called Hog Island, is a part of that group, and that is where I am."[12]

The voice was older, the speech more hesitant, but there was no mistaking Howard Hughes. As Jim Bacon observed when his turn came to ask the questions, "I have heard that voice so many times, and the minute you started talking I knew it was Howard Hughes."[13] Just as expected, Hughes handled the aviation questions with the same ease he once employed flying planes. When the subject of his design contributions to Lockheed's Constellation came up, he was prepared to speak for hours:

I remember clearly the plywood cockpit and this feature that I am discussing—Oh, and another thing there that would be clearly remembered by everyone who worked on that cockpit, was my continual complaints about the width, vertically, of the clear area of glass in the windshield. In other words, I was concerned with the visibility, and there was an everlasting struggle between the engineers of Lockheed who wanted better aerodynamic qualities, and they wanted to keep the cockpit as drag-free as possible. They kept pulling the roof of this windshield down and limiting the total amount of clear glass; do you follow me? And when we finally agreed to a compromise, which was a hard-fought battle, then I was either away from Los Angeles, or Burbank, or where the mock-up was located, for a period—or I didn't see it for a while—and when I came back, I discovered that they had taken the dimensions that I had agreed upon and made it the dimensions of the total frame itself, so that, in other words, it was not the dimensions of the clear glass at all, it was the dimensions of the clear glass plus about three-fourths of an inch, at least, maybe more, of metal into which this clear glass was clamped, which, of course, cut down the vertical arc of visibility or width of visibility appreciably.[14]

On and on Hughes talked, a memory machine.

But the machine only remembered certain things. His encyclopedic recall of the aircraft he was so closely associated with—the H-1, the D-2, the flying boat, the Constellation—overshadowed an astonishing failure to answer correctly test questions the reporters asked on a variety of nontechnical subjects.

"Here is a question, one question that we thought you might be probably the only person who would know the answer to, offhand," Gladwin Hill began. "During your development of the Constellation airplane, you were assisted at some points by a professional pilot whose last name was Martin. Do you remember what his first name was, and what his wife's occupation was?"

"I don't think I can help you with this Martin," Hughes said candidly. "I don't think I remember Mr. Martin, but I can tell you an awful lot about those [Constellation] mock-up discussions."

Hughes could not answer Wayne Thomis's test question either. "I would like to take your memory back a ways to the time of your flights in 1937 and 1938," Thomis said, "and ask you—the man who assisted you in setting up a good deal of this, particularly with the timers and the FAA, was a man who was an executive with AVCO [Aviation Corporation] and I'm wondering if you remember his name."

"No," Hughes said forthrightly. Even when Thomis supplied the man's first name, Hughes still drew a blank. And he fared no better with Marvin Miles's test question. "I'd like to ask you one identification question," Miles said. "I'm sure that you can answer very quickly, and then one other on a larger subject. At the time of your 'round-the-world flight when you—just before you took off from Floyd Bennett Field, a superstitious woman placed a traditional good luck charm on your airplane. I'd like to know if you recall what it was, and where she put it?"

"No, I don't recall, and it certainly happened without my knowledge," Hughes said.

"No, sir. You spoke of it in a speech to the Washington Press Club when you returned," Miles said. "You said that a woman placed a wad of gum on the tail."

"Well, I want to be completely honest with you. I don't remember that," Hughes said.

But perhaps the most devastating failure came when Hughes was asked whether he remembered General George, who had managed Hughes Aircraft

Company during its transition from a Hughes hobby to an important defense contractor.

"Well, he was just a friend," Hughes said. "He never worked for me, did he? I don't remember General George ever working for me."[15]

Hughes's inability to answer the test questions, although vastly puzzling at the time, was not out of character. He had possessed such charm in the early years that it was assumed by all who met him that he was like other men. If he was somewhat shy and eccentric, he seemed nonetheless to relate well to men and women. The truth is that Hughes never related at all to other people. Only mechanical objects, especially airplanes, or technical matter left an indelible mark on his mind.

Still, despite the memory lapses and the fact that Hughes had not dealt with reporters in years, he played the press conference like a seasoned politician, fielding effortlessly those questions unrelated to people, reeling off one answer after another in his low-keyed, convincing, occasionally wry style. That many times his answers bore scant resemblance to the truth no one seemed to

The 1972 telephone press conference. Around the table clockwise are Jim Bacon of the Hearst Newspapers, Marvin Miles of the *Los Angeles Times,* Vernon Scott of United Press International, Roy Neal of NBC News, Gene Handsaker of the Associated Press, Wayne Thomis of the *Chicago Tribune,* and Gladwin Hill of the *New York Times.* Dialing the telephone is Richard Hannah, a Hughes public relations man.
Wide World Photos

notice. After scoffing at published reports that when he left Las Vegas he weighed less than a hundred pounds, his hair trailed down his back, and he had exceptionally long fingernails (all of which was true), Hughes said he intended to end his self-imposed isolation to put such rumors to rest. "I will tell you one thing," he said. "I am rapidly planning to come out of it. In other words, I am not going to continue being quite as reclusive, as you call it, as I have been because it apparently has attracted so much attention that I have just got to live a somewhat modified life in order not to be an oddity. I am getting ready to embark on a program of convincing the public that these extreme statements are absurd."[16]

When questioned about rumors that he chose not to meet people personally because of a germ phobia, Hughes said, "I come in contact with everybody from here to Salt Lake City and Los Angeles and back. I have got a staff that commutes regularly across the country, and I'm in proximity to them constantly, and if I have any fear of contagion, they would certainly bring it here. Anyway, I don't think this is a particularly contagious-free area that I'm in anyway."[17]

To a proposal that he have a face-to-face meeting with the press, Hughes said, "I definitely expect to do it. I have intentions to do it." Was he considering a return to motion picture production? "I would like to. I have always thought that movies and motion pictures would be something I could do even after my last days, so to speak. I have always thought that in the later years of my life I would like very, very much to make motion pictures that would be worthwhile." Had he any plans to resume flying airplanes? "Yes. Positively. I definitely expect to recommence the program of flying."[18]

When the questioning got around to the purpose of the interview, the Clifford Irving book, Hughes expressed astonishment. "As Mr. Davis said, this must go down in history. I only wish I were still in the movie business, because I don't remember any script as wild or as stretching the imagination as this yarn has turned out to be. I'm not talking about the biography itself, because I have never read it. I don't know what's in it. But this episode is just so fantastic that it taxes your imagination to believe that a thing like this could happen." As for Clifford Irving himself, Hughes was quite explicit: "I don't know him. I never saw him. I have never even heard of him until a matter of days ago when this thing first came to my attention."[19]

Hughes professed to be at a loss to explain the motive for the Irving book, but he did rise to a question about Robert Maheu. Could, asked one reporter, the book be "a carefully structured plot by the Maheu–Hooper interests to discredit" him? Hughes replied quickly, "My attorney thinks that it could be." Such was the depth of the bitterness within the organization that Hughes's only display of anger was directed not at Irving, but at Maheu. Alluding to a lawsuit Maheu had brought against the Hughes Tool Company challenging his dismissal, Hughes charged that "everything he has done, everything short of murder, as a result of being discharged, I don't suppose any disgruntled employee who was discharged has ever even come close to Mr. Maheu's conduct." Asked why he had fired Maheu, Hughes—reflecting the stories he had been fed repeatedly over the past two years—announced flatly: "Because he's a no-good dishonest son-of-a-bitch, and he stole me blind. I don't suppose I ought to be saying that at a news conference, but I just don't know any other way to answer it. You wouldn't think it could be possible, with modern methods of bookkeeping and accounting and so forth, for a thing like the Maheu theft to have occurred, but, believe me, it did, because the money's gone and he's got it."[20]

Throughout the two-and-a-half-hour interview, this was Hughes's only serious blunder.* Otherwise, Hughes conducted himself superbly, only stumbling over those questions relating to people he had once known and long since forgotten. It had been agreed before the interview that the questions and answers would be transcribed and made public Sunday night. On Monday morning, January 10, 1972, newspapers across the country carried the Hughes interview on their front pages, and radio and television stations broadcast excerpts. Within a month, Clifford Irving acknowledged that the Hughes autobiography was the product of his own imagination.

Although Hughes had emerged with his image intact, the press conference touched off another crisis for his organization. So much publicity had

---

*A month later, on February 10, 1972, Maheu filed a $17.5-million libel and slander lawsuit against the Hughes Tool Company in the United States district court in Los Angeles. On July 1, 1974, after a four-month trial, the jury found that the Hughes Tool Company, then the Summa Corporation, was liable for Hughes' statements. A second trial to set damages followed. After hearing additional testimony, the jury awarded Maheu more than $2.8 million and a judgment for that amount was entered against Summa on December 23, 1974. Summa appealed the twin verdicts, arguing that "uncontradicted evidence regarding at least three specific incidents proves the truth of Hughes' statement" and that under California law Summa need not prove the literal truth of the allegedly defamatory remark, "so long as imputation is substantially true so as to justify the 'gist' or 'sting' of the remark." On December 27, 1977, the United States Court of Appeals for the Ninth Circuit overturned both the jury's liability finding and its damage award and sent the case back for retrial. The appellate court concluded that the presiding trial judge, Harry Pregerson, in summarizing the case before it went to the jury, had presented a favorable, "one-sided characterization of Maheu [that] came close to directing a verdict in his favor, thus denying Summa a fair trial." The court noted that Judge Pregerson described Maheu as "affable, intelligent, imaginative, articulate, a friendly man with important friends in high places" and "a man of enormous energy and drive" with the "ability to get things done." The appellate court observed that "while that description may be accurate, not all the evidence supported that view. . . . This glowing character reference failed to mention Summa's contentions that Maheu was dishonest, a thief, an embezzler, and a perjurer, a contention that was supported by a mass of very persuasive evidence." The appellate court took special note of one particular incident offered by Summa as evidence of the truth of Hughes's statement. Maheu "was supposed to provide full time guard service, around the clock, for certain properties in Tucson owned by Summa. He submitted bills for those services. On their face they showed hours of work by each guard, and an hourly rate of pay. They were false. They showed many more hours, and substantially higher rates of pay, than were in fact furnished and paid, to the tune of many thousands of dollars. Maheu did not deny that the billings were false. He said that Hughes told him to make a good profit from furnishing the guards, and to conceal from the executives of Summa the fact that he was making a profit. His explanations of other instances were equally bizarre. But they had one thing in common. They rested on private, unrecorded conversations between him and Hughes."

swirled about Hughes and his alleged autobiography that the opposition political party in the Bahamas saw an opportunity to embarrass the government of Premier Lynden O. Pindling, the Bahamas' first black ruler. Not long after the press conference, Cecil Wallace Whitfield, leader of the Free National Movement, announced that he intended to submit a series of questions to the Pindling government concerning the immigration status of Hughes and his aides. Hughes's residency permit had long ago expired. His staff did not have work permits—all foreigners employed on the islands were required to have them—and they came and left the Bahamas as they pleased. Faced with an election in the coming year, Pindling moved to squelch any controversy by sending immigration officers to the Britannia Beach Hotel to make an inquiry. But when the officials arrived at the hotel on February 15 and asked permission to enter the penthouse, the request was denied. While Hughes's guards outside the ninth-floor suite stalled for time, aides carried Hughes down an outside fire escape to a floor below. When the immigration officers finally were admitted to the rooms, they found four aides without work permits who were immediately deported. When the immigration inspectors left, the remaining aides carried Hughes back up the fire escape, placed him again in his bed, and waited while arrangements were made for an escape from the Bahamas.

Of prime importance was the need to prevent outsiders, especially hostile ones, from seeing or questioning Hughes in his present condition. This delicate task was entrusted to James O. Golden. A onetime Secret Service agent, Golden had worked in the office of Vice-President Nixon during the Eisenhower administration and had handled security for Nixon during the 1968 Republican National Convention. Later, Golden went to work for Intertel, and shortly after Intertel was retained by Gay and Davis, Golden joined the Hughes Tool Company as security chief for the Nevada properties.

To get Hughes off the islands quickly and in secret, Golden chartered an eighty-three-foot luxury yacht, the *Cygnus*, owned by a Baltimore advertising executive. At 5:50 A.M. on Wednesday, February 16, the aides placed Hughes on a stretcher and carried him down the hotel's outside fire escape to the waiting yacht. The skipper, Captain Bob Rehak, took note of Hughes's shoulder-length hair and his scraggly beard, but a white sheet covered the rest of his body. At first Hughes was left lying on the stretcher in the pilot house, but as the sea began to roll, and the stretcher with it, the aides carried Hughes to a couch in the salon. At one point, Hughes stood up and Rehak saw that he was wearing a bathrobe and nothing else. "He didn't have a damn stitch on underneath, no pajamas, nothing," Rehak said. "And that's when I first noticed his long toenails. They were so long they curled up. Never seen anything like that in my life. I had to look twice. Craziest thing I ever saw. He had on sandals."[21]

Nearly twenty-two hours after the *Cygnus* left the Bahamas, it docked at Sunset Island No. 2 in Key Biscayne Bay, where the Hughes organization had long maintained a rented house. There the boat and its secretive passengers were greeted by United States Customs agents who had been summoned under a special arrangement worked out by Golden. After a cursory inspection of the Hughes party, the agents quietly left. At 7:30 A.M., three and a half hours after its arrival in Florida, the Hughes caravan boarded a leased Eastern Airlines jet and flew to Nicaragua.

Golden had done his work well. In Managua, Turner B. Shelton, the United States ambassador to Nicaragua, had gone right to the top, securing the cooperation of that country's military strongman, President Anastasio Somoza. Delighted to be of service to one of America's most famous and wealthiest citizens, Somoza readily waived immigration and customs formalities for Hughes and his aides, an essential courtesy since Hughes did not have a valid United States passport. In addition, Somoza guaranteed that Hughes would be afforded maximum privacy. When reporters began questioning government officials after picking up rumors of Hughes's presence in the country, Nicaragua's immigration chief matter-of-factly declared that "officially, nobody named Howard Hughes has arrived."[22]

Once again, the Hughes entourage occupied an entire hotel floor, this time the eighth floor—the top, or the ninth floor, was a restaurant—of the 210-room Intercontinental Hotel located five blocks from the center of town. The hotel had been built to command a panoramic view of Lake Xolotan and the presidential palace, with mountains and smoking volcanoes in the distance. The windows in Hughes's suite were nevertheless sealed at once. The Hughes retinue remained in Managua only twenty-five days, leaving on March 13, the same day that Clifford Irving, his wife Edith, and associate Richard Suskind, pleaded guilty in New York to criminal charges growing out of their bold scheme to bilk McGraw-Hill of $750,000. Before leaving Managua, however, Hughes broke his isolation of fifteen years to meet for about an hour with two outsiders—General Somoza and Ambassador Shelton—aboard a leased airplane. George Francom, an aide present during the conversation, recalled that Hughes assured Somoza "how he liked his country and how appreciative he was of the courtesy of the invitation down there." Repeating a refrain from the telephone interview two months earlier, Hughes told the general that "he regretted he had fallen into his reclusive ways and he was definitely planning on changing his habits."[23]

When Hughes said good-bye around midnight, Shelton and Somoza left the cabin and the jet flew off toward the United States, refueling in Los Angeles —the first time Hughes had been back in that city since he left for Boston six years earlier—and took off forty-five minutes later for the final destination, Vancouver, British Columbia. When the aircraft arrived, Hughes was whisked to the twenty-story Bayshore Inn, whose top floor had been reserved. As soon as he was in his suite overlooking Vancouver harbor, the windows were, as usual, sealed.

Meanwhile, back in Nicaragua, when reporters learned that Hughes had met with two strangers, they besieged Shelton with questions. The ambassador was forthcoming. "He looks extremely well," Shelton said. "He was wearing a short beard that covers his face and builds into a Vandyke on his chin. His hair is cut short."[24] As for Hughes's isolation, Shelton said that the industrialist had explained that he was a compulsive worker and did not want to be interrupted by visitors and telephone calls.

The man Shelton saw differed markedly in appearance from the man Captain Rehak had seen on his yacht a month earlier, and there was a good explanation. Forty-eight hours before Shelton and Somoza met Hughes, Mell Stewart had cut Hughes's hair and trimmed his beard—for the first time in several years—and cut his toenails. In addition, Hughes had taken one of his infrequent showers.[25]

Following Hughes's arrival in Vancouver, Richard Hannah of Carl Byoir & Associates, whose principal responsibility as public-relations counselors to Hughes was to make certain that little information was made available about their client, issued a perfunctory press release. "Mr. Hughes is in Vancouver on a business trip," Hannah announced. "There is no indication of the nature of the business or of how long he intends to remain there."[26] As was the case with so many publicity releases distributed on Hughes's behalf, this was more than a little misleading. Whatever the reason for shipping Hughes from Managua to Vancouver, it had nothing to do with business. In fact, the groundwork for the most momentous business undertaking in the history of the Hughes empire was being laid at that time not in Vancouver, but more than a thousand miles away, in Los Angeles and Houston.

THE $350-MILLION GIVEAWAY

A decision had been reached by those now running the empire to sell the oil-tool division of the Hughes Tool Company, fountainhead of the family fortune. This family business, founded by Howard Hughes Sr. in 1909, had dominated the American oil-drilling industry for more than a half century, by 1950 controlling about 85 percent of the drill-bit market. More importantly, the oil-tool division had provided young Howard with the abundance of riches required to finance his unsuccessful ventures in filmmaking, airplane manufacturing, and hotel and casino management. No other division of the empire was significantly profitable.

The decision to sell the oil-tool division, according to testimony by Bill Gay, was made at a meeting he attended with Raymond Holliday and Chester Davis. The stated purpose of this gathering of top Hughes executives was to determine how to pay the $145.4-million judgment, plus interest, that had been entered against Hughes and in favor of TWA in the United States District Court in New York. Only a few years earlier Hughes would have had ample cash, or readily marketable securities, to cover the judgment. But no longer. His money, under the management of others, was disappearing at an alarming rate. Still, the assembling of the Hughes high command seemed premature. After all, it would be months before the TWA case was argued before the United States Supreme Court, more months until the court handed down its ruling, and of course it was possible that Hughes would win. As Gay himself put it, "We felt confident that we were going to prevail."[27] Nevertheless, Gay said, the group opted to sell the oil-tool division. Gay did not take any notes during the meeting in which the unprecedented sale plan was formulated, and he could not recall whether either of the other participants had prepared a memorandum proposing other alternatives for raising cash. "I do not believe that we prepared a white paper," he said.[28]

With the agreement to sell concluded, it fell to Holliday and Davis to tell Hughes. Although he had been representing Hughes for more than a decade now, Davis had yet to meet Hughes face-to-face, and Holliday had not seen him since the late 1950s. Even though he was the chief operating officer of all Hughes's enterprises, Holliday had not had a telephone conversation with Hughes in years, and did not even send mail directly to him. Any report or message from Holliday to Hughes was placed in an envelope and mailed to one of the aides. According to Gay, either Holliday or Davis advised Hughes of the decision to sell Hughes Tool, which one—and how—is not known. What is certain is that neither met with him. On at least two occasions that spring and summer, Holliday flew to Vancouver to discuss arrangements for the sale of the oil-tool division, and both times Hughes either refused or was mentally unable to see him. In any event, Holliday, Gay, and Davis pushed ahead, retaining Merrill Lynch, Pierce, Fenner & Smith to handle the public stock offering. By the time Hughes began to object, it was too late.

Although Hughes was doing less work than ever, Romaine Street sent another aide, James H. Rickard, to Vancouver to join the industrialist's personal staff, bringing to six the number of male attendants now looking after Hughes around the clock. Born November 20, 1919, at Powell, Wyoming, Rickard had studied mechanical engineering and business for three years at the University of Wyoming and Montana State College, and then had compiled a checkered employment career before joining Bill Gay's band of Chevrolet drivers at Romaine Street in October of 1953. After serving as a pilot during the Second World War, Rickard was a construction worker in California, ran a drive-in movie theater in Montana that was a casualty of the state's climate —"We opened on Memorial Day and it snowed about a foot and a half two weeks later"—sold life insurance in Arizona, and finally returned to California to go to work for Hughes Productions.[29] Like so many others at Romaine Street, Rickard was hired through his Mormon connections—his brother-in-law was active in church affairs with Gay. Then in 1957, after four years as a Hughes driver, Rickard took a one-year leave of absence to try his hand at managing a logging and sawmill operation in Bozeman, Montana. That business failed, too—"The lumber market price dropped about $50 about two months after we started"—and Rickard hurried back to Romaine Street.[30]

In August of 1972, the Hughes caravan, which had already moved twice in seven months, unexpectedly pulled up stakes and returned to Nicaragua, vaguely citing Canadian taxes as the reason for leaving. On Tuesday, August 29, Hughes and his aides boarded a jet and flew back to Managua, again checking in at the Intercontinental Hotel. Nicaragua's ruler was gratified by Hughes's return. "I am very pleased that Mr. Hughes has accepted my personal invitation to once again visit with us," General Somoza said, assuming that Hughes was in Managua by his own choice. "I know that all Nicaraguans will join in extending to him our traditional hospitality."[31] The general did not see Hughes this time. Nor did Raymond Holliday, who flew to Managua only to be turned away a third time.

Hughes probably lacked the strength to be truly difficult, as he would have been in healthier days, but he nevertheless made it clear that he did not want to part with the tool company. He had not visited the Houston plant, which now sprawled over eighty-four acres and employed more than four thousand people, since 1938. He had not met with any tool company officers in fifteen years. He knew almost none of the top executives. Yet his feelings for the company ran deep. He regarded it as a family monument, a living testimonial to his father. If Hughes had one unmistakable emotional concern in all his life, it was the preservation of the oil-tool division of Hughes Tool Company. In his 1925 will, Hughes had pledged to preserve the tool company and carry out the policies of his father "so long as I shall live."[32] He had dangled the tool company as bait before eager investors for three decades, but never seriously considered selling. To have done so would have betrayed the memory of the father he revered. As Hughes himself once put it, an aide recalled, "his father would probably never forgive him if he sold it."[33]

His feeble protests notwithstanding, by the late summer of 1972 Hughes was being swept along by a tide of legal and financial paperwork leading to the inevitable sale. Early in September, Securities and Exchange Commission officials in Washington exchanged memoranda on the transaction, which was subject to SEC review since it involved a public stock offering. On September 13, Raymond Holliday signed documents in Houston establishing a new Hughes Tool Company that would be publicly owned, and the following day the incorporation papers were filed with the Delaware secretary of state.

Because of recurring rumors that Hughes was incapacitated and his empire controlled by anonymous underlings, the Securities and Exchange Commission wanted firm evidence that he was alive and well and truly wanted to sell his company. Hughes was of course resisting this, and it was not until September 16, two weeks after the SEC began to study the proposed sale, and two days after the formation of the new Hughes Tool Company, that one of the aides, following a conversation with Hughes, entered this notation on the logs in Hughes's suite: "HRH said that he wanted to sell the OTD [oil-tool division] and would sign the papers in the presence of the Merrill Lynch people."[34]

Moving with unprecedented speed, the clique pushing the sale set September 24 as the date for the viewing. It was agreed that Julius H. Sedlmayr, a group vice-president of Merrill Lynch, and J. Courtney Ivey, a partner in the New York law firm of Brown, Wood, Fuller, Caldwell & Ivey, which was representing the brokerage house, would fly to Managua on Sunday, September 24, and meet with Hughes at 2 P.M.

In the four weeks leading up to the scheduled meeting, Hughes spent his time much as he had in the past two years, injecting himself with narcotics, consuming tranquilizers, and watching movies. There were a few interruptions in the routine, and the usual petty annoyances. On Sunday, September 3, Hughes fell off the toilet and injured his arm and heel. On September 7, he ordered the aides to supply him with "California and Florida orange juice, as well as the Minute Maid," so that he could make his own taste test. On September 9, he complained that the milk he was being served was not as cold as it had been in Vancouver, and that his pillows were not being folded properly. On September 10, he complained at 8:15 P.M. that his room was too warm, and seven hours later that it was too cold. On September 20 and 21, he submitted to enemas to relieve his constipation.[35]

During the four weeks, he sat and stared at thirty-five different movies at least once, including *Myra Breckinridge, Strange Bedfellows, Executive Suite,* and *Evel Knievel.* One film which had a special hold on him at the time was an hour-and-forty-minute crime thriller, *The Poppy Is Also a Flower.* Produced for the United Nations in 1966, the film is all about narcotics traffic and drug addiction, and tells the story of how U.N. agents trace the flow of narcotics through the underworld and smash a drug ring. Hughes was mesmerized by the film, with its lively scenes of narcotics agents, drug dealers, and addicts, watching it ten times in the month after he arrived in Managua. A day did not go by without an aide threading the ever-present projector and showing one or two reels of a motion picture. Even on August 29, when Hughes spent most of the day flying from Vancouver to Managua, he still squeezed one film into his schedule. But Sunday, September 24, the day he was to see Sedlmayr and Ivey, Hughes watched no movies. At 5:30 A.M., he swallowed seven of his blue, ten-milligram Valium tablets—twenty-eight times the recommended daily dose for someone his age. As might be expected, he passed out for five hours, then got up, groggily, went to the bathroom, returned to bed, and slept right through the appointed 2 P.M. meeting.[36] Sedlmayr and Ivey were then assured that Hughes would see them at 5 P.M. But at five o'clock Hughes was still sleeping, and the meeting had been pushed back to 8 P.M. At 5:30, Hughes woke up, went to the bathroom, then settled into his reclining chair, where he remained for the next three hours. Meanwhile, the aides informed Sedlmayr and Ivey that Hughes would see them at 10 P.M., but that hour, too, came and passed with Hughes still unable to face the men who were going to sell his company.[37]

Sedlmayr exploded. He told the aides that "he would call the deal off unless he and Ivey personally conferred with Hughes in time to catch a 6:45 A.M. flight back to New York."[38]

Still Hughes sat immobile in his chair. Shortly before 1 A.M. on Monday, September 25, he began watching *Man in the Middle,* a story set in India during the Second World War, depicting the fate of a psychopathic United States Army officer who empties his pistol into a British noncommissioned officer. At 3:45 A.M., Mell Stewart trimmed Hughes's beard and cleaned him up, a process that took an hour and forty-five minutes. Fifteen minutes later, Hughes, still seated in his reclining chair, received Sedlmayr and Ivey.[39] Mickey West, Hughes's tax lawyer, and Raymond Holliday, who would be the chairman of the board and chief executive officer of the new Hughes Tool Company, had accompanied the Merrill Lynch representatives to Hughes's suite, but were not invited into the bedroom. For the next thirty-five minutes they sat in the adjoining aides' office while Sedlmayr and Ivey talked with Hughes. Exactly what took place during those thirty-five minutes is uncertain, but there is no doubt about whose interests were represented and whose were not. Ivey, the Wall Street lawyer, was there to represent Sedlmayr and Merrill Lynch. Mickey West, the Houston lawyer, was there to represent the proposed publicly owned Hughes Tool Company. Only Howard Hughes, who stood to lose one of the most prosperous companies in history, and whose mental condition was diminished by years of drug addiction, was without legal representation. As West put it later, "I don't know that anyone represented Mr. Hughes personally."[40]

A year later, *Fortune* magazine reported that Sedlmayr and Ivey had "found Hughes, at sixty-six, remarkably unchanged. His black hair now carried a touch of gray and his chin bore a Vandyke that was neatly trimmed; otherwise, he looked pretty much as he had when last seen in public fifteen years earlier."[41] The magazine went on to say that Hughes talked about the tool company "with what at times struck his listeners as nostalgia. Hughes recalled how close he felt to the company and its workers. 'I want the employes to be treated well,' he stressed."[42]

At any rate, Hughes signed the necessary papers before Sedlmayr and Ivey—his signature was witnessed by Chuck Waldron and George Francom —and they left the bedroom at 6:15 A.M. As they did, Hughes called out to Raymond Holliday, a thirty-four-year veteran of the Hughes organization and the chief executive of the tool company since Noah Dietrich's firing in 1957, "Raymond, don't go away. I want to talk to you."[43] But Holliday ignored the call and accompanied Sedlmayr and Ivey to the airport. He would never see Hughes again.

His visitors gone, Hughes resumed movie watching, completing *Man in the Middle* and going on to *The Italian Job,* a comedy-suspense film built around the daylight robbery of $4 million in gold ingots from an armored van on the streets of Turin, Italy, and *The Adventurers,* a Harold Robbins account of the jet set and South American politics laced with sex and pillage. Before the day ended, however, Hughes was having second thoughts about the tool company sale. He fretted about its unseemly haste and wondered whether it might not be delayed until 1973. A postponement this year could be followed by a postponement next year. During his career, Hughes had perfected the practice of delaying decisions until the decisions became irrelevant. He summoned one of the aides and asked him to send a query to Holliday asking why it was necessary to sell the company in 1972. The aide returned to the desk in

The heart of Howard Hughes's empire, the sprawling Hughes Tool Company works in Houston, shortly before it was sold in 1972. *Wide World Photos*

the office and dutifully recorded Hughes's request in the log: "How does HRH benefit personally or how does the company benefit whether the stock is sold this year or not?"[44] Hughes might as well have whispered into the whirlwind. The scheme to sell the tool company had gained such momentum that it was beyond control. Sedlmayr and Ivey informed the Securities and Exchange Commission that Hughes himself had authorized the sale. When investigators in the agency's enforcement section raised certain questions about the transaction, the Corporation Finance Division of the SEC, which had processed the paperwork, advised them that the sale had been cleared and was out of their jurisdiction.

Monday, October 16, was like any other day for Hughes in his Nicaraguan hotel room. He watched *The Poppy Is Also a Flower* once more and *A Face in the Rain,* swallowed at least six Valium tablets, and fell asleep shortly before noon. In Washington, a registration statement was filed with the SEC providing for the sale of five million shares of stock in a new Hughes Tool Company at $28 a share. The proceeds would total $140 million—less than the company's pretax earnings over five years during the oil-industry boom of the early 1950s. Under the proposed offering, a new company was to be established called Summa Corporation. All Hughes's holdings in the existing Hughes Tool Company, including the oil-tool division, would be transferred to Summa. When the stock was to be sold to the public, the newly created Hughes Tool Company would take over the oil-tool division. Summa Corporation would retain all the remaining properties—the Nevada hotels and casinos, the Las Vegas television station, Air West, the Hughes Sports Network, a helicopter-manufacturing division, thousands of acres of undeveloped land, other real estate, and assorted investments. Raymond Holliday would become the chairman of the board and the chief executive officer of the publicly owned Hughes Tool Company. Other longtime Hughes executives also would assume corporate positions in the new company—James R. Lesch, president and chief operating officer, and Calvin J. Collier, Jr., vice-president, secretary, and treasurer. The board of directors would include Ned B. Ball, the president of Merrill Lynch, which was handling the stock offering, and Clinton F. Morse of Andrews, Kurth, Campbell & Jones.

When Hughes learned that the stock in his company was to be sold for $28 a share, he complained to his aides that it should bring $40 or $50. The aides relayed his displeasure to Holliday and Davis. Davis, in turn, "checked it out," according to Chuck Waldron, and reported back to Hughes that "it looks like we're getting what is the going price per share."[45]

As the weeks slipped by, Hughes was soothed, cajoled, and assuaged time and time again. The message was always the same—it was essential to sell the oil-tool division to satisfy the TWA judgment. No one suggested to him that the sale might not be a wise one. The attitude of Nadine Henley, whose employment with Hughes dated back to 1942, was typical. "If Mr. Hughes wanted to sell something," she explained later, "he sold it. Mine not to reason why."[46] Hughes, of course, did not want to sell. "But I think he was made to realize," George Francom said later, "that it was quite necessary or imperative that he do so."[47] Still, Hughes could not understand opposition to delaying the sale for a year. After all, the Supreme Court might overturn the TWA judgment. On December 1, a week before the stock was to be issued to the public, Hughes continued to besiege his staff with questions about postponement. In response to one inquiry, Howard Eckersley typed out a memorandum and handed it to Hughes. The memorandum began, "The OTD [oil-tool division] must be sold this year because it cannot be sold in the same year as the TWA decision."[48] Eckersley, who then was being sought by Canadian authorities in connection with his part in a uranium-mining stock-fraud case, played on Hughes's obsession with taxes and proceeded to offer a technical—and highly suspect—explanation of why he would receive certain tax benefits only if the company were sold before year's end.

On Thursday, December 7—seventeen days before Hughes's sixty-seventh birthday—the five million shares of stock in the new Hughes Tool Company were offered to investors by Merrill Lynch. The stock was snapped up at $30 a share instead of the originally announced $28, giving Hughes $150 million, less underwriting fees and taxes. One week later, on December 14, the last papers completing the transaction were signed and a new Hughes Tool Company, minus Howard Hughes for the first time, commenced business. In his Managua hotel room that day, Hughes again deviated from his customary routine, just as he had the day he was to meet with Sedlmayr and Ivey—he watched no movies. After taking six ten-milligram Valium tablets at 12:30 P.M., he spent much of the rest of the day sleeping.

When the sale of the tool company had first been announced in October, there was, as usual, no official statement from Hughes. However, a member of his staff devoted to perpetuating the Hughes legend was enthusiastic. "The old man's timing has always been good," the Hughes man asserted. "He's got some ideas we don't know about yet."[49] On the surface there was evidence to support the aide's statement, at least as far as the timing of the sale was concerned. Since 1924, when Hughes took over the tool company following his father's death, the company had produced $745.4 million in profits before taxes. But in recent years profits had declined sharply. Earnings after taxes had once reached $20 million a year, but for the years 1967 to 1971, the oil-tool division's net income averaged slightly under $5 million. The decline was accompanied by a steep downturn in the company's return on sales. Net income once ran better than 27 percent of sales, but by 1971 the figure was a dismal 5.7 percent.

Because the company's principal products were drilling bits, used primarily in the oil and gas industry, and tool joints, used to connect sections of oil- and gas-well drill pipe, its fortunes were tied to the health of the oil and gas industry.[50] From 1962 to 1971, the number of wells drilled in the United States fell from more than forty-five thousand to twenty-seven thousand—only about half the number of wells drilled during the 1950s.[51] The number of drilling rigs at work around the country plunged from 1,636 in 1962 to 975 in 1971. Two of the patents on the Hughes bit and the patent on the tool joint thread were due to expire the following year.[52]

Surely 1972 was a good time for Howard Hughes to sell his father's business. As *Newsweek* put it, "In some respects, it looked as though Hughes was unloading an albatross."[53] But business statistics can be immensely deceptive. Ever since Spindletop the oil business had run in cycles, the prosperous years followed by the lean as regularly as night follows day. Even as Merrill Lynch prepared its stock prospectus for the new Hughes Tool Company, recovery in the oil industry was well under way. Drilling activity was on the upswing, as measured by the tool company's own drilling index, the bible of the industry. And the increased drilling was already translating into rising profits. During the first seven months of 1972, the tool company's net income totaled $5.9 million—up 136 percent over its earnings of $2.5 million during the same period in 1971.

One year after Hughes's stock in the Hughes Tool Company was sold for $30 a share, it was trading at $90. In less than three years, the stock—after a 100-percent stock dividend—was selling at $50 a share. A weakened, confused, and feebly resisting Hughes by this sale had lost more than a third of a billion dollars in the short run. Over a longer span, the tool company sale was even more costly. In the five years after Hughes Tool went public, its net income amounted to $162.5 million—or $12 million more than Hughes received.

January of 1973 brought a huge but not unexpected irony that made the oil-tool division sale all the more poignant. Twenty-seven days after the sale, the United States Supreme Court ruled in favor of Hughes in his twelve-year legal war with TWA. The $145-million judgment was cancelled, and with it all necessity, or pretense, for the sale of his tool company. But Hughes's catastrophic loss was the gain of others. At fifty-eight, Raymond Holliday, the onetime accountant, severed all ties with Hughes and became chairman of the board and chief executive officer of the publicly owned Hughes Tool Company. Over the next two years, his combined salary and bonus rose 33 percent, from $204,105 to $271,324. More significantly, Holliday secured a fringe benefit that Hughes had stubbornly refused to grant—stock options. In less than three years, Holliday's options were worth more than $1.5 million. Other tool company veterans fared proportionately as well.

Now that Holliday, Calvin Collier, and other oil-tool managers were all working for the publicly owned Hughes Tool Company and no longer associated with Hughes, the top officer in Hughes's empire was Frank William Gay. The quiet Mormon had outlasted and outmaneuvered every executive who had sought the top job. His influence and power now reached all corners of the empire. He was the executive vice-president, the highest operating officer in Summa Corporation, the conglomerate that was the holding company for nearly all Hughes's enterprises. He was a director and a member of the three-member executive committee of Summa. (The others were Nadine Henley and Chester Davis.) He was half of a two-man executive committee (the other was Chester Davis) that ran the Howard Hughes Medical Institute. As the sole stockholder of Hughes Aircraft Company, the medical institute held final authority over operations at one of the country's ten largest defense contractors with annual revenue of more than $1 billion. Gay was a director of Sands, Inc., Harolds Club, Inc., Hotel Properties, Inc., Sands Country Club, Inc., Desert Inn Improvement Company, and Hughes Sports Network, Inc. He was a vice-president, director, and a member of the three-member executive committee—with Miss Henley and Davis—of Hughes Air Corporation, the company that controlled Air West. And he had further tightened his control over the channels of communication to Hughes and the aides who lived with Hughes around the clock.

Two of those aides fared quite nicely with Gay's rise in the empire. Levar Myler, the onetime burr- and milling-machine operator who had gone to work for Gay at Romaine Street in 1950, became a director of Summa. He also received a substantial raise, his combined salary and bonus jumping from $60,000 in 1972 to $75,000 in 1973 for work that still consisted largely of receiving and transmitting messages to and from Hughes. John Holmes, the onetime cigarette and wax salesman who had gone to work for Gay at Romaine Street in 1949 and who went on to become Hughes's chief narcotics courier, was elevated to the Summa board and given even a higher salary than Myler. Both Myler and Holmes were added to the gaming licenses for Hughes's casinos in Nevada.

Gay also moved other faithful Romaine Street associates into corporate positions. Kay Glenn, his general administrator, became a director of Hughes Air Corporation. Paul B. Winn, an attorney who worked out of Romaine Street and later Gay's Encino office, and Rand H. Clark, another aide who followed Gay from Romaine Street to Encino, became assistant secretaries of Hughes Air Corporation. Winn also became an assistant secretary of Summa. Like Gay, all were Mormons.

After having yielded to pressure to sell the oil-tool division, Hughes was both annoyed and puzzled by the name given to his new company. It was a sign of how little control he exercised now, as well as the contempt those running the empire had for him, that they named the company Summa Corporation without seeking Hughes's advice or consent. When he first saw a slip of paper with the name Summa on it—a name chosen by Gay—he asked, "What the hell does that mean? How do you pronounce it? I don't even know how to pronounce it, Summa, Summa, or what is it?"[54] Repeatedly, Hughes complained. He wanted the name changed. At one point he issued orders that no more stationery be printed with the name Summa. "He had in mind using his own initials" as a corporate name, recalled George Francom. The initials HRH "had a dual meaning," Francom said, "Hughes Resorts Hotels, which he thought would be good."[55] Hughes even dictated a memorandum to Chester Davis asking "why we cannot change the name Summa to HRH Properties."[56] But no one seemed to be listening.

INVALID

By now Hughes was no longer in Nicaragua, but elsewhere, routed by the forces of nature. It was 12:30 A.M. on Saturday, December 23, and Hughes had just called Jim Rickard into his Managua bedroom when the first violent earthquake tremors began to shake the pyramid-shaped Intercontinental Hotel. "He had a large speaker that we used to amplify the movie sound so he could hear and I was just walking by it when it hit," Rickard recalled later. "I would guess it would be three feet by four feet in size. It was heavy. He was sitting in a lounge chair, in a recliner, with his feet up and I figured it would fall right on his legs and break them, and I grabbed that. The movement was so violent that I probably would have fallen down had I not been holding on to that speaker. After a few minutes, two of the legs cracked off and the table it was sitting on tumbled and I threw it away from him."[57] While Hughes sat impassively in his chair, Rickard rushed back to the aides' office, where "all the desk drawers had come out and spilled, all the file drawers come out and spilled, and everything just tumbled."[58] Frantically, he placed two telephone calls, the first to his wife in Burbank, the second to Operations at Romaine

Street, asking for help. As the lights went out and the tremors continued to rock the building, sending bewildered, half-clothed guests from their rooms into the darkened streets of Managua, Rickard found a flashlight and returned to the bedroom. By this time, falling plaster covered the room and a toppled floor lamp rested across Hughes. When Rickard reappeared, Hughes looked at him and said, "Well, let's get this mess cleaned up."[59] When George Francom, Howard Eckersley, and Mell Stewart came rushing in to join Rickard, they all urged Hughes, who was wearing only his pajama tops, to get dressed and leave the hotel. "I know all about earthquakes," Hughes said confidently, "and if you live through the first jolt, then everything's going to be alright. We'll stay right here."[60] The aides had no such faith. They finally persuaded Hughes—whose calmness was no doubt due in part to his consumption of the ever-present tranquilizers—to put on a pair of slacks and a sport shirt. Placing the frail industrialist on a stretcher, they carried him down nine flights of stairs and deposited him in the back seat of a waiting Mercedes Benz, where he huddled under a blanket for the rest of the night as the earth opened up and swallowed downtown Managua. Block after block was leveled, nearly six hundred in all. Bodies and debris littered the streets. Other bodies were buried under piles of rubble reaching higher than fifteen feet. Ruptured mains shut off the water supply and fires burned out of control across a third of the city. Communications and electrical service were cut.

The next morning, Hughes's sixty-seventh birthday, aides drove the Mercedes aimlessly about nearly impassable Managua streets, passing knots of dazed and homeless victims who sat on sidewalks surrounded by their possessions. But most of the survivors clogged roads leading out of the hot, dry capital, taking with them bedding, clothing, and kettles, heading for the homes of relatives in neighboring communities or to emergency campsites being set up around the city. On Christmas Eve, American relief teams began to arrive, bringing with them emergency equipment and medical supplies. A field hospital, flown in from Fort Hood, Texas, was set up on the grounds of General Somoza's private residence. At the Las Mercedes Airport, emergency flights shuttled in and out, bringing in supplies, carrying away the injured for treatment at hospitals in neighboring Honduras and Costa Rica. One of the few planes that landed without medical equipment or other supplies was a Lear jet dispatched by Romaine Street. Hughes was loaded onto the aircraft, flown to Fort Lauderdale, Florida, and then driven to his organization's rented house on Sunset Island No. 2. On Tuesday, the day after Christmas, he was driven back to Fort Lauderdale, put on a leased Lockheed JetStar, and flown not to Los Angeles, Boston, Vancouver, or the Bahamas, but to London, where he was moved into the penthouse suite at the Inn on the Park, an elegant hotel overlooking Hyde Park and Buckingham Palace. Ninety minutes after Hughes entered his latest bedroom, he was seated in his familiar reclining chair watching a movie, *The Deserter,* the death and destruction in Managua apparently far from his thoughts. As time and distance separated Hughes and his traveling companions from the destitute survivors of the earthquake, the aides reminisced about the boss's response under stress. "He was cool, so cool," Howard Eckersley told a newspaper reporter. "Everyone was saying we must evacuate immediately, but he said no. He wanted to be sure it was absolutely necessary."[61] Although the body count was still going on at year's end, it appeared that the death toll in Nicaragua would reach six thousand, perhaps higher. Property damage rose to more than $1 billion. Neither Hughes nor those around him looked back, or offered any assistance. Hughes spent the last hours of 1972 watching *Dead Eyes of London*. Afterward, while he slept through the effects of a codeine injection and six Valium tablets, several thousand miles away a DC-7 cargo plane loaded with twenty-six tons of clothing, food, and relief supplies, lifted off the runway at an airport in Puerto Rico. As the plane headed out to sea and Managua, the engines failed and it plunged into the heaving ocean, killing all five crew members and passengers, including the leader of the mercy mission, thirty-eight-year-old Roberto Clemente, the scrappy Pittsburgh Pirate outfielder and four-time National League batting champion. In Nicaragua, the survivors mourned the death of Clemente and puzzled over the indifference of Howard Hughes, one of the world's richest men. As a friend of General Somoza lamented, "Hughes still hasn't sent a damn thing here." And then he added, perceptively, "I doubt if he will ever come back."[62]

Hughes's failure to respond to this, or indeed to any charitable cause, was consistent with a long, but concealed, tradition. Over the years, Hughes's public-relations specialists had planted stories extolling his beneficence and his —always anonymous—charitable deeds. It was one of the great Hughes legends woven from fantasy. Even when he was relatively rational, Hughes displayed an amazing lack of concern for other people, unless there was a vested interest. His charity was reserved for those who could return a favor, when the act itself would help him achieve some fleeting ambition, or when it was a legal necessity. As might be expected, his associates now followed the path that Hughes had charted in charitable affairs. On his federal income-tax return for 1965, for instance, Howard Hughes reported charitable contributions totaling $1,375 to the United Crusade, and nothing else.[63]

Hughes had no sooner settled into his ninth-floor suite at the Inn on the Park than aides began importuning him to meet with Nevada governor Mike O'Callaghan. The Hughes organization's once-cozy relationship with Nevada gaming officials and politicians had soured in 1971 after Hughes fled the United States. O'Callaghan, a Democrat, was less sympathetic than his Republican predecessor Paul Laxalt, and when Hughes lieutenants submitted revised gaming license applications containing the names of new persons representing the industrialist—notably Bill Gay, Chester Davis, and their allies—gaming officials questioned whether the changes had been made by Hughes or by someone who had seized control of his businesses. In lieu of a face-to-face meeting, they requested a letter in Hughes's handwriting, and bearing his fingerprints, naming the individuals he wanted in charge of his Nevada hotels and casinos.

Hughes submitted the letter, with his fingerprints, and for a while the Nevada authorities were placated. When the Clifford Irving fiasco broke, however, Governor O'Callaghan reiterated his demand for a personal meeting. On January 1, 1972, the aides handed Hughes a message stressing the urgency of the situation:

We are sorry to have to bring this subject up again, but we're only trying to do the best job we can for you and would not feel that we'd done our best if we hadn't given you all the facts, so you could make your decision whether you'll meet with the Governor or not. Mell Stewart has been standing by for a couple of months to do his work (haircut, trim your beard and clip toenails) before he returns home to Utah in a couple of days to see his family. The Governor said that he is planning to be in London on the 5th of January whether you meet with him or not. There can be no further delays. He has put this meeting with you off several times at your request and he now must meet with you before he goes to Legislature. Bill and Chester feels [*sic*] that if you don't meet with the Governor when he comes to London on the 5th of January, then you'd better be prepared to liquidate everything in Nevada.[64]

Hughes still balked at such a meeting. Back in Nevada, gaming officials began sounding tough. Philip P. Hannifin, chairman of the Nevada Gaming Control Board, declared that "recent events focusing upon the authenticity of Hughes' handwriting should be a clear warning to Nevada that we cannot depend upon such evidence to assure ourselves of the true desire of Hughes," a reference to the Irving book and McGraw-Hill's acceptance of a letter purportedly written by Hughes that turned out to be a forgery. Commenting on charges that the state had failed to hold Hughes to the same licensing requirements imposed on all other casino owners, Hannifin noted that "it has been reported that the State of Nevada has entered into partnership with Howard Hughes. If so, it is a partnership that has diminished the integrity and dignity of the state."[65]

Relations between the Hughes organization and Nevada officials deteriorated even further when the news media carried accounts of Hughes's midnight conversation aboard a plane in Managua with Nicaraguan president Somoza. Incensed that Hughes would meet with a Latin American dictator but not the governor of Nevada, gaming authorities refused to approve the requested amendments to the gaming licenses. The dispute dragged on for the rest of 1972 and finally, in London, Hughes consented to meet Governor O'Callaghan during the third week in March of 1973.

Although gradual changes were taking place in his daily routine, nothing major was changing for Hughes. He was consuming so many tranquilizers that no one any longer kept an accurate count. But in one six-hour period, he took at least ten of his "Blue Bombers," or ten-milligram Valium tablets—about forty times the recommended daily dose for someone his age. Not too surprisingly, then, he was sleeping more and watching fewer movies. On Saturday, March 17, the day of his appointment, Hughes started off at 3:15 A.M. by watching *Madame Sin*. He had an enema at 4 A.M. and spent the next nineteen hours in bed or in the bathroom.[66] At 11:35 P.M. Mell Stewart arrived to trim his hair and beard and clean him up, and at 1:15 A.M. on Sunday morning O'Callaghan and Hannifin were shepherded into Hughes's darkened bedroom, accompanied by two other men—Bill Gay, who had not been in Hughes's presence since Hughes placed him in "isolation" in 1958, and Chester Davis, who had never before laid eyes on Hughes. While Gay and Davis sat quietly in the background, O'Callaghan and Hannifin talked for more than an hour with Hughes, who remained seated throughout, a blanket wrapped tightly around his otherwise naked body. The governor came away from the meeting greatly impressed. He told reporters that Hughes had a "commanding personality. There was no doubt in the meeting who was telling the people what to do. When he disagreed, his voice rose. He repeated statements when he wanted to stress a point." The governor added that "there is every indication that some day he hopes to return to Nevada. It is very clear he likes the state. He has confidence in his holdings. He made the statement how he loves Nevada."[67]

After fifteen years in total seclusion, Hughes had embarked on, for him, a whirlwind of social and business intercourse. In fifteen months he had conducted a long-distance telephone interview with half a dozen newsmen, a meeting with a Merrill Lynch executive and a Wall Street lawyer, a session with the president of Nicaragua and the American ambassador, and now a personal conversation with the governor of Nevada, the state's gaming chief, his own lawyer, and even Bill Gay. What with all these person-to-person dealings after so many years of inactivity, perhaps it was time to fly once again.

With Hughes's arrival in London, there had been another addition to his personal staff. Jack Real, the former Lockheed executive so close to Hughes in the late 1950s, who had acted as liaison between Lockheed and Hughes through most of the 1960s, moved into the Inn on the Park. Real had gone to work for Hughes in 1971, but he was not an aide. Indeed, his function was difficult to define. He was there because Hughes had asked for him, which made him the first staff member to join the inner circle without being groomed by Romaine Street. His presence in London annoyed Gay and certain of the aides, but little could be done except to isolate him as much as possible, allowing him into the bedroom only when Hughes demanded to see him.

And Hughes demanded fairly often. Real talked to him about airplanes and flying, just as he had done when Hughes was passing through his mental collapse in 1957 and 1958. With his interest quickened, Hughes picked up his aviation publications again, absorbing the advances in aircraft design and performance, and in the spring of 1973, after a thirteen-year absence from the cockpit, he announced that he was about to fly again. His staff was stunned. If Hughes began to venture forth, Romaine Street might lose control. They blamed Real. "It's easier to take care of him when he is in bed," one of the aides told Real. "Go home. You're getting him alive."[68] The "aides got more and more upset and kept trying to get [Hughes] back into his chair," but

Hughes insisted he was going to fly, even if he did not have a valid pilot's license.[69]

Real pushed ahead, negotiating for an aircraft through an old friend, Tony Blackman, the chief test pilot and a salesman for Hawker Siddeley. They reached agreement on the lease-purchase of a Hawker Siddeley 748, a twin-engine turboprop similar in size to a DC-3. But there was a complication: Hughes wanted to test fly another 748, not the one he intended to buy. Hughes liked to keep the flying time on his aircraft to a minimum, Blackman recalled, "just like a fellow that goes and buys a tailor-made suit and never wears it, he keeps wearing the old suit."[70] Blackman finally secured a military demonstration aircraft for the test. The flight awaited Hughes's pleasure. Unbeknownst to Blackman as he waited for two weeks, Hughes was drugged and unable to leave his bedroom. "He looked like he was in the outer spaces," Real said.[71]

Then one day in May of 1973, Real and an aide drove Hughes to a hangar at Hatfield Airport, located on a huge farm just north of London. With Real on one side and the aide on the other, Hughes got out of the car and slowly walked around the aircraft. After he was introduced to Blackman, Hughes complained that the rivets on the fuselage were not flush with the body. Blackman explained there were flush rivets on the wing tops, where it mattered, and extended rivets on the fuselage for easier maintenance. Hughes, who had built the first flush-riveted airplane, still disapproved. When he got into the 748, Hughes inspected the cabin, entered the flight deck, and settled into the pilot's seat. Blackman said nothing. He had been told by Real that Hughes would expect to sit in the pilot's seat. Because the 748's nose-wheel steering system was on the left-hand side, Blackman was somewhat uneasy. The 748 flight manual called for two pilots. Blackman was nonetheless confident he could fly the plane unassisted, if need be. Still seated, Hughes slipped off his light-blue shirt, unfastened his dark slacks, and dropped them down to his knees. Naked and grinning, Hughes gripped the controls. It was the natural reaction not of an exhibitionist, but of one who had been unaccustomed to clothing for more than a decade.

Warned about Hughes's germ phobia, Blackman handed him a new radio headphone set still wrapped in cellophane. With Real and the aide back in the cabin and Hughes in the pilot's seat, Blackman signaled the engineers to tow the plane out of the hangar. The engines were started and Hughes taxied the plane along a zigzag course to the end of the runway. The tower gave clearance, Blackman opened the throttles, and the 748 rolled down the runway and lifted off. For the first time in thirteen years, Howard Hughes was behind the controls of a plane in flight. Blackman unobtrusively acted as a flight instructor, handling the critical maneuvers and those that Hughes neglected. When Hughes experienced difficulty keeping the 748 on course, Blackman politely turned the aircraft in the direction he wanted. They were no sooner airborne, however, than Blackman discovered that Hughes wished only to do takeoffs and landings—take off, circle the field, touch down, and take off again. Blackman had two concerns. He did not want to offend Hughes—he hoped to sell him some airplanes. Yet he wanted to stay alive. When they made the first passes at the field, Blackman, who controled the throttles throughout, kept the speed up and each time pulled up without touching down. "As we were approaching what I thought was certain disaster," he said, "I would pull the stick back and we'd bow up."[72] When Blackman took exception to one landing —they nearly ran out of runway—Hughes observed that Blackman was not the first to criticize his landings. Late that night they finally returned the 748 to its hangar.

A second flight was arranged across the English Channel to Ostend, Belgium, and back. When Hughes, Real and an aide arrived at Hatfield Airport late one night in June, it was raining and visibility was poor. Blackman tried to persuade Hughes to cancel the flight, but Hughes insisted. Blackman reluctantly agreed, but asked a friend and copilot to accompany them. The flight plan called for a stop at Stansted Airport. By the time they reached the field, the weather was so bad that the ground lights were not visible beyond fifty feet from the runway. After landing, Blackman could barely find the taxi ramp. Blackman then turned to Hughes and told him that if he wanted to fly to Belgium, he would have to go back and sit in the cabin and allow his copilot to come up to the cockpit. As the rain pelted down on the plane, Real, Hughes, and Blackman argued. When Blackman declared there would be no flight unless Hughes left the cockpit, Hughes turned to Real and said, "Well, I can fly. Tell him to get off the thing."[73] Eventually, Real convinced Hughes to leave the cockpit and he went back into the cabin and lay down. Blackman and his copilot placed the 748 on automatic pilot, flew to Ostend, turned around, and returned to Stansted.

A third flight followed in July, this time in a de Havilland 125, a twin-jet executive aircraft in which Hughes felt more comfortable. He told Blackman that the de Havilland made the 748 feel like a truck. Each time they flew, Real sent a report to Romaine Street to be included in the records that accounted for every minute Hughes spent in a plane. Real advised Romaine Street following the flight that "On July 17, HRH took off from Hatfield Airport at 1828 and landed at 2015 (he made seven takeoffs and landings at Stansted Airport). The airplane was a DH 125-400, License No. G–AYOJ."[74]

Their fourth flight late in July, again in the De Havilland, was to Woodford, northeast of London, where Blackman's club was located. As in the previous flights, Blackman backed up Hughes at the controls. But this time, despite his obvious frailty, Hughes appeared more alert than on earlier outings. When they taxied along the runway, Blackman pointed out his lodge near the landing strip. Hughes, who had given Blackman the impression that he was tired of living in hotel rooms, said he would like to visit the lodge for a few weeks. Blackman thought it could be arranged. It certainly would be more convenient, for Hughes would be living right next to his plane. After their flight that day, Blackman took Hughes to see a mock-up of a new Hawker Siddeley aircraft. Chuck Waldron, the aide who accompanied Real and

Hughes on the flight, recalled that Hughes spent some time inspecting it. "He walked up the steps into the mock-up and through the airplane and back down, around the building; checked all the different parts of that big hangar where they had their mock-up."[75] Mentally, Hughes was in fine form. It was, said Real, "the best day in the four years that I'd spent with him."[76]

But on August 9, Hughes's flying days came to an abrupt end, and with them any hope of moving from his hotel room to Blackman's lodge at Woodford or anywhere else. Exactly what happened that day is unclear, but somehow Hughes fell in his bedroom and fractured a hip. The aides later offered conflicting versions, but all said that no one was with Hughes at the time. Eckersley said Hughes "got up and went to the bathroom in the night and just tripped on a rug. There wasn't anything to trip on. He just fell down and hurt himself."[77] Francom said, "he got up to go to the bathroom and he was still in a semi-sleeping condition, and he reached for the bathroom door to open it and missed it or something and lost his balance. I think there was a sideboard or table near the door, and I think he hit his hip on that when he fell back."[78] Waldron said, "he was coming out of the bathroom and made a quick turn to turn the light off or something and popped his hip and fell down."[79]

The first non-Hughes doctors to examine the industrialist since he left Las Vegas were dismayed at his physical condition. Dr. William Young, a London radiologist, visited Hughes in his Inn on the Park bedroom on August 11 to take X-rays. When he arrived, Dr. Young said, "I observed Mr. Hughes naked in a dimly lighted room, lying on a bed and covered with paper toweling. I observed Mr. Hughes' skin to have a parchment-like quality. Mr. Hughes had long toenails and fingernails resembling that of a Chinese mandarin. Mr. Hughes was quite emaciated. In positioning Mr. Hughes for X-ray, we were instructed to keep paper toweling between Mr. Hughes, our hands and the X-ray plates, because we were told Mr. Hughes was concerned about germs." Dr. Young, who had seen Japanese prison camps during the Second World War, likened Hughes's malnourished condition to that of prisoners he had examined then.[80]

At first the aides attempted to persuade Dr. Walter C. Robinson, a prominent orthopedic surgeon, to perform the operation in Hughes's bedroom. When Dr. Robinson refused, Hughes was finally admitted to the London Clinic on August 12. Dr. E. Freeman Johnson, the anesthesiologist, described Hughes as "extremely emaciated, to an extent which would have taken some months at least to have developed. Mr. Hughes appeared to be much older than his 67 years of age and, in my opinion, Mr. Hughes would have found it very difficult to have done anything more than simply walk, even had his hip not been broken." While administering the anesthetic, Dr. Johnson said he became quite concerned about the "very poor state" of Hughes's teeth—many of which were loose—fearing that "during the surgery one of [the] teeth might break loose and be aspirated into Mr. Hughes' lung."[81] Dr. Robinson affirmed the views of his colleagues, saying that prior to surgery he found Hughes "extremely emaciated and dehydrated."[82]

Dr. Robinson inserted a steel pin in Hughes's left hip. The operation was an unqualified success and Hughes should have been up and walking within a few weeks. Instead, when he returned to his darkened bedroom at the Inn on the Park, he crawled back into bed and never left it again without assistance.

That December, in Dayton, Ohio, Hughes was inducted into the Aviation Hall of Fame, joining fifty-two other pioneers of the air who had been similarly cited, including Orville and Wilbur Wright, Edward V. Rickenbacker, William Mitchell, Henry (Hap) Arnold, Charles A. Lindbergh, Wiley Post, and Jacqueline Cochran Odlum. Hughes, naturally, was not present for the ceremony, but he was represented by Edward Lund, the flight engineer and only other surviving member of his 1938 around-the-world flight crew. Lieutenant General Ira C. Eaker, another member of the Hall of Fame and a former Hughes Tool Company executive, spoke briefly, calling Hughes "a modest, retiring, lonely genius, often misunderstood, sometimes misrepresented and libeled by malicious associates and greedy little men."[83]

CHAPTER 21

WATERGATE

UNDER FIRE

ON THE early morning of Thursday, December 20, 1973, a DC-9 left London bound for the Bahamas, carrying Howard Hughes, six of his aides, and two of his doctors. Although Hughes owned or leased a fleet of aircraft maintained in readiness at airports in Great Britain and the United States, the DC-9 was not his. It belonged to Adnan M. Khashoggi, the Middle East arms merchant who had made his millions by serving as middleman between American manufacturers of military hardware, such as Lockheed and Northrop—his Lockheed commissions alone eventually exceeded $100 million—and the Arab countries, especially Saudi Arabia, where the princes were his personal friends. It was natural that Khashoggi, the flamboyant Stanford-educated son of a Saudi palace doctor, had made his private plane available for the Hughes flight. The DC-9 had become a familiar sight at McCarran Airport in Las Vegas. Khashoggi parked it at the Hughes ground facilities on frequent trips to his favorite hotel and casino, the Hughes-owned Sands. Khashoggi, highest of the high-rollers, often ran gaming tabs into seven figures and sometimes, when he lacked ready cash to cover his losses, he arranged for the money to be transferred from the Key Biscayne Bank of his friend Bebe Rebozo.[1]

The DC-9 arrived at Freeport on Grand Bahama Island shortly after 4 A.M., and Hughes was moved into the Xanadu Princess Hotel. Because he had refused to walk since summer, after breaking his hip, he was carried to his suite at the northeast corner of the hotel, owned by Daniel K. Ludwig, the wealthy shipping magnate who was even more secretive and more publicity-shy than Hughes. Hughes's entourage had reserved the penthouse floor and the floor below it. His aides and doctors—some now being paid close to a hundred thousand dollars a year—had grown accustomed to life in splendid surroundings. They settled easily into suites with living rooms and dining rooms and kitchens, at an annual cost of a third of a million dollars.

It is uncertain who made the decision, and why, to transfer Hughes from London, where he had been living for a year, back to the Bahamas, which he had so recently fled by boat, hounded out by a hostile government. The efficiency of the move and the efficacy of its timing are plain however. The Bahamian government, displaying a remarkable change in attitude, welcomed Hughes by guaranteeing him complete privacy and assuring him that he would not be troubled again by government officials, or anyone else.

Earlier that month a Bahamian magistrate had issued an order effectively nullifying the Bahamas' extradition treaty with the United States that dated back to the 1930s. The order blocked efforts by the United States attorney's office in New York to extradite Robert L. Vesco, the fugitive financier under indictment on stock-fraud charges. Hughes would also be safe from American law-enforcement authorities—and he would need to be. One week after his arrival in Freeport, he was indicted by a federal grand jury in Las Vegas on stock-fraud charges stemming from his 1970 takeover of Air West.[2] Mysterious ties were emerging between Hughes and the unfolding Watergate scandal, and government investigators were displaying interest in his business affairs. By January of 1974, the Hughes empire was being scrutinized as never before.

The nine-count Air West indictment named as defendants Chester Davis, who had become Hughes's principal attorney; Robert Maheu; David Charnay, a Hollywood producer; and James H. Nall, a longtime Hughes employee. Two others, George Crockett, a Las Vegas businessman who had known Hughes since the 1940s, and Hank Greenspun, of the *Las Vegas Sun,* were named as unindicted co-conspirators.[3]

The indictment was largely the work of a tedious, painstaking investigation conducted by one Securities and Exchange Commission attorney, William C. Turner. It charged Hughes and his associates with engaging in a scheme "to unlawfully manipulate the market price of Air West, Inc., common stock and to instigate lawsuits against the opposing directors of Air West, Inc., to pressure the board of directors into approving Hughes' acquisition offer," and to "defraud and to obtain money and property by means of false and fraudulent pretenses and representations from shareholders of Air West."[4]

This was not the only federal inquiry Hughes faced. The Internal Revenue Service was conducting at least two investigations. One team of tax men sought to learn whether a band of former government espionage agents, who operated under the code name of the Elissa Group, had given cash to Hughes during his TWA financing difficulties in an effort to help him maintain control of the airline. According to reports by IRS informants, these operatives had raised the funds from narcotics traffic, and the money had been channeled through "certain Swiss, British, and Portuguese bank accounts."[5] Involved in one way or another, it was said, were a Wall Street brokerage house, a Far East construction company, and a Japanese bank.

Another team of IRS agents had opened a more traditional investigation, auditing Hughes's income-tax returns. At issue were some large cash contributions made in Hughes's name to various political candidates beginning in 1968, including the now-famous $100,000 that Richard Danner had delivered to Bebe Rebozo. IRS agents were also trying to trace the millions funneled into Bahamian and Swiss bank accounts by John Meier. The former Hughes executive, who had supervised acquisition of the worthless mining claims and enriched himself in the process, claimed that the cash had been sent abroad on Hughes's personal instructions.

Finally, there was the inquiry being conducted by the United States Senate Select Committee on Presidential Campaign Activities, better known as the Senate Watergate Committee. On January 16, 1974, Terry Lenzner, the committee's assistant chief counsel, wrote to Chester Davis:

As you must be aware, our investigation has now reached the stage where it is necessary to question your client, Howard R. Hughes.

Accordingly, I would appreciate it if you would speak with Mr. Hughes and make arrangements so that he will be available for questioning by the Senate Select Committee.

Please be advised that every effort will be made to accommodate Mr. Hughes with regard to the time and place where the session is to be conducted.

If you have any questions with regard to the foregoing, please do not hesitate to call.

Thank you for your prompt attention to this matter.[6]

Did the Senate Watergate Committee seriously expect to question Hughes? It is unclear whether the letter to Chester Davis was merely a formality to complete the public record, giving the appearance that the committee was pursuing all investigative leads, or whether Senator Sam J. Ervin, Jr., and his staff were truly unaware of Howard Hughes's physical and mental state at the time. What is clear is that certain government agencies, including the Central Intelligence Agency, were well aware of Hughes's condition, that he had not been in control of his empire for some time, and that he was not responsible for many acts performed in his name. They also were aware that Hughes had developed an addiction to narcotics and a dependence on tranquilizers.

Hughes, of course, seldom left his bed now, and then only to be carried to the bathroom. He spent most of his waking hours watching motion pictures over and over again or just lying in bed staring blankly upward. Confused and disoriented, he had given up all hope of returning to the United States because he had been told by those around him that IRS agents were lying in wait to question and harass him.

After he was moved to the Bahamas, Hughes expressed less interest in his business affairs, less interest in the world at large, than at any other time of his life. Where he once had devoured reports or memoranda from his lawyers and executives, he now hardly looked at them. Where he once had at least scanned the weekly news magazines, he now ignored them. Where he once would go on a "television binge," he now gave up watching TV because the reception in Freeport was so poor.[7] Even the aircraft technical manuals, his beloved plans and specifications, held little interest. "It's safe to say," George Francom understated, "that he was not aware of current events to a great extent."[8] Among the events that swirled past him largely unrecognized was Watergate. Yet it had penetrated even his hazy consciousness that he was somehow supposed to be involved. And so, while the Senate Watergate Committee sought to establish Hughes's role in Watergate, Hughes sought to determine the meaning of the word. He asked one of the aides to have Chester Davis prepare a Watergate report, setting out those activities that had been attributed to him.

On March 3, 1974, Davis dictated to an aide a memorandum recounting the more publicized connections. "We are involved in the Watergate affair to this extent," Davis said:

1. E. Howard Hunt, convicted for the Watergate break-in and in the subsequent efforts of a cover-up, was employed by Bob Bennett and his firm (our current Washington representative). In addition, Bennett was maintaining liaison with the White House through Colson, who was deeply involved in the Watergate cover-up.

2. Bennett, Ralph Winte (employed by us re: security matters) and Hunt are involved in plans to burglerize [sic] Greenspun's safe, and even though those plans were rejected and never carried out, the Government investigators see political motivation related to Watergate.

3. The political contribution by Danner to Rebozo and visits by Danner to Mitchell are claimed to be an effort for influencing Governmental decisions, including an alleged change in rulings of the Department of Justice in connection with a contemplated Dunes acquisition.

4. Payments made to Larry O'Brien and his employment has [sic] been claimed to have been a part of the possible motivation for the Watergate break-in because of White House interest in that arrangement as a possible means of embarrassing O'Brien and the Democrats.

5. The massive political contributions supposedly made by Maheu, particularly those made in cash, and as to some of which there is [sic] conflicting statements (as for example, Hubert Humphreys [sic] denial that he received $50,000 from Maheu), is part of the overall Watergate investigation dealing with the need for reform.[9]

While Davis's report was a fair, if elliptical, summation of those Hughes ties to Watergate that had received widespread attention, it did not fully report the true extent of the empire's involvement in the runaway scandal that would end with the first resignation of a president in the nation's history. In the beginning, Watergate had signified merely the break-in on June 17, 1972, at the Democratic National Committee offices and the attempted White House cover-up that followed. But by 1974 the term had taken on a much broader meaning. Now it was being applied to a wide range of unlawful and unethical political activities. For the most part, the Senate Watergate Committee, the Watergate special prosecutor's office, and the news media focused on those misdeeds that could be traced directly to President Nixon and his staff. In the

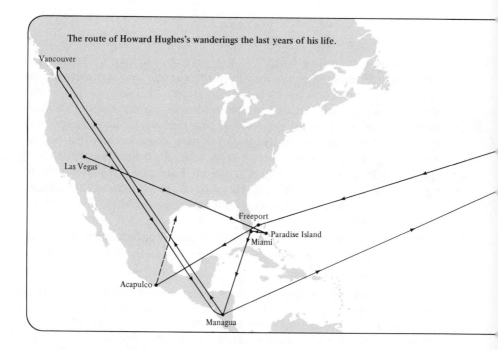

The route of Howard Hughes's wanderings the last years of his life.

Vancouver
Las Vegas
Freeport
Paradise Island
Miami
Acapulco
Managua

**THE RESIDENCES OF
HOWARD HUGHES, 1966–1976**

Below: The Desert Inn, Las Vegas,
Nov. 1966 to Nov. 1970.
United Press International

Above: The Britannia Beach Hotel,
Paradise Island, the Bahamas,
Nov. 1970 to Feb. 1972.
United Press International

Right: The Intercontinental Managua,
Managua, Nicaragua, Feb. 1972
to March 1972, and Aug. 1972 to
Dec. 1972. *Wide World Photos*

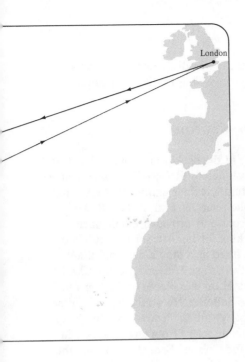

London

The Bayshore Inn, Vancouver, Canada,
March 1972 to Aug. 1972.
United Press International

Above: The Inn on the Park,
London, Dec. 1972 to Dec. 1974.
Wide World Photos

Above: The Xanadu Princess, Freeport,
the Bahamas, Dec. 1974 to Feb. 1976.
Wide World Photos

Right: The Acapulco Princess,
Acapulco, Feb. 1976 to April 1976.
Wide World Photos

process, evidence that failed to fit the pattern was discarded. So it was with an abundance of unexplained relationships involving the Hughes empire.

THE HUGHES CONNECTION

From the beginning of Watergate, lurking in the background of one incident after another was Hughes's man in Washington, Robert F. Bennett, and behind Bennett, E. Howard Hunt and Hunt's former employer the Central Intelligence Agency. It was Bennett's public-relations firm, Robert R. Mullen and Company, which served as a CIA front and provided employment for Hunt, the retired spy. Hunt had been working for Bennett's firm a little more than a year when, on July 6, 1971, he was hired as a $100-a-day consultant to the White House through his friend from the Brown University Club, Charles W. Colson, special counsel to the president. Hunt was placed on Colson's staff and given Room 338 in the Executive Office Building. He would divide his time between White House and Mullen Company duties. Pleased by Hunt's appointment, Bennett raised his Mullen Company salary from $100 to $125 a day.

The day after Hunt went to work for Colson, Bennett told him that Clifton DeMotte, who once had worked for Bennett at the Department of Transportation and now worked in Rhode Island, claimed to have damaging information about Senator Edward M. Kennedy, who then appeared to be the likely candidate for the 1972 Democratic presidential nomination. As Hunt recalled, Bennett told him "that if anybody was knowledgable of 'dirt' in the Kennedy background, it was Mr. DeMotte."[10]

Hunt passed along the information to Colson, who suggested that Hunt interview DeMotte, but under an assumed name so as to keep secret his White House connection. Working through General Robert E. Cushman, Jr., the CIA's deputy director, Hunt obtained from the intelligence agency a speech alteration device, a red wig, specially ground thick eyeglasses, and a Social Security card, a New York driver's license, a birth certificate, and various club memberships, all in the name of Edward Joseph Warren. Hunt met DeMotte in a motel near the Providence, Rhode Island, airport. Most of DeMotte's information about Kennedy drinking and Kennedy women was dated, but when DeMotte offered to look into events surrounding the drowning of Mary Jo Kopechne at Chappaquiddick, Hunt offered encouragement and expense money.

During this period Hunt also fabricated State Department cables intended to prove that President John F. Kennedy had been responsible for the overthrow and murder of South Vietnamese prime minister Ngo Dinh Diem, studied the Pentagon Papers, and planned for the burglary at the Beverly Hills office of Daniel Ellsberg's psychiatrist, Dr. Lewis J. Fielding. Working now with G. Gordon Liddy, a former FBI agent who was general counsel to the Committee for the Re-election of the President, Hunt obtained additional equipment from the CIA, a Tessina—a camera smaller than a package of cigarettes—another (black) wig, and a heel-lift device to create a limp, all of which was given to Liddy. Late in August, Hunt and Liddy flew to the West Coast to case Dr. Fielding's office, where they hoped to find information damaging to Ellsberg.

To carry out the burglary, Hunt recruited Bernard L. Barker, another onetime CIA operative living in Miami, who had worked with Hunt on the Bay of Pigs invasion. Barker recruited two Cubans, Eugenio Martinez, who had been active in the anti-Castro movement and also was on a CIA retainer, and Felipe DeDiego.* Financing for the Fielding burglary was provided by Colson—$5,000 in cash, part of the political contributions from the Associated Milk Producers, which Bennett was funneling into dummy campaign committees. On September 3, Barker and the two Cubans entered Dr. Fielding's office while Liddy stood guard outside and Hunt maintained a surveillance at the psychiatrist's apartment. But the effort was wasted. Barker and his colleagues could find no files containing Ellsberg's name.

As Hunt was tending to White House duties, Bennett called on him to do work for Hughes. One assignment: how much would it cost to have someone examine the garbage at the Westport, Connecticut, house of Clifford Irving. The novelist was rumored to be writing yet another book about Hughes, Bennett explained. There was, however, a far more likely explanation for the interest in Irving's trash. Hughes executives were obsessed with the idea that arch-enemy Robert Maheu, who was suing Hughes, was somehow behind the fraudulent Hughes book. It was a belief they had little trouble persuading Hughes himself to accept. Even after Irving and his wife pleaded guilty to the hoax, Hughes executives continued to search, without success, for evidence to link Maheu and Irving.

On another occasion, Bennett asked Hunt to find out from his CIA contacts whether Maheu had ever worked for the intelligence agency, as he had often claimed. Bennett and other Hughes lieutenants were looking into many of the stories Maheu had told Hughes, hoping to trap the former chief of Nevada operations in lies that could be used against him in the raging Maheu–Hughes legal wars. As the proprietor of a CIA front, Bennett felt sure that Maheu had never had such an association. After listening to various Hughes executives recall Maheu's tales of intelligence derring-do, Bennett was more convinced than ever. The accounts of Maheu's work "did not make much sense."[11] Hunt confirmed Bennett's instincts. He reported back that "there was no trace of Maheu having ever done anything for the CIA."[12] Bennett and Hunt were both wrong. The CIA had covered its tracks. Not only had Maheu been a freelance CIA agent since the 1950s, he had participated in at least one mission that paralleled Hunt's activities. While Hunt had been working on the Bay of Pigs project, Maheu tried to arrange the assassination of Fidel Castro.

Late in January of 1972, Bennett called Hunt into his office and told him that Hank Greenspun of the *Las Vegas Sun* "had enough information

*Both Barker and Martinez would be charged and convicted in the Watergate break-in.

on Muskie to blow Muskie out of the water."[13] Since the Maine senator was then the front-runner for the Democratic presidential nomination, Hunt felt the White House would be interested, and indeed it was. Gordon Liddy "quickly returned to me in a euphoric state," Hunt said, "indicating that the information had been well received by his superiors" and that he had been instructed "to proceed with the investigation."[14] Bennett moved with dispatch. Several days later, at another meeting in his Washington office, he introduced Hunt to Ralph Winte, a former FBI agent who was the Hughes security chief in Las Vegas. Bennett indicated that the two might have a "commonality of interest."[15] In the meeting that followed, Winte told Hunt that Greenspun probably had information in his safe at the *Sun* that would aid the Hughes Tool Company in its litigation with Maheu, as well as information damaging to Muskie's candidacy. Hunt asked Winte to obtain a diagram of Greenspun's office. He had "a team in being" that was capable of breaking into the office but would like the Hughes Tool Company to supply manpower "for lookouts, mobile surveillance and that sort of thing."[16] This seemed reasonable to Winte, who assured Hunt that he "could count on whatever assets" he might want from the Hughes organization.[17] The two men laid plans to meet later on the West Coast for another strategy session.

Late on a Friday night in February of 1972, Hunt and Liddy flew to Los Angeles and checked into the Beverly Wilshire Hotel, where the Hughes Tool Company had reserved them a suite. Winte joined them the next morning, bringing with him a diagram of the *Sun* plant. The three agreed that rather than try to photograph the documents, they would simply clean out Greenspun's safe and then board a waiting plane—to be provided by the Hughes Tool Company—and fly to some predetermined location, possibly in Baja California, where the contents of the safe would be divided. Hunt wanted to use the same team that had broken into Dr. Fielding's office, but because none of the members of that team was an experienced safe man, he had asked Barker "to locate a competent locksmith in the Miami area."[18] The next planning session was to take place in Las Vegas. In the weeks that followed, however, Hunt and Liddy were drawn into other projects. Before the burglary could be carried out, the Muskie campaign floundered. The two men lost interest and abandoned the operation.

The next project promoted by Bennett and executed by Hunt was far more successful. On February 29, 1972, the columnist Jack Anderson reported that the Nixon administration had agreed to settle an antitrust lawsuit against ITT —under terms most favorable to the company—in exchange for a $400,000 pledge to help bankroll the upcoming Republican convention. Anderson based the charge on a secret memorandum written by Dita Beard, an ITT lobbyist, and addressed to William R. Merriam, an ITT vice-president in charge of the company's Washington office. Labeled "Personal and Confidential," the memorandum, dated June 25, 1971, and typed on ITT stationery, stated, in part:

I thought you and I had agreed very thoroughly that under no circumstances would anyone in this office discuss with anyone our participation in the Convention, including me. Other than permitting John Mitchell, Ed Reinecke, Bob Haldeman and Nixon (besides Wilson, of course) no one has known from whom that 400 thousand committment [sic] had come. . . .

I am convinced, because of several conversations with Louie re Mitchell, that our noble committment [sic] has gone a long way toward our negotiations on the mergers eventually coming out as Hal wants them. Certainly the President has told Mitchell to see that things are worked out fairly. . . . If it [the convention commitment] gets too much publicity, you can believe our negotiations with Justice will wind up shot down. Mitchell is definitely helping us, but cannot let it be known.*[19]

Certain ITT officials issued an angry denial of Anderson's charges, while privately feeding lobbyist Dita Beard's memoranda and other internal documents of an embarrassing nature through a shredder. The president's staff was equally firm in its public denial, while privately scurrying from one government office to another, impounding all letters and reports dealing with the ITT case, including one document that linked Nixon to it directly.

On March 1, Anderson published another column accusing Richard G. Kleindienst, the law-and-order deputy attorney-general awaiting Senate confirmation as attorney-general, of "an outright lie" in denying that he was in any way involved in the ITT settlement.[20] The following day, at Kleindienst's request, the Senate Judiciary Committee reopened hearings on his nomination. That same day, a distraught Dita Beard, under pressure from ITT executives and about to be subpoenaed by the Senate Judiciary Committee, boarded a plane for Denver. About an hour before arriving, Mrs. Beard became ill. She complained of feeling warm and "started turning gray and blue around the mouth."[21] A stewardess gave her a nitroglycerin tablet and a shot of whisky and administered oxygen for a minute, and she seemed to recover, leaving the plane without any assistance when it landed.

The following day, though, plagued by an unremitting chest pain, Mrs. Beard checked into the Rocky Mountain Osteopathic Hospital in Denver. Heart specialists who examined the heavyset fifty-three-year-old woman concluded that she was suffering from "severe angina pectoris and an impending coronary occlusion."[22] In the days that followed, Mrs. Beard was confined to the hospital's coronary unit. Her few visitors were carefully screened. Senate Judiciary Committee members, FBI agents, White House aides, and newspaper reporters were barred.

Back in Washington, concern mounted within the Nixon administration over the political consequences of the ITT allegations, which the Democrats were using to good advantage as the Senate hearings droned on. On Monday, March 13, Robert Bennett received a telephone call from Bill Gay, the senior Hughes official now in control of the empire.

*The "Wilson" referred to in the memorandum is Robert Wilson, a California congressman; "Louie" is Louis B. Nunn, former Republican governor of Kentucky; and "Hal" is Harold S. Geneen, president of ITT.

"Hey, you know that problem that Kleindienst is having being confirmed because of the Dita Beard memo?" Gay asked.[23]

"Yes," Bennett replied.

"How would you like to know that that memo is a forgery," Gay said.

"That is fascinating. How do you know that?" Bennett asked.

"I found out today that it is forged and nobody believes that any more than they believe us about Irving," Gay declared.[24]

It was none too clear why this powerful Hughes executive was concerned about a memorandum involving an ITT political payoff or the failure of the Senate to approve Kleindienst's nomination as attorney-general. However, since the Anderson story had been published, ITT's private security firm had been working hard to find evidence to support the conglomerate's denial of the columnist's charges, and that security firm was Intertel, the same firm that handled security for Howard Hughes and his Las Vegas hotels and casinos.

Sensing the depth of Gay's interest in the ITT case as well as the political significance of his report, Bennett passed the information along to Hunt, who in turn prepared a three-paragraph memorandum for his other employer, Charles Colson. Under the heading "ITT Imbroglio," Hunt wrote:

According to Bill Gay, the Dita Beard letter is a forgery. . . . To date, the document itself has not been questioned. Since it is the crux of the matter, it should be. Any diversion or clouding of the issue at this time should be useful.[25]

Colson was ecstatic to have Hunt's message. He too believed that the Dita Beard memorandum was a forgery. He asked Hunt "to interview Mrs. Beard, to find out if the memo was in fact authentic, to tell her to tell the truth, and to assure her that if she told the truth her many friends back here in Washington would not hold it against her that she had done this thing."[26]

The problem was how to gain access to Mrs. Beard, who was still in the coronary care unit of Rocky Mountain Hospital in Denver. Other White House aides were consulted. It was suggested that Hunt should contact Mrs. Beard's daughter, Edwina McLane (Lane) Beard, who was working for the Republican National Committee. On Wednesday, March 15, Hunt drove to the Washington Monument for a meeting with Lane Beard. Wearing his CIA-issued red wig and thick glasses, Hunt introduced himself as Edward J. Hamilton—another CIA alias—"a friend of friends of her mother's, a man well placed and in a position to assist her mother out of her current situation."[27] He said that he represented the highest levels of the United States government, that he needed to speak with her mother, and that he wanted Lane to notify the hospital that he was coming. She agreed to call her mother, and Hunt flew to Denver, arriving at the hospital about 9 P.M., a box of red roses tucked under one arm.

As Mrs. Beard sat propped up in her bed, chain-smoking, surrounded by floral bouquets she had been told were bugged, Hunt, peering through his thick glasses, his head crowned with the oddly shaped red wig, began asking questions about the memorandum. She told him that the first paragraph had "a familiar ring," but that she was reasonably sure the rest was written by someone else.[28] Mrs. Beard asked what she could do. Hunt said the most useful thing "would be to have her return to Washington as soon as possible, making a brief statement, denying authorship of the memorandum—if she were able to do so in good faith—and then collapse."[29]

She insisted that in her present condition this was not possible. Yet she was sure she could not have written the memorandum and wanted to know how she could prove it. Hunt quickly volunteered "that extensive laboratory tests had determined that the memorandum was not typed last summer," when it was dated, "but had been typed this year."[30] Mrs. Beard brightened. If Hunt would provide her with the technical analysis of the document, she said, her dilemma would be solved. Hunt demurred. Finding it awkward to explain that the information had come from the Hughes organization, Hunt told her only "that it would not be appropriate for her to have such information or such a report as she would be unable to provide a plausible source for it."[31] When Mrs. Beard began to tire, Hunt left the hospital. He returned the next morning, spoke again with her briefly, then flew back to Washington to file an eight-page, single-spaced, typewritten report.

With the results of Hunt's furtive interview in the hands of the White House staff, Bennett set to work polishing a statement for Mrs. Beard denouncing the memorandum as a hoax, while Colson readied plans for a Washington press conference. Actually, the original statement was drafted by Mrs. Beard and her attorneys, the Los Angeles law firm of White, Oberhansley & Fleming. The law firm, specially retained for the assignment, also represented Orange Radio, Inc., a company in which Bill Gay was a major stockholder.

When David W. Fleming, a partner in the firm, read the text of Mrs. Beard's proposed statement over the telephone to Bennett, the Hughes Washington representative was not happy. "The statement does not really do anything for Mr. Kleindienst," Bennett told Fleming, expressing the same concern for the deputy attorney-general that Gay had exhibited. "It is a lawyer's statement. It is probably good from Dita Beard's point of view. If you want impact on the controversy, you will have to reword it."[32] Bennett, an experienced manipulator of public opinion, rewrote the statement, laboring over phrasing designed to arouse sympathy and support for Kleindienst and undermine critics of the Nixon administration and ITT. After both Fleming and Mrs. Beard approved the rewritten version, Bennett delivered it, in accordance with arrangements worked out by Colson, to the office of Senate Minority Leader Hugh Scott.

On Friday, March 17, 1972—just four days after Bill Gay called the memorandum a forgery—Mrs. Beard's attorney released the statement in Denver while Senator Scott went on national television in Washington to read the document so meticulously prepared by Bennett. Labeling the memorandum cited by Jack Anderson as a "forgery" and a "cruel fraud," Mrs. Beard said in her statement,

I did not prepare it and could not have since to my knowledge the assertions in it regarding the antitrust cases and former Attorney General Mitchell are untrue. I do not know who did prepare it, who forged my initial to it and how it got into Jack Anderson's hands or why. But I do know it is not my memo and is a hoax.[33]

Although the Senate hearings on Kleindienst's nomination dragged on through April and May, Bennett's exacting statement on Mrs. Beard's behalf marked the turning point in the controversy and defused what was becoming a serious political liability for President Nixon's reelection bid.* A story distributed by one of the national wire services the day after the release of Mrs. Beard's remarks noted:

The White House, angered by the length and the scope of Senate Judiciary Committee hearings concerning the International Telephone and Telegraph Corporation, is directing a major effort to discredit syndicated columnist Jack Anderson and the ITT memorandum he published which got the hearings started. . . .

The most dramatic success so far came Friday night when Mrs. Beard, through her attorney, released a statement calling the memo a fraud.[34]

Few seemed to notice that Dita Beard had waited nearly three weeks to call the memorandum a forgery, a claim made only after it was suggested by the Hughes organization. A few days later, it was disclosed that the FBI, following a laboratory analysis of the memorandum, had found no evidence of a forgery, and there were, in fact, some indications it was genuine. Although the examination was inconclusive, the FBI reported that the memorandum may indeed "have been prepared around June 25, 1971," as it was dated, and not at some later time as part of a hoax.[35]

As for the role of the Hughes organization in the Dita Beard episode, it remained hidden. In the style befitting a CIA-front operator, Bennett stayed inconspicuously in the background as the controversy swirled, just as he had when he became involved with Hunt in placing a spy in the campaign headquarters first of Senator Edmund S. Muskie and then of Senator George S. McGovern. Early in 1972, Bennett asked Hunt to find a job for his nephew, Robert Fletcher, at the Committee for the Re-election of the President. Hunt said that he and Liddy planned "to place agents in the offices of leading prospective Democratic nominees."[36] Fletcher rejected the offer, but he recommended a friend, Thomas J. Gregory, a senior at Brigham Young University, in Provo, Utah, who had said he was interested. A few days later Gregory received a letter from "Ed Warren," a Hunt alias, enclosing a round-trip plane ticket to Washington. About February 20, Gregory flew to the capital and met with Hunt, who told him the job would pay $175 a week. Gregory accepted, assuring Hunt that he had no qualms about passing information from the

*On June 8, 1972, the Senate approved Kleindienst's nomination as attorney-general. But the victory would prove illusory. In two years, Kleindienst would plead guilty "to a charge of failing to give accurate testimony at his 1972 confirmation hearings, regarding White House influence" on the ITT antitrust settlement, thereby becoming the first attorney-general to be convicted of a criminal offense committed while in office.

Muskie camp. Before starting work, Gregory, a twenty-five-year-old history major, returned to Provo to arrange to get credit for off-campus study. Enrolled in an "honors program for exceptionally bright and industrious students," he planned to receive sixteen credits for participating in the election campaign and writing a term paper about his experiences.*[37]

About March 1, Gregory, masquerading as a Democratic volunteer, joined the Muskie election headquarters in Washington. His assignment, according to Hunt, "was to acquire for us policy papers, working papers, advance schedules of the Muskie party, lists of contributions of contributors, bank statements."[38] Using the code name "Ruby 2," Gregory called Hunt daily with a report. At least once a week, usually on Friday, they met at a drugstore at 17th and K Streets, N.W., where they exchanged envelopes. Gregory would give Hunt an envelope containing his findings, including summaries of discussions among key Muskie aides that he had overheard. Hunt would hand Gregory an envelope containing $175 in cash. On occasion, Bennett acted as a liaison between Hunt and his student spy, transferring "packages of materials" between them.[39]

When the Muskie candidacy faltered, Hunt shifted Gregory to the McGovern campaign. There, his duties were essentially the same, with one addition: "to prepare for an electronic surveillance or electronic penetration of McGovern headquarters."[40] Initially, Gregory gave Hunt a floor plan of McGovern's office building, showing such details as the location of heating ducts and pictures in the offices of Gary Hart and Frank Mankiewicz, the senator's two chief advisers.[41] Next, Hunt introduced Gregory to James W. McCord, Jr., the onetime FBI agent and CIA operative who officially was the security coordinator for the Nixon reelection committee and the Republican National Committee, and who unofficially served as Gordon Liddy's electronics expert. On May 15, McCord went to the McGovern headquarters, posing as an out-of-town uncle of Gregory's. The student spy attempted to distract his fellow workers long enough to allow McCord to plant a listening device in Mankiewicz's office. But McCord felt rushed and the mission was aborted.

When it was decided to break into the McGovern offices to install the eavesdropping equipment, Gregory was introduced to other associates of Hunt —Bernard Barker; Gordon Liddy; Frank Sturgis, born Frank A. Fiorini, an ex-marine and soldier of fortune who participated in the Bay of Pigs invasion; and Virgilio R. Gonzalez, an anti-Castro Cuban who was a locksmith in Miami. Gregory accompanied the others on a nighttime scouting mission during which Liddy, using an air pistol, shot out a streetlight behind the McGovern headquarters. At the time Hunt's team was planning to break into the McGovern headquarters, they were also casing the Democratic National

*When Gregory's faculty adviser at Brigham Young University learned what the honors student had been doing in Washington, he told the New York Times that Gregory "won't get any credits. At least he won't get any from me. He was supposed to be working for the Democrats, not against them."

Committee offices in the Watergate, where they planned a similar bugging operation. On Thursday and Friday, May 25 and 26, two attempts to break into the Democratic National Committee offices failed. A planned break-in at the McGovern headquarters was also called off when Gregory, hiding in the building until everyone left so that he could open the door for McCord, was discovered by a watchman. On Saturday, May 27, Barker, McCord, Gonzalez, Martinez, and Sturgis finally broke into the Democratic National Committee offices. While Martinez photographed documents selected by Barker, McCord installed listening devices on the telephones of the secretary to Lawrence F. O'Brien, the national chairman of the Democratic party, and R. Spencer Oliver, the executive director of the Association of State Democratic Chairmen.

In one of those curious coincidences, both Oliver and O'Brien had Hughes connections. Oliver's father, Robert Oliver, had been the Mullen Company's "Washington lobbyist for Hughes Tool Company." O'Brien, of course, had been on the Hughes payroll until shortly after the firing of Maheu, collecting about $300,000 for his work on various Washington projects for the Hughes empire.[42]

After the burglary, a day or two went by before McCord realized that the bug on O'Brien's telephone was not working. But for the next two weeks, Oliver's phone conversations were monitored and daily logs prepared. It was then decided to enter the Watergate a second time to place another bug on O'Brien's telephone. About this time, Gregory, after more than three months of service as a political espionage agent, apparently became concerned about what he was doing. On Wednesday, June 14, he met with Bennett to talk about quitting. As Bennett recalled, Gregory told him that "they want me to bug Frank Mankiewicz's office. They want me to help them." Bennett said he replied, "Tommy, you cannot do that. You have to get out."*[43]

Gregory had already provided an office diagram to assist in the bugging; he had worked with McCord in one unsuccessful attempt to plant a bug, and had met all the Watergate burglars. Why he was suddenly uneasy is not clear. In any event, that Friday, June 16, Gregory met with Hunt and McCord at the Roger Smith Hotel and told them he was quitting. They parted on friendly terms. Hunt told Gregory that he would pay him through the end of the month.

What happened next is history. Twelve hours after Gregory resigned,

---

*According to Bennett, he gave Gregory these ethical guidelines: "If you take any money from McGovern, if you apply for, or hold any position of trust in the McGovern campaign, if you allow yourself to be put in a position where McGovern is depending upon you for anything significant, that you cannot morally discuss what you are doing with Howard Hunt and take money from him. On the other hand, if you make it clear to the McGovern people that you are simply a college student wanting the chance to watch a presidential campaign and you are willing to stuff envelopes and lick stamps in return for that privilege the question of who you talk to about experiences and who pays the expenses is your own business; that you are not doing anything all that wrong."

Bernard Barker, Virgilio Gonzalez, Eugenio Martinez, James McCord, and Frank Sturgis were arrested inside the Democratic National Committee offices and charged with burglary and wiretapping. Later, Hunt and Liddy were arrested for their part in the break-in. Within eight months, all seven Watergate defendants either pleaded guilty or were convicted and sentenced to prison. Within thirty months, nine members of the president's staff, including former Attorney-General John Mitchell, either pleaded guilty or were convicted of offenses growing out of the break-in, and the president himself resigned.

THE WELL-WIRED SOURCE

Throughout these months, there was widespread speculation about the involvement of Howard Hughes in Watergate. As *Newsweek* observed, "Almost from the beginning of the Watergate scandal, rumors have swirled around Washington that billionaire recluse Howard Hughes was somehow linked to it."[44] In his later years, however, Hughes was often improperly credited with many activities carried out in his name, and so it was with Watergate. By now, Hughes had little notion of the world outside his bedroom. His days and nights blended as he watched old movies, chewed tranquilizers, and injected himself with narcotics procured for him through illegal prescriptions.

For Hughes, then living at the Bayshore Inn in Vancouver, the week following the Watergate break-in was typical. That Sunday, June 18, 1972, he began his day at 2:15 A.M., watching television. At 2:55 A.M. an aide showed the motion picture *Captain Newman.* At 4 A.M. he began eating a piece of chicken, a chore that consumed forty-five minutes. At 5 A.M. he sat in his chair and watched a movie he had seen time and again—*Shanghai Express,* a 1932 melodrama about the adventures of a Chinese warlord, a prostitute, and an English army officer. At 5:55 A.M. Hughes began the hour-long process of eating his dessert. At 7 A.M. he went to the bathroom. At 7:25 A.M. he returned to his chair, this time to watch *The World of Suzie Wong.* At 10:20 A.M. he went to the bathroom, and at 10:35 A.M. he got into bed, where he spent the next fifteen hours sleeping or resting.[45]

During that week, Hughes would watch sixteen different motion pictures —one of them half a dozen times. And that did not count the movies he would watch on television. On Monday, it was *Unconquered, Foxfire* (a Jane Russell film), *The Night Digger, The World of Suzie Wong,* and *Shanghai Express.* On Tuesday, Hughes watched only one film, *The Wooden Horse,* as he spent most of the day sleeping after taking seven Blue Bombers—the ten-milligram Valium tablets so named by his aides because of their blue color—within less than eight hours, a quantity twenty-eight times greater than the recommended daily dose for a patient of Hughes's age and debilitated physical condition. On Wednesday, it was more movies—*VIP, Hotel Paradisio, Pleasure Seekers, Two Weeks in Another Town, Of Love and Desire,* and, once again, *Shanghai*

An excerpt from the log of Hughes's daily activities in a five-day period in July of 1972. "B/R" stands for bathroom; "bbs" means Blue Bombers, the ten-milligram Valium capsules which Hughes took in abundance; "8 E" refers to eight Empirin Compound No. 4s, a prescription drug containing codeine which he also took regularly; and "Big E" was the term Hughes's aides used for his enemas.

Express. On Thursday came *The Cincinnati Kid* and, again, *Shanghai Express,* followed by television. On Friday, *The Guns of Navarone, Two Weeks in Another Town,* and *Shanghai Express.* On Saturday, *Two Weeks in Another Town, Cafe Royal, Firecreek,* and the familiar *Shanghai Express.* On Sunday, June 25, he spent much of the day in bed after taking six Blue Bombers at 7:20 A.M., and watched only one motion picture, *Inside Daisy Clover.*[46]

And on Monday, June 26, it was more Blue Bombers, more movies. At 1:15 A.M. he began the hour-and-fifteen-minute process of eating a piece of chicken and his dessert. At 2:55 A.M. he was in the bathroom. At 3:55 A.M. he was sitting in his chair watching *Inside Daisy Clover.* At 6:20 A.M. he returned to the bathroom, and at 6:55 A.M. he was back in his chair. An aide began showing a new film, *The Grasshopper,* followed by *Shanghai Lillie,* followed by *The Guns of Navarone.* At 2:50 P.M., in the heart of the afternoon, Hughes gulped four Blue Bombers. Two hours and ten minutes later he took five more Blue Bombers. At 6 P.M. he fell asleep. When he awoke at 2:45 A.M. on Tuesday, he swallowed eight more Blue Bombers.[47] In one twelve-hour period, Hughes had taken 170 milligrams of Valium—sixty-eight times the recommended dosage.

If one thing is certain in Hughes's last years, it is that he personally had nothing whatsoever to do with Watergate. In fact, he had precious little to do with anything, notwithstanding his public image. But if Hughes himself had nothing to do with Watergate, the same could not be said for his empire, which was entangled in the scandal from its inception, beginning with the $100,000 in cash that Richard Danner delivered to Bebe Rebozo, and continuing through Bennett with an assortment of activities—the creation of phony campaign committees, the ITT matter, and the planned burglary of Hank Greenspun's safe.

Perhaps the most mysterious of the Hughes empire's ties to Watergate— one that went unnoticed throughout—was the role that Bennett played in the unraveling of the story itself, and the curious relationship that he and other Hughes lieutenants had with those authorities in charge of investigating Watergate.

From the break-in to the president's resignation, the news media, most notably the *Washington Post,* played a critical part in bringing the scandal to light and then in arousing and sustaining public interest. They did so most often through the publication of fresh disclosures of wrongdoing based on information supplied by anonymous sources. The two sources most anonymous of all were Bennett and the *Washington Post*'s still unidentified Deep Throat. Some have even suggested that Bennett was Deep Throat, a suggestion that Bennett has vigorously denied.

A lanky, garrulous, Ichabod Crane sort, Bennett enjoyed talking with newsmen, always with the understanding that he would not be identified in their articles. In the process, he pointed reporters in certain directions, steered them away from others, dropped hints of dark misdeeds by some, and neglected to mention the dark misdeeds of others, all the while helping to shape and mold the Watergate story in newspapers and magazines, on radio and television.

Like others, Bennett read about the arrest at the Democratic National Committee offices in the Sunday, June 18, 1972, *Post.* But unlike others, Bennett had every reason to believe that his colleague Howard Hunt, and quite probably the Committee for the Re-election of the President, were involved, even though the newspaper account made no mention of Hunt or Liddy. After all, Gregory had told him of the plan to bug Frank Mankiewicz's office, Gregory had met all those arrested, and Bennett had brought Hunt and Ralph Winte together to discuss burglarizing Hank Greenspun's safe. Yet Bennett made no effort to give that information to law-enforcement authorities. Instead, when he arrived at the Mullen Company on Monday morning, he went directly to Hunt's office. According to Bennett, there was only a brief conversation.

I said, "Howard, what is going on?" He said, "I don't want to talk about it. Don't say anything because the girls will hear us," meaning the girls in the secretarial pool outside his door.

I said, "What happened?" Quite obviously, his response told me that he knew what had happened. He said, "No, don't talk about it. Everything is under control. Everything will be taken care of. Those people will say nothing. There will be no damage done to the campaign. I just don't want to talk about it."

. . . At lunch time we left the office at the same time. We rode on the elevator. He said, "I may not be back. I have to get my glasses fixed. The optometrist is out in Rockville. I will be gone a long time. I may or I may not get back to the office." I said, "Fine."[48]

When Bennett returned from lunch, two FBI agents were waiting to talk with Hunt. Bennett told them that Hunt had gone to get his glasses fixed and that he might not return. They asked Bennett to have Hunt get in touch with them. He agreed, but did not question them about the purpose of the inquiry or volunteer any information about the Watergate break-in. Later in the afternoon, Hunt returned and had a longer conversation with Bennett. Bennett recalled later:

He told me that the purpose of the team was to photograph documents. He said that this was not the first time they had been in the Democratic National Committee, that they, the ubiquitous term, and he never gave me names, but that they were so titillated by what the team had found the first time, they had sent them back for more. That is what they were doing in there, he said, photographing documents.[49]

Finally, Bennett said, Hunt confided in a low tone,

"The White House wants me to get out." I don't remember if he said the country or out of town, I think that he said out of the country. He said that they wanted him to get out of the country until all of this blows over. He said, "I am leaving now. . . . John Dean will be in touch with you with some money for my wife. Will you please see that she gets it?"[50]

Bennett promised Hunt that he would pass the money along to his wife. Shortly after Hunt left, Bennett received a telephone call from Gordon Liddy.

"Where is Howard?" Liddy asked.

"I assume he is home packing," Bennett said.

"Can you get in touch with him?" Liddy asked.

"Yes, I think I can," Bennett said.

"[Tell him] the powers that be . . . are to examine the entrails one more time. They decided that he should stay put. Now, call him and tell him to stay where he is until he gets further instructions," Liddy said.[51]

Bennett called Hunt and gave him Liddy's message. "I wish that they would make up their minds," Hunt said.[52]

In the days that followed, Bennett spoke with Bob Woodward, the *Washington Post* reporter who with his colleague Carl Bernstein was responsible for breaking the Watergate story. He also talked with reporters from the *Washington Star*, the *New York Times*, the *Los Angeles Times*, and *Newsweek*, among others. He spoke with Assistant United States Attorney Earl J. Silbert, who was directing the Watergate grand-jury investigation, and with Hobart Taylor, Jr., a former Johnson administration official. Taylor was serving as a conduit to Edward Bennett Williams, the Washington lawyer representing the Democratic National Committee in a million-dollar civil lawsuit filed against Nixon's reelection committee a few days after the break-in. With some, Bennett spoke more candidly than with others. For example, the information funneled to Williams, the Democrats' lawyer, "was more extensive than the information Bennett had previously provided the grand jury."[53]

What Bennett told each is uncertain, but on July 10 he gave a detailed rundown of the Watergate incident—not to law-enforcement authorities or the news media, but to Martin Lukasky, his case officer at the CIA. "We had lunch at the Marriott Hot Shoppes Cafeteria on H Street," Bennett said later. "I briefed him on what I had told the prosecutor and what I had told the newspapers also. Then we had a general conversation about the whole situation on which, or in which, he asked me what my speculation was. I told him, that based on what I knew and felt, that I thought the chances were very good that Howard Hunt was involved in the Watergate break-in, that he would probably be charged with a crime or the crime."[54] Lukasky congratulated Bennett on his handling of the news media, indicating that "a number of people out at Langley," the CIA headquarters, were "very pleased."[*][55]

In early 1973, as reporters were attempting to establish the existence of a White House cover-up of the Watergate break-in, Bennett was still manipulating Watergate reporting. A CIA memorandum noted that "Bennett was feeding stories to Bob Woodward who was 'suitably grateful'; that he was making no attribution to Bennett; and that he was protecting Bennett and the Mullen Company." The same memorandum suggested that "Bennett took relish in implicating Colson in Hunt's activities in the press while protecting the Agency at the same time."[56] According to the CIA's summaries of meetings with the Mullen Company proprietor, "Mr. Bennett rather proudly related that he is responsible for the article 'Whispers About Colson' in the March 5, 1973, issue of *Newsweek*."[57]

The *Newsweek* story speculated about the possibility of tracing to the

---

*Because of the "sensitivity" of Bennett's information, and its bearing on other CIA operations, Lukasky carried his handwritten report of the meeting directly to Richard M. Helms, the CIA director. In addition to recounting what Bennett had said, the report contained a "mysterious reference to a 'WH flap,' indicating that if the Mullen Company cover was terminated, the Watergate could not be used as an excuse." The report also noted that "the agency might have to level with Mullen about the 'WH flap.' " Two weeks later, another secret CIA report indicated that the agency had convinced the Mullen Company "of the need to withdraw its Far East cover through an 'agreed upon scenario' which included a falsified Watergate publicity crisis." Whether the "WH flap" referred to White House, or Western Hemisphere as the CIA later insisted, only the agency knows for certain. One story put forth to explain the cryptic reference to "WH flap" was that a CIA agent who knew that the Mullen Company was a front had become a double agent and was providing information on American intelligence operations to the Soviet Union. The CIA, the story went, learned of the defection from one of its own highly placed double agents in the Soviet security organization. To close the Mullen Company without good reason, it was theorized, would tip the Russians to the existence of an American agent in their own intelligence network. Thus, it was decided to use Watergate as an excuse to close down the Mullen Company's covert operations overseas. The story was put out by the CIA and there is no evidence to support or refute it.

senior White House staff—in particular to Charles Colson—"the political espionage and sabotage operation that came to grief in last year's Watergate bugging fiasco." To support this speculation, the magazine stated that "well-wired Republican sources told *Newsweek*'s Nicholas Horrock last week that it was Colson who directed Hunt that year to work up a dossier on Senator Edward M. Kennedy, with special attention to the 1969 Chappaquiddick tragedy." The "well-wired" unnamed source was Robert Bennett, as he acknowledged later. While it was true that Colson had told Hunt to interview Clifton DeMotte about Kennedy, Bennett had provided Hunt with DeMotte's name and made the original suggestion.

The *Newsweek* article pointed out that Colson had been deeply involved in the ITT case. The magazine quoted an "insider" as saying that "Hunt relayed to Colson the theory that the centerpiece in the case—a damaging memo by ITT lobbyist Dita Beard—might have been forged. 'Hot damn!' Colson is said to have exclaimed; he decided subsequently that the White House couldn't go directly to ITT with this proposition, *Newsweek*'s source said, but with or without his promoting, Senate Minority Leader Hugh Scott made the forgery charge public." Once again, Bennett was the unnamed source for the report, and once again Bennett neglected to mention his own role—that the original source for the forgery claim was Bill Gay, his superior at the Hughes Tool Company, and that he himself had rewritten Dita Beard's statement denouncing the memo as a forgery and delivered it to Senator Scott.

Clearly, as the Watergate scandal neared the end of its first year, Bennett had, as the CIA so appreciatively noted, "handled" the press well. But in February of 1973 a new element was injected. The Senate created a seven-member Select Committee on Presidential Campaign Activities to investigate all aspects of the 1972 election campaign, and named as its chairman Senator Sam Ervin. Bennett was not concerned. An internal CIA memorandum, dated March 1, 1973, reported that "Bennett felt he could handle the Ervin Committee if the Agency could handle Hunt. Bennett even stated that he had a friend who had intervened with Ervin on the matter."[58]

Bennett lived up superbly to his billing in the CIA memorandum. The Senate Watergate Committee began its hearings at 10 A.M. on May 17, 1973. Setting a proper tone for the proceedings in his opening remarks, Senator Ervin declared that "we believe that the health, if not the survival of our social structure and of our form of government requires the most candid and public investigation of all the evidence and of all the accusations that have been leveled at any persons, at whatever level, who were engaged in the 1972 campaign."[59] From that day forward, the Senate Watergate Committee granted one favor after another to Bennett, conducting all of its investigation that touched on the Hughes empire's Washington representative in secret.

Although Bennett had been linked to half a dozen Watergate incidents —a committee lawyer acknowledged several years after the hearings that "Bennett was sort of the mystery man of the whole Watergate thing"—he was never called to testify in public before the committee.[60] Instead, he was interviewed in what amounted to casual, off-the-record sessions. Those interviews were then sealed from public inspection. One Hughes executive after another was questioned in secret—when interviewed at all. Ralph Winte, the Hughes security chief who had planned with Hunt the burglary of Hank Greenspun's safe—and who was a sometime CIA operative himself—was never questioned. Robert Maheu, involved in the distribution of hundreds of thousands of dollars in secret campaign contributions—and another CIA operative—was interviewed in private, the interview impounded. Bill Gay, who originally had volunteered that the ITT memorandum was a forgery, was interviewed in secret, and the interview sealed. Incredibly, the committee even arranged to interview in private, and grant immunity to, John Meier—the same "Dr. Meier" who had processed the worthless mining claims peddled to Hughes for millions of dollars and who later circulated bogus Hughes memoranda, some of which were initially accepted as genuine by federal courts. And so it went as more than two dozen people with information relating to ties between the Hughes empire and Watergate were questioned in private, often informally and not under oath.* The practice contrasted starkly with the spectacle in which the Senate Watergate Committee not only interrogated scores of witnesses in public, but also paraded them before television cameras.

By early 1974 only a few of the committee's staff investigators were looking into the Hughes connection, and their efforts were confined largely to the $100,000 given to Rebozo. Herbert W. Kalmbach, the president's lawyer, testifying in executive session before the Senate Watergate Committee, said that Bebe Rebozo told him on April 30, 1973, that "he had disbursed part of the funds to Rose Woods, to Don Nixon, to Ed Nixon and to unnamed others during the intervening years."[61] Kalmbach's testimony contradicted Rebozo's steadfast contention that he had placed the $100,000 in his safe-deposit box and had never touched the money until he returned it.

Interestingly, as Senate Watergate probers first pursued these leads, Hughes's attorneys were lobbying strenuously and secretly with Justice Department officials to head off a second indictment of the industrialist. In January of 1974, a month after the Air West charges had been filed, a district court judge in Nevada dismissed the indictment as defective. The SEC and the United States attorney's office in Las Vegas were preparing another, but high-level Justice Department officials in Washington had promised Hughes's lawyers that they would be given an opportunity to argue, in private, against reindictment—a courtesy not generally extended to citizens about to be charged with a federal crime. As Chester Davis, who also was named as a

*All the records compiled by the Senate Watergate Committee are stored in the National Archives but are under the control of the Senate Committee on Rules and Administration. In February of 1978, the *Philadelphia Inquirer* asked Senator Claiborne Pell, the committee chairman, for permission to examine the interviews of Hughes executives, including Bill Gay, Robert Bennett, and Nadine Henley. Pell advised the *Inquirer* that the requested material was not available for public inspection and that in a number of cases it was "not releasable because the interview is not transcribed or the interviewee is not under oath."

defendant in the original indictment, reviewed the situation for Hughes in a message dictated over the telephone on April 30, 1974, to one of the aides at the Xanadu Princess Hotel: "The Las Vegas United States Attorney is pressing another indictment. . . . The Justice Department in Washington has scheduled a conference on Thursday. I have to be in Washington tomorrow to organize our presentation, and hopefully forestall further action by the Las Vegas grand jury."[62]

This, then, was the situation in the closing days of the spring of 1974. Hughes was safely bedded down in his Bahamian hotel, mentally confused, believing that he could not return to the United States because federal agents were waiting to take him into custody. His billion-dollar empire was under the most intense scrutiny in its history. IRS agents were systematically going through his financial records. The United States attorney's office in Las Vegas and the SEC were seeking other Hughes records relating to the Air West acquisition. Robert Maheu, engaged in an acrimonious courtroom battle with the Hughes organization in Los Angeles, was seeking Hughes's records to bolster his defamation lawsuit. Senate Watergate investigators, trying to pin down the Hughes–Rebozo connection, were seeking still other documents. And through it all lurked the CIA, concerned only with protecting its own interests.

Against this background there occurred a gigantic breach in the Hughes security system. In the early morning hours of Wednesday, June 5, 1974, a team of burglars broke into Romaine Street—the Hughes command post in Hollywood so often described as a fortress. They methodically went through the records and personal papers of Hughes and his empire, and carted away thousands of documents, many of them supersensitive. If the Watergate break-in was a "third-rate burglary," the Romaine Street burglary three thousand miles away was a model of professionalism.

CHAPTER 22

HUGHESGATE

"THE BASTILLE"

IT HAD seemed a good idea in 1972 for Michael E. Davis to join the Summa Corporation as a guard at Romaine Street. His brother-in-law, Chuck Waldron, had started there in 1957 and was doing very nicely. Following service as a chauffeur, escort for budding actresses, assistant to Kay Glenn, and supervisor of the building staff, Waldron had become a personal aide to Hughes. For giving Hughes his medicine, taking and delivering messages, and performing other secretarial chores, Waldron received close to $100,000 a year. Upon marrying Waldron's sister, Davis had converted to Mormonism, the proper religious credential for a swift rise in the Hughes hierarchy. But after three years, Davis's career had stalled. Still employed as a guard, he spent his nights making the rounds inside and outside the block-long building, assuring the security of the fortress that Nadine Henley called "the Bastille."[1]

With Hughes's withdrawal from the outside world and the transfer of most executive functions to Bill Gay's Encino office, Romaine Street had declined to little more than a records center and warehouse of Hughes memorabilia. Locked away in half a dozen walk-in vaults and scores of filing cabinets and safes were negatives and prints of all Hughes's films, his pilot logs, aviation trophies, other personal mementos, and 475 scrapbooks filled with newspaper and magazine articles about Hughes from 1931 to 1975.[2] By far the most valuable contents of the building were the informal Hughes archives, a collection of Hughes's personal, business, and financial papers dating back half a century. The papers touched every phase of his career—contracts awarded to a stable of starlets, his management of TWA and RKO, his acquisition of Las Vegas hotels, casinos, and real estate. There were thousands of memoranda that Hughes had written in longhand on yellow legal tablets, expressing his wishes and views on everything from underground nuclear tests and the status of blacks in American society to detailed instructions on the handling of the TWA lawsuit and the purchase of Air West. And then there were the truly sensitive papers, messages, and memoranda, some written or dictated by Hughes, many prepared by his lieutenants, accounting for their progress on a particular assignment. There were reports on intricate schemes to avoid paying taxes and speculation about what federal agents might overlook in an audit. There were reports of secret dealings with government agencies—the Internal Revenue Service, the Justice Department, the Civil Aeronautics Board. There were summaries of negotiations or understandings reached with men in the House of Representatives, the Senate, and the White House.

Shortly before 1 A.M. on Wednesday, June 5, 1974, Michael Davis, a thirty-nine-year-old father of six children who now supplemented his income as a Hughes security guard at night by working as a car salesman during the day at Crossroads Chevrolet in North Hollywood, completed an uneventful exterior inspection of Romaine Street. As he opened one of the doors to go back inside—a door secured by both a key and a combination lock—he was suddenly grabbed from behind, shoved through the door, and ordered to "be quiet and don't look around," Davis said.[3] He did not see his assailants, he said, but he believed there were two men. They blindfolded him, taped his mouth and hands, and then pushed him into the ground-floor office of Kay Glenn. Oddly, the door to that office was ajar, although Glenn later insisted that, in keeping with his usual practice, he had locked it when he left work between seven and eight o'clock the night before.

Meanwhile, out in the hallway a clanking noise sounded as two more men arrived dragging a pair of gas tanks—one stamped "United States Navy"— and an acetylene torch. They stopped in front of a large walk-in vault across from Glenn's office and set to work. They knew exactly what they were doing. Working quietly and efficiently, they applied just the right mix of acetylene and oxygen to assure a flame that would cut quickly and leave a minimum of residue. The old Mosler safe had two outer doors secured by a combination lock and two inner doors with a relatively unsophisticated key lock. An expert safecracker, assuming that the inner doors would be locked, would have cut around the dial on the outer doors, thereby exposing the lock on the inner doors, which then could be punched out. But the Romaine Street intruders cut instead along the bottom of the vault, a faster and easier approach because it eliminated the necessity of cutting through the chromium locking bars surrounding the locking mechanism. That is, it would be a faster and easier approach if the two inner doors had been left open.

They had been.

Back in Glenn's office, after ordering Davis to stand against a wall, the other pair of burglars pried open a four-drawer filing cabinet—the top drawer was a safe—and began sifting through the contents. There were stacks of $100, $50, and $20 bills, which they pocketed, along with three Juvenia watches and a Levi Strauss stock certificate. As the men sorted through the files, scattering unwanted papers on the floor, Davis heard them mutter from time to time, "Looky here, this is it" and "Look at this."[4] Davis estimated that they remained in Glenn's office thirty to forty-five minutes, and then he was taken back into the hallway and marched west along the corridor as his captors forced open a door or two and looked into other offices. When they reached the end of the building, they turned around, retraced their steps the length of the hallway, and climbed a stairway to the second floor. At the top of the steps, they pushed Davis into the office of Lee Murrin, a forty-year veteran of the organization who oversaw Hughes's personal financial affairs. Again, Davis said, he was told to stand against the wall. After an unsuccessful attempt to pry open an old-fashioned safe, the men sent for the acetylene torch. When they began cutting through the locking bars, Davis recalled that it became "terribly smoky and extremely hot" because it was "not a great big office."[5]

In all, Davis believed he spent thirty to forty-five minutes in Murrin's office before he was ushered back out into the second-floor hallway, where they again began walking west until they reached the office of Carol Snodgrass, an accounting clerk. There, the men easily forced open another combination filing cabinet and safe. "This is a piece of cake," one said.[6] They spent about fifteen minutes shuffling through papers, and then moved Davis back to the hallway where they continued on to the office of Nadine Henley. Although Miss Henley worked out of Summa's headquarters in Encino, she also maintained an office at Romaine Street, where she had spent more than two decades. It was not necessary to force open the door of Miss Henley's locked office, for Davis heard one of the men insert a key. Inside, they ignored the wall safes, focusing their attention on documents. Davis could hear the men sorting through the papers, saying at different times "Take this" or "Don't take this."[7] After ten or fifteen minutes they left Miss Henley's office, carrying with them, in addition to certain papers, a pair of Wedgwood bowls, a collection of South American butterflies in a silver backing, and a rare Mongolian bowl.

Back in the hallway, the burglars returned to the east end of the building and a conference room which had also been left unlocked. Thousands of Hughes's personal papers were stuffed into several filing cabinets and spread across a table, where they had been assembled for cataloging and indexing. Again, Davis listened as the men ruffled through the papers, announcing to each other "Look at this" and "Take this."[8] The burglars spent about thirty minutes examining the papers, discarding some, placing others in boxes. "They seemed to know just what they wanted."[9] When the men finished packing the papers, they walked Davis back downstairs and into a warehouse room. There, he said, his ankles were taped and he was ordered not to leave. He obeyed.

"I was told to stay there, you know," Davis said. "They didn't say five minutes or five hours. So I stayed a reasonable length of time. I don't know how long with all these things, you know, going through my mind, but I stayed there what I felt was a reasonable length of time."[10] Then, he said, "I managed to roll over on the rolls of carpet onto the floor and I stood, and with the pressure on the ankles where it was taped, there was some leverage where I could move. So at that time I hobbled into Kay Glenn's office, which was out the door and the first office in the hallway."[11]

With his hands, ankles, and mouth taped, Davis said he managed to get the telephone off the hook, opening an intercom line to Operations on the west end of the second floor—the one room the burglars had carefully avoided—where Harry F. Watson, the only other staff person in the building, was manning the telephones. Following Romaine Street's standard procedure for logging all communications, Watson noted that the call came in at 4:40 A.M. Picking up the phone, he heard a muffled voice that said what sounded like "I'm bound and gagged." Watson asked the caller to repeat the message. "They have got me bound and gagged," the muffled voice said again.[12]

Watson rushed to Operations' doors to make certain they were still locked, then called Kay Glenn and the police. In the meantime, Davis said, he was able to break the tape on his ankles, and he went to the second floor and into the Xerox room adjoining Operations. He called over an intercom to Watson, announcing, "I'm outside." Watson replied, "Stay where you are. I have called the police."[13] A few minutes later the police arrived, and Davis described the burglary.

The next day, newspaper accounts of the burglary were sketchy, as they had been following the Watergate break-in. The *New York Times* reported, "A security guard at Howard R. Hughes' Hollywood message center and office building was bound and gagged by a group of men who then ransacked private papers and opened two safes, where they stole about $60,000."[14] The newspaper quoted a police spokesman as saying that "Hughes staff members would not say what papers were missing."[15]

In the days after the burglary, Hughes executives maintained their customary silence in response to questions about the break-in, not only from the news media but from the Los Angeles police as well, refusing to say exactly what private papers of Hughes, if any, had been stolen. Romaine Street's report to Hughes himself, confined to his bedroom at the Xanadu Princess Hotel in Freeport, was as vague as the report to the police.

Hughes's reaction to the break-in was ruled by his own peculiar brand of logic. His immediate concern was not what might have been stolen but who was going to determine what was stolen. He especially feared that some outsider might be allowed to rummage through his archives—perhaps an insurance adjuster. The thought chilled him, and he spelled out precise instructions to an aide, who relayed them to Miss Henley, Murrin, and Glenn:

He wants to know who is actually going to look in the various areas, vaults, and rooms at Romaine to ascertain just what is missing and presumed stolen in the robbery. He does not want some insurance investigator to take it upon himself to start opening boxes and crates when he has left such rigid instructions through the years on the handling of such sensitive items as his motion picture equipment, etc. He wants a detailed report, step by step, on just how it is intended that these searches be made. He wants this report before anything is touched.[16]

Nearly two weeks after the burglary, at 5:45 P.M. on Monday, June 17, Harry Watson received a telephone call in the Romaine Street Operations from a man who identified himself as Chester Brooks. He first asked to speak to Nadine Henley. Watson said she was not available. He then asked for Kay Glenn. Watson said he was out of town. Finally, he asked who Watson was. Watson told him and the caller announced, "Mr. Watson, it is about the burglary and it is urgent."[17]

Watson said the caller told him that

in a park in the San Fernando Valley, near your office, there is a trash can under a tree, opposite 16944 Ventura Boulevard, and on top of the trash can there would be a white envelope and it was to be seen only by Nadine Henley or Kay Glenn. . . . If they want to contact me, they should put an ad in the classified *Los Angeles Times* and it should say, "Apex okay," and should contain a phone number written backwards.[18]

Watson immediately called Miss Henley at the Encino office at 17000 Ventura Boulevard and gave her the message. She looked out the third-floor window of her office, across the street to the park the caller mentioned, and "thought that a white envelope was quite obvious in one of the trash cans."[19] She also noticed a motorcycle policeman in the street. Suspecting something more sinister than an envelope, quite possibly a letter bomb—"We have so many spurious calls that it is very difficult to tell what's what," she said later —Miss Henley sent Paul Winn, an attorney in the office, to explain the situation to the police officer and seek his help in retrieving the envelope.[20] The motorcycle policeman concluded that if the Hughes organization believed the letter might contain a bomb, he was not going to take any unnecessary risks. He placed a call for assistance to the Los Angeles Police Department's bomb squad.

A short time later, Loren C. Wells, a bomb-squad officer, arrived and carefully examined the envelope. When Wells opened it, in place of the bomb feared by Miss Henley he found a single sheet of yellow legal paper and a smaller piece of paper about four inches by five inches. On the smaller piece were the typewritten words "Air West" and "Parvin Dohrmann."* On the yellow legal paper there was a handwritten message addressed to "Bob." The note, dated June 6, 1969, said:

I would be ecstatic at the prospect of purchasing Parvin in the same manner as Air West. Do you think this really could be accomplished? I just assumed that the cries of monopoly would rule it out.

If this really could be accomplished, I think it would be a ten strike and might change all of my plans.

Please reply. Most urgent.[21]

---

*It later was determined that the words had been typed on a typewriter in the Romaine Street conference room, where Hughes's papers were being cataloged and indexed under Kay Glenn's supervision.

The message, signed "Howard," appeared to be one of Hughes's countless memoranda to Bob Maheu. The reference to Parvin concerned the Parvin–Dohrmann Company, which then owned three hotels and casinos in Las Vegas. The Hughes memorandum and the accompanying note established that the caller Watson had spoken with was someone with intimate knowledge of the burglary. He was also quite familiar with the internal workings of the Summa Corporation. For although the Encino office dated back to 1958, few outsiders knew of its existence. Even Hughes believed the office had been closed some years earlier, as he had ordered. The directory in the lobby of the three-story building bore no listing for the Summa Corporation, Howard Hughes, or Hughes employees. In fact, the directory listed no tenants at all on the third floor, where Bill Gay, Nadine Henley, Vincent Kelley—a Hughes security chief—and other Summa executives worked behind doors secured by push-button combination locks.

Responding to the directions of the mysterious Chester Brooks, Hughes officials placed a classified ad in the *Los Angeles Times,* with the Romaine Street telephone number reversed. Los Angeles police put a recording device on the telephone and everyone sat back and waited. The call for Miss Henley came three days later, on June 20.

THE MILLION-DOLLAR BURGLARY

"Mrs. Henley, this is Mr. Brooks calling, regarding the ad in the paper," said the caller.[22] After asking a few identifying questions, Brooks got down to the basics:

BROOKS: Here's what our intentions are; number one, it may please him to know that this is not part of any conspiracy through the Maheu people or anything of that nature and we wish this man no personal harm of any, any kind.

MISS HENLEY: Okay.

BROOKS: I want that clearly understood.

MISS HENLEY: Okay.

BROOKS: Number two, there was quite a bit more money that was said to be taken than actually was. You might bring that to his attention. It seems that maybe he's got some people in his own company who dabbled somewhat.

MISS HENLEY: I see.

BROOKS: Number three, the total price that we're interested in procuring is $1 million for the content. We want it in two separate drops. The first one of which will be $500,000 for half of the documents.

MISS HENLEY: Mmm, mmm.

BROOKS: The second one will follow within a three-day period.

MISS HENLEY: Mmm, mmm.

BROOKS: If there is at anytime there's any breach of trust, the negotiation will stop at once. There'll be no further attempt made to contact any of the people. We know how the Hughes [organization] operates in this type of situation, we're not fools, and we can probably trust it much more than he himself can. At any rate, we will call you tomorrow and you can either give me a yes or no at that time—

MISS HENLEY: Can I ask you what time? I did have some outside appointments tomorrow.

BROOKS: We'll call you at 12 sharp.

MISS HENLEY: That doesn't help me too much. Could you call a little later?

BROOKS: Well, give me a time, Mrs. Henley.

MISS HENLEY: Well, no, say three.

BROOKS: We'll call you at 3 o'clock and if it's satisfactory, give us your answer at that time, just as simple as that.

MISS HENLEY: Okay.

BROOKS: If not, we have other channels.

MISS HENLEY: Now it takes me a little time you know. This is not money I could just pull out of my hat, and takes me a little time to get in touch with the man, sometimes, you know.

BROOKS: Well, that's your responsibility. We won't call but one more time. Thank you very much.[23]

At 4:18 P.M. the next day, the call came into Operations. "Is Miss Henley there?" the voice asked.

"No. Who is this?" asked a Summa employee who had picked up the phone, Miss Henley's private line.

"This is Chester Brooks," replied the caller.

"She's in a meeting," said the Summa employee—an answer that carried with it the implication that neither Nadine Henley nor any other knowledgable Summa executive was much concerned about recovering Hughes's stolen papers.

"All righty. Thank you," said Chester Brooks. And he hung up.[24]

True to his word, the man who called himself Chester Brooks never telephoned again.

To the Los Angeles police there had always been something special about the Romaine Street break-in, something that set it apart from the more than thirty thousand other burglaries committed in the city thus far that year. It was a belief that was quickly reinforced. A special agent in the FBI field office in Los Angeles called to let the police know that his "home office in Washington [was] interested. They feel Watergate is involved."[25] An assistant United States attorney advised police that the burglary might have been an attempt to thwart SEC criminal and civil investigations of Hughes's purchase of Air West. A subpoena for certain Romaine Street records had been prepared just a few days before the break-in.

In a report on the theft, one of the police officers assigned to the investigation concluded "that someone within the [Summa] Corporation set up this burglary. It is not known at this time if the purpose of the burglary was for money or for certain documents that were removed."[26]

Police gave polygraph tests to seventeen Summa employes. The one notable exception was Michael Davis. "It's my firm belief that I don't believe in polygraph machines dictating whether a fellow's telling the truth or not, and

I just refused to take it," Davis said.[27] Given an ultimatum by Summa executives to take the test or be fired, Davis refused and was fired. Of the seventeen Summa employees who did take the test, one failed. He was Vincent Kelley, director of internal security for Summa in Los Angeles. Although he did not pass the examination, Kelley was retained on the Summa payroll.[28]

Some weeks after the burglary, a Summa executive called the FBI and reported, belatedly, "among the documents stolen was one that related to national security and the CIA."[29] Instead of assigning agents from the local field office, as it ordinarily would, the FBI sent two agents from Washington to confer with police in Los Angeles, informing them, rather cryptically, that "there was a national-security document involved, that if they found the document they would recognize it, and they were to forget they had ever seen it."[30] FBI agents (or CIA agents posing as FBI agents, it is not clear which) floated about Los Angeles, offering to pay $1 million for the return of the stolen Hughes papers—the same papers that just a few weeks earlier Summa executives had deemed so unimportant.

After all of this, if doubts persisted that something was peculiar about the Romaine Street burglary, they vanished with the arrival of two new characters upon the scene, both indigenous to Southern California. One was a sometime actor, screenwriter, and television scriptwriter. The other was a car salesman. They quickly emerged as the leading players in a cast that already included scores of FBI agents, private detectives, Summa executives, CIA agents, Los Angeles police, SEC investigators, Hughes security agents, Justice Department attorneys, and other official and nonofficial types who flitted in and out of the burglary case.

The actor and screenwriter was Leo Gordon, who back in the 1950s and 1960s appeared in supporting roles in an assortment of western and adventure movies. For the most part they were productions like *Man in the Shadow,* in which Gordon played the dislikable associate of a despotic rancher (Orson Welles), who was waging a private war with the courageous sheriff (Jeff Chandler). Gordon wrote screenplays for films like *Escort West, Hot Car Girl, The Cry Baby Killer,* and *All the Loving Couples.* The last movie was an X-rated production of the initiation of a new couple into a suburban wife-swapping set. Gordon's wife, Lynn Cartwright, had played one of the swap-mates. More recently, Gordon had been writing scripts for "Adam-12," a television series depicting the exploits of a pair of Los Angeles police officers.

The car salesman was Donald Ray Woolbright, who had moved to Los Angeles just three years earlier. Back in St. Louis, where he grew up in the city's slums, Woolbright had compiled a record of two dozen arrests for a variety of alleged offenses, including burglary, assault, and counterfeiting. When Woolbright moved to California in 1971, the intelligence unit of the St. Louis Police Department sent a message to the Los Angeles police advising them of his background and describing him as a "con-man, burglar and fence."[31] Soon after he came to the West Coast, Woolbright became a partner in a Woodland Hills jewelry store and a car salesman in a North Hollywood lot, just across the street from the one where Mike Davis, the Hughes security guard, sold cars.

Woolbright and Leo Gordon had known each other for about a year. Gordon had bought a car from Woolbright, and then had sent two friends to buy their cars from him. One day toward the end of July, Woolbright dropped by Gordon's Sunland home. He seemed agitated, as Gordon recalled their meeting that day. "I don't know whether I should tell you this," he said, "but I have been beating it around in my head for three days and I have been walking the walls with it. But I have something that's very big and I don't know quite how to handle it."[32] There was a pause.

Two of the characters in the drama that swirled around the burglary of Hughes's Romaine Street command post: Leo Gordon *(left),* an actor and screenwriter, and Donald Ray Woolbright, a car salesman. The Gordon photo dates from 1955 when he played the part of a warlord in *The Conqueror,* a movie produced, coincidentally, by Howard Hughes. *United Press International*

"Who is the most important man you can think of in the world today?" Woolbright asked.

"Kissinger," Gordon replied.

"How about Howard Hughes?" Woolbright offered.

"Well, I have to agree," Gordon said.

"What would you say if I told you I had two boxes of Howard Hughes' personal documents?" Woolbright asked.

"Well, where did they come from?" Gordon asked.

When Woolbright hesitated, Gordon quickly interjected, "Well, there's only one place it could have come from and that's the burglary that happened about a month and a half ago."[33]

Woolbright nodded and began to relate a bizarre tale. He was at home one night he said, when his wife answered a telephone call from a man who identified himself as Bennie from St. Louis. Woolbright said he did not know any Bennie and refused to talk. The man called again. He gave Mrs. Woolbright a message to relay to her husband: "I was at Tex and Joe's funeral in St. Louis and I saw and met you then there."[34] This time, Woolbright took the phone. Bennie from St. Louis announced that he represented the people who had Hughes's secret papers and he offered Woolbright a job as "a bag man to make a transfer of the papers and pick up the ransom for the papers."[35] Woolbright's fee as the middleman in what would be a million-dollar extortion case was fixed at a modest $15,000.

Gordon listened as Woolbright continued his story, insisting that he had not been involved in the burglary but that "there were four men brought out from St. Louis specifically to do the job."[36] He also said that the amount stolen in the burglary was considerably more than the $60,000 reported. It was "more like four times that amount," he said.[37] Gordon wondered "why would professional burglars, after taking X number of dollars, labor themselves and burden themselves down with several boxes of papers that could tie them into the crime immediately if anybody met them."[38]

"That was the reason they went there," Woolbright explained.[39] "The whole object of the burglary was to get the papers and the money was ancillary."[40] Woolbright said that after the break-in, the Hughes papers were taken to Las Vegas, where some were "taken out of the batch" by an unidentified person or persons—presumably whoever commissioned the burglary—and "the balance returned" to the thieves.[41]

Gordon was impressed by Woolbright's detailed knowledge of the burglary. Woolbright recited an inventory of items that the burglars had taken from Romaine Street in addition to the papers: a butterfly collection, Wedgwood vases, watches—items that had not been mentioned in newspaper reports published at the time of the break-in. Police later concluded that Woolbright "knew details that could only have been known by someone who did take part in the crime or was very close to someone who did take part in the crime."[42]

Gordon said Woolbright sought his advice on what to do with the stolen papers because "I'm a writer . . . and it was his idea that in view of the [Clifford]

Irving thing and everything else, that someone would pay handsomely for these documents because they are all handwritten by Mr. Hughes."[43]

Thus Leo Gordon, a onetime actor who played heavies in westerns, and Donald Woolbright, a small-time police character from St. Louis, formed an alliance to determine the fair market value of Hughes's papers. With Woolbright in tow, Gordon went to see Joanna Hayes, the wife and business manager of a novelist friend. She was not helpful. Next, they went to see a West Los Angeles attorney, Maynard Davis, the nephew of Sidney Korshak, a multimillionaire Hollywood attorney with impressive connections in the motion-picture industry, the political community, and the crime syndicate. Korshak's friends and acquaintances over the years ranged across the social scale, including the actress Jill Saint John, Robert F. Kennedy, and Chicago mobster Charles (Cherry Nose) Gioe. After listening to Gordon and Woolbright, Davis was somewhat skeptical. According to Gordon, Davis said, "I'd like to see something tangible, you know, solid, not just words, and I'll make a couple of calls."[44] It was, Gordon and Woolbright agreed, a reasonable request. After the meeting broke up, Woolbright set out alone to get the Hughes papers.

Two days later, Gordon said, Woolbright called him and reported "that he had just come back from Las Vegas in his Corvette with Bennie, and the papers were in the trunk."[45]

"Do you have some place I can put the stuff?" he asked.

"My safe," Gordon replied. But when he said the safe was a five-foot Diebold, Woolbright told him "it was not big enough."[46]

The two dealers in purloined papers returned to Maynard Davis's law office and showed him a memorandum written by Hughes concerning underground nuclear tests in Nevada. Gordon said Davis indicated that he had already contacted Greg Bautzer, the Hollywood lawyer Hughes retained in past years. Bautzer expressed an interest in the papers, Davis said, but he insisted on meeting with the burglars. On that, Woolbright was unyielding. "No way," he declared.[47] Davis then offered his visitors this parting advice, Gordon recalled, "I have a gut feeling and you guys make up your own mind. If I were you, I would drop it. You are playing with dynamite."[48]

A disheartened Woolbright and Gordon retired to a coffee shop to review their lack of progress. As Gordon remembered the conversation, Woolbright said, "We tried our best shot, and I guess we are too lightweight to handle it. It is too big for us. I'll just have to give this stuff back to the people and forget it, and it is a pity because I have already spent part of the money."[49] The two men parted company, with Gordon neglecting to mention that he had told the whole story to someone else. That person was Frank Hronek and Gordon had known him for fifteen years. Their families vacationed together. They were close personal friends. Hronek was an intelligence officer in the Los Angeles County district attorney's office.

Sometime during August, Hronek visited Gordon at his home and played a tape recording of the telephone conversation between Nadine Henley and the man who called himself Chester Brooks. There was no question in Gordon's mind. Chester Brooks was Donald Woolbright. After a meeting with another Los Angeles police officer who was in charge of the investigation of the still-unsolved Romaine Street break-in, it was suggested that Gordon should reestablish contact with Woolbright. Gordon arranged a meeting and attempted to renew Woolbright's interest in the caper by telling him that he had found a person "who is very interested in the papers. A friend of Bob Mitchum's."[50] All in all, it was a rather implausible tale the scriptwriter had come up with—"I was winging a story," he said later—and it immediately aroused Woolbright's suspicions. He wanted a few days to think it over.[51]

A second meeting was scheduled at Denny's Restaurant, at Coldwater and Ventura. Gordon alerted Hronek so that the intelligence officer could observe the meeting at a discreet distance. After Gordon arrived at Denny's, he waited about forty-five minutes for Woolbright to appear. Then the telephone rang, a waitress answered it, and asked, "Is there a Mr. Gordon here?"[52] It was Woolbright.

"I can't make it," Woolbright said. "I'm out at Sambo's at Topanga Canyon. Come out [here]."[53]

At Sambo's, Gordon said, Woolbright asked him to repeat his story. "I want to know exactly what you are doing, exactly who you are dealing with, who you are talking to, and what the whole setup is," Woolbright demanded.[54]

Gordon explained again that "Mitchum was the primary mover as far as returning these papers to Hughes, because Mitchum was a friend of Mr. Hughes."[55]

"I don't buy it," Woolbright snapped. "You are not leveling with me."

"I'm telling you all I can tell you. The less you know, the better," Gordon said.

"Nothing is going to happen until you level with me," Woolbright replied.

"All right, I'll level with you," Gordon said. "The police are on to it. The feds are on to it. They know you and they know me and all they are interested in right now is recovering those documents because national security is involved."[56]

After some persuading, Gordon said, Woolbright agreed to go along with his proposal to obtain a file of the stolen papers, which the burglars supposedly had in their possession. First, though, Gordon said Woolbright told him, "these people would want some sincere money or out front money."[57]

"What will it take?" Gordon asked.

"At least five thousand dollars," Woolbright said. "I have got seventeen hundred on me and I have got to leave some money for Joannie. I need some money for expenses."

"You put in fifteen. I'll put in thirty-five. That's five thousand," Gordon figured.[58]

Back in business once again, the pair drove to Gordon's home, where he said he took twenty-five $100 bills and two $500 bills from his safe and gave them to Woolbright. Woolbright said he planned to leave for Denver at 11:30 that night, and hastened to add, "My God, don't tell the police or the feds I'm on my way to Denver. I don't want any tails on me because if I show up with a tail, I'm a dead man. I'll be en route from there to Houston and I might have to go to Miami."[59]

Gordon said he never saw him again. There was one telephone call eleven or twelve days later, Gordon said, during which Woolbright exclaimed, "You won't believe the bills I have run up."[60]

"I don't care about the bills. I hope you are not buying cars with my money," Gordon joked.

"What kind of crack is that?" an unamused Woolbright replied.

"I'm just kidding you," Gordon said.

"Well, I'm doing the best I can," Woolbright said. "I have got to move around. I'll be in touch."[61]

Woolbright hung up and Gordon said he never heard from him again.

In the weeks following the Romaine Street burglary, both the CIA and the FBI behaved peculiarly. The FBI's initial response to the break-in had been that it related to Watergate. Interestingly, on the day of the burglary, Donald and Edward Nixon were to testify before the Senate Watergate Committee, which was continuing to look into an allegation that the Hughes $100,000 given to Rebozo had been parceled out to Nixon family members. According to newspaper accounts, "the brothers declined to answer some questions put to them at a closed session Wednesday morning and failed to appear for a scheduled afternoon session."[62] Later that month, Bebe Rebozo, whose personal and business records also were being sought by the committee, left the country before a subpoena could be served.*

In any event, the CIA established contact with the national office of the FBI following the burglary to determine what had been stolen and to monitor progress of the investigation. An internal CIA memorandum, summarizing a discussion of the burglary by top agency officials, noted that

with a background of two previous burglaries of Summa Corporation offices in the past three months, one in Las Vegas, Nevada, and one in Encino, California, as well as the court trial which has been recently completed in Los Angeles, wherein Robert A. Maheu is suing Hughes corporation for some $17 million, it was felt by all concerned that an effort should be made to determine if the FBI, in its liaison with local police, has developed any information concerning possible suspects in the perpetration of the instant burglary on 5 June 1974, or the two previous in Las Vegas and Encino.†[63]

*In its final report, the Senate Watergate Committee stated that "the principal witnesses who refused to comply fully with subpoenas and provide documents and testimony included Charles G. Rebozo—for personal documents and in his capacity as president of the Key Biscayne Bank—F. Donald Nixon and Edward Nixon and a number of Hughes' employes."

†The two other burglaries mentioned by the CIA referred to a break-in at the Summa headquarters in Las Vegas, where files were rifled, and at the Encino offices of Bill Gay and other Hughes executives, where a telephone scrambler unit was stolen. Companion units of the scrambler—a device that garbles telephone conversations to foil eavesdroppers—were at the CIA headquarters in Langley, Virginia, and the Robert Mullen Company offices, the CIA front operated by Hughes's Washington representative Robert Bennett. If the conversations between Hughes executives in Encino and the CIA operatives in Langley and Washington had been recorded by an electronic eavesdropping device, the recordings could be replayed through the scrambler, deciphered, and transcribed. It was later established that the scrambler was stolen by

The CIA memorandum also indicated the FBI had received information indicating that "a current theory existing within the LAPD [Los Angeles Police Department] that the burglars may well have been hired by the corporation itself."[64]*

By August, the CIA, which is responsible for foreign intelligence operations, had picked up leads on this domestic criminal act that not even the FBI had learned. In a three-page memorandum, dated August 5, 1974, the CIA advised the FBI:

Information has recently been brought to our attention, described as having originated from a "fairly reliable" source, which may be of interest to your Bureau. In substance, [the CIA source] has stated the following:

"The burglary in question was committed by five individuals from the Midwest and was mob-sponsored. Property taken included cash, personal notes and handwritten memoranda by Howard Hughes; correspondence between Hughes and prominent political figures; etc. The amount of cash taken is said to be approximately four times the amount publicized. The personal papers are said to be sufficient in volume to fill two foot lockers and are filed in manila-type file folders and catalogued in some fashion. The contents are said to be highly explosive from a political view and, thus, considered both important and valuable to Hughes and others as well. Efforts are now being made to sell the material which the Source believes is still being held in the Los Angeles area."
. . . The above information is transmitted for whatever action you deem necessary. If, as a result of your possible investigation, information is developed concerning the highly sensitive intelligence project involved, it is requested that prior to taking any action your Bureau coordinate with this office.[65]

Not long thereafter, when Gordon and Woolbright stumbled into the case, the FBI, with the CIA's support, prepared an elaborate scheme for buying back the stolen Hughes files, utilizing a Los Angeles Police Department informant. As the FBI field office in Los Angeles outlined the plan for Washington:

LAPD informant will introduce seller to Los Angeles attorney, who would then give name of New York attorney who had client possibly interested in stolen merchandise. Should [unknown subjects] decline to proceed further, bureau agent from L.A. division would be identified as assistant to New York attorney, and who would be available to fly to Los Angeles with $100,000 with which to negotiate a buy of merchandise. Stipulation would be not to buy package unseen, but rather to examine individual pieces

---

two associates of Robert Hall, a Los Angeles private detective, drug dealer, and wiretap specialist who at one time had performed bugging services for fugitive financier Robert Vesco. The burglars gave the stolen Hughes scrambler to Hall—who had a private library of hundreds of explosive conversations that had been secretly recorded. Hall, in turn, passed the scrambler to an old acquaintance, Vincent Kelley, the Hughes security chief at Encino. Two years later, in July of 1976, Hall was found murdered in his Burbank apartment. His two associates, who had stolen the Hughes-CIA scrambler, were later convicted.

*Equally interesting was the CIA's own list of possible explanations for the burglary set forth in an internal memorandum. The most intriguing speculation was that the burglary had been "politically motivated to aid or deter Watergate investigation/inquiry" or committed by a "foreign government—not necessarily USSR."

of merchandise and to negotiate buy of individual pieces if felt worthwhile and useful to New York attorney's client. It is believed that this procedure would enable undercover agent to examine all merchandise. Personal representative referred to above to make available $100,000 on Sept. 23, 1974, to be placed in safety deposit box in Los Angeles bank as "show money" to be utilized by undercover special agent if buy transaction. . . . At present time, no actual negotiations to make buy under way, but Los Angeles [FBI office] is currently endeavoring to make necessary arrangements to set up buy transaction and to provide appropriate cover for bureau agents and informant should individuals dealing with LAPD informant indicate access to and desire to sell stolen merchandise.[66]

The ransom of the documents was to be carried out through Gordon. But at a meeting attended by Los Angeles police officers, FBI agents, and Gordon on October 2, Gordon insisted, according to a CIA internal report, "that he must have total immunity in writing both from the federal and California jurisdictions for himself and Woolbright."[67] As another condition for cooperation, Gordon wanted a promise that "Woolbright would not have to testify before any type of judicial proceeding or be required to identify anyone involved with this matter."[68] It was during these delicate negotiations that a CIA official recorded in a memorandum information given to him by Lawrence S. Mohr, supervisor of the FBI criminal desk:

Mr. Mohr advised that Leo V. Gordon had an extensive criminal record. . . . He recalled that Gordon served 30 days in 1942 in New York; that he had been arrested as a robbery suspect in L.A. [Los Angeles] in 1944; that he had been convicted for robbery and assault with intent to commit murder in 1947, at which time he was sentenced to 11 years at San Quentin with an 11 year probation period to follow. He was arrested for assault and battery in 1952; no disposition was shown in this case. He was questioned about a robbery in L.A. in 1959, again with no disposition shown. His latest arrest was in 1968 for disturbing the peace in L.A.[69]

The scheme to buy back the Hughes papers eventually collapsed, and by November the FBI and the CIA had lost all interest in the stolen documents. Leo Gordon complained to federal agents that he was out the $3,500 he had given to Woolbright. An agent in the FBI field office in Los Angeles notified Washington that "allegedly suspect Don Woolbright has returned to the Los Angeles area and informant feels Woolbright took him for a $3,500 investment. Los Angeles [FBI office] and LAPD highly skeptical of Gordon's contention that he gave Woolbright $3,500 to go to Florida and attempt to obtain samples of pertinent material or that Woolbright ever made any such trip."[70]

After five months, the FBI was finally considering the possibility of conducting a thorough investigation of the Romaine Street burglary, but the bureau agonized over the consequences of such an investigation for a "sister agency"—the CIA. Following a joint FBI–CIA strategy conference in Los Angeles, the FBI field office there informed Washington:

Conference at Los Angeles included discussion of possibilities of embarrassment to sister federal agency in the event of direct and full field investigation of theft by

FBI. Such investigation would entail contact with Robert Maheu, Jack Hooper, Hank Greenspun, writer James Phelan, as well as Summa Corporation executives and employees. Consideration would be given for Bureau polygraphs of Summa people . . . who allegedly had specific knowledge of pertinent item being sought in this case. Consideration would also be given to direct contact with suspect Donald Woolbright and possible utilization of grand jury as weapon. The representative of sister agency plans to contact his Washington offices November 1, 1974, and contact will be made with the Bureau to arrange case conference for discussion of whether or not direct investigation should be instituted at this time. The representative requested that no immediate investigation be conducted pending the conference at Washington, D.C., and the outcome of a decision regarding the project at high levels expected in the next couple of weeks. He further requested that the money previously provided in this case be held pending arrangements to retake possession by his agency. In view of the possibilities of direct investigation and inquiry with some of the nationally known personalities involved with the Howard Hughes interests, which might lead to disclosure, it is recommended that no further investigation be conducted by the FBI unless the other interested federal agency is in agreement with the above mentioned interviews and course of action.[71]

The CIA promptly told the FBI that any investigation of the Romaine Street burglary would be damaging to national security. It was an argument reminiscent of fourteen years earlier when the agency had killed an FBI investigation of Maheu's role in the Las Vegas wiretap installed to placate mobster Sam Giancana.

So it was that later in November, CIA officials seemed gratified that the FBI and Los Angeles Police Department were not working very hard on the theft of the Hughes papers. An official who attended one meeting wrote in a memorandum:

The group covered all possible aspects of the case as to what the Agency should do at this time. It was finally decided, however, that the Agency would do nothing but monitor the case and request nothing from the FBI except what the FBI is doing, i.e., the FBI is monitoring the Los Angeles Police Department. At the current time the Los Angeles Police Department is not conducting a current investigation, so in effect they are doing nothing at this time.[72]

While the CIA watched the FBI do nothing, and the FBI watched the Los Angeles Police Department do nothing, both the Senate Watergate Committee and the Watergate special prosecutor's office ignored the Romaine Street burglary entirely. When it was suggested privately by certain law-enforcement officers that the special prosecutor's office especially had failed to look into the burglary, an indignant attorney in the office sent a letter to the FBI requesting "an inventory of documents which may have been taken in the burglary."[73] The request was delayed until nearly a year after the burglary and just before the special prosecutor's office went out of business. As for the Senate Watergate Committee, one committee investigator said, "Other than what was in the press, I don't think we got involved."[74]

Late in 1974, Donald Woolbright packed up his family, sold his house in Canoga Park, and moved back to Missouri, where he bought a small farm near Williamsville, a tiny hamlet in the Ozarks about seventeen miles northwest of Poplar Bluff.* About the same time, the Los Angeles Police Department— after the decision had been made by the CIA and FBI not to solve the burglary —turned their attention to Woolbright, not to question him about the stolen Hughes papers, but to build a case against him for receiving stolen property. Unable to identify either the burglars or those who commissioned the crime, the police and the Los Angeles County district attorney's office—which had maintained liaison with the CIA throughout—decided to settle for the person who apparently received, or at least had access to, the stolen documents.

Early in 1975, as the police and district attorney's office were putting the finishing touches on their case against Woolbright, two more characters, a veteran and a newcomer, appeared in the Romaine Street burglary scenario, spinning stories as fanciful and bizarre as those of Gordon and Woolbright. The veteran was Michael Davis, the Romaine Street guard who had been fired for refusing to take a polygraph test. The newcomer was William E. Colby, the director of the Central Intelligence Agency.

*About the same time that Woolbright moved back to Missouri, two men who lived in the same area and who, according to neighbors, visited with Woolbright a number of times, sold their homes and moved to Canada. One of the men, described as a Canadian citizen and an unemployed painter, lived in a $50,000 home. A curious law enforcement officer traced the man to a checking account maintained at a Hollywood branch office of the Bank of America by a club whose members were British intelligence officers during the Second World War. The law enforcement officer lost the trail of both men in Vancouver.

CHAPTER 23

THE CIA'S
BEST-KEPT SECRET

ON Friday afternoon, February 7, 1975, the first copies of Saturday's edition of the *Los Angeles Times* began rolling off the presses with an intriguing but cryptic front-page story under a banner headline. It began:

Howard Hughes contracted with the Central Intelligence Agency to raise a sunken Russian nuclear submarine from the North Atlantic Ocean, according to reports circulating among local law enforcement officers.

The operation reportedly was carried out, or at least attempted, by the crew of a marine mining vessel owned by Hughes' Summa Corporation and designed in super-secrecy by a Los Angeles firm.

The head of the latter firm denied any knowledge of such an operation.

Confidential files on the operation are believed to have been among the documents stolen by safecrackers from Summa's Hollywood offices at 7020 Romaine Street last June 5.

The thieves made an offer to return the sensitive documents, but the price tag initially was $1 million. The amount was negotiated downward over the subsequent months but the talks were broken off several weeks ago.

In the aftermath of the unsuccessful negotiations it was decided by authorities to take the case before the Los Angeles County Grand Jury.

Three days of hearings have been scheduled by the grand jury, beginning Tuesday. . . .

The ship involved is the Long Beach–based Glomar Explorer, the most advanced marine mining vessel in the world, even though it is still in the experimental stage. . . .

If the submarine-raising operation was indeed carried out, it is likely to have involved one of two Soviet undersea vessels:

"A nuclear-powered attack submarine of the Soviet November class which the

Pentagon believes sank off Spain in April 1970.

"Another nuclear submarine which foundered in March 1972, about 900 miles northeast of Newfoundland and which may have sunk. This submarine was equipped to carry three nuclear missiles. . . ."

Even before copies reached the streets, Dr. Franklin D. Murphy, chairman of the board of the Times Mirror Company, owner of the *Los Angeles Times,* received an urgent telephone call from an old acquaintance in Washington. He was Carl Duckett, head of the CIA's office of science and technology, which was responsible for intelligence projects ranging from secret drug experiments to the *Hughes Glomar Explorer.* It was only natural that Duckett should seek the assistance of the newspaper's board chairman. Murphy, once chancellor of UCLA, had served on the President's Foreign Intelligence Advisory Board and had known about the submarine recovery effort, code-named Project Jennifer, for several years. After listening to Duckett for a few minutes, Murphy suggested that he get in touch with William F. Thomas, the editor of the *Times.*

Duckett called Thomas. Might it not be helpful, he asked, for a CIA representative to visit the editor to explain the sensitive joint Hughes–CIA undertaking? Within an hour, a CIA agent appeared in Thomas's office, solemnly confiding that the *Hughes Glomar Explorer* had been specifically designed and built to raise a sunken Russian submarine. The mission had not been completed, he said, and the premature publicity would make it difficult, perhaps impossible, to carry it out, causing "grave harm to national security."[1] Thomas expressed his regrets. Had he known sooner he "would have killed" the article, he said.[2] He agreed to move the story off page one in later editions and promised that, although reporters were continuing their investigation, he would "exercise the full authority of his position to keep the results from ending up in the *Los Angeles Times.*"[3]

And so it was that the six-hundred-word story so unsettling to the agency moved from page one to page eighteen in later editions, where it ran alongside a photograph of the *Hughes Glomar Explorer* taken when the ship was docked in Long Beach harbor. The CIA agent, pleased with the way things were going, sent a memorandum to agency officials at Langley, Virginia, advising that "Thomas gave his personal assurances that the *Los Angeles Times* will not be the originators of any future stories regarding this program, other than the 'white' domp stories, so long as he has anything to do with editorship of paper."[4] The term "white domp" was intelligence shorthand meaning that only CIA-approved information would run in the *Los Angeles Times,* the "white" indicating that the material would be truthful as far as it went.

Thereby began a curious cover-up that was, perhaps, not a cover-up at all, at least of the information ostensibly to be concealed. In any event, Seymour Hersh, a Pulitzer Prize–winning reporter for the *New York Times,* was the next newsman prepared to write. Hersh had picked up the first faint hints of the submarine recovery project a year earlier. When Hersh called Colby with a few questions, the CIA director urged him to withhold publication. Hersh said he would relay Colby's request to his editors for a decision. Colby promptly called a top executive at the *New York Times.* "I hate to bug you on this," Colby said. "You do not bug me ever," the *New York Times* executive said. Colby then reviewed the *Los Angeles Times*'s agreement not to publish the story and recounted his conversation with Hersh. "I wanted to tip you, and I will get out of it," Colby said. "Good, I have it," the *New York Times* executive replied.[5]

The *New York Times* quickly fell in line behind the *Los Angeles Times* and embargoed the story. So did the *Washington Post.* "It is not anything we would like to get into," Katharine Graham, the *Post*'s publisher, assured Colby. "You are very kind," the CIA director told Mrs. Graham. "It is a great tribute to our journalists."[6] In the days that followed, Colby or his representatives scurried about Washington and across the country, imploring reporters and editors not to write about Project Jennifer, and at the same time providing them with elaborate briefings on the important work of the *Hughes Glomar Explorer. Time* and *Newsweek* agreed to withhold the story. So, too, did Lloyd Shearer, an editor of *Parade,* a magazine supplement distributed in about twenty million Sunday newspapers.[7]

But as the number of publications aware of Project Jennifer grew—and at least one did not know of the *Hughes Glomar Explorer's* mission until Colby thoughtfully provided a detailed explanation—the natural mistrust that exists among competing news media, the fear that a rival was about to break an exclusive story, began to take hold. The *New York Times* believed that the *Los Angeles Times* was going to violate its agreement and publish the full story of Project Jennifer. The *Los Angeles Times* believed that the *New York Times* was going to break the agreement and publish. *Parade* believed that the *Los Angeles Times,* the *New York Times,* the *Washington Post,* or some yet-unknown publication was going to rush into print.

During these four weeks of intensive news media briefings, Colby and his agents had both volunteered information and answered questions about Howard Hughes's personal involvement in Project Jennifer. When Shearer asked about Hughes's profit from the CIA operation, agents assured him "that it was quite small compared to the risk. In fact, we explained that the bulk of the Hughes profit, which was small, actually went to the Hughes Tool Company after it went public in December 1972."*[83] Colby and Carl Duckett especially

---

*The CIA has steadfastly refused to disclose either the total dollar value of the contract given to Hughes or Hughes's profit. However, records of the Securities and Exchange Commission indicate that Project Jennifer was immensely profitable for Hughes's partner, Global Marine, Inc. The Los Angeles–based company, which operates a fleet of ocean drilling rigs specializing in offshore oil and gas drilling, designed and supervised construction of the *Hughes Glomar Explorer* at the Sun Shipbuilding and Dry Dock Company in Chester, Pennsylvania, and then operated the vessel ostensibly for Hughes. From 1972 to 1974, Global Marine's operating revenue from the CIA venture totaled $35.5 million. Of that amount, the company retained $10.8 million, or 30.4 percent, as an operating profit. The three years turned out to be the most profitable in Global Marine's

emphasized Hughes's patriotism as a major reason for selecting the industrialist as a front. And another CIA operative implied that Hughes personally had been approached and had agreed to lend his name and that of his corporation. The agent, summarizing a meeting with a *Los Angeles Times* newsman, reported, "I acknowledged that the Summa Deep Ocean Mining Program is merely the facade for a CIA collection effort. . . . I told him in very general terms that . . . Mr. Hughes had agreed to perform the role."[9]

THE MELL STEWART PROBLEM

Howard Hughes had not been fit for several years to agree to anything. At the time Colby and his agents were lavishing praise on him for his part in the largest technological intelligence mission in the agency's history, Hughes was trying to decide when and if to have an enema.

In his darkened room atop the Xanadu Princess Hotel at Freeport on Grand Bahama Island, Hughes was suffering one of his prolonged periods of constipation, a chronic condition in which he would go for weeks without a successful visit to the bathroom. Not even Surfak, a stool-softening agent prescribed for patients unable to use laxatives, was having any effect, even though, as with his consumption of pain-killing drugs, tranquilizers, and narcotics, Hughes took it in massive quantities. While medical literature suggests a single Surfak capsule a day for several days, Hughes gulped upward of twenty capsules at once. Although Surfak was not known to have any dangerous side effects, the large doses reflected Hughes's approach to medication. If one capsule was recommended, then ten or fifteen or twenty would be that much better. When Surfak failed to provide relief, Hughes would resort, reluctantly, to an enema. But at that moment the one member of the Hughes entourage who specialized in enemas was home on leave with his family.

Like so many of those around Hughes, Mell Stewart was a Mormon. His first contact with the industrialist had come by way of the Mormon church, fifteen years earlier, when Stewart was operating a barbershop in Huntington Park, about five miles south of downtown Los Angeles. Stewart's wife Florence was a piano accompanist for Dallas Keller, a soloist with the Southern Califor-

---

history. The company took note of the *Hughes Glomar Explorer's* contribution to that profitability in a report filed with the SEC in April of 1974: "Since the project has thus far involved primarily engineering and management services, its relative contribution to the company's pre-tax net income has been greater than other areas of the company's business requiring substantial capital investment with related depreciation and interest expenses." Indeed, in 1972, Global Marine's operating profit from the CIA project amounted to $4.1 million, or 18 percent of the company's total operating profit of $23 million from all sources that year. During this period, the principal task of the Hughes Tool Company and later its successor, the Summa Corporation, was to provide cover for Project Jennifer, to create the illusion that Howard Hughes intended to use the *Glomar Explorer* to mine the ocean floor for minerals. In addition, the Hughes Tool Company manufactured the nearly four miles of high-tensile steel pipe, capable of lifting 6,608 long tons, that was used in the operation.

nia Mormon Choir, and also a Romaine Street journeyman. One day, Keller asked Stewart to go to the Beverly Hills Hotel to cut the hair of a mysterious stranger he could not identify. The stranger, Hughes, was apparently pleased with Stewart's work, for several days later Stewart received $1,000 for his services and was asked to be available for future calls. Over the next few years, Stewart was summoned sporadically to barber Hughes. Even after he closed his shop in Huntington Park and moved to Kearns, Utah, where he opened another shop, Stewart periodically flew to Los Angeles to cut Hughes's hair, or to stand by for haircutting sessions that never took place. Finally, in 1968 Stewart was brought to Las Vegas as a member of the permanent staff, not as one of the personal aides who had daily contact with Hughes, but as a second-level functionary who saw Hughes only when called. The calls were often separated by weeks, even months.

In the years that followed, Stewart's role changed from that of barber to male nurse, and particularly to sole administrator of Hughes's enemas. The personal aides were on duty two weeks and off two weeks, and thus able to spend regular time with their families, but Stewart had a more rigorous schedule. In fact, Hughes wanted Stewart on call all the time. In early 1975, with Hughes settled in the Bahamas, Stewart was unhappy.

"Mell had been [in Freeport] for a long time," Howard Eckersley recalled, "and he was having trouble with his wife and family for not being [home] to take care of things, and he wanted to go home. . . . and Mr. Hughes wanted him to stay for an enema and then he never would have it. So Mell was trying to get home and Hughes was trying to keep him from going home."[10] The stalemate broke when Stewart flew to Utah without permission, a development that annoyed Hughes greatly. He told one of the aides to get Stewart back at once. Instead, the aide gave Hughes the following memorandum:

Mell's wife recently has more or less given Mell an ultimatum that he must choose between his indefinite type of position or risk losing his family. As a result, Mell has practically suffered a mental breakdown and feels that after all these years, he should have been given relief by you. I would suggest that when he returns and assists next time, the two of you settle whatever it is you have in mind.[11]

Hughes was not impressed. He said he wanted Stewart at the Xanadu Princess because he wanted an enema and he wanted him immediately. The aides deluged Stewart with telephone calls, urging him to return. The calls only upset Stewart more. "Because of the pressure of his personal problems at home, and now with the additional pressure we have been putting on him to return, Mell is on the verge of a breakdown," an aide reported to Hughes. "His wife says that his stomach is tied in a knot and he has been unable to sleep since he went home."[12] Hughes remained unmoved. The aides continued to telephone Utah, but Stewart would not come. To get what he wanted, Hughes resorted to what had always worked best for him—money. He instructed an aide to tell Stewart that he would have the enema within six hours after Stewart's arrival in the Bahamas. There would be no postponements. To show his good faith, Hughes offered to pay Stewart $500 a day as long as he was kept waiting. If he did not have the enema in four days, Hughes agreed, Stewart could fly back to Utah and spend two weeks with his family. Stewart consented to the terms and arrived in Freeport late on Friday night, February 21.

The six-hour deadline passed without any word from Hughes. A day went by. Two days. Eckersley thought it time to remind Hughes of his commitment. In the adjoining room that served as an office, Eckersley wrote a note to jog Hughes's memory: "You told Mell that if he would come to Freeport he would be used within six hours. This was renegotiated to be that you would pay Mell $500 per day for each day after the six hours. That penalty time started at 4:45 A.M. Saturday morning. Mell agreed to stay a maximum of four days only, then would revert to your original agreement that he could go home for two weeks. The four days are up at 4:45 A.M. Wednesday morning. This is just a reminder."[13]

When Hughes did not respond, the aides prevailed upon Stewart to stay in Freeport beyond the four days. He would continue to receive $500 a day, in addition to his regular salary. By the middle of Stewart's second week in Freeport, as he waited for Hughes's call, the aides began grumbling among themselves about the $500-a-day agreement. On March 5—one day after the CIA advised the *Los Angeles Times* and *Parade* that the *New York Times* had agreed not to write about Hughes's secret *Glomar Explorer* mission—Eckersley handed another memorandum to Hughes about his enema.

"I am very much concerned with the large amount of money that is accruing each day to Mell Stewart," Eckersley wrote.[14] He again outlined the terms of the agreement to Hughes, adding that the situation now was creating staff unrest. "At the present time, we owe Mell $5,500 and to complicate the problem, I had to guarantee that I would follow through to see to it that he receives what the agreement calls for. I swore him to secrecy concerning this agreement but it now develops that Clyde [Crow] and others know and cannot understand why we have to pay a man $500 per day extra for doing nothing."[15]

The question of Stewart's $500 daily premium as a standby enema administrator had become the most critical issue confronting the staff of a man said to be involved in a clandestine operation for the CIA and who—at least in theory and as far as the public knew—controlled a billion-dollar empire sustained in large part by United States government contracts. The aides were annoyed that Hughes had offered to pay Stewart $500 a day for what amounted to doing nothing. They cared little how Hughes spent his money. They were upset because in their tightly controlled caste system someone at the bottom had carved out a very lucrative arrangement for himself.

Eckersley proceeded to deal diplomatically with the delicate question of how best to handle what had become a serious staff morale problem. Stopping short of suggesting that the solution might be for Hughes to have the enema, Eckersley wrote Hughes, "This problem has to be solved and I don't know how to untangle the mess. Do you have any suggestions? Why don't we send him home for a couple of days and then bring him back at his regular salary. He certainly cannot, under the circumstances, refuse to return in view of the large bonus he received."[16]

Hughes ignored Eckersley's message. More days passed and more messages flowed from the aides' office into Hughes's bedroom about the "Mell Stewart problem."[17] Warning Hughes that he faced a "revolution" if he continued to pay Stewart the "astronomical" salary, they suggested possible solutions, which included persuading Stewart to accept a lower fee.[18]

Finally, fifteen days after Stewart had returned to Freeport, Hughes was ready—not for the enema, but to begin bargaining with Stewart about his fee. Hughes scrawled across the bottom of a typewritten memorandum an aide had given him, "Pay him the $2,000 now and negotiate starting at $50." He added a warning: "Do not permit him to leave now."[19]

In the negotiations that followed, Stewart agreed to accept a $50-a-day fee—over and above his salary—with the understanding that the figure would go to $500 beginning March 13. George Francom informed Stewart that Hughes had approved the revised compensation plan. Again, though, some of the aides were dissatisfied. As the Thursday, March 13 deadline neared, one wrote Hughes, "The issue that I don't like is the switching from the $50 per day after last Sunday to the $500 per day extra starting tomorrow, and George told Mell you approved this feature. All I can do is to try to talk Mell out of this switch but I don't think I will succeed and then he will blow his top and threaten to leave the following day if not tomorrow."[20]

And so it went—offer, counteroffer, blandishment, cajolery, promises to Stewart that if he would stay in Freeport for just a few more days, Hughes would surely undergo the enema. By now, however, family pressure on Stewart was too great. After three weeks of waiting for the call that never came, Stewart again flew home without permission. It was left to one of the aides to notify an angry Hughes.

"Mell said he would not return to Freeport until next week," the aide wrote. "He said he has to spend time with his family and it makes his wife a nervous wreck having someone call him every day. He refuses any additional compensation of any kind to return here at this time. He did not buy the offer to go home for two weeks if he wasn't used within a few days. He said Clyde is here in the meantime and is perfectly capable and well trained during the past year."[21]

COVER STORY

At the height of the "Mell Stewart problem" on Grand Bahama Island, the number of news organizations with knowledge of the *Hughes Glomar Explorer's* mission continued to swell. On Tuesday morning, March 18, 1975, Colby and two associates visited the National Public Radio offices in Washington, where the "director recounted in general terms" Project Jennifer.[22] Next, they visited CBS and gave executives there a similar briefing. The cover-up was going smoothly until later in the day when Jack Anderson, the syndicated Washington columnist whom Colby had asked earlier to keep the story quiet, began having second thoughts. In his meeting with the CIA director, Anderson said, Colby had told him that "secrecy was necessary to make another recovery attempt. He said the *Los Angeles Times,* the *New York Times,* the *Washington Post,* and others were withholding the story and his obvious point, although he did not make it quite this way, was that these were responsible news organizations and they were my peers and I should do what they do."[23] But Anderson had concluded that the CIA, rather than being concerned about national security, "was merely trying to hide its embarrassment at giving Howard Hughes an estimated $350 million for a craft for a one-shot attempt to get an obsolete submarine."[24] In the past, Anderson said, he had "withheld other stories at the behest of the CIA, but this was simply a cover-up of a $350 million failure, $350 million literally went down into the ocean. I don't think the government has a right to cover up a boondoggle."[25]

And so that night, on his nine-o'clock Washington radio broadcast, Anderson related the highlights of Project Jennifer, thereby opening the media floodgates. On Wednesday, March 19, the *Los Angeles Times,* the *New York Times,* and the *Washington Post* spread across their front pages individual accounts of the CIA operation. Oddly, even though everybody had been briefed by the CIA, and at least the *Los Angeles Times* had submitted its story to the agency to check factual accuracy, the articles differed remarkably on many important details.

It was generally agreed that the Russian submarine had mysteriously exploded and sunk in 1968 in the Pacific Ocean, seven hundred miles northwest of Oahu, Hawaii, coming to rest at a depth of more than three miles, and that the purpose of the mission was to retrieve the submarine's missiles, torpedoes, and coding equipment. It also was agreed that the *Hughes Glomar Explorer* had carried out the recovery operation in tandem with a mammoth submersible barge designed by the Lockheed Aircraft Corporation and built by the National Steel and Shipbuilding Company in San Diego. "About the size of a football field and built like a floating aircraft hanger," the barge, called the HMB-1, was to be used to conceal the submarine once the *Glomar Explorer* raised it from the seabed with a giant claw attached to an arm of steel pipe more than three miles long.[26]

From there on, it was every newspaper for itself. The *New York Times* and the *Washington Post* said it was a "nuclear submarine" of the "Hotel class," the *Los Angeles Times* called it a diesel-powered submarine of the "Golf class."[27] The *Los Angeles Times,* the *New York Times, Parade,* and *Time* all said that the *Hughes Glomar Explorer* had lifted the Russian submarine intact about halfway to the surface when, as *Time* put it, "the sub's hull, already weakened and damaged by the explosion and severe water pressures, cracked into two pieces . . . the aft two-thirds, including the conning tower and the coveted missiles and code room, slipped back into the seabed. The forward third, which remained gripped firmly in the grapnels, was deposited in the still submerged barge." The *Washington Post* said the submarine "was found to be in pieces on the ocean floor, which led the CIA to attempt to raise the sunken boat piece by piece."[28]

There was no agreement either on the number of warheads brought up, nuclear or otherwise, or on the number of Soviet crewmen—reportedly from five to seventy—whose bodies were recovered and then returned to the sea in a burial videotaped by the CIA and described to several reporters and editors by Colby.

In retrospect, these differences of fact became much less important than one overwhelming reality—Project Jennifer had been a godsend to the beleaguered CIA. After a year of biting criticism from the news media and Congress on everything from Chile to Watergate, the CIA basked in the warm glow of unaccustomed praise. "Following all the painful headlines of recent months," *Newsweek* observed, "the CIA has shown it could take on a real-life Mission Impossible, and make it nearly possible after all."[29] It was, the magazine said, "a technical achievement bordering on fantasy."[30] The *New York Times,* whose recent articles had prompted the creation of government panels to investigate CIA practices, enthusiastically applauded Project Jennifer. "This complex and fascinating undersea adventure demonstrates that, once again, American technology has brought a hitherto inaccessible environment into the ambit of man's future activity," the *Times* said in an editorial. "The CIA is only to be commended for this extraordinary effort to carry out its essential mission."[31]

When there was time for sober reflection, some journalists wondered whether the CIA's deft informational campaign had not been designed all along to lead to publication of the stories, rather than their suppression. If so, was it the CIA's intention merely to generate favorable publicity for itself? Or was there some darker motive, perhaps to divert attention away from another sensitive intelligence assignment that the *Hughes Glomar Explorer* carried out? Whatever the case, all agreed that the story had leaked solely as a result of the professionally executed Romaine Street burglary in June of 1974. "If it weren't for the theft of some top-secret papers from a Hughes-owned company in Los Angeles last June," *Newsweek* reported, "the story might have gone untold."[32] The *New York Times* devoted an article to that particular point under the headline "An Easy Burglary Led to the Disclosure of Hughes–CIA Plan to Salvage Soviet Sub."[33]

It was just another of those coincidences, no doubt, but on the same day that Project Jennifer was made public, a Los Angeles County grand jury indicted Donald Ray Woolbright on charges of receiving stolen property and attempted extortion in connection with the $1-million ransom demand for the stolen Hughes papers that no one seemed to want.*

*Richard H. Kirschner, the Los Angeles attorney who represented Woolbright, maintained during the legal proceedings "that there was no victim of this alleged burglary; there was no

After nearly a year, the Romaine Street burglary, which Los Angeles police had indicated from the beginning was an inside job, remained unsolved, as mysterious as the CIA's more recent dealings with reporters and editors. Indeed, there were only questions without answers. Why, for example, did the FBI, after several weeks of intense involvement, lose all interest in the case, even though top-secret government documents supposedly had been stolen, a crime that very definitely fell under FBI jurisdiction? Why did the CIA initially make a $1-million offer for the return of the stolen Hughes papers and then abruptly withdraw that offer, indicating that it, too, had no further interest in the burglary? Why did local and federal law-enforcement authorities ignore so many prominent leads that surfaced early in the investigation and then act as though the crime defied solution? Why did Hughes executives show so little interest in the break-in or the stolen papers? Why did the CIA instruct Los Angeles police to lie to an assistant United States attorney who began asking questions about the burglary on his own? Why did Los Angeles law-enforcement authorities, at the encouragement of the CIA, press charges against Woolbright—a small-time St. Louis police character—for attempting to sell the stolen Hughes papers, when a writer for *New Times* claimed to have possession of the stolen papers and was attempting to sell them to New York publishers as the basis for a book?

And there was still more puzzlement. Two weeks after the Russian submarine raising was made public, Michael E. Davis, the guard who had been fired by the Summa Corporation when he refused to submit to a polygraph examination, sought and received immunity from the Los Angeles County district attorney's office. In exchange, he revealed information he had withheld since the burglary. Davis said that after the burglars left Romaine Street, at a time when he was still bound and gagged, he picked up two documents lying on the floor. One was a Bank of America certificate of deposit for $100,000, made payable to Kay Glenn. The other was a memorandum from Raymond Holliday to Hughes concerning the CIA–*Hughes Glomar Explorer* project.[34] Davis said that he took both documents home with him after he was questioned by police that night, and that he neglected to mention them either to investigating officers or to Hughes executives. He said that he put the CIA memorandum in an unlocked dresser drawer, where it remained for about seven months, and that he placed the $100,000 certificate of deposit "in an envelope and sealed it" and "gave it to a friend" to hold.[35] After the first *Los*

---

burglary; and in fact the entire burglary scenario was invented to absolve the Hughes corporation from the production of documents required by court order [in the SEC–Air West and Maheu–Hughes lawsuits]. It may also well have been that the CIA participated in this Hughes orchestrated burglary." In April of 1977, Woolbright was convicted by a jury of receiving stolen property and acquitted of attempted extortion. The conviction was set aside on appeal because the judge had ordered the jurors—who had been deadlocked after five days of deliberations and more than a dozen ballots—to reach a verdict. In June of 1978 Woolbright was tried a second time. The trial ended in a hung jury. Rather than seek a third trial, the Los Angeles County district attorney's office dismissed the charges against Woolbright. The Romaine Street burglary remains unsolved.

Angeles Times article about the Russian submarine operation appeared on February 8, Davis said, he took the memorandum referring to the secret government project from his drawer, "tore it up, and flushed it down the commode."[36] He destroyed the memorandum, Davis said, because it "didn't seem like it was that important to me, or to anyone else."[37] He said he reclaimed the certificate of deposit from his friend and turned it over to William Farr, one of the *Los Angeles Times* reporters who had written the first story about the *Hughes Glomar Explorer*'s secret mission.

During a forty-minute interview with Deputy District Attorney Stephen Trott and Los Angeles police officers, a nervous and stammering Davis gave this account of the contents of the memorandum he said he had flushed down a toilet:

Ah, it was a document, ah, it was to HRH from Raymond Holliday, and, ah, I'm a little vague as, ah, exactly what it said. It was in, ah, reference to the, ah, CIA contacting the, ah, Hughes people about, ah, financing the building of the Glomar. And in turn, that, ah, the IRS was going to turn their back on it. And that's, ah, that's about all I can remember about it. . . . It didn't mean that much to me at the time. Ah, and I just more or less, ah, glanced at it, ah. It said that, ah, that, ah, he, being Raymond Holliday, I assume, but I can't remember the exact words, that, ah, he was contacted by a fellow from the CIA that, ah, they were interested in financing the—this, ah, Glomar or whatever, to, ah, and one thing stuck in my mind is that, ah, they, they, he said the IRS agreed to turn their back on it. You know. Which I didn't understand at the time. . . . The document, it also, ah, mentioned President Nixon's name, that he was aware of the transaction. I forgot all about it.[38]

When Davis completed his story, Deputy District Attorney Trott asked if he would be willing to take a polygraph test. "I don't believe in 'em," said Davis. "Is it, is it admissible in court?" Davis asked.

"Well, no, but it's a helpful, it's a helpful type of a thing, you know," Trott replied.

"Well, well, being a human being, I, I feel that I would cooperate as much as I can and especially now. And that, ah, I don't, I don't want to take the polygraph," Davis said.[39]

The one consistent story that Colby and his CIA colleagues had passed along during their chats with reporters and editors was the reasoning behind their choice of Hughes as their front. As a CIA official had noted in a secret memorandum written after a meeting with *New York Times* representatives, "the individuals were impressed by the Hughes patriotism pitch."[40] But of far greater significance was the CIA's quiet assertion that the eccentric industrialist was actively pursuing an ocean mining venture. While the CIA story made a flawless cover, and the agency's version of its relationship with Hughes certainly sounded credible, neither was true.

By the time the construction of the *Hughes Glomar Explorer* was under way, everyone—the news media, scientists, mining engineers, oceanographers, corporation executives, bankers, scientific journals, and the general public—believed the vessel was going to be the country's first deep-sea mining ship.

And why not? While the average citizen might at first have been skeptical of the notion of gathering rocks from the seabed, three or four miles below the surface of the ocean, experts in mining, oceanography, and related fields knew that it was only a matter of time until ocean mining became a boom industry.

The floor of the Pacific Ocean was paved with nodules, from the size of a pea to that of a football, containing two dozen different minerals, but especially rich in manganese, nickel, cobalt, and copper. The value of those nodules could be calculated in the trillions of dollars. Strategically, the nodules were of critical importance to the United States, which already depended on foreign sources for nearly all its manganese, an essential element in steel making, and nickel.

For those few who were skeptical about the concept of ocean mining, there was the ship itself. The *Hughes Glomar Explorer* certainly looked like

The *Hughes Glomar Explorer*—the CIA spy ship—under construction near Philadelphia in 1972. *Philadelphia Inquirer*

a mining vessel, quite unlike any other ship that had ever been built. It was longer than two football fields, stretching 618 feet, 8 inches.[41] In the center of the ship, a huge steel A-frame resembling an oil derrick rose 200 feet above the deck. The derrick straddled a well in the hold of the ship that measured 199 by 74 feet. Its floor could be opened to lower pieces of machinery, or to lift objects weighing up to 14.8 million pounds, or to reel out more than three miles of pipe measuring from 12 3/4 to 15 1/2 inches in diameter.[42] The pipe, it was said, could be pulled along the ocean floor, sucking up nodules like a vacuum cleaner. On either side of the derrick were steel frames called docking legs, which could be lowered and locked into submersible equipment. An array of cranes and other equipment covered the rest of the deck. The ship had a satellite navigation system. It could fix on a preselected spot in the ocean and "maintain its position over a work site as deep as 20,000 feet while lowering or raising a heavy machine or operating the machine on the bottom."[43] The navigation system was so precise that in a gently rolling sea the 65,000-ton vessel could hold within ten feet of a fixed position. It was indeed an impressive ship.

Finally, there was the Howard Hughes connection. Who else would attempt to develop an entire industry by himself but the country's best-known eccentric, the recluse with the Midas touch, the last of the free spirits of American capitalism? Such was the power of the Hughes mythology that even the famed oceanographer Jacques Yves Cousteau became convinced that Hughes's ship was built to mine the sea. Like other experts, Cousteau had questioned whether deep-sea mining was yet economically feasible. But then, Cousteau explained, "we had to treat it seriously because we all knew that Howard Hughes does not involve himself in uneconomic undertakings."[44]

The belief that Howard Hughes was pioneering an ocean mining industry became so fixed in the public mind that even after the CIA's Project Jennifer became public, some clung to the mining myth. Two weeks after it was disclosed that the CIA had built the ship specifically to raise a submarine, *Business Week* reported that "although a few ocean miners now believe that the Glomar Explorer's well-publicized mining objectives were fabricated to cover up the CIA venture, most think Summa is still much involved in ocean mining with its Explorer."[45] The magazine went on to say that there was "evidence that the Explorer was indeed built for Hughes, not the CIA, as a mining ship and was merely used by the CIA, perhaps even on a one-shot charter arrangement."[46] Hughes executives encouraged this theory. *Business Week* said that Paul G. Reeve, the general manager of the Summa Corporation's Ocean Mining Division—a division set up expressly for the CIA project —"still claims the ship has always been part of the company's sea mining program and that the mining equipment was tested for the first time on last summer's Hawaiian cruise."[47] According to the magazine, Reeve said that the *Hughes Glomar Explorer* returned to Long Beach so that it could be "modified to solve problems encountered on the test that may have pushed its commercial operation back a year, to at least 1976. Reeve says the ship will cruise Hawaii again this summer for further tests on the mining systems."[48]

But the most prominent victim of the CIA cover story was Howard Hughes himself. The sixty-nine-year-old Hughes, like millions of other Americans, believed that the ship bearing his name would launch a trillion-dollar industry. That Hughes succumbed to the CIA cover story spun around his name was, in the end, perhaps the best-kept secret of Project Jennifer. Not only had Hughes surrendered control of his empire to others, but the CIA—aware of his narcotics addiction and mental state—took advantage of the situation by making use of his organization, with the cooperation of a few friendly executives, to serve its own needs.

On Wednesday, December 8, 1971, the day before the keel was laid for the ship carrying his name, Hughes had been blissfully unaware of the world outside his bedroom at the Britannia Beach Hotel on Paradise Island in the Bahamas. That day, he was concerned only with the condition of the pillow on his bed, so concerned that shortly before 7 A.M. he gave an aide specific instructions on the matter. The aide dutifully entered the orders in the daily diary of Hughes's activities, emphasizing their importance by typing in capital letters:

INSTRUCTION: DO NOT PUT THE SPONGE RUBBER INSIDE OF *ANY* PILLOW CASE—IN FACT HE DOES NOT WANT *ANYTHING* WHATSOEVER PUT INSIDE THE PILLOW CASE. HE WANTS THE PILLOW CASE TO BE TREATED AS IF IT WERE A SINGLE LAYER OF MATERIAL.[49]

Hughes spent much of that morning sitting in his reclining chair in the darkened bedroom. He watched *Deadlier than the Male,* a Bulldog Drummond epic featuring Elke Sommer, sadism, sex, and murder by time bomb, spear gun, dart, and exploding cigar. At 11:50 A.M., after watching the film, Hughes took four of his Blue Bombers, the ten-milligram Valium tablets. Two hours and twenty minutes later he swallowed two more Valium tablets and settled back to watch *Ten Little Indians,* an Agatha Christie murder mystery.[50]

On Thursday, December 9, the day the keel was laid for the *Hughes Glomar Explorer,* Hughes got up at 1:50 A.M., took a shower, and asked one of the aides to show *Ten Little Indians* again. At intervals throughout the night, Hughes watched the film, switching about 8:30 A.M. to *Deadlier than the Male.* In the afternoon he watched *The Wrecking Crew,* another Elke Sommer film. And that night he watched *Deadlier than the Male* once more. The next day it was more of the same. He again watched *Deadlier than the Male* and *Ten Little Indians,* as well as *Bullet for a Badman,* an Audie Murphy vehicle. In between the motion pictures, he consumed twenty-two Surfak tablets to relieve his constipation, and four Valium tablets.[51]

By March of 1974, having been moved in and out of hotel bedrooms in four different foreign countries, Hughes was back in the Bahamas, this time at the Xanadu Princess Hotel on Grand Bahama Island. The *Hughes Glomar Explorer,* after completing its sea trials, prepared to test its mining system, or so Hughes and the public thought. About this same time, Chester C. Davis, the New York lawyer who had become Hughes's most influential legal and business adviser, sent a memorandum to Hughes affirming the wondrous capabilities of his ship. The *Hughes Glomar Explorer,* Davis told Hughes, had placed him in the forefront of ocean mining technology.

The ship "is properly described in the literature on deep ocean mining as the most sophisticated deep ocean mining ship afloat," Davis wrote.[52] While indirectly acknowledging that it was still somewhat uncertain whether ocean mining was economically feasible, he assured Hughes that the ship's "accomplishment of its primary mission within three or four months should prove the feasibility of recovering" nodules at a depth as great as twenty thousand feet.[53]

Suggesting that Hughes might want to form a partnership with his friends at Lockheed, Davis said that the Lockheed Missile and Space Company, which "has been investigating for years the feasibility of deep ocean mining, is in the process of developing, with an investment of some $5 million, an improved gathering-recovery system which we believe will establish the feasibility of recovering such ore in economic commercial quantities. More importantly, they also have an exclusive on a refining process which would permit refining this recoverable ore at sea into a concentrate which would greatly reduce shipping costs when delivered for further refining on land."[54]

Referring to a mounting interest on the part of certain businesses, Davis told Hughes that "several consortiums, both national and international, are in the process of formation on the assumption that deep-sea mining is a feasible economic commercial enterprise but without having concentrated on the means of ore recovery at these depths or solved the problems involved."[55] On this particular point, Davis hastened to assure Hughes that "the current literature on the subject recognizes that we are way ahead of anyone else, through Hughes Glomar Explorer, in having developed a technique for deep ocean recoveries."[56] He added that within "the next two to three weeks Lockheed Missile and Space Company will be ready to discuss seriously some type of joint venture and the financing thereof. There is no question but that this deep ocean mining has very attractive possibilities."[57]

The *Hughes Glomar Explorer,* according to the sworn testimony of those who built and operated the ship, never possessed any special capability for ocean mining. James M. Miles, a marine superintendent at Global Marine and the ship's first master, said that the equipment on board was placed there "solely so that the ship could carry out its secret government mission. . . . The ship could not economically be utilized for exploration of oil or mineral deposits."*[58]

---

*In sworn testimony in United States district court proceedings and in appearances before government agencies, Global Marine executives and others associated with the *Hughes Glomar Explorer* project unanimously maintained that the ship could not be used in any economically viable ocean mining operation. While everyone admired the ship's enormous lifting capacity, no one, it seemed, was much interested in operating the vessel because of its staggering costs. From March to June of 1976, the General Services Administration (GSA) published advertisements inviting businesses to submit proposals for leasing the ship. By the end of the four months, the

And Howard Hughes did not even own the ship that bore his name. Nor did Summa Corporation have an option to buy it. Under the terms of a secret contract entered into by Summa, Global Marine, and the CIA, "the only role played by the Summa Corporation with respect to this vessel was to provide cover for a classified government operation."[59] All of these facts made Chester Davis's memorandum to Hughes an exceedingly puzzling and contrary document.

Was Hughes ever told the truth about his ocean mining business? Probably not. On the day Project Jennifer was made public, Hughes's personal staff in the penthouse was as surprised as everyone else. As Jim Rickard, one of the aides who controlled the flow of all information to Hughes, put it, "We thought we were going to get rich from minerals."[60]

GSA had received a total of seven bids, including a $2 offer submitted by a Lincoln, Nebraska, college student, and a $1.98 offer from a man who said he planned to seek a government contract to salvage the nuclear reactors of two sunken United States submarines. The Lockheed Missile and Space Company submitted a $3 million, two-year lease proposal contingent on the company's ability to secure financing. But the GSA had already extended the bid deadline twice to allow Lockheed to find financial backers for its project without success, and the agency concluded there was no reason to believe the company would find the funds in the near future. Although the scientific community rallied to the defense of the *Hughes Glomar Explorer,* urging the president to maintain the ship as a national asset, no agency or department of the government wanted to assume the maintenance and operating costs. So in September of 1976, the GSA turned the *Hughes Glomar Explorer* over to the navy for mothballing, and in January of 1977, after it was prepared for drydocking at a cost of more than $2 million, the ship became part of the navy's Suisun Bay Reserve Fleet. Then in September of 1978, a consortium called Ocean Minerals Company of Mountain View, California, announced that it had leased the *Hughes Glomar Explorer* and that in November the ship would begin testing a prototype deepsea mining system in the Pacific Ocean. Ocean Minerals included subsidiaries of the Standard Oil Company of Indiana, Royal Dutch Shell, and Bos Kalis Westminster Group N.V. of the Netherlands. Another partner, and the prime contractor for the group, was the Lockheed Missile and Space Company, one of the original partners in the CIA's Project Jennifer.

CHAPTER 24

THE LAST YEAR

IN 1975, Howard Hughes's seventieth year, the empire bearing his name remained neatly divided into two parts, as it had been for twenty years. The
contrast between them was the most glaring in modern American business. It
was as though IBM had deliberately established a pair of subsidiaries, one to
produce computers and profits, another to manufacture Edsels and losses.
Over one part, Hughes never exerted his authority, never interfered in its
management. This was the Hughes Aircraft Company and its record was one
of stunning achievements. The other branch of the empire, which Hughes had
personally directed for so many years before Bill Gay, Chester Davis, and
Nadine Henley assumed control, consisted of the Summa Corporation holdings, most notably the Las Vegas hotels and casinos, mining properties, and
other Nevada investments. Its record, especially after Hughes's lieutenants
subtracted the oil-tool business, was one of horrendous management and
staggering deficits.

Throughout his life, Hughes had worked in the shadow of his father,
striving at least to match his accomplishments. But after fifty years in business,
he had only a string of failures to show for his efforts. It was as if he were
missing the gene for corporate success. He was a third-rate producer of motion
pictures (with two or three exceptions), he ran RKO into the ground, he nearly
plunged TWA into bankruptcy. He posted deficits in his company's aircraft
division for more than thirty consecutive years. He had failed to put into
production either of the airplanes that he had received government contracts
to build. After fifty years, he had succeeded in exchanging a legacy worth
billions of dollars for failing businesses awash in red ink. And he had simply
frittered away more money than most people can conceive of spending. Exactly

how much is difficult to say. At least $1 billion, quite possibly twice that. Tens of millions of dollars went into maintaining his hermetic environment, while he nurtured the image of a humble millionaire who preferred budget clothing, inexpensive automobiles, and a spartan residence to the customary trappings of the rich.

To be sure, he had considerable help along the way in spending his money. All his life, Hughes seemed to attract people who learned quickly to enjoy a splendid style of living at his expense, to use his name and often his money to enhance their personal fortunes, and to give him more than his share of bad business advice. Time and again he was encouraged to spend his money unwisely. His investment in an oil-drilling venture, although modest by comparison with other undertakings, was typical. In the 1950s, someone in the organization had persuaded Hughes to invest in a Louisiana oil field. He did so and each year poured more money into wells that produced little oil. By the summer of 1961, when he was still struggling mightily to pay debts incurred during the TWA jet-buying crisis, Hughes was pressed by Bill Gay to come up with additional cash for his oil-field investment. Gay told Hughes that "our partners have recommended" setting up another drilling unit at a cost of "about $122,000 . . . all of the geologists, including our own, are convinced there is a very big field somewhere in this area and feel they have pinpointed it now to this proposed" site.[1] When Hughes received Gay's proposal, he reacted with appropriate outrage. He told Operations:

Tell Bill Gay that regarding the $122,000 of additional investment in the oil account, I should think he would be well aware that I do not have the funds for any such thing. . . . I should think that Mr. Gay, knowing my terrible shortage of funds would have been striving to develop some equitable bona fide offers for sale of these properties rather than having the audacity to present me a deal to invest an additional $122,000 in something that I have no damned business in in the first place. I have no business in the oil producing business and when Bill Gay said these properties were worth $22 or $23 million and I told that to Bank of America, the Bank of America said they could find no evidence that these properties were worth a fraction of $22 million.[2]

All his failures notwithstanding, by 1975 it was assured that the name Howard Hughes Jr. would be accorded its own niche in American business history, right alongside that of Howard Hughes Sr. The father's claim rested on his invention of the drill bit that revolutionized the oil-drilling industry around the world and provided the basis for a great fortune. The son's claim rested on the work performed by that branch of the empire to which his only contribution was a grant of autonomy—the Hughes Aircraft Company. Even though he had played no active part in the company's operations, had not visited its plants at any time in the last fifteen years, had not spoken with the company's executives in almost as many years, it was Hughes's name that would be remembered, and it was everywhere.

The world's first communications satellite launched for commercial use was Hughes's Early Bird. Placed in orbit in 1965, hovering between twenty-two and twenty-three thousand miles above the equator, the eighty-four-pound Early Bird linked the United States and Europe in a spectacular demonstration of satellite communications. It was followed over the years by successively more sophisticated Hughes satellites to form a global communications network used by United States business and industry, the military, and governmental agencies for the transmission of television signals, telephone calls, and other communications. Just two of the Hughes satellites were "capable of transmitting an average of 6,000 simultaneous two-way phone conversations or twelve simultaneous color telecasts."[3] On June 1, 1966, the United States first soft landing on the moon was made by the unmanned Hughes Surveyor spacecraft. Thirty-six minutes after settling down in the Ocean of Storms, it sent back to earth the first televised photographs of the moon's surface. Other Hughes Surveyor spacecraft followed. They transmitted thousands of photographs, conducted chemical analyses of the lunar soil, and paved the way for a manned landing. Three Hughes satellites, circling the earth 22,300 miles above the equator and west of the Galapagos Islands, provided all of Canada with color television and telephone service. Still other Hughes satellites photographed the Soviet Union, China, and other Communist countries, capturing on a single frame of film a land area larger than the state of Massachusetts and providing important data for United States intelligence agencies and the military.

The navy's F-14 Tomcat jets were equipped with a Hughes weapons-control system that enabled a pilot to launch up to six long-range air-to-air Phoenix missiles, also manufactured by Hughes, "and keep them on course while searching the skies for other possible targets."[4] The air force's F-4 Phantom jets were armed with Hughes's television-guided, eight-foot, 500-pound, air-to-ground Maverick missiles and a Hughes fire-control system that allowed a pilot to see his target on a television screen and lock the missile's guidance system to the target. Army infantry and helicopter units were equipped with Hughes's TOW heavy antitank missiles. The security of Switzerland, Japan, Belgium, the Netherlands, West Germany, and other NATO countries depended on a Hughes early-warning system that included radar stations providing "simultaneous range, bearing and height data" to a high-speed Hughes computer, which instantly sorted out friendly from unfriendly aircraft.[5]

In Los Angeles and New York, television viewers watched programs carried over Hughes's cable systems. Passengers on United States airlines listened to in-flight music systems made by Hughes. In Northern Ireland, an International Telephone and Telegraph Corporation subsidiary used a Hughes wiring analyzer to test "thirty-four different products in any of over 5,000 electrical configurations."[6] Garment manufacturers cut cloth with computerized lasers made by Hughes. Hundreds of thousands of Americans wore digital watches with Hughes modules.

In the twenty years since Hughes had given up personal control, the Hughes Aircraft Company had grown to more than thirty-six thousand employees, including a scientific and engineering technical staff of eleven thou-

An aerial view of the Hughes Aircraft Company in Culver City, California.
Hughes Aircraft Company

sand, working in some hundred buildings at eleven major locations in Southern California and Tucson, Arizona. The company had paid off Hughes-incurred debts of tens of millions of dollars, rolled up profits of that much and more, and entered the select circle of corporations with annual sales of more than $1 billion. The future promised ever-greater earnings, more technological marvels.

In stark contrast stood the other branch of the empire, the Summa Corporation, which first Hughes and then his handpicked executives ruled. From 1971 to 1974, Summa had posted losses amounting to $79.6 million.[7] Before 1975 was over, total losses would soar above $100 million. In addition, since January of 1966, half a billion dollars in cash and government securities had disappeared from Hughes and Summa bank accounts—$137,000 a day for ten years, much of it lost through improper management, unsound investments, and waste.[8]

Conditions at the Desert Inn told much about the overall state of Summa. The Desert Inn was the one Las Vegas property that Hughes had not bought.

He had leased the land and buildings in an agreement that ran until 2022 and that required him to properly maintain the facilities. The Desert Inn was twenty-five years old, and after eight years of Hughes's neglect and a heavy flow of traffic through its rooms, the nine-story main building and the adjoining low-rise structures were literally falling apart. Once the pride of the Strip, the Desert Inn was like a sagging and wrinkled dancer in a Las Vegas chorus line of youthful, seductive competitors—the Hilton International, the MGM Grand, and Caesar's Palace, among others. It needed a facelift.

Bill Gay, executive vice-president of the Summa Corporation, and other Summa officers were unwilling to order renovation of the Desert Inn on their own, even though they routinely spent millions of dollars without Hughes's permission or knowledge. Gay had once created an entire corporate division, Hughes Dynamics, without informing Hughes. But erecting or remodeling a building was quite another matter. Hughes would spend millions to lease aircraft hangars he never visited, where he stored airplanes he never flew. Yet he would not build or remodel in the normal course of business. His reluctance to expand the Hughes Aircraft Company plant at Culver City in the early 1950s had led to the revolt among scientists and engineers. In the years following Hughes's arrival there, Las Vegas entered the largest building boom in its history. Construction outlays ran into the hundreds of millions, not a penny of which was Hughes's. While this aversion to construction was eccentric, it was an eccentricity that those around Hughes had learned to take seriously. There would be no restoration work at the Desert Inn until Hughes personally approved it.

Not for a long time, however, had Hughes been capable of making such decisions. Years of half-life in his asylum, where his aberrant behavior was encouraged and none of his mental ills treated, had left the once-dashing aviator and handsome Hollywood producer a pitiful figure, as a prominent psychologist who conducted an intensive study of Hughes's behavior later concluded:

Hughes paid no attention to his personal hygiene. His teeth were not brushed or otherwise cared for . . . His hair was allowed to grow for long periods of time without cutting and it was never shampooed. His fingernails and toenails were allowed to grow without being cut. His body was not regularly cleaned or washed. As a result of his filthy hair, rotting teeth and unclean body, he had an extremely foul odor as well as an offensive appearance. [He] usually had bowel movements only once or twice a month, and then only after enemas had been administered. After an enema, he often defecated on his bed, either on papers or on the sheets. Sometimes his aides did not know when he had a bowel movement, and they would find him lying in his fecal matter.[9]

Hughes was continuing to take massive quantities of codeine and Valium. His condition "resembled that of a chronic psychotic patient in the very worst mental hospitals." Like many such psychotics, he could "carry on apparently rational conversations in specific areas," but "was incapable of caring for

himself or of surviving without the assistance of attendants. He was continuously drugged and his consciousness clouded. He was ill, emaciated, bedridden, and incapable of normal mental and physical activity. He could not have
made informed and rational judgments involving complex business and legal
affairs; nor could he have given competent assistance to those representing
him."[10]

Summa executives behaved as though dealing with a rational man. They
sent repeated messages asking what he wanted done at the Desert Inn, suggesting building alternatives, and seeking authorization to proceed. In years past,
Hughes would have picked up his blue ballpoint pen and one of the yellow legal
tablets stacked by the side of his bed and written out an answer. But the
once-prolific Hughes hand had been stilled. During his first two years at the
Desert Inn, he sometimes turned out half a dozen or more handwritten memoranda a day, some less than a page in length, others rambling on for several
detailed pages. Now he seldom wrote. Whenever a subject was to be brought
to his attention, an aide typed out a message and handed it to him. Hughes
read some messages, ignored others, apparently at random. If he had a comment, the aide returned to the adjoining office and typed a summary of what
Hughes said—there was no effort to make a verbatim record of his instructions
—and transmitted the report by telecopier or dictated it over the telephone to
the appropriate Summa official.

This new system had placed an added and potentially threatening burden
on the aides. When Hughes had given instructions in his own hand, a written
record existed and thus evidence that some of the more outrageous schemes
implemented in Hughes's name had in truth been proposed by him. Such was
no longer the case. Throughout the Hughes empire, lawyers and executives
were signing contracts with government agencies and other companies, filing
pleadings in civil and criminal lawsuits, borrowing millions of dollars—all on
the basis of verbal or typewritten communications from one of the six aides.
It was a system that had made everyone nervous, and with good reason. To
fill the authorization gap as best they could, the aides began writing memoranda of their conversations with Hughes, signing and filing them. On especially important issues, two aides would sign. A pair of typical memoranda
stated:

Today, April 9, 1975, the stockholder gave his approval to Chuck Waldron and John
Holmes for Air West to execute an agreement to purchase two Boeing 727-200s with
an option for three more.[11]

Today, June 25, 1975, the stockholder gave his approval for the purchase of
the Fort Lauderdale Convair "240" for $70,000, with the owner picking up the
cost of installing bathtub fittings, with another $5,000 budgeted for any additional
work.[12]

The first memorandum was signed by Waldron and Holmes, the second by
Waldron alone. The aides' files were packed with similar memoranda relating
to the Desert Inn.

The campaign to win Hughes's acceptance of a Desert Inn construction project had started in 1974, when the owners of the property complained about the state of their investment. They hinted broadly of a lawsuit against Hughes for failing to honor the terms of his lease. Gay presented Hughes with several building options. Hughes countered with his own. As the messages sailed back and forth between Gay in his Encino office and the aides in the Xanadu Princess Hotel in Freeport, the Desert Inn rotted away. Among the various plans under consideration were proposals to construct one high-rise, several low-rise buildings, or some combination of the two. About all that Hughes had determined was that he did not want to build on leased land. Any new structures were to be located on land that he owned adjoining the Desert Inn. At one point, when there was talk of putting up a sixty-five-story hotel, Levar Myler prepared a two-page report for Gay outlining Hughes's wishes:

Last night HRH suggested that, in his opinion, we should consider the following for the new Desert Inn. Build a foundation that would support a 65 story building, but build only the number of stories that will give us the number of rooms presently needed at the Desert Inn. The new Desert Inn should be built on land we own rather [sic] on leasehold land. It should be built within 5–10 feet of the boundary [sic] between our land and the leasehold land. It should be set back from the Strip far enough for anyone on the Strip can [sic] get the full effect of the building when it is raised to 65 stories. . . . The building should be either square or rectangular in shape and constructed with a steel framework. Between the steel network glass could be used for the outside walls. If it is necessary to use opaque material in the outside walls it should be used along the edges so we could have a ribbon of glass extending into the sky.[13]

When the sixty-five-story high-rise concept was abandoned and talks shifted to several enclosed, interconnected low-rise buildings resembling motel units, Hughes, who somehow had become enamored of people movers, indicated a desire to install one at the new Desert Inn. On June 22, 1974, Howard Eckersley wrote to Gay, "In discussion with HRH today regarding the Desert Inn improvements, HRH said that he wanted the Desert Inn to be under one roof as much as is possible. He said that this could be accomplished by connecting the buildings with covered walkways which would be air-conditioned and would accommodate both pedestrians and electric carts. He would like to see a sketch of how this could be accomplished."[14]

Gay disliked both notions. About enclosed walkways, he said, "our survey and market studies indicate that a majority of people are on a back-to-nature kick, enjoying and preferring to walk outside through a garden environment to the various activities associated with the hotel and its services. The advantage is aesthetic and convenience. The disadvantage is inclement weather when there is wind or rain."[15] As for the people mover, "at the present time there is no proven or operational people conveyor which can be functionally and aesthetically installed for the Desert Inn. However, there is a conveyor (the details of which are attached) which can be built underground to connect all the buildings. The cost of this system which would involve approximately

100 cars is estimated at $4 million. The advantages of the system are it can move people, materials, and the hotel services rapidly and efficiently in all weather. The disadvantage is it is unproven and could result in congestion, breakdown, and customer dissatisfaction as in the case of the elevators at the Landmark."[16]

The people-mover blueprint that Gay submitted to Hughes envisioned the most elaborate subway transit system ever devised for a hotel complex in which the most distant room was but several hundred yards from the lobby or casino. It provided for an automated line extending from the outlying parking garages through the hotel lobby and to the nearby motel units. Six-passenger cars traveling at fifteen miles an hour would pick up guests when they parked their automobiles, speed them to the lobby to check in, and then on to their rooms. Nonstop service to the casino would reduce a guest's travel time from his room to gaming tables. The underground rail system would be controlled by a single operator monitoring twelve closed-circuit television screens. It was pure Hughes, as pretentious as any project he himself had conceived.

Gay next sent Hughes "a revised sketch of the proposed plan for the Desert Inn addition which reflects," he said, "full useage [sic] of the low-rise building in the 'three-fingered' four-story configuration you suggested".[17]

On July 20, 1974, an aide reported to Gay that "At 7:35 Pm. [sic] on the above date the stockholder approved the starting of the demolition of the various low-rise buildings immediately."[18] The aide also allowed that there had been another change in construction plans. Instead of three-fingered, four-story buildings, there would be three-fingered, six-story buildings, with one exception:

It was suggested that each of the so called 3-fingered buildings be six stories high with the exception of the low-rise in front of the existing high-rise bldg. This would obscure the view of the golf course and he wants this to be only one story. It finally was suggested that only one swimming pool be constructed on each end of each 3-fingered bldg instead of two. However, he wants one pool to be constructed on each floor of the six-story bldg., making a total of 18 pools per bldg.[19]

But after all of this planning, there was no demolition and no construction of buildings of any height. By the end of October 1974, ninety rooms in the once-lavish Desert Inn had been closed by the Department of Health, and Hughes had become the first slum hotel owner on the glittering Las Vegas Strip.

Such confusion and financial pressure was taking its toll. Fortunately, a scapegoat was not far away, as one of the Desert Inn memoranda indicates. Although four years had gone by since the ouster of Bob Maheu, the author of the unsigned memorandum blamed the former chief of Hughes Nevada Operations for the grim financial performance of the Las Vegas properties. "Now that we have successfully overcome the old Maheu philosophy attributed to you that you were not interested in making a profit because you wanted to take advantage of the losses tax-wise," the memorandum stated, "we cannot think of anything that can be intelligently done to alter the realization of the Maheuian economic theory, except immediately build at the Desert Inn."[20]

Like so much of the information funneled to Hughes in his last bedridden years, the memorandum was misleading. Certainly, in earlier times Hughes had not been particularly interested in profits. His managers had cheerfully embraced the philosophy. When Rea Hopper, the chief executive officer of the aircraft division, was asked in the 1960s whether he wanted the division to show a profit, he replied, "I don't really care."[21] Howard Eckersley, one of the aides, said that Hughes told him "his business philosophy was to have a high gross and not necessarily high profit."[22] Hughes had developed this indifference to profits during years when the oil-tool division of the Hughes Tool Company was a nonstop money-making machine. The casual attitude toward earnings surely had to change with the sale of the oil-tool division in 1972, but it did not. By then, Hughes was no longer in control and his no-profit philosophy had become a disastrous way of life throughout the Summa Corporation.

On January 21, 1975, Gay sent another memorandum pressing Hughes to take some action at the Desert Inn. "You have been given as much valid information as we know," Gay wrote, as though Hughes were in full command of his mental faculties. "It does not mean there is not other equally valid or complete information. Neither does it mean that others would not give you different information. But even then you could not know that the other people had given you material either more or less valid, accurate or complete."[23]

Hughes responded, again, by changing his mind. Instead of pushing ahead with an ambitious construction program, he wanted to spend as little money as possible, just enough to placate the owners and forestall a lawsuit. At 5 A.M. on Saturday, January 25, Howard Eckersley recorded in a memorandum: "HRH has just said that he wants to obtain the cheapest and quickest solution to the Desert Inn lease default. . . . What he wants is an immediate short-term fix which will fully and completely stop the bleeding at the Desert Inn."[24]

For two years Gay and the aides exchanged messages about the condemned Desert Inn, lamenting its deterioration, their only discernible progress a thickening file of memoranda. There would be no construction at the Desert Inn until after Hughes's death, and then, at Gay's direction, it would proceed at a rapid pace hitherto unknown in Summa Corporation, and on leased land where Hughes had said that he would never build.

THE LAST FIGHT

The Desert Inn was not the only decaying building among Hughes's holdings. KLAS–TV was also in need of new facilities. Unlike other Hughes business interests, the television station had been managing to turn a profit, however slim, averaging a little more than $200,000 before taxes. But KLAS's share of the Las Vegas television market was eroding. A CBS affiliate, KLAS in 1971 had local billings of $1,295,000, or 36 percent of the market. By 1974, its share had fallen to 25 percent, with billings of $1,163,000.[25] Because of inadequate production facilities, KLAS could not compete in the lucrative production of commercials. Its two rivals boasted studio and production space four to five times larger. In addition, the station operated "with no back-up capacity for most of its broadcast and mechanical equipment."[26] Moreover, KLAS was housed in a building that, like the Desert Inn, was about to be condemned. Settling soil had caused the foundation to sink several inches and the walls to give way. As Levar Myler told Hughes, the building "is in terrible shape. We have been fighting to keep the county from condemning it for some time. . . . Actually, the building is unsafe."[27]

While Bill Gay did most of the corresponding on the Desert Inn, Nadine Henley held responsibility for KLAS. Before it was over, the KLAS affair, unbeknownst to the public, would become the longest-running comedy routine in Las Vegas. It had started in 1973, when Myler told Miss Henley that Hughes had approved construction of a new building. During the second week of February 1974, with the public groundbreaking ceremony scheduled for February 23, Hughes had second thoughts. He wanted it postponed and further studies made. Summa officials panicked. On February 13, Kay Glenn, Perry Lieber—his longtime publicist—and other staff members prepared a memorandum urging Hughes to reconsider:

The postponing of the groundbreaking of the new KLAS–TV building on February 23 is one of the most injurious things that can happen to us in Nevada from a public relations standpoint. Building permits have of necessity been obtained. When we filed for a variance permit from the county, our plans became a matter of public record and the Hughes family of over 6,000 employes have been excited that our first new structure is going to get underway on time and as planned. Public officials, including the governor and celebrities, have made comment on how pleased they are with our plans. . . . We do not like to call your attention to other projects that have been publicized and never started, such as the Sands project. Postponing this project for KLAS will revive the media again, stating that we are all talk and no action.[28]

The message was given to Hughes on February 14. Later that day, Myler and Eckersley signed a one-sentence memorandum: "Today, while talking to me, HRH authorized the groundbreaking for KLAS as scheduled for February 23, 1974."[29] On February 18, five days before the groundbreaking, one of the aides noted that Hughes was casting about for an excuse to delay the event. "HRH wants to build a building which could house all of our corporate offices in Las Vegas, as well as KLAS," the aide wrote. "This would give us a reason for not proceeding with present plans for groundbreaking of present building planned."[30] Hughes tossed out four possible sites for the combined corporate–KLAS offices. To relieve KLAS's dilemma, he suggested moving the station into his Landmark Hotel and Casino. There were two possible locations. The first, on the top floor of the Landmark Tower, would require transporting props and heavy equipment up and down in elevators that, as his staff observed, were "inadequate for even the people" staying there.[31] The second location, the ground floor, would require ripping out part of the casino.

Rather than cancel the ceremony, Summa officers, amid great fanfare, broke ground for a $2-million broadcast center that they knew would never be erected on that site.

While the news media speculated on whether the structure would be ready for the National Association of Broadcasters' 1975 convention in Las Vegas, Miss Henley sent Hughes a list of seven other locations for the KLAS building. After waiting more than a week, she sent a second message: "I need your response because bids are in for construction," Miss Henley said. "We must know where it is to be located to see if the building can go as bid."[32] Summa, having broken ground at a site where there would be no building, was about to award construction contracts for the erection of a building without a site.

Soon there were new concerns. By May fear grew that KLAS would be cited by health authorities because it had a defective and illegal septic system. Contractors who had bid on the new building were seeking a decision. That same month, Hughes dreamed up his own architectural rendition. He saw a building that could be moved from one spot to another, accompanied by the tons of broadcasting and air-conditioning equipment and miles of wiring that went with it. He preferred a 30,000-square-foot building of "conventional rectangular shape with corners" and recommended a site three miles west of the Strip.[33] An aide informed Miss Henley of this idea on May 25, adding that Hughes wanted the building "constructed as cheaply as possible in case we may want to move it in a few years."[34] For the rest of the year, the staff sought to talk Hughes out of his portable television station.

On February 21, 1975, Miss Henley sent an anniversary message to Hughes. "Sunday, February 23, is one year since you stopped the construction of the new KLAS–TV building," she wrote. "The station has just received the cancellation of the county work permit. . . . Is there no hope of a resolution of this problem with me?"[35] A week later, Miss Henley received a memorandum signed by Eckersley and Waldron saying that Hughes had given up on his idea of a movable TV station, and that construction on the new KLAS building should begin immediately "right on the present site for historical reasons."[36]

A large problem clouded this suggestion. "It is not possible," Miss Henley pointed out, "to get a new building covering 26,000 square feet, plus county required parking of 36,000 square feet on a 40,000-square-foot lot, while not disturbing the existing 12,000-square-foot facility that must operate during construction a minimum of twenty hours a day."[37] She added that KLAS's air conditioning had "broken down twice in recent months and much of the vital broadcast equipment is in the same decrepit condition."[38]

After more than two years of such message passing, during which KLAS's proposed home bounced about Las Vegas like the ball on a roulette wheel, Hughes and Miss Henley were still far apart, debating whether the building should be permanent or portable. In time, KLAS–TV would get its building, a nonmovable one, but construction would not begin until Hughes's last days, when he could no longer object, no longer offer just one more suggestion. As Miss Henley recalled, "It was our last fight."[39]

If the KLAS building was Miss Henley's last fight with Hughes, her harshest criticism of him came during a blitz of memoranda on a Hughes project from the 1940s: the HK-1, known variously as the flying boat, Hercules, and—to everyone but Hughes—the Spruce Goose. A plan to give the flying boat to the Smithsonian Institution was being worked out by Hughes's tax lawyers, Mickey West at Andrews, Kurth, Campbell & Jones in Houston, and Seymour Mintz at Hogan & Hartson in Washington. It was a gift dictated not by generosity or a sense of history but by federal taxes.

Since its first and only flight in 1947, for little more than one mile, the eight-engine wooden flying boat, its 320-foot wings tall enough for a man to walk inside, had been preserved in a guarded, humidity-controlled hangar at Long Beach harbor. The annual cost of keeping the flying boat in dry dock ran close to $1 million a year. As with many Hughes ventures, the American taxpayer had been underwriting a substantial portion of this expense. Hughes deducted the maintenance costs as a business expense on his federal income-tax return.* Although the plane never left the hangar, the Internal Revenue Service, in keeping with its special relationship with Hughes, had annually rubber-stamped the deductions. By 1974, however, the IRS was beginning to have second thoughts about the practice it had approved for a quarter century. When it became evident that the IRS probably would disallow the deductions —and apply the ruling retroactively to those tax returns for the past few years that were still being audited, a decision that would cost Hughes millions—his lawyers set about negotiating with the General Services Administration. The GSA actually held title to the flying boat because it had been built with government funds. Hughes had leased the plane at a nominal annual fee. By the end of 1974, the lawyers had worked out an arrangement under which the Summa Corporation would buy the flying boat from the GSA for $700,000 and then donate it and the Hughes racer to the Smithsonian Institution.

Smithsonian curators wanted very much to install the racer—in which Hughes set air-speed records in 1935 and 1937—in the National Air and Space Museum. And while they might also have displayed the flying boat, no museum building was large enough to accommodate it. So the agreement provided that the flying boat would be cut into pieces. The Smithsonian would take a fifty-one-foot section of the wing. The remaining parts would be parceled out

---

*As a rule, a deductible business expense must be incurred in an active business. It also must be an ordinary and necessary expense, necessary being defined as "appropriate and helpful" in the development and conduct of a business. The flying boat was not being used in any active business. It might once have been argued that it provided valuable technical data for the future development of aircraft. Such was hardly the case in the 1960s and 1970s. The jet age had rendered the flying boat as obsolete, technologically, as the calculator had the abacus.

to eight other museums around the country. But Hughes balked at the prospect of a dismembered flying boat.

At this point, in January of 1975, Nadine Henley wrote, in longhand, one of the strongest letters of criticism that Hughes had ever received from an employee. "It has been extremely difficult for twenty-seven years to stand by and watch the press and everyone else try to justify the government's large investment in a 'wooden' flying boat that never . . . served any purpose whatsoever, except (as the press put it) as a play-thing for a billionaire," Miss Henley wrote. "Your accountants and attorneys have struggled endlessly to give some credibility to the . . . behemoth."[40] Taking note of the IRS examination of his tax returns for the last seven years, she underscored the argument put forth by his attorneys—that donating the aircraft to the Smithsonian would not only resolve his tax problems but would assure the flying boat "a dignified place in history" rather than let it remain a "laughing stock."

This is our one chance of showing that the whole effort was sincere and productive. It is also our one chance to get IRS to let us expense seven years of maintenance (still "open")—and we are talking about six million dollars which otherwise will be charged to you personally. This could cost your company (as Mickey has pointed out to you by memos) a possible forty-two million dollars. How can you possibly keep the intensive interest and respect of your employes under such circumstances? How can we get them to watch the dollars for you when all these millions are being thrown away . . . on something we will never live down in our lifetime? . . . We implore you more for your sake and your name in history than for any other reason to take the ghost out of the hangar and allow the Smithsonian to make a shrine forever.[41]

Hughes did not respond to this no-nonsense message from Miss Henley, now nearing the end of her fourth decade as a member of the inner circle.

The agreement with the Smithsonian was to be signed on Monday, January 20. Hughes's lawyers and his staff had coordinated the transaction as they might a missile launching. Once Hughes approved, an aide would flash the decision to Seymour Mintz in Washington, and Chester Davis would have the executive committee of the Summa Corportion authorize Mintz to sign the agreement. Throughout that weekend the aides pressed Hughes for an answer. Sunday night, as one of the aides went off duty, he left a message for Eckersley and Myler outlining a course for Hughes in the hours ahead. "He said he would call Seymour as early as 5 A.M. because he had to ask him a few more questions concerning Seymour's last message," the aide wrote. "He did say that he agreed with Seymour's message. You will have to remind him around 4:30 A.M. that today is Monday and that the agreement must be signed today at 9 A.M. (Seymour actually said 10 A.M.)."[42]

Hughes would need reminding, for his thoughts were elsewhere. Some nut crumbs had remained on the plate from his last meal, and he had directed the aide on duty to store the plate, with the crumbs, in the refrigerator. As the hours slipped toward the Smithsonian deadline, an aide took down Hughes's instructions for the serving of his next dessert: "The next time he has dessert, he wants the cake put on the plate he used before which has the nut crumbs on it and which was put in the refrigerator."[43]

In any case, the signing of the Smithsonian agreement was again postponed. Hughes wanted more time. Eventually, a different agreement would be executed, containing a provision that allowed Hughes to keep the flying boat intact and to donate it to any nonprofit organization that might be interested in building a museum for it. If he could find no one to accept his airplane, it was to be cut up and the parts distributed as originally agreed. At Hughes's death, the flying boat remained in one piece.*

THE CANDYMAN

In his last full year of life Hughes was constantly harangued. Each day brought another demand upon him, more pressure to act. Build the Desert Inn. Sign the papers for a $6.5-million loan from the Texas Commerce Bank. Buy the Country Club Motel. Give away the flying boat. Buy the Rendezvous Motel. Sign the power of attorney for his personal checking account. Buy the Lucayan Beach Hotel. Invest in Nicaragua. Buy the Black Forest restaurant. Sign the papers for a $15-million loan from the Texas Commerce Bank. Buy the Country Club apartments. Open a bank safe-deposit box and authorize access. Buy the Royal Lucayan Inn. Sign a power of attorney for another lawyer to prepare the tax returns. Build a television station. Invest in Ecuador. Sign the papers for a $15-million loan from the First City National Bank, the Bank of the Southwest, and the Texas Commerce Bank. Give away the racer. Build a terminal at McCarran International Airport. Buy a de Havilland 125 jet. Accept a scrip dividend from Summa instead of cash.

The agendas for the Summa board meetings had to be reviewed, expenditures closely checked. Lights for the tennis courts at the Xanadu Princess Hotel. Dishwashers at the Frontier and Landmark Hotels. Carpet for the Garden Room at the Sands Hotel. An $11-million advance to the helicopter division. A backup air-conditioning system at the Xanadu Princess. A tractor for the ranch. New computers. There were demands from the staff, too. Increase the employee loan fund. Buy a Beechcraft King Air corporate aircraft. Then there were the employment contracts. Everyone wanted a contract, job security. The aides, Summa executives, even the doctors wanted contracts. Protection, in the event he should die in the near future. And the will. They kept pestering about the will. In all the years gone by, no one had been so

*In July of 1977, fifteen months after Hughes's death, the Summa Corporation announced it was donating the flying boat to a group of Long Beach businessmen who planned to conduct a fundraising drive and build an Air Museum of the West. One of the museum backers compared the flying boat to a work of art. "It is a beautiful sculpture," he said, "like the Pieta or Rodin's 'The Thinker' and we intend to preserve it." The museum was expected to go up not far from the *Queen Mary*, the British luxury liner that the City of Long Beach had bought ten years earlier as a tourist attraction and that had become a multimillion-dollar white elephant.

injudicious as to pressure him about his will. Now everyone asked. Who has the will? Should it not be reviewed? Does it need to be updated? Should a codicil be added? Should the executor be changed?

Hughes was sixty-nine years old and a very sick man. His mind had long ago degenerated beyond the point where he could competently manage his affairs. Now his physical degeneration was entering the final stages. He was in fact a frightening specimen of medical neglect and self-abuse. A malignant tumor was growing out of the left side of his scalp, an inch or two above his left ear. It was the size of a quarter and the scraggly gray hair no longer covered it. When he stretched out on the bed, his skin drew taut over the bony framework of his body. Suffering from malnutrition, he weighed slightly more than a hundred pounds. He had shrunk almost three inches. There were white opaque rings around the corneas of his eyes, and the eyes were glazed from drugs. His upper and lower teeth dangled from the receding jaw bone, too loose to chew solid food. His upper front teeth were completely destroyed by decay, his gums were puffy, and pus had collected around the rotting teeth. His arms and thighs were carpeted by needle marks. Anyone who looked could see these troubles. Inside the body it was worse.

Hughes's bones were wasting away as his body used more bone mass each day than it manufactured, feeding upon itself. There was a chronic peptic ulcer in the lower part of his stomach. His urinary tract was partly blocked. Although there was enough codeine in the tissues, in the blood, in the liver, in the stomach, to kill an ordinary man, through years of addiction Hughes had built up a remarkable tolerance. His prostate gland was three times larger than normal. His kidneys were about two-thirds of normal size and shrinking daily. Much of the remaining kidney tissue was dead, covered by a mass of scar tissue formed after a quarter century of drug abuse. Given his general physical condition, one might think that Hughes had not seen a doctor in years. Such was not the case. In fact, he had a personal staff of four physicians.

A rather odd medical team had been recruited to join the retinue that accompanied Hughes wherever he went. It consisted of an internist, a general practitioner, a pathologist, and a surgeon. Two of the doctors were older than their patient. The third was an international violin champion who painted watercolors and built model airplanes. The fourth, and most enigmatic, was the brother-in-law of Bill Gay, number-one man in the empire. The four physicians were drawing combined salaries and expenses well in excess of $250,000 a year, yet their joint practice was decidedly unorthodox. If any chart of Hughes's medical condition existed, at least two of the doctors were unaware of it. One doctor knew of a general file where Hughes's medical records were maintained, but he never looked at it. Another also knew of the file, but he did not know where it was. One doctor did not know the quantities of medication another doctor was prescribing, nor did he know which of his three colleagues, if any, was monitoring the medication Hughes received. None of the doctors ever gave the bedridden Hughes a complete physical examination. None treated Hughes for his kidney disease. The most frequently run medical test was a urinalysis, mainly because it was easy to get a urine specimen from Hughes. What with his disorders of the mind, Hughes was not an agreeable patient. He wanted the doctors nearby, just as he wanted Mell Stewart nearby to administer the enema he so often postponed, yet he would not submit to a physical examination. And he scorned the medical advice that he did receive.

First among the physicians, in order of age, was Dr. Lawrence Chaffin, a physically active man who looked two decades younger than his eighty-three years. He had graduated from the University of Utah in 1913 and Harvard Medical School in 1917. In 1922, he moved to Los Angeles where he began a private practice in general surgery and joined the staff of the Santa Fe Memorial Hospital, which provided medical services for employees of the Santa Fe Railroad. For the next fifty years Dr. Chaffin was a railroad doctor, becoming chief surgeon and executive officer of the Santa Fe Memorial Hospital in 1948, a dual position he held until retirement in 1971.

Dr. Chaffin, who had also been Jean Peters's doctor, first saw Hughes as a patient in 1932. He treated him again in 1946, when Hughes was nearly killed in the crash of his XF-11. Then twenty-five years went by before he saw Hughes again, this time at the Britannia Beach Hotel in Nassau, in February of 1971. Sometime after that visit, a formal association developed between Dr. Chaffin and Hughes. Unlike his colleagues, however, who would rotate shifts, spending several weeks at whatever hotel Hughes was staying at and then returning home for several weeks of leave, Dr. Chaffin refused to sit and wait for Hughes to call. He had spelled out his demands when Hughes was living in London. "He will work on the basis of $60,000 for a half year," an aide informed Hughes. "That is, he will be available when you need him for the year but does not expect to spend his whole time sitting in a hotel room waiting for a call that seldom comes. He says that if he works more than twenty-six weeks a year, using a five day week, he wants to be paid $650 per day."[44]

Of the four doctors, Chaffin had Hughes's respect but not his attention, their distance attributable in part to Chaffin's practice of telling Hughes what he did not want to hear. As Chuck Waldron recalled, "Dr. Chaffin is a very straight individual, very straight laced, and he calls it as it is and Mr. Hughes doesn't like that. He hit him between the eyes. And, 'You do this, you'll never walk,' or bam. That was Dr. Chaffin. 'Get out of that bed right now, start walking. I'll help you and we're going to do it.' But, see, the other doctors would say, 'Well, if you want to wait until tomorrow.' "[45]

The second physician was Dr. Norman Francis Crane, the internist. Born six months before Hughes on June 3, 1905, at Winter Harbor, Maine, Dr. Crane graduated from Bowdoin College in 1927 and from the Johns Hopkins University School of Medicine in 1931. Dr. Crane, had practiced internal medicine in Los Angeles since 1937, sharing offices with Dr. Verne Mason, who had been Hughes's principal physician in the 1930s and 1940s and who eventually became chairman of the Medical Advisory Board of the Howard Hughes Medical Institute. Dr. Crane had met Hughes prior to his around-the-world flight in 1938. "Dr. Mason just introduced me as an associate," he said.[46] On two or three occasions from the late 1930s until 1950, when Dr. Mason had not been available Dr. Crane treated Hughes, and in December of 1961 Hughes became Crane's full-time patient. "From then on," he said, "I made house calls on a fairly regular basis at his request."[47] With the move to Nassau in November of 1970, the demands on Dr. Crane became more persistent:

For the first nine months I was on twenty-four hour call . . . with the exception of a total of approximately ten days at home during that period. I would see him subject to his call, and somewhere in there I asked for and received relief on rotation. The first one was Dr. Clark. . . . When that rotational program started, I spent six weeks on twenty-four hour call and was relieved for two weeks by Dr. Clark, and then returned for another six-week period myself. During the time that I was there I saw him whenever he would call. . . . It might be once a day, or I might spend a month there and not be called at all. But I better be around and available.[48]

Throughout the last fifteen years of Hughes's life, Dr. Crane saw him more often than any other physician. Yet in all those years, he never conducted "a complete physical examination" of Hughes.[49]

Dr. Homer Hone Clark was the pathologist. Born November 23, 1921, at Provo, Utah, Dr. Clark graduated from Brigham Young University in 1943 and the George Washington University School of Medicine in 1948. In 1954 he joined the pathology department at Latter-day Saints Hospital in Salt Lake City. Dr. Clark's younger brother, Rand Hone Clark, was a Romaine Street graduate who had become an assistant to Bill Gay, working out of the Summa executive offices in Encino. In 1969, when Hughes needed a blood transfusion, a sample of his blood was sent to Dr. Clark in Salt Lake City. The physician matched it and shipped blood supplies to Las Vegas for the transfusion. Although he did not see Hughes in 1969, Dr. Clark performed a series of laboratory tests on blood specimens attributed to Hughes, measuring the white blood cell count, hemoglobin, and hematocrit. When Hughes was moved to Nassau, Dr. Clark, a Mormon like his brother, was asked to become a permanent member of the Hughes medical staff. In 1971 he began rotating shifts with Dr. Crane. An outgoing, loquacious man given to malapropisms and lapsed syntax, Dr. Clark described his duties:

The usual cycle of a doctor responding to a patient, the patient calls, has a question, wants some advice, has a complaint or whatever, and obviously my concourse and conduct would relate to his request. . . . I responded to calls only. Now, I don't say he called me, he called me. Do you get what I mean? But agencies presumed to be of his—his command would call me. In other words, somebody calls you on the phone and says, "Mr. so and so wants you now." You went now.[50]

Because Hughes did not easily submit to tests, even the drawing of blood, Dr. Clark relied on visual observations and urinalyses to assess the state of Hughes's health. "I remember at times when he got up and walked around," Dr. Clark said, "that I didn't examine him other than to see that he was locomote—locomote and had good balance and the whole thing."[51] He obtained urine specimens from Hughes, Clark indicated, on numerous occasions because one does not have to request—or it's not an unusual or in the least bit painful to procure any urine, as is self apparent. . . . It is a very accessible way to monitor the general health of a patient, especially a patient who is, shall we say, relatively quiescent. He wasn't out playing tennis like I was most of the day. I mean, that's an understatement in fact.[52]

What had he found in the urinalyses? "Relatively nothing, ever. There was no indication that he had a kidney problem."[53] Dr. Clark never saw any of Hughes's medical records. There was a general file that the other doctors "dropped everything in."[54] But he did not know what was in it, because "I didn't look."[55] Thus, although he was aware that Hughes was taking drugs, he said he did not know who prescribed them or why—and never asked. During the two years in Freeport, the Bahamas, Dr. Clark, who called himself a "therapeutic healist," saw Hughes about twice during each two-week tour of duty.[56] He did not give Hughes a physical examination because Hughes "just didn't request it and there was no imminent problem that required it or that would have been important to, you see."[57]

Dr. Clark did manage to treat Hughes for one ailment—bad breath caused by his rotting teeth. "He had an obvious dental odor and I did prescribe some odorous borate once. It's a mouth freshener, oxidizing agent, cleanser. . . . I think he did use it a few times, but I can't say how heroically."[58] Like his associates, Dr. Clark visited Hughes only when summoned. "You don't get in if you're not requested for an audience," he said.[59] To while away the idle hours waiting for a Hughes call, he pursued several hobbies. "I played the violin. I learned how to make violins," he said. "I've been twice international champion of violins and violas . . . so I guess I learned a little. This was entirely foreign to me prior to doing it. I painted a lot. I'm a watercolorist of some small stature. . . . I'm not one to be lonely or given to having time lay heavy on one's shoulder. I'm active doing things usually, reading, making—we made some championship model airplanes too."[60]

The fourth physician was Dr. Wilbur Sutton Thain, the general practitioner. Born on November 4, 1925, in Logan, Utah, Dr. Thain graduated from the University of Southern California School of Medicine in 1953. Two years later he began a general practice, with a secondary specialty in anesthesiology, in his hometown. The junior member of the medical team, Dr. Thain, like Dr. Clark, had a tie to the clique that now controlled the empire. Dr. Thain's older sister, Mary Elizabeth, was married to Bill Gay, the Summa Corporation's top officer. In 1972, Kay Glenn, chief assistant to Gay, invited Dr. Thain, who had worked at Romaine Street while he was in college, to join the Hughes medical group. By 1974, Dr. Thain had established with Hughes an unusual doctor–patient relationship.

Just as Hughes had a favorite aide—John Holmes—he also had a favorite physician. Throughout the 1960s and until 1974, this was Dr. Crane. It was not that Hughes had any genuine affection for either Crane or Holmes. He had long lived in an emotional wasteland, free of attachment to any other human being. Rather, it was that Dr. Crane and Holmes shared an indispensable role in Hughes's life—that of candyman. For two decades they had provided Hughes with a steady supply of narcotics, other pain-killing drugs, and tranquilizers, delivering to him tens of thousands of the white and blue tablets that damaged his kidneys and deadened his mind. From 1966 to 1970, when he lived at the Desert Inn, Hughes swallowed and dissolved and injected himself with more than thirty-three thousand codeine tablets and Empirin Compound tablets containing codeine. And that was in addition to the thousands of Valium tablets that he also took.

In the beginning, Dr. Crane had written prescriptions for Hughes's codeine in the names of different aides, who shared the job of getting them filled at pharmacies in the Los Angeles area and delivering the drugs to Hughes. But Holmes assumed an increasing responsibility for this chore, and although Dr. Crane continued to write the prescriptions in the names of other aides, Holmes got most all of them filled. Twelve years earlier, in 1963, Roy Crawford had told Dr. Crane that "he was not going to fill any more prescriptions and did not want John Holmes using his name. Dr. Crane told Crawford he understood how he felt."[61] In 1965, when George Francom noticed that his name was on one of the prescriptions, he asked Holmes about the practice. Holmes told him that "he should be able to use other names as well as his own to obtain drugs."[62] By 1974 there was a growing unease among the staff over this large-scale, illegal drug procurement. The aides no longer wanted to be involved. They did not even want to pass along Hughes's messages about drugs to Dr. Crane, fearing the day when the secrecy veil might be pierced and they would be compelled to testify in legal proceedings about Hughes's condition and their own actions. They reached an understanding that whenever Hughes spoke of drugs, he would do so with one of his doctors, who could claim the doctor–patient privilege in any lawsuit. Hughes once forgot about the agreement and an aide typed out a reminder:

You seem to have forgotten that several months ago, not only Norman but also Wilbur and Homer decided that they would not want to talk through a third party such as the six of your staff. The reasoning was because of possible testimony which we might sometime be required to give. With doctors it is privileged information and they cannot be forced to testify unless it is in a criminal case. They suggest that your staff be in the position of saying that your doctors see you occasionally and that what they talk to you about or administer to you is not known to any of us. That is also the reason that we six should not only not view any medication you have but not be in the position of giving or handing you any type of medication, even Excedrin.[63]

But even Dr. Crane, after two decades of writing illegal prescriptions, was wary. Sometime in 1974 he confided to Francom that the "drug laws were getting too harsh and he had been involved with the drugs long enough."[64] That same year Holmes told Waldron "he was afraid of getting caught and did not want to be involved any longer in obtaining drugs for Hughes."[65] It was about this time that Hughes's attachment to Dr. Crane came to an end and he chose a new favorite from among his medical staff—Dr. Thain. Abandoning Dr. Crane's cumbersome drugstore system, Dr. Thain arranged a direct supply from a New York pharmaceutical house. Not only was it more convenient, it also reduced the risk of detection.

WHERE IS THE WILL?

Hughes had often assured his aides that after such long and faithful service in the respected Hughes organization, they would have no difficulty securing good jobs in any large American corporation. "Everyone knows that the five of you have been my eyes, ears, and voice for the past five to ten years," Hughes said to Howard Eckersley, "so I am sure any one of you could get any executive position you might care to seek, and with any number of companies to choose from."[66] This typical Hughes hyperbole ignored obvious questions. What business would pay an employee $75,000 to $100,000 a year to handle telephone messages, serve meals, and operate a motion-picture projector? What business would pay its chief executive officer $400,000 a year in salary and bonuses for presiding over the dissipation of hundreds of millions of dollars in assets? The answers to those questions may have eluded Hughes. They did not elude the aides or Summa executives.

In the summer of 1975, with Hughes drugged and slowly dying, the Summa Corporation high command and the aides mounted a campaign designed to gain two objectives—corporate employment contracts and a favorable will. Without one or the other, all jobs in the Hughes hierarchy were in jeopardy.

Hughes's will was especially critical. If he had signed a will leaving his estate to the Howard Hughes Medical Institute, as he had so often said he intended to do, all would be well. Bill Gay was one member of a two-man executive committee that would run the medical institute after Hughes's death. The other was Chester Davis. Control of the empire would remain in familiar hands. Without a will, however, the estate would pass to distant, unfamiliar relatives and the future would be unpredictable. At best, those around Hughes might lose their jobs or find their salaries substantially reduced. At worst, they might be indicted or called to defend civil lawsuits relating to business transactions carried out in Hughes's name in his last years, when the fortune shrank by more than half a billion dollars. Employment contracts and consulting agreements would provide financial protection and job security. A will with the appropriate provisions would provide permanent immunity. If they could get both, so much the better. The first task was to determine whether a valid will existed, and if so its contents.

Whenever discussing his will in the past, Hughes had often confided to his listener that he just happened to be one of the lucky beneficiaries. Back in the early 1960s, when living at the Bel Air house, Hughes assured Holmes on that point, and it was a litany that he had recited to each of his aides individually—never in the presence of witnesses—at different times in later years. Even

Dr. Crane was to be blessed. "He promised me on a number of occasions that he would put me in his will," Dr. Crane said.[67]

On those rare occasions when Hughes volunteered other details about his will, the story was always the same. He had prepared a holographic, or handwritten, will while living in the "gray house" on Sarbonne Road in Bel Air during the early 1940s. "He told me he had spent a considerable amount of time writing the will," Holmes said. "He did say that in those days he was in and out of the house. It was written at the gray house behind the tenth green of the Bel Air Country Club. He said he gave it a lot of thought. He'd think about it, come home at night, rough draft a few things. In other words, it took a great deal of time. He mentioned a couple of months."[68]

In a memorandum to Howard Eckersley, Hughes was more explicit:

It was carefully written seated at a desk, and complying to all the rules governing such wills (such as no other typed or printed material on any of the pages). And to illustrate the extremity with which I complied, I did not even use paper with lines, such as this. It was all done under the supervision of my personal attorney Neil McCarthy, and I assure you no detail was overlooked.[69]

Hughes said he was so meticulous in writing the will that "I am assured it is binding as a band of steel."[70]

Despite these convincing accounts, Hughes probably never composed a holographic will. At the time he described the holographic will to Eckersley, he also confided that Eckersley was one of its beneficiaries. "You as well as other members of my staff were identified by description rather than by name," he said.[71] That would have been impossible. Hughes lived at the "gray house," where he said he wrote the will, more than a decade before he formed the personal staff of which Eckersley was a member.

There was, however, another will—a document that Hughes never discussed. This was the will so often revised by Hughes and retyped by Nadine Henley in 1947. On Hughes's orders, the draft will had been placed in a bank safe-deposit box in Hollywood, where it remained until 1974 when Miss Henley, on her own initiative, moved it to a safe in Romaine Street. Hughes had never signed the will. Those senior Hughes executives who knew of it also knew that it was not valid.

Against this background, John Holmes was given the delicate assignment of raising the subject of his employer's last will and testament. Following a suggestion by Miss Henley, Holmes first asked if Hughes might not think it wise to update his will. This brought forth the familiar rambling story of his holographic will written at the "gray house." Holmes next pursued the matter by memorandum: "Chester Davis, Seymour Mintz, Mickey West, Lee Murrin, Nadine Henley, Bill Gay have no knowledge of the existence of your will. Even Raymond Holliday said that if you had a will it would have been so old that Noah Dietrich would have been probably the administrator and chief beneficiary."[72] Furthermore, he reminded Hughes that after the death of Neil McCarthy, one of his early attorneys, Nadine Henley had obtained from

McCarthy's widow all the files relating to Hughes and they did not contain a will.

That Dietrich might be a beneficiary under an outdated will did get Hughes's attention: "Imagine me leaving that son-of-a-bitch a nickel."[73] But again Hughes affirmed to Holmes the existence of the "gray house" holographic will, which, he insisted, did not mention Dietrich. As for his attorneys and other Summa executives, Hughes said that any one of them "could have a will or a document. They'd be sworn to secrecy and they wouldn't tell you, so this doesn't mean anything saying they had no knowledge about the existence of a will, because if they did, they wouldn't tell you anyway."[74] No will was found in McCarthy's papers because "All I did is I asked Neil McCarthy a few questions," he said. "I did the holographic will. I just asked him a few questions and he had nothing to do with it besides that. I never said that he had the will."[75] In his own way, Hughes had made it clear that he did not wish to discuss his will. Pointing his finger at Holmes he said, "Don't worry. I've got the holographic will that I just told you about."[76]

As the weeks drifted by, others had a try. Waldron invoked the needs of his family. "I was explaining about my situation being the youngest individual on the staff, what security would I have upon his death, and I had to look out for my family, nobody else would," Waldron said. "At that point he explained to me that I would never have to worry, that Mr. West had assigned a lawyer to put me on his latest will, that I would be taken care of, that I didn't need

Milton H. (Mickey) West, Jr., of Houston, Hughes's tax lawyer.
Wide World Photos

to worry."[77] Waldron did not believe Hughes. He allowed a few days to pass and questioned Hughes again. "Well, you act like you don't believe me," Hughes retorted.[78]

Hughes offered a similar story to the other aides, saying that they were already included in the will or that he was in the process of adding their names. When the aides compared notes, they realized Hughes was not telling them the truth. "I knew that he'd have to go through one of us to make out a will so one of us would know," Waldron said. "We all sat there and, 'not me,' 'not me.' "[79] When George Francom asked Hughes where he kept his will, Hughes replied, "You don't think I'm going to tell you where it is, do you?"[80] By this time Hughes was "rather resentful that we would bother him with it," Francom said. "In other words, I got the impression that it was none of my business, so why keep probing him. I think perhaps he was getting a little bit perturbed at the constant probing and pressure."[81]

Stymied on the will, the aides were more sanguine about prospects for the employment contracts and consulting agreements that had been drafted in 1973. Although there were some variations, the contracts generally provided for five-year terms and the consulting agreements for a period of ten years after retirement. An employee would receive one-third of his "highest total base salary" in the three years before his resignation or retirement, with an annual cost-of-living adjustment equal to the increase in the Consumer Price Index.[82] The employee, in turn, was prohibited from working for a competitor or, more significantly, disclosing any information about Hughes or Summa.*

The contracts and agreements had already been negotiated with Miss Henley, Holmes, Myler, Waldron, Francom, Rickard, Eckersley, and Glenn. While the documents had been signed by Summa officers, they had not been approved by the Summa Board of Directors or Summa's one and only stockholder, Howard Hughes. To survive any legal challenge, the documents would have to be approved by Hughes or the Summa board, or both, since the board members were awarding themselves contracts. But Summa directors had been meeting irregularly. Hughes had refused to authorize a meeting without an opportunity to review the agenda. By September of 1975 it was decided to push through the contracts and agreements. On Tuesday, September 9, the Summa directors assembled at Milfer Farm, Chester Davis's estate near Unadilla, New York, about thirty-five miles northeast of Binghamton. All five directors—

*The secrecy provision of the consulting agreement was also intended to prevent the aides and other Hughes executives from writing or publishing any memoirs. The agreement stated: "Employee agrees that he will not at any time during or subsequent to termination of his employment by Summa, whether such termination is qualified or non-qualified, disclose any confidential records or information, nor publish nor write any material which will in any way embarrass or be harmful to Summa or any of its affiliated companies or individuals, or submit or make available any such confidential records or information to any person whomsoever which might result in its general dissemination to the public, unless such public dissemination has specifically been previously authorized in writing by Summa."

Gay, Miss Henley, Davis, Myler, and Holmes—were present for the important meeting, which would last three days. Also invited to sit in were some select Summa officers and employees—Kay Glenn, Rand Clark, and Paul Winn, all Gay lieutenants in the Encino office; William E. Rankin, vice-president, treasurer, and assistant secretary of Summa; Vern C. Olson, vice-president, controller, assistant secretary, and assistant treasurer of Summa; Howard M. Jaffe, secretary of Summa and Chester Davis's law partner; and Jack Real.

When the time came to process the employment contracts and consulting agreements, a telephone call was placed to the Xanadu Princess Hotel in Freeport and Jim Rickard, the aide on duty, was instructed to tell Hughes what actions the board planned to take. In healthier days, Hughes would have expressed a keen interest in the granting of contracts to employees worth $10 million or more. Now, after a weak objection to fixing salaries in the contracts, he was told that it had to be handled that way, and he backed down. It was not the Hughes who had hung on so tenaciously in the face of Wall Street lawyers and bankers during the bitter TWA negotiations.

By 6:30 P.M. on Wednesday, September 10, the Summa directors were ready for the ritual of voting. Davis announced that he would abstain. As Gay later explained the decision, "he was the only outside member, and he had, himself, fees due him for work which he still had to negotiate, and he did not want to be in the position of having approved agreements for members of a board to whom . . . his claims would be taken."[83] Such conflicts of interest abounded throughout Summa, and had for years. To avoid the more outrageous situation of a director presenting himself with an employment contract, it was agreed that as the board voted on a particular director's contract, that director would step outside the meeting room. When the voting was done and the parliamentary smokescreen had lifted, the Summa board had approved contracts for twelve people, including all the directors except Davis. Gay, Miss Henley, Holmes, Myler, Waldron, Francom, Rickard, Eckersley, Glenn, and Real all received contracts. So did Hughes's two drug suppliers, Dr. Crane and Dr. Thain.

During the board meeting Hughes was approached anew about his will, this time by Jim Rickard, the junior aide. Hughes had a strong sense of a pecking order among his staff. His willingness to discuss sensitive matters was proportional to an aide's years of service. Rickard, therefore, linked the question of his will to the Summa board's failure to take certain actions that Hughes wanted:

I explained to him that various board members felt quite vulnerable as to the things that they did inasmuch as he was telling them what to do and they may not agree with it and would—could possibly have to answer to the heirs of his estate for things that they had done which had been done solely at his instructions. . . . They felt that they could be held accountable to whatever was done and that it was not—it could be inferred later on by the heirs that they had acted in bad faith or that they had made foolish decisions or bad decisions and they could be held responsible for it.[84]

Once again the ploy failed. "I have a will," Hughes said. "I wrote it by hand. It's a holographic will."[85] Hughes repeated the story he had told Eckersley and Holmes—with one large difference. Finishing the story of how the will was drafted, Rickard recalled, Hughes said "that he was very willing to write a codicil to the will, and I guess I looked puzzled. I didn't know the term. And he was delighted to explain to me what a codicil was and that he knew that the will needed to be updated and that he would write a codicil."[86]

Rickard, the former drive-in movie operator and life insurance salesman, was elated. He had succeeded where Holmes and the other experienced staff members had failed. Relaying Hughes's remarks to Nadine Henley at Chester Davis's farm, Rickard asked her to forward the will so that the necessary revisions could be made. His optimism knew no bounds. "If you'll just get that information in to me," he said to Miss Henley, "I think that I can really push him on it."[87] Although Rickard never spelled it out, he quite naturally was talking about the alleged holographic will, the only will that Hughes ever referred to and the one Rickard assumed that Miss Henley had in her custody. Miss Henley, of course, knew nothing about a holographic will. She assumed that Rickard was talking about the 1947 will she had typed and Hughes had never signed. That will would require substantial revision. It could not be updated with a codicil. Several people named as executors and trustees were dead, and the medical foundation it provided for differed from the one already in existence. The misunderstanding went unnoticed, though, and before Miss Henley had a chance to send any information, Rickard returned to his home in Provo, Utah, on a two-week leave. Meanwhile, Miss Henley told Holmes that she would be sending a special message to Hughes concerning his will. In Los Angeles on September 16, she wrote a two-page letter to Hughes, placed it in a sealed envelope, put that envelope inside a second one addressed to Holmes, and gave it to Waldron to hand-carry back to the Bahamas.

The urgency of the situation notwithstanding, when Holmes received the envelope he filed it away. It was not the right time to give Hughes such a sensitive communication. Hughes had been "sleeping a lot"—a euphemism for one of his intermittent periods of drug-induced stupefaction—and staring at movies.[88] In a day or two the time seemed right. Hughes had just ordered some dessert and said that he would like to screen a movie. Walking into the bedroom, Holmes handed the still-sealed envelope to Hughes and stood quietly in the background for about forty seconds, watching Hughes open it. As soon as Hughes began reading, Holmes returned to his desk in the adjoining room and waited.

The first sentence angered Hughes, and as he continued to read the letter written by his onetime personal secretary, his anger grew.

I was told by Jim Rickard that you had inquired about your Will.

I am so glad you did because I have been worrying about it, as it needs updating very much indeed. Noah Dietrich is named as one of your executors, as well as Ralph Damon, and others you may want to re-evaluate.

You may want to change the Will substantially (after 28 years) rather than just adding a codicil.

The Will was typed and printed on blue-line and I can send you (or carry to you) the blue-line, or a copy of it to correct. Then I can retype it, or the person of your choice can do it for you.

You realize, of course, that no one else has ever seen your Will so you must instruct me as to exactly how you want me to handle it.

Awaiting your instructions.

Sincerely,

Nadine[89]

A furious Hughes summoned Holmes. "He was quite upset," Holmes said, "didn't understand this for the simple reason that he said he didn't talk to Jim Rickard about a will, he certainly didn't instruct him to call Nadine Henley about it and he was at a loss to understand why she should send him this."[90]

Hughes was especially incensed that Rickard had taken it upon himself to call Miss Henley. As the youngest member of the staff, Hughes said to Holmes, Rickard would be "the last man that I would talk to about a will. Why the hell would I—I didn't talk to him. I may have made an offhand remark about a will, but there was no instructions. . . . You've been with me longer. I'd probably talk to you about a will."[91] The words were no sooner spoken than he retracted them. "Not something that important. I would talk to Mickey or someone like that about a will personally," he said, referring to Mickey West, one of his attorneys.[92] In short, on really critical matters he would not deal with an aide.

After venting his feelings about Rickard's intervention in such a personal matter, Hughes turned on Nadine Henley: "I don't know why she seems so persistent and pushy about this subject. It seems to me you talked to me about this before," he reminded Holmes. "I told you about the holographic will."[93] For about twenty minutes Hughes droned on. Then he said something Holmes considered unusual. He apologized for taking up Holmes's time by talking about something as dull as a will. "Sorry to bother you with all this," he said. "It's boring."[94] Hughes had offered apologies before, but never for taking up someone's time talking. With that, Hughes ended the conversation. "I want to get down to eating and screening," he said.[95]

The following morning, determined to make one last effort, Holmes typed a message for Hughes, attempting to resolve which will—the holographic will that Hughes talked about or the will that Nadine Henley had in her possession —was the genuine document. That night, Holmes handed him the note, and stood by as he read it:

Re: Your Will.

While we were in Las Vegas, Nadine sent you a note. You told me that the note was about your will and that Nadine thought you should review it. You instructed me to tell Nadine that you were aware that your will should be updated but that you could not spend the time necessary at that time.

Evidently Nadine believes the will she has is the true will and she must have been given instructions in the past by you to keep it secure. If the handwritten will is the real will, it could be that you had it updated later to the one Nadine has.

At any rate, wouldn't it be prudent to have Nadine send you the one she has under sealed cover and then have whoever holds the handwritten one sent to you in the same method. You alone can then compare one with the other and make whatever changes you deem necessary in your best interests.[96]

When he finished reading, Hughes "nodded a couple of times as if he understood it."[97] He looked at Holmes. Instead of revising an old will, he said, he "would have a new will drafted." He thought some more. "I'll have Seymour Mintz do it. Mickey West. They can work together. I don't have the time and the patience that I did before when I wrote the holographic will. I'll have them draft a new will."[98]

Holmes pressed. "When?"

"We have a little time," Hughes replied. "We want to do this thing." Hughes, who had stayed in bed since injuring his hip in London more than two years earlier, added, "We have to get down to it because I want to fly before I'm 70."[99]

Holmes jotted a note on a slip of paper—"I will remind you," and handed it to Hughes.

"No, no, don't push me because this is important, too," Hughes retorted. "But give me a month and a half, two months."[100]

Hughes then launched into a stream-of-consciousness speech that was largely incoherent. He made some reference to his father's failure to "get down to it" and something about fourteen copies of his father's will. He told Holmes, "I know this is important. What the hell, you guys all know if—you have nothing to worry about. . . . You guys are afraid I'm going to fly or something, kill myself. Don't worry because, you know, I have the HHMI [Howard Hughes Medical Institute]. . . . There's an old saying, something like not an old fool—no, no, a man is a fool if he doesn't know, but he's a bigger fool if he does know, so I know how important it is. Just keep with me. We'll do it."[101]

Holmes returned to his desk, taking the note he had given Hughes, and wrote across the bottom, "Reply—Will get down to constructing new will as soon as possible. Will use West and Mintz to draft it."[102] Holmes placed the memorandum in the file that all the aides read when they came on duty. "I felt that I had better," he said. "Some people were home and they would return, they're liable to say something about a will and he might explode. I wanted them to know what was said and what his response was and so I put that in our reading file so naturally the person that relieved me, I would show it to him and tell him what happened that night, and in case he forgot by any chance to tell his relief, it would be there to see."[103] Next, Holmes put in another telephone call to Nadine Henley to bring her up to date. He read to her the memorandum he had given to Hughes and Hughes's response.

"Dearie, this is important," Miss Henley said. "Maybe I should come down and bring this document."[104]

"Nadine, it wouldn't do any good to come down here," Holmes said. "He's not going to see you about it. He's not going to bother with it right now."[105] As far as Holmes was concerned, the great Hughes will search was over for the time being. But Howard Eckersley persisted. Using a slightly different tack, Eckersley warned Hughes that "no matter how good that will was that he said he wrote, even with the codicil added to it, that it was no good to anybody unless somebody knew where it was. I told him that to my knowledge nobody on the staff knew where it was. Bill Gay didn't know where it was, Nadine Henley didn't know where it was, Chester Davis didn't know where it was. So if something happened, where was it?"[106]

But on this subject nothing could succeed. There was no reason to worry about his will, Hughes said. "It was in a place that he picked for it, and when he was ready for it to come forward, it would."[107] At last resigned to Hughes's stubbornness, the aides desisted. Hughes's intransigeance on the whereabouts of the will was the last victory in a lifetime of verbal fencing. But it was a hollow one. Hughes long ago had surrendered his empire. Now he had even lost control of his own destiny. The intricate staff and executive system designed to serve his peculiar needs and shield him from public scrutiny had turned on him and now served itself. Where he once ruled the system with unquestioned authority, the system now ruled him. The best evidence of this is a series of events that took place in 1975 and the first weeks of 1976.

First came Jack Real and the East Coast Division. Upon leaving Lockheed in 1971 to join the Hughes entourage, Real received a chilly reception from just about everyone but Hughes. The Hughes inner circle did not take kindly to outsiders—as Bob Maheu had discovered in his relatively brief tenure. But Hughes liked Real personally, considered him "one of his best friends," and wanted him around.[108] He was the only outsider with whom Hughes maintained regular contact during ten years of life in hotel rooms. The older Hughes aides and executives had no choice but to tolerate Real. In the beginning, the hours that Real spent with Hughes in his bedroom were devoted largely to his favorite topic of conversation—airplanes and aircraft technology—but gradually Real began to take an interest in Hughes's business affairs. By the time the group had moved to Freeport, Real, too, was showering Hughes with memoranda, handwritten messages on a broad assortment of subjects—from reports on his role as Hughes's envoy to General Somoza in Nicaragua to the scientific achievements of the Hughes Aircraft Company. When Hughes bought his home, the Xanadu Princess, Real oversaw management of the hotel. When negotiations began for the acquisition of the Lucayan Beach Hotel, Real acted as Hughes's representative.

Real's deep involvement in Hughes's business activities made the old-time Summa executives uneasy. Their concern was heightened by the frequent private meetings between Hughes and Real, who had his own key to the aides' office and unrestricted access to the Hughes suite—a luxury that not even Bill Gay enjoyed. With the exception of the doctors and Real, no one met with Hughes behind closed doors. Their worst fears seemed justified when Hughes let it be known that he intended to reorganize the Summa Corporation by splitting it into an East Coast Division and a West Coast Division, with Real in charge of the former. The memory of Maheu's Hughes Nevada Operations, and the diminished influence exercised by Gay and his associates was fresh in the minds of the Hughes inner circle. They did not intend to accept a new authority, or to give up the power they had worked so long and so hard to consolidate. Without warning, Real one day found a new lock on the door to Hughes's suite. He no longer had access to the aides' office or to Hughes. There were no more closed-door meetings. Summa remained intact. As one of the aides put it to Real bluntly, "Well, what do you think of your Eastern Division now, Jack?"[109]

In December of 1975, Gay, Miss Henley, and Mickey West flew to New York for an unusual meeting at Chester Davis's law office. The purpose: to work out a plan for the transfer of all Hughes's personal possessions—his prized film library, a half-century accumulation of files and records, clothing, memorabilia from his early days in aviation and Hollywood—from Romaine Street to Houston. For his own reasons, West wanted to consolidate all Hughes's papers in Houston, a city that Hughes had avoided most of his adult life. "As a matter of personal convenience to me," West said, "I preferred that the new location be accessible and convenient to me."*[110] West envisioned a facility with more amenities than the warehouselike Romaine Street building. In particular, he wanted the new Hughes archives to have bedrooms, "where if the person wanted to stay for a period of time, it would be comfortable and convenient."[111] During the meeting in Davis's office, West recalled, "there was considerable discussion about who would assume the responsibility for making the arrangements for that move, particularly with respect to the film library, and it was finally decided, Bill Gay said he would assume the responsibility for it provided the new location would offer the same humidity and atmospheric control that was presently being utilized in the so-called building at Romaine Street."[112]

This was unprecedented. Hughes was not to be told about the relocation of his personal belongings until after it had been completed. If Hughes had a sentimental attachment for anything other than airplanes, it was for the negatives and prints of his films, which were stored in specially designed, humidity-controlled vaults at Romaine Street. He had never permitted anyone to touch the films. "He had flatly turned down any notion about moving" the films in the past.[113] Earlier in the year he had rejected a

---

*West maintained that he wanted "to insulate the Summa Corporation from the reach of California income taxation." But Hughes's possessions had been in California for more than forty years, and Summa's chief corporate officers were headquartered there.

proposal to sell Romaine Street. Clearly, the relocation decision was one Hughes would not have approved.* And if anyone had made such a decision in years gone by, Hughes would have fired him. In December of 1975, however, no one paid heed to Howard Hughes. There was no reason to. He was dying.

Someone in the Hughes hierarchy, for a reason not readily discernible, decided that it would be better for Hughes to spend his last days in Mexico rather than in the Bahamas. To persuade the failing Hughes to make the move, he was told that the codeine he needed to maintain his habit was no longer available in the Bahamas, the supply had dried up. It was not true. The supplier was a New York pharmaceutical house, not a Bahamian drug merchant. But Hughes did not know that. He readily consented to the move, for the alternative seemed to be forced withdrawal from a quarter-century narcotic habit, a torturous experience for an emaciated seventy-year-old addict.

On February 10, 1976, Hughes was flown from Freeport to Acapulco and moved into a bedroom of the Acapulco Princess—his fifth foreign hotel room in five years, his 1,892nd day in exile. A fresh supply of codeine was waiting for him. With its spare furnishings, movie screen, and drawn drapes, the penthouse looked like all the other penthouses of the last ten years. Nevertheless, there were subtle differences. The food tasted strange. There were breakdowns in the electrical and air-conditioning systems. Hughes was a creature of habit. The surprise alterations in his routine unnerved him, intensified his already overactive anxieties, and hastened his decline. He stopped eating and drinking. Day by day, he wasted away. When he was finally loaded onto the plane for the flight to Houston, a ninety-three-pound skeleton clinging to life, it was too late. Fifty-five days after the move to Mexico, Howard Robard Hughes, Jr., was dead.

*The relocation effort was aborted the following year when a Houston newspaper published an article disclosing that Summa officials were considering the acquisition of a condominium. It was the kind of security breach that never seemed to occur when Hughes was in command of his organization.

CHAPTER 25

THE FIGHT
FOR THE FORTUNE

COVER-UP

THE jet carrying Howard Hughes from Mexico on April 5, 1976, touched down at Houston Intercontinental Airport at 1:50 P.M. Orderlies lifted his body out of the cabin and placed it in a green and white ambulance for the drive to Methodist Hospital, twenty-eight miles to the south. That morning an official of the Howard Hughes Medical Institute had telephoned Dr. Henry D. McIntosh, chairman of the hospital's department of internal medicine, to say that Hughes was seriously ill in Acapulco and would be flown to Houston that afternoon for hospitalization.* Methodist agreed to set aside a heavily guarded room for him where he was to be admitted under the pseudonym of John T. Conover. A handful of the hospital's staff was told the identity of the prospective patient; the rest knew only that he was a very important man.

The ambulance came to a stop at a rear dock of Methodist Hospital at 2:50 P.M. and Hughes's body was carried to the morgue in the basement. Under the supervision of Dr. Jack L. Titus, the hospital's chief pathologist, a medical team conducted a preliminary examination. Titus noted that the body was "remarkably emaciated and dehydrated."[1] Because there was "no evidence of rigor mortis," and based on other information he had been given, Titus concluded that Hughes had died less than three hours earlier.[2] Pending final arrangements, the body was placed in a cooler and guards stationed outside the laboratory door.

Since Hughes had died in Texas and "no physician licensed in Texas was

---

* Methodist Hospital is the teaching affiliate of the Baylor College of Medicine in Houston, one of a select circle of institutions to receive research grants from the Howard Hughes Medical Institute.

in attendance prior to death," Titus telephoned the office of Dr. Joseph A. Jachimczyk, the medical examiner of Harris County, to report the death, and the hospital sought to notify the next of kin.[3] Hughes's closest living relative was Annette Gano Lummis, his eighty-five-year-old Houston aunt and younger sister of his mother.* Although Mrs. Lummis had lived with Hughes and his parents for a time when he was growing up, and later looked after him following his mother's death, she had not seen her reclusive nephew since his triumphant return to Houston in 1938 following the around-the-world flight. She had corresponded with him briefly afterward until Hughes insisted that she route her personal letters to him through Nadine Henley at Romaine Street, and then she stopped writing. "I just wrote him that wasn't the way I was corresponding," she said later.[4] Other than a two-page telegram she received in 1970, congratulating her on her eightieth birthday, Mrs. Lummis never heard from her nephew. When the hospital informed her of his death, Mrs. Lummis asked her son, William Rice Lummis, who was, coincidentally, a partner in the law firm of Andrews, Kurth, Campbell & Jones, which had represented Hughes and his father before him for so many years, to make the funeral arrangements.

By late afternoon, rumor had spread through the hospital that Howard Hughes's body was in the morgue and a band of reporters had gathered outside the pathology laboratory. That night, a Methodist spokesman confirmed that Hughes had died earlier that day aboard a private plane carrying him from Mexico to Houston, but provided no details about his illness or the cause of death. "We were aware it was an emergency," the spokesman said, "but we did not know the nature of the problem and we still don't."[5] All questions were referred to a Hughes spokesman in Los Angeles.

While Hughes's death was being announced in one part of the hospital, Dr. Jachimczyk, the medical examiner, was sequestered with a group of Methodist physicians, veteran Hughes lieutenants, and Will Lummis in another office. Dr. Jachimczyk felt that an autopsy should be performed. With the family's permission, the autopsy could be done at Methodist by the hospital's pathologists, instead of transporting Hughes's body to the county morgue. The Hughes organization had hoped there would be no post mortem examination, and someone had told Lummis after he arrived at the hospital that Hughes had said he wanted to be cremated. When the meeting broke up, Lummis left for the evening to ponder Dr. Jachimczyk's suggestion and to discuss it with his mother.

The next morning he returned to the hospital and signed the form author-

---

*Hughes had no children by his two marriages. He had no brothers or sisters. His father had one sister, Greta Hughes Witherspoon, who died on February 21, 1916, at the age of forty-eight, and two brothers, Rupert Hughes, who died on September 9, 1956, at eighty-four, and Felix Hughes, who died on September 9, 1961, at eighty-six. Hughes's mother, Allene Gano Hughes, had two sisters and a brother. One sister, Martha Gano Houstoun, died on May 22, 1961, at sixty-eight, and her brother, Richard C. Gano, Sr., died on May 1, 1969, age eighty. Only her youngest sister, Annette Gano Lummis, survived him.

izing the autopsy. It was performed that afternoon by Dr. Titus and his associates while Dr. Jachimczyk, one of his assistants, and Dr. Wilbur S. Thain and Dr. Lawrence Chaffin, the two Hughes doctors who were with him when he died, and Dr. Henry McIntosh looked on. Later that afternoon, Ted Bowen, the hospital's president, told reporters who were crowded into a hospital briefing room: "The preliminary autopsy findings demonstrated that Mr. Hughes died of chronic renal disease."[6] Dr. McIntosh elaborated:

Renal means kidney, two of them. Chronic means a long time. And failure means that they don't work so well. The kidneys have the responsibility of getting rid of waste products the body makes, and they come out in the urine. The kidneys are marvelous organs, and when they don't function very well, the waste products accumulate. And unless something is done about it, the patient will die. And this is what I think has happened.[7]

At the press conference or in interviews, those who observed the autopsy or were connected with the Hughes organization sought to convey the impression there was nothing unusual about Hughes's recent lifestyle or about the circumstances of his death. Dr. McIntosh described Hughes's body as "that of a man who had lived a full life."[8] Dr. Jachimczyk assured newsmen that Hughes was simply a routine case for his office. "As far as I am concerned, it's an ordinary death," he said. "It's an extraordinary individual involved, perhaps, but the death is like any other death."[9] In answer to speculation about Hughes's mental competency, Dr. Chaffin told a reporter that Hughes's brain was not only healthy, but was "the brain of a very smart man."[10] Another member of the autopsy team discounted rumors about Hughes's long fingernails: "He had lovely, long fingers—the fingers of an artist."[11] Chuck Waldron, one of Hughes's personal aides, scoffed at suggestions that Hughes might have been mentally ill: "I can assure you he was a normal man. Just like you and me."[12]

At the press briefing, Methodist officials disclosed that Hughes weighed only ninety-three pounds at death, but other, far more telling details about his physical condition were not made public. Nor were the results of a toxicological study that followed. No mention was made of the bed sores on his back, of his separated left shoulder, or of the open sore on the left side of his head where he had knocked off a tumor a few weeks before. No mention was made that X-rays taken during the autopsy showed fragments of hypodermic needles broken off in both arms. No mention was made of the needle tracks along his arms and thighs or of the extraordinarily high level of codeine in his body. Indeed, the formal autopsy report stated that the body contained only "minimum amounts of codeine."[13] In truth, Hughes had a potentially lethal amount of codeine in him when he died. Not only was this information withheld from the news media, but much of it was withheld from Hughes's family. Lummis was not shown the X-rays of Hughes's arms or told of the high amount of codeine. The secrecy which had maintained the Hughes legend when he was alive was at work still, preserving it and safeguarding the empire now that he was gone.

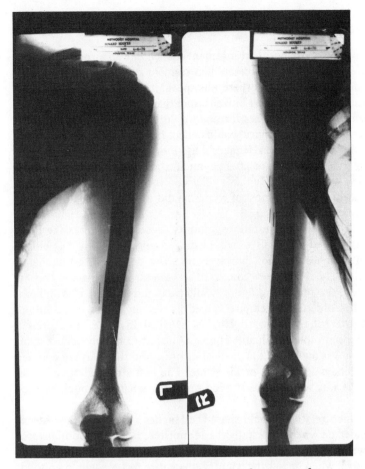

X-ray taken during Hughes's autopsy showing fragments of
hypodermic needles broken off in his arms.

Late on the afternoon of the autopsy, George H. Lewis & Sons Funeral
Home picked up Hughes's body at the hospital and prepared the $8,152 seam-
less casket that had been selected for his funeral. On Wednesday morning,
April 7, 1976—less than forty-eight hours after his death—Hughes was buried
as he had lived, privately, in a family plot alongside his father and mother in
century-old Glenwood Cemetery, amid the moss-draped oak trees. About
twenty persons, mostly distant relatives, attended the simple, eight-minute
graveside service and listened to the Very Reverend Robert T. Gibson, dean
of Christ Church Cathedral, the Episcopal church that Hughes had attended
as a child, read from the church's *Book of Common Prayer.* Quoting from
Chapter 14 of the Book of John, he said, "We brought nothing into the world
and it is certain that we will take nothing out."[14] A few hours after the funeral
caravan pulled out of the cemetery, just west of downtown Houston, and into
the morning rush-hour traffic, the flowers began to arrive for his grave: red
roses sent anonymously; a single red rose from "Karen, California"; a five-

foot-high yellow and white floral arrangement shaped like an airplane, its nose tipped toward heaven, from an unidentified resident of California.[15]

Even before Hughes's burial there was speculation that the industrialist, one of the nation's two wealthiest citizens, had died without a will.[16] If true, the chief beneficiary of the Hughes fortune would be the United States Treasury. The Internal Revenue Service would collect more than 60 percent of the estate, a last, huge irony given Hughes's life-long obsession with avoiding taxes. The remainder of the estate, after payment of expenses, claims, legal fees, and other costs, would go to Hughes's relatives, the people he had shunned the last forty years of his life, most of whom he did not know or had not seen since they were children.

The overall value of the estate was murky at best. For years the news media had exaggerated Hughes's worth, placing it anywhere from $1.5 billion to $2.5 billion. Hughes was not, however, by strict definition, a billionaire. That is, if all his assets had been converted to cash at any one time, and his debts subtracted, the remaining figure would have fallen short of $1 billion. Even so, Hughes did rule an empire valued at well in excess of $1 billion, because, as trustee of the Howard Hughes Medical Institute, he exercised control over the enormously valuable Hughes Aircraft Company. The aircraft company's stock was owned by the medical institute and thus was not counted as part of his personal holdings or his estate. The best strict estimate is that when he died he was worth at least $600 million, perhaps as much as $900 million.

Exactly which relatives would share the Hughes millions in the absence of a will depended on where the estate was administered. If it was administered under the laws of California or Nevada, the states where Hughes had lived from 1925 to 1970, when he left the country, the entire fortune would go to his closest living relative, Annette Gano Lummis. If the estate was administered under the laws of Texas, where Hughes had lived until he was twenty years old, and which he had always listed as a residence on various legal documents, the Hughes millions would be distributed among maternal and paternal relatives, down to the level of first cousins once removed. On Hughes's mother's side, there were twelve first cousins, the children or grandchildren of Allene Hughes's other sister and brother, both dead. On Hughes's father's side, there were three first cousins, all the grandchildren of Rupert Hughes, a brother of Howard Hughes Sr. Hughes's heirs ranged from affluent professionals to blue-collar workers.* Because Hughes had isolated himself from the families of both

---

*The relatives, most of whom lived in Houston, had all maintained a low profile over the years and never advertised their relationship to Hughes. Three heirs were the children of the late Mrs. Martha Houstoun, a younger sister of Hughes's mother: Mrs. Janet Davis, the wife of a Houston die-casting company executive; Mrs. Sara Lindsey, wife of a Houston insurance company executive; and James P. Houstoun, Jr., also a Houston insurance executive. Another son, William G. Houstoun, Sr., had died in 1967 at age forty and his share would go to his four surviving children, John M. Houstoun, Margot F. Houstoun, James W. Houstoun, and Richard Gano Houstoun, all of Houston. Five other maternal heirs were the children of Hughes's late uncle

The funeral. Second from left is Annette Gano Lummis, Hughes's eighty-five-year-old Houston aunt. *Wide World Photos*

his mother and father, and over the years had on a number of occasions announced his intention to leave his estate to medical research, none of the relatives had much notion of a Hughes inheritance. But when no will was produced in the days following Hughes's death, the relatives began to doubt that one existed. Within the empire, the failure to file a will presented a potential management crisis: confusion among the empire's 12,000 employees, who were unsure exactly who was in charge. With the empire adrift in uncertainty, the ruling triumvirate—Bill Gay, Chester Davis, and Nadine Henley —forged an uneasy alliance with the relatives to assure control of the organization. The maternal relatives themselves had closed ranks behind William Lummis, who would represent them.

Lummis was described as a "hard-working lawyer who did his job and did not make a lot of noise about it."[17] He had joined Andrews, Kurth after

Richard Gano, Sr. They were William K. Gano, on disability pay from his job at a Houston iron works; Richard C. Gano, Jr., of Anaheim, California, a longtime Hughes Aircraft Company employee; Mrs. Doris Gano Wallace, a Houston schoolteacher; Mrs. Annette Gragg, wife of a Houston architect; and Howard Hughes Gano, a Houston lawyer. The paternal heirs were Mrs. Elspeth De Pould of Rocky River, Ohio, the wife of a manager of a major construction company; Mrs. Agnes Roberts of Olmstead Falls, Ohio, the wife of an engineer; and Mrs. Barbara Cameron of Los Angeles, the wife of a real estate broker. The number of those who would share in the estate eventually was expanded to twenty when Mrs. Annette Lummis shared her inheritance rights with her four children. In addition to William Rice Lummis, the partner in Andrews, Kurth, her children were Mrs. Allene Russell, the wife of a Boston physician; Mrs. Annette Neff, wife of a Houston banker; and Dr. Frederick Rice Lummis, Jr., a Houston physician.

graduating from the University of Texas Law School in 1953 and had married the daughter of Palmer Bradley, a senior partner. In the years that followed, Lummis handled none of Hughes's personal business, and only "a few workmen's compensation lawsuits" for the Hughes companies back in the mid-1950s.[18] Even Andrews, Kurth's role in Hughes's legal affairs had been greatly diminished following Hughes's feud with Raymond Cook over control of the Howard Hughes Medical Institute in 1968 and 1969, and the emergence of Chester Davis as Hughes's chief lawyer after the industrialist was moved out of the country in 1970.*

With Hughes executives, lawyers, and relatives in seeming harmony, coordinated legal moves were made in Houston, Los Angeles, and Las Vegas on the same day, April 14, to assure tight control of the empire. Andrews, Kurth filed an application in Harris County Probate Court in Houston seeking appointment of Lummis and his mother as temporary co-administrators of the Hughes estate in Texas. Davis & Cox filed a similar petition in Los Angeles County Superior Court requesting the appointment of Richard C. Gano, Jr., as special administrator of the Hughes estate in California, and Andrews, Kurth, and Davis & Cox, and Morse, Foley & Wadsworth filed a petition in the Eighth Judicial District Court in Las Vegas seeking the appointment of the First National Bank of Nevada—as "the nominee of Annette Gano Lummis"—to serve as special administrator of the Hughes estate in Nevada.[19]†

In legal papers filed in Houston, simlar to those filed in Los Angeles and Las Vegas, Lummis and his mother said they believed that Hughes had "executed an effective last will and testament which, however, has not yet been located," and that they sought a "temporary administration of the estate for the purpose of facilitating location of said will."[20] In addition, they said their appointment was "essential to avoid any loss or waste to the properties comprising the estate" and to allow for continuity in the operation of Hughes's various businesses and for "the conservation, preservation and maintenance of the assets."[21] Judges in all three state courts—Kenneth P. (Pat) Gregory in Houston, Neil A. Lake in Los Angeles, and Keith C. Hayes in Las Vegas—routinely issued orders appointing Lummis and his mother administrators in Texas, Gano in California, and the First National Bank of Nevada in Nevada. (Lummis later was named co-administrator in Nevada)

---

* Raymond A. Cook and his wife Florence were killed in a car–bus collision in Brenham, Texas, on August 9, 1975. According to Brenham police, the bus struck Cook's car broadside when Cook failed to stop at an intersection. Cook was sixty years old. J. Richard Gray, another partner in Andrews, Kurth, who had represented the industrialist in many of his Las Vegas business deals, died, like Hughes, aboard an airplane. Gray suffered a heart attack on May 7, 1975, while in a plane flying over New Mexico. He was forty-nine years old.

†Under California law, the administrator of an estate must be a resident of the state. Richard C. Gano, Jr., a cousin of Lummis, lived with his wife in a modest bungalow in Anaheim. He was the only cousin employed by a Hughes company, having worked for years at Hughes Aircraft Company.

William Rice Lummis, Hughes's first cousin and son of Annette Lummis, the heir around whom other family members united after Hughes's death.
Wide World Photos

The old Hughes hands launched a well-publicized search for the will which they privately feared, or knew, did not exist. A safe and the filing cabinets at Romaine Street, locked since Hughes's visits to the communications center in the 1940s, were broken open. Davis & Cox systematically questioned every lawyer, and the partners of lawyers, who worked for Hughes. Locksmiths were engaged to open a safe, a wine vault, and miscellaneous drawers and files at the home of Neil S. McCarthy, the long-deceased Los Angeles lawyer who had severed his ties with Hughes back in 1944.

Discovery at Romaine Street of "a set of two duplicate keys on a ring," each imprinted with the number 47 and believed to fit a safe-deposit box, triggered a Cinderella-like search.[22] The scores of banks with which Hughes had dealt were contacted about safe-deposit box number 47, about long-forgotten accounts, or other safe-deposit boxes, either in his own name or in the names of nominees. The will hunt reached from the Arizona Trust Company in Tucson to the Chase Manhattan Bank in New York.

Also combed were places where Hughes had spent time in years gone by, or where there might be a Hughes connection—the Columbus Hotel in Miami, the Fairmont in San Francisco, the Goldwyn studios in Hollywood, the Hughes Aircraft Company plants, the Mizpah Hotel in Tonopah, the Waldorf-Astoria in New York, the Racquet Club in Palm Springs, and even, oddly, the Franciscan Monastery in Washington, D.C.[23] Dozens who knew or worked for Hughes, and people employed by people employed by Hughes, and their friends and family members, were interviewed, from the secretary of Frank Andrews, the senior partner in Andrews, Kurth who had died in 1936, to the widow of Neil McCarthy. A classified advertisement was placed in about forty newspapers around the country to elicit leads: "Howard Robard Hughes Jr., son of Howard Robard Hughes Sr., and Allene Gano, born Dec. 24, 1905, died April 5, 1976. Anyone having information regarding this death, please phone 213–986–7047."[24]

Not surprisingly, such a search for the last will and testament of the nation's wealthiest eccentric yielded many a bizarre tip. A Santa Monica woman, who predicted earthquakes according to a mathematical formula "based on a very ancient, archaic method of computing," calculated that the will lay in an airplane then in Acapulco but soon scheduled to fly to Bolivia.[25] Her deduction, she said, had been confirmed by a psychic, who, more precisely, had mentally located the will "in the plane's ceiling, behind a sliding panel almost all the way back in the tail section."[26] A weathered old man in tattered clothes and tennis shoes made periodic visits to the district court clerk's office in Las Vegas, insisting that he had been Howard Hughes's secret financial adviser.

The Hughes organization had hired its own psychic—Peter Hurkos. A one time Dutch house painter, Hurkos, or Peter Van der Hurk, as he had been known, billed himself as a psychometrist, "one who divines facts about an object or its owner by touching or being near the object."[27]

There are several versions of Hurkos's role in the great will search, but one part is generally agreed on. Many Hughes lieutenants supposedly still believed that the will rested in a long-forgotten safe-deposit box in a Houston bank. Hurkos advised that he could pinpoint the location of the document if they provided him with photographs of Houston banks and an article of Hughes's clothing. Andrews, Kurth detailed one of its lawyers and a secretary to photograph all the bank buildings in Houston. At one of them, a suspicious bank official notified the FBI about the amateur photographers. Eventually, the photographs and a pair of Hughes's shoes were delivered to Hurkos. But, no, the shoes would not do, said Hurkos. They had never been worn; indeed Hughes had worn no clothing in years—the fact that finally led Hurkos to withdraw the application of his psychic powers.*

Efforts to locate a will were not going well. The only evidence of wills related to those that veteran Hughes associates had long known about. The first, of course, was the will Hughes had executed in 1925, just before his marriage to Ella Rice. That will was believed to have been destroyed following the couple's divorce, and a new draft prepared in 1929. But there is no indication that the second was signed, and, in any event, no copy exists. A third draft will, prepared in 1938, which may or may not have been signed,

---

*Peter Hurkos numbered among his acquaintances John H. Meier, the "scientific adviser" to Hughes who fled to Canada after supervising the sale of mining claims to the industrialist. When a representative of the Texas attorney-general's office interviewed Hurkos in connection with the Hughes estate proceedings, Hurkos tape-recorded the interview and, according to law enforcement authorities, the tape found its way to Meier at his home in Vancouver.

apparently was placed in safe-deposit box number 3102 in the First National Bank of Houston. But Hughes's personal files contained a copy of a telegram sent to the bank on May 29, 1944, requesting that the bank "please make forceable entry into my deposit box number 3102 and send contents to me. . . ."[28] By 1976, that safe-deposit box had been rented to other bank customers for more than a quarter of a century and no trace remained of the documents put there in 1938. Finally, there was the draft will that Nadine Henley had typed and retyped as Hughes continually revised it from 1944 to 1950. That document, locked away for many years in a safe-deposit box in a Hollywood bank, then transferred to Romaine Street by Nadine Henley, had never been signed. And that was it for the Hughes wills—one signed in 1925 and presumably destroyed; one drafted in 1929, but no evidence it was ever signed, and in any event now lost; one prepared in 1938, but again no evidence it was signed, and which was also lost; and another prepared in the 1940s but never signed.

While the Hughes organization looked for a will that did not exist, in Austin, Texas, John L. Hill, the fifty-two-year-old state attorney-general, a modestly liberal—by Texas standards—populist politician with aspirations for higher office, decided that he would take an interest in the Hughes estate. If Hughes was a legal resident of Texas—and after all, he was born and raised in Texas, the source of all his wealth was a Texas-based company, and he died in Texas—then Texas was entitled to collect tens of millions of dollars in inheritance taxes. A highly regarded lawyer, Hill soon pulled together a team of attorneys led by a tenacious young assistant, Rick Harrison, chief of the taxation division in Hill's office. Within days lawyers quietly fanned out across the country to collect information on the financial holdings, business interests, and personnel of the Hughes empire. On June 10, 1976, Hill officially staked out Texas's claim, filing papers in Harris County Probate Court saying that Hughes's "domicile" throughout his life was Texas and that Texas was entitled to a "sizeable tax."[29]

About the same time that John Hill made his decision in Austin, Avis Hughes McIntyre, the stepdaughter of Hughes's uncle, Rupert Hughes, reached a similar decision at her home in Montgomery, Alabama. A sophisticated and witty woman of seventy-five, accustomed to the gracious and more civilized lifestyle of another era, Mrs. McIntyre had concluded, when it appeared that Hughes had not left a will, that it was time "to enter the rat race" with other Hughes relatives to win a share of the fortune.[30] She telephoned her lawyer, a family friend of twenty years, and instructed him to join the growing field of litigants in the Hughes estate on behalf of herself and her brother, Rush Hughes.

The lawyer was George W. Dean, Jr., who had practiced law in his hometown of Montgomery until 1966, when he moved to Destin, Florida, and settled both his family and law practice into a rambling home along the edge of Choctawhatchee Bay, an arm of the Gulf of Mexico about forty-five miles east of Pensacola. Blessed with an incisive mind, and a retentive memory that rivaled Hughes's, Dean was regarded by colleagues and adversaries alike as a brilliant legal strategist. He had been the architect of a precedent-setting civil rights legal action in the mental health field in which a United States district court ruled for the first time that persons committed involuntarily to state institutions for the mentally ill or the mentally retarded had a "constitutional right" to treatment.[31] At age forty-seven, Dean, the epitome of Old World courtliness and southern charm, possessed two characteristics that would quickly set him apart from traditional Hughes attorneys: an unflagging compulsion to seek out the truth, regardless of the consequences, and to lay it out for all to see; and an engaging sense of humor marked by, as one associate put it, a keen appreciation of the general absurdity of life.

It was no small task that Avis Hughes McIntyre had given Dean. Her inheritance rights, and those of her brother, were not clear-cut. Neither had been born into the Hughes family and neither had been adopted.

Rupert Hughes had been married three times. He and his first wife, Agnes Wheeler, had a daughter, Elspeth, born in 1897. The couple was divorced and in 1908 Rupert married Adelaide Manola Bissell, an actress with two young children by a previous marriage that had also ended in divorce. They were Avis, born in 1900, and Rush, born in 1902. Elspeth, Rupert's daughter, lived with her mother, who also remarried, in Washington, D.C., and later in Cleveland. Avis lived with her mother and Rupert. Rush lived with his father, George Bissell. About three years after Rupert and Adelaide were married, they discovered to their alarm that Rush had been placed in the House of Providence, an orphanage in Syracuse, New York. Quickly securing his release, they brought the boy to the family home, then in Bedford Hills, New York. Although Rupert wanted formally to adopt Avis and Rush, their father refused to permit it, as Mrs. McIntyre recalled.[32] Nevertheless, Rupert raised them as his own. They were known as Avis and Rush Hughes, and Rupert sent them to private schools—Avis to the exclusive Foxcroft School in Middleburg, Virginia, and Rush to the Mercersburg (Pennsylvania) Academy. Late in 1923, their mother Adelaide, in ill health and low spirits, set out alone on an around-the-world cruise to "regain her health and courage," as Rupert said later.[33] She found neither and while her ship was anchored in Haiphong harbor, Adelaide hanged herself in her cabin. Less than a year after her suicide, the fifty-two-year-old Rupert married for a third time, to Patterson Dial, an aspiring twenty-two-year-old fiction writer, two years younger than Avis. Avis was upset that Rupert had married "such a young woman," and after meeting Patterson and Rupert in New York one day in 1924, she never again saw or talked to Rupert, although they did occasionally exchange letters.[34] Rush Hughes, who became a radio announcer for NBC and played bit parts in the movies, saw Rupert on only a few occasions after Rupert's marriage to Patterson.

But establishing her right to inherit a share of the Hughes estate was not Mrs. McIntyre's only interest. For some time she had been intrigued about

Hughes's mysterious last years and why his movements had been cloaked in secrecy. She asked Dean to investigate. That assignment would prove no less challenging.

THE MORMON WILL

Late in the afternoon of April 27, 1976—before Dean and Hill began, independently, to piece together the story of Howard Hughes's life—a public relations officer of the Church of Jesus Christ of Latter-day Saints returned to his twenty-fifth floor office in the church's world headquarters building in Salt Lake City and found a Mormon church envelope on top of his desk. The handwritten address on the envelope said: "President Spencer W. Kimball, Church of Jesus Christ, Salt Lake City, Utah."

Inside the envelope was a slip of notepaper and a second sealed envelope. A handwritten message on the notepaper said: "This was found by Joseph F. Smith's house in 1972—thought you would be interested."*

The second, inner envelope bore this handwritten message:

Dear Mr. McKay,*

please see that this Will is delivered after my death to Clark County Court House, Las Vagas [sic], Nevada.

Howard R. Hughes.

And inside the second envelope was a three-page will written on yellow legal paper. It said:

Last Will and Testament.

I, Howard R. Hughes, being of sound and disposing mind and memory, not acting under duress, fraud or the undue influence of any person whomsoever, and being a resident of Las Vegas, Nevada, declare that this is to be my last Will and revolk [sic] all other Wills previously made by me—

After my death my estate is to be devided [sic] as follows—

first: one forth [sic] of all my assets to go to Hughes Medical Institute in Miami—

second: one eight [sic] of assets to be devided [sic] among the University of Texas —Rice Institute of Technology of Houston—the University of Nevada—and the University of Calif.

third: one sixteenth to Church of Jesus Christ of Latterday [sic] Saints—David O. McKay—Pre.

Forth [sic]: one sixteenth to establish a home for Orphan Cildren [sic]—

Fifth: one sixteenth of assets to go to Boy Scouts of America.

sixth: one sixteenth to be devided [sic] among Jean Peters of Los Angeles and Ella Rice of Houston—

---

*Joseph F. Smith became president of the Mormon Church in January of 1970, following the death of David O. McKay, the church's ninth president. Smith, whose grandfather Hyrum Smith was a brother of the church's founder, served as spiritual leader of the church until his death in July of 1972.

seventh: one sixteenth of assets to William R. Lommis [sic] of Houston, Texas—
eighth: one sixteenth to go to Melvin DuMar of Gabbs, Nevada—
ninth: one sixteenth to be devided [sic] amoung [sic] my personal aids [sic] at the time of my death—
tenth: one sixteenth to be used as school scholarship fund for entire Country—
the spruce goose is to be given to the City of Long Beach, Calif.
the remainder of my estate is to be devided [sic] among the key men of the company's [sic] I own at the time of my death.
I appoint Noah Dietrich as the executer [sic] of this Will—
signed the 19 day [sic] of March 1968

Howard R. Hughes.[35]

Two days after finding the will, Mormon church officials flew to Las Vegas and turned the document over to the district court. "How the envelope containing the papers was delivered to the headquarters of the church and who delivered it, we do not know," Wendell Ashton, the church's public-relations director, announced. "Circumstances surrounding delivery of the envelope frankly puzzle us after a day of extensive checking. Whether or not the will is the actual will of Mr. Hughes or is a hoax, we do not know."[36] Another church official explained that "we simply don't know whether it's a hoax or not. It came into our possession. We felt we should lay our cards on the table and let the proper authorities determine if it's authentic or a hoax."*[37]

Thereby began an elaborate hoax that would make Clifford Irving's "autobiography" of Hughes pale into insignificance. Although finally no more successful than Irving's caper, those who executed it would gain a certain satisfaction. Unlike Irving and his wife, whose misdeeds were swiftly ferreted out and who were convicted and sent to prison, the identity of the perpetrators of the counterfeit will not only would go undetected, but local, state, and federal law enforcement authorities made no serious effort to seek out and prosecute the forgers, a situation that differed markedly from the zealous pursuit of the Irvings by several law enforcement agencies. Moreover, the Mormon will hoax would prove immensely more costly than the Irving flimflam: teams of lawyers, legal secretaries, and private investigators spent millions of dollars contesting the will's authenticity and establishing it as a forgery.

---

*In the months after the Mormon will was made public, more than three dozen other "wills" of Howard Hughes were submitted to probate courts in Houston, Las Vegas, Los Angeles, and Wilmington. One left a portion of the Hughes fortune to ten "living Americans" identified only by their Social Security numbers, and to "blind and homeless children in America." Another bequeathed part of the estate to persons to be chosen at random each week and given $1 million, and yet another left $10 million to Clifford Irving and $5 million to his wife Edith. An Albuquerque, New Mexico, man who said he was the illegitimate son of Hughes and communicated with Hughes through a radio transmitter implanted in his head, filed a claim for the entire estate. And Terry Moore, the onetime Hollywood actress who had dated Hughes ("Howard was the best lover I ever had"), asserted an interest in the estate, claiming that they were married on a ship in 1949, that the marriage records were destroyed, that she gave birth to Hughes's child in Munich, Germany, in 1951, but that the baby, born prematurely, died within twenty-four hours.

In the beginning, many wanted to believe in the will, if for no other reason than the fairytale bequest it made to a Utah service station operator, Melvin Earl Dummar. A story headlined "$156 Million Good Deed" in the *Los Angeles Times* typified articles published by newspapers across the country:

A "good samaritan" deed eight years ago by a 31-year-old Utah service station owner may have earned him more than $156 million when he was named as an unexpected beneficiary in the purported last will and testament of the late billionaire Howard R. Hughes.

Melvin Dummar, owner of a service station in the small community of Willard, Utah, Thursday was named in the document as the beneficiary of a one-sixteenth share of Hughes's vast estate, estimated to be worth as much as $2.5 billion.

Reached at his home late Thursday by United Press International, Dummar said he had found a man who later said he was Hughes lying beside a road, bleeding from one ear, in January, 1968, and had lent him a quarter after giving him a ride to Las Vegas, where Hughes lived at the time.

Recalling details of the incident, Dummar said he had been driving in the Nevada desert—"in the middle of nowhere between Tonopah and Beatty—and I picked up this guy who I thought was a bum."

The man, Dummar said, had been bleeding from his ear and had been lying by the side of the road, wearing "some kind of baggy pants and tennis shoes."

Dummar said he offered to take the man, who he described as tall, skinny with a short, stubby beard and a big scar on the left side of his face, to a hospital, but the traveler refused.

As they drove along, Dummar said, the man told him he wanted to be driven to the Sands Hotel in Las Vegas.

"I dropped him off behind the Sands. He didn't tell me what happened. He didn't say nothing and wouldn't talk until we got to Las Vegas.

"That's when he told me he was Hughes."

Dummar, a Mormon, lived in Gabbs, Nev., in 1968 and worked in a magnesium mine there until moving to Willard about 18 months ago.

Dummar said the man asked "if I could loan him some money and I think I gave him a quarter."[38]

Melvin Dummar and his family adapted well to the publicity that gushed forth. Ronald B. Brown, whose mother was married to an uncle of Melvin's, flew to Willard, Utah, from his Bellflower, California, home to manage the descending hordes of newspaper, radio, and television reporters. A onetime country club greensman and marketer of new inventions, Brown made the arrangements and laid down ground rules for the media.[39] As he later described his role in dealing with reporters, "I just told them about—specifically I mentioned to them his [Melvin's] state, that they shouldn't be pressing because it would interfere with his emotional state at that point, and that if I noticed that it was pressing that I would completely cut off the interview at that time."[40]

Brown got together with Melvin's father and dashed off a rough manuscript of nearly one hundred typewritten pages recounting the early life of the Hughes heir, conferred with New York publishers, including a top official of

Melvin Dummar and his wife shortly before the trial to determine the validity of the will which named him as one of the beneficiaries of Hughes's estate.
Wide World Photos

one paperback publishing house, who sight unseen, Brown said, "expressed a real desire to have it."[41] Universal studios made arrangements with Melvin to produce a motion picture of his life—with suitable emphasis on the Hughes rescue. The studio flew Melvin and his second wife to Hollywood where they stayed at the Beverly Wilshire Hotel—"the fanciest place I ever saw," Melvin said—and signed his first wife to a contract giving her 0.25 percent of the film's profits.[42] Brown, Melvin, Melvin's father, and other family members discussed plans for "setting up a business to sell promotional items" using Melvin's name.[43] And after years of writing songs that no one would buy, Melvin, who looked like an overweight Glen Campbell, was suddenly beseiged by people who wanted to publish his music. His works included "A Dream Can Become a Reality," "Souped Up Santa's Sleigh," and "Rockview Blues," a song he wrote while driving a milk truck.[44]

Notwithstanding his fame as a Good Samaritan, Melvin Dummar had a curious background. The fourth of eight children of Arnold and Chloe Dummar, he was born on August 28, 1944, at Cedar City, Utah, and raised in Fallon, Nevada. In addition to his stint as a milk-truck driver, he sold cosmetics door to door and had worked in a magnesium mine in Nevada and in a lath and plaster business operated by his father in California. He had enlisted in the air force for four years in February 1963, but was discharged after only nine months because of his "emotional makeup."[45] In 1968, the same year that Hughes allegedly wrote his Mormon will, Melvin was arrested and charged with forging endorsement of a $251 payroll check issued by his employer, Basic Refractories Inc., in Gabbs, Nevada. When the jury could not reach a verdict, the judge dismissed the charge. A former drama student, Melvin had a knack for working his way onto television game shows. He appeared on "Let's Make a Deal" in 1970 "dressed as a hobo," and again in 1971 when, he said, he wore "orange pants and an orange sweatshirt with a string of oranges around my neck with an orange hat on it shaped like an orange."[46] Next it was "The New Price Is Right" and "Hollywood Squares" in 1974, and a repeat performance on "Let's Make a Deal" in 1975. On one occasion, Melvin used an assumed name—that of his wife's stepfather, Wayne Sisk—to go on "Let's Make a Deal," and he signed a statement saying: "I have not appeared as a contestant on any other audience participation program or game quiz show for the past year nor twice within the past five years nor have I participated on Let's Make A Deal within the past five years."*[47] As "Wayne Sisk" on "Let's Make a Deal," Melvin won an automobile, a freezer, and a range.[48] On "Hollywood Squares," he won a Pontiac Astre. Dummar's wife, Bonnie—it was the second marriage for both—was a thirty-year-old blonde, with waist-length hair, who had once served sixty days in the Orange County jail for welfare fraud. And one of Dummar's aunts had compiled material on Howard Hughes as research for a proposed magazine article.

Melvin Dummar and his family aside, there were many who fervently embraced the Mormon will and declared it authentic. "There's no question," announced Noah Dietrich, now eighty-seven, the former Hughes executive who had been fired after a bitter falling out with the industrialist in 1957 and who was named as executor in the Mormon will. "It's his handwriting and it's his signature. It's not just similar, it's the real thing."[49] A Bountiful, Utah, handwriting analyst who examined the will at the request of the Mormon church before it was turned over to the district court in Las Vegas, issued a preliminary opinion that "the document is genuine."[50] An autograph expert in New York declared that the Hughes signature on the will "is indeed genuine. . . . The signature looks exactly like Hughes and I think it would be exceedingly difficult to forge all aspects of that signature."[51] And two handwriting analysts retained by ABC News said they were sure that Hughes had written the will.

Even so, evidence mounted quickly that the will was a fraud. After examining the document, one after another of the nation's leading handwriting experts labeled it a forgery. The *New York Times* and the *Philadelphia*

---

*According to Dummar, Wayne Sisk said he, too, had met Howard Hughes. After once relating the story of picking up Hughes in the desert, Dummar said, Sisk replied that in the 1940s, while driving a cab, he had picked up Hughes "and that he was wearing a tuxedo and tennis shoes."

Inquirer printed extensive articles discrediting the document. Anyone who had studied Hughes's handwriting recognized that while the will's handwriting resembled Hughes's, it was at best an earnest imitation. And beyond the graphic similarities, there was no resemblance at all. The Mormon will contained errors in fact, spelling, grammar, and language usage completely at odds with Hughes's precise nature and the voluminous record of his known writings. The differences were most glaring when the Mormon will was placed alongside memoranda Hughes wrote both in the weeks immediately preceding and following the March 19, 1968, date on the alleged will. Although not a perfect speller, Hughes was as good as many who earn their living by the printed word. He turned out page after page of laboriously handwritten messages running to hundreds of words without making a single mistake in spelling or language usage, a pattern that suited his compulsive behavior. The 261-word Mormon will, on the other hand, was pockmarked by sixteen misspelled words—better than one in every twenty words—and another dozen errors in capitalization and style. There were mistakes that Hughes would never make, indeed, did not make before or after the date of the alleged will. The simplest words were spelled incorrectly: "Cildren" for "children," "devide" for "divide," "forth" for the number "fourth," "revolk" for "revoke," "amoung" for "among," "executer" for "executor." Even the name of his cousin, Lummis, was misspelled as "Lommis."* By referring to the Hercules as the "spruce goose," the will writer had used a term that Hughes abhorred. Those who worked for him never used it in his presence. In fact, Hughes did not own the Hercules on the date of the Mormon will. Title to the aircraft was held by the General Services Administration. On the envelope in which the will was delivered, Las Vegas was misspelled "Las Vagas."

In the face of evidence developed very early that the will was a hoax and that there had been violations of both state and federal criminal statutes, law enforcement authorities at every level either remained amazingly aloof or bungled what little work was done. Judges in state courts where the will was filed—but especially in Nevada, which retained custody of the document—failed to press criminal proceedings after their courts were drawn into the fraud. This indifference was best demonstrated when a full year went by before the Mormon will was submitted to the FBI for fingerprint analysis—a delay that almost certainly foreclosed any possibility of finding and prosecuting the persons who had committed the fraud. In April of 1977, when the Mormon will was belatedly forwarded to the FBI laboratories in Washington by Nevada attorney-general Robert List, FBI technicians found "eight latent fingerprints and two latent palm prints" on the will and the envelope in which it was delivered.[52] The FBI promptly reported its findings to List:

Eight latent fingerprints have been identified as finger impressions of Buddy Hardy. One of the latent palm prints has been identified as a palmar impression of Loretta Bowman. The remaining latent palm print was compared, insofar as possible with the submitted palm prints, but no identification was effected. Inasmuch as the submitted palm prints were not fully and clearly recorded, conclusive comparisons could not be made.[53]

Who was this Buddy Hardy, who left eight fingerprints and a palm print on the forged will and envelope? According to an FBI official, he was "a photolab technician in the police department in Las Vegas that was evidently photographing [the documents]."[54] And Loretta Bowman? She was the district court clerk in Las Vegas.

Throughout 1976, while law enforcement authorities displayed no enthusiasm for investigating the forged will, Melvin Dummar doggedly stuck to his twin stories: that he had absolutely nothing to do with writing the Mormon will or its mysterious appearance in the Mormon church headquarters, and

*The name of Melvin Dummar was also spelled incorrectly, "DuMar." In subsequent legal proceedings, Dummar testified that during the winter of 1975–76, a woman author of children's books stayed at his home one night when her car broke down. When the conversation turned to his failure to interest publishers in his music, Dummar said, the author suggested that he change the spelling of his name to "DuMar" because "it sounded more sophisticated" and might help sell his songs.

that he had picked up a man in the Nevada desert in 1968 who said he was Howard Hughes.

One night in January of 1968, "maybe an hour before the sun went down," Dummar said, he got into his blue, two-door, 1966 Chevrolet Caprice and left his home in Gabbs, Nevada, planning to drive to Las Vegas—an eight-hour trip—and then on to Cypress, California, to visit his daughter, who was living with his estranged wife.[55] When he reached Tonopah, Dummar said, he stopped for perhaps three hours, "got something to eat and gambled a little bit," and then, near midnight, continued on his way south toward Las Vegas.[56] On a lonely desert stretch of Route 95, between Tonopah and Beatty, about five miles south of the Cottontail Ranch—a legal bordello famous for its service to libidinous drivers on the dreary 450-mile trek from Las Vegas to Reno—Dummar pulled off the highway onto a rutted lane to relieve himself and rest for a few hours. He had gone "approximately a hundred yards," he said, when the headlights of his car picked up a man "lying on his stomach" in the middle of the road.[57] "When I got out of the car and started walking toward him," Dummar said, "he was trying to get up himself and he was on his hands and knees when I got to him and I just put my arm around him and helped him on up."[58] Dummar said the man, more than six feet tall, skinny, and over sixty years old, was wearing a sport shirt, slacks, and a pair of tennis shoes. He said he noticed blood coming out of the man's left ear—"the blood had dried. It wasn't fresh blood, but it had been on his collar of his shirt and partially on his neck or his hair."[59] Dummar said he also noticed a scar or "a discoloration of the skin" on the left side of his face, extending "from the temple down into his cheek."[60] His immediate reaction, Dummar said, was that the stranger "had been dumped there, that somebody had beaten him up and dumped him there."[61] During the two-hour drive to Las Vegas, Dummar said, his passenger said little. Dummar said he told the man that he once applied for a job at the Hughes Aircraft Company, and the man said "he was familiar with it because he owned it."[62] He said he was Howard Hughes. When they arrived in Las Vegas, Dummar said, "I asked him if he would like me to take him to a doctor or hospital. I could remember him telling me, no, that he would be all right."[63] Dummar said he let the man out of his car behind the Sands Hotel, handed him some change, and that he replied, "Thank you, Melvin."[64]

Although vague on many details of this experience, Dummar did not waver on the essential elements in the months following discovery of the Mormon will. Similarly, as late as December of 1976, he continued to insist that he played no part in writing the will or delivering it to the Mormon church. Questioned under oath during a deposition proceeding in December of 1976, Dummar's answers were unequivocal:

LAWYER: When was the first time you saw a copy of that purported will?

DUMMAR: . . . It was in April at the end of April and a news reporter from Salt Lake City . . . brought a copy of it up and gave it to me.

LAWYER: Prior to that time you had never seen a copy of the will?

DUMMAR: No, I hadn't.

LAWYER: Have you ever seen the original of it?

DUMMAR: No.

LAWYER: Let me ask you straightaway, Mr. Dummar, at the outset, did you write that will?

DUMMAR: No.

LAWYER: Did you have anything to do with the writing of it?

DUMMAR: No.

LAWYER: Did you write either of the envelopes and the messages, the message on either of the envelopes or the note which was included in the will. . . ?

DUMMAR: No.

LAWYER: Did you have anything to do with writing those notes or those envelopes?

DUMMAR: No.

LAWYER: Did you ever have any of those documents in your possession at any time?

DUMMAR: No.

LAWYER: Do you as of today, Mr. Dummar, have any idea how this purported will ended up on the desk of one of the Mormon Church employees on the 25th floor of the church office building headquarters?

DUMMAR: No.

LAWYER: You had nothing to do with getting the will there?

DUMMAR: No.

LAWYER: You never had your hand on this outside envelope?

DUMMAR: No.[65]

Even when Nevada attorney-general List informed Judge Keith Hayes in Las Vegas that the FBI had found Dummar's left thumb print on the outer envelope containing the Mormon will, Dummar continued to deny involvement.* "I talked to Melvin last night," one of Dummar's lawyers said following the attorney-general's disclosure. "He was crying and he told me again he didn't do it. He said if anybody anywhere has any information on how the will got to where it was found, he wishes they would come forward."[66] Harold Rhoden, the shrewd Los Angeles lawyer seeking to have the will validated, tossed out a possible explanation for the discovery of Dummar's thumb print on the envelope. "Suppose," Rhoden said, "this is a print not put there by

---

* Initially, for some strange reason, the outer envelope containing the Mormon will was turned over to the FBI for analysis, but not the inner envelope or the will itself. Nevertheless, there were occasional references in court proceedings and in the news media to an ongoing FBI study of the will. As late as January of 1977, Judge Keith Hayes observed that "there has been some delay in the FBI examination of the original will." In truth, the will still had not been delivered to the FBI. As the weeks slipped by, and as references to the FBI examination continued to appear, the FBI sent a letter on March 21, 1977, to Nevada attorney-general Robert List stating that "to date, the 'Mormon' will and the remaining envelope mentioned in your letter, have not been received in our Latent Fingerprint Section for processing. Upon their receipt, the necessary examination and comparisons will be conducted and you will be advised of the results separately." On April 12, 1977, the FBI sent another letter to List pointing out that the "Mormon" will and remaining envelope had still not been received. Late that month, the documents were finally turned over to the FBI in Washington.

human amino acid but by a Summa Xerox machine?"[67]

Two weeks later Dummar told Rhoden that he had been "lying" all along and Rhoden arranged for a special hearing before Judge Hayes to allow Dummar to recant his previous testimony in favor of a new story. Before a packed courtroom in the Clark County Court House on January 25, 1977, Dummar offered his revised version.

"About 10 o'clock in the morning" of April 27, 1976, Dummar testified, a stranger "between forty and fifty" years old, driving a blue Mercedes Benz, pulled into his service station in Willard, Utah.[68] "He asked me if I was Melvin Dummar. I told him yes," Dummar said.[69] The man said "he had been looking for me for some time."[70] Dummar said he did not ask the man's name, nor did he ask why he had been looking for him because "I didn't care," and besides, "lots of people come in and ask if I was Melvin Dummar."[71] For about half an hour, Dummar testified, the stranger followed him around while he waited on other customers and they chatted and eventually "the conversation led to what did I think of Howard Hughes dying?"[72] The stranger, Dummar said, told "me something about a will of Howard Hughes that had been found" in Salt Lake City in 1972.[73] "He said it was found somewhere around Joseph Smith's house, in his house or around it or by it."[74] Dummar said the man asked him, "wouldn't it be nice if someone like me was in a will of Howard."[75] Dummar said he told him "it would be nice."[76]

After the stranger disappeared without saying good-bye or explaining why he had been looking for him, Dummar said, he was "tinkering around" in the service station—"sweeping the floor, washing windows, I don't know what I was doing"—when he noticed an envelope on a counter top "right where my books and school work was."[77]* Dummar said the envelope bore this handwritten note: "Dear Mr. McKay, Please see that this will is delivered after my death to Clark County Court House, Las Vegas, Nevada. Howard R. Hughes."

Rather than tear the envelope open, "because I was afraid of what was in it and I didn't want anybody to know I opened it," Dummar testified, he steamed it open.[78] "I had an electric frying pan and I plugged [it] in, put water in it and turned it up as high as it would go."[79] He had opened other mail the same way, Dummar said, when he wanted to look "at letters my ex-wife had written to her boyfriend and what have you, before she could mail them."[80] When he got the envelope open, Dummar said, he found the will, read it, and returned it to the envelope. Then, he said, "I took the will back out of it because I couldn't believe what I read, and I read it again, and I done that several times."[81] Finally, he said, "I then took some other envelopes and used my finger and got some of the glue off of other envelopes and got them wet and got it transferred, the glue, onto this envelope and sealed it back up, and

---

* Dummar had been attending classes in business management at Weber State College in Ogden, Utah.

I put it in a little oven. I thought it would help seal it up."[82]

At that point, said Dummar, who was studying for the Mormon priest-hood, he decided to take the will to the president of the Mormon church, although he did not know his name. "I planned to take it and find out who the president of the church was . . ." he said.[83] "I was going to explain to the president of the church and have a word of prayer with him and tell him the story and kind of let him handle it and advise me, because I could trust him."[84]

Dummar said he waited for his wife to return with the car. When she came home, he told her he was going to school, but said nothing about the stranger who had left a will in the gas station that named him as a beneficiary of the Howard Hughes fortune. He did not mention the will, Dummar said, because his wife "had been kidding about Howard Hughes" since they were married in 1973.[85] On several occasions, he testified, she told him, "one of these days Uncle Howie is going to leave us in his will."[*][86]

Dummar said he left the gas station about 3 P.M., drove to Salt Lake City, went to the Visitor's Center on Temple Square, and asked where he could find the president of the church. He was directed to the twenty-fifth floor of the church office building across the street. On the way out of the Center he picked up a Mormon church envelope as a souvenir, he said. When he got off the elevator on the twenty-fifth floor, Dummar said he asked a woman receptionist if he "could see the president of the church."[87] Dummar said the woman told him the president "was in conference or he was busy at that time and I would have to wait."[88] He went down the hall-way to a restroom, Dummar said, took the Mormon church envelope he had picked up at the Visitor's Center, and wrote across the front: "President Spencer Kimball, Church of Jesus Christ, Salt Lake City, Utah." Next, he took a slip of notepaper and wrote, "This was found by Joseph Smith's house in 1972—thought you would be interested." He placed the envelope contain-ing the will and the note he had just written inside the Mormon church envelope addressed to President Kimball, "walked out, walked across the hallway, laid it on a guy's desk and left."[89]

Undaunted by Dummar's new story and the negative opinions of so many handwriting experts, Harold Rhoden plunged ahead in his attempt to have the will probated as authentic. A resourceful lawyer who had represented Dietrich in other lawsuits with Hughes, Rhoden had acquired a silent partner in the will campaign. In an arrangement most peculiar to a legal action that Judge Hayes had loftily declared "a search for truth," a Los Angeles stock market speculator was underwriting a substantial por-

---

*Dummar also testified that while he was talking on the telephone to the first newsman who called to tell him he was named as a beneficiary in the Hughes will, his wife called out, "Did Uncle Howard leave us anything?" Dummar testified he did not ask his wife how she knew about the will before he told her "because I love my wife."

tion of Rhoden's legal expenses.[90] He was Seymour Lazar, whose reputation for moving in and out of the market—in one year he traded more than $300 million worth of stocks by his own count—once prompted him to observe that "if I bought stock in the morning and still owned it at noon, it was a long-term investment for me."[91] This time, instead of playing the market, Lazar was gambling in the courtroom, confident that Rhoden would persuade a judge and jury that the Mormon will was genuine. The potential return on his investment was staggering. "It'll cost me $250,000 minimum," he told a reporter, "but I'm hoping for a good chunk of the attorney's fees . . . maybe in the eight-figure category, for my efforts."[92] Rhoden held out yet another possibility for his backer. "I'm told Lazar is very sophisticated financially," he said. "He could probably be very helpful in the management area [of Hughes] if we're successful."[93]

In addition to advancing cash, Lazar had spent weeks in Europe lining up handwriting analysts who would support the Mormon will, a global search made necessary when most of the recognized experts in the United States declared the will a fraud. Indeed, even handwriting authorities initially retained by Lazar in the United States had advised him and Rhoden that the Mormon will was a hoax. Such was the opinion—to name but one —of Lon H. Thomas, a former questioned-documents examiner for the United States Secret Service and retired chief of the documents section of the Central Intelligence Agency. In a December 9, 1976, letter to Rhoden, Thomas noted:

In response to request from Mr. Seymour Lazar on December 2, 1976, I have made an exhaustive and thorough examination/comparison of the handwriting on the documents listed below. He requested that an expert opinion be rendered as to whether the will was actually written by Howard R. Hughes or whether it is a forgery. . . . It is my opinion that the handwriting in the will and on the envelope was not written by Howard R. Hughes. It is my judgment that all of the questioned writing is a forgery.[94]

Rhoden's defense of the Mormon will was also complicated by Dummar's admission that he had handled the document and his amended story that it had been left at his gas station by an unidentified man driving a Mercedes Benz. But within days of Dummar's latest revelations, the mysterious stranger surfaced. Or at least a man who claimed to be the man who visited Dummar's service station and left Howard Hughes's will there. His name was LeVane Malvison Forsythe. He, too, had a curious background and told a curious story.

A burly, fifty-three-year-old construction worker, Forsythe had managed thrift stores for a mental retardation association in Los Angeles in 1969 and 1970, when he was fired following a stormy controversy with the association's board. He was accused of misusing the association's funds and placing phantom workers on the payroll, including an "investigator" who was paid in cash, or whose checks were cashed at taverns and liquor stores, sometimes by Forsythe himself, but whom no one had ever seen and Forsythe himself said he could not find. Parents of retarded children were angered that children were being paid six cents an hour for work they did, while Forsythe was drawing a $20,000-a-year salary.

Forsythe eventually drifted off to Poulsbo, Washington, where, by his own account, "for a year I did nothing but just fish," and then moved on to Anchorage, Alaska, where he became a part-owner of a construction company that was building a hospital.[95] When Rhoden introduced Forsythe as the man who had delivered the Mormon will to Melvin Dummar, Forsythe fashioned an extraordinary account of his life as a secret Hughes agent.

Forsythe said that shortly after meeting Hughes in 1946 or 1947, he began handling confidential assignments for him, delivering letters and packages around the country. Whenever Hughes had a mission for him, Forsythe said, the industrialist sometimes called his mother's home and left a message using the code name "Ventura."[96] Other times, Forsythe said, he met Hughes at different locations. In executing his missions, Forsythe said, he "generally used a fictitious name," and that over the years he assumed "more than fifty" aliases.[97] "I traveled all over the place," he said. "And everytime I was out I used different names. I had to look at the name on my suitcase to remember who I was supposed to be."[98]

Forsythe said he did not know the contents of the letters and packages he delivered, nor could he recall the names of any of the persons to whom he delivered them. But over a twenty-five-year period, he said, he made "approximately fifty of these secret deliveries."[99] In addition, Forsythe said, his "Uncle Claude" had served as a middleman, transferring packages from Hughes to Forsythe for delivery.[100]

"It was the latter part of July or August of 1972, or first part of August," Forsythe said, when he received a telephone call from Hughes asking him to come to the Bayshore Inn in Vancouver.[101] A short time later, he said, he flew to Vancouver, went to the hotel room that Hughes had given him, knocked on the door, and "was told to come in. . . . I opened the door. It was ajar; it wasn't completely closed."[102] There were no guards, no security system. Inside the room, he said, he found Hughes, wearing a bathrobe, seated in a chair, "a towel on his lap."[103] After exchanging some small talk, Forsythe said,

[Hughes] told me why I was there, why he had requested me to be there. . . . That he had a brown envelope that was laying on the table and he wanted me to—entrust me with it. And that I was—I would probably be retaining it for some time. . . . And wanted to know if I would accept that responsibility and that the document, the brown envelope, contained instructions in case of his death. And he asked me if I was willing to accept that responsibility. . . . I told him I would accept that responsibility.[104]

Forsythe said Hughes told him that "on no occasion was I to open that envelope until he had passed away. . . . He said [he] may call for it back. If he calls for it back, he didn't want it opened."[105] Forsythe said he kept the envelope for nearly four years and that on the day Hughes died, he opened it. Inside, he said, were three envelopes, one addressed to Chester Davis, one addressed to Mr. McKay, which contained the Mormon will, and a third envelope, marked "open this one," which contained $2,800 in $100 bills.[106] Forsythe said he then flew to Salt Lake City under an assumed name—"I didn't really want anyone to know LeVane Forsythe went to Salt Lake City. . . . I didn't want them to put me together."[107]

When he arrived at the airport, Forsythe said, he hired a driver and a car, which "was maybe two or three years old" and "could have been a Ford or Chevrolet."[108] When he got into the car, Forsythe said, he handed the man a slip of paper with Dummar's gas station written on it and asked the man if he knew where it was. He said "no, but he would find it."[109] They finally pulled into a gas station—Forsythe could not describe it, "to me it was not very impressive, you know what I mean? I mean it was not a new operation"—and someone pointed out Melvin Dummar to him.[110] Forsythe said he talked briefly with Dummar. "The exact conversation I don't recall," he said, "but I wanted to satisfy myself that he was Melvin Dummar. . . . I threw a couple of questions out at him. . . . 'What do you think of Howard Hughes' death,' or something of that nature."[111] Forsythe said he followed Dummar around for a while, then placed the envelope addressed to Mr. McKay on a counter top inside the service station, and left without mentioning the envelope to Dummar.

Forsythe's timely appearance on Dummar's behalf came six years after his provident appearance in another Hughes legal proceeding. Several days after Hughes had vanished from the Desert Inn in November of 1970, Hank Greenspun's *Las Vegas Sun* carried a front-page article indicating that the industrialist had been spirited away against his will and that there had been an eyewitness to the incident. At the time, of course, there was much confusion surrounding Hughes's disappearance, and the story of the eyewitness, at least in the beginning, seemed to lend credence to Bob Maheu's charge that Gay and Davis had seized control of the empire and fired him without Hughes's approval or knowledge. The eyewitness was none other than LeVane Forsythe.

In the stormy legal proceedings that followed, during which the Maheu and Gay–Davis factions battled for control of Hughes's Nevada properties, Forsythe volunteered his testimony to the district court in Las Vegas.* When

---

*Forsythe told the court that he had received a telephone call at his Torrance, California, home from a stranger who asked him to come to the Desert Inn for a special job—"primarily a little guard duty." Forsythe said he flew to Las Vegas the evening before Thanksgiving, played the slot machines in the airport, ate a grilled cheese sandwich, and drank a malt in the airport restaurant, and then took a cab to the Desert Inn. Shortly after midnight, Forsythe said, the stranger met him in the Desert Inn lobby and escorted him to the hotel parking lot, where he explained the nature of his assignment. Forsythe said the man told him: "We will be bringing someone out. I want you at this position. . . . All I want you to do is stand right here. I want you to keep anybody from interfering. We're going to be bringing someone out from the building. At this time there will be five vehicles parked at this area here. There won't be any more than that. When we bring the person out I want you to get in the fourth vehicle on the opposite side of the driver and ride with him until the destination." Forsythe told the court that the man gave him "a white button about . . . I would say inch and a quarter to inch and a half in diameter,

District Court Judge Howard W. Babcock eventually ruled that Maheu had been lawfully fired and that the proxy giving control of Hughes's Nevada properties to Gay, Davis, and Holliday was valid, he took special note of Forsythe's testimony:

Mr. Maheu . . . produced a witness, Mr. LeVane M. Forsythe, who testified concerning events which represent to his mind the departure from the Desert Inn Hotel of a person in the company of two others under circumstances which suggest mystery and intrigue. The Court observed the appearance, manner and demeanor of this witness. His testimony is not credible, it is not worthy of belief. The Court can only conclude that his testimony is fantasy, not fact.[112]

After Harold Rhoden, who was championing the Mormon will, discovered Forsythe, he counseled his prospective star witness that attorneys for the Hughes estate would attempt to discredit his story and assured Forsythe that he would produce evidence to back up his story on delivering the Mormon will to Dummar's gas station, according to a transcript of tape-recorded telephone conversations between the two men subsequently entered into the court record.

In one telephone conversation with Forsythe, Rhoden went to great lengths to assure Forsythe that Keith Hayes, the district court judge who was handling the Hughes estate in Nevada, and who would preside over the Mormon will trial, would welcome his testimony.

RHODEN: . . . We can use a judge in Las Vegas who will protect you. Who will see to
    it nothing bad happens. He's a judge extremely friendly towards us and wants that
    will to be admitted, and he'd welcome you with open arms—
FORSYTHE: Uh-huh.
RHODEN: Like a savior, because the guy's a Mormon.
FORSYTHE: Yeah.
RHODEN: To save this for his church—
FORSYTHE: Yeah.
RHODEN: So, he'd—he'd welcome you—
FORSYTHE: Yeah.
RHODEN: . . . He's very—the judge knows. He very much wants to hear your story—
FORSYTHE: Yeah.[113]

---

to wear on my left lapel and he told me that anybody else that was in this area were only to have the same buttons and anybody without them that I was to ask them in a nice way to leave the area." Forsythe said the man told him to report for duty in the parking lot at 1:30 A.M. and then disappeared. Forsythe said he returned to the Desert Inn casino, played the nickle slot machines for a while, and then at 1:30 "I put the button on and walked to the parking lot area." He said there were seven or eight other men there who also were wearing white buttons. Next, Forsythe told the court, he saw three men leave the building. "I seen two men, rather tall in stature, with one man in the center, and these two gentlemen were holding up the person in the center or walking him." Forsythe said he heard the man call out for "Bob Maheu or Pat Hyland." Forsythe said he heard another voice call out to him "get into a car," and he jumped into the fourth car in the caravan. They drove for some distance, Forsythe said, and then returned to the Desert Inn, where someone took his white button. He said he returned home on Thanksgiving Day and ate a turkey dinner with his mother.

FALLOUT

By the spring of 1977, as pretrial maneuvering over the Mormon will raged, Will Lummis moved to bring some order to the chaos that was the Hughes empire. He had the power to do so. In May of 1976, after Lummis had assumed responsibility for administering the Hughes estate, Summa Corporation, with the approval of its general counsel Chester Davis, petitioned the New Castle County Chancery Court in Wilmington to give Lummis control of the company's stock pending the outcome of the will search and the multiple estate proceedings. Chancellor William Marvel agreed and issued an order on May 11, 1976, authorizing Summa to recognize Lummis "as its sole stockholder."[114]

Shortly thereafter, Lummis gave up his law practice of twenty-three years as a partner in Andrews, Kurth, Campbell & Jones, and moved his family from Houston's quiet and exclusive River Oaks section to Las Vegas, there to become chairman of the board of Summa Corporation.* Although he received a salary of $180,000 a year as chairman, Lummis arranged with the probate courts to have that money deducted from his substantially larger fees as administrator of the estate. In keeping with his low profile, Lummis moved slowly among the ranks of veteran Hughes executives. He went far not to antagonize or challenge those who had run the empire for so many years. As a result, longtime Hughes lieutenants seriously underestimated the new man at the top. As one Summa executive put it later, "Lummis is a well-organized businessman who studies things thoroughly and then acts. I think they mistook his patience and good manners for weakness."[115]

Despite assurances to the contrary, Lummis soon realized that his famous cousin had been neither a financial genius nor in control of his business affairs when he died. Indeed, Summa was revealed as a business and financial nightmare. Nearly every operation was losing money, and corporate waste and profligate executive spending abounded. The company was spending upward of $2 million a year to lease and maintain more than a dozen aircraft around the world. Some of the planes had not been flown in years. Others were used to ferry Hughes executives and their families around the United States and Europe. Suites were maintained at the Essex House in New York and the Barclay in London for favored Hughes lieutenants. Summa built tennis courts, rented Mercedes Benzs, and handed out low-interest loans running into the hundreds of thousands of dollars to certain executives. For one fortunate executive, Summa bought his house, paid for a full-time maid, and even his food bills.

By the spring of 1977, Lummis had a firm fix on the extent of the corporate disaster over which he presided. The reports were devastating:

---

* At Hughes's death, the Summa Corporation board had five members—Bill Gay, Chester Davis, Nadine Henley, Levar Myler, and John Holmes. When Lummis became chairman of the board, two other members were added, Mickey West and William Rankin, a longtime Hughes financial officer.

From 1971 through the first nine months of 1976, Summa annually sustained net operating losses which totaled in excess of $131 million. The operations which sustained those losses were directed by Davis, Gay, and Henley. During the same period, none of the major gaming competitors of Summa in Nevada suffered any operating loss for even one of the years involved. . . . Primarily through the sale of TWA and the oil tool division, Summa had, or had received from January 1, 1966 to September 30, 1976, cash of approximately $715 million. But on September 30, 1976, its total liquid assets were only $142 million and by March 31 [1977], they had declined to $94 million. This lack of liquid assets threatened the very viability of Summa because it was only through interest earned on its cash that Summa had been able to continue to survive in the face of its regular operating losses.[116]

In December of 1976, after a series of disputes with Chester Davis, most notably over the role Summa should play in the administration of the estate, Lummis asked Davis to resign from the board. Davis refused. Now, in addition to the legal war over the legitimacy of the Mormon will, there would be a war for control of the empire, pitting the old Hughes hands against Lummis and the other Hughes relatives.

The showdown came in May of 1977. At a Summa board meeting on May 18, the Gay–Davis faction pushed through a resolution authorizing the "expenditure of up to $49,978,000" for a massive renovation program at the Desert Inn Hotel and Casino—a property that Summa did not own, but leased.[117] The resolution was approved 5 to 2—Gay, Davis, Holmes, Myler, and Henley voted in favor. Lummis and West cast the dissenting votes. Rankin abstained. At the same meeting, the Hughes veterans also rejected proposals by Lummis and his associates to retain Merrill Lynch, Pierce, Fenner & Smith —which had just completed an appraisal of Hughes's holdings for probate court—to act as financial advisers to Summa, and to declare a $32-million dividend to the estate in order to meet its mounting financial obligations. In addition, the old Hughes hierarchy also opposed setting aside funds for damages in the TWA lawsuit in Delaware and the Air West lawsuits in San Francisco. Judgments had already been entered against Hughes in both these cases. While the amount of the damages remained to be fixed, the total could reach $100 million.[118]

A week later, on May 26, Lummis removed Davis, Holmes, and Myler from the Summa board, reduced the size of the board from eight to seven directors, and elected as their successors Vernon C. Olson, Summa controller for a number of years, and E. R. Vacchina, a senior vice-president of the First National Bank of Nevada—special co-administrator of the Hughes estate in Nevada. Lummis also took over as chief executive officer of Summa, but allowed Bill Gay—who had been president since Hughes's death—to continue in that post. This was merely a reprieve for Gay, whose compensation in 1976 had been $360,523—including a bonus of $108,583 for a year in which Summa's losses exceeded $20 million. He, too, would soon be gone.

While Lummis was struggling in Las Vegas to reverse years of mismanagement in the empire, fend off challenges from veteran Hughes executives, and oversee the ongoing administration of the estate—including preparations for the upcoming Mormon will trial—George Dean and Texas attorney-general John Hill were preparing, independently, for a series of critically important pretrial proceedings that would disclose the results of intensive, year-long investigations.

Immediately after entering the Hughes estate litigation in 1976, Dean had recruited a team of lawyers to help him, first, to establish that his clients, Avis and Rush Hughes, were lawful heirs to the Hughes fortune, and second, to determine exactly what had occurred in the Hughes empire, especially during Hughes's last years. Dean's legal team included T. Norton Bond, a thirty-year-old Pensacola, Florida, lawyer with a disarmingly engaging manner and a bear-trap mind, and Robert H. Roch, who had graduated at the top of his Baylor University Law School class and was a founding partner in a young and aggressive Houston law firm, Fisher, Roch & Gallagher, which in the few years since it was formed had elevated personal injury law to an art form, its work distinguished by an unusual thoroughness in trial preparation. Dean and his associates had come up with an obscure legal concept known as "equitable adoption," which held that in certain circumstances children not formally adopted were entitled to the same inheritance rights as adopted or biological children. They contended that after Rupert Hughes had married his second wife, Avis and Rush, her two children by her first marriage, were known throughout their childhood as Avis and Rush Hughes. Because Rupert had treated them as his own—sending them to private schools, introducing them as his son and daughter, giving away Avis in marriage, and helping Rush obtain work—they were "equitably adopted children," Dean and his colleagues argued.[119] Although Rupert Hughes's three grandchildren from his first marriage at first challenged the concept, by the spring of 1977 Dean was near an understanding that Avis and Rush would share in the Hughes estate in the absence of a will.* Later that summer a new settlement agreement was drawn up providing for distribution of the Hughes fortune to the industrialist's only living aunt, Annette Gano Lummis, sixteen cousins on his mother's side of the family, and five cousins on his father's side of the family, including Avis and Rush.†

John Hill's staff had meanwhile accumulated a massive collection of Hughes's private papers and records, including 10,000 documents that had been seized by Mexican authorities at the Acapulco Princess Hotel shortly after Hughes died. To establish that Texas was Hughes's legal residence at the time of his death, and thus entitled to collect the state's 16-percent inheritance tax, Assistant Attorney-General Rick Harrison and his staff had been sifting

---

*Under the laws of intestate succession in Texas, 50 percent of an estate goes to relatives on the father's side of the family, 50 percent to relatives on the mother's side. Thus, only Rupert Hughes's three grandchildren from his first marriage had a direct interest in the claim by Avis and Rush Hughes.

†Appendix E.

through and cataloging the papers, which included memoranda to and from Hughes on many sensitive subjects, and the daily logs kept by the aides, with their enigmatic, coded entries such as "8 c," or "6 BB's," or "8 c's (23 left)," or "he took 6 of the 25 # 4's," or "E Day."

In May and June of 1977, a small army of lawyers representing various and often conflicting interests in the Hughes estate gathered in Los Angeles to take sworn testimony of the aides who had lived with Howard Hughes for nearly the last twenty years of his life. Using information gleaned from the empire's internal documents, Harrison, Dean, Roch, and other lawyers drew from the reluctant witnesses a picture of Hughes that had never before been documented: a Hughes who had been taking drugs for thirty years, who had consumed enormous quantities of narcotics without any medical reason, who had spent most of the last two decades of his life in bed or on his reclining chair, naked. The aides interpreted the cryptic references on the daily logs: "BB" stood for Blue Bombers, the name the aides gave to the blue-colored ten-milligram Valium tablets that Hughes took; "c" stood for codeine tablets he dissolved in water and injected; "# 4's stood for Empirin Compound No. 4 tablets, which also contained codeine; and "E Day" meant enema day. The aides acknowledged that the entries on the logs did not begin to tell the full story of Hughes's massive drug habit. As Waldron confided under questioning by Harrison:

HARRISON: And did you enter [in the logs] medication he received?

WALDRON: If he should ask if he took something and I said, "I don't know," he said, "Well, I just took two; go put it down." Then I would. Other than that, I wouldn't know whether he took any.

HARRISON: Did you only put down on the log medication when Mr. Hughes said to put it down?

WALDRON: That's correct. Or if I happened to be in the room and I saw him taking something. I would put it down so that the next person on would know that he had.[120]

In other words, if Hughes neglected to mention that he had administered himself narcotics or tranquilizers, or the aides did not happen to see him take the drugs, no record was made.

On June 26, 1977, the *Philadelphia Inquirer* published an article disclosing that over the years Hughes "was illegally given massive quantities of narcotics, tranquilizers and other pain killing drugs" and that "the drugs were obtained with prescriptions issued in the name of persons other than Hughes."[121] Four days later, the United States Drug Enforcement Administration launched an investigation of the Hughes drug-supply operation.

For the next few months the Texas attorney-general's office and the Dean team compiled evidence not only of Hughes's bizarre behavior, but of questionable financial, business, and legal transactions carried out in his name. Meanwhile, District Court Judge Keith Hayes in Las Vegas and Probate Court Judge Pat Gregory in Houston each set November 1977 trial dates in their respective courts to determine the authenticity of the Mormon will.

Jury selection began on Monday, November 7, in Las Vegas, and the following week in Houston. The Houston trial lasted until February 15, 1978, when the jury of three men and three women, after deliberating some ninety minutes, voted unanimously on the first ballot that the Mormon will was not written by Hughes and that Hughes was a legal resident of Texas at the time of his death, thereby requiring the estate to pay inheritance taxes. In Las Vegas, the trial progressed at a more leisurely pace, continuing through March, into May, and on to June 8, 1978, when the jury of five men and three women, after deliberating eleven hours, voted unanimously that Hughes did not write the Mormon will.

Only one serious challenge to the estate remained. The more than three dozen other "wills" submitted to various probate courts had been accepted for what they obviously were—hoaxes. But when Will Lummis began exerting a growing influence late in 1976 over the Hughes empire business operations—setting the stage for the break with Bill Gay and Chester Davis that would follow—the two veteran Hughes lieutenants responded by initiating their own will contest. In January of 1977, the Howard Hughes Medical Institute, which was controlled by Gay and Davis as members of a two-man executive commit-tee, filed a petition in Las Vegas district court seeking to have the Hughes fortune awarded to the medical institute even in the absence of a will.

In the petition, prepared by the medical institute's longtime Washington counsel Hogan & Hartson, the medical institute contended that Hughes "ex-ecuted a Last Will and Testament which was unrevoked and validly existing at the time of [Hughes's] death, the substance of which provided that the [Hughes] estate . . . be . . . bequeathed" to the medical institute.[122] The medical institute claimed that the will "has not yet been produced by the person or persons in possession thereof and the identity of such person or persons is presently unknown."[123] If the will cannot be found, the medical institute ar-gued, "then it has been lost or destroyed without the knowledge or consent of [Hughes]."[124] The institute asked the court for an opportunity to prove its theory and have the missing will "admitted to probate."[125] In effect, Gay and Davis boldly hoped to convince the court that somewhere there was a Hughes will, that the will was lost or destroyed, and that the "lost will" named the medical institute as the lone beneficiary of the Hughes estate.

The medical institute, of course, was the sole stockholder of Hughes Aircraft Company, whose sales now were running at $2 billion a year. As the institute mounted its claim, it was working quietly to resolve a critical dispute with the Internal Revenue Service. In December of 1975, the *Philadelphia Inquirer* disclosed that the IRS had neglected for six years to require the medical institute to abide by provisions of the 1969 Tax Reform Act, a failing that had saved the Hughes organization tens of millions of dollars. Under the reform act, the IRS was to designate the medical institute either a private

Jean Peters Hough arriving in Houston in January of 1978 to testify before a jury trying to decide Hughes's legal residence.
Wide World Photos

foundation or, what the institute desperately wanted, a public charity. If classed as a public charity like the United Fund, then it would be able to continue its free-wheeling practices of the past, unencumbered by the stringent regulations imposed on private foundations like Ford and Rockefeller. If classed as a private foundation, the institute's transactions would be subject to close scrutiny; business dealings between the charity and its founder, which had flourished in years gone by, would be barred; its investment income would be taxed; and it would have to sell much of its stock in Hughes Aircraft, since the reform act placed a 20 to 35 percent limitation on the amount of stock a private foundation could own in a single company. But to qualify as a public charity, the medical institute had to spend a fixed percentage of its assets (the value of its Hughes Aircraft stock) on medical research. And of the funds it had been receiving from the aircraft company, it had been spending on medical research less than one-tenth of the amount prescribed in Treasury Department regulations.

On March 6, 1976, the director of the IRS district office in Jacksonville, Florida, where the medical institute filed its annual returns, informed Hughes officials that the HHMI would be designated a private foundation. Disaster? Not quite. What happened next was a textbook study of the benefits flowing from the Hughes empire's special relationship with the nation's tax collector.

On March 27, 1976, the medical institute adopted what it called an "Expanded Medical Research Program," calling for sharply higher expenditures for medical research. Two days earlier, Hughes's lawyers had written a memorandum urging that "adoption of such a program at this time will help materially with the Court (if litigation ensues) and in any event will be helpful in our efforts to settle administratively with Treasury."[126] That year after Hughes died, Gay and Davis arranged for a Hughes Aircraft Company contribution to the medical institute of $15,750,000—more than the total amount the aircraft company had given to the medical institute over twenty of the preceding twenty-two years. In 1977, the aircraft company raised its contribution again, this time to $18,250,000.

In addition to stepped-up spending, the medical institute launched a publicity campaign that would have pleased Hughes. For two decades institute officials had seldom been available to the news media. Now they welcomed opportunities to discuss the works of the medical institute. In July of 1978, Dr. George Thorn, a professor emeritus at the Harvard Medical School and a member of the institute's medical advisory board since its inception, joined Gay and Davis on the executive committee, giving the ruling body an academic flavor, as its first outsider. In December of 1978, Thorn wrote an article for the prestigious *New England Journal of Medicine* cataloging past research efforts of the institute and painting a bright picture of the future.

At a time when funds for basic research are becoming more difficult to obtain, at a time when individual freedom by brilliant young scientists is more encumbered and particularly at a time when able scientists in clinical departments are unable to devote adequate time to important clinically related research, the unique policy and program of the Howard Hughes Medical Institute and the opportunities that it offers its scientific Investigators constitutes a national medical resource of unusual potential.[127]

Thorn also extolled the performance of the Hughes Aircraft Company:

In contrast to the portfolios of many research institutes, the Howard Hughes Medical Institute enjoys the possibility that its resources will continue to increase over the years through the skills of the Hughes Aircraft Company management chosen by the Company's Board of Directors, which the Institute has the right to designate. Thus, there is the opportunity of offsetting the erosion of endowment produced by continuing inflation.[128]

By that time, however, the IRS—at least the upper levels of the IRS bureaucracy—had already changed its mind, reversing the decision made by the IRS district director in Jacksonville two years earlier. In June of 1978, the institute was furnished a copy of a technical advice memorandum issued by the national IRS office which indicated that the HHMI was well on its way to being designated a public charity. Only a few technicalities remained. This reversal bore similarities to IRS behavior during the 1950s when the issue had been exemption for the medical institute. The self-dealing among Hughes executives and the Hughes Aircraft Company—whose operations, the medical institute insisted, it closely supervised—apparently was of little concern to the IRS. It mattered not that the company had invested the assets of a tax-exempt charity in a luxury apartment complex at Marina del Rey, built to enhance the personal fortunes of Hughes executives. Or that the company had sustained huge losses in other business dealings with friends of Hughes executives.

Although HHMI had won its dispute with the IRS and was pushing ahead with efforts to have the "lost will" declared the last will and testament of Howard Hughes, Will Lummis had initiated his own legal counterattack.* During two years as administrator of the Hughes estate and chief executive officer of Summa Corporation, Lummis had engineered a striking turnaround on the part of the Hughes holding company. After Davis, Holmes, and Myler had been dismissed from the Summa board, Lummis fired Davis as the company's chief counsel, and shortly thereafter Bill Gay resigned. Under Lummis's tight management, the years of multimillion-dollar losses at Summa ended and the company appeared to be well on its way to recording multimillion-dollar profits.

In June of 1978, Lummis filed a complaint in the New Castle County Chancery Court in Wilmington, Delaware, asking the court to appoint him trustee of the Howard Hughes Medical Institute—now run by Gay and Davis. The institute's articles of incorporation provided that it was to be controlled by a single trustee. That, naturally, was Howard Hughes. The articles of incorporation also provided that only Hughes could appoint a successor trustee. He never did. Lummis contended that as the administrator of the Hughes Estate, and therefore the legal representative of Hughes, he should be named trustee by the Delaware court. The Delaware attorney-general's office joined in this action, requesting the court to appoint, if not Lummis, then some other qualified individual or institution, as trustee, and require the medical institute to account to the court for its activities. Whatever the outcome of the twin legal proceedings, it is certain that the tide of litigation that engulfed Hughes while he was alive will not recede for many years after his death.

Indeed, the estate had inherited some sixty civil lawsuits that were pending against Hughes or his companies when he died.† The two major pieces

---

* The tax-exempt charity paid $328,673 to Hogan & Hartson during 1977 for legal services, including representation before the IRS and in the "missing will" case.

† As part of his own investigation to determine what role, if any, Hughes may have played in defending against the various legal actions brought against him, Lummis, on the recommendation of Dean, retained a prominent psychologist to assess Hughes's mental condition, with particular emphasis on the last years of his life. The psychologist was Dr. Raymond D. Fowler, Jr., professor and chairman of the Department of Psychology at the University of Alabama and the developer of the most widely used computerized system of personality test interpretation in the country, a system employed by more than a thousand mental health agencies and institutions and one-third of the psychiatrists in private practice. A slight, soft-spoken, skilled interrogator with a capacity for eliciting critical information from the most reluctant witnesses, Dr. Fowler spent months interviewing and reinterviewing those who worked for Hughes, and examining Hughes's voluminous private papers, in an effort to put together a psychiatric profile of the nation's best-known recluse. By the end of 1978, Dr. Fowler had concluded that Hughes's condition in his last years "resembled that of a chronic psychotic patient in the very worst mental hospitals," that "he was incapable of caring for himself or of surviving without the assistance of attendants," that "he was continuously drugged," and that "he could not have made informed and rational judgments involving complex business and legal affairs; nor could he have given competent assistance to those representing him."

of litigation involved Air West and, still, after seventeen years, TWA. In San Francisco, a United States district court judge had entered a default judgment against Hughes in lawsuits brought by former Air West stockholders who claimed they had been defrauded in the sale of the airline to Hughes. By the end of 1978, it appeared that the estate would reach a settlement with the stockholders, agreeing to pay about $34 million.* As for TWA, William Marvel, New Castle County chancellor, had ruled in favor of, and the Delaware Supreme Court had upheld, TWA's right to collect damages from Hughes for mismanagement of the airline. The amount of damages was still to be fixed.

DEATH BY NEGLIGENCE?

On March 16, 1978, a federal grand jury in Las Vegas returned an indictment against Dr. Norman F. Crane, one of Hughes's four personal physicians, and John Holmes, his senior aide, on charges they illegally supplied the industrialist with narcotics for twenty years. The indictment was based on the results of an investigation started the preceding year by agents of the Drug Enforcement Administration, and work by Assistant United States Attorney William C. Turner, the determined, former SEC lawyer who six years earlier, at the age of twenty-eight, had carried out the massive investigation of Hughes's acquisition of Air West that led to the filing of an SEC civil lawsuit in San Francisco, as a companion to suits brought by former stockholders.

The one-count indictment spelled out in abundant detail the secretive

---

*Hughes and four others had also been indicted by a federal grand jury in the Air West takeover. Charging that they had manipulated Air West stock and defrauded the airline's stockholders, a federal grand jury in Las Vegas indicted Hughes, Chester Davis, Robert Maheu, David Charnay, and James Nall on December 27, 1973. United States District Court Judge Bruce R. Thompson dismissed the indictment on January 30, 1974, ruling that the government failed to "state an offense." Rather than appeal Thompson's decision, the government secured a second indictment on July 30, 1974. Once again, Thompson tossed it out. In a decision handed down on November 13, 1974, Thompson again contended that the government had failed to state an offense. While observing that the conduct of the Hughes parties was "reprehensible and an abuse of the power of great wealth," the judge nevertheless ruled it did not constitute criminal misconduct. This time the Justice Department appealed Judge Thompson's order. For a year and a half the United States Court of Appeals for the Ninth Circuit carried the case on its docket. Finally, on May 7, 1976—a month after Hughes died—it ruled that Judge Thompson had erred in dismissing the indictment, ordered it reinstated, and returned the case to the district court for trial. When the case was scheduled for trial in April of 1977, the United States attorney's office requested a delay because one of its chief witnesses, George Crockett, an unindicted co-conspirator, was missing. The United States attorney advised Judge Thompson that a former director of Air West had recently talked to Crockett, who reportedly was on his fishing boat near the state of Sonora, Mexico, and that Crockett told him he intended to stay in Mexico until the indictment was dismissed. Judge Thompson denied the government's motion for a delay and, for the third and last time, dismissed the indictment.

drug-buying operation that had serviced Hughes for so many years, inventory-ing the scores of prescriptions Crane wrote in Holmes's name and the names of other aides, and describing the routine followed by Holmes in filling and delivering the prescriptions to Hughes.

Not long after the indictment was filed, Crane and Holmes indicated a willingness to plea-bargain. While Turner was successfully negotiating a tentative agreement in which the two men would enter pleas in exchange for their testimony in other criminal cases—including the expected prose-cution of Dr. Wilbur S. Thain, Hughes's drug supplier the last two years—a curious decision was made by the Drug Enforcement Administration, which in years gone by had enjoyed close relations with the old Hughes regime.* Someone decided to indict Thain, a Mormon, in Utah, thereby guaranteeing that he would be brought to trial in the heartland of the Mormon faith.† On June 6, 1978, the indictment was filed against him in the United States district court in Ogden, Utah. Compared to the detailed, six-page, one-hundred-fifty-line indictment against Crane and Holmes drafted by Turner in Las Vegas, the one-page, sixteen-line indictment of Thain, prepared by the United States attorney's office in Utah, was sketchy. It said simply that Thain distributed and dispensed codeine phos-phate "at approximately six-week intervals directly or indirectly to How-ard R. Hughes, without legitimate medical purpose by a practitioner acting in the usual course of his professional practice."[129]

Three months later, on September 13, 1978, the case went to trial before a jury in Ogden. As expected, Dr. Crane was a crucial witness. The seventy-three-year-old full-time physician to Hughes from 1961 to the industrialist's death testified that he began issuing prescriptions for codeine to Hughes in December of 1961 or early 1962.[130] Up to then, Crane said, Hughes had been taking enormous quantities of Empirin Compound No. 4, a drug containing codeine, caffeine, and phenacetin. Crane said he was concerned because studies had shown that "if the phenacetin was taken in rather large doses over long periods of time" that it could cause "a certain type of nephritis, which could be fatal."[131] He said he feared the caffeine would also aggravate another medi-cal problem of Hughes. Since the 1930s, Crane said, Hughes "had been subject to attacks of auricular paroxysmal tachycardia," a condition in which his heart would beat "over 200 times a minute in a regular fashion."[132]

Nevertheless, Crane said, he continued to give the Empirin Compound to Hughes in addition to the codeine because Hughes "insisted on it. He felt he got more of a lift out of it."[133] At first Crane prescribed oral codeine tablets, but Hughes soon demanded injectable codeine, claiming "he did not get the

---

* Crane and Holmes pleaded *nolo contendere*—a plea that has the same legal effect as a guilty plea in a criminal action—to the charges on September 11, 1978, in United States district court in Las Vegas. Both men were subsequently placed on probation.

† Thain's brother-in-law, Bill Gay, the top executive in the empire at Hughes's death, was a Mormon church leader.

effect soon enough" with the tablets.[134] Crane said he then gave a syringe to Hughes and showed him how to use it, although he conceded that that was not an "acceptable medical procedure."[135] Crane said he did not know how much codeine Hughes took, but guessed that it was "20–25, possibly 30 grains a day."[136] Over the years, Crane said Hughes had promised many times to "follow a detoxification schedule" to break his drug habit, but never did.[137] Crane said that there was no "medically recognized reason" for giving codeine to Hughes, that he never complained "of any illness or injury or pain that would have justified this kind of medication."[138]

Crane testified that he wrote his last codeine prescription for Hughes in April of 1974. He said he stopped supplying the narcotics because "I had given up hope of ever getting him to keep his promises" to give up drugs.[139] Also, he was growing fearful that law enforcement authorities would discover that he had been writing illegal prescriptions for many years. In following weeks, Crane said that while Hughes "complained that he wanted it," he did not "see any obvious withdrawal signs" and did not know whether Hughes was obtaining the drug elsewhere.[140]

In August of 1974, when Hughes was living at the Xanadu Princess Hotel in Freeport, Crane said Hughes summoned Dr. Thain and himself to his bedroom. In a meeting that lasted about six hours, Crane said, Hughes engaged in a monologue, talking about "his childhood up through the years until one or two years after he gained control of the tool company, things that I don't believe either Dr. Thain or I had heard before."[141] Eventually, Crane said, Hughes got around to his codeine, saying that "he needed more time in getting off the drugs than I had indicated I would allow him," which was two or three weeks.[142] Crane said Hughes told them "that he just couldn't get off it; that he had been on it for so many years and he couldn't get off it. All of his other pleasures were gone."[143] When Hughes complained that he needed more time to withdraw, Crane said, the indication was that "he was still taking the drug," and had been securing it from another source.[144] Crane said Dr. Thain finally agreed to provide Hughes with a decreasing volume of codeine when Hughes promised "to be detoxified and to be free of the drugs by his birthday of that year, which was Dec. 24 [1974]."[145]

Crane said that shortly afterward a new procedure was established for handling the drugs. Every eight weeks, when Thain reported for his tour of duty in the Bahamas, he would bring an eight-week supply of drugs—codeine, Valium, Empirin Compound No. 4—in eight manila envelopes that were kept in the doctors' quarters and one was given to Hughes each week. "He had dates on the outside of the envelopes as to what date they were to be delivered to Mr. Hughes," Crane said.[146] Although he assumed there were "decreasing dosages" in the envelopes, Crane testified, he never counted the drugs.[147] He said Hughes often asked him to call Thain and ask about "the messages"— the code word they used for the drugs.[148] Hughes complained, he said, "about the amounts that he found in his messages" and felt "he wasn't getting enough."[149] In any event, Hughes was not off narcotics by his birthday that year, Crane said, and continued to take drugs until he died.

On September 18, Thain took the stand in his own defense. He testified that he first learned about Hughes's drug habit in 1973 in London after Hughes had fractured his left hip:

Just shortly before surgery, Mr. Hughes called me into his room and sent everybody else out, his aides that were with him, and he told me at that time that he had been taking moderate to large quantities of codeine, both by hypo and orally. . . . He told me at that time he had been taking from 25 to 40 grains per day when he was at his maximum levels and that this had started following the F-11 accident after he had become addicted to morphine while in the hospital. He had broken that and replaced on codeine, and he had taken amounts up to this level throughout the remaining years since 1946–47.[150]

Thain said he told Hughes that his drug usage was excessive, "that he shouldn't be taking that amount, that it probably wasn't helping his pain problems, and that he should reduce himself."[151] Thain said he did not see Hughes again until August 3, 1974, the night of the meeting with Hughes, Crane, and himself.

The first part of the meeting was a discussion by Mr. Hughes where he told us a lot about his boyhood, his early childhood, his relationships with his mother and father, whom he dearly loved. As I recall, he also talked about being an amateur radio operator, a ham operator, having one of the early licenses. He talked in great detail about his flight around the world. He talked about a lot of other very personal things, his relationship with Mrs. Hughes and how much he still loved her and a lot of very personal things of that nature.[152]

When the talk got around to drugs, Thain said, Hughes "again reiterated that he had been taking from 25—this time he said as high as 45 grains per day at his maximum usage levels."[153] In addition, Thain said, Hughes told them he had been "taking an average of 7 to 15 10-milligram Valium tablets a day."[154] Contrary to Dr. Crane's testimony, Thain said Hughes contended he was in constant pain*:

He was complaining of pain, discomfort, a lot of backaches, pain in through his neck, back, and shoulders down into his shoulders and his arms, back pain, little vague stomach discomforts. He had a lot of trouble with constipation, which isn't unusual with this medication. He had a lot of difficulty urinating. He complained in great detail about his teeth bothering him and then went into a very long explanation that he was going to get his teeth fixed and we could get a dentist one of these days examine [sic] bring him down and he would get his teeth fixed. And tried to give us considerable justification as to why he was taking those large quantities. He also had a lot of trouble sleeping. And this is why he said he took the Valiums.[155]

Thain said he then tried to determine "the absolute minimum amount of medication" that Hughes thought "he could get along on and that would control his pain and discomfort."[156] Thain said Hughes indicated ten to twelve

---

* Dr. Lawrence Chaffin, another of Hughes's personal physicians, also testified that Hughes was not in pain. He told the court there never was any "legitimate medical purpose" for giving him codeine and that he took the drugs "because he wanted them."

grains of codeine a day, "which I still thought was excessive, and I agreed at that time, then, that we would then taper him down as fast as possible."[157] Thain said Hughes promised that he would be "down to no medication by his birthday in December.[158] As for Hughes's Valium consumption, Thain testified:

I told him that the amount of Valium he was taking was entirely excessive and that I would agree to let him have one or two Valium to be taken to sleep with and that he was not to take this any more frequently than every two to three days. And I agreed to give him six Valium per week, which would work out about two tablets every three days. This is the 10-milligram Valium.[159]

Thain said he continued to dispense codeine after December of 1974 because "Mr. Hughes was still having severe complaints of pain."[160] From September to November of 1974, the doses amounted to 8.46 grains per day. From November 1974 on, Thain said, he never gave him more than 6.8 grains per day, and that from January 1975 until Hughes's death, he reduced the dosage to 3.4 grains of codeine.[161] There was, Thain contended, a "legitimate medical purpose" for the medicine he prescribed.[162] Hughes suffered from "intractable pain," he said.[163] "I think this gentleman with his age and his infirmities had adequate physical problems that could cause him pain, and I gave him the medication to treat this, and I think that it was justified throughout my entire course of treatment."[164]

During cross-examination, Thain acknowledged that he did not have any medical records to show when, or what volume of drugs, Hughes actually consumed.* That led to an exchange with an assistant United States attorney:

ATTORNEY: You can't tell us precisely what drugs or the quantities that he took on any given day, can you, doctor?

THAIN: On any given day, no, sir.

ATTORNEY: The only thing you can do and the only thing you have recorded in that record is what you were delivering?

THAIN: That's correct.

ATTORNEY: As a matter of fact, you weren't even there most of the time those drugs were being administered, were you?

THAIN: I was not there in his presence at any time that he was administering them.

ATTORNEY: And you gave this quantity to an addict or a person you knew at least had been an addict of the same drug that you were giving him. Is that right?

THAIN: I was not present at the time or had knowledge of the time he was taking these excessive amounts. As to whether he was an addict or not, I don't know, sir.

ATTORNEY: In your medical judgment, sir, you know that a person cannot take those quantities of codeine without becoming addicted, don't you?

---

*The daily logs in which the aides entered the time Hughes took his various drugs, and the amount, have never been found for the period from 1974 through his death in 1976. It is not clear whether these logs are hidden away in the vast Hughes archives, or whether they were among papers fed into a shredder in the Acapulco Princess the day Hughes died, shortly before Mexican authorities seized the remainder.

THAIN: I'll have to say yes to avoid getting into an argument with you, but it is an argumentative problem, sir.[165]

Thain said he never discussed the amount of codeine and other drugs he was giving to Hughes with the other three doctors, Crane, Lawrence Chaffin, and Homer Clark. In fact, Thain acknowledged, they had no idea of the "amount of drugs" he was giving Hughes.[166] Thain said he obtained the codeine directly from a New York pharmaceutical house and did not write prescriptions for the drug, but that he "did not know" that "under the laws of the State of Utah that it's illegal for a physician to directly dispense any controlled substance [codeine] without a prescription."[167]

On September 21, 1978, after a one-week trial, the jury found Thain innocent.

Intriguing questions remain about Howard Hughes's death. Hughes died with an exceptionally high level of codeine in his body. The *Philadelphia Inquirer,* which obtained a copy of the then secret autopsy report, disclosed in June of 1977 that an analysis made by the newspaper of the toxicological results included in the autopsy showed that Hughes "had a potentially lethal amount of narcotics in his body" when he died.[168] The autopsy report listed the codeine level in his blood as 1.96 micrograms per milliliter of blood and described it as "only minimum amounts."[169] In truth, the 1.96 figure was considerably above the 1.4-microgram level found in the bodies of persons known to have died of codeine poisoning.*

During Thain's trial, Dr. Forest S. Tennant, Jr., assistant professor of public health at the UCLA School of Public Health and executive director of Community Health Projects, one of California's largest drug-abuse treatment programs, testified that based on his study of the autopsy report he concluded that Hughes had taken "anywhere from 5 to 9 grains" of codeine before his death.[170]

Other medical authorities say it is difficult to pinpoint the precise amount of codeine that Hughes may have taken, and that it could well have exceeded twenty grains. But far more significantly, Dr. Tennant testified, and pharmacologists and pathologists agree, the codeine in Hughes's body "was taken within 6 to 8 hours of death."†[171]

That was an astonishing finding, one totally ignored by federal prosecutors at Thain's trial. Hughes had been unconscious for nearly twenty-four hours before he died, according to testimony given in other legal proceedings

---

*On October 27, 1976, when Dr. Jack L. Titus, the pathologist who performed the autopsy, testified in a deposition in connection with the administration of Hughes's estate, he described the codeine levels cited in the autopsy report as "compatible with therapeutic usage." Two years later, at Dr. Thain's trial, Titus acknowledged that his previous statements were "in error" because he had misinterpreted milligrams for micrograms. Thus the level of codeine was 1,000 times greater than he originally thought.

†Codeine is a fast-acting drug which reaches a peak level in the bloodstream within one to two hours after it is administered. About one-half to two-thirds of a dose of codeine appears in the urine within six hours, and excretion is virtually complete in twenty-four hours.

by Dr. Chaffin and aides who were with him.* In other words, someone injected a large dose of codeine into Hughes while he was in a coma—an act for which, medical experts say, there would be no medical justification.

There were other nagging questions. Independent medical authorities who looked at the results of the laboratory tests of Hughes's blood and urine, performed in Acapulco on April 3, 1976, two days before his death, say they show no evidence of kidney failure. In fact, one physician observed, if he had a patient with similar readings, he would send him home and tell him to come back in a week. Others were equally insistent that the Mexican laboratory results, when considered with the autopsy report, indicated that while Hughes certainly suffered from chronic renal disease, he did not die of that.

If Hughes did not die of chronic renal disease—the cause of death listed in the autopsy report and on his death certificate—then what did he die of? There are several possibilities. No one can estimate with any certainty Hughes's tolerance for codeine. According to a medical report on codeine, the lethal dose in humans has not been established, but one study placed it at from "500 to 1,000 milligrams for an adult."[172] And a person may become addicted to the drug by taking as little as 300 milligrams a day.† If Hughes was consuming twenty grains a day, the lower estimate testified to by Dr. Crane, that would amount to 1,200 milligrams. If he was consuming forty-five grains a day, the higher estimate testified to by Dr. Thain, that would amount to 2,700 milligrams. Obviously, at one time in his life Hughes had developed a remarkable tolerance for codeine, routinely administering quantities that might well kill another person.

*Dr. Thain, who had received an employment contract and a lifetime consulting agreement from Summa Corporation in 1975, providing him with an annual salary of $60,000 for serving as one of Hughes's physicians, testified that from February until April 5, 1976, the date of Hughes's death, he saw the industrialist on only three occasions. He said he had his last conversation with Hughes toward the "end of February." Next, he said, "I saw him while he was sleeping, but not to talk to him, about the oh, middle of March, 17th or 18th." He did not see Hughes again, he said, until the morning of April 5, when he arrived at the Acapulco Princess about 8 A.M. At that time, he testified, he found Hughes "in a coma, rather flaccid. He was having seizures, multiple seizures. His pupils were dilated and fixed. His blood pressure had been stabilized in and around 100–120. His pulse wasn't too bad. He had been unconscious, I understood, since the night before. He really looked moribund, the type of person—he just looked like he was ready to die."

†Codeine addiction is so rare that medical literature contains little information about abuse of the drug. In fact, as late as the mid-1970s, medical literature suggested that codeine addiction was virtually nonexistent and the drug posed little potential for abuse because of its unpleasant side effects, not the least of which was severe constipation. As one study noted, codeine "lacks the 'thrill'-producing capacity of heroin and morphine. Codeine does not appeal to addicts of the underworld and is of practically no value in the illicit drug market. Moreover, codeine is not especially suitable for intravenous administration, the route preferred by American addicts: Intravenous injections produce effects such as intense erythema, edema, headache, even severe hypotension or vascular collapse, so that the overall sensation is at least unpleasant. Addicts found intravenous codeine unacceptable as a substitute for morphine in a study at the Addiction Research Center in Lexington, Kentucky. . . . With a few exceptions . . . pharmacology textbooks usually state that primary codeine dependence is rare among addicts as well as in clinical practice." As he had done in the movies and in aviation, Hughes rewrote the medical record books on codeine abuse, pioneering a new addiction.

But by April of 1976 Hughes was seventy years old. He was suffering from malnutrition, he was incredibly emaciated—weighing only ninety-three pounds—and severely dehydrated. Indeed, his dehydration and malnutrition were so severe that some medical authorities have suggested that Hughes died as a result of these conditions rather than kidney failure. In any event, all these factors combined would have lowered Hughes's tolerance—the level that would prove fatal to him—for the drug. And if he had become accustomed to taking smaller quantities of codeine as Thain maintained that he gave him, that would have further reduced his tolerance.

Thus, medical experts say, a dose of codeine once tolerable for Hughes could have plunged him into the coma from which he never recovered. So, too, they say, could some combination of drugs, such as codeine and the Valium that he took regularly. Then again, they say, it may have been some overall combination, the drugs, the dehydration, the malnutrition that together triggered the coma. And once he was in the coma, someone shot Hughes up one last time.

Whatever the case, neither state nor federal law enforcement authorities showed much interest in investigating the circumstances of Hughes's death, in learning whether he died of negligence or neglect. No one cared.*

*While law enforcement authorities remained indifferent to the circumstances surrounding Hughes's death, on January 24, 1979, attorneys for the estate, acting on the instructions of Will Lummis, filed what promised to be a massive lawsuit against the industrialist's longtime executives, aides, and doctors, charging that they "either negligently provided improper medical care or negligently failed to provide proper medical care to Hughes," and were involved in "deliberately destroying valuable records of Hughes while he lay on his deathbed." The legal action, filed in Nevada district court in Las Vegas, seeks damages in excess of $50 million from thirteen defendants —three of Hughes's personal physicians, Thain, Clark, and Crane; six aides, Myler, Holmes, Waldron, Eckersley, Rickard, and Francom; two corporate executives, Gay and Glenn; his chief personal and corporate lawyer, Davis; and Davis's law firm, Davis & Cox. The complaint charges that Gay and Davis, "acting in concert with the other defendants, took advantage of Hughes' age, poor physical and psychological condition, isolation and use of drugs to control and manipulate him in furtherance of their personal interests which were inimical to those of Hughes and his companies." The complaint states that each defendant "took advantage of his position of trust and power" and through "a series of self-dealing schemes and conspiracies, they controlled and manipulated Hughes and his enterprises; wrongfully converted substantial assets of Hughes and his enterprises to their own use and the use of others; wrongfully wasted substantial assets of Hughes and his enterprises; negligently represented the interests of Hughes and his enterprises in litigation. . . . " The complaint accuses the defendants of "fraudulently inducing Hughes' authorization" of certain "self-dealing" employment and consulting contracts by "misrepresenting his financial position to him; by leading him to believe that absent his authorization of these contracts he risked the loss of defendants' services who, they misled him to believe, were profitably managing his enterprises when, in truth and fact, they were not; and by means of duress and undue influence."

Epilogue

A SUMMING UP

It was money that etched Howard Hughes into the public mind. His name called forth visions of untold wealth, wealth accumulated, supposedly, through Hughes's gift for turning all he touched into gold. That he lacked this gift is now evident. If Hughes had invested the profits of the tool company, left to him by his father, in a passbook savings account, he would have died a much richer man. Hughes did not take that course, however. The mere making of money did not rule him. Rather, he always sought to make the world think he was making money. That image meant everything to him.

From the beginning, Howard Hughes had an overpowering urge to become a legend in his own lifetime. He wanted the world to notice and to marvel at what it saw. He wanted to show others that he was every bit the man his father had been. It was no accident that in his youth he ventured into the two most glamorous fields of the time—movies and aviation—where he could quickly gain notoriety. Repeatedly over the rest of his life he embarked on courses of action that subjected him to intense public curiosity and speculation. His shyness notwithstanding, the public spotlight was his oldest addiction.

In the course of his various pursuits, Hughes projected the image of an extraordinary man. Not satisfied to be judged merely a motion picture producer or a planemaker, he *had* to direct the movies he made, to test-fly the planes he built. He wanted his personal imprint on everything associated with him, for others to view him as one who could do it all—a corporate superman blessed with the Midas touch and Napoleonic daring. In that he succeeded wildly, largely due to his mastery of public relations. If Hughes realized that his life fell short of the myth he created, it caused him little concern. What mattered was the world's perception, that image compelled respect, fear, or awe. He knew only too well that history is made by reputation, not reality.

Howard Hughes was not always what he seemed, but he was nevertheless remarkable. He could read an aircraft technical manual with its dizzying array of engineering specifications and mentally test the calculations as he went along. His memory was such that he could dictate the same involved financial memorandum, word for word, on two separate occasions separated by months. It was this powerful ability for recall that convinced some who worked for Hughes, and some who came to know him, that he was a genius.

But geniuses must, like all of us, live in the real world. Hughes never learned how to convert his knowledge to practical application. Instead, he sought a perfection that assured failure. The results were there for all to see. He was to have mass-produced photo-reconnaissance planes to support the Allied cause during the Second World War, but the war ended before he had completed one. He was to have built three flying boats, but managed to turn out only one, and it was incapable of sustained flight.

While Hughes's mind was adept at absorbing complicated technical material, there was no place in it for human beings. He could remember years afterward, to the quarter-inch, the angle of the windshield in a plane he helped to design, but had entirely lost the name of the engineer who worked side by side with him for many months. From childhood on, he was never one of the boys, never able to share a joke or enjoy the camaraderie of youth or the friendship of adults. He never sought—and did not seem to need—human companionship. In both marriages, he most often lived apart from his wives. Although many would claim Hughes as a friend, in seventy years of life he quite probably had only one—his boyhood companion Dudley Sharp. The depth of his isolation can be found on an application he submitted to the FBI during the war. Next to the heading "In case of emergency notify," Hughes typed, "Howard Hall, friend, Hughes Aircraft Company."[1] Howard Hall was just another of Hughes's many lawyers.

Yet despite his inability to relate individually either to men or to women, Hughes displayed a surprising grasp of human nature. He knew what motivated people—their hunger for wealth, their thirst for power, their fascination with sex. In one way or another, he played on those drives throughout his life, from producing motion pictures designed to stir prurient interests to dangling campaign contributions before amenable politicians. And always, he assured the faithfulness of his retinue by hinting of great rewards to come.

Beginning as early as his teenage years and continuing until his death, Hughes lived in the grip of a multitude of obsessions uninfluenced by logic or reason. One of the most persistent, if least harmful, involved concocting schemes to avoid payment of state and federal income taxes. In the 1940s, he sold his home in Los Angeles—and he never owned another—to prove that he was not a resident of California and thereby escape payment of California income taxes. In the 1950s, he disrupted Hughes Aircraft Company operations when he initially refused to enlarge plant facilities, proposing instead that the company's research laboratories be shifted from Los Angeles to Las Vegas to escape the California tax collector. Again and again, Hughes made business decisions based largely on the total dollar amount of taxes he would have to pay. In the process, tax avoidance became an academic exercise without regard for the overall financial consequences. Given a choice between a financial transaction that would yield a $5-million profit and require a $2-million federal income-tax payment, or a transaction that would yield a $10-million profit and require a $4-million tax payment, Hughes would invariably choose the former.

Perhaps Hughes's deepest obsession was one that evolved into a fanatical compulsion to control every aspect of his life and environment. This control was to extend not only to his own bodily functions—to the minute when he would fall asleep, wake up, or go to the bathroom—but also to the lives of everyone around him. Early in his life, at age nineteen, he insisted on buying out the minority interest in the Hughes Tool Company owned by his father's relatives, not because he had any intention of moving into an active management position in the business—he had no such plans—but simply because he wanted total control. A few years later, when he gave $5,000 to his alma mater, Thacher School, the gift carried the stipulation that he be allowed to recommend how the money would be spent. By the 1940s and 1950s, this compulsion had turned perverse. While involved with some of Hollywood's most glamorous actresses, Hughes had many of them followed by private investigators, and detailed reports prepared on their activities. One of Robert Maheu's first assignments involved "surveillance" of Ava Gardner.[2] If a female companion fell ill, Hughes insisted that she be examined by his personal physician, Dr. Verne Mason, a practice dictated not by any special concern for the woman, but his desire to obtain—without her knowledge—a full medical report on her condition. "If a girl got sick he wouldn't want her to go to a regular doctor because he probably couldn't get the diagnosis," according to Glen Brewer, who served as a member of Hughes's "entertainment staff" during the early 1950s.[3]

Hughes's estrangement from other human beings went a long way toward explaining the demeaning way in which he treated so many people, orchestrating their daily lives down to and including instructions on what food they should eat and where they should park their cars. Instructions given to Operations in December of 1958, to be relayed to a staff man, were typical of the orders that Hughes issued daily:

Call him and tell him to come out to the bungalow. Tell him to park on Crescent and sit in the car until a man comes to show him where to park and how to get out of the car and how to get to the bungalow. When the third man has cleared the door, step inside quickly, just far enough to be inside. Do not move and do not say anything, not a single word at all. There will be a TV set directly in front of you and a wire on the floor to your left. Do not move left or right. Be sure that you instruct him to take care of all his personal chores before he leaves because he will not have any facilities at his disposal while in the bungalow. Have him park the car one foot from the curb on Crescent and have him get out of the car on the street side (do not walk on the grass at all and do not step into the gutter at all). He should make a wide step over the gutter from a point as far out toward the center road as possible.[4]

This runaway obsession with the trivial and the irrelevant accounted, in large part, for Hughes's failures as a businessman: why he ran RKO into the ground, why he nearly plunged TWA into bankruptcy and lost control of the airline, why he never successfully put an airplane into production, why his hotels and casinos lost money while those around him prospered. It was this obsession that dictated Hughes's decision to move to Las Vegas. Because of the comparatively small population of both the city and the state, and their dependence on a single industry, Hughes believed he could have his way in Nevada, whether it was an effort to "stop the Clark County School District integration plan" or arranging for a physician to be "licensed in the State of Nevada to practice medicine without having to take the examination."[5] During his first year or so in Las Vegas, Hughes succeeded, spectacularly, in having his way. But when he began suffering a setback here and there, he consulted Maheu as to other areas where they might move to gain the dictatorial control he sought. They assessed the relative merits of Puerto Rico, Curaçao, Trinidad, the British West Indies. When the Bahamas became a serious possibility, Hughes instructed Maheu that "I would expect you really to wrap that government up down there to a point where it would be—well—a captive entity in every way."[6]

Hughes's most extreme obsession was to control the dreaded flow of germs into his room. Doors and windows were sealed with masking tape. The aides who worked with him daily were required to follow a set of carefully prescribed rituals. They handed him papers or objects wrapped in "paddles," or layers of Kleenex. They spread "insulation," or layers of paper towels, on his bed, chair, and bathroom floor. They guarded against the delivery of mail to him sent by someone he feared had been exposed to contagious germs.

When all the details are considered, they reveal a classic study of the obsessive-compulsive personality in extremis. A current medical manual offers a definition that almost seems written with Howard Hughes in mind:

[Obsessives] are characterized by conscientiousness and high levels of aspiration. [They] take responsibilities seriously and often have difficulty making decisions. Their extreme concern for order and routine tends to make them rigid and unacceptable. . . . preoccupation with unlikely dangers are often prominent.[7]

They invariably develop rituals in reaction to their fears:

The most common themes concern dirt contamination and associated compulsive hand washing. . . . Irrational abhorrence of possible contamination or infection may begin with a visit to a hospital, meeting someone with a cough, or discovering a pile of dust in a corner. The patient becomes convinced that he is surrounded by sources of infection, and fears that every contact with an object belonging to someone else may have caused contamination that must be cleansed by washing. After one wash, however, the thought of contamination recurs, and the consequent anxiety can be curbed only with further washing. Failure to control the obsession with multiple washings increases the distress and anxiety, and a vicious circle develops.[8]

It is one thing to be gripped by powerful obsessions, as Hughes was by midlife, but quite another to be a hopeless psychotic as he had become in his last years. What accounted for this progression? Did he inherit a predisposition for mental disorder? Did stress prove too much for his fragile mental constitution? The questions could be richly debated by psychologists and psychiatrists for years. Hughes's mental illness could have sprung from heredity or environment, or both. His grandmother and his mother had pronounced phobias. And in times of crisis, Hughes withdrew, lost touch with reality, and displayed increasingly bizarre and chaotic thought processes.

All that can be said for certain is that Hughes cast himself into a life-role that he was ill-equipped to play. On the one hand, he aspired to greatness. But on the other, as one who hated to make decisions, who lived in fear of making a mistake, who agonized over options to the point of exhaustion, he did not have the mental and emotional toughness necessary to survive in his chosen arenas. After 1942, as Hughes's difficulties in coping with the administration of his empire mounted, his personality underwent ever-greater change. Ironically, one of the same obsessions that propelled him toward a mental collapse —his exaggerated desire for control—made it impossible for him to place himself in the care of a psychiatrist or to seek psychiatric treatment. Such a step would have been an admission of weakness, and Hughes could never do that. Since he had no close friends, there was no one to persuade him, or even to suggest, that he seek help. Had there been such a person, Hughes's life might have been quite different.

Instead of receiving treatment, Hughes passed into his own asylum. Unable to cope with adversity, to distinguish the relevant from the irrelevant, to confront the problems of everyday life, he withdrew into the security of a hospital-like environment, where he became hopelessly dependent on its controlled setting and undemanding routines. There his staff of caretakers catered to his wildest obsessions, played to his bizarre behavior, pretending with him that all his actions were normal. Isolated, feeding on fantasy and drugs, Hughes suffered a breakdown of psychotic proportions, regressing to a childlike state. It was a cruel irony that the man who wished to master everything in the end mastered nothing.

As the years passed and Hughes's mental condition continued to deteriorate, he never forgot that the outside world would not look kindly on his bizarre behavior, and so he took great pains to keep it a secret and to perpetuate the image he had so carefully nurtured. How else can his remarkable performance in the 1972 telephone press conference be explained? The Hughes who spoke to newsmen that day had spent the previous fifteen years in complete seclusion, going nude daily; allowing his hair, fingernails, and toenails to grow for months; refusing to bathe; urinating in jars, sealing the jars, and storing them in his bedroom closet; and living in mortal fear of germs. Yet when newsmen discreetly asked him to comment on wild rumors about his personal habits and appearance, Hughes chuckled and put them at ease. Yes, he too had seen a sketch of himself in a magazine showing him with hair falling about his shoulders and nails curling over the ends of his fingers. "The first thing I said was how in the hell could I sign documents that I have been signing," he told the reporters. "I would have gotten tangled up in these fingernails. . . . I have always kept my fingernails at a reasonable length. . . . I take care of them the same way I always have—the same way I did when I went around the world and times when you have seen me and at the time of the flight of the flying boat, and every other occasion I have come in contact with the press. I care for my fingernails in the same precise manner I always have in my life."[9]

In truth, we are left, finally, with two Howard Hugheses—the public and the private: the rational disguise and the world of shadows, of nightmare, of instinct to preserve and protect at any cost the image he had created. That it has taken so many years for the veil to part is tribute both to his genius and to his tragedy.

CHRONOLOGY

THE LIFE OF HOWARD HUGHES

Dec. 24, 1905—Born in Houston.

Nov. 20, 1908—Hughes's father files for patent on revolutionary oil-drilling bit.

Mid-1909—Sharp–Hughes Tool Company, a partnership, organized in Houston.

Feb. 3, 1915—Hughes Tool Company incorporated in Texas.

September 1920—Enrolls in Fessenden School, West Newton, Massachusetts, and graduates the following spring.

September 1921—Enrolls in Thacher School, Ojai, California.

March 29, 1922—Mother dies in Houston.

September 1922—Returns to Thacher, then withdraws at Christmas.

September 1923—Enrolls in Rice Institute, Houston.

Jan. 14, 1924—Father dies in Houston.

May 1924—Acquires minority interest of grandparents and uncle in the Hughes Tool Company, giving him 100 percent control.

Dec. 26, 1924—Houston judge signs order removing Hughes's "disabilities as a minor" and eliminating need for appointment of a guardian.

May 30, 1925—Executes will at age nineteen, leaving bulk of estate to medical research; believed to be the only will he ever signed.

June 1, 1925—Marries Ella Rice in Houston.

Fall 1925—Leaves Houston to live in Los Angeles.

November 1925—Hires Noah Dietrich as financial adviser in Los Angeles.

October 1927—Begins filming *Hell's Angels*.

Jan. 7, 1928—Receives first pilot's license.

January 1928—First plane crash, at Mines Field, Los Angeles, during filming of *Hell's Angels*.

Oct. 1, 1928—Ella and Hughes separate.

May 16, 1929—*Two Arabian Knights* wins Academy Award.

Dec. 2, 1929—Purchases house at 211 Muirfield Road, Los Angeles.

Dec. 9, 1929—Ella granted a divorce in Houston.

June 30, 1930—*Hell's Angels* première.

June 30, 1930—Acquires 7000 Romaine Street in Hollywood.

Spring 1932—Founds Hughes Aircraft Company in Glendale, California.

Jan. 14, 1934—Wins first air trophy, in Miami.

Sept. 13, 1935—Sets new land speed record at Santa Ana, California.

Jan. 14, 1936—Establishes new transcontinental speed record from Los Angeles to Newark of nine hours, twenty-seven minutes.

Jan. 19, 1937—Sets new transcontinental speed record from Los Angeles to Newark of seven hours, twenty-eight minutes.

July 10–14, 1938—With four crewmen, establishes new record for around-the-world flight—three days, nineteen hours, and seventeen minutes.

May 1939—First acquires stock in Transcontinental & Western Airlines, later Trans World Airlines.

Fall 1939—Begins work on experimental military aircraft, the D-2.

Spring 1940—Begins filming *The Outlaw*.

July 1941—Hughes Aircraft Company moves to new plant at Culver City, California.

Nov. 7, 1941—Air Force rejects D-2 as a military plane.

Nov. 16, 1942—Defense Plant Corporation approves $18-million contract with Kaiser–Hughes Corporation to build three flying boats to aid war effort.

May 17, 1943—Sikorsky S-43, with Hughes at the controls, crashes in Lake Mead, Nevada; two die.

Oct. 11, 1943—Air force issues letter of intent for Hughes Aircraft Company to build 101 photo-reconnaissance planes—the XF-11s.

Fall 1943—Nadine Henley becomes Hughes's private secretary.

March 27, 1944—Kaiser–Hughes contract on flying boats cancelled; Defense Plant Corporation issues new agreement with Hughes to build one flying boat.

Late 1944—Suffers first nervous breakdown.

May 29, 1945—Air force cancels contract to build 101 XF-11s; Hughes to complete two experimental planes under construction.

July 7, 1946—Critically injured in crash of XF-11 in Beverly Hills.

April 5, 1947—Successfully test-flies second XF-11 at Culver City.

August 6–10, 1947—Testifies before Senate War Investigating Committee probing his work as defense contractor in Second World War.

October 1947—Frank William Gay goes to work at Romaine Street.

Nov. 2, 1947—Test-flies the Hercules flying boat at Long Beach.

Nov. 8, 10, 11, and 14, 1947—Testifies again before the Senate War Committee.

May 10, 1948—Acquires control of RKO.

April 1951—Fires Paul Jarrico, a screenwriter, after he was subpoenaed to appear before the House Committee on Un-American Activities.

Nov. 20, 1952—Testifies in Los Angeles Superior Court in Jarrico case, his last courtroom appearance.

Sept. 23, 1952—Chicago syndicate buys control of RKO.

Feb. 10, 1953—Reassumes control of RKO after Chicago group forfeits $1.2-million downpayment.

Aug. 11, 1953—Dr. Simon Ramo and Dr. Dean Wooldridge resign at Hughes Aircraft Company, sparking crisis between Hughes and the Pentagon.

Dec. 17, 1953—Howard Hughes Medical Institute incorporated in Delaware.

March 31, 1954—Acquires 100 percent control of RKO for $23,489,478.

May 29, 1954—Jean Peters marries Stuart W. Cramer III.

Feb. 11, 1955—Takes last pilot's test, in Miami, Florida.

July 19, 1955—Sells RKO to General Tire Company for an estimated $25 million.

February 1956—Orders first jets for TWA, thirty-three Boeing 707s.

June 7, 1956—Orders thirty Convair 880s from General Dynamics.

Dec. 10, 1956—Hughes Tool Company makes $205,000 loan to F. Donald Nixon.

Jan. 12, 1957—Marries Jean Peters in Tonopah, Nevada.

May 12, 1957—Fires Noah Dietrich.

Mid-1958—Suffers second nervous breakdown.

Dec. 15, 1960—Lenders impose voting trust; Hughes loses control of TWA.

Dec. 24, 1960—Moves with Jean to Rancho Santa Fe.

Spring 1961—Hires Chester C. Davis as vice-president and general counsel of the Hughes Tool Company.

June 30, 1961—TWA files antitrust complaint against Hughes in New York.

Nov. 23, 1961—Moves with Jean to 1001 Bel Air Road, Bel Air.

Feb. 11, 1963—Refuses to appear for deposition in TWA lawsuit.

May 3, 1963—Federal judge in New York awards TWA default judgment over Hughes's refusal to give deposition.

June 21, 1964—U.S. Court of Appeals upholds the default judgment against Hughes.

May 26, 1965—Army awards contract to Hughes to build light observation helicopters, in what would become the largest single business loss of Hughes's career.

May 3, 1966—Sells his 6.5 million shares of stock in TWA for $546 million.

July 17, 1966—Leaves Los Angeles by train for Boston to stay at Ritz-Carlton Hotel.

Nov. 27, 1966—Arrives in Las Vegas by train from Boston, taking over top floor of Desert Inn.

March 31, 1967—Acquires control of Desert Inn Hotel and Casino, first step in the building of his Nevada empire.

Dec. 27, 1968—Stockholders approve sale of Air West to Hughes.

Jan. 15, 1970—Jean Peters Hughes announces she and Hughes will obtain a divorce.

April 3, 1970—Acquires Air West.

April 14, 1970—Federal court enters judgment of $145,448,141.07 against Hughes for damages to TWA in antitrust case.

July 1970—Richard Danner delivers $50,000 secret Hughes campaign contribution to "Bebe" Rebozo at San Clemente.

August 1970—Danner delivers another $50,000 to Rebozo in Key Biscayne, Florida.

Nov. 14, 1970—Hughes signs proxy giving control of his Nevada empire to Chester Davis, Raymond Holliday, and Bill Gay.

Nov. 25, 1970—Flies from Las Vegas to Paradise Island, the Bahamas, moving into the Britannia Beach Hotel.

Dec. 3, 1970—Hughes Tool Company fires Robert Maheu as chief of Hughes Nevada Operations.

January 1971—Hughes organization employs new Washington representative, Robert F. Bennett, proprietor of a CIA front; negotiations underway to use Hughes as a front for CIA Project Jennifer.

June 18, 1971—Hughes–Peters divorce made final in Hawthorne, Nevada.

Jan. 7, 1972—Conducts telephone interview from the Bahamas with newsmen in Los Angeles to refute Clifford Irving book.

Feb. 10, 1972—Robert Maheu files $17.5-million lawsuit in Los Angeles against Hughes for libel and slander.

Feb. 15, 1972—Flees the Bahamas, going by boat to Miami, then by air to Managua, Nicaragua, moving into the Intercontinental Managua.

March 13, 1972—Meets briefly with U.S. Ambassador Turner Shelton and Nicaraguan President Anastasio Somoza in Managua shortly before flying to Bayshore Inn, Vancouver, Canada.

Aug. 29, 1972—Returns to Intercontinental Managua in Nicaragua after stay in Canada.

Sept. 25, 1972—Signs papers authorizing sale of the oil-tool division of the Hughes Tool Company.

Dec. 7, 1972—Oil tool division sold to public for $150 million, becomes Hughes Tool Company; Hughes's holding company renamed Summa Corporation.

Dec. 24, 1972—Leaves Managua for London, moving into the Inn on the Park.

Jan. 10, 1973—U.S. Supreme Court overturns judgment and lower court rulings against Hughes in TWA case.

March 17, 1973—Meets with Governor O'Callaghan and Philip Hannifin in London.

Aug. 9, 1973—Falls in room at Inn on the Park, fracturing left hip.

Dec. 20, 1973—Flies from London to Freeport, Grand Bahama Island, moving into the Xanadu Princess Hotel.

Dec. 27, 1973—Federal grand jury in Nevada indicts Hughes in the acquisition of Air West.

Jan. 30, 1974—Air West indictment dismissed by federal judge.

June 5, 1974—Hughes's personal papers stolen in Romaine Street burglary.

July 30, 1974—Federal grand jury in Nevada reindicts Hughes in Air West takeover.

Nov. 13, 1974—Federal judge again dismisses Hughes indictment in Air West case; Justice Department appeals, and indictment is reinstated by U.S. Court of Appeals on May 7, 1976, a month after Hughes's death.

March 18, 1975—Hughes Glomar Explorer story disclosed.

Sept. 10, 1975—Hughes's aides and executives approve employment contracts for themselves.

Feb. 10, 1976—Hughes is flown from Freeport to Acapulco, to a penthouse of the Acapulco Princess Hotel.

April 5, 1976—Dies aboard airplane from Acapulco to Houston.

APPENDICES

APPENDIX A

IN 1954, its first full year of operation, the Howard Hughes Medical Institute received $3,609,785 to carry on its charitable work. Here is what happened to that money:

Expenditure	Amount	Percent of total
Payment to the Hughes Tool Company wholly owned by Howard R. Hughes [b]	$ 2,302,785	64
Payment to the Hughes Tool Company [c]	721,732	20
Accumulated income	539,573	15
Medical research fellowships	43,348	1
General and administrative expenses	2,347	0
TOTAL	$ 3,609,785	100

[a] SOURCE: U.S. Internal Revenue Service.
[b] Payment on real estate lease.
[c] Payment of interest on $18,043,300 loan.

APPENDIX B

TWA EARNINGS: 1946–1965
(in millions of dollars)

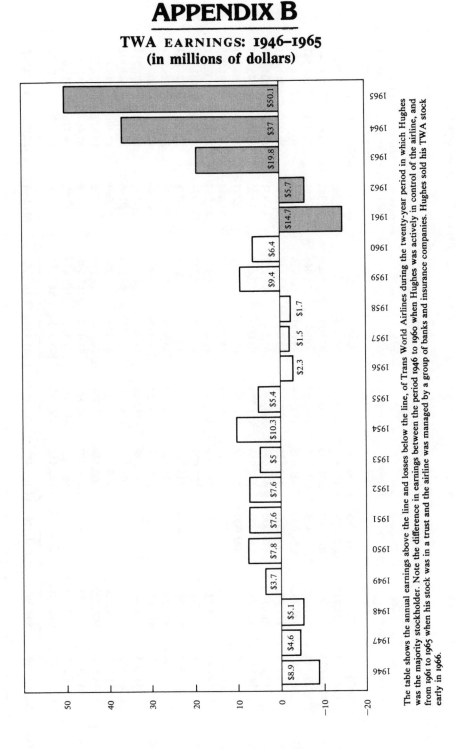

The table shows the annual earnings above the line and losses below the line, of Trans World Airlines during the twenty-year period in which Hughes was the majority stockholder. Note the difference in earnings between the period 1946 to 1960 when Hughes was actively in control of the airline, and from 1961 to 1965 when his stock was in a trust and the airline was managed by a group of banks and insurance companies. Hughes sold his TWA stock early in 1966.

APPENDIX C

THE HOWARD HUGHES MEDICAL INSTITUTE: EXPENDITURES, 1954–1975[a]

Year	Total expenditures	Interest payments on Hughes loan	Lease payments on Hughes property	Research salaries and fellowships	Laboratory supplies and expenses	Payments to officers, research directors	Employees' annuity program	Travel, subsistence expenses	Medical library	All other expenditures
1954	$ 3,070,212	$ 721,732	$ 2,302,785	$ 43,348	$—	$—	$—	$ Not Ind.	$ Not Ind.	$ 2,347
1955	4,244,702	721,732	3,035,438	122,611	—	70,000	—	46,264	11,583	237,074
1956	3,264,626	723,709	1,816,000	238,413	148,612	107,500	5,209	86,382	3,061	135,740
1957	2,719,314	721,732	1,107,428	393,860	169,693	93,000	26,465	64,258	18,311	124,567
1958	2,365,863	721,732	824,000	426,435	117,519	93,000	38,748	48,400	10,536	85,493
1959	2,371,479	721,732	660,000	417,588	173,127	93,000	23,519	49,132	13,730	219,651
1960	2,340,761	814,173	589,000	431,673	245,460	91,500	(69,228)	46,471	17,375	105,109
1961	2,274,987	811,948	580,000	432,749	135,775	93,000	10,410	53,482	16,805	140,818
1962	2,149,636	811,948	483,000	480,053	124,930	84,500	16,362	40,881	19,658	88,304
1963	2,169,883	811,948	439,424	498,611	145,188	84,000	19,809	54,464	21,534	94,905
1964	1,959,097	814,173	207,884	516,026	146,240	86,000	25,867	42,267	20,503	100,137
1965	1,755,931	811,948	—	527,027	143,221	82,000	35,737	33,974	20,696	101,328
1966	1,954,597	811,948	—	553,646	176,545	43,443	50,021	24,078	20,512	274,404
1967	1,836,808	811,948	—	538,148	215,500	44,575	53,012	24,278	20,661	128,686
1968	1,951,585	814,173	—	551,716	253,022	38,615	55,304	21,486	10,686	206,583
1969	2,158,063	992,381	—	657,269	181,956	48,245	66,723	20,292	19,462	171,735
1970	2,186,905	992,381	—	761,383	124,084	55,625	66,243	21,386	22,311	143,492
1971	2,265,252	992,381	—	854,269	74,817	64,945	89,856	21,068	22,498	145,418
1972	2,596,556	995,100	—	1,008,444	54,543	76,300	118,710	23,050	25,471	294,938
1973	2,947,911	992,381	—	1,228,050	84,974	91,450	151,004	28,279	30,664	341,109
1974	3,594,239	992,381	—	1,551,681	242,307	107,155	182,816	30,068	34,176	453,655
1975	4,220,322	992,381	—	1,868,487	336,255	113,605	245,237	47,124	41,798	575,435
TOTAL	56,398,729	18,595,962	12,044,959	14,101,487	3,293,768	1,661,458	1,281,052	827,084	422,031	4,170,928

[a] Source: U.S. Internal Revenue Service.

APPENDIX D

THE HOWARD HUGHES MEDICAL INSTITUTE: TOTAL INCOME AND PAYMENTS TO HOWARD HUGHES[a]

	INCOME		MONEY PAID BACK TO HUGHES	
Year	Income from lease on Hughes's property	Dividends or contributions from Hughes Aircraft Co.	Interest payments on Hughes loan	Lease payments on Hughes property
1954	$ 3,609,785	$ —	$ 721,732	$ 2,302,785
1955	4,619,438	—	721,732	3,035,438
1956	4,700,000	—	723,709	1,816,000
1957	2,600,000	—	721,732	1,107,428
1958	2,600,000	—	721,732	824,000
1959	2,600,000	—	721,732	660,000
1960	2,600,000	—	814,173	589,000
1961	2,600,000	—	811,948	580,000
1962	2,600,000	—	811,948	483,000
1963	2,600,000	—	811,948	439,424
1964	1,300,000	—	814,173	207,884
1965	—	—	811,948	—
1966	—	—	811,948	—
1967	—	2,000,000	811,948	—
1968	—	—	814,173	—
1969	—	2,500,000	992,381	—
1970	—	2,500,000	992,381	—
1971	—	2,500,000	992,381	—
1972	—	2,500,000	995,100	—
1973	—	3,000,000	992,381	—
1974	—	3,500,000	992,381	—
1975	—	4,250,000	992,381	—
TOTAL	$ 32,429,223	$ 22,750,000	$ 18,595,962	$ 12,044,959

[a] Source: U.S. Internal Revenue Service.

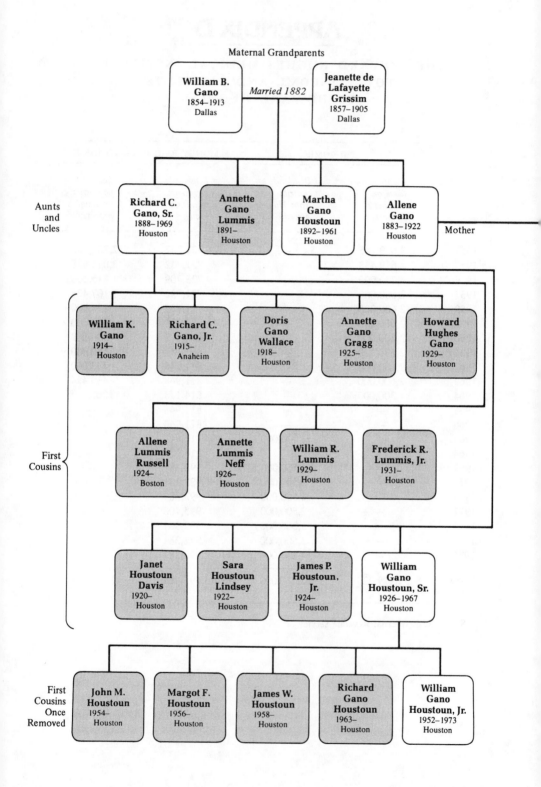

Maternal Grandparents

William B. Gano 1854–1913 Dallas — *Married 1882* — **Jeanette de Lafayette Grissim** 1857–1905 Dallas

Aunts and Uncles

Richard C. Gano, Sr. 1888–1969 Houston

Annette Gano Lummis 1891– Houston

Martha Gano Houstoun 1892–1961 Houston

Allene Gano 1883–1922 Houston — Mother

First Cousins

William K. Gano 1914– Houston

Richard C. Gano, Jr. 1915– Anaheim

Doris Gano Wallace 1918– Houston

Annette Gano Gragg 1925– Houston

Howard Hughes Gano 1929– Houston

Allene Lummis Russell 1924– Boston

Annette Lummis Neff 1926– Houston

William R. Lummis 1929– Houston

Frederick R. Lummis, Jr. 1931– Houston

Janet Houstoun Davis 1920– Houston

Sara Houstoun Lindsey 1922– Houston

James P. Houstoun, Jr. 1924– Houston

William Gano Houstoun, Sr. 1926–1967 Houston

First Cousins Once Removed

John M. Houstoun 1954– Houston

Margot F. Houstoun 1956– Houston

James W. Houstoun 1958– Houston

Richard Gano Houstoun 1963– Houston

William Gano Houstoun, Jr. 1952–1973 Houston

APPENDIX E

THE HEIRS OF
HOWARD ROBARD HUGHES, JR.
With each relative's current residence
or residence in year of death.

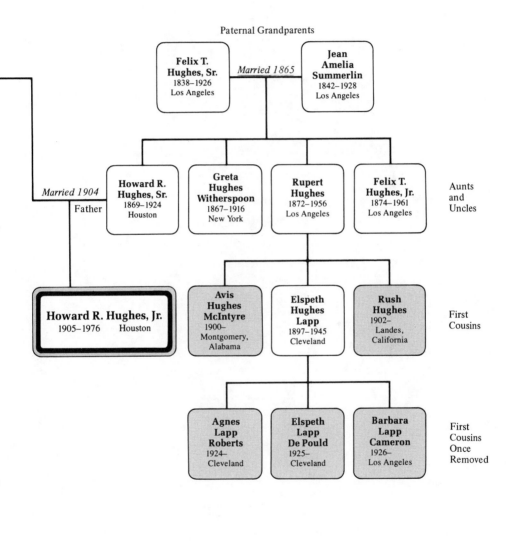

Paternal Grandparents

Felix T. Hughes, Sr.
1838–1926
Los Angeles

Married 1865

Jean Amelia Summerlin
1842–1928
Los Angeles

Married 1904

Father

Howard R. Hughes, Sr.
1869–1924
Houston

Greta Hughes Witherspoon
1867–1916
New York

Rupert Hughes
1872–1956
Los Angeles

Felix T. Hughes, Jr.
1874–1961
Los Angeles

Aunts and Uncles

Howard R. Hughes, Jr.
1905–1976   Houston

Avis Hughes McIntyre
1900–
Montgomery, Alabama

Elspeth Hughes Lapp
1897–1945
Cleveland

Rush Hughes
1902–
Landes, California

First Cousins

Agnes Lapp Roberts
1924–
Cleveland

Elspeth Lapp De Pould
1925–
Cleveland

Barbara Lapp Cameron
1926–
Los Angeles

First Cousins Once Removed

Source: Official public records in California, Iowa, Missouri, Nevada, New York, Ohio and Texas.

Beneficiaries of Hughes Estate

SOURCES

THE great majority of the records and documents used as the basis for this book were drawn from three general areas—the courts, government agencies, and private sources. Scores of civil and criminal legal actions involving Hughes, his companies, past and present Hughes executives, and others connected with the Hughes empire were examined in some two dozen different state and federal jurisdictions from New York to Los Angeles. Ten of the lawsuits have resulted in an accumulation of material running into the hundreds of thousands of pages, and thus are cited more frequently. Similarly, there are half a dozen congressional hearing records and reports mentioned more often than others. To eliminate ponderous repetition in the notes, we have abbreviated references to these sources.

There are three major cases dealing with the administration of the Hughes estate. *The Estate of Howard Robard Hughes, Jr.*, Los Angeles County Superior Court, No. 621359, is cited as "Hughes Estate California"; *In the Matter of the Estate of Howard Robard Hughes, Jr.*, Eighth Judicial District Court, Clark County, Nevada, No. 7202, is cited as "Hughes Estate Nevada"; and *The Estate of Howard Robard Hughes, Jr.*, Harris County Probate Court, Texas, No. 139, 362, is cited as "Hughes Estate Texas."

There are three significant lawsuits growing out of Hughes's takeover of Air West. *Patricia Scott Anderson et al. v. Air West Inc. et al.*, United States District Court for the Northern District of California, No. C–73–0529–AJZ, is cited as *"Anderson v. Air West"*; *Securities and Exchange Commission v. Howard R. Hughes et al.*, United States District Court for the Northern District of California, No. C–75–0589–AJZ, is cited as *"SEC v. Air West"*; and *United States Trust Company of New York et al. v. Summa Corporation et al.*, San Francisco County Superior Court, No. 643–644, is cited as *"U.S. Trust v. Summa."*

There are two lawsuits involving Robert A. Maheu, the former chief of Hughes Nevada Operations. The first, filed by Maheu immediately after he was fired by Hughes in 1970, is *Robert A. Maheu v. Chester C. Davis et al.*, Eighth Judicial District Court, Clark County, Nevada, No. A–84241, and is cited as *"Maheu v. Davis."* There is a parallel cross-action, *Hughes Tool Company v. Robert A. Maheu et al.*, Eighth Judicial District Court, Clark County, Nevada, No. 84259, but the cases and files were consolidated and so are treated as one. The second lawsuit, a defamation action brought by Maheu in 1972, is *Robert A. Maheu v. Hughes Tool Company*, United States District Court for the Central District of California, No. 72–305–HP, and is cited as *"Maheu v. Hughes Tool Company."*

There are two lawsuits stemming from Hughes's management of TWA. *Trans World Airlines v. Howard R. Hughes et al.*, United States District Court for the Southern District of New York, No. 61 Civil 2324, is cited as *"TWA v. Hughes,* New York." This case is closed and the files are now stored at the federal records center in Bayonne, New Jersey. The second lawsuit, which is still pending, is *Trans World Airlines v. Howard R. Hughes et al.*, New Castle County (Delaware) Chancery Court, Civil Action No. 1607, and is cited as *"TWA v. Hughes,* Delaware."

The 1947 Senate investigation of Hughes's wartime contracts, "Investigation of the National Defense Program, Hearings before a Special Committee Investigating the National Defense Program, United States Senate, Eightieth Congress, First Session, Parts 40 and 43," is cited as "Senate War Hearings." A 1967 House investigation of a helicopter contract awarded to Hughes, "Review of Army Procurement of Light Observation Helicopters, Hearings before the Subcommittee for Special Investigations of the Committee on Armed Services, House of Representatives, Ninetieth Congress, First Session," is cited as "Helicopter Hearings." A report issued following the hearings, "Review of Army Procurement of Light Observation Helicopters, Report of the Subcommittee for Special Investigations of the Committee on Armed Services, United States House of Representatives, Ninetieth Congress, First Session, July 18, 1967," is cited as "Helicopter Report."

The Senate investigation of Watergate, "Presidential Campaign Activities of 1972, Hearings before the Select Committee on Presidential Campaign Activities of the United States Senate, Ninety-third Congress, Second Session," is cited as "Senate Watergate Hearings." The Senate Watergate report, "The Final Report of the Select Committee on Presidential Campaign Activities, United States Senate, Ninety-third Congress, Second Session, Report No. 93–981, June 1974," is cited as "Senate Watergate Final Report." A House investigation of the CIA's role in Watergate, "Inquiry into the Alleged Involvement of the Central Intelligence Agency in the Watergate and Ellsberg Matters, Hearings before the Special Subcommittee on Intelligence of the Committee on Armed Services, House of Representatives, Ninety-fourth Congress, First Session," is cited as "House Intelligence Hearings."

Four categories of internal records of the Hughes organization referred to in the notes require further definition. First is a compilation of memoranda, dated mostly during the 1950s, assembled by the Romaine Street Operations staff and labeled the "Romaine Street Procedures Manual." Prepared as a guide for those who served Hughes's various needs, the manual offers detailed instructions on everything from how to answer the telephone at Romaine Street to how to drive a car carrying a potential Hughes starlet. The manual is cited by its official title, "Romaine Street Procedures Manual." A second collection of memoranda from the Hughes organization, designated as "Operating Memoranda," includes those messages that flowed through Romaine Street to and from Hughes and his lieutenants. These memoranda, which relate to both Hughes's business and personal affairs—from financial arrangements for the acquisition of jets to the purchase of aviation magazines he liked to read —date from the 1950s through 1966, when he moved to Las Vegas and stopped using Romaine Street as a communications center. They are cited as "Operating Memoranda." And finally, there are the Hughes organization's daily logs. Romaine Street, beginning in the late 1940s, maintained daily logs reflecting all telephone calls that came in for Hughes, as well as messages left by callers or dictated by Hughes in response to calls. These records are cited as the "Operations Logs." When Romaine Street ceased functioning as a clearing-house for all Hughes communications at the end of 1966, the aides who lived with the reclusive industrialist around the clock began keeping a daily record of his activities that differed markedly from the Operations Logs. In addition to noting any important business dealings, the aides recorded all of Hughes's personal habits—when he went to the bathroom, when he took his narcotics, what movies he watched, when and what he ate. These daily records are cited as the "Hughes Logs."

Last, a word about the source notes referring to "authors' files." While most of this book is based on the public record, it does contain certain material obtained from confidential sources. In addition, other material was obtained by the authors and the *Philadelphia Inquirer* through Freedom of Information Act requests to various federal agencies. In these cases, while the document itself is clearly identified either in the text or in the notes—such as "CIA memorandum"—the location of the document is cited as "authors' files."

NOTES

PROLOGUE. Death in Mexico

1. Deposition of Clarence A. Waldron, June 7, 1977, p. 188, Hughes Estate Texas.
2. Ibid.
3. Ibid.
4. Ibid.
5. Ibid.
6. Ibid.
7. Author's interview of confidential source.
8. Deposition of James H. Rickard, June 28, 1977, p. 107, Hughes Estate Texas.
9. Interview of Jack Real, May 16, 1978, in report to Administrator of Hughes Estate Nevada, authors' files.
10. Deposition of George A. Francom, Jr., June 30, 1977, p. 85, Hughes Estate Texas.
11. Laboratory Report, April 3, 1976, Laboratorio Central de Analasis, S.A., Acapulco, Mexico, Hughes Estate Texas.
12. Ibid.
13. Autopsy Report, Howard R. Hughes, Jr., April 7, 1976, The Methodist Hospital, Hughes Estate Texas.
14. Testimony of George A. Francom, Jan. 25, 1978, p. 207, Hughes Estate Texas.
15. Ibid.
16. Deposition of Waldron, p. 212.
17. Ibid.
18. Authors' interview of confidential source.
19. Deposition of Waldron, p. 213.
20. Authors' interview of confidential source.
21. Interview of Real, in report to Administrator of Hughes Estate Nevada.
22. Ibid.
23. Deposition of John M. Holmes, Jr., June 21, 1977, p. 323, Hughes Estate Texas.

1. The Early Years

1. Authors' interview of Mrs. Florence Stevenson, April 28, 1976.
2. Ibid.
3. Rupert Hughes, "My Mother," *American,* September 1924, p. 16.
4. Ibid.
5. Ibid.
6. Ibid.
7. Ibid.
8. Rupert Hughes, "Howard Hughes—Record Breaker," *Liberty,* Feb. 6, 1937, p. 24.
9. Ibid.
10. Authors' interview of confidential source.
11. Rupert Hughes, "Record Breaker," p. 24.
12. Records of the Class of 1897, Fourth Report, 1912, Harvard College, p. 218.
13. Ibid.
14. Ibid.
15. Ibid.
16. Ibid.
17. Ibid.
18. Rupert Hughes, "Record Breaker," p. 24.
19. Ibid.
20. *Dallas Morning News,* Jan. 27, 1972.
21. *Biographical History of Dallas County, Texas* (Chicago: Lewis Publishing, 1892), p. 1004.
22. Authors' interview of Mrs. Martha Potts, July 19, 1976.
23. Authors' interview of Dudley C. Sharp, July 1, 1976.
24. Harvard Class of 1897 report, p. 218.
25. Deposition of Annette Gano Lummis, Aug. 2, 1977, p. 8, Hughes Estate Texas.
26. Transcript of interview of Granville A.

Humason, July 7, 1953, Oral History of the Texas Oil Industry, Barker Texas History Center, University of Texas, Austin.

27. Ibid.
28. Rupert Hughes, "Record Breaker," p. 24.
29. U.S. Patent Office, patent application of H. R. Hughes, Nov. 20, 1908.
30. Harvard Class of 1897 report, p. 218.
31. *Houston Press,* July 12, 1946.
32. Jerome Beatty, "A Boy Who Began at the Top," *American,* April 1932, p. 35.
33. Rupert Hughes, "Record Breaker," p. 24.
34. Interview of Dudley Sharp.
35. Ibid.
36. Interview of Mrs. Martha Potts.
37. *Houston Chronicle,* May 2, 1971.
38. Letter, Allene Hughes to Daniel Carter Beard, June 14, 1916, Daniel Carter Beard papers, Manuscript Division, Library of Congress.
39. Letter, H. R. Hughes Sr. to Beard, June 23, 1916, Beard papers.
40. Letter, Hughes Sr. to Beard, July 8, 1916, Beard papers.
41. Letter, Beard to Hughes Sr., July 11, 1916, Beard papers.
42. Letter, Beard to Hughes Sr., Aug. 7, 1916, Beard papers.
43. Letter, Allene Hughes to Beard, Aug. 9, 1916, Beard papers.
44. Letter, Allene Hughes to Beard, Aug. 21, 1916, Beard papers.
45. Letter, Hughes Jr. to Beard, Dec. 29, 1916, Beard papers.
46. Letter, Hughes Jr. to Beard, April 22, 1917, Beard papers.
47. Letter, Allene Hughes to Beard, April 22, 1917, Beard papers.
48. Letter, Hughes Jr. to Beard, June 19, 1917, Beard papers.
49. Letter, Allene Hughes to Beard, July 16, 1917, Beard papers.
50. Letter, Allene Hughes to Lt. Aures, July 16, 1917, Beard papers.
51. Howard Hughes Jr. file, records of Daniel Beard, Beard papers.
52. Telegram, Beard to Allene Hughes, July 27, 1917, Beard papers.
53. Letter, Allene Hughes to Beard, Oct. 14, 1917, Beard papers.
54. Memorandum, Hughes to Robert Maheu, undated (about April 1968), *Maheu v. Hughes Tool Company.*
55. Letter, Allene Hughes to Beard, May 4, 1918, Beard papers.
56. Letter, Beard to Allene Hughes, May 9, 1918, Beard papers.
57. Letter, Hughes Sr. to Sherman Day Thacher, June 6, 1921, as quoted in Report to Administrator of Hughes Estate Nevada, May 29, 1978, authors' files.

58. Authors' interview of Percy Williams, May 6, 1976.
59. Ibid.
60. Ibid.
61. Ibid.
62. Ibid.
63. Ibid.
64. Ibid.
65. Ibid.
66. Letter, Hughes Sr. to Thacher, June 6, 1921, as quoted in Report to Administrator of Hughes Estate Nevada, May 29, 1978, authors' files.
67. Letter, Allene Hughes to Thacher, Oct. 19, 1921, as quoted in Report to Administrator of Hughes Estate Nevada, May 29, 1978, authors' files.
68. Rupert Hughes, "Record Breaker," p. 24.
69. Deposition of Annette Lummis, p. 21.
70. Ibid., p. 9.
71. Ibid., p. 63.
72. Letter, Thacher to Hughes Sr., Jan. 15, 1923, as quoted in Report to Administrator of Hughes Estate Nevada, May 29, 1978, authors' files.
73. Ibid.
74. Ibid.
75. Letter, Thacher to Hughes Jr., Feb. 8, 1923, as quoted in Report to Administrator of Hughes Estate Nevada, May 29, 1978, authors' files.
76. Deposition of Annette Lummis, p. 9.
77. Ibid., p. 13.
78. Deposition of Eleanor Boardman d'Arrast, March 30, 1977, p. 11, Hughes Estate Texas.
79. Ibid.
80. Deposition of Annette Lummis, pp. 16, 23–4.
81. *Houston Chronicle,* Jan. 15, 1924.
82. Deposition of Annette Lummis, p. 16.
83. *Petroleum World,* February 1924, p. 30.
84. *Estate of Howard R. Hughes (Sr.),* 11, 791, County Court of Harris County, Texas.
85. Letter, Jean Summerlin Hughes to Mary Hollingsworth, Oct. 10, 1926, authors' files.
86. Interview of Dudley Sharp.
87. Deposition of Annette Lummis, p. 65.
88. *New York News,* Sept. 19, 1948.
89. Will of Jean Hughes, Feb. 16, 1928, *Estate of Jean Hughes,* 99453, Los Angeles County Superior Court.
90. Deposition of Annette Lummis, p. 17.
91. Ibid.
92. Order of Judge Walter Montieth, Dec. 26, 1924, County Court of Harris County, Texas.
93. Ibid.
94. Deposition of Dr. Norman F. Crane, Aug. 10, 1977, p. 73, Hughes Estate Texas.
95. Deposition of Annette Lummis, pp. 60–1.
96. Ibid., pp. 17, 66.
97. Report of Richard C. Gano, Jr., Special Administrator, Regarding Will Search Activities, pp. 52–60, Hughes Estate California.
98. *Houston Chronicle,* May 31, 1925.

2. Hollywood

1. *Harper's,* May 1923, p. 694.
2. Henry F. Pringle, "Movie Magician," *Collier's,* March 19, 1932, p. 25.
•3. Bob Thomas, *Selznick* (Garden City, N.Y.: Doubleday, 1970), p. 49.
4. Charles Higham and Joel Greenberg, *The Cel-*

luloid Muse (London: Angus and Robertson, 1969), p. 148.

5. Ben Hecht, A Child of the Century (New York: Simon & Schuster, 1954), p. 487.

6. Mary Astor, A Life on Film (New York: Delacorte Press, 1967), p. 69.

7. Jerome Beatty, "A Boy Who Began at the Top," American, April 1932, p. 35 (hereinafter "Boy at the Top").

8. Bogart Rogers, "4 Million Dollars and 4 Men's Lives," Photoplay, April 1930, p. 30.

9. Ibid.

10. Ibid.

11. Noah Dietrich and Bob Thomas, Howard, the Amazing Mr. Hughes (New York: Fawcett, 1972), p. 72.

12. Transcript of interview of Don Malkames, 1958, Oral History Collection, Columbia University.

13. Transcript of interview of Roscoe Turner, 1960, Oral History Collection, Columbia University.

14. Deposition of Annette Gano Lummis, Aug. 2, 1977, p. 68, Hughes Estate Texas.

15. Beatty, "Boy at the Top," p. 34.

16. Petition of Ella Rice Hughes v. Howard R. Hughes, District Court of Harris County, Texas, Nov. 8, 1929.

17. New York World-Telegram, Feb. 13, 1937.

18. Look, March 18, 1954, p. 14.

19. Ibid.

20. Ibid.

21. Irving Shulman, Harlow (New York: Bernard Geis, 1964), p. 78.

22. Ibid.

23. Look, March 18, 1954, p. 14.

24. Ibid.

25. Shulman, Harlow, p. 91.

26. Ibid., p. 92.

27. Ibid.

28. Ibid.

29. David Thomson, Biographical Dictionary of

the Cinema (London: Secker & Warburg, 1975), p. 257.

30. Rogers, "4 Million Dollars," p. 31.

31. Beatty, "Boy at the Top," p. 34.

32. Pilot, July 1930.

33. Thomson, Biographical Dictionary of the Cinema, p. 257.

34. Rogers, "4 Million Dollars," p. 31.

35. Pilot, July 1930.

36. Rogers, "4 Million Dollars," p. 31.

37. Pilot, July 1930.

38. Pringle, "Movie Magician," p. 25.

39. Dietrich and Thomas, Amazing Mr. Hughes, p. 126.

40. Herbert Wilcox, Twenty-Five Thousand Sunsets (New York: A. S. Barnes, 1967), p. 84.

41. Ibid.

42. Beatty, "Boy at the Top," p. 34.

43. Ibid.

44. Pringle, "Movie Magician," p. 25.

45. Ibid.

46. Ibid.

47. Raoul Walsh, Each Man in His Own Time (New York: Farrar, Straus and Giroux, 1974), p. 269.

48. Ibid., p. 270.

49. Marion Davies, The Times We Had (Indianapolis: Bobbs-Merrill, 1975), p. 105.

50. Ibid , p. 106.

51. Ibid., p. 108.

52. Ibid.

53. Lewis Yablonsky, George Raft (New York: McGraw-Hill, 1974), p. 69.

54. Ibid., p. 70.

55. Beatty, "Boy at the Top," p. 34.

56. Time, Sept. 7, 1931, p. 29.

57. Photoplay, June 1931, p. 178

58. Higham and Greenberg, The Celluloid Muse, p. 156.

59. Ibid.

60. Jerome Lawrence, The Life and Times of Paul Muni (New York. Putnam's, 1974), p. 156

61. Quoted in Lawrence, Paul Muni, p. 165.

62 Ibid

3. Hero

1. Pilot, October 1932.

2. Authors' interview of Dudley C. Sharp, July 1, 1976.

3. Deposition of William Rice Lummis, Sept. 21, 1976, p. 11, Hughes Estate Nevada.

4. Authors' interview of Robert W. Rummel, Jan. 29, 1977.

5. Pilot, October 1932.

6. Interview of Robert Rummel.

7. Rush Loving, Jr., "The View from inside Hughes Tool," Fortune, December 1973, p. 106.

8. Report of Richard C. Gano, Jr., Special Administrator, Regarding Will Search Activities, pp. 79–81, Hughes Estate California.

9. Ibid.

10. Ibid.

11. Ibid., p. 82.

12. Interview of Robert Rummel.

13. Transcript of news media telephone interview of Hughes, Jan. 7, 1972, authors' files.

14. Time, Sept. 23, 1935, p. 66

15. Houston Press, March 10, 1937.

16. New York News, July 17, 1938.

17. Ibid.

18. Transcript of interview of Jacqueline Cochran, 1961, Oral History Collection, Columbia University.

19. Ibid.

20. Ibid.

21. Ibid.

22. Ibid.

23. New York Times, Jan. 15, 1936, p. 21.

24. Ibid.

25. Cochran Oral History transcript.

26. Ibid.

27. Philadelphia Inquirer, July 13, 1936.

28. Houston Chronicle, April 21, 1976.

29. Ibid.

30. Ibid.

31. New York Times, Nov. 16, 1936, p. 15.

32. Philadelphia Inquirer, Jan. 20, 1937

33. Ibid.
34. *New York Times,* Jan. 20, 1937, p. 1.
35. *Philadelphia Inquirer,* Jan. 20, 1937.
36. Ibid.
37. Ibid.
38. *New York Times,* Jan. 20, 1937, p. 1.
39. Senate War Hearings, p. 24366.
40. Letter, J. M. Johnson (assistant secretary of commerce) to Howard Hughes, July 19, 1937, Records of the Office of Airmen and Aircraft Registry, Aeronautical Center, Federal Aviation Administration, Oklahoma City.
41. Letter, J. M. Johnson to Hughes, May 23, 1938, FAA Aeronautical Center.
42. Gano Will Report, p. 89.
43. Ibid., p. 90.
44. Ibid., p. 104.
45. Ibid., p. 103.
46. *New York Times,* July 11, 1938, p. 1.
47. Ibid.
48. Ibid.
49. Ibid.
50. Ibid.
51. Ibid.
52. *New York Times,* July 12, 1938, p. 1.
53. Ibid.

54. *New York Times,* July 13, 1938, p. 1.
55. Ibid.
56. *New Republic,* July 20, 1938, p. 289.
57. *Philadelphia Inquirer,* July 18, 1938.
58. *New York Times,* July 15, 1938, p. 1.
59. Ibid.
60. Ibid.
61. Ibid.
62. *Philadelphia Inquirer,* July 18, 1938.
63. Grover A. Whalen, *Mr. New York* (New York: Putnam, 1955), p. 195.
64. Ibid.
65. Ibid., p. 196.
66. Ibid.
67. *New York Times,* July 16, 1938, p. 1.
68. Ibid.
69. Ibid., p. 3.
70. Ibid.
71. *Houston Post,* July 31, 1938.
72. Ibid.
73. Ibid.
74. Deposition of Annette Gano Lummis, Aug. 2, 1977, p. 26, Hughes Estate Texas.
75. *Houston Post,* Aug. 1, 1938.
76. *Houston Post,* July 30, 1938.
77. Ibid.

4. The War Years

1. Senate War Hearings, p. 26472.
2. Ibid., p. 24370.
3. Ibid., p. 24473.
4. Ibid., p. 24370.
5. Ibid., p. 24475.
6. Ibid.
7. Ibid., p. 24479.
8. Ibid.
9. Ibid., p. 24495.
10. *Time,* Jan. 13, 1941, p. 10.
11. James MacGregor Burns, *Roosevelt, The Soldier of Freedom* (New York: Harcourt Brace Jovanovich, 1970), p. 39.
12. *Philadelphia Inquirer,* Aug. 12, 1947.
13. Senate War Hearings, p. 24444.
14. Ibid., p. 24445.
15. Ibid., p. 24446.
16. Ibid., p. 24447.
17. Ibid.
18. Jonathan Daniels, *White House Witness* (Garden City, N.Y.: Doubleday, 1975), p. 92.
19. Bureau of the Budget, *The United States at War* (Washington, D.C.: U.S. Government Printing Office, 1946), p. 136.
20. *Oregonian* (Portland, Oregon), July 20, 1942.
21. Ibid.
22. Ibid.
23. Senate War Hearings, p. 23523.
24. *Philadelphia Inquirer,* July 22, 1942.
25. *Washington Post,* July 26, 1942.
26. Senate War Hearings, p. 23516.
27. Ibid.
28. *Philadelphia Record,* Aug. 3, 1942.
29. Senate War Hearings, p. 23508.
30. Ibid., p. 23517.
31. Ibid., p. 23608.
32. *Oregonian* (Portland, Oregon), July 20, 1942.

33. Senate War Hearings, p. 23599.
34. Ibid., p. 23644.
35. *Collier's,* Aug. 17, 1942, p. 8.
36. Ibid.
37. Senate War Hearings, p. 23551.
38. Ibid.
39. Ibid., p. 23519.
40. Ibid., p. 24429.
41. *New York World-Telegram,* Sept. 15, 1942.
42. Daniels, *White House Witness,* p. 242.
43. Senate War Hearings, p. 24439.
44. Ibid., p. 23620.
45. Ibid., p. 24391.
46. Ibid., p. 23519.
47. Ibid.
48. Ibid.
49. Ibid.
50. Ibid.
51. Ibid., p. 23524.
52. Ibid., p. 23519.
53. Igor Cassini and Jeanne Molli, *I'd Do It All Over Again: The Life and Times of Igor Cassini* (New York: Putnam, 1977), p. 87.
54. Ibid.
55. Senate War Hearings, p. 23762.
56. Ibid., p. 23761.
57. Authors' interview of Charles W. Von Rosenberg, June 24, 1977.
58. Ibid.
59. Ibid.
60. Ibid.
61. Ibid.
62. Ibid.
63. Ibid.
64. Ibid.
65. Ibid.
66. Ibid.

67. Senate War Hearings, p. 24409.
68. Ibid., p. 24448.
69. Ibid., p. 23763.
70. Ibid., p. 23729.
71. Ibid., p. 24448.
72. Ibid., pp. 24448-9.
73. Ibid., p. 23733.
74. Ibid., p. 24485.
75. Ibid., p. 23968.
76. Ibid., p. 23889.
77. Ibid.
78. Ibid., p. 23823.
79. H. H. Arnold, *Global Mission* (New York: Harper & Brothers, 1949), p 378
80. Senate War Hearings, p. 24492.
81. Ibid., p. 24493.
82. Ibid., pp. 27214-6.
83. Ibid.
84. Ibid., p. 23780.
85. Ibid., p. 26472.
86. Ibid.
87. Ibid., p. 23573.

88. Arnold, *Global Mission,* p. 479.
89. Senate War Hearings, p. 26392.
90. Ibid., p. 26474.
91. Ibid., p. 24444.
92. Ibid.
93. Ibid., p. 23706.
94. Ibid., pp. 27156-7.
95. *Newsweek,* May 13, 1946, p. 74.
96. Senate War Hearings, p. 26270.
97. Ibid., p. 26272.
98. Ibid., p. 26277.
99. Ibid.
100. Ibid., p. 26487.
101. Ibid., p. 26481.
102. Report of Richard C. Gano, Jr., Special Administrator, Regarding Will Search Activities, p. 193, Hughes Estate California.
103. Ibid.
104. Ibid., p. 195.
105. Ibid., p. 188.
106. Joe Petrali, as told to Maury Green, " 'O.K., Howard,' " *True,* February 1975, p. 16.

5. The Senate Investigation

1. Senate War Hearings, p. 26273.
2. Ibid., p. 27172.
3. Ibid., p. 27173.
4. Ibid.
5. Ibid., p. 26278.
6. Ibid., p. 27172.
7. Ibid., p. 27177.
8. Ibid., p. 26296.
9. Testimony of Jean Peters Hough, Jan. 31, 1978, p. 14, Hughes Estate Texas.
10. Senate War Hearings, p. 24507.
11. Ibid., p. 24505.
12. Ibid.
13. Message, Dr. Verne Mason to Colonel E. T. Kennedy, July 11, 1946, F-11 file, Record Group 18, "Records of the Army Air Forces," National Archives.
14. Ibid.
15. Senate War Hearings, p. 24506.
16. Ibid.
17. Message, Mason to Kennedy.
18. Ibid.
19. Senate War Hearings, p. 24507.
20. Ibid.
21. Deposition of Eleanor Boardman d'Arrast, Mar. 30, 1977, pp. 56-7, Hughes Estate Texas.
22. Authors' interview of confidential source.
23. Ibid.
24. Memorandum, Colonel George E. Price to Commanding General, Wright Field, Aug. 28, 1946, F-11 file, Record Group 18, "Records of the Army Air Forces," National Archives.
25. Senate War Hearings, p. 26792.
26. Ibid., p. 26516.
27. Ibid., p. 26517.
28. Ibid., p. 26791.
29. Ibid., p. 26516.
30. *New York Journal-American,* Aug. 1, 1947.
31. Drew Pearson, *Diaries 1949-1959,* edited by Tyler Abell (New York: Holt, Rinehart & Winston, 1974), p. 478.
32. *New York Journal-American,* Aug. 1, 1947.

33. Senate War Hearings, p. 24121.
34. Ibid., p. 24122.
35. Ibid., p. 24684.
36. Ibid., p. 24140.
37. Ibid., p. 24232.
38. Ibid., p. 24685.
39. *New York Times,* July 29, 1947, p. 8.
40. Ibid.
41. *New York Times,* July 31, 1947, p. 13.
42. *New York Journal-American,* Aug. 1, 1947.
43. Ibid.
44. Senate War Hearings, p. 23971.
45. Recording, CBS Radio Newscast, Aug. 4, 1947, National Archives.
46. Senate War Hearings, pp. 24017-8.
47. *New York Times,* Aug. 7, 1947, p. 1.
48. Senate War Hearings, p. 24114.
49. Ibid., p. 24179.
50. *Philadelphia Inquirer,* Aug. 12, 1947.
51. Senate War Hearings, pp. 24272-8.
52. Ibid., p. 24283.
53. Ibid., pp. 24344-6.
54. Ibid., p. 24345.
55. Ibid.
56. Ibid.
57. Ibid., p. 24305.
58. Ibid., p. 24364.
59. Ibid., p. 24356.
60. Ibid.
61. *Philadelphia Inquirer,* Aug. 12, 1947.
62. *New York Times,* Aug. 12, 1947, p. 1.
63. *New York Times,* Aug. 13, 1947, p. 1.
64. Joe Petrali as told to Maury Green, "O.K., Howard," *True,* March 1975, p. 31.
65. *New York Times,* Nov. 3, 1947, p. 1.
66. *Philadelphia Inquirer,* Nov. 3, 1947.
67. *New York Times,* Nov. 3, 1947, p. 1.
68. Wesley Frank Craven and James Lea Cate, eds., *The Army Air Forces in World War II* (Chicago: University of Chicago Press, 1955) 6:222.
69. Records of the Air History Center, Maxwell Air Force Base, Alabama.

6. Movies, Missiles, and Communists

1. Deposition of Frank W. Gay, July 14, 1977, p. 7, Hughes Estate Texas.
2. Ibid., pp. 7, 12.
3. Ibid., p. 8.
4. Ibid., p. 12.
5. *New York Times,* Jan. 16, 1948, p. 34.
6. Dore Schary, "I Remember Hughes," *New York Times Magazine,* May 2, 1976, p. 42.
7. Transcript of interview of Dore Schary, 1958, Oral History Collection, Columbia University.
8. Authors' interview of Jacqueline Cochran, April 18, 1977.
9. *New York Times,* May 12, 1948, p. 33.
10. Schary, "I Remember Hughes," p. 42.
11. Schary Oral History transcript.
12. Ibid.
13. Schary, "I Remember Hughes," p. 42.
14. *New York Herald-Tribune,* June 14, 1948.
15. Schary Oral History transcript.
16. Schary, "I Remember Hughes," p. 42.
17. Ibid.
18. Ibid.
19. Ibid.
20. Complaint, *Castleman v. Hughes,* 14848–BH, U.S. District Court for the Southern District of California.
21. *New York Times,* Oct. 5, 1957, p. 8.
22. Charles Higham and Joel Greenberg, *The Celluloid Muse* (London: Angus and Robertson, 1969), p. 119.
23. Louella O. Parsons, *Tell It to Louella* (New York: Putnam, 1961), p. 74.
24. Schary, "I Remember Hughes," p. 42.
25. Ibid.
26. *Hughes '76,* Hughes Aircraft Company, 1976.
27. Report of Richard C. Gano, Jr., Special Administrator, Regarding Will Search Activities, p. 116, Hughes Estate California.
28. Letter, Edward Woozley, Interior Department, to Representative Cliff Yancy, Feb. 17, 1954, Records of the Husite land exchange, Serial Patent File 1157470, National Archives.
29. Memorandum, W. L. Shafer, Interior Department field examiner, to Department of Interior regional administrator, San Francisco, Nov. 30, 1930, Husite records, National Archives.
30. Authors' interview of confidential source.
31. Ibid.
32. Ibid.
33. Memorandum, Hughes to Lee Murrin, Nadine Henley, and Bill Gay, late 1951, Hughes Estate Texas.
34. Ibid.
35. Gano Will Report, p. 152.
36. Ibid., pp. 163–164.
37. Ibid., p. 179.
38. Ibid., p. 202.
39. Ibid.
40. Deposition of Nadine Henley, June 16, 1977, p. 173, Hughes Estate Texas.
41. Gano Will Report, p. 34.
42. *Philadelphia Inquirer,* Feb. 21, 1952.
43. Deposition of Frank W. Gay, p. 37.
44. *Congressional Record,* March 19, 1953, p. A2113.
45. Ibid.
46. *Philadelphia Inquirer,* April 7, 1952.
47. Ibid.
48. *New York Journal-American,* May 5, 1952.
49. *New York Herald-Tribune,* April 18, 1952.
50. *Congressional Record,* March 19, 1953, p. A2113.
51. *New York Herald-Tribune,* Oct. 24, 1952.
52. *Time,* Feb. 9, 1953, p. 96.
53. *Philadelphia Inquirer,* Jan. 28, 1953.
54. *Congressional Record,* March 19, 1953, p. 2126.
55. Ibid., p. 2127.
56. U.S. Securities and Exchange Commission, annual report of RKO Radio Pictures Corp., 1951.
57. *Wall Street Journal,* Oct. 20, 1952.
58. *Philadelphia Inquirer,* Sept. 19, 1952.
59. Ibid., Oct. 24, 1952.
60. U.S. Securities and Exchange Commission, annual reports of RKO, 1949–1953.
61. Complaint, *Castleman v. Hughes.*

7. Revolt at Culver City

1. *Arizona Citizen,* Oct. 8, 1951.
2. *Arizona Daily Star,* Oct. 9, 1951.
3. Deposition of Frank W. Gay, July 15, 1977, p. 175, Hughes Estate Texas.
4. Authors' interview of confidential source.
5. Deposition of Nadine Henley, June 15, 1977, p. 137, Hughes Estate Texas.
6. Inventory of Green House, April 20, 1976, Hughes Estate Texas.
7. *New York Post,* Oct. 25, 1952.
8. Authors' interview of confidential source.
9. Authors' interview of confidential source.
10. *Noah Dietrich v. Howard Hughes et al.,* C–33618, Los Angeles County Superior Court.
11. Charles J. V. Murphy, "The Blowup at Hughes Aircraft," *Fortune,* February 1954, p. 116.
12. Ibid.
13. Ibid.
14. Authors' interview of Roger Lewis, Aug. 2, 1976.
15. Murphy, "The Blowup at Hughes Aircraft," p. 116.
16. Ibid.
17. *Time,* Oct. 5, 1953, p. 91.
18. Interview of Roger Lewis.
19. Ibid
20. Ibid.
21. Ibid.
22. Ibid.
23. *Aviation Week,* Oct. 5, 1953, p. 15.
24. *St. Louis Post-Dispatch,* Dec 30, 1953.
25. Ibid.

26. Ibid.
27. *Newsweek,* May 31, 1954, p. 84.
28. *Time,* May 31, 1954, p. 72.
29. *Life,* Jan. 11, 1954, p. 24.
30. *Variety,* Jan. 13, 1954.
31. Ibid.
32. Certificate of Incorporation of HHMI Corporation, Secretary of State, Delaware, December 17, 1953.
33. Certificate of Amendment of Certificate of Incorporation of HHMI Corporation, Secretary of State, Delaware, December 29, 1954.
34. Report of Richard C. Gano, Jr., Special Administrator, Regarding Will Search Activities, p. 206, Hughes Estate California.
35. Ibid., p. 217.
36. U.S., Congress, House, Subcommittee on Domestic Finance of the Committee on Banking and Currency, *Tax-Exempt Foundations and Charitable Trusts,* 93rd Cong., 1st sess., 1973, p. 152.
37. Ibid.
38. Ibid.
39. Ibid.
40. U.S., Congress, House, Chairman's Report to the Select Committee on Small Business, *Tax-Exempt Foundations and Charitable Trusts: Their Impact on Our Economy,* 87th Cong., Dec. 31, 1962, p. 74.
41. Ibid.
42. *New York Times,* Oct. 6, 1955, p. 38.

43. *Newsweek,* Oct. 17, 1955, p. 89.
44. *Time,* Oct. 17, 1955, p. 100.
45. Ibid.
46. Ibid.
47. *Congressional Record,* Aug. 20, 1962, p. 17000.
48. Gano Will Report, p. 38.
49. Ibid.
50. *Evening Bulletin* (Philadelphia), April 27, 1947.
51. Testimony of Robert A. Maheu, trial transcript, p. 8619, *Maheu v. Hughes Tool Company.*
52. U.S., Internal Revenue Service, Form 990-A, Return of Organization Exempt from Income Tax, Howard Hughes Medical Institute, 1954.
53. *Evening Bulletin* (Philadelphia), Sept. 1, 1956.
54. Assessment Rolls, 1956, Los Angeles County Assessor.
55. Debtor's Petition, F. Donald Nixon, 124460, U.S. District Court for the Southern District of California.
56. *Miami Herald,* May 12, 1955.
57. Ibid., Jan. 12, 1956.
58. Authors' interview of LeRoy Collins, Aug. 19, 1956.
59. *Miami Herald,* Feb. 2, 1956.
60. *Miami News,* April 9, 1956.
61. *New York Times,* May 1, 1976, p. 20.
62. IRS Form 990-A, Howard Hughes Medical Institute, 1957.
63. Ibid., 1955.

8. Seeds of Disaster

1. William Zeckendorf with Edward McCreary, *Zeckendorf* (New York: Holt, Rinehart and Winston, 1970), p. 156.
2. Ibid.
3. Ibid., p. 157.
4. Ibid.
5. Ibid.
6. Ibid.
7. Ibid., p. 159.
8. Ibid.
9. Ibid., p. 160.
10. Authors' interview of confidential source.
11. General Instructions, June 26, 1952, Romaine Street Procedures Manual, authors' files.
12. Special Instructions, Nov. 22, 1954, Romaine Street Procedures Manual.
13. Deposition of John M. Holmes, Jr., June 9, 1977, p. 24, Hughes Estate Texas.
14. Instruction, January 1956, Romaine Street Procedures Manual.
15. General Instructions, Oct. 5, 1949, Romaine Street Procedures Manual.
16. Affidavit of Kay G. Glenn, June 27, 1962, *TWA v. Hughes,* New York.
17. Ibid.
18. Authors' interview of LeRoy Collins, Aug. 19, 1976.
19. Affidavit of Kay Glenn.
20. Ibid.
21. Ibid.
22. Operating Memorandum, Oct. 13, 1958, Romaine Street Procedures Manual.

23. Deposition of Ron Kistler, Aug. 20, 1977, p. 139, Hughes Estate Texas.
24. Staff Memorandum No. 1, Nov. 1, 1951, Romaine Street Procedures Manual.
25. Ibid.
26. Ibid.
27. Special Instruction, Jan. 13, 1952, Romaine Street Procedures Manual.
28. Ibid.
29. Staff Memorandum No. 1, Nov. 1, 1951, Romaine Street Procedures Manual.
30. Ibid.
31. Ibid.
32. Memorandum, Hughes to Robert Rummel, May 23, 1958, *TWA v. Hughes,* New York.
33. *New York Journal-American,* July 25, 1947.
34. *Kansas City Star,* April 6, 1976.
35. Deposition of Emmett O. Cocke, Aug. 3, 1962, p. 779, *TWA v. Hughes,* New York.
36. *New York Times,* April 11, 1976, p. 13, Section F.
37. Statement of Robert W. Rummel, *TWA v. Hughes,* New York.
38. Authors' interview of Robert W. Rummel, Jan. 29, 1977.
39. Ibid.
40. Ibid.
41. Ibid.
42. Ibid.
43. Ibid.
44. Richard Austin Smith, "How a Great Corpo-

ration Got out of Control," *Fortune,* January 1962, p. 64.
45. Statement of Rummel, *TWA v. Hughes,* New York.
46. Report of Ralph S. Damon to TWA Board of Directors, Dec. 6, 1955, *TWA v. Hughes,* New York.
47. Deposition of Robert Rummel, Aug. 3, 1962, p. 1774, *TWA v. Hughes,* New York.
48. Ibid.
49. Ibid., p. 1769.
50. *Business Week,* May 19, 1956, p. 29.
51. Ibid.
52. Ibid.
53. Interview of LeRoy Collins.
54. Ibid.
55. *Miami Herald,* Jan. 12, 1956.
56. *Miami News,* April 9, 1956.
57. Operations Log, May 7, 1956, *TWA v. Hughes,* New York.
58. Ibid., May 12, 1956.
59. Ibid.

60. Smith, "How a Great Corporation Got out of Control," p. 64.
61. Letter, Raymond Cook to Noah Dietrich, Sept. 25, 1956, *TWA v. Hughes,* New York.
62. Ibid.
63. Ibid.
64. Ibid.
65. Letter, Jack Zevely to Howard Hughes, Feb. 19, 1957, *TWA v. Hughes,* New York.
66. *Fortune,* April 1957, p. 153.
67. Interview of Robert Rummel.
68. Charles J. V. Murphy and T. A. Wise, "The Problem of Howard Hughes," *Fortune,* January 1959, p. 79.
69. Deposition of Carol Dietrich, April 9, 1975, pp. 37–42, *Noah Dietrich v. Howard Hughes et al.,* C–33618, Los Angeles County Superior Court.
70. Deposition of Frank W. Gay, July 14, 1977, p. 47, Hughes Estate Texas.
71. Authors' interview of Dudley C. Sharp, July 1, 1976.
72. Ibid.

9. Breakdown

1. Deposition of Jean Peters Hough, July 26, 1977, p. 23, Hughes Estate Texas.
2. Ibid., p. 18.
3. Testimony of George A. Francom, Jan. 25, 1978, pp. 140–2, Hughes Estate Texas.
4. Testimony of Jean Peters Hough, Jan. 31, 1978, pp. 20–1, Hughes Estate Texas.
5. Memorandum, Raymond A. Cook to files, June 11, 1958, concerning meeting with Simon Taub and Noah Dietrich, authors' files.
6. Charles J. V. Murphy and T. A. Wise, "The Problem of Howard Hughes," *Fortune,* January 1959, p. 79.
7. Ibid.
8. Ibid.
9. Deposition of Frank W. Gay, July 14, 1977, p. 45, Hughes Estate Texas.
10. Deposition of John M. Holmes, Jr., June 21, 1977, p. 351, Hughes Estate Texas.
11. Ibid.
12. Ibid., p. 123.
13. Ibid., p. 128.
14. Operating Memorandum, Oct. 13, 1958, Romaine Street Procedures Manual, authors' files.
15. Deposition of John M. Holmes, June 9, 1977, p. 72, Hughes Estate Texas.
16. Deposition of Ron Kistler, Aug. 20, 1977, p. 39, Hughes Estate Texas.
17. Ibid., p. 38.
18. Ibid.
19. Ibid., p. 128.
20. Ibid., p. 41.
21. Ibid., pp. 129–30.
22. Ibid., pp. 65, 117–18.
23. Ibid., p. 132.
24. Ibid., p. 46.
25. Authors' interview of confidential source.
26. Ibid.
27. Deposition of Ron Kistler, p. 48.
28. Ibid., p. 139.

29. Memorandum, January 1958, Romaine Street Procedures Manual.
30. Ibid.
31. Ibid.
32. Operating Memorandum, Oct. 13, 1958, Romaine Street Procedures Manual.
33. Operating Memorandum, July 23, 1958, Romaine Street Procedures Manual.
34. Authors' interview of confidential source.
35. Deposition of Richmond M. Anderson, Aug. 21, 1974, pp. 9, 17, *U.S. Trust v. Summa.*
36. Operating Memorandum, Oct. 10, 1958, Romaine Street Procedures Manual.
37. Operating Memorandum, Oct. 10, 1958, Romaine Street Procedures Manual.
38. Ibid.
39. Operating Memorandum, June 20, 1958, Romaine Street Procedures Manual.
40. Operating Memorandum, July 21, 1959, Romaine Street Procedures Manual.
41. Instructions, Oct. 17, 1955, Romaine Street Procedures Manual.
42. Ibid.
43. Operating Memorandum, July 20, 1960, Romaine Street Procedures Manual.
44. Ibid.
45. Memorandum, Hughes to Gay, Jan. 13, 1961, Romaine Street Procedures Manual.
46. Ibid.
47. Ibid.
48. Ibid.
49. Memorandum, Gay to Hughes, Dec. 12, 1961, Romaine Street Procedures Manual.
50. Ibid.
51. Operating Memorandum, Feb. 20, 1958, Romaine Street Procedures Manual.
52. Operating Memorandum, Dec. 1, 1958, Romaine Street Procedures Manual.
53. Operating Memorandum, Oct. 2, 1958, Romaine Street Procedures Manual.
54. Ibid.

55. Ibid.
56. *Fortune,* July 1959, p. 112.
57. Operations Log, Feb. 27, 1959, *TWA v. Hughes,* New York.
58. *Forbes,* Aug. 1, 1974, p. 39.
59. Testimony of Robert A. Maheu, trial transcript, p. 8707, *Maheu v. Hughes Tool Company.*
60. Complaint, *Gail Ganley v. Howard Hughes et al.,* 800098, Los Angeles County Superior Court.
61. Ibid.
62. Declaration of Arthur Crowley, Dec. 10, 1963, *Arthur Crowley v. Howard Hughes et al.,* 824972, Los Angeles County Superior Court.
63. Authors' interview of Dudley C. Sharp, July 1, 1976.
64. Affidavit of J. William Bew, Jan. 31, 1963, *TWA v. Hughes,* New York.
65. Ibid.
66. Ibid.
67. Richard Austin Smith, "How a Great Corporation Got out of Control," *Fortune,* January 1962, p. 64.
68. *Fortune,* July 1959, p. 113.
69. Complaint, *TWA v. Hughes,* Delaware.
70. Ibid.
71. T. A. Wise, "The Bankers and the Spook," *Fortune,* March 1961, p. 142.
72. Operations Log, July 25, 1960, *TWA v. Hughes,* New York.
73. Ibid., June 16, 1960.
74. Ibid.
75. Ibid., Aug. 3, 1960.
76. Internal Bank of America Memorandum, Oct. 19, 1960, *TWA v. Hughes,* New York.
77. Ibid.
78. Testimony of Robert A. Maheu, trial transcript, p. 8733, *Maheu v. Hughes Tool Company.*
79. Ibid., p. 8735.
80. Ibid., p. 8737.
81. Operations Log, Oct. 28, 1960, *TWA v. Hughes,* New York.
82. Wise, "Bankers and the Spook," p. 142.
83. Operations Log, Nov. 23, 1960, *TWA v. Hughes,* New York.
84. Ibid., Nov. 25, 1960.

10. Retreat

1. Deposition of John M. Holmes, Jr., June 9, 1977, p. 65, Hughes Estate Texas.
2. T. A. Wise, "The Bankers and the Spook," *Fortune,* March 1961, p. 142.
3. Ibid.
4. Deposition of Charles C. Tillinghast, Jr., May 5, 1962, p. 112, *TWA v. Hughes,* New York.
5. Ibid., p. 67.
6. U.S., Civil Aeronautics Board, *CAB Reports,* 32: 1365.
7. Ibid.
8. Ibid.
9. Operations Log, Feb. 20, 1961, *TWA v. Hughes,* New York.
10. Complaint, *D. M. Ferry, Jr., Trustee Corporation et al. v. Chester C. Davis,* 615574, Wayne County Circuit Court, Detroit.
11. Paul Hoffman, *Lions in the Street: The Inside Story of the Great Wall Street Law Firms* (New York: Saturday Review Press, 1973), p. 90.
12. Memorandum, Hughes to Chester C. Davis, July 1, 1961, author's files.
13. Ibid.
14. Memorandum, Hughes to Davis, July 16, 1961, authors' files.
15. Ibid.
16. Memorandum, Hughes to Bautzer, July 18, 1961, authors' files.
17. Memorandum, Hughes to Gay, July 19, 1961, authors' files.
18. Memorandum, Davis to Hughes, July 21, 1961, authors' files.
19. Ibid.
20. Memorandum, Hughes to Gay, July 22, 1961, authors' files.
21. Memorandum, Hughes to Bautzer, July 27, 1961, authors' files.
22. Memorandum, Davis to Hughes, July 28, 1961, authors' files.
23. Operating Memorandum, Hughes to Gay, Aug. 6, 1961, authors' files.
24. Ibid.
25. Operating Memorandum, Hughes to Gay, Aug. 8, 1961, authors' files.
26. Ibid.
27. *CAB Reports,* 34:584.
28. U.S., Civil Aeronautics Board, transcript of meeting of Civil Aeronautics Board, Sept. 12, 1961, *Toolco-Northeast Control Case,* 11620, p. 32.
29. Ibid., pp. 42–3.
30. Ibid.
31. Ibid.
32. Ibid.
33. *New York Times,* Nov. 8, 1961, p. 51.
34. *New York Times,* Nov. 10, 1961, p. 51.
35. Authors' interview of confidential source.
36. Operating Memorandum, Hughes to Jack Price, Aug. 30, 1961, authors' files.
37. Ibid.
38. Operating Memorandum, Hughes to Gay, Sept. 5, 1961, authors' files.
39. Ibid.
40. Deposition of John Holmes, p. 135.
41. Transcript of tape-recorded telephone conversation, Hughes and Kay G. Glenn, Oct. 29, 1961, authors' files.
42. Testimony of Jean Peters Hough, Jan. 31, 1978, pp. 40–41, Hughes Estate Texas.
43. Deposition of George A. Francom, Jr., June 30, 1977, p. 5, Hughes Estate Texas.
44. *CAB Reports,* 34:584.
45. Ibid.
46. Operating Memorandum, Hughes to Raymond Cook, Dec. 14, 1961, *Toolco-Northeast Control Case,* 11620, Civil Aeronautics Board.
47. Ibid.

48. Ibid.
49. James R. Phelan, "Howard Hughes: He Is Battling for Control of a Billion-Dollar Empire," *Saturday Evening Post*, Feb. 9, 1963, p. 15.
50. Deposition of John Holmes, p. 172.
51. Ibid.
52. Ibid.
53. Ibid., pp. 172A–174.
54. Deposition of George Francom, p. 174.
55. Deposition of Levar B. Myler, June 24, 1977, p. 20, Hughes Estate Texas.
56. *United States of America v. Dr. Norman F. Crane and John Morrison Holmes*, CR LV–78–22–RDF, United States District Court for the District of Nevada.
57. Deposition of Roy E. Crawford, June 2, 1977, p. 70, Hughes Estate Texas.
58. Ibid., p. 71.
59. Deposition of John Holmes, p. 177.
60. Ibid., p. 226.
61. Thomas Thompson, "Riddle of an Embattled Phantom," *Life*, Sept. 7, 1962, p. 20.
62. Letter, Davis to Judge Charles M. Metzner, Aug. 1, 1962, *TWA v. Hughes*, New York.
63. Transcript of hearing before Judge Charles Metzner, Sept. 6, 1962, p. 7, *TWA v. Hughes*, New York.
64. Ibid., p. 12.
65. *Trans World Airlines v. Howard R. Hughes*, 32 F.R.D. 604 (1963).
66. Ibid.
67. *Trans World Airlines v. Howard R. Hughes*, 332 F. 2d 602 (1964).
68. Ibid.
69. Ibid., p. 610.
70. *New York Times*, July 31, 1964, p. 31.
71. Ibid.
72. Report of Richard C. Gano, Jr., Special Administrator, Regarding Will Search Activities, pp. 116–17, Hughes Estate California.
73. Deposition of Milton H. West, Jr., April 21, 1977, p. 352, Hughes Estate Texas.

11. A New Career

1. *New York Daily News*, Aug. 7, 1966.
2. Testimony of Jean Peters Hough, Jan. 31, 1978, p. 44, Hughes Estate Texas.
3. Ibid., p. 45.
4. Memorandum, Hughes to unidentified aide, undated, Hughes Estate Texas.
5. Operating Memorandum, Hughes to Gay, Aug. 22, 1961, Romaine Street, authors' files.
6. Memorandum, Hughes to Maheu, undated, *Maheu v. Hughes Tool Company*.
7. Testimony of Robert A. Maheu, trial transcript, p. 11461, *Maheu v. Hughes Tool Company*.
8. Ibid., p. 8867.
9. Ibid., p. 8866.
10. Ibid.
11. *Las Vegas Sun*, Dec. 2, 1966.
12. Ibid.
13. U.S., Congress, Senate, Special Committee to Investigate Organized Crime in Interstate Commerce (Kefauver Hearings), *Investigation of Organized Crime in Interstate Commerce*, 81st Cong., 2d sess., Part 2, pp. 174–75.
14. Ibid., Part 10, p. 923.
15. Ibid., Part 2, p. 175.
16. Ibid., Part 10, p. 928.
17. Deposition of Morris B. (Moe) Dalitz, May 10, 1973, p. 10, *Maheu v. Hughes Tool Company*.
18. *Las Vegas Sun*, Dec. 31, 1966.
19. Deposition of Moe Dalitz, June 1, 1973, p. 171.
20. Ibid., p. 170.
21. Ibid., p. 171.
22. Deposition of Herman M. Greenspun, Dec. 27, 1973, p. 16, *U.S. Trust v. Summa*.
23. *New York Times*, Dec. 23, 1943, p. 1.
24. Kefauver Hearings, Part 5, p. 378.
25. U.S., Congress, Senate, Interim Report of the Select Committee to Study Governmental Operations with Respect to Intelligence Activities, *Alleged Assassination Plots Involving Foreign Leaders*, 94th Cong., 1st sess., p. 74.
26. Ibid., p. 77.
27. Ibid., p. 126.
28. Ibid.
29. Ibid., p. 130.
30. Ibid., p. 131.
31. Ibid.
32. Ibid., p. 133.
33. Ibid., p. 132.
34. Ibid., p. 80.
35. Ibid.
36. Ibid.
37. Ibid., p. 81.
38. Ibid., p. 75.
39. Ibid., p. 83.
40. Testimony of Robert A. Maheu, trial transcript, p. 8836, *Maheu v. Hughes Tool Company*.
41. Senate Report on Assassination Plots, p. 75.
42. Virgil W. Peterson, *A Report on Chicago Crime for 1965*, Chicago Crime Commission, Aug. 5, 1966, p. 66.
43. Ibid.
44. Ibid., p. 67.
45. Ibid.
46. Ibid.
47. Ibid.
48. Deposition of Moe Dalitz, May 10, 1973, p. 39.
49. Ibid., p. 12.
50. Plaintiff's answers to interrogatories, filed Jul. 20, 1972, *Maheu v. Hughes Tool Company*.
51. Deposition of Moe Dalitz, June 1, 1973, p. 187.
52. Deposition of Robert A. Maheu, Jan. 29, 1973, vol. 7, p. 493, *Maheu v. Hughes Tool Company*.
53. *Las Vegas Review–Journal*, Dec. 31, 1964.
54. Ibid.
55. Deposition of Linda Gray Hollings, Nov. 5, 1976, p. 10, Hughes Estate Texas.
56. Affidavit in support of creditor's claim, filed Sept. 24, 1976, Hughes Estate Nevada.
57. Power of attorney, March 24, 1967, *Maheu v. Davis*.
58. Transcript of Nevada Gaming Control Board hearing, March 16, 1972.

59. Deposition of Thomas G. Bell, March 27, 1973, p. 568, *Maheu v. Hughes Tool Company.*
60. *Reno Evening Gazette,* Nov. 9, 1966.
61. *New York Times,* Oct. 28, 1966, p. 28.
62. Victor S. Navasky, *Kennedy Justice* (New York: Atheneum, 1971), p. 79.
63. Ed Reid and Ovid Demaris, *The Green Felt Jungle* (New York: Trident Press, 1963), p. 6.
64. Ibid., p. 5.
65. *Reno Evening Gazette,* March 28, 1967.
66. Ibid.
67. *Las Vegas Sun,* March 29, 1967.
68. *Reno Evening Gazette,* March 28, 1967.
69. Ibid.
70. Ibid.
71. Ibid.
72. Ibid., March 30, 1967.
73. *Las Vegas Sun,* April 1, 1967.
74. Deposition of Raymond M. Holliday, p. 68, *Los Angeles Airways v. Hughes Tool Company,* C–36249, Los Angeles County Superior Court.
75. Deposition of Calvin J. Collier, Jr., p. 123, *Los Angeles Airways v. Hughes Tool Company,* C–36249, Los Angeles County Superior Court.
76. Ibid., pp. 122–123.
77. Ibid., pp. 123–124.
78. Deposition of Moe Dalitz, May 10, 1973, p. 48.
79. Deposition of Moe Dalitz, June 1, 1973, p. 272.
80. Ibid., p. 241.

12. Lord of the Desert

1. Deposition of Elizabeth Peters Hough, July 26, 1977, p. 16, Hughes Estate Nevada.
2. Testimony of Jean Peters Hough, Jan. 31, 1978, p. 50, Hughes Estate Texas.
3. Ibid., p. 51.
4. Ibid., pp. 48–49.
5. Ibid., p. 50.
6. Deposition of Morris B. (Moe) Dalitz, May 10, 1973, p. 53, *Maheu v. Hughes Tool Company.*
7. Deposition of James Richard Gray, pp. 24–25, *Los Angeles Airways v. Hughes Tool Company,* C–36249, Los Angeles County Superior Court.
8. Ibid., p. 25.
9. Hearing, Harris County Probate Court, Jan. 6, 1977, p. 115, Hughes Estate Texas.
10. Deposition of Herman M. Greenspun, Feb. 23, 1973, p. 24, *Maheu v. Hughes Tool Company.*
11. Ibid., pp. 31–32.
12. Deposition of Herman Greenspun, April 10, 1973, p. 139, *Maheu v. Hughes Tool Company.*
13. Deposition of Herman Greenspun, Feb. 23, 1973, p. 32.
14. Ibid., p. 37.
15. Ibid., p. 38.
16. Ibid., p. 34.
17. Ibid.
18. Ibid.
19. Ibid.
20. Ibid., p. 35.
21. Ibid., p. 36.
22. Ibid.
23. Official transcript of SEC interview of Edward P. Morgan, June 15, 1973, p. 6, *SEC v. Air West.*
24. Ibid., p. 7.
25. Ibid., pp. 7–8.
26. Ibid., p. 10.
27. Testimony of Robert A. Maheu, trial transcript, May 15, 1974, p. 8859, *Maheu v. Hughes Tool Company.*
28. Deposition of Robert A. Maheu, July 2, 1973, p. 753, *Maheu v. Hughes Tool Company.*
29. Deposition of Herman Greenspun, Feb. 23, 1973, pp. 54–55.
30. U.S., Federal Communications Commission, Memorandum and Opinion re Application of Orange Radio Inc., Order adopted May 14, 1971, Docket No. 15752.
31. *United States of America v. Hughes Tool Company et al.,* U.S. District Court for the District of Nevada, unfiled complaint and memorandum, Senate Watergate Hearings, Book 26, p. 12799.
32. *Newsweek,* Jan. 15, 1968, p. 25.
33. Memorandum, Gray to Hughes, Oct. 2, 1967, *Las Vegas Sun v. Summa Corporation et al.,* Civil LV–76–77, U.S. District Court for the District of Nevada.
34. Ibid.
35. Ibid.
36. Wallace Turner, *Gamblers' Money* (Boston: Houghton Mifflin Company, 1965), p. 125.
37. *Las Vegas Sun,* Jan. 6, 1968.
38. *Newsweek,* Jan. 19, 1968, p. 25.
39. *Las Vegas Review–Journal,* Jan. 20, 1968.
40. Ibid., Jan. 22, 1968.
41. Ibid.
42. *Las Vegas Sun,* Jan. 26, 1968.
43. *Las Vegas Review–Journal,* Jan. 25, 1968.
44. Ibid.
45. Ibid.
46. Ibid., Sept. 10, 1967.
47. Ibid.
48. Ibid., Feb. 10, 1968.
49. *Reno Evening Gazette,* Feb. 27, 1968.
50. Ibid.
51. Memorandum, Hughes to Maheu, Feb. 10, 1968, authors' files.
52. Ibid.
53. Memorandum, Hughes to Maheu, February 1968, *Maheu v. Hughes Tool Company.*
54. Ibid.
55. Ibid.
56. Memorandum, Maheu to Hughes, March 1, 1968, *Maheu v. Hughes Tool Company.*
57. Memorandum, Hughes to Maheu, undated, *Maheu v. Hughes Tool Company.*
58. Memorandum, Hughes to Maheu, undated, *Maheu v. Hughes Tool Company.*
59. Memorandum, Hughes to Maheu, March 13, 1968, *Maheu v. Hughes Tool Company.*

60. *The Reporter,* June 9, 1953, p. 25.
61. *Las Vegas Sun,* March 16, 1968.
62. Ibid.
63. Memorandum, Hughes to Maheu, March 17, 1968, *Maheu v. Hughes Tool Company.*
64. Memorandum, Hughes to Maheu, March 26, 1968, *Maheu v. Hughes Tool Company.*
65. Memorandum, Maheu to Hughes, March 27, 1968, *Maheu v. Hughes Tool Company.*
66. Memorandum, Hughes to Maheu, March 30, 1968, *Maheu v. Hughes Tool Company.*
67. Memorandum, Hughes to Maheu, April 20, 1968, *Maheu v. Hughes Tool Company.*
68. Memorandum, James J. Coyle to Lyle L. Jones, San Francisco Office, Antitrust Division, U.S. Department of Justice, April 26, 1968, Senate Watergate Hearings, Book 26, p. 12902.
69. Ibid.
70. Ibid.
71. Ibid.
72. Ibid.
73. Memorandum, Hughes to Gray, undated, *Maheu v. Hughes Tool Company.*
74. Transcript of Nevada Gaming Commission meeting, April 30, 1968.
75. Memorandum, Hughes to Gray, undated, *Maheu v. Hughes Tool Company.*

13. Out of Control

1. Memorandum, Hughes to Maheu, undated, *Maheu v. Hughes Tool Company.*
2. Memorandum, Hughes to Maheu, April 17, 1968, *Las Vegas Sun v. Summa Corporation et al.,* Civil LV 76–77, U.S. District Court for the District of Nevada.
3. Ibid.
4. Memorandum, Hughes to Maheu, undated, *Las Vegas Sun v. Summa.*
5. Memorandum, Hughes to Maheu, April 19, 1968, *Las Vegas Sun v. Summa.*
6. Ibid.
7. Ibid.
8. Memorandum, Hughes to Gray, undated, Hughes Estate Texas.
9. Memorandum, Maheu to Hughes, June 28, 1968, Hughes Estate Texas.
10. Senate Watergate Hearings, Book 26, p. 12923.
11. Ibid.
12. Ibid., p. 12925.
13. Ibid., p. 12913.
14. Ibid., p. 12915.
15. Deposition of Morris B. (Moe) Dalitz, May 10, 1973, p. 79, *Maheu v. Hughes Tool Company.*
16. Ibid.
17. Ibid., p. 69.
18. Ibid.
19. Ibid., pp. 69–70.
20. Ibid., p. 72.
21. Ibid., p. 70.
22. Affidavit of Alan N. Gelb, *Rancho La Costa Inc. v. Penthouse International Ltd.,* C–124901, Los Angeles County Superior Court.
23. Deposition of Moe Dalitz, p. 78.
24. Deposition of Levar B. Myler, Jan. 14, 1976, p. 27, *Los Angeles Airways v. Hughes Tool Company,* C–36249, Los Angeles County Superior Court.
25. Memorandum, Hughes to unidentified aide, undated, Hughes Estate Texas.
26. Deposition of Roy Crawford, Nov. 6, 1976, p. 19, Hughes Estate California.
27. Deposition of Milton H. West, Jr., April 21, 1977, p. 206, Hughes Estate Texas.
28. Deposition of Howard L. Eckersley, May 31, 1977, pp. 41–42, Hughes Estate Texas.
29. Ibid., p. 43.
30. Ibid.
31. Deposition of Levar Myler, pp. 14–15.
32. Ibid., p. 18.
33. Deposition of Roy Crawford, p. 133.
34. Deposition of Levar Myler, p. 24.
35. Deposition of Howard Eckersley, pp. 41–2.
36. *Esquire,* March 1969, p. 73.
37. Testimony of Nadine Henley, trial transcript, p. 10936, *Maheu v. Hughes Tool Company.*
38. Testimony of Richard Ellis, trial transcript, p. 8401, *Maheu v. Hughes Tool Company.*
39. Testimony of Frank L. Doyon, trial transcript, p. 6303, *Maheu v. Hughes Tool Company.*
40. Ibid.
41. Testimony of Edwin L. Daniel, trial transcript, p. 6513, *Maheu v. Hughes Tool Company.*
42. Ibid., p. 6495.
43. Ibid., p. 6500.
44. Deposition of Henry Schwind, trial transcript, p. 6464, *Maheu v. Hughes Tool Company.*
45. Ibid., pp. 6471–2.
46. Ibid., pp. 6472–3.
47. Memorandum, Hughes to Maheu, March 1968, Hughes Estate Texas.
48. Ibid.
49. *Newsweek,* Jan. 15, 1968, p. 25.
50. Memorandum, Hughes to Maheu, March 1968, Hughes Estate Texas.
51. Ibid.
52. Memorandum, Hughes to Maheu, April 1968, Hughes Estate Texas.
53. Memorandum, Hughes to Maheu, April 1968, Hughes Estate Texas.
54. *New York Times,* Jan. 7, 1968, p. 1.
55. Memorandum, Hughes to Bautzer, February 1968, Hughes Estate Texas.
56. Ibid.
57. Ibid.
58. Memorandum, Hughes to Bautzer, Feb. 26, 1968, Hughes Estate Texas.
59. Memorandum, Hughes to Maheu, April 1968, Hughes Estate Texas.
60. Memorandum, Hughes to Maheu, April 1968, Hughes Estate Texas.
61. Ibid.
62. Ibid.
63. Ibid.
64. Ibid.
65. Ibid.

66. Ibid.
67. Memorandum, Hughes to Bautzer, June 1968, Hughes Estate Texas.
68. Ibid.
69. Memorandum, Hughes to Bautzer, June 28, 1968, Hughes Estate Texas.
70. Complaint, *American Broadcasting Companies Inc. v. Howard R. Hughes et al.*, 68 Civil 2797, U.S. District Court for the Southern District of New York.
71. Transcript of hearing, July 12, 1968, *ABC v. Hughes.*
72. Ibid.
73. Memorandum, Hughes to Maheu, undated, Hughes Estate Texas.
74. Ibid.
75. Letter, Rosel H. Hyde, FCC chairman, to Bautzer, July 3, 1968, *ABC v. Hughes.*
76. Memorandum, Hughes to Bautzer, July 16, 1968, Hughes Estate Texas.
77. *New York Times,* July 17, 1968, p. 55.
78. Deposition of Thomas G. Bell, Feb. 21, 1973, p. 18, *Maheu v. Hughes Tool Company.*
79. Ibid., p. 353.
80. Ibid., p. 489.
81. Ibid., pp. 12–21.
82. Memorandum, Hughes to Maheu, April 20, 1968, *Maheu v. Hughes Tool Company.*
83. Ibid.
84. Memorandum, Hughes to Maheu, undated, *Maheu v. Hughes Tool Company.*
85. Memorandum, Hughes to Maheu, undated, *Maheu v. Hughes Tool Company.*
86. Memorandum, Hughes to Maheu, undated, *Maheu v. Hughes Tool Company.*
87. Memorandum, Hughes to Maheu, undated, *Maheu v. Hughes Tool Company.*
88. Memorandum, Hughes to Maheu, April 1968, *Maheu v. Hughes Tool Company.*
89. Memorandum, Hughes to Maheu, April 25, 1968, *Maheu v. Hughes Tool Company.*
90. Memorandum, Hughes to Maheu, April 25, 1968, *Maheu v. Hughes Tool Company.*
91. Letter, Hughes to President Lyndon B. Johnson, April 25, 1968, Hughes Estate Texas.
92. Memorandum, Hughes to Maheu, undated, *Maheu v. Hughes Tool Company.*
93. Ibid.
94. Memorandum, Hughes to Maheu, undated, *Maheu v. Hughes Tool Company.*
95. Testimony of Gordon Judd, trial transcript, p. 4662, *Maheu v. Hughes Tool Company.*
96. Ibid., pp. 4665–7.
97. Ibid., p. 4667.
98. Testimony of Nadine Henley, trial transcript, p. 10947, *Maheu v. Hughes Tool Company.*
99. Ibid., p. 11001.
100. Ibid., p. 10980.
101. Ibid., p. 10981.
102. Testimony of Robert A. Maheu, trial transcript, p. 9176, *Maheu v. Hughes Tool Company.*
103. Ibid., p. 9177.
104. Ibid.
105. Ibid.
106. Ibid., pp. 9177–8.
107 Ibid., p. 9179.
108. Ibid.
109. Ibid., p. 9178.

14. The $90-Million Mistake

1. Letter, Hughes to President Lyndon B. Johnson, April 25, 1968, Hughes Estate Texas.
2. U.S. Department of Defense, *100 Companies and 118 Subsidiary Corporations Listed According to Net Value of Military Prime Contract Awards,* Fiscal Year 1960.
3. Helicopter Hearings, p. 483.
4. Ibid., p. 480.
5. Report, Valuation of Certain Assets of the Estate of Howard Robard Hughes, Jr., Prepared by Merrill Lynch, Pierce, Fenner & Smith, April 1977, p. 69, Hughes Estate Nevada.
6. Helicopter Report, p. 8.
7. Ibid.
8. Helicopter Hearings, p. 553.
9. Helicopter Report, p. 9.
10. Ibid.
11. Ibid.
12. Ibid., p. 10.
13. Ibid.
14. Ibid.
15. Helicopter Hearings, p. 556.
16. Helicopter Report, p. 9.
17. *New York Herald Tribune,* Aug. 3, 1947.
18. Helicopter Hearings, p. 484.
19. Ibid., p. 529.
20. Ibid., p. 532.
21. *New York Post,* Oct. 11, 1947.
22. Helicopter Hearings, p. 514.
23. Helicopter Report, p. 11.
24. Ibid.
25. Ibid., p. 12.
26. Helicopter Hearings, p. 197.
27. Ibid., p. 185.
28. Helicopter Report, p. 9.
29. Helicopter Hearings, p. 167.
30. Ibid.
31. Ibid.
32. Ibid., p. 165.
33. Ibid., p. 170.
34. Helicopter Report, p. 14
35. Helicopter Hearings, p. 320.
36. *Aviation Week,* June 28, 1965, p. 62.
37. Helicopter Hearings, p. 173.
38. Ibid., p. 518.
39. Ibid., p. 355.
40. Helicopter Hearings, p. 42.
41. Helicopter Report, p. 17.
42. Helicopter Hearings, p. 41.
43. Senate War Hearings, pp. 24456, 27173.
44. Helicopter Report, p. 17.
45. Ibid., p. 4.
46. Ibid.
47. *Aviation Week,* July 31, 1967, p. 18.
48. *Electronic News,* Oct. 2, 1967, p. 16.
49. Memorandum, Holliday, Cook, and West to Hughes, Dec. 26, 1967, Hughes Estate Texas.

50. Ibid.
51. Ibid.
52. U.S., Securities and Exchange Commission, Annual Report of Textron Inc., 1968, p. 13.
53. Memorandum, Cook to Hughes, Feb. 25, 1968, Hughes Estate Texas.
54. Memorandum, Hughes to Cook, February–March 1968, Hughes Estate Texas.

55. Memorandum, Cook to Hughes, March 1968, Hughes Estate Texas.
56. Memorandum, unidentified aide to Hughes, March 1968, Hughes Estate Texas.
57. Memorandum, Hughes to Eckersley, March 1968, Hughes Estate Texas.
58. Merrill Lynch report, p. 20.

15. The Billion-Dollar Deal

1. Memorandum, Hughes to Maheu, undated, Hughes Estate Texas.
2. Ibid.
3. Memorandum, Holliday, Cook, and West to Hughes, Dec. 26, 1967, Hughes Estate Texas.
4. Ibid.
5. Report, Valuation of Certain Assets of the Estate of Howard Robard Hughes, Jr., Prepared by Merrill Lynch, Pierce, Fenner & Smith, April 1977, Hughes Estate Nevada.
6. Ibid.
7. Ibid.
8. Deposition of Howard L. Eckersley, June 2, 1977, p. 312, Hughes Estate Texas.
9. Memorandum, Hughes to Holliday, April 25, 1968, Hughes Estate Texas.
10. Ibid.
11. Deposition of Howard Eckersley, p. 314.
12. Deposition of John M. Holmes, Jr., Dec. 10, 1976, p. 232, Hughes Estate California.
13. Memorandum, Hughes to Real, Jan. 17, 1968, Hughes Estate Texas.
14. Memorandum, Hughes to Cook, March 28, 1968, Hughes Estate Texas.
15. Memorandum, Hughes to Cook, April 3, 1968, Hughes Estate Texas.
16. Ibid.
17. Ibid.
18. Ibid.
19. Ibid.
20. Ibid.
21. Ibid.
22. Memorandum, Hughes to Cook, April 8, 1968, Hughes Estate Texas.
23. Ibid.
24. Memorandum, Real to Hughes, April 9, 1968, Hughes Estate Texas.
25. Memorandum, Hughes to Cook, April 9, 1968, Hughes Estate Texas.

26. Memorandum, Hughes to Cook. April 10, 1968, Hughes Estate Texas.
27. Memorandum, Cook to Hughes, April 13, 1968, Hughes Estate Texas.
28. Memorandum, Cook to Hughes, April 10, 1968, Hughes Estate Texas.
29. Memorandum, Hughes to Cook, April 10, 1968, Hughes Estate Texas.
30. Memorandum, Cook to Hughes, April 10, 1968, Hughes Estate Texas.
31. Memorandum, Hughes to Maheu, April 10, 1968, Hughes Estate Texas.
32. Memorandum, Cook to Hughes, April 11, 1968, Hughes Estate Texas.
33. Memorandum, Hughes to Cook, April 11, 1968, Hughes Estate Texas.
34. Memorandum, Hughes to Cook, April 13, 1968, Hughes Estate Texas.
35. Memorandum, Cook to Hughes, April 13, 1968, Hughes Estate Texas.
36. Memorandum, Hughes to Cook, April 22, 1968, Hughes Estate Texas.
37. Memorandum, Hughes to Real, April 22, 1968, Hughes Estate Texas.
38. Memorandum, Hughes to Real, April 27, 1968, Hughes Estate Texas.
39. Ibid.
40. Memorandum, Hughes to Real, undated, Hughes Estate Texas.
41. Memorandum, Hughes to Cook, May 10, 1968, Hughes Estate Texas.
42. Memorandum, Hughes to Cook, May 1968, Hughes Estate Texas.
43. Memorandum, Hughes to Cook, May 1968, Hughes Estate Texas.
44. Ibid.
45. Memorandum, Hughes to Cook, May 11, 1968, Hughes Estate Texas.
46. Ibid.

16. The Hijacking of Air West

1. *Aviation Week,* Aug. 19, 1968, p. 26.
2. Official transcript of SEC interview of Patrick J. Hillings, March 19, 1973, p. 29, *SEC v. Air West.*
3. Memorandum, Maheu to Hughes, July 30, 1968, *Anderson v. Air West.*
4. Ibid.
5. Memorandum, Hughes to Maheu, August 1968, *Anderson v. Air West.*
6. Ibid.
7. Ibid.
8. Memorandum, Maheu to Hughes, July 23, 1968, *Anderson v. Air West.*
9. Memorandum, Maheu to Hughes, Aug. 2, 1968, *Anderson v. Air West.*

10. Memorandum, Maheu to Hughes, Aug. 8, 1968, *Anderson v. Air West.*
11. Memorandum Maheu to Hughes, Aug. 8, 1968, *Anderson v. Air West.*
12. Memorandum, Maheu to Hughes, Aug. 12, 1968, *Anderson v. Air West.*
13. Memorandum, Maheu to Hughes, Aug. 9, 1968, *Anderson v. Air West.*
14. News Release of Robert Maheu and Nick Bez, Aug. 11, 1968, *Anderson v. Air West.*
15. Memorandum, Maheu to Hughes, Aug. 20, 1968, *Anderson v. Air West.*
16. Memorandum, Hughes to Maheu, Aug. 21, 1968, *Anderson v. Air West.*

17. Deposition of Joy Marie Hamann, Jan. 9, 1976, *SEC v. Air West.*
18. Press Release, Information Unlimited, undated, summer of 1968, *Anderson v. Air West.*
19. Complaint, *SEC v. Air West.*
20. *Wall Street Journal,* Sept. 19, 1968.
21. *Las Vegas Sun,* Sept. 13, 1968.
22. *Las Vegas Sun,* Oct. 16, 1968.
23. Deposition of Herman M. Greenspun, Dec. 27, 1973, pp. 40–41, *U.S. Trust v. Summa.*
24. Minutes of Board of Directors Meeting, Air West, Sept. 20, 1968, *SEC v. Air West.*
25. Letter, Joseph Martin, Jr., to W. R. Thrall, Sept. 30, 1968, *Anderson v. Air West.*
26. U.S., Civil Aeronautics Board, Joint Application of Hughes Tool Company and Air West, Inc., 20665.
27. Ibid.
28. Memorandum, Maheu to Hughes, Sept. 13, 1968, *Anderson v. Air West.*
29. U.S., Civil Aeronautics Board, transcript of proceedings before Civil Aeronautics Board, Joint Application of Hughes Tool and Air West, March 11, 1969, p. 641.
30. U.S., Civil Aeronautics Board, Proxy Statement for special meeting of stockholders, Dec. 27, 1968, Joint Application of Hughes Tool and Air West.
31. Proceedings in executive session, board of directors of Air West, Nov. 18, 1968, *SEC v. Air West.*
32. Memorandum, Maheu to Hughes, Dec. 28, 1968, *Anderson v. Air West.*
33. Office Memorandum, William C. Turner to Alfred Rusch, Securities and Exchange Commission, undated, *SEC v. Air West.*
34. Ibid.
35. Ibid.
36. Ibid.
37. Ibid.
38. Ibid.
39. Deposition of Herman Greenspun, p. 45.
40. Complaint, *SEC v. Air West.*
41. Memorandum, Turner to Rusch, undated *SEC v. Air West.*
42. Memorandum, Maheu to Hughes, Dec. 31, 1968, *Anderson v. Air West.*

43. Deposition of Gordon S. Judd, Oct. 8, 1974, p. 60, *U.S. Trust v. Summa.*
44. Memorandum, Maheu to Hughes, Jan. 1, 1969, *Anderson v. Air West.*
45. Ibid.
46. Memorandum, Maheu to Hughes, undated, about February of 1969, *Anderson v. Air West.*
47. Confidential Memorandum, Edward P. Morgan to Maheu, May 13, 1970, *Anderson v. Air West.*
48. Memorandum, Maheu to Hughes, Jan. 15, 1969, *Anderson v. Air West.*
49. Memorandum, Hughes to Maheu, Feb. 12, 1969, *Anderson v. Air West.*
50. Ibid.
51. Memorandum, Hughes to Maheu, Jan. 14, 1969, *Anderson v. Air West.*
52. U.S., Civil Aeronautics Board, Joint Application of Hughes Tool and Air West.
53. U.S., Civil Aeronautics Board, transcript of hearing before Civil Aeronautics Board, June 4, 1969, p. 82, Joint Application of Hughes Tool and Air West.
54. Order of the Civil Aeronautics Board, July 15, 1969.
55. Joint Application of Hughes Tool and Air West.
56. Memorandum, Hughes to Maheu, late summer of 1969, *Anderson v. Air West.*
57. Ibid.
58. Memorandum, Davis to Hughes, Sept. 11, 1969, *Anderson v. Air West.*
59. Memorandum, Maheu to Hughes, Oct. 14, 1969, *Anderson v. Air West.*
60. Memorandum, Hughes to Maheu, Aug. 2, 1969, *Anderson v. Air West.*
61. Memorandum, Hughes to Maheu, Nov. 9, 1969, *Anderson v. Air West.*
62. Affidavit of M. W. Odom, July 29, 1974, *U.S. Trust v. Summa.*
63. Ibid.
64. Ibid.
65. Complaint, *Anderson v. Air West.*
66. Memorandum, Hughes to Maheu, May 25, 1970, *Anderson v. Air West.*

17. Gold Fever

1. Memorandum, Maheu to Hughes, March 16, 1968, *Maheu v. Davis.*
2. Ibid.
3. Records of the Class of 1897, Fourth Report, 1912, Harvard College, p. 218.
4. *Estate of E. L. (Jack) Cleveland,* 5774, Eighth Judicial District Court, Clark County, Nevada.
5. Official transcript of SEC interview of Geraldine Cleveland, June 27, 1974, p. 73, *SEC v. Air West.*
6. *Reno Evening Gazette,* April 4, 1968.
7. Eliot Lord, *Comstock Mining and Miners* (Berkeley, Calif.: Howell-North, 1959), p. 19.
8. Storey County Recorder's Office, Virginia City, Nevada, Deed Book 66, pp. 35–37.
9. *Las Vegas Sun,* April 4, 1968.

10. *Reno Evening Gazette,* April 4, 1968.
11. *Virginia City Territorial Enterprise,* April 5, 1968.
12. *Nevada State Journal,* April 8, 1968.
13. Memorandum, Hughes to Maheu, March 16, 1968, *Maheu v. Davis.*
14. Deposition of Robert A. Maheu, Sept. 12, 1972, p. 64, *Maheu v. Hughes Tool Company.*
15. Testimony of Robert A. Maheu, trial transcript, p. 9021, *Maheu v. Hughes Tool Company.*
16. Deposition of Robert Maheu, Jan. 29, 1973, p. 673.
17. Ibid., p. 674.
18. Ibid., p. 692.
19. Ibid., p. 693.
20. Memorandum, Maheu to Hughes, April 16,

1968, *Hughes Tool Company v. Anthony Hatsis et al.*, CA–71–72, U.S. District Court for the District of Utah.
21. Ibid.
22. Memorandum, Maheu to Hughes, July 18, 1968, *Hughes Tool v. Hatsis.*
23. Memorandum, Maheu to Hughes, July 18, 1968, *Hughes Tool v. Hatsis.*
24. Government's Post Trial Brief, *U.S. v. Dennis C. Hill,* CR–LV–2771, U.S. District Court for the District of Nevada.
25. Ibid.
26. Certificate of Amendment of Articles of Incorporation, Basic Industries, Inc., March 26, 1968, Secretary of State, Nevada.
27. Deposition of Jean Beckers, p. 37, *Estate of E. L. (Jack) Cleveland.*
28. Ibid., p. 36.
29. Memorandum, John H. Meier to Maheu, Jan. 9, 1969, *Hughes Tool v. Hatsis.*
30. Ibid.
31. Ibid.
32. *Las Vegas Review–Journal,* Jan. 29, 1969.
33. Ibid.
34. *Reno Evening Gazette,* March 12, 1969.
35. *Los Angeles Times,* Feb. 16, 1969.
36. Memorandum, Meier to Maheu, Feb. 1, 1969, *Hughes Tool v. Hatsis.*
37. Memorandum, Maheu to Hughes, Feb. 5, 1969, *Hughes Tool v. Hatsis.*
38. Ibid.
39. Memorandum, Hughes to Maheu, Feb. 12, 1969, *SEC v. Air West.*
40. *Los Angeles Times,* Feb. 16, 1969.
41. Ibid.
42. Ibid.
43. Ibid.
44. U.S., Securities and Exchange Commission, Form S–3, Aztec Mining Corporation, Aug. 10, 1970.
45. Ibid.
46. *U.S. v. John H. Meier,* CR–LV–74–9, 10, U.S. District Court for the District of Nevada.
47. Senate Watergate Hearings, Book 21, pp. 10119–20.
48. Ibid., Book 22, pp. 10675–6.
49. Ibid., p. 10701.
50. Senate Watergate Hearings, Book 23, p. 11237.
51. *Las Vegas Sun,* Jan. 15, 1969.
52. Senate Watergate Hearings, Book 20, p. 9599.
53. Ibid.
54. Ibid.
55. Ibid., Book 22, p. 10707.
56. *U.S. v. Meier.*
57. Plaintiff's Answers to Interrogatories Pro-

pounded to Plaintiff, July 20, 1972, *Maheu v. Davis.*
58. Senate Watergate Hearings, Book 22, p. 10647.
59. Ibid., p. 10714.
60. Ibid.
61. Ibid.
62. Ibid., pp. 10709, 10731.
63. Affidavit of Anthony G. Hatsis, Feb. 3, 1973, *Hughes Tool v. Hatsis.*
64. Ibid.
65. Ibid.
66. U.S., Securities and Exchange Commission, Proxy Statement, American Mining Company and West Toledo Mines Company, July 23, 1968.
67. Ibid.
68. Ibid.
69. Ibid.
70. Ibid.
71. Letter, Edward P. Morgan to Maheu, Aug. 15, 1969, *Maheu v. Hughes Tool Company.*
72. Memorandum, Meier to Maheu, Sept. 2, 1969, *Hughes Tool v. Hatsis.*
73. Memorandum, Meier to Maheu, Oct. 28, 1969, *Hughes Tool v. Hatsis.*
74. Ibid.
75. Memorandum, Maheu to Hughes, Nov. 3, 1969, *Hughes Tool v. Hatsis.*
76. *Las Vegas Sun,* Nov. 3, 1969.
77. Testimony of Robert A. Maheu, trial transcript, pp. 9046–7, *Maheu v. Hughes Tool Company.*
78. Answers to Interrogatories, Aug. 27, 1973, *Hughes Tool v. Hatsis.*
79. Ibid.
80. Ibid.
81. U.S., Securities and Exchange Commission, Form 10–K, Toledo Mining Company, Fiscal Year ended Sept. 30, 1970.
82. Articles of Incorporation of Nevada Environmental Foundation, Dec. 17, 1969, Secretary of State, Nevada.
83. *U.S. v. Meier.*
84. Authors' interview of confidential source.
85. Case report, 74–15456, Alfred Netter, Nov. 30, 1974, Chief Medical Examiner's Office, Los Angeles County.
86. Authors' interview of confidential source.
87. *Wall Street Journal,* Nov. 17, 1978.
88. Ibid.
89. *Philadelphia Inquirer,* Sept. 3, 1978.
90. *Wall Street Journal,* Nov. 17, 1978.
91. Ibid.
92. Ibid.

18. Turning Point

1. *Philadelphia Inquirer,* Jan. 16, 1970.
2. Operations Logs, Dec. 4, 9, 16, and 18, 1958, authors' files.
3. Operations Log, Dec. 1, 1958, authors' files.
4. Operations Log, Dec. 16, 1958, authors' files.
5. Operating Memorandum, Oct. 2, 1958, Romaine Street Procedures Manual, authors' files.
6. Ibid.
7. Testimony of Jean Peters Hough, Jan. 31, 1978,

pp. 35–36, Hughes Estate Texas.
8. Autopsy Report, Howard R. Hughes, Jr., April 7, 1976, The Methodist Hospital, Hughes Estate Texas.
9. Deposition of Dr. Harold Lee Feikes, Nov. 3, 1977, p. 51, Hughes Estate Nevada.
10. Plaintiff's Answers to Interrogatories Propounded to Plaintiff, filed July 20, 1972, *Maheu v. Hughes Tool Company.*
11. Official transcript of SEC interview of Robert

A. Maheu, Nov. 14, 1972, p. 221, *SEC v. Air West.*

12. Ibid., p. 222.
13. Ibid., pp. 219–21.
14. Ibid., p. 220.
15. Deposition of Frank W. Gay, July 14, 1977, p. 140, Hughes Estate Texas.
16. Transcript of news media telephone interview of Hughes, Jan. 7, 1972, authors' files.
17. Deposition of Robert A. Maheu, July 2, 1973, p. 784, *Maheu v. Hughes Tool Company.*
18. *Robert Buckley v. Howard R. Hughes et al.,* 999315, Los Angeles County Superior Court.
19. Ibid.
20. Ibid.
21. Ibid.
22. Memorandum, Maheu to Hughes, Feb. 7, 1969, authors' files.
23. Certificate of Incorporation of HHMI Corporation, Dec. 17, 1953, Secretary of State, Delaware.
24. Memorandum, Hughes to Maheu and Davis, May 7, 1969, authors' files.
25. Memorandum, Eckersley to Hughes, May 13, 1970, authors' files.
26. Memorandum, Holliday to Hughes, May 20, 1970, Hughes Estate Texas.
27. Transcript of SEC interview of Maheu, p. 183.
28. Ibid.
29. Ibid., p. 178.
30. Ibid.
31. Complaint, *Los Angeles Airways Inc. v. Chester C. Davis,* 72–1070–RJK, U.S. District Court for the Central District of California.
32. *Trans World Airlines v. Howard R. Hughes,* 515 F.2d 173 (1975).
33. Ibid.
34. Ibid.
35. Senate Watergate Hearings, Book 26, p. 12937.
36. Proposed press release announcing Hughes's acquisition of Los Angeles Airways, authors' files.
37. *Los Angeles Airways v. Davis.*
38. Senate Watergate Hearings, Book 26, p. 12937.
39. Deposition of Frank W. Gay, June 28, 1973, p. 70, *Los Angeles Airways v. Davis.*
40. Ibid., pp. 70–71.
41. Ibid., pp. 71–2.
42. Deposition of Chester C. Davis, June 26, 1973, p. 113, *Los Angeles Airways v. Davis.*
43. Ibid., pp. 113–4.
44. Ibid., p. 139.
45. Ibid.
46. Deposition of Frank Gay, p. 83.
47. Ibid., p. 162.
48. Deposition of Calvin J. Collier, Jr., April 6, 1973, p. 90, *Los Angeles Airways v. Davis.*
49. Deposition of Chester Davis, p. 135.
50. Memorandum, Holliday to Hughes, June 13, 1970, authors' files.
51. Ibid.
52. Ibid.
53. Memorandum, Holliday to Maheu, Aug. 24, 1970, authors' files.
54. Deposition of Robert A. Maheu, Sept. 12, 1972, p. 9, *Maheu v. Hughes Tool Company.*
55. Ibid., p. 11.

56. Ibid., p. 12.
57. Ibid.
58. Confidential memorandum, Paul F. Smith to the files, July 25, 1968, *Maheu v. Hughes Tool Company.*
59. Testimony of Levar Myler, Trial transcript, p 726, *Maheu v. Davis.*
60. Authors' interview of confidential source.
61. Memorandum, Maheu to Hughes, Sept. 16, 1970, *Los Angeles Airways v. Davis.*
62. Deposition of Robert D. Peloquin, Sept. 24, 1973, p. 36, *Maheu v. Hughes Tool Company.*
63. Deposition of Robert D. Peloquin, April 10, 1975, pp. 19–20, *Anderson v. Air West.*
64. Resolution adopted by Hughes Tool Company Board of Directors, Oct. 16, 1968, *Maheu v. Davis.*
65. Letter, Holliday to Maheu, Oct. 17, 1968, *Maheu v. Davis.*
66. Telegram, Maheu to Davis, Nov. 6, 1970, *Maheu v. Davis.*
67. Letter, Maheu to James v. Hayes, Nov. 6, 1970, *Maheu v. Davis.*
68. Teletype, Davis to Maheu, Nov. 10, 1970, *Maheu v. Davis.*
69. Teletype, Maheu to Davis, Nov. 12, 1970, *Maheu v. Davis.*
70. Ibid.
71. Resolution adopted by Hughes Tool Company Board of Directors, Nov. 12, 1970, *Maheu v. Davis.*
72. Letter, Collier to Maheu, Nov. 13, 1970, *Maheu v. Davis.*
73. Testimony of Levar Myler, trial transcript, p. 685, *Maheu v. Davis.*
74. Ibid., p. 686.
75. Proxy, Nov. 14, 1970, *Maheu v. Davis.*
76. Memorandum, unidentified aide to Hughes, undated (about November 1966), authors' files.
77. *Las Vegas Sun,* Dec. 2, 1970.
78. *New York Times,* Dec. 3, 1970, p. 20.
79. Resolution adopted by Hughes Tool Company Executive Committee, Dec. 3, 1970, *Maheu v. Davis.*
80. Testimony of Levar Myler, trial transcript, p. 687, *Maheu v. Davis.*
81. Testimony of Richard Danner, trial transcript, p. 7816, *Maheu v. Hughes Tool Company.*
82. Ibid., p. 7817.
83. *Washington Post,* Dec. 9, 1970.
84. *New York Times,* Dec. 6, 1970, p. 1.
85. Ibid.
86. Letter, Collier to Maheu, Dec. 5, 1970, *Maheu v. Davis.*
87. *New York Times,* Dec. 6, 1970, p. 1.
88. *New York Times,* Dec. 8, 1970, p. 1.
89. *Newsweek,* Dec. 21, 1970, p. 75.
90. *St. Louis Post-Dispatch,* Dec. 7, 1970.
91. *Washington Post,* Dec. 8, 1970.
92. *New York Times,* Dec. 8, 1970, p. 1.
93. Decision and Findings of Fact and Conclusions of Law, Dec. 24, 1970, *Maheu v. Davis.*
94. Ibid.
95. Memorandum, Hughes to Gay and Davis, undated, *Maheu v. Davis.*

96. Decision and Findings of Fact and Conclusions of Law, Dec. 24, 1970, *Maheu v. Davis.*
97. Ibid.
98. Deposition of Clarence A. Waldron, June 6, 1977, p. 16, Hughes Estate Texas.
99. Ibid., p. 244.

100. Senate Watergate Hearings, Book 20, p. 9431.
101. Ibid., p. 9435.
102. Ibid., pp. 9452–3
103. Ibid., p. 9448.
104. Ibid., pp. 9436–7.
105. Ibid., p. 9435.

19. The Political Connection

1. Letter, Edwin M. Zimmerman, assistant U.S. attorney-general, to Richard Gray, Andrews, Kurth, Campbell & Jones, Dec. 20, 1968, authors' files.
2. Letter, Robert A. Hammond III, deputy assistant U.S. attorney-general, to Richard Gray, Jan. 17, 1969, authors' files.
3. Senate Watergate Hearings, Book 20, p. 9573.
4. Ibid., Book 26, p. 12851.
5. Ibid., p. 12854.
6. J. Anthony Lukas, *Nightmare: The Underside of the Nixon Years* (New York: Viking Press, 1976), p. 132.
7. Senate Watergate Hearings, Book 20, p. 9573.
8. Ibid.
9. Ibid., Book 26, p. 12878.
10. Ibid., p. 12876.
11. Memorandum, Hughes to Maheu, undated, *Maheu v. Hughes Tool Company.*
12. Testimony of Robert A. Maheu, trial transcript, p. 9474, *Maheu v. Hughes Tool Company.*
13. Senate Watergate Hearings, Book 20, p. 9534.
14. Ibid., p. 9538.
15. Ibid.
16 Ibid., p. 9539.
17. Ibid., Book 21, p. 9978.
18. Ibid., p. 9943.
19. Ibid., p. 10189.
20. Ibid., pp. 9986–7.
21. Ibid., p. 9969.
22. Ibid., p. 9989.
23. Ibid., p. 9970.
24. Senate Watergate Final Report, p. 947.
25. U.S., Congress, Joint Committee on Internal Revenue Taxation, *Examination of President Nixon's Tax Returns for 1969 through 1972,* 93d Cong., 2d sess., 1974, Senate Report 93–768, p. 38.

26. Ibid., p. A–180
27. Ibid., p. 38.
28. Weekly Compilation of Presidential Documents, Dec. 10, 1973, 9 (no. 49): 1419.
29. Brochure, "Marina City Offshore Classic Program, 1975," authors' files.
30. *Newsweek,* July 16, 1973, p. 52.
31. *Los Angeles Times,* Dec. 1, 1974.
32. *Los Angeles Times,* Dec. 20, 1970.
33. Authors' interview of confidential source.
34. *Los Angeles Times,* Feb. 22, 1974.
35. Business review letter, prepared by Arthur Young & Company, Nov. 8, 1972, authors' files.
36. Ibid.
37. U.S., Securities and Exchange Commission, Annual Report of Global Marine, Inc., 1970.
38. Ibid.
39. Senate Watergate Hearings, Book 21, p. 9747.
40. John Dean, *Blind Ambition: The White House Years* (New York: Simon and Schuster, 1976), p. 66.
41. Senate Watergate Hearings, Book 21, p. 9752.
42. Ibid., 9754.
43. Dean, *Blind Ambition,* p. 68.
44. Ibid., p. 69.
45. U.S., Congress, House, Chairman's Report to the Select Committee on Small Business, *Tax-Exempt Foundations and Charitable Trusts: Their Impact on Our Economy,* 87th Cong., 2d sess., Dec. 31, 1962, p. 71.
46. Letter, Hogan & Hartson to commissioner of Internal Revenue, June 21, 1971, authors' files.
47. Letter, Robert F. Bennett to John Dean, July 30, 1971, authors' files.
48. Ibid.
49. Ibid.
50. Ibid.
51. Letter, Dean to Bennett, undated, authors' files.

20. Life in Exile

1. Hughes Logs, Hughes Estate Texas.
2. *New York Times,* Dec. 8, 1971, p. 65.
3. Ibid.
4. *Philadelphia Inquirer,* Dec. 26, 1971.
5. *New York Times,* Dec. 8, 1971, p. 65.
6. Hughes Logs, Hughes Estate Texas.
7. Ibid.
8. Ibid.
9. Ibid.
10. Ibid.
11. Ibid.
12. Transcript of news media telephone interview of Hughes, Jan. 7, 1972, authors' files.
13. Ibid.
14. Ibid.

15. Ibid
16. Ibid.
17. Ibid.
18. Ibid.
19. Ibid.
20. Ibid.
21. *Philadelphia Inquirer,* Oct. 8, 1972.
22. *New York Times,* Feb. 19, 1972, p. 28.
23. Deposition of George A. Francom, June 30, 1977, p. 52, Hughes Estate Texas.
24. *New York Times,* March 15, 1972, p. 1
25. Hughes Logs, Hughes Estate Texas.
26. *New York Times,* March 16, 1972, p. 53.
27. Deposition of Frank W. Gay, July 14, 1977. p. 102, Hughes Estate Texas.

28. Ibid., p. 103.
29. Deposition of James H. Rickard, June 26, 1977, p. 7, Hughes Estate Texas.
30. Ibid., p. 21.
31. *New York Times*, Aug. 31, 1972, p. 26.
32. Report of Richard C. Gano, Jr., Special Administrator, Regarding Will Search Activities, p. 59, Hughes Estate California.
33. Deposition of John M. Holmes, Jr., June 23, 1977, p. 571, Hughes Estate Texas.
34. Hughes Logs, Hughes Estate Texas.
35. Ibid.
36. Ibid.
37. Ibid.
38. *Fortune*, December 1973, p. 106.
39. Hughes Logs, Hughes Estate Texas.
40. Deposition of Milton H. West, Jr., April 20, 1977, p. 568, Hughes Estate Texas.
41. *Fortune*, December 1973, p. 106.
42. Ibid.
43. Ibid.
44. Hughes Logs, Hughes Estate Texas.
45. Deposition of Clarence A. Waldron, June 6, 1977, p. 112, Hughes Estate Texas.
46. Deposition of Nadine Henley, June 15, 1977, p. 106, Hughes Estate Texas.
47. Testimony of George A. Francom, Jan. 25, 1978, p. 159, Hughes Estate Texas.
48. Memorandum, Eckersley to Hughes, Dec. 1, 1972, Hughes Estate Texas.
49. *Newsweek*, Oct. 30, 1972, p. 88.
50. U.S., Securities and Exchange Commission, Prospectus, Hughes Tool Company, 1972.
51. *Oil and Gas Journal*, March 13, 1972, p. 21.
52. Prospectus, Hughes Tool Company.
53. *Newsweek*, Oct. 30, 1972, p. 87.
54. Deposition of George Francom, p. 104.
55. Ibid., p. 196.
56. Memorandum, Hughes to Davis, undated, Hughes Estate Texas.
57. Deposition of James Rickard, p. 51.
58. Ibid., p. 54.
59. Ibid.
60. Ibid., p. 55.
61. *New York Times*, Dec. 29, 1972, p. 31.
62. Ibid., Dec. 30, 1972, p. 3.
63. Federal income-tax return, Howard R. Hughes, 1965, Hughes Estate Texas.
64. Memorandum, staff to Hughes, Jan. 1, 1972, Hughes Estate Texas.
65. *New York Times*, March 17, 1972, p. 15.
66. Hughes Logs, Hughes Estate Texas.
67. *New York Times*, March 21, 1973, p. 38.
68. Interview of Jack Real, May 16, 1978, in Report to Administrator of Hughes Estate Nevada, authors' files.
69. Ibid.
70. Interview of Tony Blackman and Jack Real, July 21, 1978, in Report to Administrator of Hughes Estate Nevada. authors' files.
71. Ibid.
72. Ibid.
73. Interview of Jack Real, May 16, 1978, in Report to Administrator of Hughes Estate Nevada, authors' files.
74. Memorandum, Real to Romaine Street, July 24, 1973, Hughes Estate Texas.
75. Testimony of Clarence A. Waldron, Jan. 25, 1978, p. 109, Hughes Estate Texas.
76. Interview of Tony Blackman and Jack Real, July 21, 1978, in Report to Administrator of Hughes Estate Nevada, authors' files.
77. Deposition of Howard L. Eckersley, May 31, 1977, p. 82, Hughes Estate Texas.
78. Deposition of George Francom, p. 63.
79. Deposition of Clarence Waldron, p. 95.
80. Affidavit of Dr. William Young, *Anderson v. Air West*.
81. Affidavit of Dr. E. Freeman Johnson, Aug. 9, 1978, in Report to Administrator of Hughes Estate Nevada, authors' files.
82. Affidavit of Dr. Walter C. Robinson, Aug. 9, 1978, in Report to Administrator of Hughes Estate Nevada, authors' files.
83. *Philadelphia Inquirer*, Dec. 15, 1973.

21. Watergate

1. Authors' interview of confidential source.
2. *United States of America v. Howard R. Hughes et al.*, CR–LV–2843, United States District Court for the District of Nevada.
3. Ibid.
4. Ibid.
5. Authors' interview of confidential source.
6. Senate Watergate Hearings, Book 26, p. 12451.
7. Deposition of George A. Francom, Jr., July 1, 1977, p. 172, Hughes Estate Texas.
8. Ibid., p. 179.
9. Memorandum, Davis to Hughes, March 3, 1974, Hughes Estate Texas.
10. House Intelligence Hearings, p. 483.
11. Ibid., p. 1110.
12. Ibid.
13. Senate Watergate Hearings, Book 20, p. 9346.
14. Ibid., p. 9356.
15. Ibid., p. 9374.
16. Ibid., pp. 9377–8.
17. Ibid., p. 9380.
18. Ibid., p. 9381.
19. U.S., Congress, Senate, Hearings before the Committee on the Judiciary on Nomination of Richard G. Kleindienst, of Arizona, to be Attorney General, 92d Cong., 2d sess., 1972, p. 447.
20. *Washington Post*, March 1, 1972.
21. U.S., Congress, House, Hearings before the Committee on the Judiciary, A resolution authorizing and directing the Committee on the Judiciary to investigate whether sufficient grounds exist for the House of Representatives to exercise its constitutional power to impeach Richard M. Nixon, President of the United States of America, 93d Cong., 2d sess., 1974, Book 5, Part 2, p. 724.
22. Ibid., p. 725.
23. House Intelligence Hearings, p. 1104.
24. Ibid.

25. Ibid., p. 598.
26. Ibid.
27. House Impeachment Hearings, Book 5, Part 2, p. 789.
28. Ibid., p. 788.
29. Ibid., pp. 789–90.
30. Ibid., p. 790.
31. Ibid., p. 791.
32. House Intelligence Hearings, p. 1104.
33. *New York Times,* March 18, 1972, p. 1.
34. *Philadelphia Inquirer,* March 19, 1972.
35. Senate Judiciary Committee hearings on Kleindienst nomination, p. 788.
36. E. Howard Hunt, *Undercover: Memoirs of an American Secret Agent* (New York: Berkley Publishing Corporation, 1974), p. 191.
37. *New York Times,* Jan. 12, 1973, p. 24.
38. Senate Watergate Hearings, Book 9, p. 3685.
39. Ibid., Book 20, p. 9367.
40. Ibid., Book 9, p. 3685.
41. Ibid.
42. Senate Watergate Final Report, p. 1123.

43. House Intelligence Hearings, p. 1089.
44. *Newsweek,* Oct. 22, 1973, p. 52.
45. Hughes Logs, Hughes Estate Texas.
46. Ibid
47. Ibid.
48. House Intelligence Hearings, p 1091.
49. Ibid., p. 1092.
50. Ibid.
51. Ibid., pp. 1092–93.
52. Ibid., p. 1093.
53. Senate Watergate Final Report, p. 1124.
54. House Intelligence Hearings, pp. 1080–81.
55. Ibid., p. 1096.
56. Senate Watergate Final Report, p 1126.
57. House Intelligence Hearings, p. 1099.
58. Senate Watergate Final Report, p. 1126.
59. *Historic Documents, 1973,* Congressional Quarterly Inc., p. 553.
60. Authors' interview of confidential source.
61. Senate Watergate Hearings, Book 21, p. 10189.
62. Memorandum, Davis to Hughes, April 30, 1974, Hughes Estate Texas.

22. Hughesgate

1. Deposition of Nadine Henley, June 16, 1977, p. 354, Hughes Estate Texas.
2. Deposition of Richard Dreher, Aug. 22, 1977, p. 112, Hughes Estate Texas.
3. Testimony of Michael E. Davis, transcript of grand jury proceedings, *State of California v. Donald Ray Woolbright,* A303305, Los Angeles County Superior Court, p. 7.
4. Ibid., p. 13.
5. Ibid., p. 17.
6. Ibid., p. 20.
7. Ibid., p. 21.
8. Ibid., p. 24.
9. Summary of evidence by Michael Brenner, transcript of Woolbright grand jury proceedings, p. 147.
10. Testimony of Michael E. Davis, transcript of Woolbright grand jury proceedings, p. 27.
11. Ibid.
12. Ibid., p. 34.
13. Ibid.
14. *New York Times,* June 6, 1974, p. 28.
15. Ibid.
16. Memorandum, Hughes to Nadine Henley, Lee Murrin, and Kay Glenn, undated, Hughes Estate Texas.
17. Testimony of Harry F. Watson, transcript of Woolbright grand jury proceedings, p. 36.
18. Ibid.
19. Testimony of Nadine Henley, transcript of Woolbright grand jury proceedings, p. 60.
20. Ibid.
21. Memorandum, Hughes to Maheu, June 6, 1969, *California v. Woolbright.*
22. Transcript of tape-recorded telephone conversation between Chester Brooks and Nadine Henley, transcript of Woolbright grand jury proceedings, p. 67
23. Ibid., pp 68–70.
24. Testimony of Sergeant Edward L. Cline, transcript of Woolbright grand jury proceedings, p. 133
25. Notice of Motion and Second Motion for

Pre-trial Discovery, filed Oct. 12, 1976, *California v. Woolbright.*
26. Motion for Continuance of Trial, filed Oct 15, 1976, *California v. Woolbright.*
27. Transcript of tape-recorded interview of Michael E. Davis by Los Angeles County Deputy District Attorney Stephen S. Trott, April 3, 1975, *California v. Woolbright.*
28. Notice of Motion and Motion for Summary Judgment, filed Sept. 30, 1976, *California v. Woolbright.*
29. Motion for Continuance of Trial, filed Oct. 15, 1976, *California v. Woolbright.*
30. Ibid.
31. *New York Times,* March 21, 1975, p 15.
32. Testimony of Leo Gordon, transcript of Woolbright grand jury proceedings, p. 78
33. Ibid., p 79
34. Ibid.
35. Ibid., p. 80
36. Ibid
37. Ibid.
38. Ibid., p 82.
39. Ibid.
40. Ibid., p. 80.
41. Ibid., p. 82.
42. Summary of evidence by Michael Brenner, transcript of Woolbright grand jury proceedings, p. 151.
43. Testimony of Leo Gordon, transcript of Woolbright grand jury proceedings, p. 84.
44. Ibid., p. 92.
45. Ibid., p. 93.
46. Ibid., p. 94.
47. Ibid., p 97
48. Ibid., p. 98.
49. Ibid.
50. Ibid., p. 105.
51. Ibid
52. Ibid., p 107.
53. Ibid.
54. Ibid.
55. Ibid., p. 108

56. Ibid.
57. Ibid., p. 109.
58. Ibid., p. 110.
59. Ibid.
60. Ibid., p. 112.
61. Ibid.
62. *Philadelphia Inquirer,* June 6, 1974.
63. CIA memorandum, July 5, 1974, authors' files.
64. Ibid.
65. Memorandum, CIA to FBI director, Aug 5, 1974, authors' files
66. Teletype, Los Angeles FBI field office to FBI director, Sept. 23, 1974, authors' files.
67. CIA memorandum, Oct. 5, 1974, authors' files.
68. Ibid.
69. Ibid.
70. Teletype, Los Angeles FBI field office to FBI director, Nov. 1, 1974, authors' files.
71. Ibid.
72. CIA memorandum, Nov. 25, 1974, authors' files.
73. Memorandum, J. E. O'Connell to Gebhardt, FBI, April 24, 1975, authors' files.
74. Authors' interview of confidential source.

23: The CIA's Best-Kept Secret

1. CIA memorandum, Feb. 8, 1975, authors' files.
2. Ibid.
3. Ibid.
4. CIA memorandum, Feb. 11, 1975, authors' files.
5. CIA transcript of telephone conversation between CIA official and *New York Times* executive, Feb. 11, 1975, authors' files.
6. CIA transcript of telephone conversation between William Colby and Katharine Graham, Feb. 13, 1975, authors' files.
7. CIA memorandum, Feb. 28, 1975, authors' files.
8. CIA memorandum, March 7, 1975, authors' files.
9. CIA memorandum, Feb. 11, 1975, authors' files.
10. Deposition of Howard L. Eckersley, June 1, 1977, p. 216, Hughes Estate Texas.
11. Memorandum, unidentified aide to Hughes, undated, Hughes Estate Texas.
12. Memorandum, unidentified aide to Hughes, undated, Hughes Estate Texas.
13. Memorandum, Eckersley to Hughes, February 1975, Hughes Estate Texas.
14. Memorandum, Eckersley to Hughes, March 3, 1975, Hughes Estate Texas.
15. Ibid.
16. Ibid.
17. Memorandum, unidentified aide to Hughes, March 8, 1975, Hughes Estate Texas.
18. Ibid.
19. Memorandum, unidentified aide to Hughes, March 8, 1975, Hughes Estate Texas.
20. Memorandum, unidentified aide to Hughes, undated, Hughes Estate Texas.
21. Memorandum, unidentified aide to Hughes, undated, Hughes Estate Texas.
22. CIA memorandum, March 18, 1975, authors' files.
23. *Los Angeles Times,* March 20, 1975.
24. Ibid.
25. *New York Times,* March 20, 1975, p. 31.
26. *Newsweek,* March 31, 1975, p. 31.
27. *New York Times,* March 19, 1975, p. 1; *Washington Post, Los Angeles Times,* March 19, 1975.
28. *Time,* March 31, 1975, p. 20; *Washington Post,* March 19, 1975.
29. *Newsweek,* March 31, 1975, p. 24.
30. Ibid.
31. *New York Times,* March 20, 1975, p. 38.
32. *Newsweek,* March 31, 1975, p. 24.
33. *New York Times,* March 27, 1975, p. 18.
34. Transcript of tape-recorded interview of Michael E. Davis by Los Angeles County Deputy District Attorney Stephen S. Trott, April 3, 1975, *State of California v. Donald Ray Woolbright,* A303305, Los Angeles County Superior Court.
35. Ibid.
36. Ibid.
37. Ibid.
38. Ibid.
39. Ibid.
40. CIA memorandum, Feb. 27, 1975, authors' files.
41. U.S., General Services Administration, *Hughes Glomar Explorer,* undated brochure.
42. Ibid.
43. Ibid.
44. *Time,* March 31, 1975, p. 20.
45. *Business Week,* April 7, 1975, p. 26.
46. Ibid.
47. Ibid.
48. Ibid.
49. Hughes Logs, Hughes Estate Texas.
50. Ibid.
51. Ibid.
52. Memorandum, Davis to Hughes, March 1974, Hughes Estate Texas.
53. Ibid.
54. Ibid.
55. Ibid.
56. Ibid.
57. Ibid.
58. *United States of America v. County of Los Angeles et al.,* CV-75-2752, U.S. District Court for the Central District of California.
59. Ibid.
60. Deposition of James H. Rickard, June 29, 1977, p. 263, Hughes Estate Texas.

24. The Last Year

1. Memorandum, Gay to Hughes, Aug. 27, 1961, authors' files.
2. Memorandum, Hughes to Gay, Aug. 27, 1961, authors' files.

3. *Hughes '75*, Hughes Aircraft Company brochure, 1975, p. 38.
4. *Armed Forces Journal*, April 4, 1970.
5. *Air Force & Space Digest*, June 1970.
6. *Aviation Week*, Feb. 3, 1975, p. 38.
7. *Summa Corporation v. First National Bank of Nevada et al.*, Civil Action No. 5058-1976, New Castle County Chancery Court, Delaware.
8. Ibid.
9. Affidavit of Dr. Raymond D. Fowler, *TWA v. Hughes*, Delaware.
10. Ibid.
11. Memorandum for the record, Waldron and Holmes, April 9, 1975, Hughes Estate Texas.
12. Memorandum for the record, Waldron, June 25, 1975, Hughes Estate Texas.
13. Memorandum, Myler to Gay, May 23, 1974, Hughes Estate Texas.
14. Memorandum, Eckersley to Gay, June 22, 1974, Hughes Estate Texas.
15. Memorandum, Gay to Hughes, July 3, 1974, Hughes Estate Texas.
16. Ibid.
17. Memorandum, Gay to Hughes, July 18, 1974, Hughes Estate Texas.
18. Memorandum, unidentified aide to Gay, July 20, 1974, Hughes Estate Texas.
19. Ibid.
20. Memorandum, unidentified aide to Hughes, Jan. 17, 1975, Hughes Estate Texas.
21. Helicopter Hearings, p. 322.
22. Deposition of Howard L. Eckersley, May 31, 1977, p. 101, Hughes Estate Texas.
23. Memorandum, Gay to Hughes, Jan. 21, 1975, Hughes Estate Texas.
24. Memorandum for the record, Eckersley, Jan. 25, 1975, Hughes Estate Texas.
25. Memorandum, Henley to Hughes, April 18, 1975, Hughes Estate Texas.
26. Ibid.
27. Memorandum, Myler to Hughes, Feb. 11, 1974, Hughes Estate Texas.
28. Memorandum, staff, Kay Glenn, and Perry Lieber to Hughes, Feb. 13, 1974, Hughes Estate Texas.
29. Memorandum for the record, Myler and Eckersley, Feb. 14, 1974, Hughes Estate Texas.
30. Memorandum for the record, author unidentified, Feb. 18, 1974, Hughes Estate Texas.
31. Memorandum, staff to Hughes, Feb. 22, 1974, Hughes Estate Texas.
32. Memorandum, Henley to Hughes, March 19, 1974, Hughes Estate Texas.
33. Memorandum, unidentified aide to Henley, May 25, 1974, Hughes Estate Texas.
34. Ibid.
35. Memorandum, Henley to Hughes, Feb. 21, 1975, Hughes Estate Texas.
36. Memorandum, Eckersley and Waldron to Henley, Feb. 28, 1975, Hughes Estate Texas.
37. Memorandum, Henley to Hughes, April 18, 1975, Hughes Estate Texas.
38. Ibid.
39. Deposition of Nadine Henley, June 15, 1977, p. 89, Hughes Estate Texas.

40. Letter, Henley to Hughes, Jan. 17, 1975, Hughes Estate Texas.
41. Ibid.
42. Memorandum, unidentified aide to Eckersley and Myler, Jan. 19, 1975, Hughes Estate Texas.
43. Ibid.
44. Memorandum, Eckersley to Hughes, Nov. 11, 1973, Hughes Estate Texas.
45. Deposition of Clarence A. Waldron, June 8, 1977, p. 448, Hughes Estate Texas.
46. Deposition of Dr. Norman F. Crane, Aug. 10, 1977, p. 14, Hughes Estate Texas.
47. Ibid., p. 17.
48. Ibid., pp. 42-4.
49. Ibid., p. 23.
50. Deposition of Dr. Homer Hone Clark, July 20, 1977, pp. 27-8, Hughes Estate Texas.
51. Ibid., p. 32.
52. Ibid., pp. 37-8.
53. Ibid., p. 72.
54. Ibid., p. 118.
55. Ibid.
56. Ibid., p. 57.
57. Ibid., p. 102.
58. Ibid., p. 51.
59. Ibid., p. 100.
60. Ibid., p. 48.
61. Indictment, *United States of America v. Dr. Norman F. Crane and John Morrison Holmes*, CR LV-78-22-RDF, United States District Court for the District of Nevada.
62. Ibid.
63. Memorandum, unidentified aide to Hughes, undated, Hughes Estate Texas.
64. Indictment, *United States of America v. Dr. Norman F. Crane and John Morrison Holmes*.
65. Ibid.
66. Memorandum, Hughes to Eckersley, undated, Hughes Estate Texas.
67. Deposition of Dr. Norman F. Crane, p. 62.
68. Deposition of John M. Holmes, Jr., June 22, 1977, p. 405, Hughes Estate Texas.
69. Memorandum, Hughes to Eckersley, undated, Hughes Estate Texas.
70. Ibid.
71. Ibid.
72. Deposition of John Holmes, p. 413.
73. Ibid., p. 415.
74. Ibid., p. 416.
75. Ibid., p. 417.
76. Ibid.
77. Deposition of Clarence Waldron, p. 327.
78. Ibid., p. 328.
79. Ibid., p. 326.
80. Deposition of George A. Francom, June 30, 1977, p. 144, Hughes Estate Texas.
81. Ibid., pp. 147-148.
82. Employment agreement, Hughes Estate Texas.
83. Deposition of Frank W. Gay, July 15, 1977, p. 290.
84. Deposition of James H. Rickard, June 29, 1977, pp. 208-9, Hughes Estate Texas.
85. Ibid., p. 214.
86. Ibid., p. 215.
87. Ibid., p. 216.

88. Deposition of John Holmes, p 420.
89. Letter, Henley to Hughes, Sept. 16, 1975, Hughes Estate Texas.
90. Deposition of John Holmes, p. 422.
91. Ibid., p. 423.
92. Ibid.
93. Ibid., p. 424.
94. Ibid., p. 425.
95. Ibid., p. 424.
96. Memorandum, Holmes to Hughes, undated, Hughes Estate Texas.
97. Deposition of John Holmes, p. 428.
98. Ibid.
99. Ibid., p. 429.
100. Ibid.
101. Ibid., p. 430.

102. Memorandum, Holmes to Hughes, undated, Hughes Estate Texas.
103. Deposition of John Holmes, p. 432
104. Ibid.
105. Ibid.
106. Deposition of Howard L. Eckersley, June 1, 1977, pp. 261–2, Hughes Estate Texas.
107. Ibid., p. 262.
108. Deposition of George Francom, p. 189.
109. Ibid., p. 77
110. Deposition of Milton H. West, Jr., April 21, 1977, p. 318, Hughes Estate Texas.
111. Ibid., p. 399.
112. Ibid., p. 315.
113. Ibid., p. 399.

25. The Fight for the Fortune

1. Autopsy Report, Howard R. Hughes, Jr., April 7, 1976, Methodist Hospital, Hughes Estate Texas.
2. Ibid.
3. Ibid.
4. Deposition of Annette Gano Lummis, Aug. 2, 1977, p. 28, Hughes Estate Texas
5. *New York Times,* April 6, 1976, p. 1.
6. Ibid., April 7, 1976, p. 18.
7. Ibid.
8. *Washington Post,* April 7, 1976.
9. *New York Times,* April 7, 1976, p. 18.
10. *Newsweek,* April 19, 1976, p. 24.
11. Ibid.
12. *Las Vegas Sun,* April 14, 1976
13. Hughes Autopsy Report
14. *Newsweek,* April 19, 1976, p. 24.
15. *Las Vegas Sun,* April 10, 1976.
16. *New York Times,* April 8, 1976, p. 1.
17. Harry Hurt III, "Howard Hughes Lives!" *Texas Monthly,* January 1977, p. 72.
18. Deposition of William Rice Lummis, Sept. 21, 1976, p. 9, Hughes Estate Nevada.
19. Petition for Special Administration and Issuance of Special Letters of Administration, filed April 14, 1976, Hughes Estate Nevada.
20. Application for Temporary Administration, filed April 14, 1976, Hughes Estate Texas.
21. Ibid.
22. Report of Richard C. Gano, Jr., Special Administrator, Regarding Will Search Activities, p. 48, Hughes Estate California.
23. Ibid., p. 260.
24. *San Francisco Examiner,* April 21, 1976.
25. *Las Vegas Sun,* May 10, 1976.
26. Ibid.
27. *New York Times,* Feb 10, 1964, p. 11.
28. Gano Will Report, p. 114.
29. Appearance of the State of Texas, filed June 10, 1976, Hughes Estate Texas.
30. Deposition of Avis Hughes McIntyre, Sept. 18, 1976, p. 154, Hughes Estate Texas.
31. *Wyatt v. Stickney,* 334 F. Supp. 1341 (1971).
32. Deposition of Avis McIntyre, p. 17.
33. *Los Angeles Times,* Dec. 15, 1923.
34. Deposition of Avis McIntyre, p. 44.
35. Hughes Estate Nevada.

36. *Las Vegas Sun,* April 30, 1976
37. Ibid.
38. *Los Angeles Times,* April 30, 1976.
39. Deposition of Ronald B. Brown, Oct 29, 1976, pp. 22, 73, Hughes Estate Nevada
40. Ibid., p. 22.
41. Ibid , p. 67
42. *Philadelphia Inquirer,* July 25, 1976.
43. Deposition of Melvin Dummar, Dec 7, 1976, p. 123.
44. *New York Times,* May 5, 1976, p. 34; Transcript of Proceedings, Jan. 27–28, 1977, p. 209, Hughes Estate Nevada.
45. Deposition of Melvin Dummar, p. 202.
46. Ibid., pp. 231–232.
47. Ibid., p. 228.
48. Ibid., p. 236.
49. *Los Angeles Times,* April 30, 1976.
50. *Santa Ana Register,* April 30, 1976.
51. *Las Vegas Sun,* May 1, 1976.
52. Letter, Richard Ash, assistant director, FBI, to Robert List, Nevada attorney-general, April 25, 1977, Hughes Estate Nevada
53. Ibid.
54. Deposition of Quintus Ferguson, June 20, 1977, p. 27, Hughes Estate Nevada.
55. Deposition of Melvin Dummar, p 33.
56. Ibid., p. 31.
57. Ibid., p. 239.
58. Ibid., pp. 239–40.
59. Ibid., p. 54.
60. Ibid., p. 53.
61. Ibid., p 240.
62. Ibid , p. 207.
63. Ibid., p. 212
64. Ibid , p. 209
65. Ibid., pp. 9–10, 65–66.
66. *Bucks County Courier Times,* Dec. 29, 1976.
67. *New York Times,* Dec. 29, 1976, p. 10.
68. Transcript of Proceedings, Jan. 25, 1977, pp. 41–42, Hughes Estate Nevada.
69. Ibid., pp. 45–46.
70. Ibid., p. 47.
71. Ibid., p. 48.
72. Ibid., p. 45.
73. Ibid., p. 51.
74. Ibid., p. 59.

75. Ibid., p. 52.
76. Ibid., p. 58
77. Ibid., pp, 61, 64.
78. Ibid., p. 62.
79. Ibid., p. 63.
80. Ibid., p. 64.
81. Ibid., p. 66.
82. Ibid.
83. Ibid , p. 68.
84. Ibid., pp 88
85. Ibid , p 69.
86. Ibid., p. 70.
87. Ibid., p. 78.
88. Ibid.
89. Ibid., p. 83
90. Ibid., p. 14
91. *New West,* Oct 11, 1976, p. 6.
92. Ibid.
93. Ibid.
94. Letter, Lon H. Thomas to Harold Rhoden, Dec. 9, 1976, Hughes Estate Nevada.
95. Deposition of LeVane Malvison Forsythe, March 9, 1977, p. 7, Hughes Estate Nevada
96. Deposition of LeVane Forsythe, April 4, 1977, p. 35, Hughes Estate Nevada.
97. Ibid., p. 39.
98. *Houston Post,* March 6, 1977.
99. Deposition of LeVane Forsythe, April 4, 1977, p. 197.
100. Ibid., pp. 197–200.
101. Deposition of LeVane Forsythe, March 9, 1977, pp. 34–35.
102. Ibid., pp. 38–39.
103. Ibid., p. 42.
104. Ibid., p. 44.
105. Ibid., pp. 21–22.
106. Ibid., pp. 55–56
107. Ibid., p. 62.
108. Ibid., p. 79.
109. Ibid.
110. Ibid., pp. 97–98.
111. Ibid., p. 105.
112 Decision and Findings of Fact and Conclusions of Law, filed Dec. 24, 1970, *Maheu v. Davis.*
113. Demurrer and Objections, Proposed Answer of Barbara Cameron to Application for Issuance of a Peremptory Writ of Prohibition. Request for Hearing of Pendant Constitutional Question. *Keith C. Hayes v. William N. Foreman,* Nevada Supreme Court.
114. Order, Chancellor William Marvel, May 11, 1976, *Summa Corporation v. First National Bank of Nevada et al.,* Civil Action 5058, Court of Chancery, New Castle County, Delaware.
115. *Fortune,* Oct. 9, 1978, p. 126.
116. Brief in Opposition to HHMI's Motion to Intervene and to Remove or Restrain Delaware Ancillary Administrator of the Hughes Estate, *Summa Corporation v. First National Bank of Nevada.*
117. Affidavit of Milton H. West, Jr., *Summa Corporation v. First National Bank of Nevada.*
118. Ibid.
119. Avis Hughes McIntyre and Rush Hughes's Reply to the Motion for Summary Judgment,

Hughes Estate Texas
120. Deposition of Clarence A. Waldron, June 6, 1977, p 144, Hughes Estate Texas
121. *Philadelphia Inquirer,* June 26, 1977
122. Petition, Howard Hughes Medical Institute, Jan 12, 1977, Hughes Estate Nevada.
123. Ibid.
124. Ibid
125 Ibid.
126 Memorandum, Davis, Mintz, and West to Hughes, March 24, 1976, authors' files.
127 *New England Journal of Medicine,* Dec. 7, 1978, p 1278.
128. Ibid.
129. Indictment, *United States of America v. Wilbur Sutton Thain,* NCR-78-00032, United States District Court for the State of Utah, Northern Division.
130. Testimony of Norman F. Crane, Sept. 13, 1978, p. 31, *U.S. v. Thain.*
131. Ibid., p. 32.
132. Ibid., p. 33.
133. Ibid., p. 52.
134. Ibid., p. 53.
135 Ibid., p. 60.
136. Ibid., p 63.
137. Ibid., p. 48.
138 Ibid., pp. 21, 60
139. Ibid., p. 90.
140. Ibid., p. 38.
141. Ibid., p. 40.
142. Ibid., p. 41.
143. Ibid., p. 42.
144. Ibid., p. 45.
145. Ibid , p 48.
146. Ibid., p. 50.
147. Ibid., p. 56.
148. Ibid., p. 58.
149. Ibid., p. 64.
150. Testimony, Wilbur S. Thain, Sept. 18, 1978, p. 662, *U.S. v. Thain.*
151. Ibid.
152. Ibid., pp 670–71.
153. Ibid., p. 671.
154. Ibid., p. 672.
155. Ibid., pp. 672–673.
156. Ibid., p. 694.
157. Ibid., p. 674.
158. Ibid.
159. Ibid., p. 675.
160. Ibid., p. 681.
161. Ibid., pp. 695, 697.
162. Ibid., p. 697.
163. Ibid., p. 790.
164. Ibid., pp. 697–99
165. Ibid., p. 801.
166. Ibid., p. 805.
167. Ibid., p. 784.
168. *Philadelphia Inquirer,* June 11, 1978
169. Hughes Autopsy Report.
170. Testimony of Dr. Forest S. Tennant, Jr , Sept 17, 1978, p. 522, *U.S. v. Thain.*
171. Ibid.
172. "Codeine: And Certain Other Analgesic and Antitusive Agents," Merck Sharp & Dohme Research Laboratories, Merck & Co., 1970.

EPILOGUE. **A Summing Up**

1. Applicant for Pilot, National Defense Program, Federal Bureau of Investigation, United States Department of Justice, Oct. 1, 1942, Hughes Estate Texas.

2. Deposition of Robert A. Maheu, Sept. 12, 1978 (1:45 P.M.), p. 21, *Los Angeles Airways v. William Lummis,* Hughes Estate Texas.

3. Deposition of Raymond Glen Brewer, June 22, 1978, p. 23, Hughes Estate Nevada.

4. Operations Log, Dec. 1, 1958, authors' files.

5. Deposition of Thomas G. Bell, Feb. 21, 1973, pp. 15 and 12, *Maheu v. Hughes Tool Company.*

6. Transcript of tape-recorded telephone conversation between Hughes and Maheu, *Maheu v. Hughes Tool Company.*

7. Robert Berkow, M.D. (ed.) and John H Talbott, M.D. (consulting ed.), *The Merck Manual of Diagnosis and Therapy* (Rahway, N.J.: Merck Sharp & Dohme Research Laboratories, 1977).

8. Ibid.

9. Transcript of news media telephone interview of Hughes, Jan. 7, 1972, authors' files.

INDEX

Major subject areas which were so much a factor in Howard Hughes's life—aviation, movies, Las Vegas, and drug usage, for example—are indexed in categories found under "Hughes, Howard Robard, Jr.," and not under their individual headings.